Second Edition

W9-AWS-397

The First HEBREW PRIMER for Adults

Biblical and Prayerbook Hebrew

Ethelyn Simon
Nanette Stahl
Linda Motzkin
Joseph Anderson

A self-teaching text designed for people who have not studied in years.

EKS Publishing Company, Oakland, California

Professor Jacob Milgrom
Professor of Hebrew and Bible
Department of Near Eastern Studies
University of California at Berkeley
Consultant to the Authors

Assistant Consultant:
Kenneth W. Shoemaker

Book Design:
Irene Imfeld

Editorial Assistant:
Ellen Hoffman

Copyright © 1983, EKS Publishing Company

Paperback, 2nd Edition, ISBN 0-939144-05-0
Library Binding, 2nd Edition, ISBN 0-939144-06-9

Third Printing, February 1987

Office Address:
5336 College Avenue
Oakland, California 94618
415-653-5183

Mailing Address:
Post Office Box 11133
Oakland, California
94611-0133

Table of Contents

לְשֵׁם שָׁמַיִם

‎. . . הוּא יַעֲשֶׂה שָׁלוֹם עָלֵינוּ וְעַל כָּל יִשְׂרָאֵל . . .

Chapter 1
The Hebrew Alphabet
Consonants

The First Hebrew Primer for Adults is designed in a simple, straightforward way to teach you this ancient language. In these 33 lessons, you will be given enough information and practice to enable you, with the aid of a Hebrew-English dictionary, to understand most Biblical texts and Hebrew prayers. As you progress, you will discover and delight in the clear, strong rhythms of original Hebrew — a joy unattainable through reading even the best of translations.

Why grammar? Because grammar is the short cut to learning a new language. The rules of grammar, in an almost magical way, make it possible to understand and compose an infinite number of sentences without learning them one by one. For example, if we know that the addition of **s** or **es** to a word changes the sense of the word from one to more than one, we immediately understand the difference between:

dog and dogs   wish and wishes

Each language has its own method of organizing and altering words to communicate meaning. Vocabulary is not enough. For instance, a three word sentence in Hebrew requires an eight word sentence to express the same idea in English:

I went to his house in the city.

הָלַכְתִּי לְבֵיתוֹ בָּעִיר.

In this book we will acquaint you with just enough grammar for you to understand how the Hebrew language works. Vocabulary is also kept to a minimum. Once you understand the organization of the language, you will be able to increase your own vocabulary at will, with the use of a dictionary. It is our intention to present this material in such an uncomplicated way that the language of Hebrew will speak directly to you.

Note to All Students

Students new to Hebrew will need to work carefully through the first three chapters covering the alphabet and the rules for pronunciation. Even those who already know how to read Hebrew are encouraged to study these chapters, both to learn new information and to review what they have previously learned.

Changes in the Second Edition

Nothing has been added and nothing of any importance has been deleted. All the changes in the Second Edition are so small that they will not prevent using this edition of the Primer along with the previous edition.

In spite of our best efforts, we made some mistakes in the first edition of this text. These minor mistakes have been corrected.

In some parts of the text, we found that we had offered too much material for beginners. Instead of deleting this information, we moved it to a separate section. Wherever we removed any information, we placed a note indicating that additional information can be found on page 272.

In some cases we have improved the original presentation by rearranging the placement of items on a page to make that page more readable.

For additional fun and practice in reading Biblical Hebrew, EKS also publishes **Tall Tales Told and Retold in Biblical Hebrew**. The tales start very simply with the grammar and vocabulary of Chapter 10 in this text and progress chapter by chapter with increased complexity.

English Alphabet

1. English is read from left to right.
2. In the English alphabet there are 26 letters: some are vowels (a, e, i, o, u.) some are consonants (b, c, d, g, etc.), and one is both (y).

Hebrew Alphabet

1. Hebrew is read from right to left.
2. In the Hebrew alphabet there are 22 letters, **all** of which are consonants. The vowels are added to the consonants in a special way which we discuss in the next chapter.

The Alphabet Chart

1. In column 1 you will find the pronunciation for each Hebrew letter. In this book we use the Sephardic pronunciation — the pronunciation officially accepted by the State of Israel.
2. In column 2 you will find the letters of the Hebrew alphabet as they will appear throughout the book. This type of lettering is called "Book Print."
3. In Hebrew, five letters of the alphabet appear in a different form when found at the end of a word. These "final forms" appear in column 3.
4. The names of the Hebrew letters are shown in column 4. We will always refer to a letter by its official name (Bet = בּ, ב).
5. In columns 5, 6, and 7, you will find the three types of lettering generally used for Hebrew. They are: Book Print, used in printed material; Block Letters, a simplified form of written Hebrew; and Script Letters, the commonly used type of written Hebrew.

In order to read these lessons it is necessary to learn to read Book Print. To write the exercises it will be necessary to learn to write either the Block or the Script Letters.

Final Forms

Five letters have a different shape when they appear at the end of a word, as noted above. They are called final forms, and are shown separately in column 3, and along with their regular forms in columns 5, 6, and 7.

Tsade	**Pey**	**Nun**	**Mem**	**Kaf**	
צ	פ	נ	מ	כ	Regular
ץ	ף	ן	ם	ך	Final

The Pronunciation of the Shin ש

There are two ways to pronounce a shin ש. When the dot is on the right side שׁ, it is pronounced **sh** as in **sh**ip; and when it is on the left שׂ, it is pronounced **s** as in **s**un.

2

Alphabet Chart

(1) Pronunciation	(2) Book Print	(3) Final Form	(4) Name of Letter	(5) Book Print	(6) Block	(7) Script
Silent letter	א		Aleph	א	א	אc
B as in **B**oy **V** as in **V**ine	בב		Bet	בב	בב	בב
G as in **G**irl	ג		Gimmel	ג	ג	ג
D as in **D**oor	ד		Dalet	ד	ד	ד
H as in **H**ouse	ה		Hey	ה	ה	ה
V as in **V**ine	ו		Vav	ו	ו	ו
Z as in **Z**ebra	ז		Zayin	ז	ז	ז
CH as in Ba**CH**	ח		Chet	ח	ח	ח
T as in **T**all	ט		Tet	ט	ט	ט
Y as in **Y**es	י		Yod	י	י	י
K as in **K**itty **CH** as in Ba**CH**	כך	ך	Kaf	כך	כך	כך
L as in **L**ook	ל		Lamed	ל	ל	ל
M as in **M**other	מ	ם	Mem	מם	מם	מם
N as in **N**ow	נ	ן	Nun	נן	נן	נן
S as in **S**un	ס		Samech	ס	ס	ס
Silent letter	ע		Ayin	ע	ע	ע
P as in **P**eople **F** as in **F**ood	פפ	ף	Pey	פפ	פף	פף
TS as in Nu**TS**	צ	ץ	Tsade	צץ	צץ	צץ
K as in **K**itty	ק		Qof	ק	ק	ק
R as in **R**obin	ר		Resh	ר	ר	ר
SH as in **SH**ape **S** as in **S**un	שש		Shin	שש	שש	שש
T as in **T**all	ת		Tav	ת	ת	ת

The Dagesh and the BeGeD-KeFeT Letters

The dagesh is a dot in the center of a letter. The dagesh performs various functions in Hebrew. The first function that we will learn concerns the letters referred to in Hebrew as the BeGeD-KeFeT letters. The word BeGeD-KeFeT בגד – כפת is simply a memory device made from the sounds of six letters: bet ב, gimmel ג, dalet ד, kaf כ, pey פ, tav ת. It is useful to remember these letters together because they all follow the same rules in relation to the dagesh. Three of these letters change their pronunciation when a dagesh is added. At one time, all the BeGeD-KeFeT letters were sounded one way with a dagesh and another way without it. Today in Sephardic Hebrew the pronunciation changes in only three of the six letters.

With a Dagesh	Without a Dagesh
B as in **B**oy = בּ	**V** as in **V**ine = ב
K as in **K**itty = כּ	**CH** as in Ba**CH** = כ
P as in **P**eople = פּ	**F** as in **F**ood = פ

The pronunciation of the other three letters remains the same, with or without the dagesh.

With a Dagesh	Without a Dagesh
G as in **G**irl = גּ	**G** as in **G**irl = ג
D as in **D**oor = דּ	**D** as in **D**oor = ד
T as in **T**all = תּ	**T** as in **T**all = ת

The Throaty Five – א, ה, ח, ע, ר

There are five letters — aleph א, hey ה, chet ח, ayin ע, and resh ר — which were, at one time, all sounded in the throat. It is almost impossible for speakers of English to pronounce all these sounds. Most speakers of English pronounce these letters as follows:

The א aleph and ע ayin are silent letters.

The ה hey is pronounced like the English H.

The ח chet is pronounced like the gutteral German **ch** as in Ba**ch**.

The ר resh should be trilled in the throat, but most speakers of English pronounce it like the English R.

The important thing to remember about the throaty five letters — א, ה, ח, ע, and ר — is that a dagesh can **never** be added to them. These are the **only** letters in the Hebrew alphabet that cannot take a dagesh.

Letters That Look Alike

Some letters look alike and may be confused by the beginning reader. You must learn to distinguish between each of the letters in the following groups.

נ – ג	ד – ך – ן	ב – כ	א – צ
נ – כ	ה – ח – ת	ז – ו – י	מ – ט
ר – ד	י – ו – ן	ס – ם	צ – ע

Letters That Sound Alike

Notice that the following letters in the Hebrew alphabet sound alike:

S as in **S**un — שׁ ס	**V** as in **V**ine — ב ו
K as in **K**itty — כּ ק	silent letter — א ע
T as in **T**all — ט ת	**CH** as in Ba**CH** — ח כ

Note: Be careful not to confuse the letters ה and ח . Though we have no English equivalent for the ח, it should not be sounded like the English **H**. Remember, the letter ח sounds like the German guttural **ch**, found in the name of the composer Ba**ch.**

Exercises

The exercises included in each chapter are designed to help you learn the material. It will be of great benefit to you to complete all the exercises before you go on to the next chapter. Choose either block or script letters to use for all the exercises in this book. We have chosen block letters.

Section A

The first eight letters: ח ,ז ,ו ,ה ,ד ,ג ,ב ,א

Exercise 1A. Write a line of each of the first eight letters. Name the letter and sound it as you write.   Example: aleph   א א א א א א א א א א א א
bet   ...ב ב ב ב ב ב ב

Exercise 2A. Repeat aloud the Hebrew names of the following letters:

ג ,ח ,ה ,ו ,ז ,א ,ב ,ד ,ב

Exercise 3A. Rearrange the letters in each group so that they are alphabetically ordered.

1. ב,א,ג,ד   2. ו,ז,ה   3. ז,ח,ו   4. ה,א,ג,ד   5. ו,ד,ז,ח,ה

Exercise 4A. Write an English word beginning with the sound of the following Hebrew letters:

Examples: goat — ג   dog — ד   ג ,ד ,ה ,ז ,ב ,ו ,ב

Section B

In this section you will be practicing the next group of letters: נ, מ, ל, כ כ, י, ט
Three of these letters have a different shape when they appear at the end of a word.

regular — כ, מ, נ   Here are some examples:

final form — ך, ם, ן   מַלְכָּה, לְךָ; שָׁמָה, שָׁם; נֵר, בֵּן

Exercise 1B. Write a line of each of the second group of letters, including the final forms. Name the letter and sound it as you write.

Example: tet   ט ט ט ט ט ט ט ט . . .

Exercise 2B. Repeat the Hebrew names of these letters.   מ, י, ט, נ, כ, ל

Exercise 3B. Rearrange the letters in each group so that they are alphabetically ordered.

1. ט, י, כ
2. נ, ל, מ
3. כ, מ, ן, ט, ל, י
4. ל, ז, ך, ה, י, ח, ו, ט, ד
5. ט, ו, י, ח, ה, ל, ד, ם, ב, ז, כ, א, ג

Exercise 4B. Write an English word beginning with the sound of the following Hebrew letters. Examples: can — כ   near — נ   י, ל, מ, ט, נ, כ

Section C

In this section we learn the end of the alphabet: ת ,שׁ שׂ, ר, ק, צ, פ פ, ע, ס
Two of these letters have a different shape when they appear at the end of a word.

regular — פ, צ   Here are some examples:

final form — ף, ץ   טַפֵּל, טַף; רָצָה, רָץ

Remember that the letter שׁ can be pronounced two ways, depending on where the dot on top of the letter appears.

שׁ — **sh** as in **sh**ip   שׂ — **s** as in **s**un

Exercise 1C. Write a line of each letter from this group. Name the letter and sound it as you write.

Example: samech   ס ס ס ס ס ס ס ס . . .

Exercise 2C. Repeat aloud the following letters.   צ, ת, ק, ס, פ, ר, שׁ

Exercise 3C. Rearrange the letters in each group so that they are alphabetically ordered.

1. פ, ס, ע, צ   2. ק, ר, שׁ, ת   3. ס, ץ, פ, ע   4. ץ, ק, ר, ך, ע, ס, ת, שׁ

6

Exercise 4C. Write an English word beginning with the sound of the following Hebrew letters:

Examples: pan – **פּ**   river – **ר**   פ, ר, שׂ, פ, ק, תּ, שׁ, ס

Exercise 5C. Fill in the missing letters so that each group of letters is alphabetically arranged.

1. ע, _, צ, ק
2. ק, ר, _, ת
3. ס, _, פ, _, ק, _, שׁ, _
4. כ, ל, _, נ, _, ע, פ, _, _, שׁ
5. ה, ו, _, _, ט, _, כ, _, נ, ס, ע, _, _, ק, _, שׁ, _
6. א, ב, ג, _, ה, _, _, ח, _, _

Exercise 6C. Alphabetize the following words according to the first letter of each word.

טוב, מות, חטא, כל, רק, גאל, תורה, צד, למה, שמים, עלה,
בחר, אב, נתן, פנים, דרך, זקן, יד, ספר, וו, קול, הנה

Exercise 7C. List the five letters that cannot take a dagesh.

Exercise 8C. Which three letters are pronounced differently with and without a dagesh?

Exercise 9C. Which five letters have a different shape at the end of a word?

Exercise 10C. Copy each of these words into script or block print, whichever you have chosen.

רגל	_רגל_	כבוד	_כבוד_	אשה	_אשה_
שלום	_שלום_	לאה	_לאה_	בית	_בית_
תפלה	_תפלה_	מספר	_מספר_	גדול	_גדול_
אנחנו	_אנחנו_	נביא	_נביא_	דודה	_דודה_
ברית	_ברית_	ספר	_ספר_	ההיא	_ההיא_
גבור	_גבור_	עבדה	_עבדה_	זקן	_זקן_
דרך	_דרך_	פנים	_פנים_	חדש	_חדש_
הר	_הר_	צוה	_צוה_	טוב	_טוב_
זרע	_זרע_	קדוש	_קדוש_	יעקב	_יעקב_

Chapter 2
Vowels

In Hebrew the vowels are added to the consonants by means of dots and dashes. Usually these are found written below the letter, but sometimes you may see one written above or to the side of a letter. The following chart shows the sounds of the vowels. When discussing the vowels, we will use the sign **X** as a substitute for the consonant, which could be any Hebrew letter.

Name	Vowel Sound	Vowel Sign
qamets	**a** as in y**a**cht	X̞
patach	**a** as in y**a**cht	X̠
chireq	**ee** as in b**ee**	X̣
chireq with yod	**ee** as in b**ee**	יX̣
tsere	**ay** as in h**ay**	X̤
tsere with yod	**ay** as in h**ay**	יX̤
segol	**eh** as in b**e**d	X
cholem	**o** as in r**o**w	‘X
cholem with vav	**o** as in r**o**w	וX
qamets chatuf	**o** as in d**o**g	X̞*
qibbuts	**oo** as in p**oo**l	X
shureq	**oo** as in p**oo**l	וX

Vowel names are listed for your information only. You need not memorize them.

*Rarely used.

How to Read the Vowel Signs with the Consonants

A. The vowel signs in Hebrew usually appear below the consonant, as in דַ. One utters first the sound of the letter, and then the sound of the vowel. The sound produced is thus d + a = **da**.

B. The vowels אֹ and אוֹ are placed after the consonant. Remember that Hebrew is read from right to left. These vowels are sounded with the letters that precede them.
Example: רוּת is pronounced **root** — the Hebrew name for Ruth.

Vowel-letters — the Vav and the Yod

In English, the letter **y** can be either a consonant as in **y**ellow, or a vowel, as in pretty. In the same way, the Hebrew letter vav ו can function as a consonant or a vowel. When the vav is a consonant, it sounds like **v** as in **v**ine, and usually has a vowel sign under it.

וֶ the consonant with the vowel **eh**, as in **ve**teran
וֵ the consonant with the vowel **ay**, as in **va**cation
וִ the consonant with the vowel **ee**, as in **ve**al

When the vav functions as a vowel, it has the sound of **o** as in **ro**w or the sound of **oo** as in **pool**.

The vav is **not** a vowel and a consonant at the same time. When a vav functions as a vowel, sounded **o** or **oo**, it does not have the sound of **v** as in **v**ine.

With a dot above it, the vav sounds like **o** as in **ro**w: וֹ
With a dot in its center, the vav sounds like **oo** as in p**oo**l: וּ
Note: This dot in the center of the vav is not a dagesh.

The yod י is a consonant, and may also function as **part** of a vowel. When it is a consonant it has the sound of **y** as in **y**ellow, and is pronounced together with the vowel under or beside it:

יַ the consonant with the vowel **a**, as in **ya**cht
יֵ the consonant with the vowel **ay**, as in **yea**
יֶ the consonant with the vowel **e**, as in **ye**ll
יוּ the consonant with the vowel **oo**, as in **you**

The Vowel Sounds

Not all of the words in the following exercises are actual Hebrew words.

The vowel sound a— X̲ , X̞ .

The vowel sound **a**, as in **ya**cht, is shown by the signs **X̲** or **X̞**. At one time, the vowel **X̞** was pronounced as a longer sound than the vowel **X̲**. However, most people today do not distinguish between these vowels.   Exercises for **X̲** and **X̞**. Read the following.

רַק, בַּת, רָץ, הָמָה, זָכַר, כַּמָּה, הָבָה, חַזָּן, תָּלָה, שָׁלַח, שַׁבָּת, קַיָּם

The vowel sound ee— X̞ , ʾX̞ .

The vowel sound **ee**, as in b**ee**, is shown by the signs **X̞** or **ʾX̞**. The addition of the yod does not change the sound of the vowel. There is no difference in the pronunciation of **עִיר** and **עִר**. Both sound like the English word **ear**. Exercises for **X̲**, **X̞**, **ʾX̞**, and **X̞**.

שִׁשִׁי, מִלִּים, חַיִּים, אִמָּא, לִבָּם, בְּמָה, גַּלִי, סִירָה, דַּפִּים, צָעִיר, מַיִם, בַּיִת

The vowel sound ay— X̤ , ʾX̤ .

The vowel sound **ay**, as in h**ay**, is shown by the signs **X̤** or **ʾX̤**. The addition of the yod does not change the sound of the vowel. There is no difference in the pronunciation of **שֵׁם** and **שֵׁים**. Both sound like the English word **shame**. Exercises for **X̲**, **X̞**, **X̞**, **ʾX̞**, **X̤**, and **ʾX̤**.

שֵׁם, עֵת, קֵץ, עֵין, אֲשֶׁר, אַחֵר, עֵצִים, בֵּין, רַבִּי, דִּבֵּר, עֵינַי, לָתֵת, אַיֵּה, הָרֵגָה

The vowel sound eh— X̶ .

The vowel sound **eh**, as in b**e**d, is shown by the sign **X̶**. The Hebrew form **שֵׁד** is pronounced **shed**. Exercises for **X̲**, **X̞**, **X̞**, **ʾX̞**, **X̤**, **ʾX̤**, and **X̶**.

אֵל, שֶׁקֶל, עֵבֶר, פֶּרַח, אָשֵׁר, קֶשֶׁר, קֶבֶר, פֶּתַח, סֶדֶר, אֶחָד, אֵין, בָּתֵי, עֵוֵר

The vowel sound o— ʿX , וֹX .

The vowel sound **o**, as in r**o**w, is shown by the sign **ʿX** or **וֹX**, and appears after the letter. The sound is the same whether the vowel has the **vav** with the dot, or just the dot. Therefore, both **עוֹד** and **עֹד** sound like the English word **ode**.
Exercises for **X̲**, **X̞**, **X̞**, **ʾX̞**, **X̤**, **ʾX̤**, **X̶**, **ʿX**, and **וֹX**.

לֹא, מוֹלִי, יוֹם, גֹּרֶן, בּוֹאִי, תּוֹרַת, שָׁלוֹם, בְּעֹז, בֹּקֶר, בּוֹרֵא, כּוֹתֶבֶת, אֹם, בֵּיתִי

The vowel sound oo— אוּ, אֻ.

The vowel sound **oo**, as in p**oo**l, is shown by the signs אוּ or אֻ. The vowel sign אוּ is written after the consonant; the vowel sign אֻ is written beneath it. Both vowels have the same sound. There is no difference in pronunciation between רוּת and רֻת. Both sound like the English word **root**. Exercise for all the vowels.

סֻכּוֹת, אָחֵין, חֲנֻכָּה, הַהוּא, הַרֲגָה, בָּרוּר, קֹדֶשׁ, סוּפוֹת, אֵימָה, שָׂדֶה

אָמֹר, מוּמוֹ, כַּפַּיִם, יֻלַּד, סֻלָּם, עֶבֶד, נֹעַם, תּוֹרָה, יוֹמַיִם, וָעֵד, תָּמִיד, שׁוֹפֵט

The Silent Letters — א and ע

Since the letters א and ע are silent, they take the sound of the vowels that are either under or beside them. Here are some English words written in Hebrew letters to show you how to sound the vowels with the silent letters. These words will help you read the sounds correctly.

Examples: ear—אִיר, עֵר   eat—עִית, אֵט   odd—אָד, עַד

egg—אֶג, עֶג   co-ed—קוֹעֵד, קוֹאֵד

The following are examples of English words spelled with **Hebrew** letters. Practice reading the sounds correctly.

coat	—	קוֹת	rain	—	רֵין	mama	—	מַמַה
rule	—	רֻל	need	—	נִיד	red	—	רֶד
suit	—	סוּט	goat	—	גֹט	shame	—	שֵׁם

Exercises

Exercise 1. Combine each letter of the alphabet with each of the vowel signs, sounding the letters with the vowels as you write them.

Example: אוּ אֻ אוֹ אִי אֵ אֵי אֶ אָ אַ אֲ

etc. בִּ בֵ בֵי בִי בֶ בָ בַ בֲ בָ

Exercise 2. Read the following words aloud. Copy them down and then read aloud the words that you have written.

בָּנִים, דּוֹד, רָעֵב, רֶגֶל, חֹדֶשׁ, בַּת, יָד, נֵר, אֵל, פַּעַם, קוּם, חֲנֻכָּה, נַעַר

Exercise 3. In each of the following groups of three words, one word does not sound like the other two. Pick out the word that is different.

5. תָּמִיד, תָּמָר, טָמֵד   3. שׁוֹפֵט, שְׁפִית, שָׁלוֹם   1. נַעַר, נָעַר, דּוֹר

6. עָכֵן, אָחֵין, אֹכֶל   4. אֵם, עִים, אִם   2. סוּכָּה, לָמָה, שָׁקָה

11

Exercise 4a. In each of the following pairs of words, there is one word in which the vav is a consonant, and another in which it is a vowel. Pick out the word in which the vav is a consonant.

1. מָוֶת – לָמוּת   2. עֵוֵר – אוֹר   3. קוּם – וַתָּקָם   4. דָּוִד – דּוֹד

Exercise 4b. In each of the following pairs of words, there is one word in which the yod is a consonant, and another in which it is part of a vowel. Pick out the words in which the yod is a consonant.

1. קַיָם – הָקִים   2. מִין – מַיִם   3. יָלַד – לִין   4. בֵּית – בַּיִת   5. יֵשׁ – אִישׁ

Exercise 5. In each of the following words there are letters that have a dagesh. Circle only those letters in each word whose sound changes by the addition of the dagesh.

בָּנוֹת, אִשָּׁה, וַתָּקָם, גִּבּוֹר, פָּקַד, כַּלָּה, שָׁלֵם, הֵמָּה

Exercise 6. Circle the letters in the following words that never take a dagesh.

בֹּעַז, רוּת, לֶחֶם, וַתֵּהֹם, גֹּרֶן, אֵיפָה, תַּחַת, עַמִּי, רָאָה

Exercise 7. Practice reading the following words aloud. Be careful not to confuse the letters that look alike but sound different.

נַד	–	גַּן	קוּ	–	כֵּן
עָם	–	צָם	כָּך	–	לָן
נָחַם	–	נָהָר	עִיר	–	לֵץ

דָּם	–	רָם
שָׂכַר	–	שָׁבַר
גֻּבָּס	–	גַּם

Exercise 8. The following Hebrew forms approximate actual English words. However, they have no meaning in Hebrew. Practice reading and pronouncing the Hebrew. Find the English word in the list below which matches each Hebrew form.

25. קָר	21. כֵּיב	17. בִּיד	13. נֵם	9. פָּד	5. יַט	1. אַד
26. מִית	22. דָּף	18. טָר	14. רֵד	10. לוֹן	6. גֻּט	2. סַד
27. זוּם	23. רֵיט	19. תֵּא	15. נֶת	11. הֵית	7. דוֹז	3. שִׁיט
28. קִיא	24. לוּם	20. עֵז	16. טֵל	12. עֵץ	8. בֶּד	4. סִין

English Words: tell, yacht, loom, name, pod, car, bed, key, tar, doze, bead, lone, seen, raid, sheets, goat, hate, two, seed, odd, cave, deaf, meat, rate, zoom, net, ooze, oats

Exercise 9. Write the following English words using Hebrew letters and vowels. Many words can be written several ways.

1. cots   3. date   5. seam   7. Bach   9. bell   11. mean   13. pane
2. so   4. head   6. goof   8. nose   10. room   12. got   14. yes

Chapter 3
Syllables
More Vowels and Odd Endings

Hebrew Syllables

A syllable in Hebrew never begins with a vowel. It always consists of either:

A. a **consonant** plus a **vowel**　　Example: sha　שָׁ

B. a **consonant** plus a **vowel** plus a **consonant**　　Example: teesh　תִּשׁ

It is often easier to read Hebrew words that have many letters when they are broken down into syllables.

Examples:

ta/meed	תָּ/מִיד	=	תָּמִיד
ay/leem	אֵ/לִים	=	אֵלִים
sha/lom	שָׁ/לוֹם	=	שָׁלוֹם
ha/a/rehts	הָ/אָ/רֶץ	=	הָאָרֶץ
sho/meh/reht	שׁוֹ/מֶ/רֶת	=	שׁוֹמֶרֶת

The Sheva

A sheva is a half-vowel written as two vertical dots under the consonant **אְ**. It is called a half-vowel because it is pronounced so quickly that it is hard to hear.

A.　The Sheva at the Beginning of a Word

When the sheva appears under the first letter of a word, it has a short, quick sound, like the **a** in **a**mong or the **o** in **o**ccur. We call this a **short-sound sheva**.

Examples:　　k'tov　כְּתוֹב　　　d'var　דְּבַר　　　sh'ma　שְׁמַע

B.　The Sheva in the Middle of a Word

1. When a sheva appears under the second consonant of a consonant-vowel-consonant syllable such as תִּשׁ , it marks the end of that syllable and is not pronounced. This sheva is called a **silent sheva**.

Examples: teesh/mor　תִּשְׁ/מֹר　=　תִּשְׁמֹר　　　yeeg/dal　יִגְ/דַּל　=　יִגְדַּל

Occasionally a sheva in the middle of a word is a short-sound sheva. We will point out these special cases when they occur.

2. When two consecutive consonants in the middle of a word both have a sheva, the first sheva is always a silent sheva, and the second is always a short-sound sheva.

Examples:

yeesh/m'roo   יִשְׁ / מְרוּ = יִשְׁמְרוּ

teech/t'voo   תִּכְ / תְּבוּ = תִּכְתְּבוּ

C. The Sheva at the End of the Word

Sometimes the sheva appears at the end of a word; when it does, the sheva is silent.

Examples:

at   אַתְּ

ay/naych   עֵי/נֵךְ = עֵינֵךְ

do/da/taych   דוֹ/דָ/תֵךְ = דוֹדָתֵךְ

Sheva Reading Exercises

זְמַן, תַּלְמִידִי, לְבַד, כְּלִי, מַלְכָּה, בְּלִי, תּוֹךְ, יִכְתְּבוּ, לְמִי, שִׂמְלָה, מַרְבִּים

Rules About BeGeD-KeFeT Letters and the Dagesh

A. BeGeD-KeFeT Letters at the Beginning of a Word

When a BeGeD-KeFeT letter ת ,פ ,כ ,ד ,ג ,ב begins a word, it **always** takes a dagesh.

Examples:

bayn   בֵּן

pa/neem   פָּ/נִים = פָּנִים

ga/dol   גָּ/דוֹל = גָּדוֹל

de/rech   דֶּ/רֶךְ = דֶּרֶךְ

B. BeGeD-KeFeT Letters in the Middle of a Word

When a BeGeD-KeFeT letter appears in the middle of a word, it takes a dagesh if it is preceded by a silent sheva. If you see a dagesh in a BeGeD-KeFeT letter following a sheva, you know that this sheva is a silent sheva.

Examples:

ehch/tov   אֶכְ/תֹּב = אֶכְתֹּב

leesh/pot   לִשְׁ/פֹּט = לִשְׁפֹּט

teev/kehh   תִּבְ/כֶּה = תִּבְכֶּה

C. BeGeD-KeFeT Letters at the End of a Word

When a BeGeD-KeFeT letter appears at the end of a word it rarely takes a dagesh.

Exercise for BeGeD-KeFeT Letters

In the following words, add a dagesh to the BeGed-KeFet letters where required by the BeGeD-KeFeT rule. All shevas here are silent shevas. When you have finished, practice reading the words aloud.

כּוֹס, פָּנִים, תּוֹרָה, לִזְכֹּר, דָּבָר, אִישׁ, תִּכְתֹּב, בָּרוּךְ, יִגְדַּל

Combination Vowels

Of the **throaty five** — א, ה, ח, ע, ר — the א, ה, ע and ח are difficult to pronounce with sheva. In words where these four letters have a sheva, a full vowel is added to this sheva to make it easier to sound the syllable.

Only three full vowels may be added to the sheva to form a combination vowel. The combination vowels are אֱ, אֲ and אֳ. The combination vowel אֲ sounds like the אַ, the combination vowel אֱ sounds like the vowel אֶ, but the combination vowel אֳ is pronounced **o** as in **dog**.

Examples:

eh/meht	אֱ/מֶת =	אֱמֶת
a/cha/ray	אַ/חֲ/רֵי =	אַחֲרֵי
o/nee	אֳ/נִי =	אֳנִי

Combination Vowel Exercises

Circle the combination vowel in the following words, and read the word aloud.

6. לֶאֱכֹל   5. שׁוֹאֲלִים   4. אֳנִיָּה   3. לַעֲמֹד   2. אֱנוֹשׁ   1. עֲבוֹדָה

Odd Endings

The Furtive Patach— אַ

You have learned that the vowel sign appearing under a word is read **after** the consonant. However, this rule does not apply when the last consonant of a word is ח and the vowel underneath it is אַ — חַ. When you see ח at the end of a word, the vowel is pronounced first: **ach** not **cha**.

Examples:

roo/ach	רוּ/חַ =	רוּחַ
ko/ach	כֹּ/חַ =	כֹּחַ

Additional information on this subject can be found on page 272, note 1.

The "Eye" Ending

When the last vowel of a word is the אַ vowel followed by a yod—אַי, the two are pronounced together to form the vowel sound **eye** as in **tie**.

Examples: do/die   דּוֹ/דַי = דּוֹדַי   a/lie   עָ/לַי = עָלַי

Exercises

Exercise 1. The following words have been broken down into syllables. Read them aloud and copy them without the syllable divisions.

5. מְשׁ/פָּ/חָה   4. מָ/קוֹם   3. מוֹ/אָב   2. מַחְ/לוֹן   1. אִשׁ/תּוֹ

10. מוֹ/אָ/בִי   9. אֱ/לִי/מֶ/לֶךְ   8. זָ/קַנְ/תִּי   7. יַלְ/בְּשׁוּ   6. נַ/עַר

Exercise 2. Divide the following words into syllables.

5. אֶכְתֹּב   4. נָשׁוּב   3. שָׁפַט   2. מֵתִים   1. בָּנוֹת

10. יַעֲקֹב   9. הוֹלֶכֶת   8. יִכְתְּבוּ   7. אֶרֶץ   6. אַבְרָהָם

Exercise 3. The following are the names of Hebrew letters written in Hebrew. Write them in alphabetical order.

דָּלֶת, רֵישׁ, מֵם, שִׁין, הֵא, לָמֶד, נוּן, בֵּית, יוֹד, תָּו, סָמֶךְ, גִּמֶל, זַיִן, אָלֶף,
פֵּא, חֵית, וָו, צָדִי, טֵית, קוֹף, עַיִן, כַּף

Exercise 4. Read aloud the opening sentence from the book of Ruth.

וַיְהִי בִּימֵי שְׁפֹט הַשֹּׁפְטִים וַיְהִי רָעָב בָּאָרֶץ.

Exercise 5. Read aloud the following blessing from the prayerbook which is recited when the Torah is taken from the Ark.

בָּרוּךְ שֶׁנָּתַן תּוֹרָה לְעַמּוֹ יִשְׂרָאֵל.

Exercise 6. If you have a prayerbook or Bible available, practice reading Hebrew as much as possible.

Chapter 4
The Sentence
Nouns and Verbs

Each chapter will begin with a vocabulary list in Hebrew alphabetical order. The words in the vocabulary lists have been selected for two reasons: first, they appear very frequently in the Bible and the prayerbook, and second, they help to introduce the material of each chapter. Memorize the vocabulary words. Other Hebrew in the chapter need not be memorized.

Vocabulary

man	. . . .	אִישׁ	eesh
Abraham *man's name*	. . . .	אַבְרָהָם	av/ra/ham
Boaz *man's name*	. . . .	בֹּעַז	bo/az
David *man's name*	. . . .	דָּוִד	da/veed
he	. . . .	הוּא	hoo
went, walked	. . . .	הָלַךְ	ha/lach
remembered	. . . .	זָכַר	za/char
Jacob *man's name*	. . . .	יַעֲקֹב	ya/a/kov
wrote	. . . .	כָּתַב	ka/tav
lad, young man	. . . .	נַעַר	na/ar

Note 1: The accent usually falls on the last syllable of a Hebrew word. If the accent falls on another syllable, an accent mark $\check{X}$ will be written over that syllable the first time that word appears.

Note 2: In Hebrew there is no word for **a**. The **a** can be assumed before a noun, e.g. (a) man, (a) lad.

The Sentence

In both English and Hebrew, a sentence is one or more words arranged to express a complete thought. Normally, a sentence has at least two parts: a subject and a verb.

Verb	Subject	
זָכַר remembered	בֹּעַז Boaz	← Remember Hebrew reads from right to left.
כָּתַב wrote	אִישׁ a man	

17

In English, the verb normally follows the subject.

	Subject	**Verb**
Example 1.	Boaz	remembered.
Example 2.	He	wrote.

In Hebrew, the verb may be placed before or after the subject.

Verb	**Subject**
הָלַךְ.	בֹּעַז

Subject	**Verb**
בֹּעַז.	הָלַךְ

These are both translated into English as "Boaz went".

The Noun, the Pronoun, and the Subject of a Sentence

A **noun** is a word which names a person, object or idea. The nouns in the vocabulary of this chapter are:

Boaz	בֹּעַז	Abraham	אַבְרָהָם
David	דָּוִד	man	אִישׁ
lad, young man	נַעַר	Jacob	יַעֲקֹב

A **pronoun** is a word used in place of a noun: he, she, it. The vocabulary of this chapter introduces the pronoun he — הוּא.

The **subject of the sentence** is what, or who, the sentence is about. In Example 1, "Boaz remembered", **Boaz** is the subject of the sentence. In Example 2, "He wrote", **he** is the subject of the sentence. Usually the subject of a sentence is either a noun or a pronoun.

The Verb

The **verb** describes the action or state of being of the subject in the sentence. The verbs in the vocabulary of this chapter are:

(he) went, walked	הָלַךְ
(he) remembered	זָכַר
(he) wrote	כָּתַב

Note that all of these verbs describe action completed in the past. In English there are many ways to describe action in the past. The Hebrew sentence בֹּעַז כָּתַב can be translated in any of the five ways listed below.

Boaz wrote.
Boaz did write.
Boaz was writing. } בֹּעַז כָּתַב
Boaz has written.
Boaz had written.

The **perfect tense** is the name given to verb forms that describe actions that have been completed and/or have happened in the past. Therefore, the verb in the sentence בֹּעַז כָּתַב is in the perfect tense. All the verb forms introduced in this chapter are in the perfect tense.

Exercises

Exercise 1. Rewrite the sentences below, replacing the underlined word with each word in the list that follows. Read the sentences aloud. Translate.   Example: זָכַר בֹּעַז.

זָכַר דָּוִד. A.

1. זָכַר בֹּעַז.
A. דָּוִד   B. נַעַר   C. הוּא   D. אַבְרָהָם   E. יַעֲקֹב   F. בֹּעַז

2. הוּא כָּתַב.
A. הָלַךְ   B. זָכַר   C. כָּתַב

Exercise 2. Translate the following sentences into English.

1. בֹּעַז זָכַר.
2. אַבְרָהָם הָלַךְ.
3. כָּתַב אִישׁ.
4. נַעַר זָכַר.
5. יַעֲקֹב כָּתַב.
6. הוּא הָלַךְ.
7. זָכַר דָּוִד.
8. הוּא כָּתַב.
9. אַבְרָהָם זָכַר.

Exercise 3. Pick out the words in Exercise 2 that have BeGeD-KeFeT letters.

Exercise 4. Pick out the words in Exercise 2 that have one or more of the throaty five letters.

Exercise 5. Translate the following sentences into Hebrew.

1. Abraham remembered.
2. A man went.
3. He went.
4. David remembered.
5. Boaz wrote.
6. A lad went.

Exercise 6. Add the vowels and then translate.

1. דוד כתב.   2. הלך נער.   3. אברהם זכר.   4. הוא הלך.   5. יעקב כתב.

Chapter 5
Feminine Nouns and Verbs
The Definite Article

Vocabulary

woman, wife *n, f*	. . . .	אִשָּׁה	ee/shah
she *pro*	. . . .	הִיא	hee
gift *n, f*	. . . .	מִנְחָה	meen/chah
family *n, f*	. . . .	מִשְׁפָּחָה	meesh/pa/chah
Naomi *woman's name*	. . . .	נָעֳמִי	na/o/mee
young woman, maiden *n, f*	. . . .	נַעֲרָה	na/a/rah
book *n, m*	. . . .	סֵפֶר	šay/fehr
Ruth *woman's name*	. . . .	רוּת	root
sent *vb*	. . . .	שָׁלַח	sha/lach
Sarah *woman's name*	. . . .	שָׂרָה	sa/rah

Note 1: In the vocabulary lists of the following chapters, we will use these abbreviations — *n* for noun, *vb* for verb, *pro* for pronoun, *m* for masculine, *f* for feminine.

Note 2: When there is an unexplained dagesh in a vocabulary word, as in אִשָּׁה above, consider it part of the spelling.

Each chapter will introduce approximately ten new vocabulary words. These vocabulary words will be easy to memorize if you start to make flash cards now. Flash cards are very simple to make. You can use ordinary 3 × 5 index cards. On one side of the index card, write the word in Hebrew. On the other side of the card, write the English translation, along with any other information about the word that you need to know, such as whether it is a verb or noun, masculine or feminine, etc. As you learn additional Hebrew forms of the word, you may add these to the Hebrew side of the flash card. With these cards you will be able to drill yourself or use a partner to help you review your vocabulary.

The Gender of Nouns

In English, nouns are usually masculine or feminine **only** when they refer to living beings, for example: boy, man, lady. In Hebrew, **all** nouns are either masculine or feminine, even though many have no male or female qualities.

Examples: A **book** סֵפֶר is masculine and follows the rules for masculine forms.

A **family** מִשְׁפָּחָה is feminine and follows the rules for feminine forms.

There is nothing male or female about either a family or a book. The gender of objects may have been established by chance alone. The important thing to know is that every Hebrew noun is either masculine or feminine, and that you must remember which gender it is.

The Feminine Singular Noun

1. There are two endings characteristic of feminine singular nouns. These are general rules; there are, of course, exceptions.

    a. Nouns with ָX under the next to the last letter, followed by a hey — ָX ה

        Examples: young woman *n, f* . . . . נַעֲרָה

        woman *n, f* . . . . אִשָּׁה

    b. Nouns ending with the letter tav — ת

        Examples: sister *n, f* . . . . אָחוֹת

        truth *n, f* . . . . אֱמֶת

2. Names of cities or countries are always feminine.

    Examples: Jerusalem *n, f* . . . . יְרוּשָׁלַיִם

    Judah *n, f* . . . . יְהוּדָה

3. Parts of the body found in pairs are usually feminine.

    Examples: eye *n, f* . . . . עַיִן

    hand *n, f* . . . . יָד

The Masculine Singular Noun

There is no ending characteristic of the masculine singular noun. If a singular noun does not have a feminine ending, it is probably masculine singular. However, there are many exceptions. The only absolute way to determine the gender of a noun is to look it up in a Hebrew dictionary. We will indicate the gender of each noun in the vocabulary of each chapter and in the glossary in the back of this book. All nouns introduced in Chapter 4 are masculine nouns.

The Gender of Verbs

In English, verb forms are neither masculine nor feminine. The same verb form is used with males, females, and objects.

Example: Boaz went.   Ruth went.   It went.

However, in Hebrew, every verb has both masculine and feminine forms. In the last chapter, all the verbs were used in their masculine singular form, and they all followed the same pattern.

The general pattern for the masculine singular verb in the perfect tense is:

$$\text{X}\underset{\text{-}}{\text{X}}\underset{\text{T}}{\text{X}} \; .$$

Examples: (he) wrote כָּתַב   (he) remembered זָכַר   (he) walked הָלַךְ

To make the feminine singular form of these verbs, a hey ה is added to the three letters of the masculine singular verb, and the vowels under the letters change.

The general pattern for the feminine singular verb in the perfect tense is:

$$\text{הX}\underset{\text{:}}{\text{X}}\underset{\text{T}}{\text{X}} \; .$$

Examples: (she) wrote כָּתְבָה   (she) remembered זָכְרָה   (she) walked הָלְכָה

Additional information on this subject can be found on page 272, note 2.

Agreement of Subject and Verb

In Hebrew, the subject and verb in a sentence must agree in gender.
1.   If the subject is masculine, it must take the masculine form of the verb.
2.   If the subject is feminine, it must take the feminine form of the verb.

Examples: Boaz wrote   בֹּעַז כָּתַב

                                       Ruth wrote   רוּת כָּתְבָה

                                       He wrote   הוּא כָּתַב

                                       She wrote   הִיא כָּתְבָה

The Definite Article

In English there is an indefinite article: **a** or **an**, as in "a man" or "an eye". In Hebrew there is **no** indefinite article. Therefore, the word נַעַר can mean either "lad" or "a lad", depending on the context. In both English and Hebrew there is a definite article, which indicates a definite, specific subject. In English, the definite article is a separate word, **the**. In Hebrew, the definite article attaches itself to the specified word and cannot stand alone.

The definite article in Hebrew is a **hey** ה with a ֲ under it, followed by a **dagesh** in the next letter.

$$\text{the} = \text{הַX}$$

Definite Noun	=	Indefinite Noun	+	Definite Article
the family	=	family	+	the
הַמִּשְׁפָּחָה	=	מִשְׁפָּחָה	+	הַX
the book	=	book	+	the
הַסֵּפֶר	=	סֵפֶר	+	הַX
the lad	=	lad	+	the
הַנַּעַר	=	נַעַר	+	הַX
the gift	=	gift	+	the
הַמִּנְחָה	=	מִנְחָה	+	הַX

Variations of the Definite Article

As you have already learned, these letters א, ה, ח, ע, ר — the throaty five — cannot take a dagesh. Therefore, a problem arises when the definite article comes before a word that begins with one of the throaty five letters. When this happens, the vowel of the definite article הַX usually changes. The following variations need not be memorized.

1. Before words beginning with the letters א, ע, ר, the article הַX becomes הָX.
   Examples: the man הָאִישׁ   the tree הָעֵץ   the friend הָרֵעַ

2. Before words beginning with הָ, חָ, עָ, the article הַX becomes הֶX.
   Examples: the rich man הֶעָשִׁיר   the mountains הֶהָרִים

3. When a word begins with a ה or a ח which does not have a qamets ֲ under it, the article הַX usually remains הַ, but the dagesh is omitted.
   Example: the life הַחַיִּים

23

Below is a chart summarizing the rules for the vowels of the definite article הַX. You can refer to this chart whenever you add the definite article הַX to a Hebrew word.

Examples	Vowel	Before Consonants
הַנַּעַר, הַסֵּפֶר	הַX	regular
הָאִישׁ, הָעֵץ, הָרֵעַ	הָX	ר, ע, א
הֶהָרִים, הֶחָכָם, הֶעָשִׁיר	הֶX	הָ, חָ, עָ
הַחַיִּים	הַX	ה, ח

Exercises

Exercise 1. Rewrite the sentences below, replacing the underlined word with each word in the list that follows. Read the sentences aloud. Translate.

Example: <u>נָעֳמִי</u> כָּתְבָה.

נַעֲרָה – נַעֲרָה כָּתְבָה.

1. <u>הָאִשָּׁה</u> כָּתְבָה.

A. רוּת   B. נַעֲרָה   C. הִיא   D. שָׂרָה   E. מִשְׁפָּחָה   F. הַנַּעֲרָה

2. <u>יַעֲקֹב</u> הָלַךְ.

A. אַבְרָהָם   B. דָּוִד   C. הוּא   D. הָאִישׁ   E. בֹּעַז   F. הַנַּעַר

In sentence 3, be sure to change the verb to agree with each new subject.

3. <u>נָעֳמִי</u> כָּתְבָה סֵפֶר.

A. רוּת   B. אַבְרָהָם   C. הָאִשָּׁה   D. בֹּעַז

E. הַנַּעֲרָה   F. יַעֲקֹב   G. הַנַּעַר   H. הַמִּשְׁפָּחָה

Exercise 2. Translate the following sentences.

1. הַמִּשְׁפָּחָה שָׁלְחָה נַעַר.   3. רוּת זָכְרָה מִנְחָה.   5. זָכַר הָאִישׁ סֵפֶר.

2. הָלַךְ בֹּעַז.   4. הָאִשָּׁה הָלְכָה.   6. הִיא שָׁלְחָה אִישׁ.

Exercise 3. Add the definite article to the following words, and translate.

1. נַעַר   3. מִשְׁפָּחָה   5. מִנְחָה   7. נַעֲרָה

2. סֵפֶר   4. אִישׁ   6. אִשָּׁה

Exercise 4.   Circle the correct form of the verb. The first word of each sentence is the subject.

5. דָּוִד (שָׁלַח, שָׁלְחָה) נַעַר.

6. הָאִישׁ (הָלַךְ, הָלְכָה).

7. הַנַּעֲרָה (כָּתַב, כָּתְבָה) סֵפֶר.

8. נָעֳמִי (זָכַר, זָכְרָה) אִישׁ.

1. אַבְרָהָם (כָּתַב, כָּתְבָה) סֵפֶר.

2. הָאִשָּׁה (שָׁלַח, שָׁלְחָה) מִנְחָה.

3. הַנַּעַר (זָכַר, זָכְרָה) נַעֲרָה.

4. שָׂרָה (הָלַךְ, הָלְכָה).

Exercise 5.   Translate the following sentences into Hebrew.

1. A lad wrote a book.
2. The lad wrote a book.
3. Naomi wrote a book.
4. She wrote a book.
5. A man sent a gift.
6. The man sent a gift.
7. He sent a book.
8. Boaz sent a young man.
9. The family sent a gift.
10. Abraham went.

Exercise 6.   Add the vowels to these sentences and translate.

3. האשה שלחה מנחה.

4. אברהם שלח נער.

1. המשפחה הלכה.

2. דוד זכר ספר.

Exercise 7.   Unscramble and translate the following sentences.

4. זָכַר – הָאִישׁ – מִשְׁפָּחָה

5. סֵפֶר – כָּתַב – הַנַּעַר

6. אִשָּׁה – שָׁלְחָה – הִיא

1. שָׁלְחָה – מִנְחָה – שָׂרָה

2. יַעֲקֹב – סֵפֶר – זָכַר

3. נַעֲרָה – הוּא – שָׁלַח

Exercise 8.   Construct as many sentences as you can from the words below. Make all necessary changes.

Example: הִיא שָׁלְחָה מִנְחָה.

סֵפֶר	שׁ.ל.ח	אַבְרָהָם
מִנְחָה	ז.כ.ר	הִיא
מִשְׁפָּחָה	כ.ת.ב	הַנַּעֲרָה
אִשָּׁה		הָאִישׁ

25

Chapter 6
Plural Nouns and Verbs
The Conjunction "and"

Vocabulary

house *n, m*	בַּיִת	ba/yeet
road, way *n, m or f*	דֶּרֶךְ	deh/rehch
they *pro, m*	הֵם, הֵמָּה	haym, hay/mah
they *pro, f*	הֵן, הֵנָּה	hayn, hay/nah
and *conj*	וְ	
shoe *n, f*	נַעַל	na/al

Note 1: New abbreviation — *conj* conjunction

Note 2: The pronoun הֵן appears only in post-Biblical Hebrew.

Nouns — Plural Form

English nouns are normally made plural by adding **s** or **es** to the singular form.

Examples: book — books   wish — wishes

The plural of masculine nouns in Hebrew is formed by adding the plural ending אִים.
The vowels often change when the plural ending is added.

Examples:		**Plural**		**Singular**
n'a/reem	נַעַר + אִים = נְעָרִים		lad	נַעַר
s'fa/reem	סֵפֶר + אִים = סְפָרִים		book	סֵפֶר

The plural of feminine nouns in Hebrew is formed by dropping the אָהor ת ending and
adding the plural ending אוֹת. The vowels often change when the plural ending is added.

Examples:		**Plural**		**Singular**
meesh/pa/chot	מִשְׁפָּחָה – אָה + אוֹת = מִשְׁפָּחוֹת		family	מִשְׁפָּחָה
n'a/rot	נַעֲרָה – אָה + אוֹת = נְעָרוֹת		maiden	נַעֲרָה
cha/ta/ot	חַטָּאת – ת + אוֹת = חַטָּאוֹת		sin	חַטָּאת

Dual Endings

In addition to the plural endings, there is also a dual ending in Hebrew, which is used specifically to indicate a pair of things. Dual endings are used with:

1. Parts of the body that are in pairs — hands, feet, etc.
2. Some objects that are naturally in pairs — shoes, for example
3. Units of time — two days, two months, etc.

The same dual ending is used for both masculine and feminine nouns. The dual ending is אַֽיִם. The accent is on the next to the last syllable.

	Plural	**Dual**	**Singular**
Examples:	more than two shoes	a pair of shoes	a shoe
	נְעָלִים	נַעֲלַֽיִם	נַֽעַל
	more than two days	a pair of days	a day
	יָמִים*	יוֹמַֽיִם	יוֹם
		a pair of hands	a hand
		יָדַֽיִם	יָד

*The plural of יוֹם is irregular.

Noun Chart

The following is a chart of all the nouns introduced through Chapter 6, showing the singular, plural, and dual forms. Unfortunately, in Hebrew as in English, a great number of the most common nouns have irregular plurals. All the forms in this chart must be memorized.

Translation	Gender	Dual	Plural	Singular
man	m		אֲנָשִׁים	אִישׁ
woman	f		נָשִׁים	אִשָּׁה
house	m		בָּתִּים	בַּיִת
road, way	f		דְּרָכִים	דֶּרֶךְ
gift	f		מְנָחוֹת	מִנְחָה
family	f		מִשְׁפָּחוֹת	מִשְׁפָּחָה
shoe	f	נַעֲלַֽיִם	נְעָלִים	נַֽעַל
lad, young man	m		נְעָרִים	נַֽעַר
maiden, young woman	f		נְעָרוֹת	נַעֲרָה
book	m		סְפָרִים	סֵֽפֶר

Note: the plural of man, אֲנָשִׁים, can also be translated **people**.

27

Verbs — Plural Form

You have already learned in the last two chapters a masculine and feminine singular form of the verb in the perfect tense.

Example: he wrote XXX כָּתַב ka/tav   she wrote XXXה כָּתְבָה kat/vah

The vowel pattern for the plural form is XXXוּ, and it is the same for both masculine and feminine.

Examples:
they wrote	כָּתְבוּ	kat/voo
they remembered	זָכְרוּ	zach/roo
they went, walked	הָלְכוּ	hal/choo
they sent	שָׁלְחוּ	shal/choo

Additional information on this subject can be found on page 272, note 3.

Below is a chart of all the forms of the verbs that we have learned thus far.

	walked, went	remembered	sent	wrote
he	הָלַךְ	זָכַר	שָׁלַח	כָּתַב
she	הָלְכָה	זָכְרָה	שָׁלְחָה	כָּתְבָה
they *m*	הָלְכוּ	זָכְרוּ	שָׁלְחוּ	כָּתְבוּ
they *f*	הָלְכוּ	זָכְרוּ	שָׁלְחוּ	כָּתְבוּ

The Conjunction "and"

In both English and Hebrew, the conjunction **and** is used to connect words, phrases, clauses and sentences.

However, in Hebrew, the conjunction **and** is not written as a separate word. It is the letter וֹ added to the beginning of a word. The conjunction וֹ ordinarily takes the sheva vowel —וְ.

Examples:
Boaz and Ruth and Naomi   בֹּעַז וְרוּת וְנָעֳמִי

Boaz wrote and went.   בֹּעַז כָּתַב וְהָלַךְ.

Abraham wrote and a young man remembered.   אַבְרָהָם כָּתַב וְנַעַר זָכַר.

Variations on the Conjunction "and"

The following variations need not be memorized. You can refer to this list whenever you add the conjunction וְ to a Hebrew word.

1. When the first letter of a word has a sheva, the וְ becomes וּ — sounded **oo** and not **voo**.

    Examples: young men and young women   נְעָרִים וּנְעָרוֹת

    good and large   טוֹבָה וּגְדוֹלָה

2. When the first letter of a word is one of the following: פ , מ , ב , the וְ becomes וּ .
    Using the sounds of these letters to form **Boomf** — בּוּמְף — is a good memory device for this rule.

    Examples: Ruth and Boaz   רוּת וּבֹעַז

    Naomi and Machlon   נָעֳמִי וּמַחְלוֹן

3. When the first letter of a word is a yod with a sheva under it — as in יְרוּשָׁלַיִם Jerusalem
    — the וְ becomes וִ — sounded **vee** — and the yod loses its sheva, becoming part of the
    ee vowel וִי , as in וִירוּשָׁלַיִם .

    Example: Hebron and Jerusalem   חֶבְרוֹן וִירוּשָׁלַיִם

4. When the first letter of a word has a combination vowel, as do the words people אֲנָשִׁים
    and truth אֱמֶת, the וְ takes the same sound as the combination vowel that follows it.

    Examples: and people   וַאֲנָשִׁים

    and truth   וֶאֱמֶת

Exercises

Exercise 1. Rewrite the sentences below, replacing the underlined word with each word in
the list that follows, and making the necessary changes in the rest of the sentence. Read the
sentences aloud. Translate.

1. <u>יַעֲקֹב וּבֹעַז</u> הָלְכוּ וְזָכְרוּ.

E. הֵמָּה	D. הָאֲנָשִׁים	C. הִיא	B. שָׂרָה וְרוּת	A. אַבְרָהָם
J. הַנַּעַר	I. הֵנָּה	H. הוּא	G. הַנָּשִׁים	F. הַנַּעֲרָה

2. <u>שָׂרָה שָׁלְחָה</u> סְפָרִים וּנְעָלִים.

E. נָעֳמִי	D. אַבְרָהָם	C. הַמִּשְׁפָּחָה	B. הַנְּעָרוֹת	A. הֵם
J. הַנְּעָרִים	I. הֵן	H. יַעֲקֹב	G. רוּת	F. הֵמָּה

Exercise 2. Fill in the blanks with the correct form of the conjunction **and**.

8. סֵפֶר__מִנְחָה   5. הוּא__הִיא   1. אִישׁ__אִשָּׁה.

9. הָאִישׁ__הַמִּשְׁפָּחָה   6. דָּוִד__בֹּעַז   2. יַעֲקֹב__אַבְרָהָם

10. הַמִּנְחָה__הַסֵּפֶר   7. נָעֳמִי__שָׂרָה   3. נַעַר__מִשְׁפָּחָה

4. בֵּית לֶחֶם__יְרוּשָׁלַיִם.

Exercise 3. Read aloud and translate the following sentences into English.

6. הַנְּעָרִים כָּתְבוּ סֵפֶר.

7. הַנַּעֲרָה שָׁלְחָה מְנָחוֹת.

8. נָעֳמִי זָכְרָה דֶּרֶךְ.

9. רוּת וּבֹעַז שָׁלְחוּ נַעֲלַיִם.

10. אַבְרָהָם זָכַר אִשָּׁה.

1. הָאִשָּׁה כָּתְבָה.

2. דָּוִד כָּתַב.

3. דָּוִד וְהָאִישׁ הָלְכוּ.

4. הַמִּשְׁפָּחָה הָלְכָה.

5. הָאֲנָשִׁים וְהַנָּשִׁים זָכְרוּ בָּתִּים.

Exercise 4. Circle the correct form of the verb.

4. הַנָּשִׁים וְהָאֲנָשִׁים (הָלְכוּ, הָלְכָה, הָלַךְ).

5. רוּת (שָׁלַח, שָׁלְחָה, שָׁלְחוּ) מִנְחָה.

6. הַנָּשִׁים (זָכַר, זָכְרָה, זָכְרוּ) בַּיִת.

1. יַעֲקֹב (כָּתְבוּ, כָּתַב, כָּתְבָה) סְפָרִים.

2. אִישׁ וְנַעַר (שָׁלַח, שָׁלְחָה, שָׁלְחוּ) נַעֲלַיִם.

3. הַנַּעֲרָה (זָכְרָה, זָכְרוּ, זָכַר) מִשְׁפָּחָה.

Exercise 5. Change all the nouns and verbs in the following sentences from singular to plural.

3. הוּא כָּתַב סֵפֶר.

4. הָאִשָּׁה שָׁלְחָה מִנְחָה.

1. הָאִישׁ שָׁלַח נַעֲרָה.

2. הַנַּעֲרָה זָכְרָה דֶּרֶךְ.

Exercise 6. Change all the nouns in the following sentences from plural to singular, making the necessary changes in the rest of the sentence.

3. הַנְּעָרוֹת הָלְכוּ וְזָכְרוּ.

4. הֵמָּה זָכְרוּ דְּרָכִים.

1. הֵנָּה כָּתְבוּ סְפָרִים.

2. הַנָּשִׁים וְהָאֲנָשִׁים שָׁלְחוּ מְנָחוֹת.

Exercise 7. Translate the following sentences into Hebrew.
1. The young man and the young woman went.
2. The people sent gifts.
3. They ƒ remembered a family.
4. Jacob and Abraham sent a pair of shoes.
5. The man wrote books.
6. The families remembered a house.

Exercise 8. Add the correct vowels to the following sentences. Translate:

3. נעמי כתבה ספרים.

4. הנשים זכרו.

1. יעקב ובעז הלכו.

2. רות והאשה שלחו מנחות.

Chapter 7
Prepositions

Vocabulary

to, into, towards *prep*	אֶל
in, with *prep*	‐בְּ
as, like *prep*	‐כְּ
to, for *prep*	‐לְ
from *prep*	מִן
upon, about *prep*	עַל
with *prep*	עִם

Place Names

Bethlehem	בֵּית לֶחֶם
Judah	יְהוּדָה
Jerusalem	יְרוּשָׁלַיִם

Note 1: New abbreviation — *prep* preposition

Note 2: In the Bible, Jerusalem is spelled יְרוּשָׁלַם and יְרוּשָׁלָם.
In post-Biblical Hebrew, it is spelled יְרוּשָׁלַיִם. Since the post-
Biblical spelling יְרוּשָׁלַיִם is easier to read, we will use this spelling.

Prepositional Phrases

Hebrew prepositions, like English prepositions — on, about, to, from, etc. — introduce a
phrase which describes the **when, where,** or **how** of a noun or verb.

Examples: in the morning   in a house   with a family

In this chapter we have introduced seven prepositions.

Four are called independent prepositions: with עִם , to אֶל , from מִן , upon or about עַל

Three are called inseparable prepositions: in, with ‐בְּ , as, like ‐כְּ , to, for ‐לְ

The Independent Prepositions

The independent Hebrew prepositions are separate words which function like prepositions in English.

Examples:

with the family	עִם הַמִּשְׁפָּחָה	with	עִם
to the house	אֶל הַבַּיִת	to	אֶל
from the road	מִן הַדֶּרֶךְ	from	מִן
about men	עַל אֲנָשִׁים	about	עַל

The Inseparable Prepositions

The inseparable prepositions are prefixes, which cannot exist as separate words.

Examples:

like Boaz	כְּבֹעַז	as, like	־כְּ
in Moab	בְּמוֹאָב	in, with	־בְּ
for Ruth	לְרוּת	to, for	־לְ

The Vowels for the Inseparable Prepositions

The inseparable prepositions ordinarily take a sheva.

Examples: in Moab בְּמוֹאָב   to Ruth לְרוּת   like a lad כְּנַעַר

The following variations need not be memorized. You can refer to this list whenever you add an inseparable preposition to a Hebrew word.

1. When the first letter of a word has a sheva, the preposition takes the ֲ vowel — בְּ, ל, כְּ

    Examples:

    | in books | like books | to books | books |
    | בִּסְפָרִים | כִּסְפָרִים | לִסְפָרִים | סְפָרִים |

2. When a word begins with the letter yod י with a sheva under it, as in יְהוּדָה, the preposition takes the ֲ vowel and the yod loses its sheva, becoming part of the אִי vowel, לִי, as in לִיהוּדָה.

    Examples:

    | as Judah | Judah | to Jerusalem | Jerusalem |
    | כִּיהוּדָה | יְהוּדָה | לִירוּשָׁלַיִם | יְרוּשָׁלַיִם |

3. When a word begins with a combination vowel, as do the words people אֲנָשִׁים and truth אֱמֶת, the preposition takes the same sound as the combination vowel that follows it.

    Examples: to people לַאֲנָשִׁים   in truth בֶּאֱמֶת

The Inseparable Prepositions and the Definite Article

When an inseparable preposition בְּ, כְּ, or לְ combines with a definite article, the following changes take place.

1. The definite article הַ· is dropped.
2. The אַ vowel of the definite article is transfered to the inseparable preposition.
3. A dagesh is placed in the letter following the inseparable preposition.

$$בַּ·א \quad = \quad הַ·א + בְּ$$
$$כַּ·א \quad = \quad הַ·א + כְּ$$
$$לַ·א \quad = \quad הַ·א + לְ$$

Listed below are examples showing how inseparable prepositions combine with both indefinite and definite nouns.

house	בַּיִת	a book	סֵפֶר
to a house	לְבַיִת	in a book	בְּסֵפֶר
the house	הַבַּיִת	the book	הַסֵּפֶר
to the house	לַבַּיִת	in the book	בַּסֵּפֶר

Variations

The same changes in the vowels that occur in the definite article הַ· when it is followed by one of the throaty five letters, א, ה, ח, ע, ר (see chapter 5, page 6. "Variations of the Definite Article") also occur when the definite article combines with the preposition.

Examples:	to the man	לָאִישׁ	the man	הָאִישׁ
	as the rich man	כֶּעָשִׁיר	the rich man	הֶעָשִׁיר
	in the life	בַּחַיִּים	the life	הַחַיִּים

Exercise with the Inseparable Preposition and the Definite Article

Add the inseparable preposition to the following **definite** nouns. Remember to drop the definite article.

5. ב + הַדֶּרֶךְ

6. כ + נַעֲלַיִם

7. ב + הַמִּשְׁפָּחָה

1. ל + הַנַּעַר

2. כ + הַבַּיִת

3. ב + הַסֵּפֶר

4. ל + הָאִשָּׁה

The Preposition מִן

The preposition מִן has two forms. It can appear fully spelled as the word מִן, and it can also be contracted and attached to the following word in the form מָ·x — the mem with the dagesh in the following letter. The full spelling מִן is used only when followed by a definite noun. The contracted form מָ·x can be followed by both definite and indefinite nouns. You have already learned that definite nouns in Hebrew are words that have the definite article הַ·x added to them. In addition to this, person and place names are definite nouns. There are still other types of definite nouns in Hebrew, which you will learn in a later chapter.

Examples: **only** with definite nouns   from the house   מִן הַבַּיִת

                                                   from the man   מִן הָאִישׁ

                        both definite and indefinite nouns   from a house   מִבַּיִת

                                                      from Moab   מִמּוֹאָב

Variations

1. Before the throaty five — א ה ח ע ר — the contracted form מָ·x becomes מֵ·x.
    Examples: from a man מֵאִישׁ   from a city מֵעִיר   from Ruth מֵרוּת

2. Before the definite article hey הַ·x the contracted form מָ·x becomes מֵ·x. This form is used interchangeably with the full spelling מִן.
    Examples: from the house   מֵהַבַּיִת   or   מִן הַבַּיִת

                       from the man   מֵהָאִישׁ   or   מִן הָאִישׁ

How to Use a Prepositional Phrase

In Hebrew, prepositional phrases may be placed anywhere in the sentence.

Examples: Boaz went **with the lad.**   בֹּעַז הָלַךְ עִם הַנַּעַר.

            Boaz sent a pair of shoes **to Bethlehem.**   בֹּעַז שָׁלַח נַעֲלַיִם אֶל בֵּית לָחֶם.

            The man **in Jerusalem** wrote **like Abraham..** הָאִישׁ בִּירוּשָׁלַיִם כָּתַב כְּאַבְרָהָם.

When a prepositional phrase appears at the beginning of a sentence, it is generally followed by the verb.

Examples: Ruth wrote **about the women.**   רוּת כָּתְבָה עַל הַנָּשִׁים.

            Ruth wrote **about the women.**   עַל הַנָּשִׁים כָּתְבָה רוּת.

Note that the prepositional phrase עַל הַנָּשִׁים can be translated upon the women, or about (concerning) the women. The context will often help you determine the correct meaning.

Exercises

Exercise 1. Rewrite the sentences below, replacing the underlined word with each word in the list that follows, making the necessary changes in the rest of the sentence. Read the sentences aloud. Translate.

١. הָאִישׁ שָׁלַח נַעַר מִבֵּית לֶחֶם אֶל יְרוּשָׁלַיִם.

D. נָעֳמִי וּבֹעַז   C. אֲנָשִׁים   B. הַנָּשִׁים   A. הַמִּשְׁפָּחָה

G. אִשָּׁה   F. שָׂרָה   E. הֵן

٢. הַנַּעַר וְהַנַּעֲרָה הָלְכוּ לַבָּיִת.

D. רוּת   C. הֵמָּה   B. יַעֲקֹב וְדָוִד   A. אַבְרָהָם וְדָוִד

G. הִיא   F. הֵנָּה   E. הוּא

٣. רוּת כָּתְבָה עַל דָּוִד.

D. רוּת וְנָעֳמִי   C. הָאִישׁ   B. הַנְּעָרִים   A. הַמִּשְׁפָּחוֹת

G. יַעֲקֹב   F. הַנָּשִׁים   E. שָׂרָה וּבֹעַז

٤. הָאִישׁ הָלַךְ כְּאַבְרָהָם.

D. הִיא   C. הֵנָּה   B. הוּא   A. הַנְּעָרוֹת

G. יַעֲקֹב   F. הַנַּעַר וְהַנַּעֲרָה   E. הֵם

Exercise 2. Fill in the blanks in the sentences below with an appropriate preposition. There may be more than one correct answer for each sentence. Translate.

١. רוּת הָלְכָה _____ הַבָּיִת.

٢. הָאִישׁ _____ יְרוּשָׁלַיִם כָּתַב סֵפֶר.

٣. הַנְּעָרִים הָלְכוּ _____ הַנְּעָרוֹת אֶל הַדֶּרֶךְ.

٤. הַמִּשְׁפָּחוֹת _____ בֵּית לֶחֶם שָׁלְחוּ מִנְחוֹת.

٥. _____ אַבְרָהָם כָּתְבָה שָׂרָה.

٦. הָאֲנָשִׁים שָׁלְחוּ נָשִׁים _____ הַבָּיִת.

٧. דָּוִד וּבֹעַז זָכְרוּ נְעָרוֹת _____ הַדֶּרֶךְ.

Exercise 3. Add the inseparable prepositions בְּ, כְּ, and לְ to the following words. Pay attention to the vowels. Translate.

Example: הַנָּשִׁים

בַּנָּשִׁים   with the women
כַּנָּשִׁים   as, like the women
לַנָּשִׁים   to, for the women

٧. יְרוּשָׁלַיִם   ٥. הַנַּעֲלַיִם   ٣. הַסֵּפֶר   ١. מִשְׁפָּחוֹת

٨. הַבָּתִּים   ٦. אֲנָשִׁים   ٤. דְּרָכִים   ٢. מִנְחָה

Exercise 4. Translate the following sentences into English.

‏1a.‏ בֹּעַז כָּתַב סֵפֶר.

‏1b.‏ בֹּעַז כָּתַב לַנַּעֲרָה.

‏1c.‏ בֹּעַז כָּתַב לַנַּעֲרָה בִּירוּשָׁלַיִם.

‏1d.‏ בֹּעַז כָּתַב עַל הַמִּשְׁפָּחָה לַנַּעֲרָה בִּירוּשָׁלַיִם.

‏1e.‏ רוּת וּבֹעַז כָּתְבוּ עַל הַמִּשְׁפָּחָה לַנַּעֲרָה בִּירוּשָׁלַיִם.

‏2a.‏ שָׂרָה הָלְכָה אֶל הַדֶּרֶךְ.

‏2b.‏ שָׂרָה הָלְכָה מֵהַבַּיִת אֶל הַדֶּרֶךְ.

‏2c.‏ שָׂרָה וְיַעֲקֹב הָלְכוּ מֵהַבַּיִת אֶל הַדֶּרֶךְ.

‏2d.‏ שָׂרָה וְיַעֲקֹב הָלְכוּ עִם דָּוִד מֵהַבַּיִת אֶל הַדֶּרֶךְ.

Exercise 5. Translate the following sentences into Hebrew.

1.   The family in Bethlehem sent a gift.
2.   The family in Bethlehem sent a gift to the man in Jerusalem.
3.   The family in Bethlehem sent a gift from Ruth to the man in Jerusalem.
4.   The family in Bethlehem sent a lad with a gift from Ruth to the man in Jerusalem.
5.   The family in Bethlehem sent a lad with books as a gift to the man in Jerusalem.

Exercise 6. Add the correct vowels to the following sentences.

‏3.‏ הם שלחו נערה מן הבית.   ‏1.‏ דוד זכר דרך לירושלים.

‏4.‏ נעמי הלכה כאשה.   ‏2.‏ הנה כתבו לנשים בבית לחם.

Exercise 7. Underline the prepositional phrase or phrases in the sentences below.

‏1.‏ הַנְּעָרִים מִבֵּית לֶחֶם הָלְכוּ אֶל יְרוּשָׁלַיִם.

‏2.‏ רוּת הָלְכָה עִם בֹּעַז.

‏3.‏ שָׂרָה וְיַעֲקֹב שָׁלְחוּ סֵפֶר לְאַבְרָהָם.

‏4.‏ הַנָּשִׁים כָּתְבוּ כִּנְעָרוֹת עַל הַנְּעָרִים.

‏5.‏ הוּא הָלַךְ מִמּוֹאָב אֶל יְהוּדָה.

‏6.‏ אַבְרָהָם וּבֹעַז זָכְרוּ אִשָּׁה בִּירוּשָׁלַיִם.

Chapter 8
Subject Pronouns
Perfect Tense of the Pa'al פָּעַל Pattern

Vocabulary

we common	אֲנַֿחְנוּ, אָֿנוּ
I common	אֲנִי, אָנֹכִי
you f, sg	אַתְּ
you m, sg	אַתָּה
you m, pl	אַתֶּם
you f, pl	אַתֶּן

Place Names

Israel — both a place and a people	יִשְׂרָאֵל
Moab	מוֹאָב

Note 1: New abbreviations — *sg* singular, *pl* plural

Note 2: The pronoun אָֿנוּ appears only in post-Biblical Hebrew.

Subject Pronouns

Pronouns which are used to replace a noun as the subject of a sentence are called subject pronouns.

Examples:	1.	Boaz wrote.	בֹּעַז כָּתַב.
		He wrote.	הוּא כָּתַב.
	2.	The young woman remembered.	הַנַּעֲרָה זָכְרָה.
		She remembered.	הִיא זָכְרָה.

The masculine singular pronoun הוּא, he, replaces the masculine singular noun בֹּעַז as the subject of the first sentence. The feminine singular pronoun הִיא, she, replaces the feminine singular noun הַנַּעֲרָה as the subject of the second sentence.

Subject Pronoun Chart

Singular

I common	אֲנִי, אָנֹכִי	1st person
you *m, sg*	אַתָּה	2nd person
you *f, sg*	אַתְּ	2nd person
he *m, sg*	הוּא	3rd person
she *f, sg*	הִיא	3rd person

Plural

we common	אֲנַֿחְנוּ, אָֿנוּ	1st person
you *m, pl*	אַתֶּם	2nd person
you *f, pl*	אַתֶּן	2nd person
they *m, pl*	הֵם, הֵֿמָּה	3rd person
they *f, pl*	הֵן, הֵֿנָּה	3rd person

Notes on the Subject Pronouns

1. In Hebrew, subject pronouns are used only as the subject of a sentence.

2. There is no pronoun **it** in Hebrew. All pronouns are either masculine or feminine, depending upon the gender of the noun that they replace in the sentence.

3. Some pronouns have two forms which may be used interchangeably.

| they *m, pl* | הֵם, הֵֿמָּה | | I common | אֲנִי, אָנֹכִי |
| they *f, pl* | הֵן, הֵֿנָּה | | we *common* | אֲנַֿחְנוּ, אָֿנוּ |

4. The first person singular pronouns are the same for both masculine and feminine: I — אֲנִי, אָנֹכִי. The pronouns for the first person plural are also the same for both masculine and feminine: we — אָֿנוּ, אֲנַֿחְנוּ. The term "common" is used to refer to pronouns which are the same for both masculine and feminine. We will refer to the common pronouns with the following abbreviations: *1 c sg* — first person, common, singular and *1 c pl* — first person, common, plural.

5. The second and third person pronouns in the singular and plural have distinct forms for the masculine and feminine. We will refer to them with the following abbreviations: *2 m sg, 2 f sg, 3 m sg, 3 f sg, 2 m pl, 2 f pl, 3 m pl, 3 f pl.*

Roots

Most words in Hebrew come from what is called a root. A root is a combination of letters — usually three — which expresses a general idea. Words — nouns, adjectives, verbs, etc. — can be built upon the basic root structure. For example, the English word **part,** meaning **a portion of the whole,** is a root word. From the word **part,** we build the following words: partition, particle, parts, participate, parting, partial, partly, partisan, partake, partner. As you can see, each of these words maintains the basic idea of **part** or **portion of the whole.** It is often difficult to identify the roots of words in English.

In Hebrew, roots are the unit **central** to the construction of the whole language. Hebrew roots follow two general rules.

1. No matter how a word is formed, the root letters normally remain.
2. A word which derives from the root usually carries the basic meaning of that root.

An example of building from the root is found in the word Amen, an English word that comes from the Hebrew word אָמֵן. Amen is used as an expression of assent and, in English, means "so be it" or "so it shall be". The Hebrew root is א.מ.ן, which means confirm or support. From that root, the following words are formed.

faithful	נֶאֱמָן	believed	הֶאֱמִין
foster mother	אֹמֶנֶת	so it shall be	אָמֵן
pillars	אֲמֹנוֹת	faith	אֱמוּנָה
		truly	אָמְנָם

Notice the starred (*) letters in each word. As you can see, they are the root letters א.מ.ן .

Verb Roots

Every verb in Hebrew has a root, generally composed of three letters. In chapters 4 and 5 we introduced the following verbs.

(he) walked — הָלַךְ	(he) remembered — זָכַר
(he) wrote — כָּתַב	(he) sent — שָׁלַח

The three consonants which combine to make each of these verbs are the root letters for that verb. In this book we will always write the root of a verb with dots between the consonants and without vowels.

כ.ת.ב is the root for write   ה.ל.ך is the root for walk

ש.ל.ח is the root for send   ז.כ.ר is the root for remember

39

The Perfect Tense of the Pa'al פָּעַל Verb Pattern

Conjugating a verb means altering its basic form in order to indicate tense, person, and number. In Hebrew verbs are conjugated by altering the root with the addition of prefixes and suffixes and/or by changing the vowels. A **prefix** is one or more letters added to the beginning of a root. A **suffix** is one or more letters added to the end of a root.

In this chapter you will learn the conjugation in the perfect tense of the Pa'al פָּעַל verb pattern. The Pa'al פָּעַל verb pattern is one of seven Hebrew verb patterns. In the perfect tense of the Pa'al פָּעַל pattern, verb roots are conjugated by adding suffixes to the basic form. The perfect tense is the verb tense that describes actions that have been completed and/or have happened in the past. In the following chart you will find the regular verb כ.ת.ב, (write), conjugated in the perfect tense of the Pa'al פָּעַל pattern. Read this chart aloud. Memorize it.

English	Verb	Pronoun	
I wrote	כָּתַבְתִּי	אֲנִי, אָנֹכִי	1 c sg
you wrote	כָּתַבְתָּ	אַתָּה	2 m sg
you wrote	כָּתַבְתְּ	אַתְּ	2 f sg
he wrote	כָּתַב	הוּא	3 m sg
she wrote	כָּתְבָה	הִיא	3 f sg
we wrote	כָּתַבְנוּ	אֲנַחְנוּ, אָנוּ	1 c pl
you wrote	כְּתַבְתֶּם	אַתֶּם	2 m pl
you wrote	כְּתַבְתֶּן	אַתֶּן	2 f pl
they wrote	כָּתְבוּ	הֵם, הֵמָּה	3 m pl
they wrote	כָּתְבוּ	הֵן, הֵנָּה	3 f pl

Notes on the Conjugation

1. The verbs שׁ.ל.ח and ז.כ.ר are conjugated in the perfect tense exactly like the verb כ.ת.ב. The verb ה.ל.ך is conjugated like כ.ת.ב in all forms except the second person plural. The vowel pattern of the second person plural of ה.ל.ך is different: הֲלַכְתֶּן and הֲלַכְתֶּם.

2. In the perfect tense in Hebrew it is not necessary, except for emphasis, to use the subject pronouns for the first and second person singular and plural. The suffixes of these verbs include the subject pronoun. The single word כָּתַבְתִּי stands alone as the complete sentence "I wrote."

3. The accent falls on the next to last syllable in the first and second person singular and in the first person plural. Remember, unless otherwise stated, the accent in Hebrew is on the last syllable.

4. The verb form is the same for masculine and feminine in the third person plural.

Exercises

Exercise 1. Conjugate ש.ל.ח and ז.כ.ר in the perfect tense of the Pa'al פָּעַל verb pattern.

Exercise 2. Rewrite the sentences below, replacing the underlined word with each word in the list that follows, and making the necessary changes in the rest of the sentence. Read the sentences aloud. Translate.

1. אֲנִי הָלַכְתִּי אֶל הַבַּיִת.

A. אַתָּה   B. אַתְּ   C. הוּא   D. הִיא   E. אֲנַחְנוּ
F. אַתֶּם   G. אַתֶּן   H. הֵם   I. הֵנָּה

2. הוּא שָׁלַח נַעֲלַיִם אֶל הַנָּשִׁים.

A. הֵם   B. אַתְּ   C. אָנוּ   D. אַתֶּן   E. הִיא
F. אַתָּה   G. הֵנָּה   H. אֲנִי   I. הֵמָּה   J. אָנֹכִי

3. אַתְּ זָכַרְתְּ אִישׁ מִבֵּית לָחֶם.

A. אַתֶּם   B. אָנוּ   C. הוּא   D. הֵם   E. אַתָּה
F. הֵן   G. אֲנִי   H. אַתֶּן

Exercise 3a. Rewrite the following sentences, changing the subjects and verbs from the singular to the plural.

1. הָלַכְתִּי מִן הַדֶּרֶךְ אֶל הַבַּיִת.
2. הִיא שָׁלְחָה נַעַר אֶל בֹּעַז.
3. אַתָּה כָּתַבְתָּ סֵפֶר עַל מוֹאָב.
4. הוּא זָכַר נַעֲרָה.
5. כָּתַבְתְּ אֶל הַנָּשִׁים וְאֶל הָאֲנָשִׁים מִבֵּית לָחֶם.
6. הוּא שָׁלַח סְפָרִים לְרוּת.

Exercise 3b. Rewrite the following sentences, changing the subjects and verbs from the plural to the singular.

1. כְּתַבְתֶּן עַל בֹּעַז וְעַל נָעֳמִי.
2. הֵנָּה שָׁלְחוּ נַעֲלַיִם אֶל הַנַּעַר מִן מוֹאָב.
3. זְכַרְתֶּם דֶּרֶךְ אֶל הַבַּיִת.
4. הָלַכְנוּ עִם הָאֲנָשִׁים מִירוּשָׁלַיִם.
5. הֵמָּה כָּתְבוּ אֶל הַנָּשִׁים עַל בֵּית לָחֶם.
6. זָכְרוּ אִישׁ כְּבֹעַז.

Exercise 4. In the following sentences, fill in the blanks with the correct form of the verb root given.

1. ה.ל.ך   אֲנִי   _____ עִם הָאִישׁ אֶל מוֹאָב.

2. ש.ל.ח   שָׂרָה   _____ מִנְחָה אֶל הַנָּשִׁים מִן יְהוּדָה.

3. ז.כ.ר   אַתֶּם   _____ מִשְׁפָּחוֹת עִם נְעָרוֹת.

4. כ.ת.ב   הִיא   _____ עַל הַדֶּרֶךְ מִירוּשָׁלַיִם.

5. ה.ל.ך   אֲנַחְנוּ   _____ עִם הָאֲנָשִׁים אֶל הַבַּיִת.

6. ש.ל.ח   הֵנָּה   _____ נַעֲלַיִם אֶל רוּת וְנָעֳמִי.

7. ז.כ.ר   הוּא   _____ דֶּרֶךְ אֶל הַבַּיִת.

8. כ.ת.ב   אַתְּ   _____ עַל הַסְּפָרִים מִן יְהוּדָה.

9. ה.ל.ך   הֵם   _____ אֶל בֵּית לֶחֶם עִם נַעַר וְעִם נַעֲרָה.

10. ש.ל.ח   אַתֵּן   _____ מִנְחוֹת אֶל הַמִּשְׁפָּחָה.

Exercise 5. Combine the two parts of each sentence below into one simple sentence. Use the appropriate pronoun. Make all other necessary changes. When combining a masculine and feminine pronoun, the masculine plural form is used.

Example: הוּא כָּתַב סֵפֶר וְהִיא כָּתְבָה סֵפֶר.

הֵם כָּתְבוּ סֵפֶר.

1. אָנֹכִי שָׁלַחְתִּי נַעֲלַיִם וְאַתָּה שָׁלַחְתָּ נַעֲלַיִם.

2. אַתָּה זָכַרְתָּ אִישׁ וְהוּא זָכַר אִישׁ.

3. אַתְּ כָּתַבְתְּ אֶל דָּוִד וְהִיא כָּתְבָה אֶל דָּוִד.

4. הִיא הָלְכָה אֶל הַבַּיִת וְנָעֳמִי הָלְכָה אֶל הַבַּיִת.

5. אַבְרָהָם שָׁלַח מִנְחָה וְיַעֲקֹב שָׁלַח מִנְחָה.

6. הוּא זָכַר נְעָרִים מִמּוֹאָב וְהִיא זָכְרָה נְעָרִים מִמּוֹאָב.

Exercise 6. Translate the following sentences into Hebrew.

1. We sent a pair of shoes from Moab.
2. You *f, sg* sent books to a family.
3. I remembered a man and a woman.
4. You *m, pl* wrote to a woman about the gift.
5. They went with Sarah and Jacob to Jerusalem.

Exercise 7. Add the vowels and then translate.

3. היא הלכה אל הבית.   1. הם כתבו על האיש.

4. שלחת מנחה עם אברהם.   2. אתם זכרתם ספרים.

Chapter 9
The Definite Direct Object Marker אֵת/אֶת
The Negative Sentence

Vocabulary

land *n, f* . . . . *pl* אֲרָצוֹת , *sg* אֶרֶץ
son *n, m* . . . . *pl* בָּנִים , *sg* בֵּן
daughter *n, f* . . . . *pl* בָּנוֹת , *sg* בַּת
thing, word *n, m* . . . . *pl* דְּבָרִים , *sg* דָּבָר
day *n, m* . . . . *dual* יוֹמַיִם , *pl* יָמִים , *sg* יוֹם
not . . . . לֹא
city *n, f* . . . . *pl* עָרִים , *sg* עִיר
field *n, m* . . . . *pl* שָׂדוֹת , *sg* שָׂדֶה
judge *n, m* . . . . *pl* שׁוֹפְטִים, שֹׁפְטִים , *sg* שׁוֹפֵט, שֹׁפֵט

Idiom

today . . . . הַיּוֹם

Note 1: When the definite article הָ is added to אֶרֶץ , it becomes
הָאָרֶץ .

Note 2: In Biblical Hebrew, spelling is not always fixed. Notice in the
above vocabulary that the Hebrew word for judge is spelled two
ways. **Both** forms are correct.

The Direct Object

You have already learned the simple sentence, consisting of a subject and a verb, such as
Boaz remembered or **Boaz sent**. However, most sentences are not this simple. A more
complex sentence can be formed by indicating **what** or **whom** Boaz sent, such as:

Boaz sent a book.   בֹּעַז שָׁלַח סֵפֶר.

Boaz sent young women.   בֹּעַז שָׁלַח נְעָרוֹת.

The **direct object** is the noun or pronoun which indicates the thing or person to which the
verb is directed. In the examples above, **book** and **young women** are direct objects of the
verb **sent**. They complete the meaning of the sentences by answering the question **what** or
whom the subject, Boaz, sent.

The Indefinite Direct Object

In the preceding examples, the direct objects סֵפֶר and נְעָרוֹת are indefinite nouns; they refer to books and young women generally. When a direct object is an indefinite noun, it is called an indefinite direct object.

The Definite Direct Object

When a direct object refers to a specific noun (**the** book, **the** young woman), it is called a definite direct object. In Hebrew the definite direct object **must** be preceded by the word אֵת. There are two ways to spell this word: אֶת and אֵת. The word אֵת has no meaning in English: rather, it **signals** the definite direct object of the sentence. Every time אֵת appears in a sentence, it is followed by the definite direct object of the verb. Since word order is not fixed in Biblical Hebrew, the marker word אֵת helps to determine the meaning of a sentence.

Examples:

Boaz sent the book.	בֹּעַז שָׁלַח אֶת הַסֵּפֶר.
Boaz sent the young man.	בֹּעַז שָׁלַח אֶת הַנַּעַר.
Boaz sent the young man.	אֶת הַנַּעַר שָׁלַח בֹּעַז.

Notes on the Definite Direct Object

1. Names of people and places — proper nouns — are considered to be definite. Therefore, when a name is the direct object, it is preceded by אֵת.
    Example: Ruth sent Naomi.   רוּת שָׁלְחָה אֶת נָעֳמִי.

2. If there is more than one definite direct object in a sentence, אֵת precedes each one.
    Example: בֹּעַז זָכַר אֶת הָאִישׁ וְאֶת הַבֵּן וְאֶת הַבַּת.
    Boaz remembered the man, the son and the daughter.

3. In Biblical Hebrew, the direct object does not always follow the verb. The direct object may be placed elsewhere in the sentence.

Subject	Verb	Object

Example: Boaz remembered the young man.   בֹּעַז.   זָכַר   אֶת הַנַּעַר

No matter where the definite direct object appears in the Hebrew sentence, it is preceded by the direct object marker אֵת.

Verbs That Cannot Take Direct Objects

Some verbs **cannot** take a direct object. In both English and Hebrew an example of a verb which cannot take a direct object is the verb **went** — ה.ל.ך. We cannot say **Boaz went the judges** — בֹּעַז הָלַךְ אֶת הַשּׁוֹפְטִים. However, we can use a prepositional phrase and say **Boaz went with the judges** — בֹּעַז הָלַךְ עִם הַשּׁוֹפְטִים. When the verb of a sentence cannot take a direct object, the word אֵת will not appear.

44

Object of a Preposition

A definite or indefinite noun which follows a preposition is called the object of the preposition.

Example: Ruth walked with the lad.   רוּת הָלְכָה עִם הַנַּעַר.

In the example above, the noun הַנַּעַר is the object of the preposition עִם. The object of a preposition should never be confused with the direct object of a verb. The direct object marker אֶת appears before the definite direct object of a verb; however, it **never** appears before the object of a preposition.

Examples:

1. **Object of a Preposition**

   Indefinite noun: Ruth walked with **a lad**.   רוּת הָלְכָה עִם נַעַר.

   Abraham wrote to **a woman**.   אַבְרָהָם כָּתַב לְאִשָּׁה.

   Definite noun: Ruth walked with **the lad**.   רוּת הָלְכָה עִם הַנַּעַר.

   Abraham wrote to **the woman**.   אַבְרָהָם כָּתַב לָאִשָּׁה.

2. **Direct object of a verb**

   Indefinite noun: Boaz sent **a family** to the city.   בֹּעַז שָׁלַח מִשְׁפָּחָה אֶל הָעִיר.

   Definite noun: Boaz sent **the family** to the city.   בֹּעַז שָׁלַח אֶת הַמִּשְׁפָּחָה אֶל הָעִיר.

How to Make a Statement Negative in Hebrew

Statements are usually made negative in Hebrew by using the word לֹא — not.

1. When the word לֹא is placed before the verb, it makes the action of the sentence negative.

   Positive — Ruth sent the shoes.   רוּת שָׁלְחָה אֶת הַנְּעָלִים.

   Negative — Ruth did not send the shoes.   רוּת לֹא שָׁלְחָה אֶת הַנְּעָלִים.

2. When the word לֹא is placed before the subject, it makes the subject of the sentence negative.

   Positive — Jacob wrote to Boaz.   יַעֲקֹב כָּתַב לְבֹעַז.

   Negative — (It was) not Jacob (who) wrote to Boaz.   לֹא יַעֲקֹב כָּתַב לְבֹעַז.

3. When the word לֹא is placed before a prepositional phrase, it makes the prepositional phrase negative.

   Positive — Jacob went to the city.   יַעֲקֹב הָלַךְ אֶל הָעִיר.

   Negative — (It was) not to the city (that) Jacob went.   לֹא אֶל הָעִיר הָלַךְ יַעֲקֹב.

4. When the word לֹא is placed before the direct object, it makes the direct object negative.

   Positive — Ruth sent the shoe.   רוּת שָׁלְחָה אֶת הַנַּעַל.

   Negative — (It was) not the shoe (that) Ruth sent.   לֹא אֶת הַנַּעַל שָׁלְחָה רוּת.

Exercises

Exercise 1. Rewrite the sentences below, replacing the underlined word with each word in the list that follows, and making the necessary changes in the rest of the sentence. Read the sentences aloud. Translate.

1. בֹּעַז שָׁלַח אֶת הַנְּעָרוֹת אֶל מוֹאָב.

   E. בַּת   D. הַנְּעָרִים   C. רוּת   B. נְעָלִים   A. הַסֵּפֶר

                I. דָּבָר   H. אֲנָשִׁים   G. הַבָּנִים   F. נָעֳמִי

2. הִיא הָלְכָה אֶל הַבַּיִת.

   E. יְהוּדָה   D. הַדֶּרֶךְ   C. בֵּית לֶחֶם   B. הַבֵּן   A. עִיר

                H. הַשָּׂדֶה   G. הַבָּנוֹת   F. נַעַר

3. הַבַּת זָכְרָה אֶת הַדְּבָרִים בָּאָרֶץ.

   E. הֵנָּה   D. הֵם   C. אַתָּה   B. אֲנִי   A. הַנַּעַר

                I. אַתֶּן   H. אֲנַחְנוּ   G. אַתְּ   F. אַתֶּם

4. הוּא כָּתַב אֶת הַסֵּפֶר וְלֹא שָׁלַח אֶת הַסֵּפֶר לְרוּת.

   E. אַתָּה   D. אֲנַחְנוּ   C. הִיא   B. אַתֶּן   A. אֲנִי

                I. הֵמָּה   H. אַתְּ   G. הֵן   F. אַתֶּם

Exercise 2. Rewrite the sentences below, making the direct object definite and adding אֵת/אֶת.

5. הוּא זָכַר שׁוֹפֵט מִן הָאָרֶץ.   1. הִיא כָּתְבָה סְפָרִים.

6. זְכַרְתֶּם אִשָּׁה מִן הַבַּיִת.   2. הָאִישׁ שָׁלַח נַעֲרָה אֶל בֵּית לֶחֶם.

7. הַיּוֹם זָכַרְתִּי שָׂדוֹת בְּמוֹאָב.   3. רוּת וְאַבְרָהָם זָכְרוּ דֶּרֶךְ.

                                               4. שָׁלַחְתְּ נַעֲלִים לְרוּת.

Exercise 3. Fill in the blanks in the following sentences with the word אֵת when it is necessary. Translate.

1. בֹּעַז שָׁלַח _____ נַעַר אֶל הַשָּׂדֶה.

2. רוּת כָּתְבָה _____ סֵפֶר עַל יְהוּדָה.

3. הָאִישׁ שָׁלַח _____ הַמִּשְׁפָּחָה אֶל מוֹאָב.

4. הַבֵּן זָכַר _____ דֶּרֶךְ וְעִיר.

5. נָעֳמִי שָׁלְחָה _____ הַנַּעַר וְ _____ הַנַּעֲרָה.

Exercise 4. Translate into Hebrew.

1a. Ruth walked to a city.

1b. Ruth walked to the city.

1c. Ruth walked in a city.

1d. Ruth walked in the city.

1e. Ruth did not walk in the city.

1f. (It was) not Ruth (who) walked in the city.

1g. (It was) not in the city (that) Ruth walked.

2a. Boaz wrote a book about houses.

2b. Boaz wrote the book about houses.

2c. Boaz did not write the book about houses.

2d. (It was) not Boaz (who) wrote the book about houses.

2e. (It was) not about houses (that) Boaz wrote.

Exercise 5. Unscramble and translate the following sentences.

4. אֶל יַעֲקֹב הָלַךְ הָעִיר   1. מִן רוּת הָלְכוּ הָעִיר וְנָעֳמִי

5. בֵּית לֶחֶם זָכְרָה אֶת הִיא   2. כָּתְבָה לַבָּנִים רוּת וְלַבָּנוֹת

3. זָכַר הַדָּבָר הָאִישׁ אֶת

Exercise 6. Turn the sentences in Exercise 5 into negative statements.

Exercise 7. Translate the following sentences.

1. הַבֵּן זָכַר אֶת הָאִשָּׁה וְאֶת הַנַּעַר הַיּוֹם.

2. הוּא שָׁלַח נַעֲלַיִם וְסֵפֶר אֶל הַנְּעָרוֹת.

3. הֵנָּה לֹא הָלְכוּ עִם נָעֳמִי וְרוּת מִן הַבַּיִת אֶל הַדֶּרֶךְ הַיּוֹם.

4. אֶת הַדְּבָרִים כָּתַב הַשֹּׁפֵט וְלֹא דָוִד.

5. זָכְרָה הָאִשָּׁה אֶת הַיָּמִים בִּירוּשָׁלַיִם.

Exercise 8. Using the above sentences, identify: a. the definite direct object b. the indefinite direct object c. the object of the preposition.

Exercise 9. Read and translate. Notice the conjugated verbs used without subject pronouns.
זָכַרְנוּ אֶת הַיָּמִים בְּבֵית לֶחֶם. זָכַרְתִּי אֶת הָעִיר וְאֶת הַשָּׂדוֹת. זָכַרְתְּ אֶת הָאֲנָשִׁים וְאֶת הַמִּשְׁפָּחוֹת. אַבְרָהָם וּבֹעַז לֹא זָכְרוּ אֶת הָעִיר וְלֹא זָכְרוּ אֶת הָאֲנָשִׁים; הֵם זָכְרוּ אֶת הַנְּעָרוֹת.

God's Name

The Bible and the prayerbook use more than one name to refer to God. The most sacred is יְהֹוָה – יהוה — the personal name of the God of the people of Israel. Because of the particular sacredness of this name, it is **never** pronounced.

Other names used to refer to God are אֵל, אֱלֹהִים, אֲדֹנָי. The names אֵל and אֱלֹהִים may refer to pagan gods as well as the God of Israel. When אֱלֹהִים refers to the God of Israel it is always singular in concept, even though it has a masculine plural ending.

Another form of God's most sacred name, יְהֹוָה, is יְיָ. Like the name יְהֹוָה, it is never pronounced. Whenever the names יְהֹוָה and יְיָ appear in the Bible or prayerbook, they should be pronounced אֲדֹנָי — **Adonai**. The name אֲדֹנָי derives from the Hebrew word for **lord** — אָדוֹן — and is used in this form specifically to refer to God.

From this chapter on we will introduce a prayer or a part of a prayer in every chapter. We will use God's name **only** when quoting a prayer or when quoting from the Bible. When we quote a passage which includes God's name, we will write it as it appears in the original. Always remember, however, to pronounce God's name אֲדֹנָי — **Adonai** — when it is written either יהוה— יְהֹוָה — or יְיָ .

From the Prayerbook

Prayerbook Vocabulary

Bless!. . . . . בָּרְכוּ   the one who is blessed. . . . . הַמְבֹרָךְ
both forms come from the root ב.ר.ך

Selection from the Prayerbook

Person called to the Torah recites: בָּרְכוּ אֶת יְיָ הַמְבֹרָךְ.

First try to translate the prayer in your own words, then read the translations quoted below.

Prayerbook Translations

"Bless the Lord who is blessed."

Daily Prayer Book, Philip Birnbaum, 1977, p. 124

"Praise the Lord, to whom our praise is due!"

Gates of Prayer, the New Union Prayerbook, 1975, p. 438

Notice the use of the direct object marker אֶת which indicates that יְיָ is the definite direct object of the verb בָּרְכוּ.

Chapter 10
The Verb "be" in the Perfect Tense

Vocabulary

eat *vb*	א.כ.ל
food *n, m*	אֹכֶל
say *vb*	א.מ.ר
that, who, which	אֲשֶׁר
be *vb*.	ה.י.ה
because, that	כִּי
bread *n, m*	לֶחֶם
famine *n, m*	רָעָב
there, in that place	שָׁם
guard, keep *vb*.	ש.מ.ר

Note 1: The words אֹכֶל, לֶחֶם, רָעָב are used only in the singular.

How to Use the Verb ה.י.ה

The Hebrew verb ה.י.ה is different from all other verbs introduced in this book.

1. The verb ה.י.ה describes a state of being rather than an action.

    Examples: Boaz walked in the city.   בֹּעַז הָלַךְ בָּעִיר.
                    (action)

                    Boaz was in the city.   בֹּעַז הָיָה בָּעִיר.
                    (state of being)

2. The verb ה.י.ה cannot take a direct object.

    Examples: A. Boaz sent the man.   בֹּעַז שָׁלַח אֶת הָאִישׁ.
                    B. Boaz was the man.   בֹּעַז הָיָה הָאִישׁ.

In Example A, **the man** — הָאִישׁ — is the direct object of the verb **sent** — שָׁלַח — and therefore is preceded by the direct object marker אֶת. In Example B, **the man** is a description of the subject, Boaz, rather than the direct object. Therefore, the direct object marker אֶת is not used.

The Verb ה.י.ה in the Perfect Tense

The conjugation of the verb ה.י.ה **be** in the perfect tense of the Pa'al פָּעַל pattern is irregular. The conjugation of this root varies from the regular pattern of the פָּעַל perfect because the first and third root letters are ה, one of the throaty five letters. It is therefore necessary to memorize this irregular verb separately.

Below is a chart comparing the conjugations of the irregular verb ה.י.ה and the regular verb כ.ת.ב in the perfect tense of the פָּעַל pattern.

English	be ה.י.ה	write כ.ת.ב	
I was	הָיִיתִי	כָּתַבְתִּי	1 c sg
you were	הָיִיתָ	כָּתַבְתָּ	2 m sg
you were	הָיִית	כָּתַבְתְּ	2 f sg
he was	הָיָה	כָּתַב	3 m sg
she was	הָיְתָה	כָּתְבָה	3 f sg
we were	הָיִינוּ	כָּתַבְנוּ	1 c pl
you were	הֱיִיתֶם	כְּתַבְתֶּם	2 m pl
you were	הֱיִיתֶן	כְּתַבְתֶּן	2 f pl
they were	הָיוּ	כָּתְבוּ	3 m pl
they were	הָיוּ	כָּתְבוּ	3 f pl

Notes on the Conjugation

1. The third root letter ה drops out of the conjugation in the perfect tense except in the third person masculine singular.
2. The second root letter י takes the ee אִ vowel in the first and second person. This explains the existence of two yods.
3. A tav ת is added to the conjugation of the third person feminine singular — הָיְתָה.
4. The first root letter ה in the second person plural masculine and feminine takes the combination vowel אֱ — הֱיִיתֶם — הֱיִיתֶן.

The Difference Between כִּי and אֲשֶׁר

The words כִּי and אֲשֶׁר, which appear in the vocabulary of this chapter, both can be translated as the English word **that**. However, these words do not mean the same thing and **cannot** be used interchangeably.

The Use of כִּי

The word כִּי can be translated as **that** or **because**, depending on the context. No matter which meaning it has, it is always used to join together two separate ideas into a single sentence. It could be omitted from the sentence, and two separate complete sentences would remain.

Examples:
The man remembered that Naomi went to Bethlehem.   הָאִישׁ זָכַר כִּי נָעֳמִי הָלְכָה לְבֵית לָחֶם.

1. The man remembered.   הָאִישׁ זָכַר.
2. Naomi went to Bethlehem.   נָעֳמִי הָלְכָה לְבֵית לָחֶם.

The man wrote to Ruth because she was in Jerusalem.   הָאִישׁ כָּתַב לְרוּת כִּי הִיא הָיְתָה בִּירוּשָׁלַיִם.

1. The man wrote to Ruth.   הָאִישׁ כָּתַב לְרוּת.
2. She was in Jerusalem.   הִיא הָיְתָה בִּירוּשָׁלַיִם.

The Use of אֲשֶׁר

The word אֲשֶׁר can be translated as **that** or **who** or **which**. It is used to join together two related ideas by combining them into one sentence. It replaces a noun in one of the sentences.

Example:
1. The men ate the food.   הָאֲנָשִׁים אָכְלוּ אֶת הָאֹכֶל.
2. The men went.   הָאֲנָשִׁים הָלְכוּ.

The men, who ate the food, went. (that)   הָאֲנָשִׁים אֲשֶׁר אָכְלוּ אֶת הָאֹכֶל הָלְכוּ.

In the above example, when the two sentences are combined, the word **who** — אֲשֶׁר — replaces **the men** — הָאֲנָשִׁים — in one of the sentences. Therefore, unlike the word כִּי, the word אֲשֶׁר cannot be omitted from the sentence and leave two separate, complete sentences.

Guided Reading

Guided reading is a device to lead you step by step to understand and practice material that has been introduced. As you will see, it is self-correcting so that you can learn and absorb at your own speed. The following guided reading will show you action verbs with and without direct objects, the uses of the verb ה.י.ה, and the difference between כִּי and אֲשֶׁר.

How to Use the Guided Reading

With a plain piece of paper, cover the entire page beneath these instructions. Slide the paper down, exposing Hebrew Box 1 in the right hand column. Read and translate the Hebrew in Hebrew Box 1. Expose the next line of boxes and check your translation by looking at the English in English Box 1 in the left hand column. Then read the Hebrew sentence in Hebrew Box 2 in the right hand column and continue.

English Boxes	**Hebrew Boxes**
	Box 1. אַבְרָהָם כָּתַב אֶת הַסֵּפֶר.
Box 1. Abraham wrote the book. *action verb with direct object*	Box 2. אַבְרָהָם כָּתַב עַל הַסֵּפֶר.
Box 2. Abraham wrote on the book. *action verb without direct object*	Box 3. אַבְרָהָם הָיָה הָאִישׁ עִם הַסֵּפֶר.
Box 3. Abraham was the man with the book. *verb describing state of being*	Box 4. זָכַרְתִּי כִּי הָיִיתָ בַּשָּׂדֶה עִם בֹּעַז.
Box 4. I remembered that you were in the field with Boaz. *use of* כִּי	Box 5. הֵם הָיוּ הָאֲנָשִׁים אֲשֶׁר הָלְכוּ אֶל בֵּית לָחֶם.
Box 5. They were the people who went to Bethlehem. *use of* אֲשֶׁר	

"There was" and "there were" in Hebrew

The third person of the verb ה.י.ה in the perfect tense, הָיָה, הָיְתָה, הָיוּ, is also used to mean **there was** or **there were**. Notice that ה.י.ה agrees in gender and number with the subject.

Examples:	**There was** a famine in the land.	הָיָה רָעָב בָּאָרֶץ.
	There was a woman in the house.	הָיְתָה אִשָּׁה בַּבַּיִת.
	There were men in the field.	הָיוּ אֲנָשִׁים בַּשָּׂדֶה.

The negative **there was not** or **there were no** is expressed by adding לֹא before the verb.

Examples:	**There was not** famine in the land.	לֹא הָיָה רָעָב בָּאָרֶץ.
	There were no women in the house.	לֹא הָיוּ נָשִׁים בַּבַּיִת.

The Verbs ה.ל.ך, א.כ.ל, א.מ.ר

The first root letters of the verb roots ה.ל.ך, א.כ.ל, א.מ.ר are א and ה, two of the throaty five letters. These verbs are conjugated in the perfect tense exactly like the verbs you learned in the previous chapter, except for the second person plural. Since the א and the ה cannot take a sheva ְ , the sheva ְ is changed to a combination vowel: ֲ .

א and ה as First Root Letter		Regular	
א.מ.ר	ה.ל.ך	כ.ת.ב	
אָמַרְתִּי	הָלַכְתִּי	כָּתַבְתִּי	1 c sg
אָמַרְתָּ	הָלַכְתָּ	כָּתַבְתָּ	2 m sg
אָמַרְתְּ	הָלַכְתְּ	כָּתַבְתְּ	2 f sg
אָמַר	הָלַךְ	כָּתַב	3 m sg
אָמְרָה	הָלְכָה	כָּתְבָה	3 f sg
אָמַרְנוּ	הָלַכְנוּ	כָּתַבְנוּ	1 c pl
•אֲמַרְתֶּם	•הֲלַכְתֶּם	כְּתַבְתֶּם	2 m pl
•אֲמַרְתֶּן	•הֲלַכְתֶּן	כְּתַבְתֶּן	2 f pl
אָמְרוּ	הָלְכוּ	כָּתְבוּ	3 m pl, 3 f pl

Exercises

Exercise 1. Conjugate the following verbs in the perfect tense of the פָּעַל Pa'al pattern.

‏1. א.כ.ל‎   ‏2. א.מ.ר‎   ‏3. ש.מ.ר‎

Exercise 2. Rewrite the sentences below, replacing the underlined word with each word in the list that follows, and making the necessary changes in the rest of the sentence. Read the sentences aloud. Translate.

‏1. הָאִישׁ הָיָה עִם הַשֹּׁפֵט.‎

E. אָנוּ	D. בֹּעַז וְנָעֳמִי	C. אַתָּה	B. רוּת	A. אֲנִי
J. הַבֵּן	I. אַתֶּם	H. אַתְּ	G. אַתֵּן	F. הַנְּעָרִים

‏2. הַשֹּׁפֵט שָׁמַר אֶת הָאֹכֶל כִּי הָיָה רָעָב בָּעִיר.‎

E. הָאֲנָשִׁים	D. הִיא	C. הֵנָּה	B. אַתָּה	A. אָנוּ
		H. אַתֶּם	G. אָנֹכִי	F. אַתֵּן

‏3. הַנָּשִׁים אָמְרוּ: "הַמִּנְחָה הָיְתָה בַּבַּיִת."‎

E. הוּא	D. הֵנָּה	C. אֲנַחְנוּ	B. רוּת	A. אַתָּה
		H. אַתְּ	G. אָנֹכִי	F. הֵם

‏4. הַמִּשְׁפָּחָה אֲשֶׁר הָיְתָה מִמּוֹאָב אָכְלָה אֶת הַלֶּחֶם הַיּוֹם.‎

E. אֲנַחְנוּ	D. אַתְּ	C. אַתֵּן	B. אֲנִי	A. אַבְרָהָם
		H. הַבָּנוֹת	G. אַתָּה	F. הֵמָּה

Exercise 3. Identify the person, gender, and number of the following verb forms. Write the appropriate subject pronoun.

Example: אָכַלְנוּ **אֲנַחְנוּ**

13. שָׁלַחְנוּ	9. הָיִיתִי	5. אָמַרְתְּ	1. זְכַרְתֶּן
14. הֱיִיתֶם	10. אָכְלָה	6. שָׁלַח	2. שָׁמְרָה
15. שָׁמְרוּ	11. זָכְרוּ	7. הָלַכְתְּ	3. הָיוּ
16. כָּתַבְנוּ	12. הֲלַכְתֶּן	8. אֲמַרְתֶּם	4. כָּתַבְתִּי

Exercise 4. Fill in the blanks with the correct conjugation of the root shown at the beginning of the sentence. Translate.

‏1. ה.ל.ך – הַשֹּׁפֵט _____ מִבֵּית לֶחֶם אֶל מוֹאָב.‎

‏2. ה.י.ה – אֲנַחְנוּ _____ בַּשָּׂדוֹת.‎

‏3. ש.מ.ר – הִיא _____ אֶת הַדֶּרֶךְ יוֹמַיִם.‎

‏4. ה.י.ה – אַבְרָהָם _____ בֶּן וְנָעֳמִי _____ בַּת.‎

‏5. ק.ת.ב – בֹּעַז וְדָוִד _____ עַל הָאֹכֶל.‎

6. ה.י.ה – אַתֶּם _____ עִם הַשּׁוֹפְטִים שָׁם.

7. ש.מ.ר – אַתְּ לֹא _____ אֶת הַנְּעָלִים.

8. א.כ.ל – אַתֶּם _____ עִם הַמִּשְׁפָּחָה.

9. ה.י.ה – הֵנָּה _____ עִם הַנָּשִׁים.

10. ז.כ.ר – הַנַּעַר _____ אֶת הַדְּבָרִים בִּירוּשָׁלַיִם.

11. ה.י.ה – אָנֹכִי לֹא _____ עִם רוּת בַּשָּׂדֶה כִּי רוּת _____ בְּבֵית לֶחֶם.

12. א.כ.ל – אַתֶּן _____ עִם דָּוִד שָׁם.

13. א.מ.ר – יַעֲקֹב _____ אֶל הָאִישׁ: "לֹא הַיּוֹם."

14. ש.מ.ר – אֲנִי לֹא _____ אֶת הַדָּבָר.

Exercise 5. Exercise with the words כִּי and אֲשֶׁר. Translate the following sentences.

1. לֹא הָיוּ אֲנָשִׁים בָּאָרֶץ כִּי הָיָה רָעָב שָׁם.

2. כָּתַבְנוּ לְיַעֲקֹב כִּי אַבְרָהָם הָיָה בִּירוּשָׁלַיִם.

3. דָּוִד הָיָה הָאִישׁ אֲשֶׁר שָׁמַר אֶת הֶעָרִים.

4. אַבְרָהָם כָּתַב לְבֹעַז כִּי בֹּעַז הָיָה שׁוֹפֵט.

5. הַנַּעֲרָה אֲשֶׁר הָיְתָה בַּבַּיִת, הָלְכָה אֶל הַשָּׂדֶה.

6. הַבָּנִים אָכְלוּ בָּעִיר כִּי הָיָה שָׁם לֶחֶם.

7. שָׂרָה זָכְרָה אֶת הַנַּעַר אֲשֶׁר הָלַךְ אֶל בֵּית לֶחֶם.

8. הָאִישׁ שָׁלַח סְפָרִים לַבַּת בִּירוּשָׁלַיִם כִּי לֹא הָיוּ סְפָרִים שָׁם.

9. הָאִישׁ הָיָה כְּבֵן לְאַבְרָהָם כִּי הוּא שָׁמַר אֶת הַבַּיִת.

From the Prayerbook

Prayerbook Vocabulary

blessed . . . . בָּרוּךְ　king of. . . . . מֶלֶךְ

our God . . . . אֱלֹהֵינוּ　the universe . . . . הָעוֹלָם

the one who brings out . . . . הַמּוֹצִיא

Selection from the Prayerbook

בָּרוּךְ אַתָּה יְיָ אֱלֹהֵינוּ מֶלֶךְ הָעוֹלָם, הַמּוֹצִיא לֶחֶם מִן הָאָרֶץ.

First try to translate the prayer in your own words, then read the translations quoted below.

Prayerbook Translations

"Blessed art thou, O Lord our God, King of the universe, who bringest forth bread from the earth."
Daily Prayer Book, Joseph Hertz, 1948, p. 962

"Blessed is the Lord our God, Ruler of the universe, who causes bread to come forth from the earth."
Gates of Prayer, the New Union Prayerbook, 1975, p. 722

Introduction to Ruth — Guided Reading

As you may have guessed from the names we have used — Ruth, Naomi, and Boaz — we will be reading the Book of Ruth. We have chosen this book because it is short, simple and beautiful. In this chapter you will be reading most of the first two verses. In the beginning of this Primer, the Hebrew text will be simplified, but as we progress, the text will approach the original. Before we finish the Book of Ruth, you will be reading the actual Biblical text.

	1. ‏בַּיָמִים אֲשֶׁר הָיוּ שֹׁפְטִים . . .‏
1. In the days that there were judges . . .	2. ‏הָיָה רָעָב בָּאָרֶץ.‏
2. there was a famine in the land.	3. ‏הָלַךְ אִישׁ מִבֵּית לֶחֶם יְהוּדָה . . .‏
3. A man from Bethlehem, Judah went . . .	4. to live ‏לָגוּר‏ fields of ‏שְׂדֵי‏ ‏לָגוּר בִּשְׂדֵי מוֹאָב,‏
4. to live in the fields of Moab,	5. his wife ‏אִשְׁתּוֹ‏ two ‏שְׁנֵי‏ ‏הוּא וְאִשְׁתּוֹ וּשְׁנֵי בָנִים.‏
5. he and his wife and two sons.	6. ‏הָאִישׁ הָיָה אֱלִימֶלֶךְ וְאִשְׁתּוֹ הָיְתָה נָעֳמִי . . .‏
6. The man was Elimelech and his wife was Naomi . . .	7. ‏וְהַבָּנִים הָיוּ מַחְלוֹן וְכִלְיוֹן.‏
7. and the sons were Machlon and Kilyon.	8. name of a people Ephrathites ‏אֶפְרָתִים‏ ‏הֵם הָיוּ אֶפְרָתִים מִבֵּית לֶחֶם יְהוּדָה . . .‏
8. They were Ephrathites from Bethlehem, Judah . . .	9. ‏אֲשֶׁר הָלְכוּ אֶל שְׂדֵי מוֹאָב וְהָיוּ שָׁם.‏
9. who went to the fields of Moab and they were there.	

‏בַּיָמִים אֲשֶׁר הָיוּ שֹׁפְטִים הָיָה רָעָב בָּאָרֶץ. הָלַךְ אִישׁ מִבֵּית לֶחֶם יְהוּדָה לָגוּר בִּשְׂדֵי מוֹאָב, הוּא וְאִשְׁתּוֹ וּשְׁנֵי בָנִים. הָאִישׁ הָיָה אֱלִימֶלֶךְ וְאִשְׁתּוֹ הָיְתָה נָעֳמִי וְהַבָּנִים הָיוּ מַחְלוֹן וְכִלְיוֹן. הֵם הָיוּ אֶפְרָתִים מִבֵּית לֶחֶם יְהוּדָה אֲשֶׁר הָלְכוּ אֶל שְׂדֵי מוֹאָב וְהָיוּ שָׁם.‏

Chapter 11
Adjectives
Sentences Without Verbs

Vocabulary

father *n, m* . . . . *pl* אָבוֹת ,*sg* אָב
one *adj* . . . . .אַחַת ,אֶחָד
mother *n, f* . . . . *pl* אִמּוֹת ,*sg* אֵם
big, great *adj* . . . . .גְּדוֹלוֹת ,גְּדוֹלִים ,גְּדוֹלָה ,גָּדוֹל
old *adj* . . . . זְקֵנוֹת ,זְקֵנִים ,זְקֵנָה ,זָקֵן
good *adj* . . . . טוֹבוֹת ,טוֹבִים ,טוֹבָה ,טוֹב
sit, stay, settle *vb* . . . . .י.שׁ.ב
king *n, m* . . . . *pl* מְלָכִים ,*sg* מֶלֶךְ
holy *adj* . . . . קְדוֹשׁוֹת ,קְדוֹשִׁים ,קְדוֹשָׁה ,קָדוֹשׁ
evil, bad *adj* . . . . .רָעוֹת ,רָעִים ,רָעָה ,רַע

Note 1: New abbreviation — *adj* — adjective

Note 2: The adjective זָקֵן — *old* — is used to describe people only.
It is never used to describe non-living things.

Adjectives

An adjective is a word used to describe or limit a noun.

Examples: a big man   good shoes   a bad king

In English, the adjective comes **before** the noun that it describes, but in Hebrew the
adjective comes **after** the noun that it describes.

Examples: an old man   אִישׁ זָקֵן   a bad king   מֶלֶךְ רַע

a big house   בַּיִת גָּדוֹל   a good judge   שֹׁפֵט טוֹב

a good father   אָב טוֹב   a big lad   נַעַר גָּדוֹל

Matching Gender and Number

In Hebrew, adjectives must agree in gender and number with the nouns they describe. The
forms for adjectives correspond to the four possible combinations of gender and number.

Adjective Chart

	Feminine Plural	Masculine Plural	Feminine Singular	Masculine Singular
big, great	גְּדוֹלוֹת	גְּדוֹלִים	גְּדוֹלָה	גָּדוֹל
old (people)	זְקֵנוֹת	זְקֵנִים	זְקֵנָה	זָקֵן
good	טוֹבוֹת	טוֹבִים	טוֹבָה	טוֹב
holy	קְדוֹשׁוֹת	קְדוֹשִׁים	קְדוֹשָׁה	קָדוֹשׁ
evil, bad	רָעוֹת	רָעִים	רָעָה	רַע

As you can see from the chart above, adjectives generally have the same endings as the regular nouns. Therefore, if the noun is regular, the adjective describing it will generally rhyme with all forms except the masculine singular.

Examples: a good family מִשְׁפָּחָה טוֹבָה   a good word דָּבָר טוֹב

good families מִשְׁפָּחוֹת טוֹבוֹת   good words דְּבָרִים טוֹבִים

When a noun has irregular endings, its adjective must still agree with the gender and number of the noun. Notice that the nouns אֶרֶץ and עִיר are feminine, even though neither one has the feminine ending ָה or ת. Although the adjectives will not rhyme, they still must agree in gender and number with the irregular nouns.

Examples: big fields שָׂדוֹת גְּדוֹלִים   a good land אֶרֶץ טוֹבָה

old women נָשִׁים זְקֵנוֹת   a holy city עִיר קְדוֹשָׁה

Matching with Definite Nouns

In Hebrew adjectives must be made definite when the nouns they describe are definite. When the noun is definite, its adjective **always** takes the definite article הַ‧.

Examples: the big house הַבַּיִת הַגָּדוֹל   the good fields הַשָּׂדוֹת הַטּוֹבִים

If a noun is naturally definite, as with the name of a person or place, its adjective must take the definite article. Example: old Ruth רוּת הַזְּקֵנָה

Sentences Without Verbs: The Noun Sentence

In English, every sentence must have a subject and a verb; in Hebrew, it is possible to construct a sentence with a number of words and **no apparent** verb. There is no word in Hebrew that can be translated as **is, am,** or **are.** This is because there is no present tense in Hebrew for the verb **be** — ה.י.ה. Whenever these verbs are needed to translate a Hebrew sentence into proper English, they must be supplied.

Examples: Boaz (is) a man. בֹּעַז אִישׁ.   We (are) women. אֲנַחְנוּ נָשִׁים.

In English, "Boaz a man." or "We women." is not a sentence. Therefore the verb **to be** must be inserted in the English translation.

A Hebrew sentence which has at least one noun and any number of other words, but no apparent verb is called a **noun sentence.**

Since there is no verb in the noun sentence, there is also no indication of time frame (yesterday, today, or tomorrow). The Hebrew sentence בֹּעַז אִישׁ may be translated as: Boaz is a man; Boaz was a man; Boaz will be a man. The time of the noun sentence is determined by the context. If no time frame is indicated, the sentence is understood to be in the present.

The Guided Reading will show you how to determine the time frame from the context.

	Box 1. רוּת בַּבַּיִת.
Box 1. Ruth (is) in the house.	Box 2. בֹּעַז הָלַךְ לַבַּיִת כִּי רוּת בַּבַּיִת.
Box 2. Boaz went to the house because Ruth (was) in the house.	Box 3. הָיִיתִי בַּשָּׂדֶה עִם יַעֲקֹב.
Box 3. I was in the field with Jacob.	Box 4. אֲנִי בַּשָּׂדֶה עִם יַעֲקֹב.
Box 4. I (am) in the field with Jacob.	Box 5. הָיָה אִישׁ מִמּוֹאָב וְהָאִישׁ בֹּעַז.
Box 5. There was a man from Moab and the man (was) Boaz.	

Simple Types of Noun Sentences

1. A noun sentence can consist of two nouns.
    Examples: David (is) a king. — or — David (is) king.   דָּוִד מֶלֶךְ.
                Ruth (is) a mother.   רוּת אֵם.

2. A noun sentence can consist of many nouns.
    Examples: Boaz and Abraham and Jacob (are) lads.   בֹּעַז וְאַבְרָהָם וְיַעֲקֹב נְעָרִים.
                David (is) a king and Boaz (is) a judge.   דָּוִד מֶלֶךְ וּבֹעַז שׁוֹפֵט.

3. A noun sentence can consist of nouns and prepositional phrases.
    Examples: The man (is) in the house.   הָאִישׁ בַּבַּיִת.
                Naomi and Ruth (are) with the king   נָעֳמִי וְרוּת עִם הַמֶּלֶךְ בִּירוּשָׁלַיִם.
                in Jerusalem.

4. A noun sentence can consist of nouns and adjectives.
    Examples: The man (is) good.   הָאִישׁ טוֹב.
                The women (are) old.   הַנָּשִׁים זְקֵנוֹת.

59

How to Distinguish an Adjective Phrase from a Noun Sentence

A single noun described by an adjective is an adjective phrase. Adjective phrases should not be confused with noun sentences containing adjectives.

1. If the noun and the adjective are both definite, it is probably an adjective phrase. In an adjective phrase, the adjective **must** follow the noun.

   Examples:

The big house	הַבַּיִת הַגָּדוֹל
The old woman	הָאִשָּׁה הַזְּקֵנָה
The holy man	הָאִישׁ הַקָּדוֹשׁ

2. If the noun is definite and the adjective is indefinite, it is a noun sentence. In a noun sentence, the adjective may be placed either before or after the noun.

   Examples:

The house is big.	הַבַּיִת גָּדוֹל.
The woman is old.	הָאִשָּׁה זְקֵנָה.
The man is holy.	קָדוֹשׁ הָאִישׁ.

3. If the noun and the adjective are both indefinite, it may be an adjective phrase or it may be a noun sentence. The actual meaning must be determined from the context.

   Examples:

A famine is great.	— or —	a great famine	רָעָב גָּדוֹל
Food is good.	— or —	good food	אֹכֶל טוֹב
Men are bad.	— or —	bad men	אֲנָשִׁים רָעִים

Exercises

Exercise 1. Rewrite the sentences below, replacing the underlined word with each word in the list that follows, and making the necessary changes in the rest of the sentence. Read the sentences aloud. Translate.

1. הִיא יָשְׁבָה בְּאֶרֶץ טוֹבָה.

   A. אֲנַחְנוּ   B. הַמֶּלֶךְ   C. הֵנָּה   D. אַתֶּן   E. אַתָּה וְדָוִד
   F. יַעֲקֹב וְאַבְרָהָם   G. אַתְּ

2. הָאִישׁ הַטּוֹב הָלַךְ אֶל הָעִיר.

   A. הָאֵם   B. הַנְּעָרוֹת   C. הָאָב   D. הַבָּנִים   E. הַבַּת

3. הַשֹּׁפֵט הַזָּקֵן בַּבַּיִת הַגָּדוֹל הַיּוֹם.

   A. בַּשָּׂדֶה   B. בָּעִיר   C. בַּשָּׂדוֹת   D. בַּדְּרָכִים

4. הָאָבוֹת מְמוֹאָב אֲנָשִׁים קְדוֹשִׁים.

E. הַבָּנוֹת   D. הַמְּלָכִים   C. הַשׁוֹפֵט   B. הָאִמּוֹת   A. הָאִשָּׁה

5. הַמֶּלֶךְ הָיָה אִישׁ רַע.

E. הִיא   D. אַתֶּן   C. הֵמָּה   B. רוּת וְנָעֳמִי   A. אֲנַחְנוּ

I. אַתְּ   H. אַתֶּם   G. אַתָּה   F. אֲנִי

Exercise 2. Circle the correct adjective.

1. הָאִישׁ זָכַר סֵפֶר (קָדוֹשׁ, קְדוֹשָׁה, קְדוֹשִׁים, קְדוֹשׁוֹת).
2. הָאִמּוֹת הָיוּ נָשִׁים (זָקֵן, זְקֵנָה, זְקֵנִים, זְקֵנוֹת).
3. הַבָּנִים בְּמוֹאָב (רַע, רָעָה, רָעִים, רָעוֹת).
4. הַיּוֹם הָלַךְ דָּוִד לְעִיר (גָּדוֹל, גְּדוֹלָה, גְּדוֹלִים, גְּדוֹלוֹת).
5. הַנַּעֲרָה שָׁלְחָה נַעֲלַיִם (טוֹב, טוֹבָה, טוֹבִים, טוֹבוֹת).
6. יְרוּשָׁלַיִם עִיר (קָדוֹשׁ, הַקָּדוֹשׁ, קְדוֹשָׁה, הַקְּדוֹשָׁה, קְדוֹשִׁים, הַקְּדוֹשׁוֹת).
7. הַשָּׂדוֹת בִּיהוּדָה (גָּדוֹל, גְּדוֹלָה, גְּדוֹלִים, גְּדוֹלוֹת).
8. בֹּעַז זָכַר אֶת הַיָּמִים (טוֹב, הַטּוֹבָה, טוֹבָה, טוֹבִים, הַטּוֹבִים, טוֹבוֹת).
9. רוּת יָשְׁבָה בְּבַיִת (אֶחָד, אַחַת) וְאָמְרָה דָּבָר טוֹב לְנָעֳמִי.
10. הִנֵּה כָּתְבוּ סְפָרִים (טוֹב, טוֹבָה, טוֹבִים, טוֹבוֹת) עַל יְרוּשָׁלַיִם.
11. הֵמָּה אָכְלוּ עִם אִישׁ (הַזָּקֵן, זָקֵן, הַזְּקֵנָה, זְקֵנִים, הַזְּקֵנִים, זְקֵנוֹת).

Exercise 3. Read and translate. Pay attention to the difference between noun sentences and adjective phrases.

1b. מִנְחָה טוֹבָה	1a. אִישׁ זָקֵן
2b. הַמִּנְחָה טוֹבָה	2a. הָאִישׁ זָקֵן
3b. הַמִּנְחָה הַטּוֹבָה	3a. הָאִישׁ הַזָּקֵן
1d. אִישׁ קָדוֹשׁ בְּבַיִת גָּדוֹל	1c. מְלָכִים גְּדוֹלִים
2d. הָאִישׁ הַקָּדוֹשׁ גָּדוֹל	2c. גְּדוֹלִים הַמְּלָכִים
3d. הָאִישׁ הַקָּדוֹשׁ וְהַגָּדוֹל בַּבַּיִת	3c. הַמְּלָכִים הַגְּדוֹלִים רָעִים

Exercise 4. Change the following sentences to the perfect tense using the verb ה.י.ה.

1. רוּת נַעֲרָה וְנָעֳמִי אִשָּׁה.
6. אַתְּ כְּאֵם לְרוּת.

2. הַמֶּלֶךְ וְהַשׁוֹפְטִים בַּדֶּרֶךְ הָאַחַת לְמוֹאָב.
7. אַתָּה אָב לְיַעֲקֹב.

3. אָנוּ בַּבַּיִת וְהֵם בַּשָּׂדֶה.
8. שָׂרָה נַעֲרָה מִיהוּדָה.

4. הִיא עִם הַנָּשִׁים כִּי אַתֶּם עִם הַמֶּלֶךְ.
9. שׁוֹפֵט אֶחָד בַּשָּׂדֶה עִם דָּוִד.

5. הַלֶּחֶם הַטּוֹב בַּבַּיִת.

Exercise 5. Change the following sentences into noun sentences.

.5 הָיִית אֵם לְיַעֲקֹב וּבַת לְאַבְרָהָם.   .1 הָיִינוּ עִם אַבְרָהָם בַּדֶּרֶךְ לְמוֹאָב.

.6 דָּוִד הָיָה בַּבַּיִת הַגָּדוֹל.   .2 הַדְּבָרִים הָיוּ מֵעִיר בִּיהוּדָה.

.7 אִשָּׁה אַחַת הָיְתָה בַּשָּׂדֶה.   .3 הָיִיתָ בְּמוֹאָב כִּי לֶחֶם בַּשָּׂדוֹת שָׁם.

.4 הֱיִיתֶן עִם הַנָּשִׁים הַטּוֹבוֹת בִּירוּשָׁלַיִם.

Exercise 6. Compose as many noun sentences as you can with the following words. You may use inseparable prepositions and the definite article. Translate.

עָרִים, טוֹבָה, שָׂרָה, דֶּרֶךְ, אֵם, יַעֲקֹב, יוֹמַיִם, בַּיִת, רַע, אָנוּ, בֵּן, זְקֵנִים, קְדוֹשׁוֹת

Exercise 7.

1. Read and translate.

הָיְתָה מִשְׁפָּחָה אֲשֶׁר יָשְׁבָה בִּיהוּדָה. הָאֵם הַזְּקֵנָה שָׂרָה וְהָאָב הַזָּקֵן בֹּעַז. הַבַּת בַּמִּשְׁפָּחָה, רוּת, הָיְתָה טוֹבָה וְהַבֵּן, יַעֲקֹב, רַע. הָיָה רָעָב גָּדוֹל בִּיהוּדָה וְלֹא הָיָה לָהֶם לֶחֶם. שָׂרָה וּבֹעַז שָׁלְחוּ אֶת רוּת וְאֶת יַעֲקֹב אֶל מוֹאָב כִּי הָיָה שָׁם אֹכֶל. כַּאֲשֶׁר when הָיְתָה רוּת בְּמוֹאָב, הִיא זָכְרָה אֶת הַמִּשְׁפָּחָה וְהִיא שָׁלְחָה אֹכֶל לַמִּשְׁפָּחָה וְלָאֲנָשִׁים בִּיהוּדָה. יַעֲקֹב הָרַע לֹא זָכַר אֶת הָאָב וְאֶת הָאֵם וְלֹא שָׁלַח אֹכֶל לִיהוּדָה. כַּאֲשֶׁר הָיָה לֶחֶם בִּיהוּדָה, רוּת הָלְכָה מִמּוֹאָב אֶל הַמִּשְׁפָּחָה בִּיהוּדָה. יַעֲקֹב הָרַע יָשַׁב בְּמוֹאָב.

2. List all adjectives in the above reading.
4. List all definite direct objects.
3. List all noun sentences.
5. List all indefinite direct objects.

From the Prayerbook

Prayerbook Vocabulary

hear *vb, imperative* שְׁמַע .... ש.מ.ע.   Our God..................... אֱלֹהֵינוּ

Selection from the Prayerbook

שְׁמַע יִשְׂרָאֵל יְיָ אֱלֹהֵינוּ יְיָ אֶחָד

First try to translate the prayer in your own words, then read the translations quoted below.

Prayerbook Translations

''Hear, O Israel: the Lord our God, the Lord is One.''

Sabbath and Festival Prayer Book, The Rabbinical Assembly of America, 1946, p. 92

''Hear, O Israel, the Lord is our God, the Lord is One.''

Daily Prayer Book, Philip Birnbaum, 1977, p. 76

Notice that the first translation assumes that there is only one noun sentence in the Hebrew, while the second translation assumes that there are two noun sentences.

Guided Reading from Ruth

	died מֵת .1 מֵת אֱלִימֶלֶךְ
1. Elimelech died	remained נִשְׁאֲרָה .2 שְׁנֵי two וְנָעֳמִי נִשְׁאֲרָה עִם שְׁנֵי הַבָּנִים.
2. and Naomi remained with the two sons.	married נָשְׂאוּ .3 Moabite מֹאֲבִיּוֹת הֵם נָשְׂאוּ נָשִׁים מֹאֲבִיּוֹת.
3. They married Moabite women.	second שֵׁנִית .4 אַחַת עָרְפָּה וְהַשֵּׁנִית רוּת.
4. One (was) Orpa and the second (was) Ruth.	ten עֶשֶׂר .5 שָׁנִים years וְהֵם יָשְׁבוּ שָׁם כְּעֶשֶׂר שָׁנִים.
5. And they dwelled there about ten years.	

מֵת אֱלִימֶלֶךְ וְנָעֳמִי נִשְׁאֲרָה עִם שְׁנֵי הַבָּנִים. הֵם נָשְׂאוּ נָשִׁים מֹאֲבִיּוֹת.
אַחַת עָרְפָּה וְהַשֵּׁנִית רוּת. וְהֵם יָשְׁבוּ שָׁם כְּעֶשֶׂר שָׁנִים.

Chapter 12
The Construct State

Vocabulary

morning *n, m*	בֹּקֶר, בְּקָרִים
kindness *n, m*	חֶסֶד, חֲסָדִים
hand *n, f*	יָד, יָדַיִם
all, every, the whole *n, m*	כֹּל, כָּל
night *n, m*	לַיְלָה *or* לֵיל, לֵילוֹת
very *adv*	מְאֹד
place *n, m*	מָקוֹם, מְקוֹמוֹת
still, yet *adv*	עוֹד
eye *n, f*	עַיִן, עֵינַיִם
nation, people *n, m*	עַם, עַמִּים

Note 1: New abbreviation *adv* adverb

Note 2: The *sg* and *pl* abbreviations will no longer be used in the vocabulary lists. Hebrew nouns will be listed in the singular, and then in the plural. If a dual form exists, it will be listed last.

Note 3: יָדַיִם and עֵינַיִם are dual forms. There is no plural form of עַיִן. The plural of יָד does not refer to human hands in the Bible.

Note 4: The ָ vowel in כָּל is pronounced **o** as in **dog**.

The Use of the Preposition מִן "from" for Comparisons

In English, comparisons are formed by adding the ending "er" to an adjective, followed by the word "than." Examples: Boaz is bigger than Ruth. Naomi is older than Sarah.

In Hebrew, comparisons are formed by using the preposition מִן, from, with any adjective.

Examples: Literally: Boaz is big from Ruth.   בֹּעַז גָּדוֹל מֵרוּת.

      or: Boaz is bigger than Ruth.

     Literally: Naomi is old from Sarah.   נָעֳמִי זְקֵנָה מִשָּׂרָה.

      or: Naomi is older than Sarah.

The Construct State

In Biblical Hebrew there is no word to express the English word **of** when it means either

possession: The house **of** Ruth

or description: A word **of** kindness

However, in Hebrew, when two nouns are linked together to create a single idea, the **first** noun carries with it the meaning of **of**. This noun is in what is called the **construct state**. The construct state expresses the word **of** in both its possessive and descriptive functions. A word in the construct state should always be translated with **of** following it.

Examples: The **mother of** Jacob   אֵם יַעֲקֹב

                  The **daughter of** the man   בַּת הָאִישׁ

                  A **man of** kindness   אִישׁ חֶסֶד

The examples above are literal translations of the construct state. When the construct state expresses possession, you can turn the phrase around after translating it literally and express the same idea in ordinary English.

Examples: Step 1. The mother of Jacob   אֵם יַעֲקֹב
                  Step 2. Jacob's mother

                  Step 1. The daughter of the man   בַּת הָאִישׁ
                  Step 2. The man's daughter

Additional information on this subject can be found on page 272, note 4.

How to Form Nouns in the Construct State

Some nouns, such as those shown in the previous examples, remain unchanged when they appear in the construct state. However, many nouns have a changed form in the construct state. Following are some general rules on how nouns change when they appear in the construct state.

Masculine Singular Nouns

There are no general rules for forming masculine singular nouns in the construct state. Some masculine singular nouns have a changed form, but some are completely unchanged when they appear in the construct state. The only sure way to determine the construct form of a masculine singular noun is to look it up in the glossary of this book or in a Hebrew dictionary.

Masculine Plural Nouns

The אִים ending of regular masculine plural nouns changes to יִX in the construct state. The other vowels of the noun often change.

Examples:

	Construct Ending		Plural Ending
judges of	שׁוֹפְטֵי	judges	שׁוֹפְטִים
sons of	בְּנֵי	sons	בָּנִים
people of	אַנְשֵׁי	people	אֲנָשִׁים
words of, things of	דִּבְרֵי	words, things	דְּבָרִים

Feminine Singular Nouns

The אָה ending of regular feminine singular nouns changes to אַת in the construct state. The other vowels of the noun often change.

Examples:

	Construct Ending		Feminine Ending
present of	מִנְחַת	present	מִנְחָה
young woman of	נַעֲרַת	young woman	נַעֲרָה
family of	מִשְׁפַּחַת	family	מִשְׁפָּחָה

Feminine Plural Nouns

The אוֹת ending of regular feminine plural nouns remains the same in the construct state. (However, the vowels of the noun often change.)

Examples:

	Construct Ending		Feminine Plural Ending
mothers of	אִמּוֹת	mothers	אִמּוֹת
daughters of	בְּנוֹת	daughters	בָּנוֹת
families of	מִשְׁפְּחוֹת	families	מִשְׁפָּחוֹת

Rules for the Construct State

Definite Nouns in the Construct State

Two nouns which are joined together in the construct state are made definite by adding the definite article הX· to the **second** noun.

Example: **Indefinite**   **a** mother of **a** girl — or — **a** girl's mother   אֵם נַעֲרָה

          Definite   **the** mother of **the** girl — or — **the** girl's mother   אֵם הַנַּעֲרָה

If the second noun is a person or place name, the construct unit is definite.

Example: **The** nation of Israel   עַם יִשְׂרָאֵל

          The house of Ruth — or — Ruth's house   בֵּית רוּת

Adjectives and Nouns in the Construct State

Nouns that are joined together in the construct state are almost never separated. Adjectives, whether they are describing the first or the second noun, are added after the construct unit.

Examples: The large gift of Jacob — or —   מִנְחַת יַעֲקֹב הַגְּדוֹלָה

          Jacob's large gift

          The good bread of the woman — or —   לֶחֶם הָאִשָּׁה הַטּוֹב

          The woman's good bread

There are some cases where the adjective may refer to either the first or second noun.

Example: מִנְחַת הָאִשָּׁה הַגְּדוֹלָה

May be translated as: The great gift of the woman — or — The gift of the great woman

When such ambiguities occur, they are to be understood in context.

The Construct Chain

More than two nouns can be joined together in the construct state to form a construct chain. When this occurs, every word except the last word of the chain is in the construct state.

Examples: The **house of** the **father of** Ruth — or — Ruth's father's house   בֵּית אֲבִי רוּת

          The **gift of** the **judges of** the city   מִנְחַת שׁוֹפְטֵי הָעִיר

Notice that the definite article הַ·אX is added only to the **last** noun in the construct chain.

Agreement with the Verb

When a construct unit appears as the subject of a sentence, the **first** noun must agree with the verb.

Example: The daughter of Boaz remembered the family.   בַּת בֹּעַז זָכְרָה אֶת הַמִּשְׁפָּחָה.

Using the Glossary

You will need to be able to recognize nouns appearing in the construct state, but you do not need to memorize all the forms. The singular and plural construct forms of each noun are listed in the glossary at the end of this book.

Example from the Glossary: mother *n. f* ...... אֵם, אִמּוֹת, אֵם־, אִמּוֹת־, אִמִּי, אִמּוֹתַי

The construct forms are listed after the plural form of the noun. A hyphen is written after the construct forms to distinguish them from other forms of the noun. You will learn the two forms listed after the construct forms in later chapters.

Exercises

Exercise 1. Rewrite the sentences below, replacing the underlined word with each word in the list that follows. Every word or grammatical form in the sentence that agrees with the underlined word should be changed to agree with the newly substituted words. Read the sentences aloud. Translate.

١. אַנְשֵׁי הַמָּקוֹם שָׁמְרוּ אֶת שְׂדֵה הָאִשָּׁה הַזְּקֵנָה מְאֹד.

E. נַעֲרַת   D. נְעָרוֹת   C. מֶלֶךְ   B. נַעֲרֵי   A. שׁוֹפֵט

٢. כָּל הַלַּיְלָה אֲבִי הָאִשָּׁה הָיָה בְּבֵית אַבְרָהָם.

E. אַתָּה   D. הֵמָּה   C. אֲנִי   B. בַּת הַמִּשְׁפָּחָה   A. אֲנַחְנוּ
H. הֵן   G. אַתֶּן   F. אַתְּ

٣. אֵם יַעֲקֹב הַזְּקֵנָה אָכְלָה עִם מִשְׁפַּחַת רוּת כָּל בֹּקֶר.

E. הַקְּדוֹשָׁה   D. הַגָּדוֹל   C. הָרָעָה   B. הַטּוֹב   A. הַזָּקֵן

٤. אַנְשֵׁי יְהוּדָה עוֹד זָכְרוּ אֶת יְמֵי דָוִד הַמֶּלֶךְ.

E. עַם יִשְׂרָאֵל   D. אַתְּ   C. אַתֶּם   B. אֲנִי   A. נַעֲרוֹת הָעִיר
H. בַּת הַשֹּׁפֵט   G. אַתָּה   F. אֲנַחְנוּ

٥. אַתְּ כָּתַבְתְּ כִּי רַע הָאִישׁ הַזָּקֵן מִבְּעוֹ.

E. אֲנִי   D. אַתֶּן   C. אַתָּה   B. כָּל נְשֵׁי הַמָּקוֹם   A. אֲנַחְנוּ
I. בֶּן אַבְרָהָם   H. אַתֶּם   G. אֵשֶׁת יַעֲקֹב   F. שׁוֹפְטֵי יְהוּדָה

٦. בַּבֹּקֶר הוּא לֹא הָלַךְ וְלֹא יָשַׁב כְּאִישׁ זָקֵן.

E. אַתֶּם   D. נַעַר הַשָּׂדֶה   C. אֵם שָׂרָה   B. אַתְּ   A. אֲנִי

Exercise 2. Using the construct forms in the glossary, combine the following pairs of nouns into a construct unit. Translate.

Example:	מִנְחָה/אַבְרָהָם	**מִנְחַת אַבְרָהָם**	the gift of Abraham

Singular nouns

7. שׁוֹפֵט/אִישׁ   4. בֶּן/שׁוֹפֵט   1. בַּיִת/מֶלֶךְ

8. אֹכֶל/שָׂרָה   5. אֵם/נְעָרוֹת   2. חֶסֶד/מְלָכִים

9. בַּת/אִשָּׁה   6. שׁוֹפֵט/אֲנָשִׁים   3. עִיר/דָוִד

Plural nouns

16. יָדַיִם/בֹּעַז   13. מִשְׁפָּחוֹת/עָרִים   10. בָּתִּים/אֲנָשִׁים

17. חֲסָדִים/אָבוֹת   14. עֵינַיִם/אַבְרָהָם   11. דְּבָרִים/שׁוֹפְטִים

15. אָבוֹת/נְעָרִים   12. אֲנָשִׁים/מָקוֹם

Nouns with the definite article

18. מָקוֹם/הַנְּעָרוֹת   21. דְּבָרִים/הָאָבוֹת   24. בָּנִים/הָעָם

19. יָד/הַנַּעַר   22. נַעֲלַיִם/הָאִשָּׁה   25. דְּרָכִים/הָאָרֶץ

20. סְפָרִים/הַשּׁוֹפְטִים   23. חֲסָדִים/הַמֶּלֶךְ

Exercise 3. Translate the following construct units literally. If the construct unit expresses possession, turn the phrase around into ordinary English.

Example: סִפְרֵי הָאָב   the books of the father   the father's books

1. מִנְחוֹת הַנָּשִׁים   4. בֵּית הָאֵם   7. אֵשֶׁת אַבְרָהָם

2. עָרֵי יְהוּדָה   5. אֲבִי הַנַּעַר   8. עַם יִשְׂרָאֵל

3. יְמֵי רָעָב   6. בֶּן הַמֶּלֶךְ   9. אַנְשֵׁי הַמָּקוֹם

Exercise 4. Change the construct units listed in the above exercise into separate nouns.

Example: סְפָרִים/הָאָב to סִפְרֵי הָאָב

Exercise 5. Translate into English.

1. בֶּן הָאִישׁ

2. בֶּן הָאִישׁ הַטּוֹב

3. בֶּן הָאִישׁ טוֹב.

4. בֶּן הָאִישׁ הַטּוֹב בָּעִיר.

5. בְּנֵי הָאִישׁ הַטּוֹב בָּעִיר הַגְּדוֹלָה.

6. בְּנֵי הָאִישׁ הַטּוֹבִים בָּעִיר הַגְּדוֹלָה.

7. בְּנֵי הָאֲנָשִׁים הַטּוֹבִים בָּעִיר הַגְּדוֹלָה הַיּוֹם.

8. בְּנֵי הָאֲנָשִׁים הַטּוֹבִים טוֹבִים.

Exercise 6. Translate into Hebrew.

1. A king's family
2. The king's family
3. The great king's family
4. The king's large family
5. The king's family is large.
6. The king's large family is not in the field.
7. The great king's family is large.

Exercise 7. Translate the following sentences. Circle the construct units.

1. הַמָּקוֹם טוֹב מְאֹד בְּעֵינֵי רוּת.

2. מְקוֹמוֹת קְדוֹשִׁים הָיוּ בִּידֵי עַם יְהוּדָה.

3. עַם גָּדוֹל מְאֹד עוֹד יָשַׁב בְּאֶרֶץ יִשְׂרָאֵל.

4. הָאֹכֶל עוֹד הָיָה בַּבַּיִת כִּי הָאֲנָשִׁים עוֹד הָיוּ בַּשָּׂדֶה.

5. כָּל בֹּקֶר נַעֲרֵי בֹּעַז אָכְלוּ לֶחֶם בְּמָקוֹם טוֹב.

6. בַּלַּיְלָה כָּל נַעֲרוֹת הַמֶּלֶךְ הָלְכוּ אֶל בֵּית הַמֶּלֶךְ.

7. בַּלַּיְלָה רוּת אָמְרָה "לֹא" וּבַבֹּקֶר רוּת עוֹד אָמְרָה "לֹא".

8. כָּל מִנְחוֹת הַמֶּלֶךְ הָיוּ בִּידֵי אַנְשֵׁי הָעִיר.

9. כָּתַבְתִּי עַל חַסְדֵי הַשּׁוֹפֵט אֶל שָׂרָה.

10. אֵשֶׁת דָּוִד הָלְכָה בַּדֶּרֶךְ לְבֵית לֶחֶם כָּל הַלַּיְלָה.

11. עֵינֵי נָעֳמִי הָיוּ גְּדוֹלוֹת מְאֹד.

From the Prayerbook

Prayerbook Vocabulary

blessed	בָּרוּךְ
our God	אֱלֹהֵינוּ
our fathers	אֲבֹתֵינוּ
Isaac	יִצְחָק
mighty	גִּבּוֹר
awesome	נוֹרָא
supreme	עֶלְיוֹן
construct form of אֱלֹהִים	אֱלֹהֵי

Selection from the Prayerbook (from the Amidah service)

בָּרוּךְ אַתָּה, יְיָ אֱלֹהֵינוּ וֵאלֹהֵי אֲבוֹתֵינוּ, אֱלֹהֵי אַבְרָהָם, אֱלֹהֵי יִצְחָק, וֵאלֹהֵי יַעֲקֹב, הָאֵל הַגָּדוֹל, הַגִּבּוֹר
וְהַנּוֹרָא, אֵל עֶלְיוֹן ...

First try to translate the prayer in your own words, then read the translations quoted below.

Prayerbook Translations

"Blessed is the Lord our God and God of all generations, God of Abraham, God of Isaac and God of Jacob; great, mighty and exalted."

Gates of Prayer, the New Union Prayerbook, 1975, p. 339

"Blessed art thou, Lord our God and God of our fathers, God of Abraham, God of Isaac and God of Jacob; great, mighty and revered God, sublime God."

Daily Prayer Book, Philip Birnbaum, 1977, p. 82

Notice the frequent use of the construct state in the above prayer.

Guided Reading from Ruth

	מֵׁתוּ died .1
	מֵתוּ מַחְלוֹן וְכִלְיוֹן
1. Machlon and Kilyon died	נִשְׁאֲרָה remained bereft .2
	שְׁנֵי two
	יְלָדֶיהָ her children
	וְהָאִשָּׁה נִשְׁאֲרָה מִן שְׁנֵי יְלָדֶיהָ
	וּמִן אֱלִימֶלֶךְ.
2. and the woman remained bereft of her two children and Elimelech.	קָׁמוּ they arose .3
	כַּלֹּתֶיהָ her daughters-in-law
	קָמוּ הִיא וְכַלֹּתֶיהָ
3. She and her daughters-in-law arose	שָׁבָה she returned .4
	וְהִיא שָׁבָה מִשְׂדֵי מוֹאָב,
4. And she returned from the fields of Moab	שָׁמְעָה she heard .5
	כִּי שָׁמְעָה בִּשְׂדֵי מוֹאָב
5. because she heard in the fields of Moab	עַמּוֹ his people .6
	כִּי זָכַר יְהוָה אֶת עַמּוֹ,
6. that the Lord remembered his people	לָתֵת to give .7
	לָהֶם to them
	לָתֵת לָהֶם לָחֶם.
7. to give bread to them.	

מֵתוּ מַחְלוֹן וְכִלְיוֹן וְהָאִשָּׁה נִשְׁאֲרָה מִן שְׁנֵי יְלָדֶיהָ וּמִן אֱלִימֶלֶךְ.
קָמוּ הִיא וְכַלֹּתֶיהָ וְהִיא שָׁבָה מִשְׂדֵי מוֹאָב, כִּי שָׁמְעָה בִּשְׂדֵי
מוֹאָב כִּי זָכַר יְהוָה אֶת עַמּוֹ, לָתֵת לָהֶם לָחֶם.

Chapter 13
Possessive Pronoun Endings
for Singular Nouns

Vocabulary

also	גַּם
beloved, uncle *n, m*	דּוֹד, דּוֹדִים
aunt *n, f*	דּוֹדָה
as, when *conj*	כַּאֲשֶׁר
seat, throne *n, m*	כִּסֵּא, כִּסְאוֹת
what?	מַה, מֶה, מָה
who?	מִי
voice, sound *n, m*	קוֹל
lie down *vb*	שׁ.כ.ב
name *n, m*	שֵׁם, שֵׁמוֹת

Note 1: While in the Bible דּוֹד means both uncle and beloved, the feminine form of the word, דּוֹדָה, means only aunt and not beloved woman. There is no plural form for דּוֹדָה in the Bible.

Note 2: The noun קוֹל — **voice** has no plural form. When the plural of קוֹל is used in the Bible, it means thunder.

Note 3: The word כַּאֲשֶׁר means **when** as a conjunction.

Example: I ate when I wrote.   אָכַלְתִּי כַּאֲשֶׁר כָּתַבְתִּי.

Possessive Pronouns

Possessive pronouns are pronouns which are used to describe belonging or possession. In English, possessive pronouns are separate words which precede the nouns that are described.

Examples: **my** book   **your** family   **his** fields

our city   **their** names   **her** house

In Hebrew, possessive pronouns are not separate words. They are endings which are attached to the nouns that are described.

Possessive Pronoun Endings With Masculine Singular Nouns

The possessive pronoun endings are attached to regular masculine singular nouns. Below is a chart showing the possessive pronoun endings and how they are added to the regular masculine singular noun דּוֹד.

	Translation	Noun with Endings		Possessive Endings		Masculine Noun
1 c sg	my beloved	דּוֹדִי	=	אִי	+	דּוֹד
2 m sg	your beloved	דּוֹדְךָ	=	אֲךָ	+	דּוֹד
2 f sg	your beloved	דּוֹדֵךְ	=	אֵךְ	+	דּוֹד
3 m sg	his beloved	דּוֹדוֹ	=	אוֹ	+	דּוֹד
3 f sg	her beloved	דּוֹדָהּ	=	אָהּ	+	דּוֹד
1 c pl	our beloved	דּוֹדֵנוּ	=	אֵנוּ	+	דּוֹד
2 m pl	your beloved	דּוֹדְכֶם	=	אֲכֶם	+	דּוֹד
2 f pl	your beloved	דּוֹדְכֶן	=	אֲכֶן	+	דּוֹד
3 m pl	their beloved	דּוֹדָם	=	אָם	+	דּוֹד
3 f pl	their beloved	דּוֹדָן	=	אָן	+	דּוֹד

Possessive Pronoun Endings With Feminine Singular Nouns

When possessive pronoun endings are attached to a feminine singular noun ending in אָה, the ה changes to ת. Possessive pronoun endings are attached directly to all other feminine singular nouns. Below is a chart showing the possessive pronoun endings and how they are added to the regular feminine singular noun נַעֲרָה.

	Translation	Noun with Endings		Possessive Endings		Feminine Noun
1 c sg	my maiden	נַעֲרָתִי	=	אִי	+	נַעֲרָה – נַעֲרַת
2 m sg	your maiden	נַעֲרָתְךָ	=	אֲךָ	+	נַעֲרָה – נַעֲרַת
2 f sg	your maiden	נַעֲרָתֵךְ	=	אֵךְ	+	נַעֲרָה – נַעֲרַת
3 m sg	his maiden	נַעֲרָתוֹ	=	אוֹ	+	נַעֲרָה – נַעֲרַת
3 f sg	her maiden	נַעֲרָתָהּ	=	אָהּ	+	נַעֲרָה – נַעֲרַת
1 c pl	our maiden	נַעֲרָתֵנוּ	=	אֵנוּ	+	נַעֲרָה – נַעֲרַת
2 m pl	your maiden	נַעֲרַתְכֶם	=	אֲכֶם	+	נַעֲרָה – נַעֲרַת
2 f pl	your maiden	נַעֲרַתְכֶן	=	אֲכֶן	+	נַעֲרָה – נַעֲרַת
3 m pl	their maiden	נַעֲרָתָם	=	אָם	+	נַעֲרָה – נַעֲרַת
3 f pl	their maiden	נַעֲרָתָן	=	אָן	+	נַעֲרָה – נַעֲרַת

Changes in Nouns Caused by Possessive Pronoun Endings

Some nouns, such as those shown in the previous examples, remain unchanged when the possessive pronoun endings are attached. However, many nouns have a changed form when the possessive pronoun endings are attached. This changed form remains the same no matter which possessive pronoun ending is attached.

Example: בַּיִת house   changes to   בֵּיתִי my house

Once you know this change, you know how to form:

בֵּיתְךָ your house   בֵּיתוֹ his house   etc.

You can find this changed form in the glossary at the end of this book.

Using the Glossary

In the glossary at the end of this book, the singular form of each noun is shown with the first person possessive pronoun ending attached. All the other possessive pronoun endings are attached to this same form of the noun. You can look up this form when you need to use the possessive pronoun endings.

Example from the Glossary:

house *n m* . . . . בַּיִת, בָּתִּים, בֵּית, בָּתֵּי, בֵּיתִי, בָּתַּי

The possessive form of the singular noun is listed after the plural construct form. The last form that is listed is the possessive form of the plural noun and will be taught in a later chapter.

Irregular Possessives

Some Hebrew nouns are irregular when the possessive pronoun endings are attached. These nouns are listed as irregular possessives — *irr p* — in the glossary, and no possessive forms are shown. Instead, there is a separate chart listing these forms in the back of the book.

The Mappiq

There is a dot in the ה in the third person feminine singular pronoun ending.

Examples: דּוֹדָהּ — her beloved   נַעֲרָתָהּ — her maiden

This is **not** a dagesh. It is part of the spelling of the possessive pronoun ending and is called a **mappiq**. The mappiq helps to distinguish the third person possessive ending ָהּ — **her** — from a simple feminine noun with a ָה ending.

Examples:

her lad	נַעֲרָהּ
a maiden	נַעֲרָה
her beloved, her uncle	דּוֹדָהּ
an aunt	דּוֹדָה

74

Definite Nouns

You have already learned that indefinite nouns are made definite by adding the definite article הַ to them. Indefinite nouns can also be made definite by attaching the possessive pronoun endings.

Example: house בַּיִת   the house הַבַּיִת   my house בֵּיתִי

Both **the house** — הַבַּיִת — and **my house** — בֵּיתִי — refer to a definite, specific house. However, nouns can never take both the definite article and the possessive pronoun endings at the same time. In both Hebrew and English, it is impossible to say:

הַבֵּיתִי   the my house

Since nouns with possessive pronoun endings attached are definite, they follow all the rules for definite nouns.

1. Whenever a noun is used as a direct object of a verb, and that noun has a personal pronoun ending attached, it is preceded by אֶת.

   Examples: He guarded my house.   הוּא שָׁמַר אֶת בֵּיתִי.
              Abraham ate your bread.   אַבְרָהָם אָכַל אֶת לַחְמְךָ.

2. Whenever a noun is the second noun of a construct unit, and that noun has a personal pronoun ending attached to it, the construct unit is definite.

   Examples: **The** house of **our** father — or — **Our** father's house   בֵּית אָבִינוּ
              The field of **his** family — or — **His** family's field   שְׂדֵה מִשְׁפַּחְתּוֹ

3. Adjectives, describing nouns with possessive pronoun endings attached, take the definite article הַ.

   Examples: I guarded my good father.   שָׁמַרְתִּי אֶת אָבִי הַטּוֹב.
              She walked to her big field.   הִיא הָלְכָה אֶל שָׂדֵה הַגָּדוֹל.

Exercises

Exercise 1. Add the possessive pronoun endings to the following nouns. Check the glossary to see whether the nouns change form.

3. אֶרֶץ   2. מִנְחָה   1. עִיר

Exercise 2. Rewrite the sentences below, replacing the underlined word with each word in the list that follows. Make the necessary grammatical changes and match pronoun endings to the newly substituted words. Read the sentences aloud. Translate.

1. מִי בְּבֵיתִי עִם בְּנִי?

A. בְּבֵיתְךָ   B. בְּבֵיתוֹ   C. בְּבֵיתֵנוּ   D. בְּבֵיתְכֶם   E. בְּבֵיתָהּ

F. בְּבֵיתְכֶן   G. בְּבֵיתֵךְ   H. בְּבֵיתָן   I. בְּבֵיתָם

‫2. מַה בְּיָדִי? סְפָרַי בְּיָדִי.‬

E. בְּיֶדְכֶם	D. בְּיָדָן	C. בְּיָדֵנוּ	B. בְּיָדְךָ	A. בְּיָדָם
	I. בְּיֶדְכֶן	H. בְּיָדָהּ	G. בְּיָדֵךְ	F. בְּיָדוֹ

‫3. לֹא זָכַרְתִּי אֶת בָּתֵּי הַטּוֹבָה.‬

E. מַלְכֵּנוּ	D. הָאָרֶץ	C. הַמֶּלֶךְ	B. אִמּוֹ	A. בְּנָהּ
		G. הָאֲנָשִׁים	F. אֲבִיכֶם	

‫4. שְׁמוֹ גָּדוֹל בָּאָרֶץ כִּי הוּא אִישׁ טוֹב.‬

E. שִׁמְכֶם	D. שְׁמִי	C. שִׁמְךָ	B. שְׁמָהּ	A. שְׁמֵנוּ
			F. שְׁמָן	

‫5. הָאִישׁ שָׁכַב בְּבֵיתוֹ וְזָכַר אֶת מְקוֹם מִשְׁפַּחְתּוֹ.‬

E. דּוֹדְכֶם	D. אֲנַחְנוּ	C. בְּנֵךְ	B. בִּתִּי	A. רוּת
			F. הַנָּשִׁים	

Exercise 3. Fill in the blank with the form of the underlined noun which agrees with the subject of the second half of the sentence.

Example: ‫הִיא הָלְכָה אֶל בֵּיתָהּ וְאָנוּ הָלַכְנוּ אֶל ___בֵּיתֵנוּ___.‬

‫1. אָכַלְתָּ אֶת אָכְלְךָ וְהוּא אָכַל אֶת _____.‬

‫2. הוּא הָלַךְ לְדַרְכּוֹ כַּאֲשֶׁר הֲלַכְתֶּם לְ_____.‬

‫3. הֵם כָּתְבוּ אֶת סִפְרָם וְאָנֹכִי כָּתַבְתִּי אֶת _____.‬

‫4. אָנוּ הָלַכְנוּ עִם מִשְׁפַּחְתֵּנוּ כַּאֲשֶׁר הָלַכְתְּ עִם _____.‬

‫5. הִיא אָמְרָה שָׁלוֹם אֶל מַלְכָּהּ וְאַתָּה לֹא אָמַרְתָּ שָׁלוֹם אֶל _____.‬

‫6. אַתֶּן זְכַרְתֶּן אֶת נַעֲרְכֶן כַּאֲשֶׁר הוּא זָכַר אֶת _____.‬

‫7. הָיִיתִי עִם בִּתִּי וֶהֱיִיתֶם עִם _____.‬

‫8. שְׁמִי שָׂרָה וְ_____ רוּת.‬

‫9. אַבְרָהָם שָׁמַר אֶת בְּנוֹ וְהִיא לֹא שָׁמְרָה אֶת _____.‬

‫10. הָיִינוּ בְּאַרְצֵנוּ וְהִנֵּה הָיוּ בְּ_____.‬

‫11. כַּאֲשֶׁר הָיָה רָעָב, דּוֹדָתִי הַזְּקֵנָה לֹא אָכְלָה אֶת לַחְמָהּ וְגַם דָּוִד לֹא אָכַל אֶת _____.‬

Exercise 4. Translate the following into English.

9. מַה שְּׁמֶךָ?	5. מִי אָבִיו?	1. אִשְׁתּוֹ
10. בֵּית אִמִּי	6. נַעֲלוֹ	2. מִי בִּתָּהּ?
11. אַרְצֵנוּ הַטּוֹבָה	7. מַה בְּיָדוֹ?	3. מִשְׁפַּחְתִּי
12. קוֹל שׁוֹפְטָן	8. דּוֹדָם	4. מַלְכֵּנוּ

76

Exercise 5. Read and translate.

Vocabulary for Reading Selection

second	שֵׁנִי	bear n, m	דֹב, דֻבִּים
third	שְׁלִישִׁי	bear n, f	דֻבָּה
bed n, m	מִשְׁכָּב, מִשְׁכָּבִים	three	שְׁלֹשָׁה
she slept	יָשְׁנָה	she came	בָּאָה
they loved	אָהֲבוּ	they came	בָּאוּ
forever	עַד עוֹלָם	table n, m	שֻׁלְחָן

This vocabulary is included to help you read the following story. These words are not part of your regular vocabulary and need not be memorized.

גּוֹלְדִילַקְס וּשְׁלֹשָׁה הַדֻּבִּים

הָיוּ שְׁלֹשָׁה דֻבִּים אֲשֶׁר יָשְׁבוּ בְּבֵיתָם בְּשָׂדֶה גָּדוֹל. בְּמִשְׁפַּחַת הַדֻּבִּים הָיוּ אַב־דֹב, אֵם־דֻבָּה, וּבֶן־דֹב. בַּבֹּקֶר הָלְכוּ הַדֻּבִּים אֶל שָׂדֶם הַגָּדוֹל וְלֹא הָיָה דֹב בְּבֵית הַדֻּבִּים.

בָּעִיר הָיְתָה נַעֲרָה וּשְׁמָה גּוֹלְדִילַקְס. הִיא הָלְכָה מִבֵּיתָהּ בָּעִיר אֶל הַשָּׂדוֹת. הִיא הָלְכָה וְהָלְכָה וּבָאָה אֶל בֵּית הַדֻּבִּים. בַּבַּיִת הָיָה שֻׁלְחָן וְעַל הַשֻּׁלְחָן הָיָה אֹכֶל. הָיוּ גַם שְׁלֹשָׁה כִּסְאוֹת. גּוֹלְדִילַקְס יָשְׁבָה עַל כִּסֵּא אֶחָד וְהַכִּסֵּא הָיָה גָּדוֹל מְאֹד. הִיא יָשְׁבָה עַל הַכִּסֵּא הַשֵּׁנִי וְהַכִּסֵּא הַשֵּׁנִי גַם גָּדוֹל. הִיא יָשְׁבָה עַל הַכִּסֵּא הַשְּׁלִישִׁי וְהַכִּסֵּא הָיָה טוֹב. גּוֹלְדִילַקְס יָשְׁבָה עַל הַכִּסֵּא וְאָכְלָה אֶת הָאֹכֶל אֲשֶׁר הָיָה עַל הַשֻּׁלְחָן. בַּבַּיִת הָיוּ שְׁלֹשָׁה מִשְׁכָּבִים. גּוֹלְדִילַקְס שָׁכְבָה עַל מִשְׁכָּב אֶחָד וְהַמִּשְׁכָּב הָיָה גָּדוֹל מְאֹד. הִיא שָׁכְבָה עַל הַמִּשְׁכָּב הַשֵּׁנִי וְגַם הוּא הָיָה גָּדוֹל. הִיא שָׁכְבָה עַל הַמִּשְׁכָּב הַשְּׁלִישִׁי וְהַמִּשְׁכָּב הָיָה טוֹב. גּוֹלְדִילַקְס יָשְׁנָה שָׁם. הַדֻּבִּים בָּאוּ מִשָּׂדָם אֶל בֵּיתָם. הֵם הָלְכוּ אֶל הַשֻּׁלְחָן.

אַב־דֹב אָמַר בְּקוֹלוֹ הַגָּדוֹל מְאֹד: "מִי אָכַל אֶת אָכְלִי?"

אֵם־דֻבָּה אָמְרָה בְּקוֹלָהּ הַגָּדוֹל: "מִי אָכַל אֶת אָכְלִי?"

בֶּן־דֹב אָמַר בְּקוֹל לֹא גָּדוֹל: "מִי אָכַל אֶת אָכְלִי?"

הַדֻּבִּים יָשְׁבוּ עַל הַכִּסְאוֹת.

אַב־דֹב אָמַר בְּקוֹלוֹ הַגָּדוֹל מְאֹד: "מִי יָשַׁב עַל כִּסְאִי?"

אֵם־דֻבָּה אָמְרָה בְּקוֹלָהּ הַגָּדוֹל: "מִי יָשַׁב עַל כִּסְאִי?"

בֶּן־דֹב אָמַר בְּקוֹל לֹא גָּדוֹל: "מִי יָשַׁב עַל כִּסְאִי?"

הַדֻּבִּים הָלְכוּ אֶל הַמִּשְׁכָּבִים.

אַב־דֹב אָמַר בְּקוֹלוֹ הַגָּדוֹל מְאֹד: "מִי שָׁכַב עַל מִשְׁכָּבִי?"

אֵם־דֻבָּה אָמְרָה בְּקוֹלָהּ הַגָּדוֹל: "מִי שָׁכַב עַל מִשְׁכָּבִי?"

בֶּן־דֹב אָמַר בְּקוֹל לֹא גָּדוֹל: "מִי שָׁכַב עַל מִשְׁכָּבִי? נַעֲרָה שָׁכְבָה בְּמִשְׁכָּבִי וְהִיא עוֹד בְּמִשְׁכָּבִי!!!"

הַדֻּבִּים אָהֲבוּ אֶת גּוֹלְדִילַקְס וְהִיא יָשְׁבָה עִם מִשְׁפַּחַת הַדֻּבִּים עַד עוֹלָם.

Exercise 6. Fill in the proper form of the verb in the last column and translate.

Root	Number	Gender	Person	Tense	Pattern	Word	
ז.כ.ר	sg	c	1	perfect	פָּעַל		1
כ.ת.ב	sg	c	1	perfect	פָּעַל		2
י.שׁ.ב	sg	c	1	perfect	פָּעַל		3
א.כ.ל	sg	c	1	perfect	פָּעַל		4
א.מ.ר	pl	c	1	perfect	פָּעַל		5
ז.כ.ר	pl	c	1	perfect	פָּעַל		6
כ.ת.ב	pl	c	1	perfect	פָּעַל		7
שׁ.ל.ח	pl	c	1	perfect	פָּעַל		8
א.כ.ל	pl	m	2	perfect	פָּעַל		9
א.כ.ל	pl	f	2	perfect	פָּעַל		10
א.מ.ר	pl	m	2	perfect	פָּעַל		11
ה.י.ה	pl	f	2	perfect	פָּעַל		12

From the Prayerbook

Prayerbook Vocabulary   Lord . . . . אָדוֹן

Selection From the Prayerbook (from the Torah service)

אֶחָד אֱלֹהֵינוּ, גָּדוֹל אֲדוֹנֵינוּ, קָדוֹשׁ שְׁמוֹ.

First try to translate the prayer in your own words, then read the translations quoted below.

Prayerbook Translations

"Our God is One; Our Lord is great; holy is His name."

Gates of Prayer, The New Union Prayerbook, 1975, p. 532

"One is our God; great is our Lord; holy is His name."

Sabbath and Festival Prayerbook, Rabbinical Assembly of America, 1946, p. 217

Notice that this prayer consists of three noun sentences. Each one includes a noun with a possessive pronoun ending.

Guided Reading from Ruth

	1. וְהִיא הָלְכָה מִן הַמָּקוֹם אֲשֶׁר הָיְתָה שָׁם
1. And she went from the place where she was (Literally: from the place that she was there)	2. שְׁתֵּי two כַּלֹּתֶיהָ her daughters-in-law עִם שְׁתֵּי כַלֹּתֶיהָ.
2. with her two daughters-in-law.	3. לָשׁוּב to return וְהִנֵּה הָלְכוּ בַדֶּרֶךְ לָשׁוּב אֶל אֶרֶץ יְהוּדָה.
3. And they went on the road to return to the land of Judah.	4. אָמְרָה נָעֳמִי לִשְׁתֵּי כַלֹּתֶיהָ,
4. Naomi said to her two daughters-in-law,	5. לֵכְנָה Go! *command form of* ה.ל.ךְ שֹׁבְנָה Return! *command form of* שׁ.ו.ב "לֵכְנָה שֹׁבְנָה אִשָּׁה לְבֵית אִמָּהּ.
5. "Go! Return! Each woman to the house of her mother (Literally: a woman to the house of her mother).	6. ע.שׂ.ה do *verb* יַעֲשֶׂה *3 m sg* (he) shall do עִמָּכֶן with you יַעֲשֶׂה יהוה עִמָּכֶן חֶסֶד
6. God shall deal kindly (do kindness) with you	7. עֲשִׂיתֶן you did *perfect tense* *2 f pl of* ע.שׂ.ה מֵתִים dead ones עִמִּי with me כַּאֲשֶׁר עֲשִׂיתֶן עִם הַמֵּתִים וְעִמִּי."
7. as you did with the dead ones and with me."	

וְהִיא הָלְכָה מִן הַמָּקוֹם אֲשֶׁר הָיְתָה שָׁם עִם שְׁתֵּי כַלֹּתֶיהָ. וְהִנֵּה הָלְכוּ בַדֶּרֶךְ לָשׁוּב אֶל אֶרֶץ יְהוּדָה. אָמְרָה נָעֳמִי לִשְׁתֵּי כַלֹּתֶיהָ, "לֵכְנָה שֹׁבְנָה אִשָּׁה לְבֵית אִמָּהּ. יַעֲשֶׂה יהוה עִמָּכֶן חֶסֶד כַּאֲשֶׁר עֲשִׂיתֶן עִם הַמֵּתִים וְעִמִּי."

79

Chapter 14
The Active and Passive Participle
of the פָּעַל Pattern

Vocabulary

after, behind *prep*	אַחַר *or* אַחֲרֵי
before, in the presence of *prep*	לִפְנֵי
take *vb*	ל.ק.ח
reign, rule *vb*	מ.ל.ךְ
open *vb*	פ.ת.ח
harvest *vb*.	ק.צ.ר
hear *vb*	שׁ.מ.ע
gate *n, m*	שַׁעַר, שְׁעָרִים
judge *vb*	שׁ.פ.ט
under, instead of *prep*	תַּחַת

The Participle

A participle is a word that can be used as a verb, a noun, or an adjective.

Examples: walking, writing, sitting, going

In Hebrew also, the same word may be used in each of these three ways: as a verb, as a noun or as an adjective. We will discuss further how to use the participle in Hebrew after we show you how to form the participle from the root letters.

The Active Participle in the פָּעַל Pattern

	write — כ.ת.ב — **Participle**	**Participle Pattern**
masculine singular	כּוֹתֵב	אוֹXֵX
	כֹּתֵב	XֹXֵX
feminine singular	כּוֹתֶּבֶת *or* כּוֹתְבָה	אוֹXֶֶXת *or* אוֹXְXָה
	כֹּתֶבֶת כֹּתְבָה	XֹXֶֶXת XֹXְXָה
masculine plural	כּוֹתְבִים	אוֹXְXִים
	כֹּתְבִים	XֹXְXִים
feminine plural	כּוֹתְבוֹת	אוֹXְXוֹת
	כֹּתְבוֹת	XֹXְXוֹת

Notes on the Formation of the Participle

1. The participle in the פָּעַל pattern is made by placing the אֹ or אֵ vowel between the first and second root letters. Both forms are used interchangeably: כּוֹתֵב = כֹּתֵב, etc.
2. The masculine singular has the אֵ vowel under the second root letter: כֹּתֵב / כּוֹתֵב
3. The feminine singular has two endings which are used interchangeably: כּוֹתֶבֶת / כּוֹתְבָה
4. The masculine plural is formed by adding the אִים ending: כּוֹתְבִים
5. The feminine plural is formed by adding the אוֹת ending: כּוֹתְבוֹת

Variations

When the third root letter of a verb is ח or ע, as in the roots שׁ.מ.ע, פ.ת.ח, ל.ק.ח, שׁ.ל.ח, the active participle is formed somewhat differently in the masculine and feminine singular.

Example:	Third Root Letter ח or ע	Regular Verb
	שׁוֹלֵחַ	זוֹכֵר
	שׁוֹלַחַת/שׁוֹלְחָה	זוֹכֶרֶת/זוֹכְרָה
	שׁוֹלְחִים	זוֹכְרִים
	שׁוֹלְחוֹת	זוֹכְרוֹת

1. The third root letter in the masculine singular form of the participle takes the אַ vowel. Examples: שׁוֹמֵעַ, לוֹקֵחַ, פּוֹתֵחַ. This vowel is called a **furtive patach.** When a furtive patach אַ appears under the letter ח — חַ — it is pronounced "ach" and not "cha" (see Chapter 3, Odd Endings).
2. The second and third root letters in the feminine singular take the אַ vowel. Examples: שׁוֹמַעַת, פּוֹתַחַת, לוֹקַחַת.

The Participle as Verb

As we have seen, the verb ה.י.ה — **be** — has no present tense (see Chapter 11). In actuality, in Biblical Hebrew **there is no present** tense as we understand it. When the participle is used as a verb it usually describes an action that is continuing, an action in progress, or an action in the immediate future.

Example:	He (is) walking to his house.	הוּא הוֹלֵךְ לְבֵיתוֹ.
	(is) about to walk to his house.	
	(is) continuing to walk to his house.	

As in the noun sentence, the verb **be** is absent from these sentences. If translated literally, they read: He walking to his house.

Since the verb ה.י.ה, **be,** is absent from these sentences, they can be translated in any time frame. For example, "He is walking . . ." or "He was walking . . ." or "He will be walking . . .". However, unless there is a specific time frame required by context, the participle should be translated as action in progress or action about to happen.

The Participle as Adjective

The participle can be used as an adjective to describe a noun.
The rules that govern adjectives also govern participles as adjectives.

Without a Definite Article	Adjective	a good man	אִישׁ טוֹב
	Participle	a writing man —	אִישׁ כּוֹתֵב
		or — a man who is writing	
With a Definite Article	Adjective	the good man	הָאִישׁ הַטּוֹב
	Participle	the writing man —	הָאִישׁ הַכּוֹתֵב
		or — the man who is writing	
Agreement with Noun	Adjective	the good women	הַנָּשִׁים הַטּוֹבוֹת
	Participle	the writing women —	הַנָּשִׁים הַכּוֹתְבוֹת
		or — the women who are writing	

It is often best to translate the participle when it is used as an adjective with a phrase beginning with "who". "The writing man" is often best translated "The man who is writing", although both translations are correct.

The Participle as Noun

The participle can be used as a noun and is governed by the same rules as any Hebrew noun.

Without a Definite Article	Noun	a lad	נַעַר
	Participle	a guarding one — or — a guard	שׁוֹמֵר
With a Definite Article	Noun	the lad	הַנַּעַר
	Participle	the guarding one — or — the guard	הַשׁוֹמֵר
In the Construct State	Noun	the lad of the city	נַעַר הָעִיר
	Participle	the guard of the city	שׁוֹמֵר הָעִיר
		the guards of the city	שׁוֹמְרֵי הָעִיר
		the sons of the guard	בְּנֵי הַשׁוֹמֵר
With Pronoun Endings	Noun	his lad	נַעֲרוֹ
	Participle	his guarding one — or — his guard	שׁוֹמְרוֹ

The Passive Participle in the פָּעַל Pattern

There are two types of participles in Biblical Hebrew: the active participle and the passive participle. Until now we have covered the active participle. The passive participle is used to describe a person or thing that is acted upon.

	Active Participle	Passive Participle
Examples: Verb	הוּא שׁוֹמֵר אֶת הָאִישׁ.	הָאִישׁ שָׁמוּר.
	He (is) guarding the man.	The man (is) guarded.
Adjective	הוּא אִישׁ שׁוֹמֵר.	הוּא אִישׁ שָׁמוּר.
	He (is) a guarding man.	He (is) a guarded man.
Noun	הוּא הַשּׁוֹמֵר.	הוּא הַשָּׁמוּר.
	He (is) the guarding one.	He (is) the guarded one.
	— or — He (is) the guard.	

The best known Hebrew passive participle is the word בָּרוּךְ. It comes from the root ב.ר.ך. —**bless**— and it means **blessed**. The passive participle only occurs in the פָּעַל pattern.

How to Form the Passive Participle

		Passive Participle	Passive Participle Pattern
	write — כ.ת.ב —	Participle	
masculine singular		כָּתוּב	XXוX
feminine singular		כְּתוּבָה	XְXוXָה
masculine plural		כְּתוּבִים	XְXוXִים
feminine plural		כְּתוּבוֹת	XְXוXוֹת

The passive participle is made by placing וּ between the second and third root letters.

In Biblical Hebrew, the passive participle is less common than the active. Not all verbs have a passive participle. Of those you have learned, only the following have a passive participle.

ז.כ.ר–זָכוּר, כ.ת.ב–כָּתוּב, ל.ק.ח–לָקוּחַ, פ.ת.ח–פָּתוּחַ, ק.צ.ר–קָצוּר, שׁ.מ.ר–שָׁמוּר

Adjectives as Nouns

You have learned that in Hebrew, as in English, adjectives are used to describe nouns.

Examples: The old man   הָאִישׁ הַזָּקֵן   The good women   הַנָּשִׁים הַטּוֹבוֹת

In Hebrew, adjectives can be used also by themselves, as nouns.

Examples: The old one   הַזָּקֵן   The good ones   הַטּוֹבוֹת

From now on, the adjectives that you have learned will be used as both adjectives and nouns.

Examples: **The old men** sat under the tree.   הָאֲנָשִׁים הַזְּקֵנִים יָשְׁבוּ תַּחַת הָעֵץ.

           The old ones sat under the tree.   הַזְּקֵנִים יָשְׁבוּ תַּחַת הָעֵץ.

Guided Reading to Show Uses of the Participle

		אַנְשֵׁי מוֹאָב הוֹלְכִים אֶל יְרוּשָׁלַיִם. .1
1.	The people of Moab (are) going to Jerusalem. *Participle as verb of action continuing or in immediate future*	אַנְשֵׁי מוֹאָב יוֹשְׁבִים לִפְנֵי שֹׁפְטֵי הָעִיר. .2
2.	The people of Moab (are) sitting in the presence of the judges of the city. *Participle as verb of continuing action*	נְשֵׁי מוֹאָב שׁוֹלְחוֹת אֶת הַנְּעָרִים מִירוּשָׁלַיִם. .3
3.	The women of Moab (are) sending the lads from Jerusalem. *Participle as verb of continuing action with object.*	הָאִישׁ הַכּוֹתֵב שָׁלַח אֶת סִפְרוֹ. .4
4.	The man who is writing (the writing man) sent his book. *Participle as adjective describing the subject "man"*	הָאִשָּׁה הַהוֹלֶכֶת זְקֵנָה. .5
5.	The woman who is walking is old. *Participle as adjective describing the subject "woman"*	בַּבֹּקֶר פָּתַח הַקּוֹצֵר אֶת הַשְּׁעָרִים וְהָלַךְ לַשָּׂדוֹת. .6
6.	In the morning the harvesting one (the harvester) opened the gates and went to the fields. *Participle as noun*	בַּבֹּקֶר פָּתְחוּ קוֹצְרֵי הָעִיר אֶת הַשְּׁעָרִים וְהָלְכוּ לַשָּׂדוֹת. .7
7.	In the morning the harvesters of the city opened the gates and went to the fields. *Participle as noun in the construct state*	בַּבֹּקֶר פָּתַח קוֹצְרוֹ אֶת הַשְּׁעָרִים וְהָלַךְ לַשָּׂדוֹת. .8
8.	In the morning his harvesting one (his harvester) opened the gates and went to the fields. *Participle as noun with pronoun ending*	בֶּן רוּת זָכוּר בְּאֶרֶץ יִשְׂרָאֵל. .9
9.	The son of Ruth is remembered in the land of Israel. *Passive participle*	

Exercises

Exercise 1.

1. Give the four active participle forms of the following roots:

ש.מ.ע   ש.כ.ב   פ.ת.ח   ל.ק.ח   ז.כ.ר   א.כ.ל

ש.פ.ט   ש.ל.ח   ק.צ.ר   מ.ל.ך   י.שׁ.ב   ה.ל.ך

2. Give the four passive participle forms of the following roots:

ק.צ.ר   פ.ת.ח   ל.ק.ח   ז.כ.ר   שׁ.מ.ר

Exercise 2. Rewrite the sentences below, replacing the underlined word with each word in the list that follows. Every word or grammatical form in the sentence that agrees with the underlined word should be changed to agree with the newly substituted words. Read the sentences aloud. Translate.

1. הַמֶּלֶךְ הַזָּקֵן מָלַךְ וְהוּא עוֹד מוֹלֵךְ.

   E. שָׁכַב   D. יָשַׁב   C. שָׁמַע   B. כָּתַב   A. שָׁמַר

2. בֹּעַז פּוֹתֵחַ אֶת שַׁעֲרֵי עִירוֹ תַּחַת אַבְרָהָם.

   E. אֲנִי   D. הֵנָּה   C. אַתָּה   B. אֲנַחְנוּ   A. נָעֳמִי

   H. אַתֶּם   G. אַתְּ   F. אַתֶּן

3. הָאִשָּׁה הַקּוֹצֶרֶת לָקְחָה אֶת הַמִּנְחָה מִן בֹּעַז.

   E. אֲנַחְנוּ   D. דָּוִד   C. הַנָּשִׁים   B. הַבֵּן   A. הַנְּעָרִים

4. בְּנִי שׁוֹמֵעַ אֶת קוֹלִי כָּל הַלַּיְלָה.

   E. הַנָּשִׁים   D. הַשּׁוֹמֵר   C. הַנַּעֲרָה   B. הֵם   A. בִּתֵּנוּ

5. הָאִישׁ הָרַע לוֹקֵחַ אֶת הָאֹכֶל מִתַּחַת בֵּיתֵנוּ.

   E. אֲנָשִׁים   D. הַשּׁוֹמְרִים   C. הַנְּעָרוֹת   B. דּוֹדָתָהּ   A. שָׂרָה

6. בֵּית הַמֶּלֶךְ שָׁמוּר כָּל הַיּוֹם וְכָל הַלַּיְלָה.

   E. מָקוֹם   D. כִּסֵּא   C. בָּנוֹת   B. שָׂדַי   A. נַעֲלַי

Exercise 3. In the following sentences, fill in the blanks with the appropriate form of the passive participle. Use the same root as the active participle given in the first part of the sentence. Example:

אַבְרָהָם פּוֹתֵחַ אֶת הַשַּׁעַר; הַשַּׁעַר פָּתוּחַ.

1. הָאִישׁ הַזָּקֵן לָקַח אֶת הָאֹכֶל מֵאַחַר הַבַּיִת: הָאֹכֶל _____.

2. אֵשֶׁת יַעֲקֹב שָׁלְחָה אֶת הַמִּנְחוֹת; הַמִּנְחוֹת _____.

3. הַמֶּלֶךְ פּוֹתֵחַ אֶת כָּל סְפָרָיו; סְפָרָיו _____.

4. נָעֳמִי זֹכֶרֶת אֶת יַעֲקֹב; יַעֲקֹב _____.

5. אָנוּ שׁוֹמְרִים אֶת הָעִיר; הָעִיר _____.

6. הַמֶּלֶךְ זוֹכֵר אֶת הַנְּעָרוֹת הַטּוֹבוֹת; הַנְּעָרוֹת _____.

7. בֹּעַז פּוֹתֵחַ אֶת הַשַּׁעַר; הַשַּׁעַר _____.

8. אַתְּ כּוֹתְבָה אֶת שְׁמֵנוּ; שְׁמֵנוּ _____.

9. כַּאֲשֶׁר רוּת בְּבֵית לֶחֶם, הִיא שׁוֹמֶרֶת אֶת מִשְׁפַּחְתָּהּ הַגְּדוֹלָה מְאֹד; מִשְׁפַּחְתָּהּ _____.

10. מִי זֹכֵר אֶת חַסְדֵי רוּת אֲשֶׁר הָלְכָה בַּדֶּרֶךְ אַחַר נָעֳמִי?   חַסְדֵי רוּת _____.

Exercise 4. In the following sentences, change the participles to the appropriate form of the verb in the perfect tense. Translate.

1. דָּוִד שׁוֹמֵר עַל הַבַּיִת תַּחַת יַעֲקֹב.

2. אָנוּ פּוֹתְחוֹת אֶת הַשַּׁעַר בַּבֹּקֶר לִפְנֵי אַנְשֵׁי הָעִיר.

3. הוּא מֹלֵךְ עַל כָּל הָאָרֶץ.

4. אַתְּ הוֹלֶכֶת לָעִיר תַּחַת אִמֵּךְ.

5. הַנָּשִׁים שׁוֹמְעוֹת אֶת הָאִישׁ הַקָּדוֹשׁ בְּבֵית לֶחֶם.

6. הַמֶּלֶךְ הַזָּקֵן שׁוֹפֵט אֶת הָאִישׁ הָרַע לִפְנֵי הָעָם.

7. הֵנָּה לוֹקְחוֹת אֶת הַלֶּחֶם תַּחַת הַפְּרִי.

8. אֲנִי הֹלֵךְ אַחֲרֵי הַקּוֹצְרִים.

Exercise 5. Translate the following sentences into Hebrew.

1. I am eating with my mother.
2. You *m, sg* are writing from his house.
3. She is remembering the people in her city.
4. The food from her city is remembered.
5. The good food from our house is guarded.
6. Ruth is taking her aunt to the big city.
7. Boaz took his son to his city.

Exercise 6. Read and translate.

Vocabulary for Reading Selection

stand . . . . ע.מ.ד   alone . . . . לְבַד

Name That Tune!

הַקּוֹצֵר בַּשָּׂדֶה, הַקּוֹצֵר בַּשָּׂדֶה, הַי הוֹ הַדְּראוֹ, הַקּוֹצֵר בַּשָּׂדֶה.

הַקּוֹצֵר לוֹקֵחַ אִשָּׁה, הַקּוֹצֵר לוֹקֵחַ אִשָּׁה, הַי הוֹ הַדְּראוֹ, הַקּוֹצֵר לוֹקֵחַ אִשָּׁה.

הָאִשָּׁה לוֹקַחַת בֵּן, הָאִשָּׁה לוֹקַחַת בֵּן, הַי הוֹ הַדְּראוֹ, הָאִשָּׁה לוֹקַחַת בֵּן.

הַבֵּן לוֹקֵחַ נַעֲרָה, הַבֵּן לוֹקֵחַ נַעֲרָה, הַי הוֹ הַדְּראוֹ, הַבֵּן לוֹקֵחַ נַעֲרָה.

הַנַּעֲרָה לוֹקַחַת לֶחֶם, הַנַּעֲרָה לוֹקַחַת לֶחֶם, הַי הוֹ הַדְּראוֹ, הַנַּעֲרָה לוֹקַחַת לֶחֶם.

הַלֶּחֶם עוֹמֵד לְבַד, הַלֶּחֶם עוֹמֵד לְבַד, הַי הוֹ הַדְּראוֹ, הַלֶּחֶם עוֹמֵד לְבַד.

Exercise 7. Fill in the proper form of the verb in the last column and translate.

Root	Number	Gender	Person	Tense	Pattern	Word
כ.ת.ב	sg	m	3	perfect	פָּעַל	1
כ.ת.ב	sg	m	—	active participle	פָּעַל	2
כ.ת.ב	sg	m	—	passive participle	פָּעַל	3
פ.ת.ח	pl	m	3	perfect	פָּעַל	4
פ.ת.ח	pl	m	—	active participle	פָּעַל	5
פ.ת.ח	pl	m	—	passive participle	פָּעַל	6
ק.צ.ר	sg	f	2	perfect	פָּעַל	7
ז.כ.ר	pl	f	2	perfect	פָּעַל	8
ז.כ.ר	pl	f	—	active participle	פָּעַל	9
א.כ.ל	pl	f	3	perfect	פָּעַל	10
א.כ.ל	sg	f	—	active participle	פָּעַל	11
א.כ.ל	sg	m	—	active participle	פָּעַל	12
ש.מ.ר	sg	c	1	perfect	פָּעַל	13
ש.מ.ר	pl	c	1	perfect	פָּעַל	14
ש.מ.ר	pl	f	2	perfect	פָּעַל	15
ש.מ.ר	sg	f	—	active participle	פָּעַל	16
ש.ל.ח	sg	f	—	active participle	פָּעַל	17
ל.ק.ח	sg	f	—	active participle	פָּעַל	18
פ.ת.ח	sg	f	—	active participle	פָּעַל	19
פ.ת.ח	sg	f	—	passive participle	פָּעַל	20
ש.מ.ע	sg	f	—	active participle	פָּעַל	21
ש.מ.ע	sg	f	3	perfect	פָּעַל	22
ש.מ.ע	pl	f	3	perfect	פָּעַל	23
ש.מ.ע	pl	m	—	active participle	פָּעַל	24

From the Prayerbook

Prayerbook Vocabulary bestow ..... גּוֹמֵל – ג.מ.ל   master...... קוֹנֶה – ק.נ.ה

Selection From the Prayerbook (from the Amidah service)

גּוֹמֵל חֲסָדִים טוֹבִים, וְקוֹנֵה הַכֹּל, וְזוֹכֵר חַסְדֵי אָבוֹת. . . .

First try to translate the prayer in your own words, then read the translations quoted below.

Prayerbook Translations

"Who bestowest lovingkindnesses, and art master of all things; who rememberest the pious deeds of the patriarchs. . . ."   *Daily Prayer Book, Joseph H. Hertz, 1975, p. 131*

"Who bestowest lovingkindness, and art Master of all things; who rememberest the good deeds of our fathers. . . ."   *Daily Prayer Book, Philip Birnbaum, 1977, p. 82*

Notice that this prayer includes three participles.

Guided Reading from Ruth

	1. find *command form* מְצֶאןָה rest, peace מְנוּחָה נָעֳמִי אָמְרָה: "מְצֶאןָה מְנוּחָה אִשָּׁה בֵּית אִישָׁהּ".
1. Naomi said: "Find rest, (each) woman (in) the house of her husband".	2. kiss נ.שׁ.ק נָעֳמִי נָשְׁקָה לְרוּת וּלְעָרְפָּה
2. Naomi kissed Ruth and Orpah	3. raise נ.שׂ.א (they) wept בָּכוּ וְהֵנָּה נָשְׂאוּ אֶת קוֹלָן וַבָּכוּ.
3. and they raised their voices and wept.	4. הֵנָּה אָמְרוּ לְנָעֳמִי:
4. They said to Naomi:	5. with you אִתָּךְ we will return נָשׁוּב "אִתָּךְ נָשׁוּב לְעַמֵּךְ".
5. "We will return with you to your people".	

נָעֳמִי אָמְרָה: "מְצֶאןָה מְנוּחָה אִשָּׁה בֵּית אִישָׁהּ". נָעֳמִי נָשְׁקָה לְרוּת וּלְעָרְפָּה וְהֵנָּה נָשְׂאוּ אֶת קוֹלָן וַבָּכוּ.
הֵנָּה אָמְרוּ לְנָעֳמִי: "אִתָּךְ נָשׁוּב לְעַמֵּךְ".

Chapter 15
The Demonstratives
אֵין and יֵשׁ
The Preposition לְ with Pronoun Endings

Vocabulary

there is not	אֵין
these *dem, c, pl*	אֵלֶּה
that *dem, m, sg*	הוּא
that *dem, f, sg*	הִיא
those *dem, m, pl*	הֵם, הֵמָּה
those *dem, f, pl*	הֵן, הֵנָּה
this *dem, f, sg*	זֹאת
this *dem, m, sg*	זֶה
there is	יֵשׁ

Note 1: New abbreviation — *dem* demonstrative

Note 2: The demonstratives הֵנָּה, הֵם, הֵמָּה, הִיא, הוּא, **that**, and הֵן, **those**, are the third person subject pronouns. The correct translation must be determined from the context.

The Demonstratives

The demonstratives are words that call attention to specific nouns. In English, the demonstratives are: this, these, that, those. In Hebrew, the demonstratives are:

that *m, sg*	הוּא	this *m, sg*	זֶה
that *f, sg*	הִיא	this *f, sg*	זֹאת
those *m, pl*	הֵם, הֵמָּה	these *c, pl*	אֵלֶּה
those *f, pl*	הֵן, הֵנָּה		

Uses of the Demonstratives

In both English and Hebrew, the demonstratives can be used in two ways.

1. They can be used as adjectives.
    Examples: this man   הָאִישׁ הַזֶּה   that maiden   הַנַּעֲרָה הַהִיא
2. They can be used as pronouns.   Example: This is a man.   זֶה אִישׁ.

Demonstratives as Adjectives

When a demonstrative is used as an adjective, it follows the noun and agrees with it in number and gender. Since a demonstrative is a word that calls attention to a definite, specific noun, the noun that it describes must be definite. Therefore, both the noun and the demonstrative adjective take the definite article הַX.

Examples:	that lad	הַנַּעַר הַהוּא	this lad	הַנַּעַר הַזֶּה
	that maiden	הַנַּעֲרָה הַהִיא	this maiden	הַנַּעֲרָה הַזֹּאת
	those lads	הַנְּעָרִים הָהֵם	these lads	הַנְּעָרִים הָאֵלֶּה
	those maidens	הַנְּעָרוֹת הָהֵן	these maidens	הַנְּעָרוֹת הָאֵלֶּה

If a noun is described by both an adjective and a demonstrative, the demonstrative follows the adjective.

Examples:	this old man	הָאִישׁ הַזָּקֵן הַזֶּה
	those good shoes	הַנַּעֲלִים הַטּוֹבוֹת הָהֵנָּה

Demonstratives as Pronouns

When a demonstrative is used as a pronoun, it replaces a noun or a pronoun in the sentence. If it is used as a pronoun at the beginning of a sentence, it forms a noun sentence.

Examples:	This is the book.	זֶה הַסֵּפֶר.
	This is a woman.	זֹאת אִשָּׁה.
	These are the books.	אֵלֶּה הַסְּפָרִים.
	These are women.	אֵלֶּה נָשִׁים.

Notice that the demonstrative pronoun must agree in number and gender with the noun to which it refers. However, the demonstrative pronoun never takes a definite article, even if the noun is definite.

How to Distinguish Between a Demonstrative Adjective and a Demonstrative Pronoun

1. A demonstrative adjective always takes the definite article הַX; a demonstrative pronoun never takes the definite article הַX.
2. A demonstrative adjective and a noun form an adjective phrase; a demonstrative pronoun and a noun form a noun sentence.

Examples:	Adjective	This road . . .	הַדֶּרֶךְ הַזֹּאת . . .
	Pronoun	This is the road.	זֹאת הַדֶּרֶךְ.
	Adjective	This judge . . .	הַשּׁוֹפֵט הַזֶּה . . .
	Adjective	This judge is old.	הַשּׁוֹפֵט הַזֶּה זָקֵן.
	Pronoun	This is an old judge.	זֶה שׁוֹפֵט זָקֵן.

The Use of יֵשׁ and אֵין

You have already learned in Chapter 10 that the third person of the verb ה.י.ה in the perfect tense is used to mean **there was** or **there were** and **there was not** or **there were not**.

Examples: There was food in the house.	הָיָה אֹכֶל בַּבַּיִת.
There were no people in the field.	לֹא הָיוּ אֲנָשִׁים בַּשָּׂדֶה.

1. The word יֵשׁ means **there is** or **there are**.

Examples: There is a man in the field.	יֵשׁ אִישׁ בַּשָּׂדֶה.
There are men in the field.	יֵשׁ אֲנָשִׁים בַּשָּׂדֶה.

2. The word אֵין means **there is not** or **there are not.** The word אֵין is always the negation of יֵשׁ. You cannot use לֹא to negate יֵשׁ.

Examples: There is not a man in the field.	אֵין אִישׁ בַּשָּׂדֶה.
There are not men in the field.	אֵין אֲנָשִׁים בַּשָּׂדֶה.

Notice that the words יֵשׁ and אֵין do not agree with the nouns to which they refer. Unlike the verb ה.י.ה which must agree with the number and gender of the subject, the words יֵשׁ and אֵין do not change form.

Prepositions with Pronoun Endings

In both English and Hebrew, a subject pronoun cannot follow a preposition. It is impossible to say:

to I לְ אֲנִי   — or —   with we עִם אֲנַחְנוּ

In Hebrew, pronoun endings are attached to the preposition. In this chapter, only the inseparable preposition לְ — **to** will be shown with pronoun endings. Other prepositions with pronoun endings will be introduced in later chapters.

לְ with Pronoun Endings

to us, for us	לָנוּ	to me, for me	לִי
to you, for you *m pl*	לָכֶם	to you, for you *m sg*	לְךָ
to you, for you *f pl*	לָכֶן	to you, for you *f sg*	לָךְ
to them, for them *m pl*	לָהֶם	to him, for him	לוֹ
to them, for them *f pl*	לָהֶן	to her, for her	לָה

Notice that the pronoun endings attached to the preposition are very similar to the possessive pronoun endings.

"Have" in Hebrew

There is no verb in Hebrew to express the English verb **have**. Therefore, a statement of possession is made indirectly by using the inseparable preposition לְ.

"Have" in a Noun Sentence

The inseparable preposition לְ can be used in two ways to express the English verb **have** in a Hebrew noun sentence.

1. It may be attached to the noun or pronoun that is the possessor.

    Examples: Literally: To Abraham books.
                or: Abraham has books.   לְאַבְרָהָם סְפָרִים.

                Literally: To us a son.
                or: We have a son.   לָנוּ בֵּן.

2. It may be attached to the noun or pronoun that is the possessor and used together with the word יֵשׁ. However, this way of expressing possession is rarely used in the Bible.

    Examples: Literally: There are to Abraham books.
                or: Abraham has books.   יֵשׁ לְאַבְרָהָם סְפָרִים.

                Literally: There is to us a son.
                or: We have a son.   יֵשׁ לָנוּ בֵּן.

"Have" with the Perfect Tense

The inseparable preposition לְ is used with the perfect tense of the verb ה.י.ה to express possession in the past. The verb ה.י.ה must agree in gender and number with the subject.

Examples: Literally: **There were** to Abraham books.
            or: Abraham had books.   הָיוּ לְאַבְרָהָם סְפָרִים.

            Literally: **There was** to us a son.
            or: We had a son.   הָיָה לָנוּ בֵּן.

Note that in the literally translated sentences above, **there were** and **there was** are the subject clauses of the sentences.

How to Express "not have" in Hebrew

There is only one way to express **not have** in a Hebrew noun sentence. The inseparable preposition לְ is attached to the noun or pronoun and used together with the word אֵין. The word לֹא is never used to express **not have** in a noun sentence.

Examples: Literally: There are not to Abraham books.
            or: Abraham does not have books.   אֵין לְאַבְרָהָם סְפָרִים.
            or: Abraham has no books.

	Literally:	There is not to us a son.	אֵין לָנוּ בֵּן.
	or:	We do not have a son.	
	or:	We have no son.	

However, the word לֹא is used with the inseparable preposition לְ and the perfect tense of the verb ה.י.ה to express lack of possession in the past. The word אֵין is not used with the perfect tense. Notice that the verb ה.י.ה must agree in gender and number with the subject.

Examples:	Literally:	There were not to Abraham books.	לֹא הָיוּ לְאַבְרָהָם סְפָרִים.
	or:	Abraham did not have books.	
	or:	Abraham had no books.	
	Literally:	There was not to us a son.	לֹא הָיָה לָנוּ בֵּן.
	or:	We did not have a son.	
	or:	We had no son.	

Exercises

Exercise 1. Rewrite the sentences below, replacing the underlined word with each word in the list that follows. Make the necessary grammatical changes and match pronoun endings to the newly substituted words. Read the sentences aloud. Translate.

1. זֶה עַם גָּדוֹל וְטוֹב.

E. עָרִים	D. שָׂדוֹת	C. חֶסֶד	B. אֶרֶץ	A. מָקוֹם

2. אֵין לָנוּ אֹכֶל כִּי יֵשׁ רָעָב בָּעִיר הַהִיא.

E. לָכֶם	D. לָהֶן	C. לוֹ	B. לָכֶן	A. לִי
	I. לָךְ	H. לָהֶם	G. לְךָ	F. לָהּ

3. יַעֲקֹב שָׁמַע אֶת קוֹל הָאִשָּׁה הָרָעָה הַזֹּאת.

E. הַנָּשִׁים	D. הָאָבוֹת	C. הַדּוֹדָה	B. הַשּׁוֹפְטִים	A. הַמֶּלֶךְ

4. יֵשׁ לוֹ סְפָרִים אֲשֶׁר הוּא לוֹקֵחַ מִמִּשְׁפַּחְתּוֹ.

E. לָךְ	D. לָכֶם	C. לָהּ	B. לַבָּנִים	A. לִי
	I. לָנוּ	H. לָכֶן	G. לְךָ	F. לָהֶן

5. אֵלֶּה הַשּׁוֹפְטִים אֲשֶׁר פָּתְחוּ אֶת הַשְּׁעָרִים הָהֵמָּה.

E. הַדּוֹד	D. הָאִמּוֹת	C. הַמִּשְׁפָּחָה	B. הָאֲנָשִׁים	A. הַבַּת

6. אַתָּה אָמַרְתָּ דְּבָרִים טוֹבִים עַל אִמְּךָ.

E. הוּא	D. הֵנָּה	C. הִיא	B. אַתֶּם	A. אָנֹכִי
	I. הֵם	H. אַתְּ	G. אַתֶּן	F. אֲנַחְנוּ

93

Exercise 2. Change the following sentences from the perfect tense to noun sentences using
יֵשׁ or אֵין. Make all necessary changes. Translate.

Example: הָיוּ נָשִׁים זְקֵנוֹת בַּשָּׂדֶה.　יֵשׁ נָשִׁים זְקֵנוֹת בַּשָּׂדֶה.

1. הָיוּ לִי סְפָרִים בַּבַּיִת.
2. הָיָה בַּיִת גָּדוֹל לָאֲנָשִׁים הָהֵמָּה.
3. הָיוּ לַנַּעַר מְמוֹאָב עֵינַיִם רָעוֹת וְיָדַיִם גְּדוֹלוֹת.
4. כָּל בֹּקֶר וְכָל לַיְלָה הָיוּ אֲנָשִׁים בַּדֶּרֶךְ.
5. בַּיּוֹם הַהוּא, לֹא הָיָה לֶחֶם בָּעִיר.
6. בְּבֵית לֶחֶם הָיְתָה אִשָּׁה אֲשֶׁר יָשְׁבָה בְּבַיִת גָּדוֹל.
7. הָיְתָה לְדָוִד מִנְחָה מִמִּשְׁפַּחְתּוֹ בִּירוּשָׁלַיִם.
8. לֹא הָיוּ לִי בָּתִּים בְּבֵית לֶחֶם.

Exercise 3. Change the following sentences from noun sentences to the perfect tense. Make
all the necessary changes. Translate.

Example: יֵשׁ לִי סֵפֶר בַּבַּיִת.　הָיָה לִי סֵפֶר בַּבַּיִת.

1. יֵשׁ לָנוּ נַעֲלַיִם גְּדוֹלוֹת מְאֹד.
2. אֵין קוֹצְרִים בַּשָּׂדֶה הַיּוֹם.
3. בַּמָּקוֹם הַהוּא אֵין לְנָעֳמִי שָׂדֶה גָּדוֹל.
4. לִפְנֵי אַבְרָהָם יֵשׁ שַׁעַר פָּתוּחַ.
5. יֵשׁ בָּאָרֶץ הַהִיא מֶלֶךְ טוֹב.
6. יֵשׁ לְךָ שֵׁם טוֹב בַּמָּקוֹם הַזֶּה.

Exercise 4. In the following sentences, fill in the blanks with the appropriate perfect tense
form of the verb shown. Translate. Then rewrite each sentence, using the appropriate form
of the participle in place of the perfect.

Example: (ש.ל.ח) אַתָּה ____שָׁלַחְתָּ____ מְנָחוֹת לַמֶּלֶךְ.　אַתָּה שׁוֹלֵחַ מְנָחוֹת לַמֶּלֶךְ.

1. (ה.ל.ךְ) אֲבִי יַעֲקֹב _____ הַיּוֹם אַחֲרֵי אִשְׁתּוֹ.
2. (א.כ.ל) הַקּוֹצְרִים הָהֵמָּה _____ לֶחֶם עִם הַנָּשִׁים הָהֵן.
3. (כ.ת.ב) הַנְּעָרוֹת הָהֵנָּה _____ דְּבָרִים רָעִים תַּחַת דְּבָרִים טוֹבִים.
4. (ז.כ.ר) מָה אַתְּ עוֹד _____ עַל הַמָּקוֹם הַזֶּה?
5. (ש.כ.ב) כַּאֲשֶׁר אֲנִי _____ בַּלַּיְלָה, אֲנִי (ש.מ.ע) _____ אֶת קוֹל אִמִּי.
6. (א.מ.ר) מִי _____ דְּבַר חֶסֶד אֶל הָאִשָּׁה הַזְּקֵנָה הַהִיא?
7. (מ.ל.ךְ) מֶלֶךְ אֶחָד _____ עַל הֶעָרִים הַקְּדוֹשׁוֹת וְגַם עַל מוֹאָב.

Exercise 5. Translate the following sentences into Hebrew.
1. This man is evil.
2. This evil man is from Moab.
3. That evil man from Moab is his father.
4. These are good women.
5. Those good women are the mothers of the lads.
6. There are great men in my city.
7. There are no evil men in this city.

Exercise 6. Read and translate.

Vocabulary for Reading Selection

weep . . . . *participle* בּוֹכָה   ב.כ.ה   kill . . . . ה.ר.ג.

"This is the House that . . ."

זֶה הַבַּיִת אֲשֶׁר בִּשְׂדֵה יְהוּדָה.

זֶה הָאִישׁ הַיּוֹשֵׁב בַּבַּיִת אֲשֶׁר בִּשְׂדֵה יְהוּדָה.

וֹאת הָאִשָּׁה הַיּוֹשֶׁבֶת

עִם הָאִישׁ הַיּוֹשֵׁב בַּבַּיִת אֲשֶׁר בִּשְׂדֵה יְהוּדָה.

אֵלֶּה הַבָּנוֹת אֲשֶׁר לָאִשָּׁה הַיּוֹשֶׁבֶת

עִם הָאִישׁ הַיּוֹשֵׁב בַּבַּיִת אֲשֶׁר בִּשְׂדֵה יְהוּדָה.

אֵלֶּה הַנְּעָרִים הַלּוֹקְחִים אֶת הַבָּנוֹת אֲשֶׁר לָאִשָּׁה הַיּוֹשֶׁבֶת

עִם הָאִישׁ הַיּוֹשֵׁב בַּבַּיִת אֲשֶׁר בִּשְׂדֵה יְהוּדָה.

זֶה הַשּׁוֹפֵט הַשּׁוֹמֵר אֶת הַנְּעָרִים הַלּוֹקְחִים אֶת הַבָּנוֹת אֲשֶׁר לָאִשָּׁה הַיּוֹשֶׁבֶת

עִם הָאִישׁ הַיּוֹשֵׁב בַּבַּיִת בִּשְׂדֵה יְהוּדָה.

זֶה הָרָעָב הַהוֹרֵג אֶת הַשּׁוֹפֵט הַשּׁוֹמֵר

אֶת הַנְּעָרִים הַלּוֹקְחִים אֶת הַבָּנוֹת אֲשֶׁר לָאִשָּׁה הַיּוֹשֶׁבֶת

עִם הָאִישׁ הַיּוֹשֵׁב בַּבַּיִת אֲשֶׁר בִּשְׂדֵה יְהוּדָה.

זֶה הָעָם הַבּוֹכָה עַל הָרָעָב הַהוֹרֵג אֶת הַשּׁוֹפֵט הַשּׁוֹמֵר

אֶת הַנְּעָרִים הַלּוֹקְחִים אֶת הַבָּנוֹת אֲשֶׁר לָאִשָּׁה הַיּוֹשֶׁבֶת

עִם הָאִישׁ הַיּוֹשֵׁב בַּבַּיִת אֲשֶׁר בִּשְׂדֵה יְהוּדָה.

Exercise 7. Fill in the proper form of the verb in the last column and translate.

Root	Number	Gender	Person	Tense	Pattern	Word	
א.כ.ל	sg	c	1	perfect	פָּעַל		1
א.כ.ל	sg	m	—	active participle	פָּעַל		2
ז.כ.ר	pl	c	1	perfect	פָּעַל		3
ז.כ.ר	pl	m	—	active participle	פָּעַל		4
ה.ל.ך	sg	f	2	perfect	פָּעַל		5
ה.ל.ך	sg	f	—	active participle	פָּעַל		6
כ.ת.ב	pl	f	2	perfect	פָּעַל		7
כ.ת.ב	pl	f	—	active participle	פָּעַל		8
כ.ת.ב	pl	f	—	passive participle	פָּעַל		9
שׁ.מ.ע	sg	m	2	perfect	פָּעַל		10
שׁ.מ.ע	sg	f	—	active participle	פָּעַל		11
שׁ.ל.ח	pl	m	2	perfect	פָּעַל		12
שׁ.ל.ח	pl	m	—	active participle	פָּעַל		13
שׁ.פ.ט	pl	m	3	perfect	פָּעַל		14
שׁ.פ.ט	pl	m	2	perfect	פָּעַל		15
ק.צ.ר	pl	f	2	perfect	פָּעַל		16
ק.צ.ר	pl	f	—	active participle	פָּעַל		17
ל.ק.ח	sg	f	3	perfect	פָּעַל		18
ל.ק.ח	sg	f	—	active participle	פָּעַל		19
מ.ל.ך	sg	m	2	perfect	פָּעַל		20
מ.ל.ך	sg	m	3	perfect	פָּעַל		21
שׁ.כ.ב	sg	m	—	active participle	פָּעַל		22
שׁ.כ.ב	pl	m	—	active participle	פָּעַל		23
שׁ.כ.ב	pl	m	3	perfect	פָּעַל		24

From the Prayerbook

Prayerbook Vocabulary

deliverer, savior . . . . **מוֹשִׁיעַ**   blessed . . . . **בָּרוּךְ**

Selection from the Prayerbook (sung at the conclusion of the Sabbath services)

אֵין כֵּאלֹהֵינוּ, אֵין כַּאדוֹנֵינוּ, אֵין כְּמַלְכֵּנוּ, אֵין כְּמוֹשִׁיעֵנוּ.

מִי כֵאלֹהֵינוּ, מִי כַאדוֹנֵינוּ, מִי כְמַלְכֵּנוּ, מִי כְמוֹשִׁיעֵנוּ . . .

בָּרוּךְ אֱלֹהֵינוּ, בָּרוּךְ אֲדוֹנֵינוּ, בָּרוּךְ מַלְכֵּנוּ, בָּרוּךְ מוֹשִׁיעֵנוּ . . . .

First try to translate the prayer in your own words, then read the translation quoted below.

Prayerbook Translation

"There is none like our God; there is none like our Lord; there is none like our King; there is none like our Deliverer.

Who is like our God? Who is like our Lord? Who is like our King? Who is like our Deliverer?

Blessed be our God; blessed be our Lord; blessed be our King; blessed be our Deliverer."

Daily Prayer Book, Philip Birnbaum, 1977, p. 408

Notice the use of אֵין, מִי, and בָּרוּךְ in noun sentences.

Guided Reading from Ruth

	return שֹׁבְנָה .1
	my daughters בְּנֹתַי
	נָעֳמִי אָמְרָה: "שֹׁבְנָה בְּנֹתַי.
1. Naomi said: "Return, my daughters.	
	why לָמָה .2
	you will go (ה.ל.ך) תֵּלַכְנָה
	with me עִמִּי
	לָמָה תֵלַכְנָה עִמִּי?
2. Why will you go with me?	
	my womb מֵעַי .3
	עוֹד לִי בָנִים בְּמֵעַי . . .
3. Do I still have sons in my womb . . .	
	will be (ה.י.ה) יִהְיוּ .4
	אֲשֶׁר יִהְיוּ לָכֶן לַאֲנָשִׁים?"
4. who will be husbands for you?"	

נָעֳמִי אָמְרָה: "שֹׁבְנָה בְּנֹתַי. לָמָה תֵלַכְנָה עִמִּי? עוֹד לִי בָנִים בְּמֵעַי אֲשֶׁר יִהְיוּ לָכֶן לַאֲנָשִׁים?"

97

Chapter 16
The Imperfect Tense of the פָּעַל Pattern
The Interrogative הֲ

Vocabulary

brother *n, m*	אָח, אַחִים
if *conj*	אִם
between, among *prep*	בֵּין
lo! behold!	הִנֵּה
mountain, hill *n, m*	הַר, הָרִים
sea *n, m*	יָם, יַמִּים
couch, bed *n, m*	מִשְׁכָּב, מִשְׁכָּבִים
as far as, until *prep*	עַד
head *n, m*	רֹאשׁ, רָאשִׁים

Idioms

to obey	שׁ.מ.ע בְּקוֹל
Example: I obeyed him.	שָׁמַעְתִּי בְּקוֹלוֹ.
the top of the mountain	רֹאשׁ הָהָר

Note 1: The preposition בֵּין when used to mean "between" is usually
placed before each noun.   בֵּין בֹּעַז וּבֵין רוּת

Note 2: The ָX vowel in רָאשִׁים, heads, is pronounced **o** as in d**o**g.

The Imperfect Tense

There are two main tenses in Biblical Hebrew. You have already learned one, the perfect
tense, which describes actions that are completed.

Examples: He wrote.   He did write.   He had written.

The second tense is the **imperfect tense**, which describes actions or states that are not completed. The imperfect tense includes:

1.   simple future   Example: He will write.
2.   habitual or customary   Example: He usually writes.
3.   potential or probable   Example: He might write.

A Hebrew verb which appears in the imperfect tense can be translated with any of these meanings. All these possibilities should be kept in mind when translating the Bible. However, for the purposes of learning, the simple future will generally be used in this book.

How to Form the Imperfect Tense of Regular פָּעַל Verbs

The following is a chart of the verb ש.מ.ר, conjugated in the imperfect tense. Read this chart aloud. Memorize it.

	ש.מ.ר — Verb	Pattern	
I will guard	אֶשְׁמֹר	XXXֶא	1 c sg
you will guard	תִּשְׁמֹר	XXXתִּ	2 m sg
you will guard	תִּשְׁמְרִי	XXXִיתִּ	2 f sg
he will guard	יִשְׁמֹר	XXXיִ	3 m sg
she will guard	תִּשְׁמֹר	XXXתִּ	3 f sg
we will guard	נִשְׁמֹר	XXXנִ	1 c pl
you will guard	תִּשְׁמְרוּ	XXXוּתִּ	2 m pl
you will guard	תִּשְׁמֹרְנָה	XXXָנָהתִּ	2 f pl
they will guard	יִשְׁמְרוּ	XXXוּיִ	3 m pl
they will guard	תִּשְׁמֹרְנָה	XXXָנָהתִּ	3 f pl

Notes on the Conjugation of Regular פָּעַל Verbs in the Imperfect Tense

1. The main characteristic of a verb form in the imperfect tense is the prefix added to the root. Every verb form in the imperfect tense has a prefix.
2. The first person singular prefix א takes the X vowel. All other prefixes take the X vowel.
3. The second person masculine singular and the third person feminine singular forms are the same:

you will guard	תִּשְׁמֹר
she will guard	תִּשְׁמֹר

4. The second and third person feminine plural forms are the same:

you will guard	תִּשְׁמֹרְנָה
they will guard	תִּשְׁמֹרְנָה

Additional information on this subject can be found on page 272, note 5.

Most regular verbs are conjugated in the imperfect tense in the same way as ש.מ.ר. They follow this general vowel pattern: XXXX. However, some verbs follow a different vowel pattern when they are conjugated in the imperfect tense: XXXX.

99

Following is a chart comparing the conjugation of the verb שׁ.מ.ר with the conjugation of the verb שׁ.ל.ח in the imperfect tense. Notice the differences in the vowel pattern. Read this chart aloud. Memorize it.

Pattern	שׁ.ל.ח — Verb		שׁ.מ.ר —Verb
אֶXXַX	אֶשְׁלַח	1 c sg	אֶשְׁמֹר
תִּXXַX	תִּשְׁלַח	2 m sg	תִּשְׁמֹר
תִּXXְאִי	תִּשְׁלְחִי	2 f sg	תִּשְׁמְרִי
יִXXַX	יִשְׁלַח	3 m sg	יִשְׁמֹר
תִּXXַX	תִּשְׁלַח	3 f sg	תִּשְׁמֹר
נִXXַX	נִשְׁלַח	1 c pl	נִשְׁמֹר
תִּXXְאוּ	תִּשְׁלְחוּ	2 m pl	תִּשְׁמְרוּ
תִּXXֹאְנָה	תִּשְׁלַחְנָה	2 f pl	תִּשְׁמֹרְנָה
יִXXְאוּ	יִשְׁלְחוּ	3 m pl	יִשְׁמְרוּ
תִּXXֹאְנָה	תִּשְׁלַחְנָה	3 f pl	תִּשְׁמֹרְנָה

Some of the verb roots that you have already learned are conjugated in imperfect tense with the XXַXX vowel pattern. Others are conjugated in the imperfect tense with the XXֹXX vowel pattern. Following is a chart showing the regular verbs you have learned and the vowel pattern that they follow when conjugated in the imperfect tense. As you learn new regular verbs in this book, we will tell you to which vowel pattern they belong.

XXַXX	XXֹXX
פ.ת.ח	ז.כ.ר
שׁ.כ.ב	כ.ת.ב
שׁ.ל.ח	מ.ל.ךְ
שׁ.מ.ע	שׁ.מ.ר
	שׁ.פ.ט
	ק.צ.ר

The chart above does not include all of the verb roots that you have learned. Some of the roots that you have learned are regular in the perfect tense and the participle, but irregular in the imperfect tense. The imperfect tense of those verbs will be taught in later chapters.

Negatives in the Imperfect Tense

A verb in the imperfect tense is made negative by placing the word לֹא before the verb.

Example: We will write   נִכְתֹּב

                               We will not write.   לֹא נִכְתֹּב.

The Interrogative הַ

In Hebrew, a question may be introduced with the prefix הַ. This prefix is called the interrogative הַ and should not be confused with the definite article הַX. The interrogative ה usually takes the X vowel, and there is no dagesh in the following letter.

Examples:

	Question	Statement
	הֲנַעַר הוּא?	נַעַר הוּא.
	Is he a lad?	He is a lad.
	הֲדָוִד שָׁם?	דָּוִד שָׁם.
	Is David there?	David is there.

There are variations in the vowels pattern of the interrogative הַ which we will not discuss in this book. However, you will be able to distinguish from context between the definite article and the interrogative.

Exercises

Exercise 1. Conjugate the following verb roots in the perfect, imperfect and participle forms.

ח.ת.פ .3   ק.צ.ר .2   כ.ת.ב .1

Exercise 2. Rewrite the sentences below, replacing the underlined word with each word in the list that follows. Every word or grammatical form in the sentence that agrees with the underlined word should be changed to agree with the newly substituted words. Read the sentences aloud. Translate.

1. הוּא יִשְׁמֹר אֶת שַׁעֲרֵי הָעִיר.

A. אַתֶּן	B. הֵם	C. הִיא	D. אָנֹכִי	E. אַתֶּם
F. הֵנָּה	G. אַתָּה	H. אָנוּ	I. אַתְּ	

2. עֵינֵי רוּת לֹא כְּעֵינֵי אִמָּהּ.

A. נְעָלִים	B. כִּסְאוֹת	C. סֵפֶר	D. קוֹל	E. אֹכֶל

3. הֲעוֹד אַתָּה תִזְכֹּר אֶת שֹׁפְטֵי הַמָּקוֹם הַהוּא?

A. אַתֶּן	B. הַנָּשִׁים	C. הַנַּעֲרָה	D. אַתֶּם	E. אַתְּ
F. הָאַחִים	G. אֲנַחְנוּ	H. אֲנִי		

4. אִם לֹא תִכְתֹּב בַּסֵּפֶר, לֹא תִזְכֹּר אֶת הַדְּבָרִים הָאֵלֶּה.

A. יִכְתֹּב	B. תִּכְתֹּבְנָה	C. נִכְתֹּב	D. תִּכְתְּבוּ	E. אֶכְתֹּב
F. תִּכְתְּבִי	G. יִכְתְּבוּ			

5. אֵין לְאַבְרָהָם שָׂדוֹת בֵּין הֶהָרִים הַהֵם וּבֵין הָעִיר הַהִיא.

A. מָקוֹם	B. שָׂדֶה	C. דְּרָכִים	D. בַּיִת

101

6. הִנֵּה הָאִישׁ הַהוּא הַיּוֹשֵׁב בִּירוּשָׁלַיִם יִשְׁלַח מִנְחָה אֶל מַלְכּוֹ.

A. בְּנוֹת אַבְרָהָם   B. הַמִּשְׁפָּחָה   C. הָאָבוֹת   D. הַשּׁוֹמֵר   E. בְּנֵי נָעֳמִי

Exercise 3. Fill in the blanks with the appropriate imperfect tense form of the verb shown. Translate. Then change each verb form to the perfect tense and the participle.

1. (ק.צ.ר) אַתָּה _____ בַּבֹּקֶר בַּשָּׂדֶה.

2. (ש.כ.ב) בַּלַּיְלָה _____ אֵשֶׁת אַבְרָהָם עַל מִשְׁכָּבָהּ בְּבֵית רוּת.

3. (ש.ל.ח) אַחֲרֵי הָרָעָב _____ אֲחֵי שָׂרָה אֹכֶל אֶל אֲבִיהֶם בִּיהוּדָה.

4. (ש.מ.ע) הַנָּשִׁים מִמּוֹאָב _____ אֶת הַדְּבָרִים הָאֵלֶּה מֵהַמֶּלֶךְ.

5. (כ.ת.ב) הִנֵּה רֹאשׁ הַבַּיִת _____ אֶל הַנְּעָרוֹת הֵהֵנָּה.

6. (ז.כ.ר) אַתֶּן _____ אֶת שֵׁם הָאִשָּׁה הַיּוֹשֶׁבֶת לִפְנֵי הָאֲנָשִׁים הָהֵמָּה.

Exercise 4. Change the verb(s) in each sentence from the perfect to the imperfect tense.

1. נָעֳמִי שָׁמְעָה אֶת קוֹל אִשָּׁהּ.   4. הִנֵּה הַנָּשִׁים שָׁלְחוּ לֶחֶם לְכָל אִישׁ בָּעִיר.

2. הֲקָצַרְתָּ מֵהַבֹּקֶר עַד הַלַּיְלָה?   5. כַּאֲשֶׁר מָלַךְ הַמֶּלֶךְ הָרַע בְּאַרְצֵנוּ לֹא שָׁמַעְנוּ בְּקוֹלוֹ.

3. זָכַרְנוּ אֶת אֲחֵי יַעֲקֹב.

Exercise 5. Translate the following sentences into Hebrew.

1. The maiden will remember the evil man.
2. The maiden's brother will hear the voice of the evil man.
3. The maiden's father and uncle will guard the evil men.
4. There was an evil man in that land.
5. There are no evil men in our house.
6. Will you *f sg* remember the good men of our city?

Exercise 6. Read and translate.

1. אִם אֶשְׁלַח אֶת רוּת לְרֹאשׁ הָהָר, הֲתִשְׁלָחִי אֶת שָׂרָה?

2. אִם תִּשְׁפֹּט בֵּין הָאַחִים, הֲתִשְׁפֹּט גַּם בֵּין הַנַּעַר הַזֶּה וּבֵין אָבִיו?

3. אִם נִקְצֹר בַּשָּׂדֶה, לֹא נִשְׁמַע אֶת דִּבְרֵי הַנָּשִׁים בָּאֹהֶל.

4. הֲיִשְׁמְעוּ בְּקוֹל הַמֶּלֶךְ, אִם הוּא מֶלֶךְ רַע?

5. אִם תִּשְׁכַּב עַל מִשְׁכָּבְךָ כָּל הַיּוֹם, לֹא תִּכְתֹּב אֶת סִפְרְךָ.

Exercise 7. Read and translate.

Vocabulary for Reading Selection

I will be . . . . *imperfect of* ה.י.ה אֶהְיֶה   peace . . . . שָׁלוֹם

אָמַר הַנַּעַר: כַּאֲשֶׁר אֲנִי אֶהְיֶה אִישׁ, אֶמְלֹךְ עַל כָּל אַרְצִי. אֶמְלֹךְ מִן הֶהָרִים עַד הַיָּם בְּשָׁלוֹם. אֶשְׁלַח שׁוֹפְטִים טוֹבִים אֶל כָּל הֶעָרִים וְהֵם יִשְׁפְּטוּ אֶת הָאֲנָשִׁים הָרָעִים. בַּיּוֹם הַהוּא יִשְׁלְחוּ אֶת הָאֲנָשִׁים הָהֵמָּה מֵהָאָרֶץ. אֶזְכֹּר אֶת מִשְׁפַּחְתִּי: אָבִי וְאִמִּי וְאָחִי וְדוֹדִי וְדוֹדָתִי. אֶשְׁלַח לָהֶם לֶחֶם. תִּשְׁמַעְנָה כָּל הַנָּשִׁים בְּקוֹלִי. יִשְׁלַח לִי עַמִּי מְנָחוֹת. אֲנָשִׁים גְּדוֹלִים יִשְׁמְרוּ עַל בֵּיתִי. אֶשְׁכַּב בְּמִשְׁכָּב טוֹב מִכָּל הַמִּשְׁכָּבִים בְּאַרְצִי. כַּאֲשֶׁר אֶהְיֶה אִישׁ אֶהְיֶה הַמֶּלֶךְ, כִּי הַיּוֹם אָנֹכִי נַעַר וְאָבִי הַמֶּלֶךְ.

Exercise 8. Fill in the proper form of the verb in the last column and translate.

Root	Number	Gender	Person	Tense	Pattern	Word	
שׁ.כ.ב	sg	m	3	perfect	פָּעַל		1
שׁ.כ.ב	sg	m	3	imperfect	פָּעַל		2
שׁ.כ.ב	sg	m	—	active participle	פָּעַל		3
פ.ת.ח	sg	f	3	perfect	פָּעַל		4
שׁ.מ.ר	sg	f	3	imperfect	פָּעַל		5
שׁ.מ.ר	sg	f	—	active participle	פָּעַל		6
שׁ.מ.ע	sg	f	2	perfect	פָּעַל		7
שׁ.מ.ע	sg	f	2	imperfect	פָּעַל		8
שׁ.מ.ע	sg	f	—	active participle	פָּעַל		9
ז.כ.ר	pl	c	1	imperfect	פָּעַל		10
ז.כ.ר	pl	m	2	imperfect	פָּעַל		11
ז.כ.ר	sg	m	3	imperfect	פָּעַל		12
ז.כ.ר	pl	f	3	imperfect	פָּעַל		13
ז.כ.ר	pl	m	—	active participle	פָּעַל		14
ז.כ.ר	pl	m	3	perfect	פָּעַל		15
שׁ.פ.ט	sg	m	2	imperfect	פָּעַל		16
שׁ.פ.ט	sg	f	3	imperfect	פָּעַל		17
שׁ.פ.ט	sg	f	3	perfect	פָּעַל		18
שׁ.פ.ט	sg	f	2	imperfect	פָּעַל		19
כ.ת.ב	pl	c	1	perfect	פָּעַל		20
כ.ת.ב	pl	c	1	imperfect	פָּעַל		21
כ.ת.ב	pl	m	—	passive participle	פָּעַל		22
כ.ת.ב	pl	f	2	imperfect	פָּעַל		23
כ.ת.ב	pl	f	3	imperfect	פָּעַל		24

From the Prayerbook

Prayerbook Vocabulary

for ever and ever . . . . לְעֹלָם וָעֶד   give . . . *3 m sg imperfect irregular* נ.ת.ן יִתֵּן

strength . . . . עֹז   bless . . . . *3 m sg imperfect* ב.ר.ך יְבָרֵךְ

peace . . . . שָׁלוֹם

Selection from the Prayerbook (from the Torah service)

יְיָ מֶלֶךְ, יְיָ מָלָךְ, יְיָ יִמְלֹךְ לְעֹלָם וָעֶד.
יְיָ עֹז לְעַמּוֹ יִתֵּן, יְיָ יְבָרֵךְ אֶת עַמּוֹ בַשָּׁלוֹם.

First try to translate the prayer in your own words, then read the translations quoted below.

Prayerbook Translations

"The Lord is King; the Lord was King; the Lord shall be King forever and ever. The Lord will give strength to his people; the Lord will bless his people with peace."

Daily Prayer Book, Philip Birnbaum, 1977, p. 362

"The Lord reigneth, the Lord hath reigned, the Lord will reign for ever and ever. May the Lord give strength unto His people; may the Lord bless His people with peace."

Sabbath and Festival Prayer Book, Rabbinical Assembly of America, 1946, p. 117

Notice that the first phrase is a noun sentence, the second phrase is in the perfect tense and the third phrase is in the imperfect tense. The verbs in the second sentence are in the imperfect tense.

Guided Reading from Ruth

	return! שֹׁבְנָה .1
	my daughters בְּנֹתַי
	go! לֵכְןָ
	"שֹׁבְנָה בְּנֹתַי לֵכְןָ!
1. "Return, my daughters, go!	become old ז.ק.ן .2
	to be *from* ה.י.ה לִהְיוֹת
	זָקַנְתִּי לִהְיוֹת לְאִישׁ.

2. I have become (too) old to be a man's (wife).	3. כִּי *best translated here as* if תִּקְוָה hope כִּי אָמַרְתִּי: 'יֶשׁ לִי תִּקְוָה
3. If I said: 'I have hope,	4. אֶהְיֶה I will be ה.י.ה *imperfect form of* אֶהְיֶה הַלַּיְלָה לְאִישׁ
4. I will be a man's (wife) tonight	5. י.ל.ד give birth אֵלֵד I will give birth to וְגַם אֵלֵד בָּנִים',
5. and I will also give birth to sons',	6. תְּשַׂבֵּרְנָה you will wait עַד אֲשֶׁר until ג.ד.ל grow up הֲלָהֶם תְּשַׂבֵּרְנָה עַד אֲשֶׁר יִגְדָּלוּ?
6. will you wait for them until they will grow up? *Notice the interrogative* הַ *in the word* הֲלָהֶם.	7. אַל don't אַל בְּנוֹתַי,
7. Don't, my daughters,	8. מַר bitter, bitterness מִכֶּן than you כִּי מַר לִי מְאֹד מִכֶּן."
8. because I am much more bitter than you." *Notice the use of* מִכֶּן *as a comparative.*	

"שֹׁבְנָה בְּנוֹתַי לֵכְנָה! זָקַנְתִּי לִהְיוֹת לְאִישׁ. כִּי אָמַרְתִּי:

'יֶשׁ לִי תִּקְוָה, אֶהְיֶה הַלַּיְלָה לְאִישׁ וְגַם אֵלֵד בָּנִים',

הֲלָהֶם תְּשַׂבֵּרְנָה עַד אֲשֶׁר יִגְדָּלוּ? אַל בְּנוֹתַי, כִּי מַר לִי מְאֹד מִכֶּן."

Chapter 17
The Imperative of the פָּעַל Pattern

Vocabulary

don't	אַל
garment, clothing *n, m*	בֶּגֶד, בְּגָדִים
choose *vb* . . . . (xxxx)	ב.ח.ר
trust *vb* . . . . (xxxx)	ב.ט.ח
steal *vb* . . . . (xxxx)	ג.נ.ב
wise *adj*	חָכָם, חֲכָמָה, חֲכָמִים, חֲכָמוֹת
know *vb* . . . . *irreg*	י.ד.ע
put on, wear *vb* . . . . (xxxx)	ל.ב.ש
fruit *n, m*	פְּרִי
forget *vb* . . . . (xxxx)	ש.כ.ח

Idiom

I went on my way.	הָלַכְתִּי לְדַרְכִּי
He went on his way, etc.	הָלַךְ לְדַרְכּוֹ

Note 1: The singular word פְּרִי can refer to fruit as a group.

Note 2: The vowel pattern of the imperfect tense of each verb root above is shown following the verb root.

The Imperative

The imperative is the strongest type of command and is used only with the second person (you). In English, the imperative is usually shown by leaving out the subject and putting an exclamation point at the end of the sentence. Examples: Write! Remember these words! In Hebrew, the imperative is formed by dropping the prefix ת from the second person forms of the imperfect tense and by changing some of the vowels. Thus, there are four imperative forms for each verb.

Imperative			**Imperfect**			
	write!	כְּתֹב		you will write	תִּכְתֹּב	*2 m sg*
	write!	כִּתְבִי		you will write	תִּכְתְּבִי	*2 f sg*
	write!	כִּתְבוּ		you will write	תִּכְתְּבוּ	*2 m pl*
	write!	כְּתֹבְנָה		you will write	תִּכְתֹּבְנָה	*2 f pl*

106

The Formation of the Imperative

Masculine Singular

The imperfect tense prefix ת is dropped in the imperative, and no other changes are made. A dagesh is added to the first root letter when it is one of the BeGeD-KeFeT letters.

	Imperative		Imperfect
guard!	שְׁמֹר	you will guard	תִּשְׁמֹר
open!	פְּתַח	you will open	תִּפְתַּח

Feminine Singular

The imperfect tense prefix ת is dropped in the imperative. Since it is difficult to pronounce two shevas at the beginning of a word, the sheva under the first root letter changes to a אֲ vowel. A dagesh is added to the first root letter when it is one of the BeGeD-KeFeT letters.

	Imperative		Imperfect
guard!	שִׁמְרִי	you will guard	תִּשְׁמְרִי
open!	פִּתְחִי	you will open	תִּפְתְּחִי

Masculine Plural

The imperfect tense prefix ת is dropped in the imperative. The sheva under the first root letter changes to a אֲ vowel, as in the feminine singular imperative. A dagesh is added to the first root letter when it is of the BeGeD-KeFeT letters.

	Imperative		Imperfect
guard!	שִׁמְרוּ	you will guard	תִּשְׁמְרוּ
open!	פִּתְחוּ	you will open	תִּפְתְּחוּ

Feminine Plural

The imperfect tense prefix ת is dropped in the imperative, and no other changes are made. A dagesh is added to the first root letter when it is one of the BeGeD-KeFeT letters.

	Imperative		Imperfect
guard!	שְׁמֹרְנָה	you will guard	תִּשְׁמֹרְנָה
open!	פְּתַחְנָה	you will open	תִּפְתַּחְנָה

Notice that those verbs whose vowel pattern in the imperfect is XXXX retain that vowel pattern in the imperative, and those verbs whose vowel pattern is XXXX retain that vowel pattern in the imperative.

The Negative Command

In Hebrew, the imperative is not used to express negative commands. Negative commands are expressed by using the imperfect tense with negative words. There are two ways to express a negative command in Hebrew.

1. The negative word לֹא is used with an imperfect tense form of the verb to express permanent prohibition. The second half of the Ten Commandments is the best example of this type of negative command. Example: You shall not steal.   לֹא תִגְנֹב.

2. The negative word אַל is used with an imperfect tense form of the verb to express immediate and temporary prohibitions. Example: Don't open the gate. אַל תִּפְתַּח אֶת הַשַּׁעַר.

The Indirect Imperative

The imperative form that has been introduced thus far in this chapter is used to express direct commands. There also exists in both Hebrew and English an indirect imperative form, which is used to express wishes and indirect commands. In English, the indirect imperative is usually shown by using the word "may" or "let".

Examples: May you have happiness.   Let's go to the city.

The First Person Indirect Imperative

The first person indirect imperatives "let me" and "let us" are formed by adding the suffix אָה to the first person singular and plural forms of the imperfect tense. The ẋ vowel or the x vowel of the second root letter in the imperfect tense becomes a sheva in the indirect imperative.

	Indirect Imperative		**Imperfect**	
Singular	let me guard	אֶשְׁמְרָה	I will guard	אֶשְׁמֹר
Plural	let us open	נִפְתְּחָה	we will open	נִפְתַּח

The Second and Third Person Indirect Imperative

The second person indirect imperative "may you" and the third person indirect imperative "may he" or "let him" are usually the same forms as in the imperfect tense.

	Indirect Imperative		**Imperfect**	
2nd person	may you guard	תִּשְׁמֹר	you will guard	תִּשְׁמֹר
3rd person	let them open — or — may they open	יִפְתְּחוּ	they will open	יִפְתְּחוּ

Since usually the imperfect tense and the indirect imperative are exactly the same for the second and third person the meaning of the sentence is determined from context. For example, in the prayerbook selection in Chapter 16, one translator prefers "may he . . ." and another prefers "he will . . .".

Irregular Verbs in the Imperfect and Imperative

The verbs י.ד.ע, ל.ק.ח, י.ש.ב, ה.ל.ך are irregular in both the imperfect tense and the imperative. Because they are very common verbs, we include a chart of these verbs conjugated in the imperfect tense and the imperative. It is important that you memorize the conjugations of these verbs, because they appear so frequently in the Bible and prayerbook.

Imperfect

know	take	sit	go	
י.ד.ע	ל.ק.ח	י.ש.ב	ה.ל.ך	
אֵדַע	אֶקַּח	אֵשֵׁב	אֵלֵךְ	1 c sg
תֵּדַע	תִּקַּח	תֵּשֵׁב	תֵּלֵךְ	2 m sg
תֵּדְעִי	תִּקְחִי	תֵּשְׁבִי	תֵּלְכִי	2 f sg
יֵדַע	יִקַּח	יֵשֵׁב	יֵלֵךְ	3 m sg
תֵּדַע	תִּקַּח	תֵּשֵׁב	תֵּלֵךְ	3 f sg
נֵדַע	נִקַּח	נֵשֵׁב	נֵלֵךְ	1 c pl
תֵּדְעוּ	תִּקְחוּ	תֵּשְׁבוּ	תֵּלְכוּ	2 m pl
תֵּדַ֫עְנָה	תִּקַּ֫חְנָה	תֵּשַׁ֫בְנָה	תֵּלַ֫כְנָה	2 f pl
יֵדְעוּ	יִקְחוּ	יֵשְׁבוּ	יֵלְכוּ	3 m pl
תֵּדַ֫עְנָה	תִּקַּ֫חְנָה	תֵּשַׁ֫בְנָה	תֵּלַ֫כְנָה	3 f pl

Imperative

י.ד.ע	ל.ק.ח	י.ש.ב	ה.ל.ך	
דַּע	קַח	שֵׁב	לֵךְ	m sg
דְּעִי	קְחִי	שְׁבִי	לְכִי	f sg
דְּעוּ	קְחוּ	שְׁבוּ	לְכוּ	m pl
דַּ֫עְנָה	קַ֫חְנָה	שֵׁ֫בְנָה	לֵ֫כְנָה	f pl

The Verb ב.ח.ר

The verb root ב.ח.ר was introduced in the vocabulary for this chapter. The conjugation of this verb is slightly irregular because the middle root letter is ח, one of the throaty five letters. This letter usually does not take a sheva. Therefore, whenever a sheva appears under the second root letter in the regular conjugation, the combination vowel אֲ appears under the letter ח in the verb ב.ח.ר.

Note on the Use of Prepositions

Verbs do not always take the same prepositions in Hebrew as they take in English. Therefore, prepositions cannot always be literally translated.

Example 1.   We trusted the man.   בָּטַחְנוּ בָּאִישׁ.

In English, "trust" takes a direct object, however in Hebrew ב.ט.ח takes the preposition בְּ , literally: We trusted in the man.

Example 2.   He chose the maiden.   הוּא בָּחַר אֶת הַנַּעֲרָה. — or — הוּא בָּחַר בַּנַּעֲרָה.

In English, the verb "choose" takes a direct object, but in Hebrew the verb ב.ח.ר may take either a direct object or the preposition בְּ . The correct translation of prepositions can usually be determined from the context.

Exercises

Exercise 1. Conjugate the following verb roots in the perfect tense, the imperfect tense, the participle, the imperative, and the indirect imperative of the פָּעַל pattern.

1. ג.נ.ב   2. שׁ.כ.ב   3. י.ד.ע

Exercise 2. Rewrite the sentences below, replacing the underlined word with each word in the list that follows. Every word or grammatical form in the sentence that agrees with the underlined word should be changed to agree with the newly substituted words. Read the sentences aloud. Translate.

1. (אַתָּה) קַח אֶת דָּוִד לַמֶּלֶךְ תַּחַת הָאִישׁ הָרָע הַזֶּה.

   A. (אַתְּ)   B. (אַתֶּן)   C. (אַתֶּם)

2. (אַתֶּם) אַל תִּבְטְחוּ בְּדִבְרֵי הַשּׁוֹפְטִים.

   A. (אַתָּה)   B. (אַתְּ)   C. (אַתֶּן)

3. נִגְנְבָה בְּגָדִים וְנַעֲלַיִם מִבֵּית מִשְׁפַּחְתֵּנוּ.

   A. ל.ב.שׁ   B. ב.ח.ר   C. שׁ.ל.ח   D. ז.כ.ר

4. לֵךְ וְשֵׁב בְּבֵיתְךָ וּשְׁמַע בְּקוֹל אִמְּךָ.

   A. לְכִי   B. לְכוּ   C. לֵכְנָה

5. אַבְרָהָם יִקַּח אֶת מִנְחָתוֹ אֶל הָאִישׁ הֶחָכָם הַיּוֹשֵׁב בַּשָּׂדֶה.

   A. הַנַּעֲרָה   B. רָאשֵׁי הָעָם   C. אַתָּה   D. אֲנִי   E. נְשֵׁי יְרוּשָׁלַיִם

   F. אֲנַחְנוּ   G. אַתֶּן   H. אַתֶּם   I. אַתְּ

Exercise 3. In the following sentences, fill in the blanks with the appropriate imperative form of the verb root shown. Translate. Then write the negative command form using אַל.

1. (ל.ב.שׁ) (אַתָּה) _____ אֶת בְּגָדֶיךָ.

110

2. _____ מֵעִירְכֶן אֶל הָעִיר הַהִיא. (ה.ל.ך)

3. (אַתֶּם) _____ אֶת הַבְּגָדִים כִּי הַנָּקֵן שָׁמַר אֶת הַבַּיִת. (ג.נ.ב)

4. (אַתְּ) _____ אֶת פְּרִי הָאָרֶץ. (ל.ק.ח)

5. (אַתֶּן) _____ אֶת הַדְּבָרִים אֲשֶׁר אָמַרְתִּי. (ש.כ.ח)

6. _____ בְּחֶסֶד אָחִיךָ. (ב.ט.ח)

7. (אַתֶּם) _____ בְּקוֹלוֹ. (ש.מ.ע)

8. (אַתָּה) _____ אֶת כָּל אַנְשֵׁי הָאָרֶץ. (ש.פ.ט)

9. (אַתָּה) _____ בַּנַּעֲרָה הַהִיא לְאִשָּׁה. (ב.ח.ר)

Exercise 4. Change the verbs in the following sentences into the imperative form. Remember that the first and third persons can be changed into the indirect imperative only. Translate.

1. תֵּלְכוּ אֶל רֹאשׁ הָהָר.

2. תִּשְׁלַח פְּרִי מֵאַנְשֵׁי הָעִיר אֶל רֹאשׁ הָעִיר.

3. הַנַּעַר יִשְׁכַּב בַּלַּיְלָה בְּבֵית מִשְׁפַּחְתּוֹ.

4. הַנָּשִׁים הַחֲכָמוֹת תִּקַּחְנָה לָהֶן פְּרִי.

5. נִקְצֹר בַּבֹּקֶר בַּשָּׂדוֹת הַגְּדוֹלִים.

6. אֶכְתֹּב סֵפֶר כְּסֵפֶר דּוֹדִי.

7. תֵּלְכִי בַּדֶּרֶךְ בֵּין הֶהָרִים עַד הַיָּם.

8. תֵּדְעוּ אֶת שְׁמוֹת פְּרִי אֶרֶץ יִשְׂרָאֵל.

Exercise 5. Read and translate. "A Modern Solomon Story"

Vocabulary for Reading Selection

between us . . . . בֵּינֵינוּ	
they came . . . . בָּאוּ	Solomon . . . . שְׁלֹמֹה
together . . . . יַחְדָּו	two . . . . שְׁתֵּי
to see . . . . לִרְאוֹת	she does not . . . . אֵינֶנָּה

אַחֲרֵי דָּוִד הַמֶּלֶךְ, מָלַךְ שְׁלֹמֹה בְּנוֹ עַל אֶרֶץ יִשְׂרָאֵל. הוּא חָכָם מְאֹד וְהוּא גַּם שׁוֹפֵט טוֹב. בַּיָּמִים הָהֵם עַם יִשְׂרָאֵל הָלַךְ אֶל יְרוּשָׁלַיִם לִרְאוֹת אֶת שְׁלֹמֹה הַמֶּלֶךְ. בֵּין כָּל הָאֲנָשִׁים אֲשֶׁר הָלְכוּ לִירוּשָׁלַיִם הָיוּ שְׁתֵּי נָשִׁים. שֵׁם הָאַחַת שָׂרָה וְשֵׁם הַשֵּׁנִית עָרְפָּה. הָיָה נַעַר אֶחָד בֵּין שָׂרָה וּבֵין עָרְפָּה כַּאֲשֶׁר בָּאוּ לִפְנֵי הַמֶּלֶךְ.

שָׂרָה אָמְרָה לִשְׁלֹמֹה: "הַנַּעַר הַזֶּה לֹא בְּנִי, הוּא בֶּן הָאִשָּׁה הַזֹּאת."

שָׂרָה אָמְרָה לְעָרְפָּה: "קְחִי אֶת בְּנֵךְ."

עָרְפָּה אָמְרָה: "הוּא לֹא בְּנִי, אֵין לִי בָּנִים! הֲלֹא תֵּדְעִי כִּי הוּא בְּנֵךְ? אַל תִּשְׁכְּחִי אֶת בְּנֵךְ."

שָׂרָה אָמְרָה: "אֲנִי זוֹכֶרֶת אֶת מִשְׁפַּחְתִּי וְהַנַּעַר הַזֶּה לֹא מִמִּשְׁפַּחְתִּי."

שְׁתֵּי הַנָּשִׁים אָמְרוּ לִשְׁלֹמֹה: "שְׁפֹט בֵּינֵינוּ; בְּחַר אֶת אֵם הַנַּעַר!"

שְׁלֹמֹה הַמֶּלֶךְ אָמַר אֶל הַנָּשִׁים: "בָּטַחְנָה בְּדִבְרֵי מַלְכְּכֶן. שְׁבְנָה וּשְׁמַעְנָה בְּקוֹלִי. אֵין אֵם בְּאַרְצִי אֲשֶׁר אֵינֶנָּה זוֹכֶרֶת אֶת בְּנָהּ. אִם אַתֶּן לֹא זוֹכְרוֹת אֶת הַנַּעַר הַזֶּה, הוּא לֹא בְּנְכֶן. לֵכְנָה לְדַרְכְּכֶן. יֵשֵׁב הַנַּעַר בְּבֵיתִי."

הַמֶּלֶךְ אָמַר לַנַּעַר: "שְׁכַח אֶת הַנָּשִׁים הָרָעוֹת הָאֵלֶּה! שֵׁב בְּבֵיתִי עִם מִשְׁפַּחְתִּי וּלְבַשׁ בִּגְדֵי בֶּן מֶלֶךְ!"

שְׁתֵּי הַנָּשִׁים אָמְרוּ יַחְדָּו: "בְּנִי הוּא, בְּנִי הוּא!"

הַמֶּלֶךְ אָמַר לַנַּעַר: "אָנֹכִי שְׁפַטְתִּי! הַנַּעַר יֵשֵׁב בְּבֵיתִי, לֵכְנָה לְבֵיתְכֶן!"

111

Exercise 6. Fill in the proper form of the verb in the last column and translate.

Root	Number	Gender	Person	Tense	Pattern	Word	
שׁ.פ.ט	sg	m	2	imperfect	פָּעַל		1
שׁ.פ.ט	sg	m	2	imperative	פָּעַל		2
שׁ.ל.ח	pl	f	2	imperfect	פָּעַל		3
שׁ.ל.ח	pl	f	2	imperative	פָּעַל		4
פ.ת.ח	sg	f	2	imperfect	פָּעַל		5
פ.ת.ח	sg	f	2	imperative	פָּעַל		6
ג.נ.ב	pl	m	2	imperfect	פָּעַל		7
ג.נ.ב	pl	m	2	imperative	פָּעַל		8
ה.ל.ך	pl	m	3	imperfect	פָּעַל		9
ה.ל.ך	pl	m	2	imperative	פָּעַל		10
ה.ל.ך	sg	m	3	imperfect	פָּעַל		11
י.שׁ.ב	sg	m	3	imperfect	פָּעַל		12
ל.ק.ח	sg	m	3	imperfect	פָּעַל		13
י.ד.ע	sg	m	3	imperfect	פָּעַל		14
ה.ל.ך	sg	f	2	imperative	פָּעַל		15
י.שׁ.ב	sg	f	2	imperative	פָּעַל		16
ל.ק.ח	sg	m	2	imperative	פָּעַל		17
י.ד.ע	sg	m	2	imperative	פָּעַל		18
שׁ.מ.ע	pl	f	2	imperative	פָּעַל		19
שׁ.מ.ע	sg	m	2	imperative	פָּעַל		20
שׁ.מ.ע	sg	f	2	imperative	פָּעַל		21
שׁ.מ.ע	pl	m	2	imperative	פָּעַל		22
ה.ל.ך	pl	f	2	imperative	פָּעַל		23
ל.ק.ח	pl	f	2	imperative	פָּעַל		24

From the Prayerbook

Prayerbook Vocabulary

hosts, armies . . . . צְבָאוֹת

fullness . . . . מְלֹא   honor, glory . . . . כָּבוֹד

Selection from the Prayerbook (from the Kedushah)

קָדוֹשׁ, קָדוֹשׁ, קָדוֹשׁ יְיָ צְבָאוֹת; מְלֹא כָל הָאָרֶץ כְּבוֹדוֹ . . . בָּרוּךְ כְּבוֹד יְיָ מִמְּקוֹמוֹ.

First try to translate the prayer in your own words, then read the translations quoted below.

Prayerbook Translations

"Holy, holy, holy is the Lord of hosts; The whole earth is full of his glory. . . Blessed be the glory of the Lord from his abode."
Daily Prayer Book, Philip Birnbaum, 1977, p. 393

"Holy, Holy, Holy is the Lord of Hosts; the fullness of the whole earth is His glory! . . . Blessed is the glory of God in heaven and earth."
Gates of Prayer, the New Union Prayerbook, 1975, p. 308

Guided Reading from Ruth

	1. נ.שׂ.א raise
	בָּכוּ they wept
	הֵנָּה נָשְׂאוּ אֶת קוֹלָן וְעוֹד בָּכוּ.
1. They raised their voices and still wept.	2. נ.שׁ.ק kiss
	חָמוֹת mother-in-law
	וְעׇרְפָּה נָשְׁקָה לַחֲמוֹתָהּ
2. And Orpah kissed her mother-in-law	3. ד.ב.ק cling
	וְרוּת דָּבְקָה בַּחֲמוֹתָהּ.
3. and Ruth clung to her mother-in-law.	4. שָׁבָה she has returned
	יְבֶמֶת sister-in-law
	וַנָּעֳמִי אָמְרָה: "הִנֵּה יְבִמְתֵּךְ שָׁבָה . . .
4. And Naomi said: "Behold, your sister-in-law has returned. . . .	5. אֱלֹהֶיהָ her gods
	אֶל עַמָּהּ וְאֶל אֱלֹהֶיהָ.
5. to her people and to her gods.	6. שׁוּבִי return *f sg imperative*
	שׁוּבִי אַחֲרֵי יְבִמְתֵּךְ."
6. Return after your sister-in-law."	

הֵנָּה נָשְׂאוּ אֶת קוֹלָן וְעוֹד בָּכוּ. וְעׇרְפָּה נָשְׁקָה לַחֲמוֹתָהּ וְרוּת דָּבְקָה בַּחֲמוֹתָהּ. וַנָּעֳמִי אָמְרָה: "הִנֵּה יְבִמְתֵּךְ שָׁבָה אֶל עַמָּהּ וְאֶל אֱלֹהֶיהָ. שׁוּבִי אַחֲרֵי יְבִמְתֵּךְ."

Chapter 18
The Infinitive of the פָּעַל Pattern

Vocabulary

be able *vb*	י.כ.ל.
tree, wood *n, m*	עֵץ, עֵצִים
mouth *n, m*	פֶּה
face *n, m*	פָּנִים
small *adj*	קָטֹן, קְטַנָּה, קְטַנִּים, קְטַנּוֹת
heavens, sky *n, m*	שָׁמַיִם
sun *n, m or f*	שֶׁמֶשׁ
midst	(תָּוֶךְ), תּוֹךְ־

Note 1: The plural form of פֶּה is rare.

Note 2: The word שָׁמַיִם, heavens, has no singular form.

Note 3: The word פָּנִים, face, appears only in the plural form, although it has a singular meaning.

Note 4: The word עֵץ, tree, can refer to trees as a group.

Note 5: The word שֶׁמֶשׁ, sun, is both masculine and feminine in the Bible. The plural form is rarely used.

Note 6: The word תָּוֶךְ, midst, usually appears in its construct form תּוֹךְ with the inseparable preposition בְּ added. The form בְּתוֹךְ means "in the midst of".

The Infinitive

In both Hebrew and English the infinitive form of the verb is "infinite" in the sense of having no limits with regards to person, gender, number or tense. It·does not need to agree with any other word in the sentence. In English, the infinitive is formed by placing the word "to" before the unconjugated form of the verb.

Examples: I went to guard.   We are going to guard.   She will go to guard.

In the above sentences, the word "guard" is an infinitive. As you can see, it has no person, gender, number, or tense and does not agree with any other word in the sentence.

In Hebrew, there are two infinitive forms of the verb: the **infinitive construct** and the **infinitive absolute.** The infinitive construct is the form to which pronouns and prepositions are attached, and the infinitive absolute is the form which always stands alone.

The Infinitive Construct

The infinitive construct is built around the three root letters of the verb. Generally the vowel pattern of the infinitive construct is ẊX̣X. Examples: זְכֹר שְׁמֹר כְּתֹב
When the third root letter of a verb is ח or ע , the vowel pattern of the infinitive construct is X̣X̣X. Examples: פְּתֹחַ שְׁמֹעַ שְׁלֹחַ

How the Infinitive Construct is Used

The infinitive construct can be used with prepositions attached, with pronoun endings attached, or with both prepositions and pronoun endings attached.

With Prepositions Attached

The inseparable prepositions, בְּ , לְ , כְּ , and the preposition מִ can be attached to the infinitive construct. The preposition most frequently used with the infinitive construct is לְ . This version of the Hebrew infinitive is closest in meaning to the English infinitive.
Examples: to guard   לִשְׁמֹר   to open   לִפְתֹּחַ
When the preposition בְּ is added to the infinitive construct, it usually expresses the English word "when" or "while".
Example: while guarding the house, the man . . .   . . . בִּשְׁמֹר הָאִישׁ אֶת הַבַּיִת
When the preposition כְּ is added to the infinitive construct, it usually expresses the English word "as" or "while".
Example: as the king opens the gate . . .   כִּפְתֹּחַ הַמֶּלֶךְ אֶת הַשַּׁעַר
The sheva under the inseparable prepositions בְּ , כְּ , לְ becomes a X̣ vowel when the prepositions are attached to the infinitive construct because it is difficult to pronounce two shevas at the beginning of a word.
Examples: בִּכְתֹב   כִּשְׁפֹּט   לִפְתֹּחַ
Additional information on this subject can be found on page 272, note 6.

With Pronoun Endings Attached

The pronoun endings that are used with singular nouns and participles can also be attached to the infinitive construct.   Example: שָׁמְרִי my guarding
When pronoun endings are added to the infinitive construct, the sheva under the first root letter changes to a X̣ vowel, and the Ẋ of the second root letter changes to X̣.

With Both Prepositions and Pronoun Endings Attached

Both a preposition and a pronoun ending can be attached to an infinitive construct at the same time. This unit forms a phrase which is difficult to translate into English.

Examples: Literally: in my writing the book . . .   בְּכָתְבִי אֶת הַסֵּפֶר . . .
or: when I write the book . . .

Literally: as our remembering the road . . .   כְּנָכְרֵנוּ אֶת הַדֶּרֶךְ . . .
or: while we remember the road . . .

Verbs That Have an Irregular Infinitive Construct

Some of the verbs you have learned have an irregular infinitive construct. They are listed below. Memorize them.

to be	לִהְיוֹת	ה.י.ה	to sit	לָשֶׁבֶת	י.ש.ב
to go	לָלֶכֶת	ה.ל.ך	to take	לָקַחַת	ל.ק.ח
to know	לָדַעַת	י.ד.ע	to lie down	לִשְׁכַּב	ש.כ.ב

The Infinitive Absolute

The infinitive absolute never takes any prefixes or suffixes.

How to Form the Infinitive Absolute

The vowels of the infinitive absolute of regular verbs in the פָּעַל pattern are XîXX̱.
Examples: כָּתוֹב, שָׁמוֹר, זָכוֹר
When the third root letter of a verb is ח or ע, the vowel pattern is XîXX̱.
Examples: שָׁמוֹעַ, שָׁלוֹחַ

How the Infinitive Absolute is Used

The infinitive absolute is most commonly used to emphasize the main verb in a sentence. The infinitive absolute form of the verb is placed immediately before the conjugated form of the verb, doubling the verb in the sentence. The infinitive absolute may be translated as "really, closely, certainly, surely, etc."

Examples: I really heard the words.   שָׁמוֹעַ שָׁמַעְתִּי אֶת הַדְּבָרִים.
You guarded the women closely.   שָׁמוֹר שָׁמַרְתָּ אֶת הַנָּשִׁים.

There are other uses for the infinitive absolute which we will not teach in this book.

The Completion of the פָּעַל Pattern

Now you have learned every form in the conjugation of regular פָּעַל verbs. There are some irregular verbs in the פָּעַל pattern, as well as additional verb patterns, which will be introduced later. Following is a chart showing all the forms in the conjugation of the regular verb root כ.ת.ב in the פָּעַל pattern.

VERB CHART		Verb Pattern פָּעַל		Root כ.ת.ב write

Perfect		**Imperfect**		**Active Participle**	
כָּתַבְתִּי	1 c sg	אֶכְתֹּב	m sg		כּוֹתֵב
כָּתַבְתָּ	2 m sg	תִּכְתֹּב	f sg		כּוֹתְבָה, כּוֹתֶבֶת
כָּתַבְתְּ	2 f sg	תִּכְתְּבִי	m pl		כּוֹתְבִים
כָּתַב	3 m sg	יִכְתֹּב	f pl		כּוֹתְבוֹת
כָּתְבָה	3 f sg	תִּכְתֹּב			
כָּתַבְנוּ	1 c pl	נִכְתֹּב	**Imperative**		
כְּתַבְתֶּם	2 m pl	תִּכְתְּבוּ	m sg		כְּתֹב
כְּתַבְתֶּן	2 f pl	תִּכְתֹּבְנָה	f sg		כִּתְבִי
כָּתְבוּ	3 m pl	יִכְתְּבוּ	m pl		כִּתְבוּ
כָּתְבוּ	3 f pl	תִּכְתֹּבְנָה	f pl		כְּתֹבְנָה

Infinitive		**First Person Indirect Imperative**	
absolute	כָּתוֹב	1 c sg	אֶכְתְּבָה
construct	כְּתֹב לִכְתֹּב	1 c pl	נִכְתְּבָה

Passive Participle	f pl כְּתוּבוֹת	f sg כְּתוּבִים	m pl כְּתוּבָה	m sg כָּתוּב

117

The Irregular Verb י.כ.ל "be able"

The verb י.כ.ל means "be able" and frequently appears followed by an infinitive construct. The verb י.כ.ל does not have either a participle or imperative form. The conjugation of י.כ.ל in the perfect and imperfect tenses is irregular and should be memorized.

	Perfect	**Imperfect**
1 c sg	יָכֹ֫לְתִּי	אוּכַל
2 m sg	יָכֹ֫לְתָּ	תּוּכַל
2 f sg	יָכֹ֫לְתְּ	תּוּכְלִי
3 m sg	יָכֹל	יוּכַל
3 f sg	יָכְלָה	תּוּכַל
1 c pl	יָכֹ֫לְנוּ	נוּכַל
2 m pl	יְכָלְתֶּם	תּוּכְלוּ
2 f pl	יְכָלְתֶּן	תּוּכַ֫לְנָה
3 m pl	יָכְלוּ	יוּכְלוּ
3 f pl	יָכְלוּ	תּוּכַ֫לְנָה

Infinitive Construct

rarely used

Infinitive Absolute

יָכוֹל

Note: The אֳ in the perfect tense 2nd plural is a qamets chatuf and is pronounced **o** as in d**o**g.

Exercises

Exercise 1. Write the infinitive construct and the infinitive absolute forms of each of the following verb roots.

ז.כ.ר   כ.ת.ב   שׁ.פ.ט   ב.ט.ח   ל.ק.ח   שׁ.ל.ח   ה.ל.ך   מ.ל.ך   י.ד.ע

Exercise 2. Rewrite the sentences below, replacing the underlined word with each word in the list that follows. Every word or grammatical form in the sentence that agrees with the underlined word should be changed to agree with the newly substituted words. Read the sentences aloud. Translate.

1. הָאַחִים יָכְלוּ לִקְצֹר בְּתוֹךְ הַשָּׂדֶה.

A. שׁ.מ.ר   B. שׁ.כ.ב   C. י.שׁ.ב   D. ה.ל.ך   E. ה.י.ה

2. זָכוֹר תִּזְכֹּר אֶת בֵּית אָבִיךָ.

A. שָׁכוֹחַ   B. יָדוֹעַ   C. בָּחוֹר   D. שָׁמוֹר

3. הוּא שָׁמוֹר שָׁמַר אֶת הַדְּבָרִים הָאֵלֶּה.

A. אַתְּ   B. אֲנַחְנוּ   C. הֵנָּה   D. הִיא   E. הֵם

118

4. כְּלָבֵשׁ הַנַּעֲרָה אֶת בִּגְדָהּ, יָשְׁבָה עַל כִּסְאָהּ.

A. אַבְרָהָם   B. שָׂרָה   C. הַזְּקֵנָה   D. בִּתִּי   E. הָאֵם

5. בְּפָתְחוֹ אֶת הַשַּׁעַר, שָׁמַע הַשּׁוֹמֵר אֶת קוֹל אַנְשֵׁי עִירוֹ.

A. הֵמָּה   B. אַתָּה   C. נָעֳמִי   D. אֲנַחְנוּ   E. הַנְּעָרוֹת

F. אַתֶּם   G. אַתְּ   H. אַתֶּן   I. אֲנִי

6. הַנַּעַר יוּכַל לִשְׁכַּב תַּחַת הָעֵץ הַקָּטֹן.

A. אֲנִי   B. הֵמָּה   C. אַתֶּן   D. רוּת   E. אַתָּה וְדָוִד

F. אָנוּ   G. אַתָּה   H. אַתְּ   I. הֵן

Exercise 3. Add the appropriate form of י.כ.ל to the following sentences, changing the verb in each sentence to the infinitive. Pay attention to the gender, number, and tense of the verb. Translate.

Examples: הָאִשָּׁה שָׁמְעָה   הָאִשָּׁה יָכְלָה לִשְׁמֹעַ.

הַשּׁוֹפְטִים יִשְׁפְּטוּ. הַשּׁוֹפְטִים יוּכְלוּ לִשְׁפֹּט.

1. הַבָּנִים הָלְכוּ מֵהַיָּם עַד רֹאשׁ הָהָר.
2. הֱיִיתֶם בֵּין הַקּוֹצְרִים בַּמָּקוֹם הַהוּא.
3. נִזְכֹּר אֶת פְּנֵי בִּנְךָ.
4. שָׁכַבְתָּ בַּלַּיְלָה בַּשָּׂדֶה תַּחַת הַשָּׁמַיִם.
5. הֲתֵשֵׁב בֵּין הָאֲנָשִׁים הָאֵלֶּה?

Exercise 4. Fill in the blanks with the appropriate infinitive form (absolute or construct) of the verbs shown at the beginning of each sentence. Add inseparable prepositions to the infinitive construct where necessary. Translate.

1. (ש.כ.ח) הוּא לֹא יָכֹל _____ אֶת פְּנֵי הַנַּעֲרָה.
2. (ב.ט.ח) לֹא יָדַעְנוּ אִם יָכֹלְנוּ _____ בַּשּׁוֹפֵט הַזֶּה.
3. (ק.צ.ר) הוּא הָלַךְ בַּבֹּקֶר _____ בַּשָּׂדֶה.
4. (מ.ל.ך) _____ תִּמְלֹךְ עַל כָּל אֲשֶׁר תַּחַת הַשָּׁמַיִם.
5. (ש.מ.ר) הַנָּשִׁים לֹא יָכְלוּ _____ אֶת בֵּיתָן וְהַנְּעָרִים גָּנְבוּ אֶת הַכֹּל.
6. (ג.נ.ב) כְּ_____ הָאֲנָשִׁים אֶת הָאֹכֶל לֹא לָקְחוּ אֶת הַפְּרִי.
7. (י.ש.ב) כַּאֲשֶׁר הַשֶּׁמֶשׁ בְּתוֹךְ הַשָּׁמַיִם, תּוּכַל בִּתֵּנוּ _____ תַּחַת הָעֵץ.
8. (פ.ת.ח) _____ תִּפְתַּח אֶת שַׁעַר הָעִיר הַיּוֹם, אַל תִּשְׁכַּח.

119

Exercise 5. Read and translate.

Vocabulary for Reading Selection

they will die	יָמ֫וּתוּ	camel	גָּמָל, גְּמַל-
he came	בָּא	by	אֵ֫צֶל
only	רַק	in you *with 2 m sg pronoun ending*	בְּךָ
but	אַךְ	to bring	לְהָבִיא
weary	עָיֵף	to rest	לָנ֫וּחַ
they came	בָּ֫אוּ	hot	חַמָּה

said in his heart, to himself .... אָמַר בְּלִבּוֹ

"הַגָּמָל הַקָּטָן אֲשֶׁר יָכֹל"

בְּעִיר אֲשֶׁר הָיְתָה עַל רֹאשׁ הָהָר הָיָה רָעָב וְלָאֲנָשִׁים שָׁם לֹא הָיָה לֶחֶם. הֵ֫מָּה שָׁלְחוּ אִישׁ מֵהָעִיר עַל הָהָר אֶל עִיר אֲשֶׁר הָיְתָה אֵ֫צֶל הַיָּם.

בְּשָׁלְחָם אֶת הָאִישׁ אָמְרוּ לוֹ: "קַח אֶת גְּמַלְךָ וְלֵךְ אֶל הָעִיר הַהִיא כִּי שָׁמַ֫עְנוּ כִּי יֵשׁ אֹ֫כֶל שָׁם. אַל תִּשְׁכַּח כִּי בָּטַ֫חְנוּ בְּךָ לְהָבִיא לָ֫נוּ לֶחֶם."

הָאִישׁ הָלַךְ עִם גְּמַלּוֹ אֶל הָעִיר אֵ֫צֶל הַיָּם וְלָקַח מִשָּׁם אֹ֫כֶל. בְּקַחְתּוֹ אֶת הָאֹ֫כֶל הוּא עוֹד זָכַר אֶת הָרָעָב בְּעִירוֹ וְלֹא שָׁכַב לָנ֫וּחַ. הוּא הָלַךְ עִם גְּמַלּוֹ בַּדֶּ֫רֶךְ אֶל הֶהָרִים. וְהַשֶּׁ֫מֶשׁ בַּשָּׁמַ֫יִם הָיְתָה חַמָּה מְאֹד. אַחֲרֵי הָלְכוּ כָּל הַבֹּ֫קֶר, שָׁכַב הַגָּמָל עַל הַדֶּ֫רֶךְ וְלֹא יָכֹל עוֹד לָלֶ֫כֶת.

הָאִישׁ אָמַר אֶל גְּמַלּוֹ: "אַל תִּשְׁכַּב עַל הַדֶּ֫רֶךְ! שְׁמַע בְּקוֹלִי! אַנְשֵׁי הָהָר בּוֹטְחִים בְּךָ!" הַגָּמָל אָמַר לוֹ: "לֹא אוּכַל לָלֶ֫כֶת". הַגָּמָל עוֹד שָׁכַב.

הָאִישׁ אָמַר בְּלִבּוֹ: "אִם לֹא אֶקַּח אֹ֫כֶל לָאֲנָשִׁים בָּהָר, הֵם יָמ֫וּתוּ." וְהִנֵּה בָּא גָּמָל גָּדוֹל מְאֹד בַּדֶּ֫רֶךְ.

הָאִישׁ אָמַר לַגָּמָל הַגָּדוֹל: "יֵשׁ רָעָב בָּעִיר בֶּהָרִים וְאַנְשֵׁי הָעִיר יָמ֫וּתוּ אִם לֹא אוּכַל לְהָבִיא לָהֶם אֶת הָאֹ֫כֶל הַזֶּה. גְּמַלִּי שָׁכוֹב שָׁכַב בַּדֶּ֫רֶךְ וְלֹא יוּכַל לָלֶ֫כֶת. הַאַתָּה תּוּכַל לָקַ֫חַת אֶת הָאֹ֫כֶל וְלָלֶ֫כֶת לְרֹאשׁ הָהָר?"

הַגָּמָל הַגָּדוֹל מְאֹד פָּתַח אֶת פִּיו וְאָמַר: "מָה אַתָּה אוֹמֵר לִי?" אֲנִי גָּמָל גָּדוֹל מְאֹד! אֲנִי הוֹלֵךְ כָּל יוֹם וְכָל לַ֫יְלָה לְעָרִים גְּדוֹלוֹת מְאֹד. לֹא אֵלֵךְ אֶל עָרִים קְטַנּוֹת אֲשֶׁר בֶּהָרִים!" וְהוּא הָלַךְ לְדַרְכּוֹ.

וְהִנֵּה בָּא גְּמַל הַמֶּ֫לֶךְ בַּדֶּ֫רֶךְ. הָאִישׁ אָמַר אֶל גְּמַל הַמֶּ֫לֶךְ: "שְׁמַע גָּמָל! יֵשׁ רָעָב בָּעִיר בֶּהָרִים וְאַנְשֵׁי הָעִיר יָמ֫וּתוּ אִם לֹא אוּכַל לְהָבִיא לָהֶם אֶת הָאֹ֫כֶל הַזֶּה. גְּמַלִּי שָׁכוֹב שָׁכַב בַּדֶּ֫רֶךְ וְלֹא יוּכַל לָלֶ֫כֶת. הֲתוּכַל אַתָּה לָקַ֫חַת אֶת הָאֹ֫כֶל וְלָלֶ֫כֶת לְרֹאשׁ הָהָר?"

גְּמַל הַמֶּ֫לֶךְ פָּתַח אֶת פִּיו וְאָמַר: "מָה אַתָּה אֹמֶר לִי? אֲנִי גְּמַל הַמֶּ֫לֶךְ! אֲנִי הוֹלֵךְ כָּל יוֹם וְכָל לַ֫יְלָה לָקַ֫חַת רַק אֶת הַמֶּ֫לֶךְ." וְהוּא הָלַךְ לְדַרְכּוֹ.

וְהִנֵּה בָּא גָּמָל קָטָן מְאֹד בַּדֶּ֫רֶךְ. הָאִישׁ אָמַר בְּלִבּוֹ: "גְּמַלִּי גָּדוֹל וְהוּא לֹא יָכֹל לָלֶ֫כֶת בַּדֶּ֫רֶךְ הַזֹּאת. הַגָּמָל הַזֶּה קָטָן מְאֹד. הוּא לֹא יוּכַל לָלֶ֫כֶת עַד רֹאשׁ הָהָר." אַךְ הָאִישׁ פָּתַח אֶת פִּיו וְאָמַר אֶל הַגָּמָל הַקָּטָן: "שְׁמַע, גָּמָל קָטָן! יֵשׁ רָעָב בָּעִיר בֶּהָרִים. אַנְשֵׁי הָעִיר יָמ֫וּתוּ אִם לֹא תֵּלֵךְ עַד רֹאשׁ הָהָר לְהָבִיא לָהֶם אֹ֫כֶל. הֲתוּכַל לָלֶ֫כֶת עַד רֹאשׁ הָהָר עִם הָאֹ֫כֶל?"

הַגָּמָל הַקָּטָן אָמַר: "יָכוֹל אוֹכַל!" הַגָּמָל הַקָּטָן לָקַח אֶת הָאֹכֶל מֵהַגָּמָל הַשּׁוֹכֵב, וְהוּא וְהָאִישׁ הָלְכוּ בַּדֶּרֶךְ לֶהָרִים. הַשֶּׁמֶשׁ בַּשָּׁמַיִם הָיְתָה חַמָּה מְאֹד וְהֵמָּה הָלְכוּ וְהָלְכוּ. הַגָּמָל הַקָּטָן אָמַר בְּלִבּוֹ: "יָכוֹל אוֹכַל! יָכוֹל אוֹכַל!"

וְהַשֶּׁמֶשׁ בַּשָּׁמַיִם הָיְתָה חַמָּה מְאֹד וְהֵמָּה עוֹד הָלְכוּ. הַגָּמָל הַקָּטָן אָמַר בְּלִבּוֹ: "יָכוֹל אוֹכַל!" אַךְ הוּא עָיֵף מְאֹד.

בַּלַּיְלָה הֵם בָּאוּ אֶל הָעִיר בֶּהָרִים. כָּל אַנְשֵׁי הָעִיר אָכְלוּ מִן הָאֹכֶל אֲשֶׁר הָיָה עַל הַגָּמָל הַקָּטָן. הַגָּמָל הַקָּטָן אָמַר בְּלִבּוֹ: "הַגָּמָל הַגָּדוֹל לֹא יָכֹל, הַגָּמָל הַגָּדוֹל מְאֹד לֹא יָכֹל, גַּם גְּמַל הַמֶּלֶךְ לֹא יָכֹל, אַךְ אָנֹכִי יָכוֹל יָכֹלְתִּי!"

From the Prayerbook

Prayerbook Vocabulary

and you shall speak . . . . וְדִבַּרְתָּ   of them . . . . בָּם

rise up . . . . ק.ו.ם

Selection from the Prayerbook (from the "Ve-ahavta")

וְדִבַּרְתָּ בָּם בְּשִׁבְתְּךָ בְּבֵיתֶךָ, וּבְלֶכְתְּךָ בַדֶּרֶךְ, וּבְשָׁכְבְּךָ וּבְקוּמֶךָ.

First try to translate the prayer in your own words, then read the translations quoted below.

Prayerbook Translations

"and you shall speak of them when you are sitting at home and when you go on a journey, when you lie down and when you rise up."

Daily Prayer Book, Philip Birnbaum, 1977 p. 76

"and shalt talk of them when thou sittest in thine house, and when thou walkest by the way, and when thou liest down, and when thou risest up."

Daily Prayer Book, Joseph H. Hertz, 1975 p. 441

In this prayer, the words "of them" בָּם refer to the following words: "You shall love the Lord your God with all your heart, and with all your soul, and with all your might."

Notice the list of infinitive constructs with the inseparable preposition בְּ and the pronoun ending ךָ .

Guided Reading from Ruth

	1. פ.ג.ע. entreat
	בִּי me
	לְעָזְבֵךְ to leave you
	רוּת אָמְרָה לְנָעֲמִי: "אַל תִּפְגְּעִי בִּי לְעָזְבֵךְ,
1. Ruth said to Naomi: "Do not entreat me to leave you,	2. שׁ.ו.ב. return
	לָשׁוּב מֵאַחֲרָיִךְ.
2. to return from (going) after you.	3. אֶל אֲשֶׁר where
	כִּי אֶל אֲשֶׁר תֵּלְכִי אֵלֵךְ
3. Because where you will go, I will go	4. ל.י.ן. lodge
	בַּאֲשֶׁר where
	וּבַאֲשֶׁר תָּלִינִי אָלִין.
4. and where you will lodge, I will lodge.	5. אֱלֹהַיִךְ your God
	אֱלֹהָי my God
	עַמֵּךְ עַמִּי וֵאלֹהַיִךְ אֱלֹהָי.
5. Your people will be my people and your God will be my God. *Remember that the tense of noun sentences is determined from the context.*	6. מ.ו.ת. die
	ק.ב.ר. bury
	אֶקָּבֵר I will be buried
	בַּאֲשֶׁר תָּמוּתִי אָמוּת וְשָׁם אֶקָּבֵר.
6. Where you will die, I will die, and there I will be buried.	7. כֹּה thus
	ע.שׂ.ה. do
	יוֹסִיף add
	כֹּה יַעֲשֶׂה יהוה לִי וְכֹה יוֹסִיף
7. Thus may God do to me and thus add	8. הַמָּוֶת death
	יַפְרִיד will separate
	בֵּינִי בֵּינֵךְ בֵּין *with pronoun ending*
	כִּי הַמָּוֶת יַפְרִיד בֵּינִי וּבֵינֵךְ."
8. that (only) death will separate me and you (Literally: between me and you)."	

רוּת אָמְרָה לְנָעֲמִי: "אַל תִּפְגְּעִי בִּי לְעָזְבֵךְ לָשׁוּב מֵאַחֲרָיִךְ. כִּי אֶל אֲשֶׁר תֵּלְכִי אֵלֵךְ וּבַאֲשֶׁר תָּלִינִי אָלִין. עַמֵּךְ עַמִּי וֵאלֹהַיִךְ אֱלֹהָי. בַּאֲשֶׁר תָּמוּתִי אָמוּת וְשָׁם אֶקָּבֵר. כֹּה יַעֲשֶׂה יהוה לִי וְכֹה יוֹסִיף כִּי הַמָּוֶת יַפְרִיד בֵּינִי וּבֵינֵךְ."

Chapter 19
Direct Object Pronouns
Pronoun Endings for Plural Nouns

Vocabulary

stone *n, f* . . . . אֶֽבֶן, אֲבָנִים

tent *n, m* . . . . אֹֽהֶל, אֹהָלִים

light *n, f* . . . . אוֹר

beast, animal *n, f.* . . . . בְּהֵמָה, בְּהֵמוֹת

nation, people *n, m* . . . . גּוֹי, גּוֹיִם

darkness *n, m* . . . . חֹֽשֶׁךְ

wilderness, desert *n, m.* . . . . מִדְבָּר

dwelling place, tabernacle *n, m.* . . . . מִשְׁכָּן, מִשְׁכָּנוֹת

only *adv* . . . . רַק

regularly *adv* . . . . תָּמִיד

Note 1: חֹֽשֶׁךְ, darkness, and מִדְבָּר, wilderness, have no plural.

Note 2: The plural form of אוֹר is very rarely used.

Direct Object Pronouns

Direct object pronouns are pronouns that are used to replace a noun as the direct object of a verb.

Example: Boaz sent **the lad** to Moab.

Boaz sent **him** to Moab.

In English, the direct object pronouns are: me, you, him, her, it, us, you, them. In Hebrew, the direct object pronouns are formed from the direct object marker אֶת/אֵת with pronoun endings attached.

Examples: Boaz sent **him** to Moab.   בֹּֽעַז שָׁלַח אֹתוֹ אֶל מוֹאָב.

We remembered **them.**   זָכַֽרְנוּ אֹתָם.

There is no direct object pronoun **it** in Hebrew. All direct object pronouns are either masculine or feminine, depending upon the gender of the noun that they replace in the sentence.

Examples: Boaz sent **the gift** to Moab.   בֹּֽעַז שָׁלַח אֶת הַמִּנְחָה לְמוֹאָב.

Boaz sent **it** to Moab.   בֹּֽעַז שָׁלַח אוֹתָהּ לְמוֹאָב.

123

Object Pronoun Chart

Following is a chart of the direct object pronouns formed by adding the pronoun endings to the direct object marker אֶת/אֵת. Memorize it.

	Plural		**Singular**	
us	אֹתָ֫נוּ	me	אֹתִי	1 c
you	אֶתְכֶם	you	אֹתְךָ	2 m
you	אֶתְכֶן	you	אֹתָךְ	2 f
them	אֹתָם	him	אֹתוֹ	3 m
them	אֹתָן	her	אֹתָהּ	3 f

Notice that the direct object marker אֶת/אֵת changes to אֹת with the addition of pronoun endings in all forms except the second person plural אֶתְכֶם and אֶתְכֶן.

Adding Pronoun Endings to Verbs

Direct object pronouns can be expressed in two ways in Hebrew. They can be expressed by adding pronoun endings to the direct object marker אֶת/אֵת as shown above. They can also be expressed by adding pronoun endings to the verb.

Example: הוּא שָׁמַר אֹתִי.

He guarded me. — or —

הוּא שְׁמָרַ֫נִי.

The pronoun endings which are added to verbs are almost the same as those which are attached to a noun or a preposition. In this book, we will not teach the rules for attaching pronoun endings to verbs. However, since verbs often appear in the Bible with pronoun endings, we want you to be aware that these forms exist. We hope you recognize them when you see them.

Possessive Pronoun Endings with Masculine Plural Nouns

You have already learned the possessive pronoun endings for singular masculine and feminine nouns (see Chapter 13). There are also possessive pronoun endings for plural masculine and feminine nouns.

When possessive pronoun endings are attached to masculine plural nouns, the masculine plural ending ים is dropped and the pronoun endings are attached to the base form of the noun. Following is a chart showing the nouns with possessive pronoun endings and how they are attached to the regular masculine plural noun דּוֹדִים.

				Possessive Endings		Base Form	Masculine Plural Noun
1 c sg	my uncles	דּוֹדַי	=	אַי	+	דּוֹד	דּוֹדִים
2 m sg	your uncles	דּוֹדֶיךָ	=	אֶיךָ	+	דּוֹד	דּוֹדִים
2 f sg	your uncles	דּוֹדַיִךְ	=	אַיִךְ	+	דּוֹד	דּוֹדִים
3 m sg	his uncles	דּוֹדָיו	=	אָיו	+	דּוֹד	דּוֹדִים
3 f sg	her uncles	דּוֹדֶיהָ	=	אֶיהָ	+	דּוֹד	דּוֹדִים
1 c pl	our uncles	דּוֹדֵינוּ	=	אֵינוּ	+	דּוֹד	דּוֹדִים
2 m pl	your uncles	דּוֹדֵיכֶם	=	אֵיכֶם	+	דּוֹד	דּוֹדִים
2 f pl	your uncles	דּוֹדֵיכֶן	=	אֵיכֶן	+	דּוֹד	דּוֹדִים
3 m pl	their uncles	דּוֹדֵיהֶם	=	אֵיהֶם	+	דּוֹד	דּוֹדִים
3 f pl	their uncles	דּוֹדֵיהֶן	=	אֵיהֶן	+	דּוֹד	דּוֹדִים

Notes on the Chart

1. The letter י after the base form of the noun is the characteristic feature of plural possessive pronoun endings.

2. The yod is silent in all forms except the first person singular, where it is part of a vowel combination pronounced "eye" (see Chapter 3), and the second person feminine singular where it is a consonant.

Comparison Chart

Below is a chart comparing the possessive pronoun endings for the singular and plural forms of the regular masculine noun דּוֹד.

	דּוֹדִים		דּוֹד
my uncles	דּוֹדַי	my uncle	דּוֹדִי
your uncles	דּוֹדֶיךָ	your uncle	דּוֹדְךָ
your uncles	דּוֹדַיִךְ	your uncle	דּוֹדֵךְ
his uncles	דּוֹדָיו	his uncle	דּוֹדוֹ
her uncles	דּוֹדֶיהָ	her uncle	דּוֹדָהּ
our uncles	דּוֹדֵינוּ	our uncle	דּוֹדֵנוּ
your uncles	דּוֹדֵיכֶם	your uncle	דּוֹדְכֶם
your uncles	דּוֹדֵיכֶן	your uncle	דּוֹדְכֶן
their uncles	דּוֹדֵיהֶם	their uncle	דּוֹדָם
their uncles	דּוֹדֵיהֶן	their uncle	דּוֹדָן

Possessive Pronoun Endings with Feminine Plural Nouns

When possessive pronoun endings are attached to feminine plural nouns, the feminine plural ending אוֹת remains and the pronoun endings are attached to the plural form of the noun. Below is a chart showing the possessive pronoun endings and how they are attached to the regular feminine plural noun נְעָרוֹת.

		Feminine Plural Noun	Base Form		Possessive Endings		
1 c sg	my maidens	נַעֲרוֹתַי	=	אַי	+	נַעֲרוֹת	נְעָרוֹת
2 m sg	your maidens	נַעֲרוֹתֶיךָ	=	אֶיךָ	+	נַעֲרוֹת	נְעָרוֹת
2 f sg	your maidens	נַעֲרוֹתַיִךְ	=	אַיִךְ	+	נַעֲרוֹת	נְעָרוֹת
3 m sg	his maidens	נַעֲרוֹתָיו	=	אָיו	+	נַעֲרוֹת	נְעָרוֹת
3 f sg	her maidens	נַעֲרוֹתֶיהָ	=	אֶיהָ	+	נַעֲרוֹת	נְעָרוֹת
1 c pl	our maidens	נַעֲרוֹתֵינוּ	=	אֵינוּ	+	נַעֲרוֹת	נְעָרוֹת
2 m pl	your maidens	נַעֲרוֹתֵיכֶם	=	אֵיכֶם	+	נַעֲרוֹת	נְעָרוֹת
2 f pl	your maidens	נַעֲרוֹתֵיכֶן	=	אֵיכֶן	+	נַעֲרוֹת	נְעָרוֹת
3 m pl	their maidens	נַעֲרוֹתֵיהֶם	=	אֵיהֶם	+	נַעֲרוֹת	נְעָרוֹת
3 f pl	their maidens	נַעֲרוֹתֵיהֶן	=	אֵיהֶן	+	נַעֲרוֹת	נְעָרוֹת

Notice that when possessive pronoun endings are added to נְעָרוֹת, the vowel pattern changes to נַעֲרוֹת. Many nouns have a changed form when the possessive pronoun endings are added. You can find this changed form in the glossary at the back of the book.

Comparison Chart

Below is a chart comparing the possessive pronoun endings for the singular and plural forms of the regular feminine noun נַעֲרָה.

	נְעָרוֹת		נַעֲרָה
my maidens	נַעֲרוֹתַי	my maiden	נַעֲרָתִי
your maidens	נַעֲרוֹתֶיךָ	your maiden	נַעֲרָתְךָ
your maidens	נַעֲרוֹתַיִךְ	your maiden	נַעֲרָתֵךְ
his maidens	נַעֲרוֹתָיו	his maiden	נַעֲרָתוֹ
her maidens	נַעֲרוֹתֶיהָ	her maiden	נַעֲרָתָהּ
our maidens	נַעֲרוֹתֵינוּ	our maiden	נַעֲרָתֵנוּ
your maidens	נַעֲרוֹתֵיכֶם	your maiden	נַעֲרַתְכֶם
your maidens	נַעֲרוֹתֵיכֶן	your maiden	נַעֲרַתְכֶן
their maidens	נַעֲרוֹתֵיהֶם	their maiden	נַעֲרָתָם
their maidens	נַעֲרוֹתֵיהֶן	their maiden	נַעֲרָתָן

Using the Glossary

Until now we have explained the following.

1.   The first word listed for each entry is the singular.
2.   The second word is the plural.
3.   The third word is the singular construct form.
4.   The fourth word is the plural construct form.
5.   The fifth word is the singular possessive with the first person possessive pronoun ending attached. If the singular possessive is irregular, you will see: *irr, s, p.*

Plural Possessives

The sixth and final word listed for each entry is the plural possessive with the first person pronoun ending attached. All the other plural possessive pronoun endings are attached to this same form of the noun. You can look up this form when you need to use the possessive pronoun endings. In order to identify the correct ending you can refer to the charts in this chapter.

Examples from the glossary:

stone *n, f* . . . . אֶבֶן, אֲבָנִים, אֶבֶן, אַבְנֵי־, אַבְנִי, אֲבָנַי

house *n, m* . . . . בַּיִת, בָּתִּים, בֵּית־, בָּתֵּי־, בֵּיתִי, בָּתַּי

Irregular Plural Possessives

Some Hebrew nouns are irregular when the plural possessive pronoun endings are attached. These nouns are listed as irregular plural possessives — *irr, pl, p* — in the glossary, and no plural possessive form is shown. Instead, there is a separate chart listing these forms on page 274.

Examples from the glossary:

thing, word *n, m.* . . . . דָּבָר, דְּבָרִים, דְּבַר־,
irr, pl, p, דִּבְרֵי־, דְּבָרִי

book *n, m* . *irr, pl, p,* סֵפֶר, סְפָרִים, סֵפֶר־, סִפְרֵי־, סִפְרִי

Irregular Possessives

If both the singular and the plural possessive forms are irregular, you will see: *irr, p.* There is a chart listing these forms on page 273.

The Complete Conjugation of the Verb ה.י.ה

You have already learned the conjugation of the verb ה.י.ה in the perfect tense and the infinitive. Because this verb appears very frequently in the Bible, you need to learn all of its forms. Below is a chart showing the complete conjugation of the irregular verb ה.י.ה. There is no participle of ה.י.ה. Memorize this chart.

	Perfect	Imperfect		Imperative
1 c sg	הָיִיתִי	אֶהְיֶה	m sg	הֱיֵה
2 m sg	הָיִיתָ	תִּהְיֶה	f sg	הֲיִי
2 f sg	הָיִית	תִּהְיִי	m pl	הֱיוּ
3 m sg	הָיָה	יִהְיֶה	f pl	הֱיֶינָה
3 f sg	הָיְתָה	תִּהְיֶה		
1 c pl	הָיִינוּ	נִהְיֶה		**Infinitive**
2 m pl	הֱיִיתֶם	תִּהְיוּ	abs	הָיֹה
2 f pl	הֱיִיתֶן	תִּהְיֶינָה	const	הֱיוֹת (לִהְיוֹת)
3 m pl	הָיוּ	יִהְיוּ		
3 f pl	הָיוּ	תִּהְיֶינָה		

"There will be" in Hebrew

You have already learned that the third person of the verb ה.י.ה in the perfect tense is used to mean "there was" or "there were". Similarly, the third person of the verb ה.י.ה in the imperfect tense is used to mean "there will be."

Examples: There will be people in the field.   יִהְיוּ אֲנָשִׁים בַּשָּׂדֶה.

There will not be food in the house.   לֹא יִהְיֶה אֹכֶל בַּבַּיִת.

Notice that the verb ה.י.ה must agree with the gender and number of the subject.

"Have" and "not have" in the Imperfect Tense

The verb ה.י.ה is used in the imperfect tense to express possession the same way that it is used in the perfect tense (see Chapter 15).

Examples: Literally: There will be to Abraham a son.   יִהְיֶה לְאַבְרָהָם בֵּן.

or: Abraham will have a son.

These statements of possession are made negative with the word לֹא.

Examples: Literally: There will not be to Abraham a son.   לֹא יִהְיֶה לְאַבְרָהָם בֵּן.

or: Abraham will not have a son. — or — Abraham will have no son.

Notice that the verb ה.י.ה must agree in gender and number with the subject.

Exercises

Exercise 1. Translate the following words into English. Pay attention to singular and plural possessive pronoun endings.

16. אֹהָלַי	11. גּוֹיְכֶן	6. מִשְׁכָּנְךְ	1. נַעֲרוֹ
17. שַׁעֲרָם	12. לַחְמָה	7. אֲבָנֶיהָ	2. אִשְׁתְּךָ
18. אוֹרֵנוּ	13. בָּנֶיךָ	8. אַרְצֵנוּ	3. מְנֻחוֹתֵיהֶם
19. אִמְּכֶם	14. עֵינָיו	9. בַּהֲמוֹתַי	4. סְפָרֵינוּ
20. אָבִי	15. יָדֶיךָ	10. אֲבוֹתֵיהֶן	5. בֵּיתְכֶם

Exercise 2a. Change the following direct object pronouns to subject pronouns.

Example: אֹתָנוּ **אֲנַחְנוּ**

6. אֶתְהֶן	5. אֹתִי	4. אֶתְכֶן	3. אֹתָהּ	2. אֹתָם	1. אֹתְךָ
		9. אֹתָךְ	8. אֶתְכֶם	7. אֹתוֹ	

Exercise 2b. Change the following subject pronouns to direct object pronouns.

6. אַתֶּן	5. אָנֹכִי	4. הֵנָּה	3. הוּא	2. אַתֶּם	1. אַתְּ
		10. אָנוּ	9. אַתָּה	8. הֵם	7. הִיא

Exercise 3. Rewrite the sentences below, replacing the underlined word with each word in the list that follows. Every word or grammatical form in the sentence that agrees with the underlined word should be changed to agree with the newly substituted words. Read the sentences aloud. Translate.

1. (אַתָּה) רַק שָׁכַחְתָּ אֶת נְעָלֶיךָ. <u>(אַתָּה)</u>

E. הִיא	D. (אֲנַחְנוּ)	C. (אֲנִי)	B. (אַתֶּם)	A. הוּא
	I. (אַתְּ)	H. הֵנָּה	G. (אַתֶּן)	F. הֵם

2. <u>תֵּלֵךְ</u> לַמִּדְבָּר לָשֶׁבֶת שָׁם עִם בָּנֶיךָ.

E. הָלַכְנוּ	D. יֵלֵךְ	C. אֵלֵךְ	B. יֵלְכוּ	A. תֵּלְכִי
			G. הָלַכְתִּי	F. תֵּלַכְנָה

3. <u>הַשּׁוֹפְטִים</u> לָקְחוּ רַק אֶת בִּגְדֵיהֶם לִשְׁלֹחַ אֹתָם אֶל מִשְׁפְּחוֹתֵיהֶם.

E. רוּת	D. אַתֶּם	C. אָנֹכִי	B. הֵנָּה	A. אַבְרָהָם
	I. אַתֶּן	H. אַתְּ	G. אָנוּ	F. הַזְּקֵנִים

4. <u>(אֲנִי)</u> זָכַרְתִּי אֹתְךָ וְאַתָּה לֹא זָכַרְתָּ אֹתִי.

E. נְשֵׁי הָעִיר	D. הוּא	C. אִמְּךָ	B. (אָנוּ)	A. בָּנַי

129

5. כָּל דִּבְרֵיהֶן הָיוּ בְּבָתֵּי אֲבָנִים וְהֵן לָקְחוּ אֹתָם לְבָתֵּי עֵץ.

A. דְּבָרֶיךָ   B. דִּבְרֵיהֶם   C. דְּבָרָיו   D. דִּבְרֵיכֶם   E. דְּבָרַיִךְ

6. אֶהְיֶה בְּמִשְׁכָּנִי הַיּוֹם וְאֶשְׁמֹר אֶת בָּנַי.

A. יִשְׁמְרוּ   B. תִּשְׁמְרִי   C. שָׁמַרְנוּ   D. תִּשְׁמֹרְנָה (אַתֶּן)   E. שָׁמְרָה

F. תִּשְׁמְרוּ   G. תִּשְׁמֹרְנָה (הֵנָּה)   H. תִּשְׁמֹר (אַתָּה)   I. יִשְׁמֹר

Exercise 4. Fill in the blanks with the direct object pronoun which correctly substitutes for the word given in parenthesis. Translate.

Example: (בְּהֵמוֹת) הַנְּעָרִים שָׁמְרוּ _____ אֹתָן _____.

1. (פְּרִי) הֵנָּה אוֹכְלוֹת _____.
2. (הַדְּבָרִים) אַל תִּשְׁכַּח כִּי אֲנִי זוֹכֵר _____.
3. (בִּגְדֵיכֶן) תִּלְבַּשְׁנָה _____.
4. (אִשְׁתּוֹ) בַּחֹשֶׁךְ הוּא שָׁכַב בַּמִּדְבָּר וְזָכַר _____.
5. (אֲנַחְנוּ) הוּא תָּמִיד יִשְׁמֹר _____.
6. (אַתֶּן) בְּתוֹךְ הָעִיר הַהִיא יִהְיוּ חֲכָמִים וְהֵמָּה יִשְׁפְּטוּ _____.
7. (הַסֵּפֶר) הוּא כָּתַב לְאוֹר הַשֶּׁמֶשׁ _____.
8. (הַמִּדְבָּר) הַגּוֹיִם בָּחֲרוּ _____ וַיֵּשְׁבוּ שָׁם.

Exercise 5. Translate the following sentences into Hebrew.
1a. He sent the men to his house.
1b. He sent them to their house.
1c. He sent them to their houses.
2a. The lads took their gift and sent it to their mother.
2b. The lads took their gifts and sent them to their mother.
2c. The lads took their gifts and sent them to their mothers.
3a. The woman will sit in her place and will hear the word of her son.
3b. The woman will sit in her place and will hear the words of her sons.
3c. The woman will sit in her place and will hear them.
4a. In the day there is light and in the night there will be darkness.
4b. This nation will go only in the light and will not walk in the darkness.
4c. This nation walked from the wilderness to the sea.

Exercise 6. Read and translate.

Vocabulary for Reading Selection

how	כַּמָּה	Red Riding Hood	כִּפָּה אֲדֻמָּה
to see	לִרְאוֹת	old one, "grandmother"	זְקֵנָה
to eat	לֶאֱכֹל	strangers	זָרִים
it got up	קָמָה	it saw, she saw	רָאֲתָה
it did	עָשְׂתָה	in its heart	בְּלִבָּהּ
my belly	בִּטְנִי	where	אָנָה
sick	חוֹלָה	another	אַחֶרֶת
they came out	יָצְאוּ	she came	בָּאָה
they ran	רָצוּ	come!	בּוֹאִי

"כִּפָּה–אֲדֻמָּה–הַקְּטַנָּה"

הָיְתָה נַעֲרָה קְטַנָּה וּשְׁמָהּ כִּפָּה–אֲדֻמָּה–הַקְּטַנָּה כִּי הִיא תָּמִיד לָבְשָׁה כִּפָּה אֲדֻמָּה. הִיא יָשְׁבָה בְּתוֹךְ הָעִיר עִם אִמָּהּ וְאָחִיהָ בְּבֵית אֲבָנִים קָטָן.

אִמָּהּ אָמְרָה לָהּ: "לְכִי אֶל אֹהֶל זְקֵנְתֵּךְ אֲשֶׁר בַּמִּדְבָּר לָקַחַת לָהּ לֶחֶם וּפְרִי. לְכִי רַק עַל הַדֶּרֶךְ וְלֹא בַּשָּׂדוֹת וְאַל תִּבְטְחִי בְּזָרִים."

כִּפָּה–אֲדֻמָּה–הַקְּטַנָּה אָמְרָה: "אֶשְׁמַע בְּקוֹלֵךְ" וְהִיא הָלְכָה לְדַרְכָּהּ.

וְהִנֵּה בְּהֵמָה רָעָה בְּתוֹךְ הַמִּדְבָּר. כְּלֶכֶת כִּפָּה–אֲדֻמָּה–הַקְּטַנָּה בַּדֶּרֶךְ בַּמִּדְבָּר, הַבְּהֵמָה הָרָעָה רָאֲתָה אֹתָהּ וְהִיא אָמְרָה בְּלִבָּהּ: "מִי הַנַּעֲרָה הַקְּטַנָּה הַזֹּאת? וּמָה הַדְּבָרִים אֲשֶׁר בְּיָדֶיהָ?"

הַבְּהֵמָה הָלְכָה אֶל הַנַּעֲרָה וְאָמְרָה לָהּ: "מָה הַדְּבָרִים אֲשֶׁר בְּיָדֵךְ? וְאָנָה אַתְּ הוֹלֶכֶת?"

כִּפָּה–אֲדֻמָּה–הַקְּטַנָּה שָׁכְחָה אֶת כָּל אֲשֶׁר אִמָּהּ אָמְרָה לָהּ.

הִיא אָמְרָה: "אֲנִי הוֹלֶכֶת אֶל אֹהֶל זְקֵנְתִּי לָקַחַת לָהּ לֶחֶם וּפְרִי."

הַבְּהֵמָה הָרָעָה אָמְרָה בְּלִבָּהּ: "אֵלֵךְ שָׁם לָקַחַת אֶת הַכֹּל: הַזְּקֵנָה, הָאֹכֶל, וְכִפָּה–אֲדֻמָּה–הַקְּטַנָּה." הַבְּהֵמָה הָלְכָה בְּדֶרֶךְ אַחֶרֶת אֶל אֹהֶל הַזְּקֵנָה.

כִּפָּה–אֲדֻמָּה–הַקְּטַנָּה הָלְכָה לְדַרְכָּהּ וְהִיא בָּאָה אֶל אֹהֶל זְקֵנְתָּהּ. הִיא אָמְרָה: "זְקֵנְתִּי! הִנֵּה אֹכֶל טוֹב!" הִיא שָׁמְעָה קוֹל מִתּוֹךְ הָאֹהֶל. "כִּפָּה–אֲדֻמָּה–הַקְּטַנָּה! בּוֹאִי וְאֶקַּח אֹתוֹ מִיָּדֵךְ."

כִּפָּה–אֲדֻמָּה–הַקְּטַנָּה לֹא זָכְרָה אֶת הַקּוֹל הַזֶּה וְאָמְרָה: "הַאַתְּ זְקֵנְתִּי?"

וְהִנֵּה הִיא שָׁמְעָה קוֹל מֵהָאֹהֶל: "בּוֹאִי לָאֹהֶל וְתֵדְעִי כִּי אֲנִי זְקֵנְתֵּךְ."

כִּפָּה–אֲדֻמָּה–הַקְּטַנָּה הָלְכָה אֶל תּוֹךְ הָאֹהֶל. כַּאֲשֶׁר הָיְתָה בָּאֹהֶל הִיא רָאֲתָה אֶת הַבְּהֵמָה בְּמִשְׁכַּב זְקֵנְתָּהּ. כִּפָּה–אֲדֻמָּה–הַקְּטַנָּה לֹא יָדְעָה כִּי הַבְּהֵמָה אָכְלָה אֶת זְקֵנְתָּהּ וְלָבְשָׁה אֶת בְּגָדֶיהָ.

כִּפָּה–אֲדֻמָּה–הַקְּטַנָּה אָמְרָה: "כַּמָּה גְּדוֹלוֹת עֵינַיִךְ!"

הַבְּהֵמָה אָמְרָה: "בְּעֵינַי הַגְּדוֹלוֹת אוּכַל לִרְאוֹת אֹתָךְ."

כִּפָּה–אֲדֻמָּה–הַקְּטַנָּה אָמְרָה: "כַּמָּה גְּדוֹלוֹת יָדַיִךְ!"

הַבְּהֵמָה אָמְרָה: "בְּיָדַי הַגְּדוֹלוֹת אוּכַל לָקַחַת אֶת הַלֶּחֶם וְאֶת הַפְּרִי אֲשֶׁר בְּיָדֶיךָ".

כַּפָּה־אֲדָמָה־הַקְּטַנָּה אָמְרָה "כַּמָּה גָּדוֹל פִּיךָ!"

הַבְּהֵמָה אָמְרָה: "בְּפִי הַגָּדוֹל אוּכַל לֶאֱכֹל אֶת הָאֹכֶל . . . וְגַם אֹתָךְ! אֲנִי תָּמִיד אוֹכֶלֶת נְעָרוֹת בַּבֹּקֶר!"

כְּשָׁמַע כַּפָּה־אֲדָמָה־הַקְּטַנָּה אֶת הַדְּבָרִים הָאֵלֶּה, רָאֲתָה כִּי הַבְּהֵמָה לֹא זְקֶנְתָּהּ. הַבְּהֵמָה קָמָה מֵהַמִּשְׁכָּב וְלָקְחָה אֹתָהּ בְּיָדֶיהָ וְאָכְלָה אֹתָהּ. כַּאֲשֶׁר הַבְּהֵמָה אָכְלָה אֶת כַּפָּה־אֲדָמָה־הַקְּטַנָּה, הִיא יָדְעָה כִּי הַדָּבָר אֲשֶׁר הִיא עָשְׂתָה לֹא הָיָה טוֹב.

הַבְּהֵמָה אָמְרָה בְּלִבָּהּ: "זֶה לֹא טוֹב! עֵינַי גְּדוֹלוֹת מִבִּטְנִי! אֲנִי חוֹלָה מְאֹד. לֹא טוֹב לֶאֱכֹל גַּם זְקֵנָה וְגַם נַעֲרָה בְּיוֹם אֶחָד."

וְהִנֵּה כַּפָּה־אֲדָמָה־הַקְּטַנָּה וּזְקֶנְתָּהּ יָצְאוּ מִפִּי הַבְּהֵמָה. הַבְּהֵמָה שָׁכְבָה עַל הָאֲדָמָה וְכַפָּה־אֲדָמָה־הַקְּטַנָּה וּזְקֶנְתָּהּ רָצוּ לָעִיר.

From the Prayerbook

Prayerbook Vocabulary

come . . . . ב.ו.א		be good, be pleasing . . . . ט.ו.ב
1 c sg imperfect (I will come) . . . . אָבֹא		*3 c pl perfect tense* . . . . טוֹבוּ
or indirect imperative (let me come)		abundant . . . . רֹב

Selection from the Prayerbook (said when entering the synagogue)

מַה טֹּבוּ אֹהָלֶיךָ יַעֲקֹב, מִשְׁכְּנֹתֶיךָ יִשְׂרָאֵל. וַאֲנִי בְּרֹב חַסְדְּךָ אָבֹא בֵיתֶךָ.

First try to translate the prayer in your own words, then read the translations quoted below.

Prayerbook Translations

"How lovely are your tents, O Jacob, your dwelling-places, O Israel! In Your abundant loving-kindness, O God, let me enter Your house."

Gates of Prayer, the New Union Prayerbook, 1975, p. 283

"How goodly are thy tents, O Jacob, thy dwelling places, O Israel! As for me, in the abundance of thy lovingkindness will I come into thy house."

Daily Prayer Book, Joseph Hertz, 1975, p. 5

Notice that both singular and plural possessive pronoun endings appear in the prayer above.

Guided Reading from Ruth

1. רָאֲתָה *see 3 f sg perfect*
   מִתְאַמֶּצֶת *insistent*
   אִתָּה *with her*
   נָעֳמִי רָאֲתָה כִּי מִתְאַמֶּצֶת הִיא לָלֶכֶת אִתָּה

---

1. Naomi saw that she was insistent to go with her

2. ח.ד.ל *cease*
   לְדַבֵּר *to speak infinitive*
   אֵלֶיהָ *to her*
   וַהִיא חָדְלָה לְדַבֵּר אֵלֶיהָ.

---

2. and she ceased to speak to her.

3. שְׁתֵּיהֶן *the two of them*
   וּשְׁתֵּיהֶן הָלְכוּ אֶל בֵּית לָחֶם.

---

3. The two of them went to Bethlehem.

4. בָּאוּ *come 3 f pl perfect*
   כַּאֲשֶׁר הֵנָּה בָּאוּ לְבֵית לָחֶם,

---

4. When they came to Bethlehem,

5. נְשֵׁי הָעִיר אָמְרוּ: "הֲזֹאת נָעֳמִי!?"

---

5. the women of the city said: "Is this Naomi!?"

6. תִּקְרֶאנָה *call 3 f pl imperfect*
   נ.ע.ם *be pleasant, lovely*
   נָעֳמִי אָמְרָה: "אַל תִּקְרֶאנָה לִי נָעֳמִי.

---

6. Naomi said: "Don't call me Naomi (pleasant).

7. מָרָא *bitter*
   קְרֶאנָה לִי מָרָא,

---

7. Call me Mara (bitter),

8. הֵמַר *has shown bitterness*
   שַׁדַּי *the Almighty*
   כִּי הֵמַר שַׁדַּי לִי מְאֹד.

---

8. because the Almighty has shown me much bitterness.

9. מְלֵאָה *full*
   אֲנִי מְלֵאָה הָלַכְתִּי

---

9. I went (out) full

10. רֵיקָם *empty*
    הֵשִׁיב *brought back*
    וְרֵיקָם הֵשִׁיב אֹתִי יהוה."

---

10. and the Lord brought me back empty."

נָעֳמִי רָאֲתָה כִּי מִתְאַמֶּצֶת הִיא לָלֶכֶת אִתָּה וַהִיא חָדְלָה לְדַבֵּר אֵלֶיהָ. וּשְׁתֵּיהֶן הָלְכוּ אֶל בֵּית לָחֶם.
כַּאֲשֶׁר הֵנָּה בָּאוּ לְבֵית לָחֶם, נְשֵׁי הָעִיר אָמְרוּ: "הֲזֹאת נָעֳמִי!?" נָעֳמִי אָמְרָה: "אַל תִּקְרֶאנָה לִי נָעֳמִי.
קְרֶאנָה לִי מָרָא, כִּי הֵמַר שַׁדַּי לִי מְאֹד. אֲנִי מְלֵאָה הָלַכְתִּי וְרֵיקָם הֵשִׁיב אֹתִי יהוה."

Chapter 20
The Reversing Vav

Vocabulary

ground, land *n, f* . . . . אֲדָמָה

covenant *n, f* . . . . בְּרִית

life *n, m* . . . . חַיִּים

utensil, vessel *n, m* . . . . כְּלִי, כֵּלִים

silver, money *n, m* . . . . כֶּסֶף

heart, mind *n, m* . . . . לֵב, לֵבָב

soul, living being *n, f* . . . . נֶפֶשׁ, נְפָשׁוֹת

now *adv* . . . . עַתָּה

Idiom

He said to himself (He said in his heart) הוּא אָמַר בְּלִבּוֹ

    She said to herself, etc. . . . . הִיא אָמְרָה בְּלִבָּהּ

Note 1: The plural forms of אֲדָמָה, land, and כֶּסֶף, silver, are rare.

Note 2: The word בְּרִית, covenant, has no plural form.

Note 3: The word חַיִּים, life, has no singular form.

Note 4: There are two Hebrew forms for the word "heart" or "mind" which can be used interchangeably: לֵב and לֵבָב. The plural forms of both of these words are rarely used.

The Reversing Vav

In the Bible, sequences of verbs are commonly used to recount events.

Example: The king **went** to his house and **sat** there and **wrote** to his wife.

When such sequences of verbs appear, the Bible usually uses a device called the **reversing vav**. The reversing vav is the letter ו , which is attached to the verbs which make up a sequence and reverse their tense. When a verb is in the imperfect tense, the addition of the reversing vav changes its meaning to that of the perfect tense. When a verb is in the perfect tense, the addition of the reversing vav changes its meaning to that of the imperfect tense. The reversing vav is used only with verb forms in the perfect tense and the imperfect tense.

Verbs in the Imperfect with the Reversing Vav		**Verbs in the Imperfect**	
and he wrote	וַיִּכְתֹּב	he will write	יִכְתֹּב
and you heard	וַתִּשְׁמְעִי	you will hear	תִּשְׁמְעִי
and they guarded	וַיִּשְׁמְרוּ	they will guard	יִשְׁמְרוּ

Verbs in the Perfect with the Reversing Vav		**Verbs in the Perfect**	
and he will write	וְכָתַב	he wrote	כָּתַב
and you will hear	וְשָׁמַעְתָּ	you heard	שָׁמַעְתָּ
and they will guard	וְשָׁמְרוּ	they guarded	שָׁמְרוּ

The use of the reversing vav is a distinguishing feature of Biblical Hebrew.

How to Translate the Reversing Vav

The reversing vav is usually translated into English as "and". Since the reversing vav serves to link sequences of events, it can also be translated into English as "then", "so", "now", "when", etc., depending on the context.

Past Events

When a sequence of verbs recounts events that took place in the past, the first verb is in the **perfect** tense. All other verbs following in the sequence are in the **imperfect** tense, with a reversing vav attached to them. The sentence should be translated as if all the verbs were in the **perfect** tense.

Example: The king went to his house and sat there and wrote to his wife.
הַמֶּלֶךְ הָלַךְ לְבֵיתוֹ וַיֵּשֶׁב שָׁם וַיִּכְתֹּב לְאִשְׁתּוֹ.

Future Events

When a sequence of verbs recounts events that will take place in the future, the first verb is in the **imperfect** tense. All other verbs following in the sequence are in the **perfect** tense, with a reversing vav attached to them. The sentence should be translated as if all the verbs were in the **imperfect** tense.

Example: The king will go to his house and will sit there and will write to his wife.
הַמֶּלֶךְ יֵלֵךְ לְבֵיתוֹ וְיָשַׁב שָׁם וְכָתַב לְאִשְׁתּוֹ.

Since the reversing vav is used so often in the Bible, sometimes it even appears attached to the first verb in a verb sequence. When this occurs, the reversing vav reverses the tense of the first verb in addition to that of all the verbs in the sequence which follows.

The Vowel Pattern of the Reversing Vav

With Verbs in the Imperfect Tense

When the reversing vav is attached to a verb in the imperfect tense, the vowel is ‎וַX in all forms except the first person singular.

Examples: וַתִּשְׁמַע   וַנִּכְתֹּב

Before a first person singular verb, the vowel of the reversing vav is ‎וָ.

Examples: וָאֶשְׁמַע   וָאֶכְתֹּב

With Verbs in the Perfect Tense

When the reversing vav is attached to a verb in the perfect tense, the vowel is ‎וְ.

Examples: וְשָׁמַע   וְכָתַבְנוּ

Before a verb that begins with a "boomf" letter — ‎ב, ‎ו, ‎מ, ‎פ — or one that has a sheva under the first letter, the vowel of the reversing vav is ‎וּ.

Examples: וּשְׁמַעְתֶּם   וּכְתַבְתֶּם   וּבָטַחְתִּי

The Reversing Vav and the Conjunction "and"

Do not confuse the reversing vav with the conjunction "and". The conjunction "and" **never** reverses the tense of a verb to which it is attached. When the verb is in the imperfect tense, the reversing vav can be distinguished from the conjunction "and" because of the difference in vowel pattern.

Example:	**Conjunction "and"**		**Reversing Vav**	
	and he will write	וְיִכְתֹּב	and he wrote	וַיִּכְתֹּב

When the verb is in the perfect tense, both the reversing vav and the conjunction "and" take the ‎X vowel —‎וְ.

Example:	**Conjunction "and"**		**Reversing Vav**	
	and he wrote	וְכָתַב	and he will write	וְכָתַב

However, the context will usually indicate whether a ‎וְ attached to a verb in the perfect tense is the reversing vav or the conjunction "and".

The Use of the Word וַיְהִי

Biblical narratives often begin with the word וַיְהִי. The word וַיְהִי is a shortened form of the word יִהְיֶה with a reversing vav attached. The word וַיְהִי is often translated "and it came to pass." Similarly, the word הָיָה with the reversing vav וְהָיָה is often translated "and it shall come to pass".

Exercises

Exercise 1. Add a reversing vav with the appropriate vowel to the following verbs. Pay attention to the tense of the verb. Translate.

21. תִּשְׁכַּבְנָה	17. תִּכְתֹּב	13. תִּשְׁמְרִי	9. אֶשְׁפֹּט	5. יִזְכְּרוּ	1. נִקְצֹר
22. אֶשְׁלַח	18. אֶקַּח	14. נִבְטַח	10. יִהְיֶה	6. אֶשְׁמַע	2. גָּנַבְתִּי
23. זָכַרְנוּ	19. מָלַךְ	15. יָדְעוּ	11. שָׁכַחְתִּי	7. הָלְכָה	3. תִּלְבַּשׁ
24. תִּקְצֹרְנָה	20. פָּתַחְתָּ	16. יְשַׁבְתֶּם	12. אֲמַרְתֶּם	8. תִּבְחַרְנָה	4. אָכַל

Exercise 2. Rewrite the sentences below, replacing the underlined word with each word in the list that follows. Every word or grammatical form in the sentence that agrees with the underlined word should be changed to agree with the newly substituted words. Read the sentences aloud. Translate.

1. הִיא שָׁמְעָה אֶת דִּבְרֵי הַבְּרִית וַתִּזְכֹּר אֹתָם וַתִּשְׁמֹר אֹתָם.

A. וַיִּזְכְּרוּ   B. וָאֶזְכֹּר   C. וַתִּזְכֹּרְנָה (הֵנָּה)   D. וַתִּזְכֹּר (אַתָּה)   E. וַנִּזְכֹּר

F. וַתִּזְכֹּרְנָה (אַתֶּן)   G. וַיִּזְכֹּר   H. וַתִּזְכְּרִי   I. וַתִּזְכְּרוּ

2. עַתָּה אֶקַּח אֶת הַכֵּלִים וְאֵלֵךְ לְאָהֳלִי.

A. יִקַּח   B. נִקַּח   C. תִּקַּחְנָה   D. תִּקַּח   E. יִקְחוּ

F. תִּקְחִי

3. הֵם יִלְבְּשׁוּ אֶת בִּגְדֵיהֶם וּפָתְחוּ אֶת הַשַּׁעַר וְהָלְכוּ לְבֵיתָם.

A. הֲלַכְתֶּם   B. הָלַךְ   C. הֲלַכְתֶּן   D. הָלַכְתְּ   E. הָלְכוּ (הֵנָּה)

F. הָלַכְנוּ   G. הָלְכָה   H. הָלַכְתִּי   I. הָלַכְתָּ

4. (אַתָּה) תִּהְיֶה מֶלֶךְ טוֹב וְשָׁפַטְתָּ אֶת עַמֶּךָ.

A. אַתֶּם   B. הוּא   C. הֵם   D. אֲנִי   E. אָנוּ

5. יָשַׁבְתִּי עַל אַדְמָתִי וְאֶכְתֹּב סֵפֶר לְמִשְׁפַּחְתִּי.

A. הִיא יָשְׁבָה   B. יְשַׁבְתֶּן   C. יָשַׁבְתְּ   D. יָשַׁבְנוּ   E. הֵנָּה יָשְׁבוּ

F. יָשַׁבְתָּ   G. יְשַׁבְתֶּם   H. הֵם יָשְׁבוּ   I. הוּא יָשַׁב

6. עַתָּה אֲנִי בֹּטֵחַ בְּבָנַי בְּכָל לְבָבִי.

A. אַתֶּם   B. אֲנַחְנוּ   C. אַתָּה   D. הֵמָּה   E. בֹּעַז

F. הִיא   G. אַתְּ

Exercise 3. Translate the following sentences into English.

‎1. וַיְהִי בִּימֵי הַשּׁוֹפְטִים וַיְהִי רָעָב בָּאָרֶץ.

‎2. הַנַּעַר גָּנַב אֶת כָּל הַכֶּסֶף וַיִּקַּח אֶת הַכֶּסֶף לְאָחִיו.

‎3. נִזְכֹּר אֶת חַסְדְּךָ וּבָחַרְנוּ אֹתְךָ לִהְיוֹת מֶלֶךְ.

‎4. אָכַלְנוּ אֶת הַלֶּחֶם וַנִּשְׁכַּב עַל מִשְׁכָּבֵנוּ.

‎5. נִשְׁלַח אֶת הַבֶּגֶד אֶל אָבִינוּ וְהוּא יִלְבַּשׁ אֹתוֹ.

‎6. חַכְמֵי יְהוּדָה יָדְעוּ אֶת דִּבְרֵי הַבְּרִית וְשָׁמְרוּ אוֹתָם.

Exercise 4a. Rewrite the following sentences, changing the verbs that appear in the imperfect tense with a reversing vav to perfect tense verbs with the conjunction "and". Translate.

Example:

הָאִישׁ שָׁכַב עַל הָאֲדָמָה וַיִּשְׁמַע אֶת קוֹל אִשְׁתּוֹ.

הָאִישׁ שָׁכַב עַל הָאֲדָמָה וְשָׁמַע אֶת קוֹל אִשְׁתּוֹ.

‎1. הִיא אָכְלָה מִפְּרִי הָעֵץ וַתִּקַּח מֵהַפְּרִי גַּם לְאִישָׁהּ.

‎2. דָּוִד בָּטַח בְּדִבְרֵי אָבִיו וַיִּבְחַר בְּאִשָּׁה טוֹבָה לִהְיוֹת לוֹ לְאִשָּׁה.

‎3. הָלַכְנוּ אֶל רֹאשׁ הָהָר וַנִּשְׁמַע אֶת קוֹל הַשּׁוֹפֵט.

‎4. וַיְהִי אוֹר בַּמִּדְבָּר בַּלַּיְלָה וַיֵּדְעוּ הָאֲנָשִׁים כִּי אֹהֶל שָׁם.

Exercise 4b. Rewrite the following sentences, changing the verbs that appear in the perfect tense with a reversing vav to imperfect tense verbs with the conjunction "and". Translate.

Example:

הַשּׁוֹפֵט יִשְׁפֹּט אֶת הָאֲנָשִׁים הָרָעִים וְשָׁלַח אֹתָם מִן הָאָרֶץ.

הַשּׁוֹפֵט יִשְׁפֹּט אֶת הָאֲנָשִׁים הָרָעִים וַיִּשְׁלַח אֹתָם מִן הָאָרֶץ.

‎1. הַנְּעָרִים יִגְנְבוּ אֶת כְּלֵי הַמִּשְׁכָּן וְלָקְחוּ אֹתָם לְאֶרֶץ מוֹאָב.

‎2. הַזָּקֵן יֵשֵׁב בְּבֵיתוֹ כָּל הַלַּיְלָה וְכָתַב אֶת סִפְרוֹ עַד הַבֹּקֶר.

‎3. יִמְלֹךְ הַמֶּלֶךְ עַל כָּל הָאָרֶץ וְשָׁפַט בְּחֶסֶד.

‎4. בָּנֶיךָ יִהְיוּ טוֹבִים וְזָכְרוּ אֹתְךָ וּבָחֲרוּ לָלֶכֶת בְּדַרְכְּךָ.

Exercise 5. Translate the following singular and plural nouns with pronoun endings into English.

‎17. רֹאשׁוֹ	‎13. בְּהֵמְתְּכֶם	‎9. אָהֳלֵיהֶם	‎5. בְּרִיתֵנוּ	‎1. אַדְמָתְךָ
‎18. מְקוֹמוֹתַיִךְ	‎14. פָּנֵינוּ	‎10. לְבָבְךָ	‎6. לִבּוֹ	‎2. כֵּלֶיהֶן
‎19. עֵינִי	‎15. בִּגְדֵיהֶן	‎11. מִשְׁכָּנֶךָ	‎7. נַפְשָׁהּ	‎3. כַּסְפּוֹ
‎20. יָדֶיהָ	‎16. אֲחִיכֶם	‎12. פִּיו	‎8. אַבְנֵכֶם	‎4. חַיַּי

Exercise 6. Read and translate.

בִּימֵי הַשּׁוֹפְטִים אִישׁ זָקֵן יָשַׁב בְּאֶרֶץ יִשְׂרָאֵל וּשְׁמוֹ דָּן. הָיוּ לוֹ בְּהֵמוֹת וְשָׂדוֹת וּבָתִּים וְרַק בֵּן אֶחָד וּשְׁמוֹ יוֹסֵף. לְיוֹסֵף לֹא הָיְתָה אִשָּׁה. וַיִּשְׁלַח דָּן אִישׁ אֶל אֶרֶץ אֲבוֹתָיו לִבְחֹר אִשָּׁה לִבְנוֹ. וַיִּקַּח הָאִישׁ בְּיָדוֹ מִנְחוֹת, כֶּסֶף וּבְגָדִים, וַיֵּלֶךְ לְאֶרֶץ אֲבוֹת דָּן. בָּאָרֶץ הַהִיא הָיְתָה אִשָּׁה וּשְׁמָהּ דִּינָה. הִיא לֹא הָיְתָה אֵשֶׁת אִישׁ וַתֵּשֶׁב בְּבֵית אָבִיהָ. הָאִישׁ אֲשֶׁר שָׁלַח דָּן אֶל בֵּית מִשְׁפַּחַת דִּינָה וַיִּבְחַר הָאִישׁ בְּדִינָה לְאִשָּׁה לְיוֹסֵף. וַיִּשְׁמַע אֲבִי דִּינָה אֶת דְּבָרָיו וַיֹּאמֶר בְּלִבּוֹ: "לֹא טוֹב הַדָּבָר. אִם תֵּלֵךְ דִּינָה עִם הָאִישׁ אֶל אֶרֶץ יִשְׂרָאֵל, לֹא תִהְיֶה עוֹד עִם מִשְׁפַּחְתָּהּ כָּל יְמֵי חַיֶּיהָ." וַתִּשְׁמַע דִּינָה אֶת דִּבְרֵי הָאִישׁ וַתֵּדַע כִּי הָיוּ לְדָן בְּהֵמוֹת וְשָׂדוֹת וּבָתִּים. וַתֵּדַע דִּינָה כִּי דָן אִישׁ גָּדוֹל. אִם תֵּלֵךְ לִהְיוֹת אִשָּׁה לְיוֹסֵף, יִהְיוּ לָהּ בְּגָדִים וְאֹכֶל טוֹב כָּל יְמֵי חַיֶּיהָ. וַתֵּלֶךְ דִּינָה עִם הָאִישׁ אֶל אֶרֶץ יִשְׂרָאֵל וַיִּקַּח אֹתָהּ יוֹסֵף לוֹ לְאִשָּׁה. אַחֲרֵי קַחַת יוֹסֵף אֶת דִּינָה לְאִשָּׁה הָיוּ לָהּ בְּגָדִים וְאֹכֶל טוֹב וְגַם בָּנִים וּבָנוֹת.

Exercise 7. Fill in the chart.

Root	Number	Gender	Person	Tense	Pattern	Word	
ה.ל.ך	pl	f	2	perfect	פָּעַל		1
י.ד.ע	—	—	—	infinitive absolute	פָּעַל		2
ל.ק.ח	sg	f	—	active participle	פָּעַל		3
ה.י.ה	pl	f	3	imperfect	פָּעַל		4
י.ד.ע	sg	m	—	imperative	פָּעַל		5
ש.מ.ע	—	—	—	infinitive construct	פָּעַל		6
ה.ל.ך	sg	c	1	imperfect	פָּעַל		7
ה.י.ה	sg	c	1	imperfect	פָּעַל		8
ב.ט.ח	pl	f	—	imperative	פָּעַל		9
א.מ.ר	sg	f	3	perfect	פָּעַל		10
ש.כ.ב	pl	c	1	imperfect	פָּעַל		11
						יִבְטְחוּ	12
						לָקַחַת	13
						שָׁמֹרְנָה	14
						הָלְכוּ	15
						יִהְיוּ	16

From the Prayerbook

Prayerbook Vocabulary

love . . . . א.ה.ב.　　　command . . . . צ.ו.ה.

מְאֹד *as noun with pronoun ending* מְאֹדֶךָ　　　I am commanding you *participle* אָנֹכִי מְצַוְּךָ

Selection from the Prayerbook (from the ''Ve-ahavta'')

וְאָהַבְתָּ אֵת יְיָ אֱלֹהֶיךָ בְּכָל לְבָבְךָ וּבְכָל נַפְשְׁךָ וּבְכָל מְאֹדֶךָ. וְהָיוּ הַדְּבָרִים הָאֵלֶּה אֲשֶׁר אָנֹכִי מְצַוְּךָ הַיּוֹם עַל לְבָבֶךָ.

Prayerbook Translations

''You shall love the Lord your God with all your heart, and with all your soul, and with all your might. And these words which I command you today shall be in your heart.''

Daily Prayer Book, Philip Birnbaum, 1977, p. 344

''You shall love the Lord your God with all your mind, with all your strength, with all your being. Set these words, which I command you this day, upon your heart.''

Gates of Prayer, the New Union Prayerbook, 1975, p. 251

Notice that both the sentences in the prayer begin with a reversing vav.

Guided Reading from Ruth

	came *3 c pl perfect* בָּאוּ .1
	הֵנָּה בָּאוּ אֶל בֵּית לָחֶם
1. They came to Bethlehem	
	beginning תְּחִלָּה .2
	harvest קָצִיר
	barley שְׂעֹרִים
	בִּתְחִלַּת קְצִיר שְׂעֹרִים.
2. at the beginning of the barley harvest.	
	kinsman מוֹדַע .3
	strong and valorous גִּבּוֹר חַיִל
	וּלְנָעֳמִי מוֹדָע לְאִישָׁהּ, אִישׁ גִּבּוֹר חַיִל
	מִמִּשְׁפַּחַת אֱלִימֶלֶךְ וּשְׁמוֹ בֹּעַז.

3. And Naomi had a kinsman of her hus-band, a strong and valorous man from Elimelech's family, and his name was Boaz.	and she said *from* וַתֹּאמֶר א.מ.ר .4 glean ל.ק.ט grains שִׁבֳּלִים וַתֹּאמֶר רוּת לְנָעֳמִי: "אֵלְכָה אֶל הַשָּׂדֶה וַאֲלַקֳטָה בַשִּׁבֳּלִים	
4. And Ruth said to Naomi: "Let me go to the field, and let me glean among the grains *Notice the use of the first person indirect imperative.*	find מ.צ.א .5 *1 c sg imperfect* אֶמְצָא favor חֵן אַחַר אֲשֶׁר אֶמְצָא חֵן בְּעֵינָיו".	
5. after him in whose eyes I will find favor".	וַתֵּלֶךְ וַתְּלַקֵּט בַּשָּׂדֶה אַחֲרֵי הַקֹּצְרִים .6	
6. And she went, and gleaned in the field after the harvesters	come *3 f sg imperfect* תָּבוֹא .7 וַתָּבוֹא לְשָׂדֶה בֹּעַז אֲשֶׁר מִמִּשְׁפַּחַת אֱלִימֶלֶךְ.	
7. and she came to the field of Boaz, who was from the family of Elimelech.	come *m sg participle* בָּא .8 with you *m pl* עִמָּכֶם וְהִנֵּה בֹעַז בָּא מִבֵּית לֶחֶם וַיֹּאמֶר לַקֹּצְרִים: "יהוה עִמָּכֶם".	
8. And behold Boaz came from Bethlehem and he said to the harvesters: "The Lord be with you."		

הִנֵּה בָאוּ אֶל בֵּית לֶחֶם בִּתְחִלַּת קְצִיר שְׂעֹרִים.

וּלְנָעֳמִי מוֹדַע לְאִישָׁהּ, אִישׁ גִּבּוֹר חַיִל מִמִּשְׁפַּחַת אֱלִימֶלֶךְ וּשְׁמוֹ בֹּעַז.

וַתֹּאמֶר רוּת לְנָעֳמִי: "אֵלְכָה אֶל הַשָּׂדֶה וַאֲלַקֳטָה בַשִּׁבֳּלִים אַחַר אֲשֶׁר אֶמְצָא חֵן בְּעֵינָיו".

וַתֵּלֶךְ וַתְּלַקֵּט בַּשָּׂדֶה אַחֲרֵי הַקּוֹצְרִים וַתָּבוֹא לְשָׂדֶה בֹּעַז אֲשֶׁר מִמִּשְׁפַּחַת אֱלִימֶלֶךְ.

וְהִנֵּה בֹעַז בָּא מִבֵּית לֶחֶם וַיֹּאמֶר לַקּוֹצְרִים: "יהוה עִמָּכֶם".

Chapter 21
Prepositions with Pronoun Endings

Vocabulary — Review of Prepositions

after, behind *prep*	אַחַר, אַחֲרֵי
to, into, towards *prep*	אֶל
in, with *prep*	בְּ־
between, among *prep*	בֵּין
as, like *prep*	כְּ־
to, for *prep*	לְ־
before, in the presence of *prep*	לִפְנֵי
from *prep*	מִן
as far as, until *prep*	עַד
upon, about *prep*	עַל
with *prep*	עִם
under, instead of *prep*	תַּחַת

Prepositions with Pronoun Endings

In Hebrew, a preposition can **never** be followed by a separate pronoun. The only way to express "him", "her", or any other pronoun following a preposition is to attach a pronoun ending to the preposition. Every preposition in Hebrew takes pronoun endings.

In Chapter 15, you learned the inseparable preposition לְ with pronoun endings: לִי, לְךָ, לָךְ, לוֹ, לָה, לָנוּ, etc.

The pronoun endings which are attached to prepositions are almost the same as the possessive pronoun endings which are attached to nouns. Although prepositions are neither singular nor plural, some prepositions take pronoun endings similar to those of singular nouns, and other prepositions take the same pronoun endings as plural nouns.

Prepositions with Singular Pronoun Endings

in	בְּ–	with	עִם
in me	בִּי	with me	עִמִּי
in you *m, s*	בְּךָ	with you *m, s*	עִמְּךָ
in you *f, s*	בָּךְ	with you *f, s*	עִמָּךְ
in him	בּוֹ	with him	עִמּוֹ
in her	בָּהּ	with her	עִמָּהּ
in us	בָּנוּ	with us	עִמָּנוּ
in you *m, pl*	בָּכֶם	with you *m, pl*	עִמָּכֶם
in you *f, pl*	בָּכֶן	with you *f, pl*	עִמָּכֶן
in them *m*	בָּהֶם/בָּם	with them *m*	עִמָּהֶם/עִמָּם
in them *f*	בָּהֶן	with them *f*	עִמָּהֶן/עִמָּן

These pronoun endings are almost exactly the same as the possessive pronoun endings for singular nouns. Notice that only the third person plural endings have a different form.

Prepositions with Plural Pronoun Endings

upon	עַל	to	אֶל
upon me	עָלַי	to me	אֵלַי
upon you *m, sg*	עָלֶיךָ	to you *m, sg*	אֵלֶיךָ
upon you *f, sg*	עָלַיִךְ	to you *f, sg*	אֵלַיִךְ
upon him	עָלָיו	to him	אֵלָיו
upon her	עָלֶיהָ	to her	אֵלֶיהָ
upon us	עָלֵינוּ	to us	אֵלֵינוּ
upon you *m, pl*	עֲלֵיכֶם	to you *m, pl*	אֲלֵיכֶם
upon you *m, pl*	עֲלֵיכֶן	to you *f, pl*	אֲלֵיכֶן
upon them *m*	עֲלֵיהֶם	to them *m*	אֲלֵיהֶם
upon them *f*	עֲלֵיהֶן	to them *f*	אֲלֵיהֶן

These pronoun endings are exactly the same as the possessive pronoun endings for plural nouns.

Variations

The prepositions מִן and ־כְּ do not follow either of the two patterns shown above when pronoun endings are attached. Following is a chart showing the forms of these prepositions. Notice the unusual endings.

from	מִן	**like**	־כְּ
from me	מִמֶּנִּי	like me	כָּמוֹנִי
from you m, sg	מִמְּךָ	like you m, sg	כָּמוֹךָ
from you f, sg	מִמֵּךְ	like you f, sg	כָּמוֹךְ
from him	מִמֶּנּוּ	like him	כָּמוֹהוּ
from her	מִמֶּנָּה	like her	כָּמוֹהָ
from us	מִמֶּנּוּ	like us	כָּמוֹנוּ
from you m, pl	מִכֶּם	like you m, pl	כְּמוֹכֶם
from you f, pl	מִכֶּן	like you f, pl	כְּמוֹכֶן
from them m	מֵהֶם	like them m	כְּמוֹהֶם
from them f	מֵהֶן	like them f	כְּמוֹהֶן

The Other Prepositions

This book will not list every Hebrew preposition and its endings. However, it is not difficult to recognize prepositions when they appear with pronoun endings. Most Hebrew prepositions take pronoun endings similar to those of singular or plural nouns.

Examples:

after you, behind you m, sg	אַחֲרֶיךָ	after, behind	אַחַר
between you, among you m, sg	בֵּינְךָ	between, among	בֵּין
before you, in the presence of you m, sg	לְפָנֶיךָ	before, in the presence of	לִפְנֵי
until you, as far as you m, sg	עָדֶיךָ	until, as far as	עַד
under you, instead of you m, sg	תַּחְתֶּיךָ	under, instead of	תַּחַת

The Preposition עַל Meaning "must"

The preposition עַל can be used with a pronoun ending attached to express the idea of "obligation" or "must". When the preposition עַל has this meaning, it is followed by an infinitive.

Examples: Literally: (It is) upon us to guard our daughters.   עָלֵינוּ לִשְׁמֹר אֶת בְּנוֹתֵינוּ.

           or: We must guard our daughters.

           Literally: (It is) upon him to write to them.   עָלָיו לִכְתֹּב לָהֶם.

           or: He must write to them.

אֵין with Pronoun Endings

The word אֵין also takes pronoun endings although it is not a preposition. The word אֵין with pronoun endings attached is used in Biblical Hebrew to make noun sentences and participles negative. It is not used to negate verbs in the perfect tense or the imperfect tense.

אֵין with Noun Sentences

Noun sentences can be made negative by using either the single word לֹא or the word אֵין with pronoun endings attached.

Example: I am not in my house.   אֵינֶנִּי בְּבֵיתִי. —or— אֲנִי לֹא בְּבֵיתִי.

אֵין with Participles

Participles are usually made negative by using the word אֵין with pronoun endings attached. The word לֹא is rarely used in Biblical Hebrew to make a participle negative.

Example: I am not guarding. —or— I am not a guard.   אֵינֶנִּי שׁוֹמֵר.

The word אֵין with pronoun endings attached is used only with participles or in noun sentences. It cannot be used with verbs in the perfect tense or the imperfect tense.

	there is not אֵין		אֵין
we are not	אֵינֶנּוּ	I am not	אֵינֶנִּי
you are not	אֵינְכֶם	you are not	אֵינְךָ
you are not	אֵינְכֶן	you are not	אֵינֵךְ
they are not	אֵינָם	he is not	אֵינֶנּוּ
they are not	אֵינָן	she is not	אֵינֶנָּה

עוֹד with Pronoun Endings

The word עוֹד, like the word אֵין, takes pronoun endings when it is used with a participle or in a noun sentence.

Examples: I am still in my house.   עוֹדֶנִּי בְּבֵיתִי.
            I am still guarding. — or — I am still a guard.   עוֹדֶנִּי שׁוֹמֵר.

The word עוֹד cannot be used with verbs in the perfect tense or the imperfect tense when it has pronoun endings attached.

	still עוֹד		עוֹד
we are still	עוֹדֶנּוּ	I am still	עוֹדֶנִּי, עוֹדִי
you are still	עוֹדְכֶם	you are still	עוֹדְךָ
you are still	עוֹדְכֶן	you are still	עוֹדָךְ
they are still	עוֹדָם	he is still	עוֹדֶנּוּ
they are still	עוֹדָן	she is still	עוֹדֶנָּה, עוֹדָה

Exercises

Exercise 1. Translate the following prepositions with pronoun endings.

1. בְּךָ	6. לָכֶן	11. עָלֵינוּ	16. לִי	21. עָלֶיךָ	26. מִמֶּךָ	31. עִמָּנוּ
2. עִמָּכֶם	7. עִמָּהֶן	12. עִמָּנוּ	17. עָלֶיךָ	22. מִמֶּנּוּ	27. כָּמוֹהוּ	32. בָּם
3. בּוֹ	8. לָךְ	13. אֲלֵיכֶן	18. אֲלֵיהֶם	23. כָּמוֹהָ	28. לוֹ	33. כְּמוֹכֶם
4. בָּהֶם	9. בָּהּ	14. בָּנוּ	19. מֵהֶם	24. בָּכֶן	29. עָלַי	34. אֲלֵיהֶן
5. עִמִּי	10. אֵלָיו	15. עָלֶיהָ	20. כָּמוֹנִי	25. אֲלֵיכֶן	30. מִכֶּן	35. מִמֶּנָּה

Exercise 2. Rewrite the sentences below, replacing the underlined word with each word in the list that follows. Every word or grammatical form in the sentence that agrees with the underlined word should be changed to agree with the newly substituted words. Read the sentences aloud. Translate.

1. <u>עוֹדֶנּוּ</u> בַּמִּדְבָּר וְאֵינֶנּוּ הֹלְכִים מִשָּׁם לַיָּם.

A. עוֹדְךָ	B. עוֹדְכֶן	C. עוֹדֶנּוּ	D. עוֹדֶנִּי	E. עוֹדָם
F. עוֹדָךְ	G. עוֹדְכֶם	H. עוֹדֶנָּה	I. עוֹדָן	

2. הֵם יִבְטְחוּ בִּי כִּי הֵם זוֹכְרִים <u>אֹתִי</u>.

A. אֹתָנוּ	B. אֹתָךְ	C. אֹתָם	D. אֹתוֹ	E. אֶתְכֶן
F. אֹתָךְ	G. אֹתָהּ	H. אֶתְכֶם		

3. הַמֶּלֶךְ יִקַּח אֶת בְּנֵיכֶם מִכֶּם וְגָנַב גַּם אֶת <u>כַּסְפְּכֶם</u>.

A. כַּסְפִּי	B. כַּסְפֵּנוּ	C. כַּסְפָּהּ	D. כַּסְפְּכֶן	E. כַּסְפָּם
F. כַּסְפּוֹ	G. כַּסְפֵּךְ	H. כַּסְפָּן	I. כַּסְפְּךָ	

4. <u>עָלֶיהָ</u> לִבְחֹר נָשִׁים חֲכָמוֹת לִשְׁמֹר אֶת בְּנוֹתֶיהָ.

A. עָלֵינוּ	B. עָלֶיךָ	C. עֲלֵיכֶם	D. עֲלֵיהֶן	E. עָלַי
F. עָלָיו	G. עָלַיִךְ			

5. הִנֵּה הָלְכוּ <u>אֵלֶיךָ</u> לָשֶׁבֶת עִמְּךָ וַתִּשְׁמַעְנָה בְּקוֹלְךָ וַתִּשְׁמֹרְנָה אֹתָךְ.

A. אֵלֵינוּ	B. אֲלֵיהֶם	C. אֵלַי	D. אֵלֶיהָ	E. אֲלֵיכֶן
F. אֵלָיו	G. אֲלֵיכֶם	H. אֵלַיִךְ		

Exercise 3. Change sentences 2, 3, 4, and 5 into the imperfect tense. Translate all the sentences into English.

1. עַתָּה עָלֶיהָ לִכְתֹּב לְאִמָּהּ.

2. הָלַכְתְּ עִמָּנוּ עַד הָעִיר.

3. הוּא גָּנַב מִמֶּנִּי אֶת הַכֹּל.

4. בָּחַרְנוּ בְּךָ מִכָּל הַנְּעָרִים.

5. הֵם הָלְכוּ אַחֲרַיִךְ בַּדֶּרֶךְ לְבֵית לָחֶם.

146

Exercise 4a. Substitute אֵין for עוֹד in the following sentences. For all the following exercises, refer to the charts in the chapter to locate the correct form. Translate.

Example: אֵינֶנּוּ בִּשְׂדֵי אֲבוֹתֵינוּ.   עוֹדֶנּוּ בִּשְׂדֵי אֲבוֹתֵינוּ.

3. עוֹדָן אֹכְלוֹת אֶת הַפְּרִי.   1. עוֹדֶנִּי בָּאֹהֶל עִמָּהֶן.

4. עוֹדָהּ זוֹכֶרֶת אֶת פְּנֵי אִישָׁהּ.   2. עוֹדֶנּוּ בַחֹשֶׁךְ עִם הַבְּהֵמוֹת בַּמִּדְבָּר.

Exercise 4b. Substitute עוֹד for אֵין in the following sentences. Translate.

3. אֵינֶנּוּ עִם הַקְּדוֹשִׁים בַּמִּשְׁכָּן.   1. אֵינְכֶם אֲנָשִׁים טוֹבִים.

4. אֵינָם שׁוֹכְבִים בְּאָהֳלֵיהֶם הַיּוֹם.   2. אֵינֶנִּי יוֹדֵעַ אֶת הַדְּבָרִים הָאֵלֶּה.

Exercise 5. In the following sentences, choose the correct preposition from those shown in parenthesis to fill in the blanks. Translate.

1. הָאֲנָשִׁים הָלְכוּ אֶל בֵּית הַנַּעֲרָה וַיִּגְנְבוּ כֶּסֶף _____ . (עָלֶיךָ, אֵלֵינוּ, בִּי, מִמֶּנָּה)

2. _____ , אַתֶּם מִמִּשְׁפַּחַת יַעֲקֹב. (בָּהּ, כָּמוֹנִי, עוֹדָם, עֲלֵיכֶן)

3. נִבְטַח _____ וְזָכַרְנוּ אֶת דְּבָרָיו. (עִמִּי, עָלֶיהָ, בּוֹ, מִמְּךָ)

4. הוּא יָשַׁב עַל כִּסְאוֹ וַיִּמְלֹךְ _____ . (עָלֵינוּ, בָּם, מִמֶּנִּי, אֵינְךָ)

5. הֵנָּה בָּחֲרוּ בָּךְ וַתֵּלַכְנָה _____ . (עָלַי, עוֹדֶנּוּ, עִמְּךָ, אֵינֵךְ)

Exercise 6. Translate the following sentences into Hebrew.

1. I am still on my land.
2. You *m, sg* are still on your land.
3. We are still on our land.
4. She is sitting with us.
5. I am sitting with them *m.*
6. You *f, pl* are sitting with him.
7. They *m, pl* are not like me.
8. You *f, sg* are not like them *f.*
9. I went to my house with my mother and sat there.
10. You *m, sg* went to your house with your mother and you sat in her chair.
11. He went to his big house with his old mother and his old father.
12. We went to our mother's big house when she was there.

From the Prayerbook

Prayerbook Vocabulary

gods . . . . אֵלִם   glorious. . . . . נֶאְדָּר

holiness. . . . . קֹדֶשׁ

Selection from the Prayerbook (said before the Amidah)

מִי כָמֹכָה בָּאֵלִם יְיָ; מִי כָמֹכָה נֶאְדָּר בַּקֹּדֶשׁ.

First try to translate the prayer in your own words, then read the translations quoted below.

Prayerbook Translations

"Who is like thee, O Lord, among the mighty?
Who is like thee, glorious in holiness?"

Daily Prayer Book, Philip Birnbaum, 1977, p. 350

"Who is like You, Eternal One, among the gods that are worshipped?
Who is like You, majestic in holiness?"

Gates of Prayer, The New Union Prayerbook, 1975, p. 196

Notice the use of the preposition כְּ with pronoun endings. The form כָמֹכָה is an alternate spelling for the form כָּמוֹךָ.

Guided Reading from Ruth

	he was in charge of נִצָּב 1.
	and he said וַיֹּאמֶר
	וַיֹּאמֶר בֹּעַז לְנַעֲרוֹ אֲשֶׁר נִצָּב עַל הַקּוֹצְרִים:
1. And Boaz said to his lad (servant) who was in charge of the harvesters:	2. "לְמִי הַנַּעֲרָה הַזֹּאת?"
2. To whom does this maiden belong?"	and he answered וַיַּעַן 3.
	וַיַּעַן הַנַּעַר וַיֹּאמַר: "נַעֲרָה מוֹאֲבִיָּה הִיא . . .

148

3. The servant (lad) answered and said: "She is a Moabite maiden . . .	return *3 f sg perfect* שָׁבָה 4. אֲשֶׁר שָׁבָה עִם נָעֳמִי מִשְּׂדֵי מוֹאָב.
4. who returned with Naomi from the fields of Moab.	glean ל.ק.ט 5. please נָא וַתֹּאמֶר: 'אֲלַקֳטָה נָא
5. And she said (to me): 'Please let me glean	gather א.ס.ף 6. sheaves עֳמָרִים וְאָסַפְתִּי בָעֳמָרִים אַחֲרֵי הַקּוֹצְרִים.'
6. and I will gather among the sheaves after the harvesters.'	come *3 f sg imperfect* תָּבוֹא 7. stand *3 f sg imperfect* תַּעֲמוֹד וַתָּבוֹא וַתַּעֲמוֹד מֵהַבֹּקֶר עַד עַתָּה."
7. And she came and stood from the morning until now."	another אַחֵר 8. וַיֹּאמֶר בֹּעַז אֶל רוּת: "אַל תֵּלְכִי לִלְקֹט בְּשָׂדֶה אַחֵר.
8. Boaz said to Ruth: "Do not go to glean in another field.	and thus וְכֹה 9. stay with ד.ב.ק וְכֹה תִּדְבְּקִי עִם נַעֲרוֹתַי.
9. And thus you will stay with my young women (harvesters).	עֵינַיִךְ בַּשָּׂדֶה אֲשֶׁר תִּקְצֹרְנָה וְהָלַכְתְּ אַחֲרֵיהֶן. 10.
10. Your eyes will be on the field where they will harvest, and you will go after them.	I commanded צִוִּיתִי 11. touch נ.ג.ע צִוִּיתִי אֶת הַנְּעָרִים לֹא לִנְגֹּעַ בָּךְ.
11. I commanded the young men not to touch you.	be thirsty *2 f sg perfect* צָמֵאת 12. drink *2 f sg perfect* שָׁתִית וְצָמֵאת וְהָלַכְתְּ אֶל הַכֵּלִים וְשָׁתִית."
12. And (when) you will be thirsty, you will go to the vessels and will drink."	

וַיֹּאמֶר בֹּעַז לְנַעֲרוֹ אֲשֶׁר נִצָּב עַל הַקּוֹצְרִים: "לְמִי הַנַּעֲרָה הַזֹּאת?" וַיַּעַן הַנַּעַר וַיֹּאמֶר: "נַעֲרָה מוֹאֲבִיָּה הִיא אֲשֶׁר שָׁבָה עִם נָעֳמִי מִשְּׂדֵי מוֹאָב. וַתֹּאמֶר: 'אֲלַקֳטָה נָא וְאָסַפְתִּי בָעֳמָרִים אַחֲרֵי הַקּוֹצְרִים.' וַתָּבוֹא וַתַּעֲמוֹד מֵהַבֹּקֶר עַד עַתָּה." וַיֹּאמֶר בֹּעַז אֶל רוּת: "אַל תֵּלְכִי לִלְקֹט בְּשָׂדֶה אַחֵר. וְכֹה תִּדְבְּקִי עִם נַעֲרוֹתַי. עֵינַיִךְ בַּשָּׂדֶה אֲשֶׁר תִּקְצֹרְנָה וְהָלַכְתְּ אַחֲרֵיהֶן. צִוִּיתִי אֶת הַנְּעָרִים לֹא לִנְגֹּעַ בָּךְ. וְצָמֵאת וְהָלַכְתְּ אֶל הַכֵּלִים וְשָׁתִית."

Chapter 22
Final ה Verbs

Vocabulary

build *vb*	ב.נ.ה.
wine *n, m*	יַ֫יִן
water *n, m*	מַ֫יִם
go up, ascend *vb*	ע.ל.ה.
answer *vb*	ע.נ.ה.
evening *n, m* . . . . *du* עֶ֫רֶב, עַרְבַּ֫יִם	
do, make *vb*	ע.שׂ.ה.
see *vb*	ר.א.ה.
drink *vb*	שׁ.ת.ה.

Idiom

at dusk	בֵּין הָעַרְבַּ֫יִם

Note 1: The word יַ֫יִן — wine has no plural form.
Note 2: The word מַ֫יִם — water has no singular form.
Note 3: The word עֶ֫רֶב — evening has no plural form.
The word עַרְבַּ֫יִם is a dual form.

Final ה Verbs

You have learned the complete conjugation of regular verbs in the פָּעַל pattern. As you have seen, there are some variations in the conjugation which occur when ה or ע is the last root letter, as in the verbs שׁ.ל.ח. and שׁ.מ.ע. There are other Hebrew letters that cause major variations in verb conjugations when they are part of the verb root. The letter ה is one that causes major variations when it is the last letter of the verb root. Verbs which have ה as their final root letter are called **final ה verbs.**

All the verbs introduced in the vocabulary of this chapter are final ה verbs. In this chapter, you will learn the complete conjugation of final ה verbs in the פָּעַל pattern.

The Perfect Tense of Final ה Verbs

Notice the difference between the conjugation of the regular verb כ.ת.ב and the final ה verb ב.נ.ה in the perfect tense.

build — ב.נ.ה		write — כ.ת.ב
בָּנִיתִי	1 c sg	כָּתַבְתִּי
בָּנִיתָ	2 m sg	כָּתַבְתָּ
בָּנִית	2 f sg	כָּתַבְתְּ
בָּנָה	3 m sg	כָּתַב
בָּנְתָה	3 f sg	כָּתְבָה
בָּנִינוּ	1 c pl	כָּתַבְנוּ
בְּנִיתֶם	2 m pl	כְּתַבְתֶּם
בְּנִיתֶן	2 f pl	כְּתַבְתֶּן
בָּנוּ	3 c pl	כָּתְבוּ

1. The third root letter ה disappears in all forms except the third person singular.
2. The ◌ַ vowel under the second root letter becomes an ◌ִי vowel in all forms except the third person. The letter י of the ◌ִי vowel appears in place of the third root letter ה.

The Imperfect Tense of Final ה Verbs

Notice the difference between the conjugation of the regular verb כ.ת.ב and the final ה verb ב.נ.ה in the imperfect tense.

build — ב.נ.ה		write — כ.ת.ב
אֶבְנֶה	1 c sg	אֶכְתֹּב
תִּבְנֶה	2 m sg	תִּכְתֹּב
תִּבְנִי	2 f sg	תִּכְתְּבִי
יִבְנֶה	3 m sg	יִכְתֹּב
תִּבְנֶה	3 f sg	תִּכְתֹּב
נִבְנֶה	1 c pl	נִכְתֹּב
תִּבְנוּ	2 m pl	תִּכְתְּבוּ
תִּבְנֶינָה	2 f pl	תִּכְתֹּבְנָה
יִבְנוּ	3 m pl	יִכְתְּבוּ
תִּבְנֶינָה	3 f pl	תִּכְתֹּבְנָה

1. The third root letter ה remains in the forms which have no endings added.
2. The third root letter ה disappears when an ending is added.
3. The basic vowel pattern is ◌ְ◌ֶ , instead of ◌ֹ◌ְ or ◌ְ◌ֹ .

The Participle of Final ה Verbs

Notice the difference between the participle of the regular verb כ.ת.ב and the participle of the final ה verb ב.נ.ה.

build — ב.נ.ה		write — כ.ת.ב
בּוֹנֶה/בָּנָה	m sg	כָּתַב/כּוֹתֵב
בּוֹנָה/בָּנָה	f sg	כָּתְבָה/כּוֹתֶבֶת, כּוֹתְבָה/כּוֹתֶבֶת
בּוֹנִים/בָּנִים	m pl	כָּתְבִים/כּוֹתְבִים
בּוֹנוֹת/בָּנוֹת	f pl	כָּתְבוֹת/כּוֹתְבוֹת

1. The third root letter ה remains in the singular forms but disappears in the plural.
2. The vowel pattern of the singular forms is different. Notice that the feminine singular form takes only the ָ vowel and not the ֶת ending.

The Imperative of Final ה Verbs

Notice the difference between the imperative of the regular verb כ.ת.ב and the imperative of the final ה verb ב.נ.ה.   The third root letter ה remains in the masculine singular form but disappears in the other three forms.

build — ב.נ.ה		write — כ.ת.ב
בְּנֵה	m sg	כְּתֹב
בְּנִי	f sg	כִּתְבִי
בְּנוּ	m pl	כִּתְבוּ
בְּנֶינָה	f pl	כְּתֹבְנָה

The indirect imperative forms of final ה verbs will not be taught in this book.

The Infinitive Construct of Final ה Verbs

Notice the difference between the infinitive construct of the regular verb כ.ת.ב and the infinitive construct of the final ה verb ב.נ.ה. The third root letter ה is replaced by the וֹת ending.

build — ב.נ.ה	write — כ.ת.ב
(לְ) בְּנוֹת לִבְנוֹת	לִכְתֹּב

The Infinitive Absolute of Final ה Verbs

Notice the difference between the infinitive absolute of the regular verb כ.ת.ב and the infinitive absolute of the final ה verb ב.נ.ה.

build — ב.נ.ה	write — כ.ת.ב
בָּנֹה	כָּתוֹב

Final ה Verbs with ע as First Root Letter

When the first root letter of a final ה verb is ע, some minor changes occur in the vowel pattern. The verbs ע.ל.ה, ע.נ.ה, and ע.ש.ה introduced in this chapter are examples of this type of final ה verb. Following are charts showing the complete conjugation of this type of verb. Notice the differences between the conjugation of the regular final ה verb ב.נ.ה and the slightly irregular final ה verb ע.ש.ה.

Perfect Tense

ע.ש.ה	ב.נ.ה	
עָשִׂיתִי	בָּנִיתִי	1 c sg
עָשִׂיתָ	בָּנִיתָ	2 m sg
עָשִׂית	בָּנִית	2 f sg
עָשָׂה	בָּנָה	3 m sg
עָשְׂתָה	בָּנְתָה	3 f sg
עָשִׂינוּ	בָּנִינוּ	1 c pl
עֲשִׂיתֶם	בְּנִיתֶם	2 m pl
עֲשִׂיתֶן	בְּנִיתֶן	2 f pl
עָשׂוּ	בָּנוּ	3 m pl
עָשׂוּ	בָּנוּ	3 f pl

Imperfect Tense

ע.ש.ה	ב.נ.ה	
אֶעֱשֶׂה	אֶבְנֶה	1 c sg
תַּעֲשֶׂה	תִּבְנֶה	2 m sg
תַּעֲשִׂי	תִּבְנִי	2 f sg
יַעֲשֶׂה	יִבְנֶה	3 m sg
תַּעֲשֶׂה	תִּבְנֶה	3 f sg
נַעֲשֶׂה	נִבְנֶה	1 c pl
תַּעֲשׂוּ	תִּבְנוּ	2 m pl
תַּעֲשֶׂינָה	תִּבְנֶינָה	2 f pl
יַעֲשׂוּ	יִבְנוּ	3 m pl
תַּעֲשֶׂינָה	תִּבְנֶינָה	3 f pl

Imperative

ע.ש.ה	ב.נ.ה	
עֲשֵׂה	בְּנֵה	m sg
עֲשִׂי	בְּנִי	f sg
עֲשׂוּ	בְּנוּ	m pl
עֲשֶׂינָה	בְּנֶינָה	f pl

Infinitive Construct

ע.ש.ה		ב.נ.ה
עֲשׂוֹת לַעֲשׂוֹת		בְּנוֹת

The participle and the infinitive absolute of final ה verbs that have the first root letter ע are formed in the same way as the participle and the infinitive absolute of regular final ה verbs.

Final ה Verbs with the Reversing Vav

When a reversing vav is added to a final ה verb, the third root letter ה disappears in some forms of the imperfect tense.

Examples:	With Reversing Vav	Regular Form	Root
	וַיִּבֶן	יִבְנֶה	ב.נ.ה
	וַיַּעַל	יַעֲלֶה	ע.ל.ה
	וַיַּעַן	יַעֲנֶה	ע.נ.ה

This shortened form of the final ה verb occurs in the imperfect tense only when the reversing vav is attached. Shortened forms often appear in the Bible. If you see an imperfect tense verb form with a reversing vav attached which seems to have only two root letters, remember that this verb could be a shortened form of a final ה verb.

Exercises

Exercise 1. Conjugate the following verb roots in all forms of the פָּעַל pattern.

ש.מ.ר .1   ש.ת.ה .2   ע.ל.ה .3

Exercise 2. Rewrite the sentences below, replacing the underlined word with each word in the list that follows. Every word or grammatical form in the sentence that agreed with the underlined word should be changed to agree with the newly substituted words. Read the sentences aloud. Translate.

1. אֲנַחְנוּ רָאִינוּ אֶת הַמִּשְׁכָּן אֲשֶׁר בְּנֵי יִשְׂרָאֵל בָּנוּ בַּמִּדְבָּר.

A. הוּא   B. אַתְּ   C. הַקּוֹצְרִים   D. אַתֶּן   E. אֲנִי

F. אַתָּה   G. שָׂרָה   H. הֵנָּה   I. אַתֶּם

2. בֵּין הָעַרְבַּיִם הִיא שָׁתְתָה יַיִן מֵהַכְּלִי וְאָמְרָה "לְחַיִּים!"

A. אֲנִי   B. אַתֶּם   C. הֵנָּה   D. הוּא   E. אַתְּ

F. אֲנַחְנוּ   G. הֵמָּה   H. אַתֶּן   I. אַתָּה

3. (אַתֶּם) עֲלוּ עַל הָאֲדָמָה לִבְנוֹת אֶת בָּתֵּיכֶם.

A. (אַתְּ)   B. (אַתֶּן)   C. (אַתָּה וְדָוִד)   D. (אַתָּה)   E. (אַתְּ וְנָעֳמִי)

4. אַתָּה תִּרְאֶה זָקֵן אֲשֶׁר הָלַךְ בַּדֶּרֶךְ וּבָטַחְתָּ בּוֹ וּפָתַחְתָּ לוֹ אֶת שַׁעֲרֵי עִירְךָ.

A. אַתֶּן   B. אֲנַחְנוּ   C. הוּא   D. הֵמָּה   E. אַתְּ

F. הִיא   G. אַתֶּם   H. הֵנָּה   I. אֲנִי

5. הָאִישׁ הַקָּדוֹשׁ אָמַר אֵלֵינוּ "תַּעֲשׂוּ חֶסֶד כַּאֲבוֹתֵכֶם" וְשָׁמַעְנוּ בְּקוֹלוֹ.

A. אֵלַי   B. אֵלֶיךָ   C. אֲלֵיכֶן   D. אֲלֵיהֶם   E. אֵלַיִךְ

F. אֲלֵיהֶן   G. אֵלֶיהָ   H. אֲלֵיכֶם

Exercise 3. In the following sentences, replace the underlined verb with the appropriate form of the verb root given. Translate.

Example: הָאִשָּׁה שָׁתְתָה ...   (ש.ת.ה) הָאִשָּׁה אָכְלָה מֵהַכְּלִי וַתַּעַל לְבֵיתָה.

1. (ע.נ.ה) אַתָּה אָמַר "כָּל אֲשֶׁר תַּחַת הַשָּׁמַיִם רַע" וַאֲנִי אוֹמֶרֶת לְךָ "לֹא".
2. (ע.ל.ה) תֵּלְכוּ עִמִּי בָּעֶרֶב מֵהַיָּם עַד הָרֵי יְרוּשָׁלַיִם.
3. (ב.נ.ה) אֶבְחַר בָּאֲנָשִׁים הָאֵלֶּה לִשְׁמֹר אֶת בֵּיתִי.
4. (ר.א.ה) שְׁמַע אֶת הַדְּבָרִים הַכְּתוּבִים הָאֵלֶּה וְאַל תִּשְׁכַּח אֹתָם.
5. (ע.שׂ.ה) הֵמָּה נָכוֹר יִזְכְּרוּ אֶת כָּל אֲשֶׁר עָשׂוּ אֲבוֹתֵיהֶם.

Exercise 4. Rewrite the following sentences, filling in the blanks with all forms of the verb root shown that will yield a meaningful sentence. Translate.

‎1. (ע.ל.ה) כָּל הַגּוֹי הַזֶּה _____ מֵהַמִּדְבָּר אֶל אֶרֶץ יִשְׂרָאֵל.

‎2. (ש.ת.ה) שְׁבִי עִם מִשְׁפַּחְתֵּךְ בַּשָּׂדֶה וּ_____ רַק אֶת הַמַּיִם.

‎3. (ע.שׂ.ה) אַתֶּם _____ אֶת הָרַע בְּעֵינֵי הַשּׁוֹפֵט.

‎4. (ע.נ.ה) אָמַרְתִּי לוֹ: "הִנֵּה לֶחֶם וְיַיִן וּפְרִי" וְהוּא _____: "אֶזְכֹּר אֶת חַסְדְּךָ."

‎5. (ב.נ.ה) אֲנַחְנוּ _____ אֶת שַׁעֲרֵי עִירֵנוּ.

‎6. (ע.שׂ.ה) אֲנִי _____ יַיִן מֵהַפְּרִי לְמִשְׁפַּחְתִּי לִשְׁתּוֹת בְּעֶרֶב שַׁבָּת.

‎7. (ש.ת.ה) כַּאֲשֶׁר תֵּלֵךְ לְמוֹאָב, אַל _____ אֶת הַמַּיִם. _____ רַק אֶת הַיַּיִן!

‎8. (ר.א.ה) אַתֶּן _____ אֶת פְּנֵי הַנַּעַר תָּמִיד.

Exercise 5. Read and translate the following sentences. Underline all verb forms that are shortened by the addition of a reversing vav.

‎1. אָכַלְנוּ אֶת הָאֹכֶל וַנֵּשְׁתְּ מַיִם וַנֵּשֶׁב בְּאָהֳלֵנוּ בֵּין הָעַרְבַּיִם.

‎2. הָאִישׁ עָלָה לִירוּשָׁלַיִם וַיַּרְא שָׁם אֶת דּוֹדוֹ.

‎3. וַיְהִי חֹשֶׁךְ וַתֵּלַכְנָה הַנָּשִׁים אֶל בֵּיתָן.

‎4. עֲלֵיהֶם לִבְנוֹת עִיר בְּתוֹךְ הַמִּדְבָּר וְהֵם יִבְנוּ אֹתָהּ.

Exercise 6. Using the list of verb roots at the bottom of this exercise, identify the roots of the following verb forms. Translate each verb form.

16. וָאֶשְׁתְּ	13. וַתִּבֶן	10. שׁוֹתִים	7. הֱיוֹת	4. בְּנִיתֶם	1. פָּתַחְתִּי
17. עָנִינוּ	14. קַח	11. אֵלֵךְ	8. וַנַּעַשׂ	5. וָאֶשְׁכַּח	2. לֵךְ
18. עֲשִׂי	15. רְאוּ	12. וַיְהִי	9. לַעֲנוֹת	6. וַתֵּרֶא	3. תִּקַּח

ב.נ.ה, ה.י.ה, ה.ל.ך, ע.נ.ה, ל.ק.ח, פ.ת.ח, ר.א.ה, ש.כ.ח, ש.ת.ה.

Exercise 7. The following phrases are taken directly from the Bible. You now know enough Hebrew grammar to understand them. Read and translate.

Vocabulary for Reading Selection

וַיַּבְדֵּל .... and he divided   ‎-שֶׁ prefix .... *a shortened form of* אֲשֶׁר

ק.ר.א .... call, name   חָדָשׁ .... new

1. from the first day of the Creation story, Genesis 1:4-5

וַיַּרְא אֱלֹהִים אֶת הָאוֹר כִּי טוֹב.
וַיַּבְדֵּל אֱלֹהִים בֵּין הָאוֹר וּבֵין הַחֹשֶׁךְ.
וַיִּקְרָא אֱלֹהִים לָאוֹר יוֹם וְלַחֹשֶׁךְ קָרָא לָיְלָה.
וַיְהִי עֶרֶב וַיְהִי בֹקֶר יוֹם אֶחָד.

3. from Ecclesiastes 1:9

מַה שֶּׁהָיָה הוּא שֶׁיִּהְיֶה ...
וְאֵין כָּל חָדָשׁ תַּחַת הַשָּׁמֶשׁ.

2. from Song of Songs 2:16

דּוֹדִי לִי וַאֲנִי לוֹ.

Exercise 8. Fill in the proper form of the verb in the last column and translate.

Root	Number	Gender	Person	Tense	Pattern	Word	
כ.ת.ב	sg	c	1	perfect	פָּעַל		1
ב.נ.ה	sg	c	1	perfect	פָּעַל		2
ע.ל.ה	sg	c	1	perfect	פָּעַל		3
שׁ.ת.ה	pl	m	2	perfect	פָּעַל		4
שׁ.מ.ר	pl	m	2	perfect	פָּעַל		5
ע.שׂ.ה	pl	m	2	perfect	פָּעַל		6
שׁ.פ.ט	sg	m	3	imperfect	פָּעַל		7
ר.א.ה	sg	m	3	imperfect	פָּעַל		8
ע.שׂ.ה	sg	m	3	perfect	פָּעַל		9
ה.י.ה	sg	m	3	perfect	פָּעַל		10
ע.שׂ.ה	sg	f	—	active participle	פָּעַל		11
כ.ת.ב	sg	f	—	active participle	פָּעַל		12
י.שׁ.ב	pl	f	2	perfect	פָּעַל		13
ע.ל.ה	pl	f	2	perfect	פָּעַל		14
ז.כ.ר	pl	f	2	imperfect	פָּעַל		15
ר.א.ה	pl	f	2	imperfect	פָּעַל		16
ע.נ.ה	pl	f	2	imperfect	פָּעַל		17
ב.ט.ח	sg	m	—	imperative	פָּעַל		18
שׁ.ת.ה	sg	m	—	imperative	פָּעַל		19
ע.שׂ.ה	sg	m	—	imperative	פָּעַל		20
ע.שׂ.ה	—	—	—	infinitive construct	פָּעַל		21
ה.ל.ך	—	—	—	infinitive construct	פָּעַל		22
ב.נ.ה	—	—	—	infinitive construct	פָּעַל		23
כ.ת.ב	—	—	—	infinitive construct	פָּעַל		24

From the Prayerbook

Prayerbook Vocabulary

peace . . . . שָׁלוֹם   high place. . . . . מָרוֹם

אִמְרוּ . . . . *m pl imperative of* א.מ.ר

Selection from the Prayerbook (from the Kaddish)

עֹשֶׂה שָׁלוֹם בִּמְרוֹמָיו, הוּא יַעֲשֶׂה שָׁלוֹם עָלֵינוּ וְעַל כָּל יִשְׂרָאֵל, וְאִמְרוּ אָמֵן.

First try to translate the prayer in your own words, then read the translations quoted below.

Prayerbook Translations

"He who creates peace in his celestial heights, may he create peace for us and for all Israel; and say, Amen."

Daily Prayer Book, Philip Birnbaum, 1977, p. 416

"He who maketh peace in his high places, may he make peace for us and for all Israel; and say ye, Amen."

Daily Prayer Book, Joseph Hertz, 1975, p. 555

Notice that the first word עֹשֶׂה is a *m sg* participle used as a noun, and that the word יַעֲשֶׂה is translated in both prayer books as an indirect imperative and not as the *3 m sg* form of the imperfect tense.

Guided Reading from Ruth

	and she fell וַתִּפֹּל .1 and she bowed down וַתִּשְׁתַּחוּ וַתִּפֹּל עַל פָּנֶיהָ וַתִּשְׁתַּחוּ וַתֹּאמֶר אֵלָיו:
1. And she fell (down) on her face, and bowed down, and said to him:	why מַדּוּעַ .2 find מ.צ.א favor חֵן "מַדּוּעַ מָצָאתִי חֵן בְּעֵינֶיךָ
2. "Why have I found favor in your eyes,	pay attention to לְהַכִּיר .3 foreign woman נָכְרִיָּה לְהַכִּיר אֹתִי וְאָנֹכִי נָכְרִיָּה?"

3. to pay attention to me, when I am a foreign woman?"	4. חָמוֹת mother-in-law וַיַּעַן בֹּעַז וַיֹּאמֶר לָהּ: "שָׁמַעְתִּי אֶת כָּל אֲשֶׁר עָשִׂית עִם חֲמוֹתֵךְ
4. And Boaz answered and said to her: "I have heard all that you have done with your mother-in-law	5. מוֹת death of אַחֲרֵי מוֹת אִישֵׁךְ,
5. after the death of your husband,	6. ע.ז.ב. leave מוֹלֶדֶת kindred, birth וַתַּעַזְבִי אֶת אָבִיךְ וְאֶת אִמֵּךְ וְאֶת אֶרֶץ מוֹלַדְתֵּךְ
6. when you left your father and your mother and the land of your birth	7. וַתֵּלְכִי אֶל עַם אֲשֶׁר לֹא יָדַעַתְּ.
7. and you went to a people that you did not know.	8. יְשַׁלֵּם may he reward פֹּעַל deed יְשַׁלֵּם יהוה פָּעֳלֵךְ
8. May the Lord reward your deed	9. מַשְׂכֹּרֶת reward שְׁלֵמָה complete, full מֵעִם from prep וּתְהִי מַשְׂכֻּרְתֵּךְ שְׁלֵמָה מֵעִם יהוה אֱלֹהֵי יִשְׂרָאֵל
9. and may your reward be full from the Lord, God of Israel	10. בָּאת come 2 f sg perfect ח.ס.ה. seek refuge כָּנָף wing אֲשֶׁר בָּאת לַחֲסוֹת תַּחַת כְּנָפָיו."
10. under whose wings you came to seek refuge." (Literally: whom you came to seek refuge under his wings)	

וַתִּפֹּל עַל פָּנֶיהָ וַתִּשְׁתַּחוּ וַתֹּאמֶר אֵלָיו: "מַדּוּעַ מָצָאתִי חֵן בְּעֵינֶיךָ לְהַכִּירֵנִי וְאָנֹכִי נָכְרִיָּה?". וַיַּעַן בֹּעַז וַיֹּאמֶר לָהּ: "שָׁמַעְתִּי אֶת כָּל אֲשֶׁר עָשִׂית עִם חֲמוֹתֵךְ אַחֲרֵי מוֹת אִישֵׁךְ, וַתַּעַזְבִי אֶת אָבִיךְ וְאֶת אִמֵּךְ וְאֶת אֶרֶץ מוֹלַדְתֵּךְ וַתֵּלְכִי אֶל עַם אֲשֶׁר לֹא יָדַעַתְּ. יְשַׁלֵּם יהוה פָּעֳלֵךְ וּתְהִי מַשְׂכֻּרְתֵּךְ שְׁלֵמָה מֵעִם יהוה אֱלֹהֵי יִשְׂרָאֵל אֲשֶׁר בָּאת לַחֲסוֹת תַּחַת כְּנָפָיו."

Chapter 23
Hollow Verbs

Vocabulary

come, go *vb* . . . . ב.ו.א

turn aside *vb* . . . . ס.ו.ר

arise, stand up *vb* . . . . ק.ו.ם

run *vb* . . . . ר.ו.ץ

return *vb* . . . . ש.ו.ב

put, set, place *vb* . . . . ש.י.ם

sing *vb* . . . . ש.י.ר

year *n, f* . . . . *du* שְׁנָתַיִם ,שָׁנִים ,שָׁנָה

Idioms

He paid attention to . . . . אֶל (לְבָבוֹ) הוּא שָׂם לִבּוֹ

   She paid attention to, etc. אֶל (לְבָבָהּ) הִיא שָׂמָה לִבָּהּ

day by day, daily . . . . יוֹם יוֹם

every year . . . . שָׁנָה בְּשָׁנָה

Hollow Verbs

You have just learned that the letter ה causes major variations in the conjugation of a verb when it is the last letter of the root. Similarly, the letters ו and י cause major variations when either one is the middle letter of a verb root. In the conjugation of such verbs, the middle root letter ו or י is never pronounced as a consonant. Therefore, these verbs are called **hollow verbs**. All the verbs introduced in the vocabulary of this chapter are hollow verbs. In this chapter, you will learn the conjugation of hollow verbs in the פָּעַל pattern.

The Perfect Tense of Hollow Verbs

Notice the difference between the conjugation of the regular verb כ.ת.ב and the hollow verbs ש.ו.ב and ש.י.ם in the perfect tense. Hollow verbs with the middle root letter ו usually follow the same conjugation as the verb root ש.ו.ב. Hollow verbs with the middle root letter י usually follow the same conjugation as the verb root ש.י.ם.

159

The Perfect Tense of Hollow Verbs

	put — שׂ.י.ם	return — שׁ.ו.ב	write — כ.ת.ב
1 c sg	שַׂ֫מְתִּי	שַׁ֫בְתִּי	כָּתַ֫בְתִּי
2 m sg	שַׂ֫מְתָּ	שַׁ֫בְתָּ	כָּתַ֫בְתָּ
2 f sg	שַׂמְתְּ	שַׁבְתְּ	כָּתַבְתְּ
3 m sg	שָׂם	שָׁב	כָּתַב
3 f sg	שָׂ֫מָה	שָׁ֫בָה	כָּתְבָה
1 c pl	שַׂ֫מְנוּ	שַׁ֫בְנוּ	כָּתַ֫בְנוּ
2 m pl	שַׂמְתֶּם	שַׁבְתֶּם	כְּתַבְתֶּם
2 f pl	שַׂמְתֶּן	שַׁבְתֶּן	כְּתַבְתֶּן
3 c pl	שָׂ֫מוּ	שָׁ֫בוּ	כָּתְבוּ

1. The middle root letter וֹ or י disappears in the perfect tense.
2. The accent is on the first syllable in all forms except the second person plural forms.

The Imperfect Tense of Hollow Verbs

Notice the difference between the conjugation of the regular verb כ.ת.ב and the hollow verbs שׁ.ו.ב and שׂ.י.ם in the imperfect tense.

	put — שׂ.י.ם	return — שׁ.ו.ב	write — כ.ת.ב
1 c sg	אָשִׂים	אָשׁוּב	אֶכְתֹּב
2 m sg	תָּשִׂים	תָּשׁוּב	תִּכְתֹּב
2 f sg	תָּשִׂ֫ימִי	תָּשׁ֫וּבִי	תִּכְתְּבִי
3 m sg	יָשִׂים	יָשׁוּב	יִכְתֹּב
3 f sg	תָּשִׂים	תָּשׁוּב	תִּכְתֹּב
1 c pl	נָשִׂים	נָשׁוּב	נִכְתֹּב
2 m pl	תָּשִׂ֫ימוּ	תָּשׁ֫וּבוּ	תִּכְתְּבוּ
2 f pl	תְּשִׂימֶ֫ינָה/תָּשֵׂ֫מְנָה	תְּשׁוּבֶ֫ינָה/תָּשֹׁ֫בְנָה	תִּכְתֹּ֫בְנָה
3 m pl	יָשִׂ֫ימוּ	יָשׁ֫וּבוּ	יִכְתְּבוּ
3 f pl	תְּשִׂימֶ֫ינָה/תָּשֵׂ֫מְנָה	תְּשׁוּבֶ֫ינָה/תָּשֹׁ֫בְנָה	תִּכְתֹּ֫בְנָה

1. The middle root letter וֹ or י appears as a vowel in the imperfect tense. When the middle root letter is a וֹ, it usually appears as an אוֹ vowel. The verbs ס.ו.ר, ק.ו.ם, and ר.ו.ץ introduced in the vocabulary of this chapter all have an אוֹ vowel in the imperfect tense. When the middle root letter is a י, it usually appears as an אִי vowel. The verb שׂ.י.ר introduced in the vocabulary of this chapter has an אִי vowel in the imperfect tense.
2. There are two second and third f pl forms.
3. The vowel of the prefix is אָ in most forms of the imperfect tense.

The Participle of Hollow Verbs

Notice the difference between the participle of the regular verb כ.ת.ב and the hollow verbs שׁ.ו.ב and שׂ.י.ם.

	put — שׂ.י.ם	return — שׁ.ו.ב	write — כ.ת.ב
m sg	שָׂם	שָׁב	כּוֹתֵב/כֹּתֵב
f sg	שָׂמָה	שָׁבָה	כּוֹתֶבֶת/כֹּתֶבֶת כּוֹתְבָה/כֹּתְבָה
m pl	שָׂמִים	שָׁבִים	כּוֹתְבִים/כֹּתְבִים
f pl	שָׂמוֹת	שָׁבוֹת	כּוֹתְבוֹת/כֹּתְבוֹת

1. The middle root letter ו or י disappears in the participle.
2. The masculine and feminine singular participles of hollow verbs are spelled the same as the third person singular of the perfect tense.

The Imperative of Hollow Verbs

Notice the difference between the imperative of the regular verb כ.ת.ב and the hollow verbs שׁ.ו.ב and שׂ.י.ם.

	put — שׂ.י.ם	return — שׁ.ו.ב	write — כ.ת.ב
m sg	שִׂים	שׁוּב	כְּתֹב
f sg	שִׂימִי	שׁוּבִי	כִּתְבִי
m pl	שִׂימוּ	שׁוּבוּ	כִּתְבוּ
f pl	שֵׂמְנָה	שֹׁבְנָה	כְּתֹבְנָה

The middle root letter ו or י appears as a vowel in the imperative just as it does in the imperfect tense.

The Infinitive Construct of Hollow Verbs

Notice the difference between the infinitive construct of the regular verb כ.ת.ב and the hollow verbs שׁ.ו.ב and שׂ.י.ם.

	put —שׂ.י.ם	return — שׁ.ו.ב	write —כ.ת.ב
	שִׂים לָשִׂים (לְ)	שׁוּב לָשׁוּב (לְ)	כְּתֹב לִכְתֹּב (לְ)

The middle root letter ו or י appears as a vowel in the infinitive construct.

The Infinitive Absolute of Hollow Verbs

Notice the difference between the infinitive absolute of the regular verb כ.ת.ב and the hollow verbs שׁ.ו.ב and שׂ.י.ם.

	put — שׂ.י.ם	return — שׁ.ו.ב	write — כ.ת.ב
	שׂוֹם	שׁוֹב	כָּתוֹב

The middle root letter ו or י always becomes an וֹ vowel in the infinitive absolute.

The Indirect Imperative of Hollow Verbs

The indirect imperative forms of hollow verbs will not be taught in this book.

Hollow Verbs with the וּ Vowel

Most hollow verbs with the middle root letter ו follow the same conjugation as the verb שׁ.ו.ב. However, some hollow verbs with the middle root letter ו follow a slightly different conjugation, in which the middle root letter ו appears as the וֹ vowel instead of the וּ vowel in the imperfect tense, imperative, and infinitive construct. The verb ב.ו.א is the only example of this type of verb introduced in this book.

Following are charts showing the complete conjugation of the verb ב.ו.א. The conjugation of the verb ב.ו.א is slightly irregular because, in addition to the middle vowel ו, the third root letter of ב.ו.א is א, one of the throaty five letters. Notice the differences between the conjugation of the regular hollow verb שׁ.ו.ב and the slightly irregular hollow verb ב.ו.א.

Perfect			Imperfect			Participle		
ב.ו.א	שׁ.ו.ב		ב.ו.א	שׁ.ו.ב		ב.ו.א	שׁ.ו.ב	
בָּ֫אתִי	שַׁ֫בְתִּי	1 c sg	אָבוֹא	אָשׁוּב		בָּא	שָׁב	m sg
בָּ֫אתָ	שַׁ֫בְתָּ	2 m sg	תָּבוֹא	תָּשׁוּב		בָּאָה	שָׁבָה	f sg
בָּאת	שַׁבְתְּ	2 f sg	תָּבֹ֫אִי	תָּשׁ֫וּבִי		בָּאִים	שָׁבִים	m pl
בָּא	שָׁב	3 m sg	יָבוֹא	יָשׁוּב		בָּאוֹת	שָׁבוֹת	f pl
בָּ֫אָה	שָׁ֫בָה	3 f sg	תָּבוֹא	תָּשׁוּב				
בָּ֫אנוּ	שַׁ֫בְנוּ	1 c pl	נָבוֹא	נָשׁוּב				
בָּאתֶם	שַׁבְתֶּם	2 m pl	תָּבֹ֫אוּ	תָּשׁ֫וּבוּ				
בָּאתֶן	שַׁבְתֶּן	2 f pl	תְּבוֹאֶ֫ינָה/תָּבֹ֫אנָה	תְּשׁוּבֶ֫ינָה/תָּשֹׁ֫בְנָה				
בָּ֫אוּ	שָׁ֫בוּ	3 m pl	יָבֹ֫אוּ	יָשׁ֫וּבוּ				
בָּ֫אוּ	שָׁ֫בוּ	3 f pl	תְּבוֹאֶ֫ינָה/תָּבֹ֫אנָה	תְּשׁוּבֶ֫ינָה/תָּשֹׁ֫בְנָה				

Imperative			Infinitive Absolute			Infinitive Construct		
ב.ו.א	שׁ.ו.ב		ב.ו.א	שׁ.ו.ב		ב.ו.א	שׁ.ו.ב	
בּוֹא	שׁוּב	m sg	בּוֹא	שׁוֹב		לָבוֹא (לְ) בּוֹא	לָשׁוּב (לְ) שׁוּב	
בֹּ֫אִי	שׁ֫וּבִי	f sg						
בֹּ֫אוּ	שׁ֫וּבוּ	m pl						
בֹּ֫אנָה	שֹׁ֫בְנָה	f pl						

Hollow Verbs with the Reversing Vav

When a reversing vav is added to a hollow verb, the middle root letter ו or י disappears in some forms of the imperfect tense, and the vowel pattern changes.

	With Reversing Vav	Regular Form	Root	
Examples:	וַתָּשָׁב	תָּשׁוּב	שׁ.ו.ב	*2 m sg*
	וַיָּשֶׂם	יָשִׂים	שׂ.י.ם	*3 m sg*
	וַתָּקָם	תָּקוּם	ק.ו.ם	*3 f sg*

Exercises

Exercise 1. Conjugate the following verb roots in all forms of the פָּעַל pattern.

‏1. ז.כ.ר‏   ‏2. ק.ו.ם‏   ‏3. שׁ.י.ר‏   ‏4. ע.נ.ה

Exercise 2. Rewrite the sentences below, replacing the underlined word with each word in the list that follows. Every word or grammatical form in the sentence that agrees with the underlined word should be changed to agree with the newly substituted words. Read the sentences aloud. Translate.

‏1. (אֲנִי) קַמְתִּי בַּבֹּקֶר וָאֶשְׁכַּב בָּעֶרֶב.

A. הִיא   B. אַתֶּן   C. אָנוּ   D. אַתְּ   E. הוּא
F. הֵנָּה   G. אַתֶּם   H. אַתָּה   I. הֵם

‏2. יָסוּר הָאִישׁ מֵהַדֶּרֶךְ וְרָץ לָקַחַת אֶת הָאֹכֶל מֵהָאֹהֶל.

A. אֵשֶׁת בֹּעַז   B. אֲנַחְנוּ   C. הַנְּעָרִים   D. אַתֶּם   E. נְשֵׁי יְרוּשָׁלַיִם
F. אַתָּה   G. אַתְּ   H. אַתֶּן   I. אֲנִי

‏3. קַמְתִּי וּבָאתִי אֶל הָאִישׁ הַקָּדוֹשׁ לִשְׁמֹעַ אֶת דְּבָרָיו.

A. קַמְנוּ   B. יָקוּם   C. קַמְתֶּם   D. אָקוּם   E. תָּקוּמִי

‏4. בְּשׁוּב הַקּוֹצְרִים מֵהַשָּׂדֶה אֶל בָּתֵּיהֶם יָשְׁבוּ וְאָכְלוּ וְשָׁתוּ יַיִן וְשָׁרוּ.

A. בְּשׁוּב הָאִישׁ   B. בְּשׁוּבִי   C. בְּשׁוּבְכֶם   D. בְּשׁוּבְךָ   E. בְּשׁוּב הַנָּשִׁים
F. בְּשׁוּבֵנוּ   G. בְּשׁוּבָהּ   H. בְּשׁוּבְכֶן   I. בְּשׁוּבֵךְ

‏5. (אֲנַחְנוּ) נָשִׂים לְפָנָיו מִנְחוֹת וְכֶסֶף שָׁנָה בְּשָׁנָה וְהוּא יִשְׁמֹר אֹתָנוּ מִכָּל רַע.

A. הוּא   B. אַתֶּם   C. הֵנָּה   D. אַתָּה   E. אֲנִי
F. אַתֶּן   G. הִיא   H. אַתְּ   I. הֵמָּה

163

Exercise 3. Rewrite the following sentences, filling in the blanks with all forms of the verb root shown that will yield a meaningful sentence. Translate.

Example: שׁ.וּ.ב (אַתָּה) _____ אֶל הָאֹהֶל בָּעֶרֶב.

תָּשׁוּב אֶל הָאֹהֶל בָּעֶרֶב.

אַתָּה שָׁב אֶל הָאֹהֶל בָּעֶרֶב.

שַׁבְתָּ אֶל הָאֹהֶל בָּעֶרֶב.

שׁוּב תָּשׁוּב אֶל הָאֹהֶל בָּעֶרֶב.

שׁוּב שַׁבְתָּ אֶל הָאֹהֶל בָּעֶרֶב.

שׁוּב אֶל הָאֹהֶל בָּעֶרֶב.

1. ב.ו.א (הֵמָּה) _____ לִקְצֹר יוֹם יוֹם.

2. ס.ו.ר (אַתְּ) _____ מֵרַע וּלְכִי בַּדֶּרֶךְ הַטּוֹב.

3. ק.ו.ם (אֲנַחְנוּ) _____ לַעֲלוֹת עַל הָהָר.

4. שׂ.י.ם (הוּא) _____ לִבּוֹ לְקוֹל אִמּוֹ.

5. ר.ו.ץ (אֲנִי) כְּשׁוּב אָחִי אֶל אַדְמָתָם, _____ לִרְאוֹת אֹתָם.

6. שׁ.י.ר הִיא תָּמִיד _____ בָּעֶרֶב עִם מִשְׁפַּחְתָּהּ.

Exercise 4a. Rewrite the following sentences, changing the verb forms from the perfect tense to the imperfect tense. Translate.

1. שַׂמְתֶּם אֶת דִּבְרֵי הַבְּרִית עַל לְבַבְכֶם וְעַל נַפְשְׁכֶם.

2. הוּא שָׁב לְאַרְצוֹ וּבָנָה שָׁם בַּיִת מֵאָבֶן.

3. הֵם סָרוּ מֵהַבְּרִית וְעָשׂוּ אֶת הָרַע בְּעֵינֵי אֲבִיהֶם.

4. אָכַלְנוּ וְשָׁתִינוּ וְקַמְנוּ לָלֶכֶת אֶל אָהֳלֵינוּ.

Exercise 4b. Rewrite the following sentences, changing the verb forms from the imperfect tense to the perfect tense. Translate.

1. נַעֲשֶׂה כְּלֵי כֶסֶף וְנָשִׂים אֹתָם בַּמִּשְׁכָּן.

2. הֵמָּה יַעֲנוּ "נָבוֹא לִרְאוֹת אֶתְכֶם".

3. הִיא תָּשׁוּב אֶל בֵּית אָבִיהָ שָׁנָה בְּשָׁנָה.

4. אַתֶּן תָּשֵׁרְנָה עִם כָּל אַנְשֵׁי הָעִיר.

Exercise 5. Read and translate the following sentences. Underline all verb forms that are shortened by the addition of a reversing vav.

1. וַיֵּלֶךְ הַזָּקֵן וַיָּבוֹא אֶל הָהָר הַקָּדוֹשׁ וַיַּעַל עָלָיו.

2. שָׁמַעְתָּ קוֹל בְּהֶמָה וַתֵּרֶא אֹתָהּ וַתָּסַר מֵהַדֶּרֶךְ.

3. וַתָּשָׁב רוּת עִם נָעֳמִי אֶל אֶרֶץ יִשְׂרָאֵל וַתֵּשֶׁב עִמָּהּ שָׁם.

4. וַיִּבֶן לוֹ כִּסֵּא מֵעֵץ וַיָּשֶׂם אֶת הַכֶּסֶף תַּחְתָּיו וַיֵּשֶׁב עָלָיו.

5. וַיְהִי בַבֹּקֶר וַתָּקָם הַנַּעֲרָה מִמִּשְׁכָּבָהּ וַתִּלְבַּשׁ אֶת בְּגָדֶיהָ וַתֵּלֶךְ אֶל בֵּית אָחִיהָ.

6. אָשִׂים לִבִּי אֶל דִּבְרֵי הַחֲכָמִים וְסָרְתִּי מִיַּיִן וְנָשִׁים.

Exercise 6. Complete the following story, using the Hebrew grammar and vocabulary you have learned.

הָיָה אִישׁ אֲשֶׁר יָשַׁב בְּאֹהֶל בַּמִּדְבָּר. הָיוּ לוֹ בָּנִים וּבָנוֹת, וְלֹא הָיָה לוֹ כֶּסֶף. וַיְהִי הַיּוֹם וְלֹא הָיָה לְמִשְׁפַּחְתּוֹ אֹכֶל . . .

Exercise 7. Fill in the proper form of the verb in the last column and translate.

Root	Number	Gender	Person	Tense	Pattern	Word	
שׁ.ו.ב	sg	m	2	perfect	פָּעַל		1
ע.שׂ.ה	sg	m	2	perfect	פָּעַל		2
ז.כ.ר	sg	m	2	perfect	פָּעַל		3
ב.ו.א	sg	m	2	perfect	פָּעַל		4
ר.ו.ץ	pl	c	1	imperfect	פָּעַל		5
ע.ל.ה	pl	c	1	imperfect	פָּעַל		6
ס.ו.ר	pl	c	1	imperfect	פָּעַל		7
שׁ.מ.ר	pl	c	1	imperfect	פָּעַל		8
ב.ו.א	sg	f	—	active participle	פָּעַל		9
ב.נ.ה	sg	f	—	active participle	פָּעַל		10
ב.ו.א	sg	f	3	perfect	פָּעַל		11
כ.ת.ב	sg	f	3	perfect	פָּעַל		12
ה.י.ה	sg	f	3	perfect	פָּעַל		13
ה.י.ה	pl	f	3	imperfect	פָּעַל		14
ק.ו.ם	pl	f	3	imperfect	פָּעַל		15
שׁ.י.ר	pl	m	3	imperfect	פָּעַל		16
שׂ.י.ם	sg	m	2	perfect	פָּעַל		17
שׁ.י.ר	sg	m	—	imperative	פָּעַל		18
ק.ו.ם	pl	m	—	imperative	פָּעַל		19
ק.ו.ם	sg	c	1	imperfect	פָּעַל		20
ב.ו.א	sg	c	1	imperfect	פָּעַל		21

From the Prayerbook

Prayerbook Vocabulary

grace . . . . חֵן		bless . . . . ב.ר.ך
mercy . . . . רַחֲמִים		blessing n, f . . . . בְּרָכָה
all of us . . . . כֻּלָּנוּ		bless us . . . . בָּרְכֵנוּ

Selection from the Prayerbook (from the Amidah)

שִׂים שָׁלוֹם טוֹבָה וּבְרָכָה חֵן וָחֶסֶד וְרַחֲמִים עָלֵינוּ וְעַל כָּל יִשְׂרָאֵל עַמֶּךָ. בָּרְכֵנוּ אָבִינוּ כֻּלָּנוּ כְּאֶחָד בְּאוֹר פָּנֶיךָ.

First try to translate the prayer in your own words, then read the translations quoted below.

Prayerbook Translations

"Grant peace, welfare, blessing, grace, loving kindness and mercy unto us and unto all Israel, thy people. Bless us, O our Father, even all of us together, with the light of thy countenance."
Daily Prayer Book, Joseph Hertz, 1975, p. 465

"O grant peace, happiness, blessing, grace, kindness and mercy to us and to all Israel thy people. Bless us all alike, our Father, with the light of thy countenance."
Daily Prayer Book, Philip Birnbaum, 1977, p. 404

Notice that the first word of this prayer is the imperative of the hollow verb שׂ.י.ם.

Guided Reading from Ruth

	find מ.צ.א .1
	favor חֵן
	lord אָדוֹן
	וַתֹּאמֶר: "אֶמְצָא חֵן בְּעֵינֶיךָ אֲדֹנִי,
1. And she (Ruth) said: "Let me find favor in your eyes, my lord,	comfort, console נ.ח.ם .2
	2 m sg perfect נִחַמְתָּ
	כִּי נִחַמְתָּ אֹתִי
2. because you have comforted me	speak ד.ב.ר .3
	2 m sg perfect דִּבַּרְתָּ
	maid-servant שִׁפְחָה
	וְכִי דִבַּרְתָּ אַל לֵב שִׁפְחָתֶךָ

3. and because you have spoken to the heart of your maid-servant	4. וְאָנֹכִי לֹא אֶהְיֶה כְּאַחַת שִׁפְחֹתֶךָ".
4. (though) I am not as one of your maid-servants."	5. עֵת time וַיֹּאמֶר לָה בֹּעַז לְעֵת הָאֹכֶל:
5. Boaz said to her at mealtime: (Literally: at the time of the food)	6. אִכְלִי א.כ.ל *f sg imperative of* "בֹּאִי! אִכְלִי מִן הַלֶּחֶם!"
6. "Come! Eat from the bread!"	7. מִצַּד at the side of צ.ב.ט reach, hold out קָלִי parched grain וַתֵּשֶׁב מִצַּד הַקֹּצְרִים וַיִּצְבָּט לָה קָלִי.
7. And she sat at the side of the harvesters, and he held out to her parched grain.	8. ש.ב.ע be satisfied וַתֹּתַר and she left over וַתֹּאכַל וַתִּשְׂבַּע וַתֹּתַר.
8. And she ate, and was satisfied, and left over (some of the food).	9. ל.ק.ט glean וַיְצַו and he commanded וַתָּקָם לְלַקֵּט וַיְצַו בֹּעַז אֶת נְעָרָיו:
9. And she arose to glean, and Boaz commanded his lads (servants):	10. עֳמָרִים sheaves תַכְלִימוּ you will humiliate "גַּם בֵּין הָעֳמָרִים תְּלַקֵּט וְלֹא תַכְלִימוּ אֹתָהּ.
10. "Also among the sheaves let her glean, and do not humiliate her.	11. ש.ל.ל draw out תָּשֹׁלּוּ *2 m pl imperfect* צְבָתִים bundles of grain תָּשֹׁלּוּ לָהּ מִן הַצְּבָתִים
11. You will draw out (some grain) for her from the bundles of grain	12. ע.ז.ב leave ג.ע.ר rebuke וַעֲזַבְתֶּם וְלִקְּטָה וְלֹא תִגְעֲרוּ בָהּ".
12. and you will leave, and she will glean, and do not rebuke her."	13. ח.ב.ט beat out (grain) וַתְּלַקֵּט בַּשָּׂדֶה עַד הָעָרֶב. וַתַּחְבֹּט אֵת אֲשֶׁר לִקֵּטָה

13. And she gleaned in the field until evening. Then she beat out that which she had gleaned	אֵיפָה *ephah a grain-measure* 14. שְׂעֹרִים *barley* וַיְהִי כְּאֵיפָה שְׂעֹרִים.
14. and it was about an ephah of barley.	נ.שׂ.א. *lift, carry* 15. תִּשָּׂא *3 f sg imperfect* וַתִּשָּׂא וַתָּבוֹא אֶל הָעִיר
15. And she carried (it) and she came to the city	חָמוֹת *mother-in-law* 16. וַתֵּרֶא חֲמוֹתָהּ אֵת אֲשֶׁר לִקֵּטָה
16. and her mother-in-law saw what she had gleaned	וַתּוֹצֵא *and she took out* 17. הוֹתִרָה *she had left over* וַתִּתֶּן *and she gave* וַתּוֹצֵא וַתִּתֶּן לָהּ אֵת אֲשֶׁר הוֹתִרָה.
17. and she (Ruth) took out and she gave to her (Naomi) what she had left over (from her midday meal).	

וַתֹּאמֶר: "אֶמְצָא חֵן בְּעֵינֶיךָ אֲדֹנִי, כִּי נִחַמְתָּ אֹתִי וְכִי דִבַּרְתָּ אֶל לֵב שִׁפְחָתֶךָ וְאָנֹכִי לֹא אֶהְיֶה כְּאַחַת שִׁפְחֹתֶךָ." וַיֹּאמֶר לָהּ בֹּעַז לְעֵת הָאֹכֶל: "בּוֹאִי! אִכְלִי מִן הַלֶּחֶם!" וַתֵּשֶׁב מִצַּד הַקֹּצְרִים וַיִּצְבָּט לָהּ קָלִי. וַתֹּאכַל וַתִּשְׂבַּע וַתֹּתַר. וַתָּקָם לְלַקֵּט וַיְצַו בֹּעַז אֶת נְעָרָיו: "גַּם בֵּין הָעֳמָרִים תְּלַקֵּט וְלֹא תַכְלִימוּ אֹתָהּ. תָּשֹׁלּוּ לָהּ מִן הַצְּבָתִים וַעֲזַבְתֶּם וְלִקְּטָה וְלֹא תִגְעֲרוּ בָהּ." וַתְּלַקֵּט בַּשָּׂדֶה עַד הָעֶרֶב. וַתַּחְבֹּט אֶת אֲשֶׁר לִקֵּטָה וַיְהִי כְּאֵיפָה שְׂעֹרִים. וַתִּשָּׂא וַתָּבוֹא אֶל הָעִיר וַתֵּרֶא חֲמוֹתָהּ אֵת אֲשֶׁר לִקֵּטָה וַתּוֹצֵא וַתִּתֶּן לָהּ אֵת אֲשֶׁר הוֹתִרָה.

Chapter 24
Additional Irregular פָּעַל Verbs
The ה of Direction

Vocabulary

love *vb*	א.ה.ב.
love *n, f*	אַהֲבָה
truth, faithfulness *n, f*	אֱמֶת
deed, work *n, m*	מַעֲשֶׂה, מַעֲשִׂים
give *vb*	נ.ת.ן.
much, many, great *adj*	רַב, רַבָּה, רַבִּים, רַבּוֹת
compassion *n, m*	רַחֲמִים
week *n, m*	שָׁבוּעַ, שָׁבוּעוֹת, שְׁבֻעַיִם *du*
law, Torah *n, f*	תּוֹרָה, תּוֹרוֹת

Place Names

Jordan *river*	יַרְדֵּן
Canaan	כְּנַעַן
Egypt	מִצְרַיִם

Note 1: The words אַהֲבָה, love, and אֱמֶת, truth, have no plurals.

Note 2: The word רַחֲמִים, compassion, has no singular form.

Additional Irregular פָּעַל Verbs

This is the last chapter which will contain charts of irregular verb conjugations in the פָּעַל pattern. In this chapter, you will learn the conjugations of the irregular verbs א.ה.ב, א.כ.ל, א.מ.ר, and נ.ת.ן, which appear frequently in the Bible and the prayerbook.

The Perfect Tense of א.מ.ר, א.כ.ל, א.ה.ב, and נ.ת.ן

You have already learned the conjugation of the verbs א.מ.ר and א.כ.ל in the perfect tense and the participle. These two verbs are conjugated the same way in all forms; therefore, only the conjugation of the verb א.מ.ר will be shown. Notice the difference between the conjugation of the regular verb שׁ.מ.ר and the irregular verbs א.מ.ר, א.ה.ב, and נ.ת.ן.

The Perfect Tense of א.מ.ר, א.ה.ב, and נ.ת.ן

	say — א.מ.ר	love — א.ה.ב	give — נ.ת.ן	guard — ש.מ.ר
1 c sg	אָמַ֫רְתִּי	אָהַ֫בְתִּי	נָתַ֫תִּי	שָׁמַ֫רְתִּי
2 m sg	אָמַ֫רְתָּ	אָהַ֫בְתָּ	נָתַ֫תָּ	שָׁמַ֫רְתָּ
2 f sg	אָמַרְתְּ	אָהַבְתְּ	נָתַתְּ	שָׁמַרְתְּ
3 m sg	אָמַר	אָהַב	נָתַן	שָׁמַר
3 f sg	אָמְרָה	אָהֲבָה	נָתְנָה	שָׁמְרָה
1 c pl	אָמַ֫רְנוּ	אָהַ֫בְנוּ	נָתַ֫נּוּ	שָׁמַ֫רְנוּ
2 m pl	אֲמַרְתֶּם	אֲהַבְתֶּם	נְתַתֶּם	שְׁמַרְתֶּם
2 f pl	אֲמַרְתֶּן	אֲהַבְתֶּן	נְתַתֶּן	שְׁמַרְתֶּן
3 c pl	אָמְרוּ	אָהֲבוּ	נָתְנוּ	שָׁמְרוּ

Notice that the third root letter נ of the verb נ.ת.ן disappears in the first and second person. Whenever a נ disappears in the conjugation of נ.ת.ן, a dagesh appears in the following letter.

The Imperfect Tense of א.מ.ר, א.ה.ב, and נ.ת.ן

Notice the difference between the conjugation of the regular verb ש.מ.ר and the irregular verbs א.מ.ר, א.ה.ב, and נ.ת.ן in the imperfect tense.

	say — א.מ.ר	love — א.ה.ב	give — נ.ת.ן	guard — ש.מ.ר
1 c sg	אֹמַר	אֹהַב	אֶתֵּן	אֶשְׁמֹר
2 m sg	תֹּאמַר	תֶּאֱהַב	תִּתֵּן	תִּשְׁמֹר
2 f sg	תֹּאמְרִי	תֶּאֱהֲבִי	תִּתְּנִי	תִּשְׁמְרִי
3 m sg	יֹאמַר	יֶאֱהַב	יִתֵּן	יִשְׁמֹר
3 f sg	תֹּאמַר	תֶּאֱהַב	תִּתֵּן	תִּשְׁמֹר
1 c pl	נֹאמַר	נֶאֱהַב	נִתֵּן	נִשְׁמֹר
2 m pl	תֹּאמְרוּ	תֶּאֱהֲבוּ	תִּתְּנוּ	תִּשְׁמְרוּ
2 f pl	תֹּאמַ֫רְנָה	תֶּאֱהַ֫בְנָה	תִּתֵּ֫נָּה	תִּשְׁמֹ֫רְנָה
3 m pl	יֹאמְרוּ	יֶאֱהֲבוּ	יִתְּנוּ	יִשְׁמְרוּ
3 f pl	תֹּאמַ֫רְנָה	תֶּאֱהַ֫בְנָה	תִּתֵּ֫נָּה	תִּשְׁמֹ֫רְנָה

1. Notice that the first root letter נ of the verb נ.ת.ן disappears in all forms, and a dagesh appears in the following letter ת.

2. The basic vowel pattern of each of these verbs differs from the regular X̧X̧X̧X or X̧XXX imperfect patterns, as shown with the regular verb ש.מ.ר. The basic vowel pattern of נ.ת.ן is X̧XX̧. The basic vowel pattern of א.מ.ר is X̧XX̧X.

3. The verb א.ה.ב has no basic vowel pattern in the imperfect tense.

The Participle of ר.מ.א, א.ה.ב, and נ.ת.ן

Compare the participle of the regular verb ש.מ.ר with the participles of the verbs ר.מ.א, א.ה.ב, and נ.ת.ן. The participles of verbs ר.מ.א and נ.ת.ן are regular. The participles of the verb א.ה.ב has a slight change in the vowel pattern in the plural forms. Remember that participles in the פָּעַל pattern may be spelled with or without the vav.

	say — א.מ.ר	love — א.ה.ב	give — נ.ת.ן	guard — ש.מ.ר
m sg	אוֹמֵר	אוֹהֵב	נוֹתֵן	שׁוֹמֵר
f sg	אוֹמֶרֶת/אוֹמְרָה	אוֹהֶבֶת	נוֹתֶנֶת/נוֹתְנָה	שׁוֹמֶרֶת/שׁוֹמְרָה
m pl	אוֹמְרִים	אוֹהֲבִים	נוֹתְנִים	שׁוֹמְרִים
f pl	אוֹמְרוֹת	אוֹהֲבוֹת	נוֹתְנוֹת	שׁוֹמְרוֹת

The Imperative of ר.מ.א, א.ה.ב, and נ.ת.ן

Notice the difference between the imperative of the regular verb ש.מ.ר and the imperatives of the irregular verbs ר.מ.א, א.ה.ב, and נ.ת.ן.

	say — א.מ.ר	love — א.ה.ב	give — נ.ת.ן	guard — ש.מ.ר
m sg	אֱמֹר	אֱהַב	תֵּן	שְׁמֹר
f sg	אִמְרִי	אֶהֱבִי	תְּנִי	שִׁמְרִי
m pl	אִמְרוּ	אֶהֱבוּ	תְּנוּ	שִׁמְרוּ
f pl	אֱמֹרְנָה	אֱהַבְנָה	תֵּנָּה	שְׁמֹרְנָה

Notice that the first root letter נ of the verb נ.ת.ן disappears in all forms.

The Infinitive Construct of ר.מ.א, א.כ.ל, א.ה.ב, and נ.ת.ן

Notice the difference between the infinitive construct of the regular verb ש.מ.ר and the infinitive constructs of the irregular verbs ר.מ.א, א.כ.ל, א.ה.ב, and נ.ת.ן. Although the infinitive construct of the verbs ר.מ.א and א.כ.ל are the same, they differ when the inseparable preposition לְ is attached. Therefore, both verbs are shown below.

eat — א.כ.ל	say — א.מ.ר	love — א.ה.ב	give — נ.ת.ן	guard — ש.מ.ר
אֱכֹל (לֶאֱכֹל)	אֱמֹר (לֵאמֹר)	אֱהֹב (לֶאֱהֹב)	תֵּת (לָתֵת)	שְׁמֹר (לִ)

1. The word לֵאמֹר usually appears before a direct quote and serves as a quotation mark. It is best translated into English as "saying".
2. The first and last root letters נ of the verb נ.ת.ן disappear and the letter ת is added.

The Infinitive Absolute of א.מ.ר, א.ה.ב, and נ.ת.ן

Compare the infinitive absolute of the regular verb ש.מ.ר with the infinitive absolute of the verbs א.מ.ר, א.ה.ב, and נ.ת.ן. The infinitive absolute of these verbs is regular.

guard — ש.מ.ר	give — נ.ת.ן	love — א.ה.ב	say — א.מ.ר
שָׁמוֹר	נָתוֹן	אָהוֹב	אָמוֹר

Irregular Verbs with the Reversing Vav

You have already learned that the forms of some verbs are shortened when a reversing vav is added. Many verbs which do not have disappearing root letters have their vowels change with the addition of a reversing vav. Even with the changes in vowel pattern, such verbs can be recognized.

Example:	With Reversing Vav	Regular Form	Root
	וַיֹּאמֶר	יֹאמַר	א.מ.ר

The ה of Direction

When the ending הָ is attached to a noun, it can mean "direction" or "motion toward". Examples:

toward the heavens — or — heavenwards	הַשָּׁמַיְמָה	the heavens	הַשָּׁמַיִם
toward the city — or — citywards	הָעִירָה	the city	הָעִיר
toward Egypt — or — Egyptwards	מִצְרַיְמָה	Egypt	מִצְרַיִם
toward there — or — thither	שָׁמָּה	there	שָׁם

The ה of direction does not appear with all nouns. However, you should be able to recognize it when it does appear.

Exercises

Exercise 1. Conjugate the following verb roots in all forms of the פָּעַל pattern.

1. א.כ.ל   2. שׁ.י.ם   3. ע.שׂ.ה   4. שׁ.פ.ט

Exercise 2. Rewrite the sentences below, replacing the underlined word with each word in the list that follows. Every word or grammatical form in the sentence that agrees with the underlined word should be changed to agree with the newly substituted words. Read the sentences aloud. Translate.

1. הוּא אָמַר בְּלִבּוֹ: "הֵם יָסוּרוּ מִמַּעֲשֵׂיהֶם הָרָעִים".

A. אֲנִי   B. הִיא   C. הוּא   D. הֵנָּה   E. בָּנַי

‎2. הִיא תִּתֵּן לָהֶם מַיִם מֵהַיַּרְדֵּן בָּעֶרֶב וְהֵם יִשְׁתּוּ אֹתָם.

E. אַתְּ	D. הוּא	C. אֲנִי	B. הֵנָּה	A. אַתֶּם
I. אֲנַחְנוּ	H. אַתָּה	G. אַתֵּן		F. הֵמָּה

‎3. וַיֹּאמֶר דָּוִד אֶל אִמּוֹ לֵאמֹר: "אֲנִי אֹכַל אֶת הַפְּרִי".

E. אָנוּ	D. בִּתֵּךְ	C. הַנְּעָרוֹת	B. הַבָּנִים	A. אַבְרָהָם
		G. אַתְּ		F. אַנְשֵׁי מִצְרַיִם

‎4. (אַתָּה) תֶּאֱהַב אֶת מַלְכְּךָ בְּכָל לִבְּךָ וְתַעֲשֶׂה מַעֲשִׂים רַבִּים בִּשְׁמוֹ.

E. הוּא	D. אֲנַחְנוּ	C. הֵמָּה	B. אַתֵּן	A. הִיא
I. אַתֶּם	H. הֵנָּה	G. אֲנִי		F. אַתְּ

‎5. (אֲנַחְנוּ) נָתַנּוּ לַזָּקֵן אֶת הַלֶּחֶם וְאֶת הַיַּיִן.

E. הִיא	D. הֵמָּה	C. אַתֵּן	B. הוּא	A. אַתְּ
I. אַתֶּם	H. הֵנָּה	G. אֲנִי		F. אַתָּה

‎6. הוּא לָקַח אֶת סִפְרֵי הַתּוֹרָה וַיִּתֵּן אֹתָם לְבָנָיו.

E. אַתֶּם	D. אַתְּ	C. אֲנִי	B. הַנָּשִׁים	A. שָׂרָה
I. אַתָּה	H. אַתֵּן	G. הָאֲנָשִׁים		F. אֲנַחְנוּ

‎7. הַגּוֹיִם יֹאמְרוּ: "בְּנֵי יִשְׂרָאֵל עָשׂוּ מַעֲשֵׂי חֶסֶד וְרַחֲמִים כִּי לָהֶם תּוֹרַת אֱמֶת."

E. אַתֵּן	D. אַתָּה	C. אַתֶּם	B. נְשֵׁי מוֹאָב	A. כָּל הָעָם
I. אֲנִי	H. אַתְּ	G. אֲנַחְנוּ		F. הִיא

Exercise 3. Rewrite the following sentences, filling in the blanks with all forms of the verb root shown that will yield a meaningful sentence. Translate.

Example: ‎(ה.ל.ך) (אַתֶּם) _____ מִצְרַיְמָה.

אַתֶּם הוֹלְכִים מִצְרַיְמָה.	הָלוֹךְ הֲלַכְתֶּם מִצְרַיְמָה.	הֲלַכְתֶּם מִצְרַיְמָה.
לְכוּ מִצְרַיְמָה.	הָלוֹךְ תֵּלְכוּ מִצְרַיְמָה.	תֵּלְכוּ מִצְרַיְמָה.

‎1. (ש.י.ם) (אַתָּה) _____ אֶת אַהֲבַת הַתּוֹרָה בְּתוֹךְ בְּנֵי יִשְׂרָאֵל.

‎2. (נ.ת.ן) (הוּא) _____ כֵּלִים רַבִּים לְאִשְׁתּוֹ.

‎3. (א.ה.ב) (אַתֶּם) _____ אֶת הָאֱמֶת וְאֶת אֹכֶל אִמְּכֶם.

‎4. (א.כ.ל) שָׁבוּעַ בְּשָׁבוּעַ, תָּבוֹאִי אֶל בֵּיתִי וּ_____ אֶת אָכְלִי.

‎5. (ע.שׂ.ה) (אֲנִי) _____ מַעֲשֵׂי חֶסֶד וְרַחֲמִים יוֹם יוֹם כִּי אֲנִי טוֹב מִכָּל אַנְשֵׁי עִירִי.

‎6. (א.מ.ר) (אַתְּ) _____ לִבְנוֹתַיִךְ לֵאמֹר: "שִׁמְעַתֶּן רַק דִּבְרֵי אֱמֶת מִפִּי אִמְּכֶן".

Exercise 4. Read the following sentences. Change the nouns that have a ה of direction attached into simple nouns, making the necessary changes. Translate.

Example:

הָאִישׁ הָלַךְ אֶל מִצְרַיִם.   הָאִישׁ הָלַךְ מִצְרַיְמָה.

1. בַּשָּׁבוּעַ הַבָּא הַנְּעָרִים יָרוּצוּ יְרוּשָׁלַיְמָה לָתֵת לַאֲבוֹתֵיהֶם כֶּסֶף רַב.

2. וַיַּעַל יַעֲקֹב הָהָרָה לִשְׁכֹּחַ אַהֲבַת נָשִׁים.

3. וַיֹּאמֶר הַזָּקֵן אֲלֵיהֶם: "לְכוּ שָׁמָּה לַעֲשׂוֹת מַעֲשֵׂי חֶסֶד וְרַחֲמִים.

4. וַיִּשְׁלַח הַמֶּלֶךְ אֶת הַשּׁוֹפֵט הָעִירָה וַיֹּאמֶר אֵלָיו: "שִׂים לִבְּךָ לְמַעֲשֵׂי עַמִּי וּשְׁפֹט אֹתָם בְּחָסֶד.

5. עָלֵינוּ לָשׁוּב אַרְצָה אַחֲרֵי הָרָעָב.

Exercise 5. Read the following story, filling in the blanks with the appropriate form of the verb root shown under the blank.

וַתְּהִי אִשָּׁה אֲשֶׁר _____ בְּאֶרֶץ כְּנַעַן וּשְׁמָהּ שָׂרָה. וַיִּהְיוּ אֲנָשִׁים רַבִּים אֲשֶׁר _____
[א.ה.ב]   [י.שׁ.ב]

_____ אֹתָהּ. הֵם _____ יוֹם יוֹם לְ_____ אֹתָהּ וְהִיא לֹא _____
[שׁ.י.ם]   [ר.א.ה]   [ב.ו.א]

_____ לִבָּהּ לְדִבְרֵיהֶם. שָׂרָה אָמְרָה לָהֶם: "_____ ! _____ מִמֶּנִּי וְ_____
[שׁ.ו.ב]   [ה.ל.ך]   [ס.ו.ר]

לְבָתֵּיכֶם!" הֵמָּה _____ בְּקוֹלָהּ וְ_____ לְדַרְכֵיהֶם.
[שׁ.מ.ע]   [ה.ל.ך]

אִישׁ אֶחָד _____ לְבֵיתָהּ כָּל שָׁבוּעַ. הוּא _____ לָהּ: "אֲנִי _____
[שׁ.ו.ב]   [א.מ.ר]   [א.ה.ב]

אֹתָךְ בְּכָל לְבָבִי! (אֲנִי) _____ לָךְ אֶת כָּל אֲשֶׁר _____ _____ !"
[נ.ת.ן]   [י.כ.ל]   [נ.ת.ן]

שָׂרָה _____ כִּי הוּא אִישׁ טוֹב. הִיא _____ אֹתוֹ וְ_____ לוֹ
[ר.א.ה]   [א.ה.ב]   [ה.י.ה]

לְאִשָּׁה.

Exercise 6. Using the list of verb roots at the bottom of this exercise, identify the roots of the following verb forms. Translate each verb form.

16. עוֹנֶה	11. בָּא	6. שִׂימוּ	1. אָהַבְנוּ
17. תִּכְתֹּבְנָה	12. אוֹמְרוֹת	7. בָּחַרְתְּ	2. אֶכְתֹּב
18. בּוֹאוּ	13. תִּתֵּן	8. עָנִינוּ	3. אֹהַב
19. תִּבְחֲרוּ	14. יְשַׁבְתֶּם	9. תֹּאמְרִי	4. קוּם
20. תְּנִי	15. נָשִׂים	10. לָשֶׁבֶת	5. נְתַתֶּן

א.ה.ב, א.מ.ר, ב.ו.א, ב.ח.ר, י.שׁ.ב, כ.ת.ב, נ.ת.ן, ע.נ.ה, ק.ו.ם, שׁ.י.ם

174

Exercise 7. Fill in the chart. Translate.

Root	Number	Gender	Person	Tense	Pattern	Word	
א.מ.ר	sg	f	3	perfect	פָּעַל		1
א.ה.ב	sg	f	3	perfect	פָּעַל		2
נ.ת.ן	sg	f	3	perfect	פָּעַל		3
כ.ת.ב	sg	f	3	perfect	פָּעַל		4
ר.א.ה	sg	f	3	perfect	פָּעַל		5
ש.י.ם	sg	f	3	perfect	פָּעַל		6
א.מ.ר	pl	m	3	imperfect	פָּעַל		7
א.ה.ב	pl	m	3	imperfect	פָּעַל		8
נ.ת.ן	pl	m	3	imperfect	פָּעַל		9
ש.מ.ר	pl	m	3	imperfect	פָּעַל		10
ע.ש.ה	pl	m	3	imperfect	פָּעַל		11
י.ש.ב	pl	m	3	imperfect	פָּעַל		12
						תֹּאמְרִי	13
						יָאֶהֱבוּ	14
						יֵשֵׁב	15
						לָתֵת	16
						נָתַן	17
						זָכְרָת	18
						תִּתְּנוּ	19
						נְתַתָּן	20
						נָשִׁים	21
						בְּנִיתֶם	22
						עֲשִׂינָה	23
						נִבְנֶה	24

From the Prayerbook

Prayerbook Vocabulary

for ever and ever .... לְעוֹלָם וָעֶד   bless *m pl imperative of* ב.ר.ך ...... בָּרְכוּ

plant *vb* .... נ.ט.ע   the one who is blessed .... הַמְבֹרָךְ

Selection from the Prayerbook (recited by the person called to the Torah)

Before the Torah reading

בָּרְכוּ אֶת יְיָ הַמְבֹרָךְ.

בָּרוּךְ יְיָ הַמְבֹרָךְ לְעוֹלָם וָעֶד.

בָּרוּךְ אַתָּה, יְיָ אֱלֹהֵינוּ, מֶלֶךְ הָעוֹלָם, אֲשֶׁר בָּחַר בָּנוּ מִכָּל הָעַמִּים וְנָתַן לָנוּ אֶת תּוֹרָתוֹ. בָּרוּךְ אַתָּה,

יְיָ, נוֹתֵן הַתּוֹרָה.

After the Torah reading

בָּרוּךְ אַתָּה, יְיָ אֱלֹהֵינוּ, מֶלֶךְ הָעוֹלָם, אֲשֶׁר נָתַן לָנוּ תּוֹרַת אֱמֶת וְחַיֵּי עוֹלָם נָטַע בְּתוֹכֵנוּ. בָּרוּךְ אַתָּה,

יְיָ, נוֹתֵן הַתּוֹרָה.

First try to translate the prayer in your own words, then read the translations quoted below.

Prayerbook Translations

"Bless the Lord who is blessed.

Blessed be the Lord who is blessed forever and ever.

Blessed art thou, Lord our God, King of the universe, who hast chosen us from all peoples, and hast given us thy Torah.

Blessed art thou, O Lord, Giver of the Torah."

"Blessed art thou, Lord our God, King of the universe, who hast given us the Torah of truth, and hast planted everlasting life in our midst.

Blessed art Thou, O Lord, Giver of the Torah."

Daily Prayer Book, Philip Birnbaum, 1977, p. 124

"Praise the Lord, to whom our praise is due!

Praised be the Lord, to whom our praise is due, now and for ever!

Blessed is the Lord our God, Ruler of the universe, who has chosen us from all peoples by giving us His Torah. Blessed is the Lord, Giver of the Torah."

"Blessed is the Lord our God, Ruler of the universe, who has given us a Torah of truth, implanting within us eternal life.

Blessed is the Lord, Giver of the Torah."

Gates of Prayer, The New Union Prayerbook, 1975, p. 419

Guided Reading from Ruth

	1. חָמוֹת mother-in-law אֵיפֹה where? ל.ק.ט glean וַתֹּאמֶר לָהּ חֲמוֹתָהּ: "אֵיפֹה לָקַטְתְּ הַיּוֹם?
1. And her mother-in-law said to her: "Where did you glean today?	2. יְהִי may he be מַכִּיר the one who recognized יְהִי הַמַּכִּיר אֹתָךְ בָּרוּךְ".
2. May the one who recognized you be blessed."	3. וַתַּגֵּד and she told ע.שׂ.ה translate as "work" וַתַּגֵּד לַחֲמוֹתָהּ אֵת אֲשֶׁר עָשְׂתָה עִמּוֹ.
3. And she told her mother-in-law with whom she had worked. (Literally: the one that she had worked with him.)	4. וַתֹּאמֶר: "שֵׁם הָאִישׁ אֲשֶׁר עָשִׂיתִי עִמּוֹ הַיּוֹם בֹּעַז".
4. And she said: "The name of the man with whom I worked today is Boaz."	5. כַּלָּה daughter-in-law וַתֹּאמֶר נָעֳמִי לְכַלָּתָהּ: "בָּרוּךְ הוּא לַיהוה".
5. And Naomi said to her daughter-in-law: "Blessed be he to the Lord."	6. קָרוֹב close, related וַתֹּאמֶר לָהּ נָעֳמִי: "קָרוֹב הָאִישׁ לָנוּ.
6. And Naomi said to her: "The man is related to us.	7. ג.א.ל redeem, act as kinsman גֹּאֵל one who acts as a kinsman *participle used as noun* מִגֹּאֲלֵנוּ הוּא".
7. He is from our kinsmen." (Literally: from those who act as kinsmen for us.")	8. מוֹאֲבִיָּה Moabitess וַתֹּאמֶר רוּת הַמּוֹאֲבִיָּה: "הוּא אָמַר אֵלַי:
8. And Ruth the Moabitess said: "He said to me:	9. ד.ב.ק stay close 'עִם הַנְּעָרִים אֲשֶׁר לִי תִּדְבָּקִי
9. 'You will stay close to my lads (harvesters)	10. כִּלּוּ they have completed קָצִיר harvest *n* עַד כִּלּוּ אֵת כָּל הַקָּצִיר אֲשֶׁר לִי'."
10. until they have completed all of my harvest.'"	11. וַתֹּאמֶר נָעֳמִי אֶל כַּלָּתָהּ:

11. And Naomi said to her daughter-in-law:	go out א.צ.י.12 *2 f sg imperfect* תֵּצְאִי "טוֹב בִּתִּי כִּי תֵצְאִי עִם נַעֲרוֹתָיו
12. "(It is) good, my daughter, that you will go out with his young women (harvesters)	bother ע.ג.פ.13 אַחֵר another וְלֹא יִפְגְּעוּ בָךְ בְּשָׂדֶה אַחֵר."
13. and they will not bother you in another field."	14.וַתִּדְבַּק בְּנַעֲרוֹת בֹּעַז לְלַקֵּט
14. And she stayed close to Boaz' young women to glean	end of כְּלוֹת.15 barley שְׂעֹרִים wheat חִטִּים עַד כְּלוֹת קְצִיר הַשְּׂעֹרִים וּקְצִיר הַחִטִּים.
15. until the end of the barley harvest and the wheat harvest.	16.וַתֵּשֶׁב עִם חֲמוֹתָהּ.
16. And she dwelt with her mother-in-law.	

וַתֹּאמֶר לָהּ חֲמוֹתָהּ: "אֵיפֹה לָקַטְתְּ הַיּוֹם? יְהִי הַמַּכִּיר אַתָּךְ בָּרוּךְ." וַתַּגֵּד לַחֲמוֹתָהּ אֵת אֲשֶׁר עָשְׂתָה עִמּוֹ. וַתֹּאמֶר: "שֵׁם הָאִישׁ אֲשֶׁר עָשִׂיתִי עִמּוֹ הַיּוֹם בֹּעַז".

וַתֹּאמֶר נָעֳמִי לְכַלָּתָהּ: "בָּרוּךְ הוּא לַיהוה." וַתֹּאמֶר לָהּ נָעֳמִי: "קָרוֹב הָאִישׁ לָנוּ. מִגֹּאֲלֵנוּ הוּא." וַתֹּאמֶר רוּת הַמּוֹאֲבִיָּה: "הוּא אָמַר אֵלַי: 'עִם הַנְּעָרִים אֲשֶׁר לִי תִּדְבָּקִין עַד אֵם כִּלּוּ אֵת כָּל הַקָּצִיר אֲשֶׁר לִי.' " וַתֹּאמֶר נָעֳמִי אֶל כַּלָּתָהּ: "טוֹב בִּתִּי כִּי תֵצְאִי עִם נַעֲרוֹתָיו וְלֹא יִפְגְּעוּ בָךְ בְּשָׂדֶה אַחֵר." וַתִּדְבַּק בְּנַעֲרוֹת בֹּעַז לְלַקֵּט עַד כְּלוֹת קְצִיר הַשְּׂעֹרִים וּקְצִיר הַחִטִּים. וַתֵּשֶׁב עִם חֲמוֹתָהּ.

Chapter 25
The Pi'el פִּעֵל Pattern

Vocabulary

seek *vb* . . . . (פִּעֵל)	ב.ק.שׁ
grow up, become great *vb* . . . . (פָּעַל)	ג.ד.ל
cause to grow, bring up *vb* . . . . (פִּעֵל)	
speak *vb* . . . . (פִּעֵל)	ד.ב.ר
number *n, m* . . . . מִסְפָּר, מִסְפָּרִים	
commandment *n, f* . . . . מִצְוָה, מִצְוֹת	
count *vb* . . . . (פָּעַל)	ס.פ.ר
recount, relate *vb* . . . . (פִּעֵל)	
command, order *vb* . . . . (פִּעֵל)	צ.ו.ה

Note 1: The plural noun **מִצְוֹת** is pronounced ''meetsvot''. The letter וֹ should be regarded as the consonant ו with the vowel ֹX following it.

Note 2: Vocabulary listings will not always include every pattern in which a verb root appears. In this book, you will only need to learn the patterns of the verb root which are shown in the vocabulary.

The Hebrew Verb Patterns

There are seven verb patterns in Hebrew. You have already learned the first verb pattern, the פָּעַל pattern. All the verb roots that you have learned thus far were introduced in the פָּעַל pattern. Some of these roots, such as כ.ת.ב and שׁ.מ.ר, have a regular conjugation. Other verb roots, such as the final ה verbs and the hollow verbs, have major variations in their conjugations. However, all the verbs were conjugated in the פָּעַל pattern. In this chapter, you will learn a second Hebrew verb pattern: the Pi'el פִּעֵל pattern.

A single Hebrew verb root may be conjugated in more than one of the seven verb patterns. Most of the Hebrew verb roots do appear in more than one pattern. The specific meaning of the verb changes as it is conjugated in the different patterns, but the central meaning of the verb root remains.

The Pi'el פָּעֵל Verb Pattern

When a root can be conjugated in both the פָּעַל and the פָּעֵל verb patterns, the meaning of the verb in the פָּעֵל pattern is usually different from its meaning in the פָּעַל pattern. Verb roots conjugated in the פָּעַל pattern usually express simple action, while the same roots conjugated in the פָּעֵל pattern often express an intensification or repetition of that simple action.

Examples:	**Meaning in** פָּעֵל	**Meaning in** פָּעַל	**Root**
	send away, set free	send	שׁ.ל.ח
	recount, narrate	count	ס.פ.ר

Many roots appear in the פָּעֵל pattern but do not appear in the פָּעַל pattern. Such פָּעֵל verbs often have the same simple active meaning as do verbs in the פָּעַל pattern.

Examples:		**Meaning in** פָּעֵל	**Root**
	No פָּעַל	seek	ב.ק.שׁ
	No פָּעַל	command, order	צ.ו.ה

Similarly, many roots appear in the פָּעַל pattern but do not appear in the פָּעֵל pattern. Most of the פָּעַל verbs that you have already learned do not appear in the פָּעֵל pattern. The roots ג.ד.ל and ס.פ.ר are the only verbs you will be taught in both the פָּעַל and the פָּעֵל patterns.

The Conjugation of Verbs in the פָּעֵל Pattern

Following are charts showing the conjugation of the regular verb ד.ב.ר in the פָּעֵל pattern. Compare this to the conjugation of the regular verb שׁ.מ.ר in the פָּעַל pattern. The important characteristic of the פָּעֵל pattern is the dagesh which appears in the second root letter. This dagesh will help you to recognize verbs conjugated in the פָּעֵל pattern. Read aloud the conjugations of both ד.ב.ר and שׁ.מ.ר so that you can hear the differences between the פָּעַל and the פָּעֵל patterns.

The Perfect Tense

	speak — (פִּעֵל) ד.ב.ר		guard — (פָּעַל) ש.מ.ר
1 c sg	XְXַ֫Xְתִּי	דִּבַּ֫רְתִּי	שָׁמַ֫רְתִּי
2 m sg	XְXַ֫Xְתָּ	דִּבַּ֫רְתָּ	שָׁמַ֫רְתָּ
2 f sg	XְXַXְתְּ	דִּבַּרְתְּ	שָׁמַרְתְּ
3 m sg	XִXֵX	דִּבֶּר	שָׁמַר
3 f sg	XְXְXָה	דִּבְּרָה	שָׁמְרָה
1 c pl	XְXַ֫Xְנוּ	דִּבַּ֫רְנוּ	שָׁמַ֫רְנוּ
2 m pl	XְXַXְתֶּם	דִּבַּרְתֶּם	שְׁמַרְתֶּם
2 f pl	XְXַXְתֶּן	דִּבַּרְתֶּן	שְׁמַרְתֶּן
3 c pl	XְXְXוּ	דִּבְּרוּ	שָׁמְרוּ

1. In the perfect tense, the first root letter takes an X֫ vowel.
2. The second root letter takes the dagesh characteristic of the פִּעֵל pattern.
3. The endings in the perfect tense of the פִּעֵל pattern are exactly the same as the endings in the perfect tense of the פָּעַל pattern.
4. ד.ב.ר cannot be conjugated in פָּעַל .

The Imperfect Tense

	speak — (פִּעֵל) ד.ב.ר		guard — (פָּעַל) ש.מ.ר
1 c sg	אֲXַXֵX	אֲדַבֵּר	אֶשְׁמֹר
2 m sg	תְּXַXֵX	תְּדַבֵּר	תִּשְׁמֹר
2 f sg	תְּXַXְXִי	תְּדַבְּרִי	תִּשְׁמְרִי
3 m sg	יְXַXֵX	יְדַבֵּר	יִשְׁמֹר
3 f sg	תְּXַXֵX	תְּדַבֵּר	תִּשְׁמֹר
1 c pl	נְXַXֵX	נְדַבֵּר	נִשְׁמֹר
2 m pl	תְּXַXְXוּ	תְּדַבְּרוּ	תִּשְׁמְרוּ
2 f pl	תְּXַXֵ֫Xְנָה	תְּדַבֵּ֫רְנָה	תִּשְׁמֹ֫רְנָה
3 m pl	יְXַXְXוּ	יְדַבְּרוּ	יִשְׁמְרוּ
3 f pl	תְּXַXֵ֫Xְנָה	תְּדַבֵּ֫רְנָה	תִּשְׁמֹ֫רְנָה

1. The basic vowel pattern is XְXַXֵX , instead of the XִXְXֹX or the XְXַXֹX pattern of regular פָּעַל verbs.
2. The second root letter takes the dagesh characteristic of the פִּעֵל pattern.
3. The prefix and suffix consonants in the imperfect tense of the פִּעֵל pattern are exactly the same as the prefix and suffix consonants in the imperfect tense of the פָּעַל pattern.

The Participle

		speak — ד.ב.ר (פִּעֵל)		guard — ש.מ.ר (פָּעַל)
m sg	מְXַXֵX	מְדַבֵּר		שׁוֹמֵר/שֹׁמֵר
f sg	מְXַXֶXֶת	מְדַבֶּרֶת		שׁוֹמֶרֶת/שֹׁמֶרֶת, שׁוֹמְרָה/שֹׁמְרָה
m pl	מְXַXְXִים	מְדַבְּרִים		שׁוֹמְרִים/שֹׁמְרִים
f pl	מְXַXְXוֹת	מְדַבְּרוֹת		שׁוֹמְרוֹת/שֹׁמְרוֹת

1. The participle in the פִּעֵל pattern always begins with the prefix מְ.
2. The second root letter takes the dagesh characteristic of the פִּעֵל pattern.

The Imperative

		speak — ד.ב.ר (פִּעֵל)		guard — ש.מ.ר (פָּעַל)
m sg	XַXֵX	דַּבֵּר		שְׁמֹר
f sg	XַXְXִי	דַּבְּרִי		שִׁמְרִי
m pl	XַXְXוּ	דַּבְּרוּ		שִׁמְרוּ
f pl	XַXֵXְנָה	דַּבֵּרְנָה		שְׁמֹרְנָה

The second root letter takes the dagesh characteristic of the פִּעֵל pattern.

The Infinitive

		speak — ד.ב.ר (פִּעֵל)		guard — ש.מ.ר (פָּעַל)
absolute	XַXֵX	דַּבֵּר		שָׁמוֹר
construct	לְXַXֵX	(לְ) דַּבֵּר		לִשְׁמֹר

The second root letter takes the dagesh characteristic of the פִּעֵל pattern.

The Final ה Verb in the פִּעֵל

The verb צ.ו.ה is a final ה verb, and therefore it is conjugated differently from the regular פִּעֵל conjugation. Following is a chart showing the verb צ.ו.ה conjugated in the פִּעֵל pattern, together with the conjugations of the regular verb ד.ב.ר in the פִּעֵל pattern, and the final ה verb ב.נ.ה in the פָּעַל pattern.

Notice that the verb צ.ו.ה is **not** a hollow verb. There are no hollow verbs in the פִּעֵל pattern. The vav in the verb צ.ו.ה is a full consonant. The dagesh in the vav is the dagesh characteristic of the פִּעֵל pattern and is not an וּ vowel.

You will need to memorize the conjugation of this verb.

The Perfect Tense

	build — (פִּעֵל) ב.נ.ה	command — (פִּעֵל) צ.ו.ה	speak — (פִּעֵל) ד.ב.ר
1 c sg	בָּנִֽיתִי	צִוִּֽיתִי	דִּבַּֽרְתִּי
2 m sg	בָּנִֽיתָ	צִוִּֽיתָ	דִּבַּֽרְתָּ
2 f sg	בָּנִית	צִוִּית	דִּבַּרְתְּ
3 m sg	בָּנָה	צִוָּה	דִּבֶּר
3 f sg	בָּנְתָה	צִוְּתָה	דִּבְּרָה
1 c pl	בָּנִֽינוּ	צִוִּֽינוּ	דִּבַּֽרְנוּ
2 m pl	בְּנִיתֶם	צִוִּיתֶם	דִּבַּרְתֶּם
2 f pl	בְּנִיתֶן	צִוִּיתֶן	דִּבַּרְתֶּן
3 c pl	בָּנוּ	צִוּוּ	דִּבְּרוּ

1. As in regular פָּעַל verbs, the first root letter takes the X̱ vowel and the second root letter takes the dagesh characteristic of the פִּעֵל pattern.

2. As in final ה verbs, the second root letter takes the X̣י vowel and the final ה disappears in all forms except the third person singular.

3. צָוּוּ is pronounced tsee/voo. The first ו is a consonant and the second ו is a vowel.

4. ה.ו.צ cannot be conjugated in פָּעַל .

The Imperfect Tense

	build — (פִּעֵל) ב.נ.ה	command — (פִּעֵל) צ.ו.ה	speak — (פִּעֵל) ד.ב.ר
1 c sg	אֶבְנֶה	אֲצַוֶּה	אֲדַבֵּר
2 m sg	תִּבְנֶה	תְּצַוֶּה	תְּדַבֵּר
2 f sg	תִּבְנִי	תְּצַוִּי	תְּדַבְּרִי
3 m sg	יִבְנֶה	יְצַוֶּה	יְדַבֵּר
3 f sg	תִּבְנֶה	תְּצַוֶּה	תְּדַבֵּר
1 c pl	נִבְנֶה	נְצַוֶּה	נְדַבֵּר
2 m pl	תִּבְנוּ	תְּצַוּוּ	תְּדַבְּרוּ
2 f pl	תִּבְנֶֽינָה	תְּצַוֶּֽינָה	תְּדַבֵּֽרְנָה
3 m pl	יִבְנוּ	יְצַוּוּ	יְדַבְּרוּ
3 f pl	תִּבְנֶֽינָה	תְּצַוֶּֽינָה	תְּדַבֵּֽרְנָה

1. The basic vowel pattern is X̱X̱Xֶ̣ה , which is the same as the X̱X̱X̱X̣ pattern of regular פָּעַל verbs, except for the last vowel Xֶ̣ה, which is the same as that of final ה verbs.

2. The second root letter takes the dagesh characteristic of the פִּעֵל pattern.

3. The *2 m pl* form תְּצַוּוּ is pronounced t'tsah/voo. The *3 m pl* form יְצַוּוּ is pronounced y'tsah/voo. The first ו is a consonant and the second ו is a vowel.

183

The Participle

	build — (פָּעַל) ב.נ.ה	command — (פָּעַל) צ.ו.ה	speak — (פָּעַל) ד.ב.ר
m sg	בּוֹנֶה	מְצַוֶּה	מְדַבֵּר
f sg	בּוֹנָה	מְצַוָּה	מְדַבֶּרֶת
m pl	בּוֹנִים	מְצַוִּים	מְדַבְּרִים
f pl	בּוֹנוֹת	מְצַוּוֹת	מְדַבְּרוֹת

1. As in regular פָּעַל verbs, the participle begins with the prefix מְ, and the second root letter takes the dagesh characteristic of the פָּעַל pattern.

2. As in final ה verbs, the last vowel in the *m sg* form is אֶה and in the *f sg* form is אָה, and the final ה disappears in the plural forms.

The Imperative

	build — (פָּעַל) ב.נ.ה	command — (פָּעַל) צ.ו.ה	speak — (פָּעַל) ד.ב.ר
m sg	בְּנֵה	צַוֵּה	דַּבֵּר
f sg	בְּנִי	צַוִּי	דַּבְּרִי
m pl	בְּנוּ	צַוּוּ	דַּבְּרוּ
f pl	בְּנֶינָה	צַוֶּינָה	דַּבֵּרְנָה

1. As in regular פָּעַל verbs, the first root letter takes the אַ vowel and the second root letter takes the dagesh characteristic of the פָּעַל pattern.

2. As in final ה verbs, the final ה remains in the *m sg* form, but disappears in the other three forms.

3. The *m pl* form צַוּוּ is pronounced tsah/voo. The first ו is a consonant and the second ו is a vowel.

The Infinitive

	build — (פָּעַל) ב.נ.ה	command — (פָּעַל) צ.ו.ה	speak — (פָּעַל) ד.ב.ר
absolute	בָּנֹה	צַוֵּה	דַּבֵּר
construct	(לְ) בַּנּוֹת לִבְנוֹת	(לְ) צַוּוֹת לְצַוּוֹת	(לְ) דַּבֵּר לְדַבֵּר

1. As in regular פָּעַל verbs, the first root letter takes the אַ vowel and the second root letter takes the dagesh characteristic of the פָּעַל pattern.

2. As we have seen in final ה verbs in פָּעַל, the third root letter ה is replaced by the וֹת ending in the infinitive construct.

Exercises

Exercise 1. Conjugate the following roots in all forms of the verb pattern given.

‏1. ס.פ.ר (פָּעַל)‏   ‏2. ס.פ.ר (פִּעֵל)‏   ‏3. ב.ק.שׁ (פִּעֵל)‏

Exercise 2. Rewrite the sentences below, replacing the underlined word with each word in the list that follows. Every word or grammatical form in the sentence that agrees with the underlined word should be changed to agree with the newly substituted words. Read the sentences aloud. Translate.

‏1. הָאֵם גִּדְּלָה אֶת הַנַּעַר וְהוּא גָּדַל.‏

E. הָאִישׁ	D. אֲנַחְנוּ	C. אַתֶּן	B. הָאָבוֹת	A. אַתְּ
	I. הַנָּשִׁים	H. אַתֶּם	G. אֲנִי	F. אַתָּה

‏2. הָיוּ בְּהֵמוֹת רַבּוֹת בַּשָּׂדֶה וַיִּסְפֹּר הַנַּעַר אֹתָן.‏

E. הֵם	D. אַתְּ	C. אַתֶּם	B. אֲנִי	A. הַבָּנוֹת
	I. שָׂרָה	H. אַתֶּן	G. אַתָּה	F. אֲנַחְנוּ

‏3. אָבִינוּ יִזְכֹּר אֶת מַעֲשָׂיו הַטּוֹבִים וְהוּא יְסַפֵּר לָנוּ עֲלֵיהֶם.‏

E. הֵנָּה	D. אַתֶּם	C. הִיא	B. אַתָּה	A. הַזְּקֵנִים
		G. אַתֶּן		F. אַתְּ

‏4. וַיֹּאמֶר הָאִישׁ לֵאמֹר: "אֲנִי מְצַוֶּה אֶתְכֶם לַעֲשׂוֹת אֶת כָּל הַמִּצְוֹת".‏

D. אֲנַחְנוּ	C. אֵשֶׁת דָּוִד	B. הַזְּקֵנוֹת	A. הַשּׁוֹפְטִים

‏5. הִיא בִּקְשָׁה אֶת הָאֱמֶת וְצִוְּתָה אֶת הָאֲנָשִׁים לֵאמֹר, "דַּבְּרוּ אֵלַי".‏

E. אֲנַחְנוּ	D. אַתְּ	C. הֵנָּה	B. אַתֶּם	A. אֲנִי
	I. הֵמָּה	H. הוּא	G. אַתֶּן	F. אַתָּה

‏6. (אֲנִי) סָפַרְתִּי אֶת כָּל כֵּלַי, וּמִסְפָּרָם לֹא גָּדוֹל.‏

E. אַתֶּם	D. הֵן	C. שָׂרָה	B. אֲנַחְנוּ	A. דָּוִד
	I. אַתֶּן	H. הֵמָּה	G. אַתָּה	F. אַתְּ

Exercise 3. Translate the following verb forms.

‏1. יָבוֹא, בָּאָה, לָבוֹא, בָּאתִי, בָּאִים, בּוֹאִי‏
‏2. לְבַקֵּשׁ, בִּקַּשְׁנוּ, תְּבַקֵּשְׁנָה, מְבַקְשִׁים, בַּקֵּשׁ, נְבַקֵּשׁ‏
‏3. רְאִיתֶם, תֵּרְאִי, רוֹאָה, לִרְאוֹת, רָאוּ‏
‏4. אֶתֵּן, תְּנוּ, נָתַתְּ, נוֹתְנוֹת, נָתְנָה, לָתֵת‏
‏5. תְּצַוֶּה, צַו, מְצַוֶּה, לְצַוּוֹת, צַוִּי, צִוִּיתֶן, אֲצַוֶּה‏

185

6. מְדַבֶּרֶת, דַּבֵּר, דִּבַּרְתָּ, לְדַבֵּר, דַּבְּרוּ, אֲדַבֵּר, תְּדַבְּרוּ

7. סִפֵּר, סָפַר, סָפַרְתִּי, סִפַּרְתִּי, לִסְפֹּר, לְסַפֵּר, יִסְפְּרוּ, יְסַפְּרוּ, סוֹפֵר, מְסַפֶּרֶת

8. מְגַדְּלִים, תִּגְדְּלוּ, תְּגַדֵּלְנָה, לְגַדֵּל, גָּדוֹל, גִּדֵּל, גָּדַל, יִגְדַּל, גָּדְלָה, גָּדַלְנוּ, גָּדְלוּ

Exercise 4. Rewrite the following sentences, filling in the blanks with all forms of the verb root shown that will yield a meaningful sentence. Translate.

Example: ד.ב.ר (אַתְּ) _____ אֶל הַשּׁוֹפְטִים עַל הַמִּצְוֹת.

תְּדַבְּרִי אֶל הַשּׁוֹפְטִים עַל הַמִּצְוֹת.   דַּבֵּר דִּבַּרְתָּ אֶל הַשּׁוֹפְטִים עַל הַמִּצְוֹת.

דִּבַּרְתְּ אֶל הַשּׁוֹפְטִים עַל הַמִּצְוֹת.   דַּבְּרִי אֶל הַשּׁוֹפְטִים עַל הַמִּצְוֹת.

דַּבֵּר תְּדַבְּרִי אֶל הַשּׁוֹפְטִים עַל הַמִּצְוֹת.   אַתְּ מְדַבֶּרֶת אֶל הַשּׁוֹפְטִים עַל הַמִּצְוֹת.

1. ס.פ.ר (אַתֶּם) _____ לַגּוֹיִם עַל הַבְּרִית.

2. ב.ק.שׁ בְּשׁוּבְךָ מִן הַמִּדְבָּר _____ אֶת מִשְׁפַּחְתְּךָ.

3. צ.ו.ה הוּא _____ אֶת בָּנָיו לֵאמֹר: "תְּנוּ מַיִם מֵהַיַּרְדֵּן לַזְּקֵנִים".

4. ג.ד.ל הֵמָּה _____ בְּהֵמוֹת רַבּוֹת בְּמִצְרַיִם.

5. ס.פ.ר (אֲנַחְנוּ) _____ לָהֶם עַל הָאֲנָשִׁים אֲשֶׁר _____ אֶת הַכֶּסֶף.

6. ב.נ.ה (אֲנִי) _____ עִיר גְּדוֹלָה בִּכְנַעַן.

7. שׁ.ו.ב הִיא _____ מִמִּצְרַיִם לִרְאוֹת אֶת אִמָּהּ.

8. ב.ק.שׁ יַעֲקֹב _____ לָדַעַת אֶת מִסְפַּר אֹהָלָיו.

Exercise 5. Translate the following sentences into Hebrew.

1. I spoke many words to the people of the city.
2. You *m, sg* spoke many words to the people of the city.
3. You *m, sg* will speak many words to the people of the city.
4. They *f* are still seeking the truth.
5. We are still seeking the truth.
6. You *f, sg* are still seeking the truth.
7. I commanded her, saying: ''Go!''
8. She commanded him, saying: ''Go!''
9. We commanded them *m*, saying: ''Go!''

Exercise 6. Using the list of roots at the bottom of this exercise, identify the roots of the following verb forms. Circle all פִּעֵל forms. Translate.

17. תֵּת	13. לֶאֱהֹב	9. צַוֵּינָה	5. וַתַּעַשׂ	1. כָּתְבָה
18. וַיֵּרָא	14. עֲשִׂיתֶם	10. גָּדוֹל	6. וָאֹהַב	2. קָמָה
19. דִּבַּרְתָּ	15. מְצֻוִּים	11. נָתַתְּ	7. לָדַעַת	3. מִסַפְּרוֹת
20. תֵּדְעוּ	16. אֲגַדֵּל	12. תְּדַבֵּרְנָה	8. נָבוֹא	4. רְאִי

א.ה.ב, ב.ו.א, ג.ד.ל, ד.ב.ר, י.ד.ע, כ.ת.ב, נ.ת.ן, ס.פ.ר, ע.שׂ.ה, צ.ו.ה, ק.ו.ם, ר.א.ה

Exercise 7. Read and translate.

Vocabulary for Reading Selection

why? . . . . לָמָה   fish n, m . . . . דָּג

gods . . . . אֵלִים   fish, catch fish vb . . . . ד.ו.ג

                                          fisherman . . . . דַּיָּג

הַדַּיָּג וְאִשְׁתּוֹ

הָיָה דַיָּג אֲשֶׁר יָשַׁב בְּבַיִת קָטָן מְאֹד עִם אִשְׁתּוֹ וְלֹא הָיָה לָהֶם כֶּסֶף. הָלַךְ הָאִישׁ יוֹם יוֹם אֶל הַיָּם לָדוּג וְשָׁב בָּעֶרֶב אֶל בֵּיתוֹ לָתֵת אֹכֶל לְאִשְׁתּוֹ. וַיְהִי בַּבֹּקֶר וַיֵּלֶךְ הַדַּיָּג אֶל הַיָּם וַיָּדוּג שָׁם. וַיְהִי בָּעֶרֶב וַיָּדוּג הַדַּיָּג דָּג גָּדוֹל.

וַיֹּאמֶר הַדָּג אֶל הַדַּיָּג: "אָשׁוּבָה אֶל בֵּיתִי תַּחַת הַמַּיִם וְאֶתֵּן לְךָ כָּל אֲשֶׁר תְּבַקֵּשׁ מִמֶּנִּי".

וַיַּעַן הַדַּיָּג לַדָּג לֵאמֹר: "עָלַי לָתֵת לְאִשְׁתִּי אֹכֶל. אִם תִּתֵּן לִי אֹכֶל תַּחְתֶּיךָ, אֶשְׁלַח אוֹתְךָ אֶל בֵּיתְךָ תַּחַת הַמַּיִם.

וַיִּתֵּן הַדָּג לַדַּיָּג יַיִן וְלֶחֶם וּפְרִי וַיָּשָׁב הָאִישׁ לְבֵיתוֹ.

וַתֹּאמֶר לוֹ אִשְׁתּוֹ: "מַה הָאֹכֶל הַזֶּה?" וַיְסַפֵּר לְאִשְׁתּוֹ אֶת כָּל אֲשֶׁר הַדָּג עָשָׂה לוֹ.

וַתְּצַו אוֹתוֹ אִשְׁתּוֹ: "שׁוּב יָמָּה! צַוֵּה אֶת הַדָּג לִבְנוֹת לָנוּ בַּיִת גָּדוֹל וְלָתֵת לָנוּ כָּסֶף."

וַיֵּלֶךְ הַדַּיָּג וַיָּבוֹא אֶל הַיָּם וַיֹּאמַר: "דָּג, בּוֹא! עֲלֵה אֵלַי!"

וַיַּעַל הַדָּג וַיֹּאמֶר: "מַה אַתָּה מְבַקֵּשׁ מִמֶּנִּי?"

וַיְסַפֵּר לַדָּג אֶת כָּל אֲשֶׁר אִשְׁתּוֹ אָמְרָה.

וַיֹּאמֶר הַדָּג: "שׁוּב אֶל בֵּיתְךָ וְאֶעֱשֶׂה כָּל אֲשֶׁר בִּקַּשְׁתָּ".

וַיָּשָׁב הַדַּיָּג אֶל בֵּיתוֹ, וְהִנֵּה הַכֹּל הָיָה כַּאֲשֶׁר בִּקֵּשׁ מֵהַדָּג.

וַתֹּאמֶר אֵלָיו אִשְׁתּוֹ: "שׁוּב יָמָּה! צַוֵּה אֶת הַדָּג לַעֲשׂוֹת אוֹתָנוּ כִּמְלָכִים וְנִמְלֹךְ עַל כָּל הָאָרֶץ."

וַיֵּלֶךְ הַדַּיָּג וַיָּבוֹא אֶל הַיָּם וַיֹּאמַר: "דָּג, בּוֹא! עֲלֵה אֵלַי!"

וַיַּעַל הַדָּג וַיֹּאמֶר: "מָה אַתָּה מְבַקֵּשׁ מִמֶּנִּי?" וַיְסַפֵּר לַדָּג אֶת כָּל אֲשֶׁר אִשְׁתּוֹ אָמְרָה.

וַיֹּאמֶר הַדָּג: "שׁוּב אֶל בֵּיתְךָ וְהַכֹּל יִהְיֶה כַּאֲשֶׁר בִּקַּשְׁתָּ".

וַיָּשָׁב הַדַּיָּג לְבֵיתוֹ, וְהִנֵּה הַכֹּל הָיָה כְּדִבְרֵי הַדָּג.

וַתֹּאמֶר אֵשֶׁת הַדַּיָּג אֵלָיו לֵאמֹר: "עַתָּה אָנוּ כִּמְלָכִים. לָמָה לֹא נִהְיֶה אֵלִים? שׁוּב יָמָּה! צַוֵּה אֶת הַדָּג לַעֲשׂוֹת אוֹתָנוּ אֵלִים וְנִמְלֹךְ גַּם עַל הָאָרֶץ וְגַם עַל הַשָּׁמַיִם."

וַיַּעַן הַדַּיָּג לְאִשְׁתּוֹ: "אֲנַחְנוּ כִּמְלָכִים. עָלֵינוּ לְבַקֵּשׁ רַק דְּבָרִים אֲשֶׁר לַאֲנָשִׁים. לֹא אֵלֵךְ לְבַקֵּשׁ מִן הַדָּג אֶת הַדָּבָר הַזֶּה."

וְהָאִשָּׁה לֹא שָׁמְעָה לְבָהּ לִדְבָרָיו וַתֹּאמֶר אֵלָיו: "שׁוּב יָמָּה! עֲשֵׂה אֶת אֲשֶׁר צִוִּיתִי אֹתְךָ!"

וַיֵּלֶךְ הַדַּיָּג וַיָּבוֹא אֶל הַיָּם וַיֹּאמַר: "דָּג, בּוֹא! עֲלֵה אֵלַי!"

וַיַּעַל הַדָּג וַיֹּאמֶר: "מָה עוֹד אַתָּה מְבַקֵּשׁ מִמֶּנִּי?" וַיְסַפֵּר לַדָּג אֶת כָּל אֲשֶׁר אִשְׁתּוֹ אָמְרָה.

וַיֹּאמֶר הַדָּג: "לֹא טוֹב בִּקַּשְׁתָּ! אִישׁ לֹא יוּכַל לִהְיוֹת אֵל. עַתָּה לֹא תִהְיוּ אֵלִים וְגַם לֹא תִּהְיוּ מְלָכִים וְגַם אֶת הַבַּיִת וְאֶת הַכֶּסֶף אֶקַּח מִכֶּם. שׁוּב אֶל אִשְׁתְּךָ הָרָעָה! בְּבַקָּשַׁתְכֶם אֶת הַכֹּל וְעַתָּה לֹא יִהְיֶה לָכֶם דָּבָר."

וַיָּשָׁב הַדַּיָּג אֶל בֵּיתוֹ הַקָּטָן וְהַדָּג לֹא עָלָה אֵלָיו מִן הַיָּם עוֹד.

Exercise 8. Fill in the proper form of the verb in the last column and translate.

Root	Number	Gender	Person	Tense	Pattern	Word	
שׁ.מ.ר	sg	m	2	perfect	פָּעֵל		1
ד.ב.ר	sg	m	2	perfect	פָּעֵל		2
כ.ת.ב	pl	c	1	perfect	פָּעֵל		3
ב.ק.שׁ	pl	c	1	perfect	פָּעֵל		4
ב.ג.ה	pl	c	1	perfect	פָּעֵל		5
צ.ו.ה	pl	c	1	perfect	פָּעֵל		6
שׁ.מ.ר	sg	f	3	imperfect	פָּעֵל		7
ד.ב.ר	sg	f	3	imperfect	פָּעֵל		8
כ.ת.ב	pl	m	3	imperfect	פָּעֵל		9
ב.ק.שׁ	pl	m	3	imperfect	פָּעֵל		10
ב.ג.ה	pl	m	2	imperfect	פָּעֵל		11
צ.ו.ה	pl	m	2	imperfect	פָּעֵל		12
שׁ.מ.ר	pl	m	2	imperfect	פָּעֵל		13
ד.ב.ר	sg	f	—	participle	פָּעֵל		14
כ.ת.ב	sg	f	—	participle	פָּעֵל		15
ב.ק.שׁ	pl	m	—	participle	פָּעֵל		16
ב.ג.ה	pl	m	—	participle	פָּעֵל		17
צ.ו.ה	sg	m	2	imperfect	פָּעֵל		18
ד.ב.ר	sg	m	2	imperfect	פָּעֵל		19
ד.ב.ר	sg	f	3	perfect	פָּעֵל		20
ב.ק.שׁ	sg	m	3	perfect	פָּעֵל		21
ב.ק.שׁ	sg	m	3	imperfect	פָּעֵל		22
צ.ו.ה	sg	m	3	perfect	פָּעֵל		23
צ.ו.ה	sg	m	3	imperfect	פָּעֵל		24

From the Prayerbook

Prayerbook Vocabulary

שֶׁ— .... shortened form of אֲשֶׁר

form, shape *vb* .... (פִּעֵל) י.צ.ר

שׁ.ב.ח (פִּעֵל) .... praise *vb*

in the beginning .... בְּרֵאשִׁית

גְּדֻלָּה .... greatness

Prayerbook Selection

עָלֵינוּ לְשַׁבֵּחַ לַאֲדוֹן הַכֹּל, לָתֵת גְּדֻלָּה לְיוֹצֵר בְּרֵאשִׁית, שֶׁלֹּא עָשָׂנוּ כְּגוֹיֵי הָאֲרָצוֹת, וְלֹא שָׂמָנוּ כְּמִשְׁפְּחוֹת הָאֲדָמָה ...

First translate the prayer into your own words, then read the translations.

Prayerbook Translations

"It is our duty to praise the Lord of all things, to ascribe greatness to him who formed the world in the beginning; since he hath not made us like the nations of other lands, and hath not placed us like other families of the earth. . ." *Daily Prayer Book, Joseph Hertz, 1975, p. 397*

"It is our duty to praise the Master of all, to exalt the Creator of the universe, who has not made us like the nations of the world and has not placed us like the families of the earth. . ." *Daily Prayer Book, Philip Birnbaum, 1977, p. 278*

Notice the use of the פִּעֵל infinitive לְשַׁבֵּחַ, and the use of the participle יוֹצֵר as a noun. Also, notice the use of the idiom עָלֵינוּ לְ–.

Guided Reading from Ruth

	1. חָמוֹת mother-in-law
	וַתֹּאמֶר לָהּ נָעֳמִי חֲמוֹתָהּ:
1. And Naomi, her mother-in-law, said to her:	2. מָנוֹחַ rest, security
	יִיטַב it will be good
	"בִּתִּי הֲלֹא אֲבַקֶּשׁ לָךְ מָנוֹחַ אֲשֶׁר יִיטַב לָךְ?
2. "My daughter, shall I not seek for you rest which will be good for you? *Notice the use of the interrogative הֲ in the word הֲלֹא.*	3. מֹדַעַת kindred
	וְעַתָּה הֲלֹא בֹעַז מֹדַעְתָּנוּ
3. And now is not Boaz our kindred	4. אֲשֶׁר הָיִית עִם נַעֲרוֹתָיו?
4. whose young women you were with? (Literally: that you were with his young women?)	5. ז.ר.ה (פָּעַל) winnow
	גֹּרֶן threshing floor
	שְׂעֹרִים barley
	הִנֵּה הוּא זֹרֶה אֶת הַשְּׂעֹרִים בְּגֹרֶן הַלָּיְלָה.

5. Behold, he is winnowing the barley at the threshing floor tonight.	6. ר.ח.ץ (פָּעַל) bathe ס.ו.ך (פָּעַל) anoint שִׂמְלֹתַיִךְ your clothing וְרָחַצְתְּ נָסַכְתְּ וְשַׂמְתְּ אֶת שִׂמְלֹתַיִךְ עָלַיִךְ
6. You shall bathe and anoint (yourself) and put your clothing upon yourself	7. י.ר.ד (פָּעַל) go down וְיָרַדְתְּ אֶל הַגֹּרֶן.
7. and you will go down to the threshing floor.	8. תִּוָּדְעִי make yourself known כ.ל.ה (פָּעַל) complete, finish כַּלֹּתוֹ his finishing *infinitive construct* אַל תִּוָּדְעִי לָאִישׁ עַד כַּלֹּתוֹ לֶאֱכֹל וְלִשְׁתּוֹת.
8. Don't make yourself known to the man until he has finished eating and drinking. (Literally: until his finishing to eat and to drink.)	9. וְהָיָה בְשָׁכְבוֹ וְיָדַעַתְּ אֶת הַמָּקוֹם אֲשֶׁר יִשְׁכַּב שָׁם.
9. And it will be when he lies down, you will know the place in which he will lie there.	10. ג.ל.ה (פָּעַל) uncover מַרְגְּלֹת place of the feet וּבָאת וְגִלִּית מַרְגְּלֹתָיו וְשָׁכָבְתְּ
10. And you shall come and uncover the place of his feet and lie down	11. יַגִּיד he will tell וְהוּא יַגִּיד לָךְ אֵת אֲשֶׁר תַּעֲשִׂי."
11. and he will tell you what you shall do."	12. וַתֹּאמֶר אֵלֶיהָ: "כֹּל אֲשֶׁר תֹּאמְרִי אֶעֱשֶׂה."
12. And she (Ruth) said to her (Naomi): "All that you say, I will do."	13. תֵּרֶד she will go down וַתֵּרֶד אֶל הַגֹּרֶן וַתַּעַשׂ כֹּל אֲשֶׁר צִוְּתָה אֹתָהּ חֲמוֹתָהּ.
13. And she went down to the threshing floor, and she did everything that her mother-in-law had commanded her.	

וַתֹּאמֶר לָהּ נָעֳמִי חֲמוֹתָהּ: "בִּתִּי הֲלֹא אֲבַקֶּשׁ לָךְ מָנוֹחַ אֲשֶׁר יִיטַב לָךְ? וְעַתָּה הֲלֹא בֹעַז מֹדַעְתָּנוּ אֲשֶׁר הָיִית עִם נַעֲרוֹתָיו? הִנֵּה הוּא זֹרֶה אֶת הַשְּׂעֹרִים בַּגֹּרֶן הַלָּיְלָה. וְרָחַצְתְּ נָסַכְתְּ וְשַׂמְתְּ אֶת שִׂמְלֹתַיִךְ עָלַיִךְ וְיָרַדְתְּ אֶל הַגֹּרֶן. אַל תִּוָּדְעִי לָאִישׁ עַד כַּלֹּתוֹ לֶאֱכֹל וְלִשְׁתּוֹת. וְהָיָה בְשָׁכְבוֹ וְיָדַעַתְּ אֶת הַמָּקוֹם אֲשֶׁר יִשְׁכַּב שָׁם. וּבָאת וְגִלִּית מַרְגְּלֹתָיו וְשָׁכָבְתְּ וְהוּא יַגִּיד לָךְ אֵת אֲשֶׁר תַּעֲשִׂי." וַתֹּאמֶר אֵלֶיהָ: "כֹּל אֲשֶׁר תֹּאמְרִי אֶעֱשֶׂה." וַתֵּרֶד אֶל הַגֹּרֶן וַתַּעַשׂ כֹּל אֲשֶׁר צִוְּתָה אֹתָהּ חֲמוֹתָהּ.

Chapter 26
The Hif'il הִפְעִיל Pattern

Vocabulary

grow up, become great *vb* . . . . (פָּעַל)	ג.ד.ל
cause to grow, bring up *vb* . . . . (פִּעֵל)	
make great, magnify *vb* . . . . (הִפְעִיל)	
remember *vb* . . . . (פָּעַל)	ז.כ.ר
cause to remember, remind, mention *vb* (הִפְעִיל)	
new *adj* . . . . חָדָשׁ, חֲדָשָׁה, חֲדָשִׁים, חֲדָשׁוֹת	
put on, wear (clothing) *vb* . . . . (פָּעַל)	ל.ב.שׁ
cause to wear, dress *vb* . . . . (הִפְעִיל)	
reign, rule *vb* . . . . (פָּעַל)	מ.ל.ך
cause to reign, make king, crown *vb* . . . (הִפְעִיל)	
tell, declare *vb* . . . . (הִפְעִיל)	נ.ג.ד
deliver, rescue *vb* . . . . (הִפְעִיל)	נ.צ.ל
throw, cast *vb* . . . . (הִפְעִיל)	שׁ.ל.ך

The Hif'il הִפְעִיל Pattern

You have already learned two Hebrew verb patterns: the פָּעַל pattern and the פִּעֵל pattern. The third verb pattern that you will learn is the Hif'il הִפְעִיל pattern.

When a root appears in both the פָּעַל and the הִפְעִיל patterns, it usually has a simple active meaning when conjugated in the פָּעַל pattern and a causative meaning when conjugated in the הִפְעִיל pattern. Following is a chart of all the verb roots you have learned which appear in both the פָּעַל and הִפְעִיל patterns. This chart is included to help you see the causative meaning of verbs in the הִפְעִיל pattern. However, many of these verbs are irregular and will not be used in the הִפְעִיל pattern in this book.

Root	Meaning in פָּעַל	Meaning in הִפְעִיל
א.כ.ל	eat	cause to eat, feed
ב.ו.א	go, come	cause to come, bring
ב.ט.ח	trust	cause to trust, make secure
ג.ד.ל	grow up, become great	make great, magnify
ה.ל.ך	go, walk	cause to go, lead, bring
ז.כ.ר	remember	cause to remember, remind, mention
י.ד.ע	know	cause to know, make known, declare
י.שׁ.ב	sit, stay, settle	cause to sit, cause to dwell
ל.ב.שׁ	put on, wear	cause to wear, dress
מ.ל.ך	reign, be king	cause to reign, make king, crown
ס.ו.ר	turn aside	cause to turn aside, remove, take away
ע.ל.ה	go up, ascend	cause to ascend, bring up
ק.ו.ם	arise, stand up	cause to arise, cause to stand, set up, establish
ר.א.ה	see	cause to see, show
שׁ.ו.ב	return, turn back	cause to return, bring back
שׁ.כ.ב	lie down	cause to lie down
שׁ.מ.ע	hear	cause to hear, proclaim

Some verb roots appear in the הִפְעִיל pattern, but do not appear in the פָּעַל pattern. Such הִפְעִיל verbs often have the same simple active meaning as verbs in the פָּעַל pattern.

Examples:

		Root	Meaning in הִפְעִיל
No	פָּעַל	נ.ג.ד	tell
No	פָּעַל	נ.צ.ל	rescue
No	פָּעַל	שׁ.ל.ך	throw

The Conjugation of Verbs in the הִפְעִיל Pattern

Following are charts showing the conjugation of the regular verb שׁ.ל.ך in the הִפְעִיל pattern. Compare this to the conjugation of the regular verb שׁ.מ.ר in the פָּעַל pattern.

The two important characteristics of the הִפְעִיל pattern are the prefix ה, which appears in the perfect tense, the imperative, and both infinitives, and the אִי vowel, which appears under the second root letter in almost every form.

Read aloud the conjugations of both שׁ.ל.ך and שׁ.מ.ר so that you can hear the differences between the פָּעַל and the הִפְעִיל patterns.

The Perfect Tense

	throw — (הִפְעִיל) ש.ל.ך		guard — (פָּעַל) ש.מ.ר
1 c sg	הִשְׁלַכְתִּי	הִאָאַֿתִי	שָׁמַֿרְתִּי
2 m sg	הִשְׁלַכְתָּ	הִאָאַֿתָ	שָׁמַֿרְתָּ
2 f sg	הִשְׁלַכְתְּ	הִאָאַֿתְּ	שָׁמַרְתְּ
3 m sg	הִשְׁלִיךְ	הִאָאִיא	שָׁמַר
3 f sg	הִשְׁלִיכָה	הִאָאִיאָה	שָׁמְרָה
1 c pl	הִשְׁלַֿכְנוּ	הִאָאַֿאנוּ	שָׁמַֿרְנוּ
2 m pl	הִשְׁלַכְתֶּם	הִאָאַתֶם	שְׁמַרְתֶּם
2 f pl	הִשְׁלַכְתֶּן	הִאָאַתֶן	שְׁמַרְתֶּן
3 c pl	הִשְׁלִֿיכוּ	הִאָאִֿיאו	שָׁמְרוּ

1. The prefix ה takes the ַX vowel in the perfect tense.
2. The ִיX vowel, characteristic of the הִפְעִיל pattern, appears in the third person forms.
3. The endings in the perfect tense of the הִפְעִיל pattern are exactly the same as the endings in the perfect tense of the פָּעַל pattern.

The Imperfect Tense

	throw — (הִפְעִיל) ש.ל.ך		guard — (פָּעַל) ש.מ.ר
1 c sg	אַשְׁלִיךְ	אַאִֿיא	אֶשְׁמֹר
2 m sg	תַּשְׁלִיךְ	תַּאִֿיא	תִּשְׁמֹר
2 f sg	תַּשְׁלִֿיכִי	תַּאִֿיאִי	תִּשְׁמְרִי
3 m sg	יַשְׁלִיךְ	יַאִֿיא	יִשְׁמֹר
3 f sg	תַּשְׁלִיךְ	תַּאִֿיא	תִּשְׁמֹר
1 c pl	נַשְׁלִיךְ	נַאִֿיא	נִשְׁמֹר
2 m pl	תַּשְׁלִֿיכוּ	תַּאִֿיאו	תִּשְׁמְרוּ
2 f pl	תַּשְׁלֵֿכְנָה	תַּאֵֿאנָה	תִּשְׁמֹֿרְנָה
3 m pl	יַשְׁלִֿיכוּ	יַאִֿיאו	יִשְׁמְרוּ
3 f pl	תַּשְׁלֵֿכְנָה	תַּאֵֿאנָה	תִּשְׁמֹֿרְנָה

1. The basic vowel pattern ַXִיXX , instead of XXֹX or the XַXֹX pattern of regular פָּעַל verbs.
2. The prefix ה disappears in the imperfect, and the prefix and suffix consonants which are added in the הִפְעִיל pattern are the same as the imperfect tense prefix and suffix consonants of the פָּעַל pattern.
3. The ִיX vowel, characteristic of the הִפְעִיל pattern, appears under the second root letter in all forms except the feminine plural.

The Participle

	throw — ש.ל.ך (הִפְעִיל)		guard — ש.מ.ר (פָּעַל)
m sg	מַשְׁלִיךְ	מַxְxִיא	שׁוֹמֵר/שָׁמֵר
f sg	מַשְׁלִיכָה/מַשְׁלֶכֶת	מַxְxִיאָה/מַxְxֶאֶת	שׁוֹמֶרֶת/שָׁמֶרֶת, שׁוֹמְרָה/שְׁמָרָה
m pl	מַשְׁלִיכִים	מַxְxִיאִים	שׁוֹמְרִים/שְׁמָרִים
f pl	מַשְׁלִיכוֹת	מַxְxִיאוֹת	שׁוֹמְרוֹת/שְׁמָרוֹת

1. The prefix ה is replaced by the prefix מ in the participle.
2. The אִי vowel, characteristic of the הִפְעִיל pattern, appears under the second root letter in all forms.
3. The endings of the participle in the הִפְעִיל pattern are exactly the same as the endings of the participle in the פָּעַל pattern.

The Imperative

	throw — ש.ל.ך (הִפְעִיל)		guard — ש.מ.ר (פָּעַל)
m sg	הַשְׁלֵךְ	הַxְxֵx	שְׁמֹר
f sg	הַשְׁלִיכִי	הַxְxִיxִי	שִׁמְרִי
m pl	הַשְׁלִיכוּ	הַxְxִיxוּ	שִׁמְרוּ
f pl	הַשְׁלֵכְנָה	הַxְxֵxְנָה	שְׁמֹרְנָה

1. The prefix ה takes the x vowel in the imperative.
2. The אִי vowel, characteristic of the הִפְעִיל pattern, appears under the second root letter in the f sg and m pl forms.

The Infinitive

	throw — ש.ל.ך (הִפְעִיל)		guard — ש.מ.ר (פָּעַל)
absolute	הַשְׁלֵךְ	הַxְxֵx	שָׁמוֹר
construct	(לְ) הַשְׁלִיךְ לְהַשְׁלִיךְ	לְהַxְxִיא	לִשְׁמֹר

1. The prefix ה takes the x vowel in both infinitives.
2. The אִי vowel, characteristic of the הִפְעִיל pattern, appears under the second root letter in the infinitive construct.

The הִפְעִיל Pattern for Verbs Starting with נ

When the first root letter of a verb is נ, the נ disappears in the הִפְעִיל pattern and a dagesh is placed in the second root letter. This dagesh will help you recognize verbs in the הִפְעִיל pattern whose first root letter is a נ. The verbs נ.ג.ד and נ.צ.ל introduced in this chapter are examples of this type of הִפְעִיל verb. Since these two verbs appear quite often in the Bible, we are including a chart of the verb נ.ג.ד conjugated in the הִפְעִיל pattern. The verb נ.צ.ל is conjugated the same way. Compare this to the conjugation of the regular הִפְעִיל verb ש.ל.ך.

The Perfect Tense

tell — (הִפְעִיל) נ.ג.ד	throw — (הִפְעִיל) ש.ל.ך	
הִגַּדְתִּי	הִשְׁלַכְתִּי	1 c sg
הִגַּדְתָּ	הִשְׁלַכְתָּ	2 m sg
הִגַּדְתְּ	הִשְׁלַכְתְּ	2 f sg
הִגִּיד	הִשְׁלִיךְ	3 m sg
הִגִּידָה	הִשְׁלִיכָה	3 f sg
הִגַּדְנוּ	הִשְׁלַכְנוּ	1 c pl
הִגַּדְתֶּם	הִשְׁלַכְתֶּם	2 m pl
הִגַּדְתֶּן	הִשְׁלַכְתֶּן	2 f pl
הִגִּידוּ	הִשְׁלִיכוּ	3 m pl
הִגִּידוּ	הִשְׁלִיכוּ	3 f pl

The Imperfect Tense

tell — (הִפְעִיל) נ.ג.ד	throw — (הִפְעִיל) ש.ל.ך	
אַגִּיד	אַשְׁלִיךְ	1 c sg
תַּגִּיד	תַּשְׁלִיךְ	2 m sg
תַּגִּידִי	תַּשְׁלִיכִי	2 f sg
יַגִּיד	יַשְׁלִיךְ	3 m sg
תַּגִּיד	תַּשְׁלִיךְ	3 f sg
נַגִּיד	נַשְׁלִיךְ	1 c pl
תַּגִּידוּ	תַּשְׁלִיכוּ	2 m pl
תַּגֵּדְנָה	תַּשְׁלֵכְנָה	2 f pl
יַגִּידוּ	יַשְׁלִיכוּ	3 m pl
תַּגֵּדְנָה	תַּשְׁלֵכְנָה	3 f pl

The Participle

tell — (הִפְעִיל) נ.ג.ד	throw — (הִפְעִיל) ש.ל.ך	
מַגִּיד	מַשְׁלִיךְ	m sg
מַגִּידָה, מַגֶּדֶת	מַשְׁלִיכָה, מַשְׁלֶכֶת	f sg
מַגִּידִים	מַשְׁלִיכִים	m pl
מַגִּידוֹת	מַשְׁלִיכוֹת	f pl

The Imperative

tell — (הִפְעִיל) נ.ג.ד	throw — (הִפְעִיל) ש.ל.ך	
הַגֵּד	הַשְׁלֵךְ	m sg
הַגִּידִי	הַשְׁלִיכִי	f sg
הַגִּידוּ	הַשְׁלִיכוּ	m pl
הַגֵּדְנָה	הַשְׁלֵכְנָה	f pl

The Infinitive

	tell — נ.ג.ד (הִפְעִיל)	throw — ש.ל.ך (הִפְעִיל)
absolute	הַגֵּד	הַשְׁלֵךְ
construct	(לְ) הַגִּיד לְהַגִּיד	(לְ) הַשְׁלִיךְ לְהַשְׁלִיךְ

הַפְעִיל Verbs with the Reversing Vav

When a reversing vav is added to a הַפְעִיל verb, the vowel pattern often changes in the imperfect tense and the אִי vowel disappears.

Examples:	Imperfect with Reversing Vav	Imperfect	Root
	וַיַּשְׁלֵךְ	יַשְׁלִיךְ	שׁ.ל.ך
	וַיַּגֵּד	יַגִּיד	נ.ג.ד

Exercises

Exercise 1. Conjugate the following roots in all forms of the verb pattern given.

‏1. ז.כ.ר (פָּעַל)   2. ז.כ.ר (הִפְעִיל)   3. נ.צ.ל (הִפְעִיל)

Exercise 2. Rewrite the sentences below, replacing the underlined word with each word in the list that follows. Every word or grammatical form in the sentence that agrees with the underlined word should be changed to agree with the newly substituted words. Read the sentences aloud. Translate.

‏1. הַבָּנִים הִשְׁלִיכוּ אֲבָנִים אֶל תּוֹךְ הַיַּרְדֵּן.

E. אַתֶּם	D. הוּא	C. אֲנַחְנוּ	B. אַתְּ	A. הַנְּעָרוֹת
I. אַתָּה	H. אַתֶּן	G. אֲנִי		F. הִיא

‏2. הַנָּשִׁים הָאֵלֶּה מַלְבִּישׁוֹת אֶת בְּנוֹתֵיהֶן בַּבֹּקֶר.

E. הִיא	D. אַתְּ	C. אַתֶּן	B. הוּא	A. אֲנִי
I. אַתָּה	H. אֲנַחְנוּ	G. אַתֶּם		F. הֵם

‏3. (אָנוּ) נַמְלִיךְ אֹתוֹ וּמָלַךְ עָלֵינוּ כָּל יְמֵי חַיָּיו.

E. אַתֶּן	D. אֲנִי	C. אַתֶּם	B. אַנְשֵׁי כְּנַעַן	A. הָעָם
I. הִיא	H. הֵנָּה	G. אַתָּה		F. אַתְּ

‏4. הָאָב גִּדֵּל אֶת הַנַּעַר וְכַאֲשֶׁר גָּדַל הַנַּעַר גָּדַל הוּא הִגְדִּיל אֶת בֵּית מִשְׁפַּחְתּוֹ.

E. אֹתָנוּ	D. אֹתְךָ	C. אֶתְכֶן	B. אֹתִי	A. אֶת הַבָּנִים
I. אֶת הַנַּעֲרָה	H. אֹתָךְ	G. אֶתְכֶם		F. אֶת הַבָּנוֹת

‏5. וַיַּגֵּד הָאִישׁ לָהֶם לֵאמֹר: "אֶת מַעֲשֵׂי אֲבוֹתֵיכֶם (אֲנִי) אַזְכִּיר לָכֶם וְזָכוֹר תִּזְכְּרוּ אֹתָם."

E. הוּא	D. הִיא	C. הֵנָּה	B. אֲנַחְנוּ	A. הֵמָּה

‎6. <u>יַעֲקֹב הִצִּיל</u> אֶת אַנְשֵׁי הָעִיר הַהִיא.

E. אֲנַחְנוּ	D. הִיא	C. אַתָּה	B. הֵנָּה	A. אֲנִי
	I. אַתֶּם	H. אַתְּ	G. הֵמָּה	F. אַתֶּן

Exercise 3. Rewrite the following sentences, filling in the blanks with all forms of the verb root shown that will yield a meaningful sentence. Translate.

Example: ‎נ.ג.ד (אַתָּה) _____ לָהּ אֶת כָּל לִבְּךָ.

‎הִגַּדְתָּ תַּגִּיד לָהּ אֶת כָּל לִבְּךָ.   הִגַּדְתָּ לָהּ אֶת כָּל לִבְּךָ.
‎אַתָּה מַגִּיד לָהּ אֶת כָּל לִבְּךָ.   הַגֵּד הִגַּדְתָּ לָהּ אֶת כָּל לִבְּךָ.
‎הַגֵּד לָהּ אֶת כָּל לִבְּךָ.   תַּגִּיד לָהּ אֶת כָּל לִבְּךָ.

‎1. ש.ל.ך (אַתְּ) _____ אֶת וְעָלַיִךְ עַל הָאֲדָמָה.
‎2. נ.צ.ל (אַתֶּם) _____ אֶת הַנָּשִׁים מֵהָאֲנָשִׁים הָרָעִים.
‎3. מ.ל.ך _____ הָעָם אֶת דָּוִד כְּמֶלֶךְ עַל יִשְׂרָאֵל.
‎4. ז.כ.ר (אַתָּה) _____ לַזְּקֵנִים אֶת בֵּית לֶחֶם וְהֵם _____ אֶת הָאֲנָשִׁים שָׁם.
‎5. ב.ק.שׁ (אַתֶּן) _____ לְהַצִּיל אֶת הַנַּעֲרָה מִתּוֹךְ הַיָּם.
‎6. נ.ת.ן (הֵם) _____ בְּגָדִים חֲדָשִׁים לַנָּשִׁים לְהַלְבִּישׁ אֶת בְּנֵיהֶן.
‎7. ק.ו.ם (אֲנַחְנוּ) _____ לְהַגִּיד לְכָל הָעִיר אֶת הָאֱמֶת.

Exercise 4. Read and translate the following sentences. Underline all verb forms that are shortened by the addition of a reversing vav.

‎1. וַיָּרָץ הַנַּעַר הָעִירָה וַיַּגֵּד לָאֲנָשִׁים אֶת כָּל אֲשֶׁר רָאָה.
‎2. וַתֵּרֶא אֶת מַעֲשָׂיו הַטּוֹבִים וַתַּמְלֵךְ אֹתוֹ.
‎3. וַתִּתֵּן הָאֵם לִבְנָהּ מַיִם לִשְׁתּוֹת וַתַּלְבֵּשׁ אֹתוֹ בְּגָדִים חֲדָשִׁים.
‎4. וַיִּשְׁמַע קוֹל אִשָּׁה וַיֵּרֶא אַתָּה בַּמַּיִם נִסַר מֵהַדֶּרֶךְ וַיַּצֵּל אֹתָהּ וַיִּקַּח אֹתָהּ לְבֵית אָבִיהָ.

Exercise 5. Using the list of verb roots at the bottom of this exercise, identify the roots and the verb pattern of the following verb forms. Translate.

13. שָׂרָה	10. מְגַדְּלִים	7. לְהַשְׁלִיךְ	4. יִבְנֶה	1. אַגְדִּל
14. אֲדַבֵּר	11. הִצַּלְנוּ	8. הִזְכַּרְתִּי	5. דִּבַּרְנוּ	2. מַצִּיל
15. הִשְׁלִיכוּ	12. מַזְכִּירוֹת	9. בּוֹנָה	6. הִגְדַּלְנָה	3. לָשִׁיר

‎ב.נ.ה, ג.ד.ל, ד.ב.ר, ז.כ.ר, נ.צ.ל, שׁ.י.ר, שׁ.ל.ך

Exercise 6. Complete the following sentences in your own words.

‎1. בַּשָּׁבוּעַ הַבָּא יַמְלִיכוּ אֹתִי כִּי . . .
‎2. שָׁנָה בְּשָׁנָה אַגִּיד לְמִשְׁפַּחְתִּי . . .
‎3. יוֹם יוֹם אֲנִי מַגְדִּיל אֶת שְׁמִי כִּי . . .
‎4. אַחַי הִשְׁלִיכוּ אֲבָנִים עָלַי כִּי . . .
‎5. הִצַּלְתָּ אֶת הַנַּעַר אֲשֶׁר . . .

Exercise 7. Fill in the blanks in the following story with the correct form of the verb root given. Read and translate.

Vocabulary for Reading Selection

to kill	לְהָמִית	Aaron *man's name*	אַהֲרֹן
but	אַךְ	naked	עָרֹם

אִישׁ רַע אֲשֶׁר _____ כֶּסֶף רַב וּשְׁמוֹ אַהֲרֹן. וַיְהִי הַיּוֹם וְאַהֲרֹן
ה.י.ה   ב.ק.שׁ

_____ לְעִיר גְּדוֹלָה. בָּעִיר הַהִיא מֶלֶךְ אֲשֶׁר _____
ל.ב.שׁ   ה.י.ה   ב.ו.א

בְּגָדִים חֲדָשִׁים תָּמִיד. וַיֵּלֶךְ אַהֲרֹן אֶל בֵּית הַמֶּלֶךְ וַיֹּאמֶר: "אוּכַל לְ_____ לְךָ בְּגָדִים
ע.שׂ.ה

אֲשֶׁר אֵין כְּמוֹהֶם בְּכָל אַרְצְךָ. רַק אֲנָשִׁים חֲכָמִים _____ לְ_____ אֶת
י.כ.ל   ר.א.ה

הַבְּגָדִים הָאֵלֶּה." הַמֶּלֶךְ אָמַר בְּלִבּוֹ: _____ לִי כֶּסֶף וְ_____ לְךָ אֹתָם."
נ.ת.ן   ע.שׂ.ה

"אֶהְיֶה מֶלֶךְ גָּדוֹל מְאֹד. אוּכַל _____ מִי חָכָם וּמִי אֵינֶנּוּ חָכָם."
י.ד.ע

וַיַּעַן הַמֶּלֶךְ לֵאמֹר: "הִנֵּה הַכֶּסֶף, וְעַתָּה _____ לִי אֶת הַבְּגָדִים הָאֵלֶּה וְ(אֲנִי) _____
ע.שׂ.ה   ל.ב.שׁ

אֹתָם וְ_____ אֶת שְׁמִי בָּאָרֶץ." אַהֲרֹן _____ אֶת כֶּסֶף הַמֶּלֶךְ וַיֵּלֶךְ
ג.ד.ל   ל.ק.ח

לַעֲשׂוֹת אֶת הַבְּגָדִים לַמֶּלֶךְ. אַחַר הַדְּבָרִים הָאֵלֶּה _____ הַמֶּלֶךְ אֶת נַעֲרוֹ אֶל אַהֲרֹן
שׁ.ל.ח

לְ_____ אֶת הַבְּגָדִים אֲשֶׁר הוּא עָשָׂה. כְּבוֹא הַנַּעַר אֶל בֵּית אַהֲרֹן וַיַּרְא כִּי לֹא _____
ר.א.ה   ה.י.ה

בְּגָדִים שָׁם. וַיֹּאמֶר הַנַּעַר בְּלִבּוֹ: "אֲנִי לֹא _____ אֶת הַבְּגָדִים." הַנַּעַר _____
ר.א.ה   י.ד.ע

כִּי רַק אֲנָשִׁים חֲכָמִים _____ לְ_____ אֶת הַבְּגָדִים. וַיֹּאמֶר הַנַּעַר אֶל
י.כ.ל   ר.א.ה

אַהֲרֹן: "אֲנִי רוֹאֶה אֶת הַבְּגָדִים הַחֲדָשִׁים. אֵין כְּמוֹהֶם בְּכָל הָאָרֶץ." וְ_____ הַנַּעַר אֶל
שׁ.ו.ב

מַלְכּוֹ וְ_____ לוֹ כִּי רָאָה אֶת בִּגְדֵי הַמֶּלֶךְ הַחֲדָשִׁים. הַמֶּלֶךְ _____ אֶת
נ.ג.ד   ה.ו.צ

כָּל עַמּוֹ לֵאמֹר: "בַּשָּׁבוּעַ הַבָּא _____ אֶת בִּגְדֵי הַחֲדָשִׁים. עֲלֵיכֶם לְ_____
ל.ב.שׁ   ר.א.ה

לְ_____ אֹתִי."
ר.א.ה

כָּל הָעָם _____ כִּי רַק אֲנָשִׁים חֲכָמִים _____ לְ_____ אֶת
י.ד.ע   י.כ.ל   ר.א.ה

הַבְּגָדִים הָאֵלֶּה. בַּשָּׁבוּעַ הַהוּא _____ הָעָם אֶל בֵּית הַמֶּלֶךְ. וְהִנֵּה כָּל הָעָם _____
ב.ו.א   ר.א.ה

כִּי לֹא הָיוּ עַל הַמֶּלֶךְ בְּגָדִים. כָּל אִישׁ _____ בְּלִבּוֹ "אֵינֶנִּי חָכָם כִּי אֲנִי לֹא רוֹאֶה אֶת
א.מ.ר

בִּגְדֵי הַמֶּלֶךְ. בֵּין כָּל הָאֲנָשִׁים _____ נַעֲרָה אֲשֶׁר _____ עִם אָבִיהָ. הִיא
ה.י.ה   ב.ו.א

אָמְרָה: "רְאוּ! אֵין לַמֶּלֶךְ בְּגָדִים!" כָּל הָאֲנָשִׁים יָדְעוּ כִּי הַנַּעֲרָה _____ אֶת הָאֱמֶת. הַמֶּלֶךְ
נ.ג.ד

כִּי הוּא עָרֹם וַיָּרָץ אֶל תּוֹךְ בֵּיתוֹ. הוּא _____ אֶת נְעָרָיו לְ_____
ר.א.ה   צ.ו.ה   ב.ק.שׁ

אֶת אַהֲרֹן וּלְהָמִית אֹתוֹ. אַךְ אַהֲרֹן לֹא הָיָה בָּעִיר. הוּא _____ וְכָל כֶּסֶף הַמֶּלֶךְ עִמּוֹ.
ה.ל.ךְ

198

Exercise 8. Fill in the proper form of the verb in the last column and translate.

Root	Number	Gender	Person	Tense	Pattern	Word
פ.ת.ח	sg	m	2	perfect	פָּעַל	1
שׁ.ל.ך	sg	m	2	perfect	הִפְעִיל	2
נ.צ.ל	sg	m	2	perfect	הִפְעִיל	3
ז.כ.ר	pl	f	—	active participle	פָּעַל	4
ז.כ.ר	pl	f	—	participle	הִפְעִיל	5
נ.ג.ד	pl	f	—	participle	הִפְעִיל	6
מ.ל.ך	sg	f	3	imperfect	פָּעַל	7
מ.ל.ך	sg	f	3	imperfect	הִפְעִיל	8
נ.ג.ד	sg	f	3	imperfect	הִפְעִיל	9
ג.ד.ל	—	—	—	infinitive construct	פָּעַל	10
ג.ד.ל	—	—	—	infinitive construct	פָּעַל	11
ג.ד.ל	—	—	—	infinitive construct	הִפְעִיל	12
ל.ב.שׁ	sg	m	—	active participle	פָּעַל	13
ל.ב.שׁ	sg	m	—	participle	הִפְעִיל	14
נ.צ.ל	sg	m	—	participle	הִפְעִיל	15
כ.ת.ב	sg	c	1	imperfect	פָּעַל	16
ס.פ.ר	sg	c	1	imperfect	פָּעַל	17
שׁ.ל.ך	sg	c	1	imperfect	הִפְעִיל	18
ס.ו.ר	sg	c	1	imperfect	פָּעַל	19
ר.א.ה	sg	c	1	imperfect	פָּעַל	20
צ.ו.ה	sg	c	1	imperfect	פָּעַל	21
נ.צ.ל	sg	c	1	imperfect	הִפְעִיל	22
שׁ.מ.ע	sg	m	—	active participle	פָּעַל	23
מ.ל.ך	sg	m	—	participle	הִפְעִיל	24

From the Prayerbook

Prayerbook Vocabulary

tabernacle, shelter . . . . סֻכָּה   cause to stand, raise up . . . ע.מ.ד (הִפְעִיל)

cause to lie down . . . . ש.כ.ב (הִפְעִיל)   spread out . . . . פ.ר.ש (פָּעַל)

Selection from the Prayerbook (from the evening service for the Sabbath and festivals)

הַשְׁכִּיבֵנוּ יְיָ אֱלֹהֵינוּ לְשָׁלוֹם וְהַעֲמִידֵנוּ מַלְכֵּנוּ לְחַיִּים . . .

בָּרוּךְ אַתָּה יְיָ הַפּוֹרֵשׂ סֻכַּת שָׁלוֹם עָלֵינוּ וְעַל כָּל עַמּוֹ יִשְׂרָאֵל וְעַל יְרוּשָׁלָיִם.

First translate the prayer into your own words, then read the translations quoted below.

Prayerbook Translations

"Grant, O Eternal God, that we may lie down in peace, and raise us up, O Sovereign, to life renewed . . .

Blessed is the Lord, whose shelter of peace is spread over us, over all His people Israel, and over Jerusalem."

Gates of Prayer, the New Union Prayerbook, 1975, p. 133

"Grant, Lord our God, that we lie down in peace, and that we rise again, O our King, to life . . .

Blessed art thou, O Lord, who spreadest the shelter of peace over us and over all thy people Israel and over Jerusalem."

Daily Prayer Book, Philip Birnbaum, 1977, pp. 262-264

Notice the use of the הִפְעִיל forms of ע.מ.ד and ש.כ.ב. Also notice the use of direct object suffixes with these verbs: הַשְׁכִּיבֵנוּ = הַשְׁכִּיב אֹתָנוּ (see Chapter 18).

Biblical Punctuation

In the guided readings from the Book of Ruth, we have been using English punctuation marks: periods, commas, quotation marks, etc., to help you read. The Bible does not have these punctuation marks, but uses a different system of punctuation. Beginning with this chapter, we will use the following Biblical punctuation marks in the Hebrew section of the guided reading.

The Sof Pasuq סוֹף פָּסוּק

The end of a verse in the Bible is shown by the sof pasuq סוֹף פָּסוּק which looks very much like an English colon : . The sof pasuq appears after the last word in the verse.

Example: וַתֹּאמֶר אֵלֶיהָ כֹּל אֲשֶׁר תֹּאמְרִי אֶעֱשֶׂה׃   Ruth 3:5

The Etnachta אֶתְנַחְתָּא

Each Biblical verse is divided into two parts by the etnachta אֶתְנַחְתָּא ֑ . The etnachta appears below the last word of the first part of a verse and indicates a pause in the reading.

Example: וַתֹּאמֶר אֵלֶיהָ כֹּל אֲשֶׁר תֹּאמְרִי אֶעֱשֶׂה׃ Ruth 3:5

The sof pasuq and the etnachta may cause slight spelling changes in the words to which they are added.

In the guided reading for this chapter and the rest of the book, you will be reading the actual Biblical text of the book of Ruth. From now on, the guided readings will include chapter and verse numbers, and the Biblical punctuation marks introduced above. The spelling of words in the Bible is often unusual, and we will use these unusual spellings as they appear in the Biblical text.

Guided Reading from Ruth	
	Ruth 3:7 .1
	(he) was glad וַיִּיטַב
	וַיֹּאכַל בֹּעַז וַיֵּשְׁתְּ וַיִּיטַב לִבּוֹ
1. And Boaz ate and drank, and his heart was glad,	end קָצֶה .2
	grain-heap עֲרֵמָה
	וַיָּבֹא לִשְׁכַּב בִּקְצֵה הָעֲרֵמָה
2. and he came to lie down at the end of the grain-heap.	secretly בַּלָּט .3
	and she uncovered וַתְּגַל
	place of the feet מַרְגְּלוֹת
	וַתָּבֹא בַלָּט וַתְּגַל מַרְגְּלֹתָיו וַתִּשְׁכָּב׃
3. And she (Ruth) came secretly and uncovered the place of his feet and lay down.	Ruth 3:8 .4
	middle חֲצִי
	tremble, start ח.ר.ד (פָּעַל)
	he twisted himself, turned over וַיִּלָּפֵת
	וַיְהִי בַּחֲצִי הַלַּיְלָה וַיֶּחֱרַד הָאִישׁ וַיִּלָּפֵת
4. And it came to pass in the middle of the night (that) the man trembled and he turned over,	וְהִנֵּה אִשָּׁה שֹׁכֶבֶת מַרְגְּלֹתָיו׃ .5
5. and behold! a woman (was) lying at the place of his feet.	Ruth 3:9 .6
	וַיֹּאמֶר מִי אָתְּ .7
6. And he said: "Who are you?"	maidservant אָמָה .7
	וַתֹּאמֶר אָנֹכִי רוּת אֲמָתֶךָ

201

7. And she said: "I am Ruth, your maid-servant.	8. פ.ר.שׂ (פָּעַל) spread out כָּנָף wing, corner of garment וּפָרַשְׂתָּ כְנָפֶךָ עַל אֲמָתְךָ
8. Spread out the corner of your garment over your maidservant,	9. גֹּאֵל kinsman, redeemer כִּי גֹאֵל אָתָּה:
9. for you are a kinsman." (a relative who is eligible to act as a husband or redeemer of property)	10. Ruth 3:10 ב.ר.ך (פָּעַל) bless וַיֹּאמֶר בְּרוּכָה אַתְּ לַיהוה בִּתִּי
10. And he said: "You are blessed to the Lord, my daughter;	11. הֵיטַבְתְּ you have made good אַחֲרוֹן last רִאשׁוֹן first הֵיטַבְתְּ חַסְדֵּךְ הָאַחֲרוֹן מִן הָרִאשׁוֹן
11. you have made your last kindness better than your first,	12. לְבִלְתִּי not בָּחוּר young man לְבִלְתִּי לֶכֶת אַחֲרֵי הַבַּחוּרִים
12. not to go after the young men,	13. דַּל poor עָשִׁיר rich אִם דַּל וְאִם עָשִׁיר:
13. whether poor or rich.	14. Ruth 3:11 י.ר.א (פָּעַל) be afraid וְעַתָּה בִּתִּי אַל תִּירְאִי כֹּל אֲשֶׁר תֹּאמְרִי אֶעֱשֶׂה לָּךְ
14. And now, my daughter, do not fear. All that you will say I will do for you,	15. כָּל שַׁעַר עַמִּי everybody (Literally: every gate of my people) חַיִל valor כִּי יוֹדֵעַ כָּל שַׁעַר עַמִּי כִּי אֵשֶׁת חַיִל אָתְּ:
15. because everybody knows that you are a woman of valor."	

Ruth 3:7 וַיֹּאכַל בֹּעַז וַיֵּשְׁתְּ וַיִּיטַב לִבּוֹ וַיָּבֹא לִשְׁכַּב בִּקְצֵה הָעֲרֵמָה וַתָּבֹא בַלָּט וַתְּגַל מַרְגְּלֹתָיו וַתִּשְׁכָּב:

Ruth 3:8 וַיְהִי בַּחֲצִי הַלַּיְלָה וַיֶּחֱרַד הָאִישׁ וַיִּלָּפֵת וְהִנֵּה אִשָּׁה שֹׁכֶבֶת מַרְגְּלֹתָיו:

Ruth 3:9 וַיֹּאמֶר מִי אָתְּ וַתֹּאמֶר אָנֹכִי רוּת אֲמָתֶךָ וּפָרַשְׂתָּ כְנָפֶךָ עַל אֲמָתְךָ כִּי גֹאֵל אָתָּה:

Ruth 3:10 וַיֹּאמֶר בְּרוּכָה אַתְּ לַיהוה בִּתִּי הֵיטַבְתְּ חַסְדֵּךְ הָאַחֲרוֹן מִן הָרִאשׁוֹן לְבִלְתִּי לֶכֶת אַחֲרֵי הַבַּחוּרִים אִם דַּל וְאִם עָשִׁיר: Ruth 3:11 וְעַתָּה בִּתִּי אַל תִּירְאִי כֹּל אֲשֶׁר תֹּאמְרִי אֶעֱשֶׂה לָּךְ כִּי יוֹדֵעַ כָּל שַׁעַר עַמִּי כִּי אֵשֶׁת חַיִל אָתְּ:

Chapter 27
Hollow Verbs in the הִפְעִיל Pattern

Vocabulary

come, go *vb*........................	ב.ו.א (פָּעַל)
cause to come, bring *vb*..............	(הִפְעִיל)
understand *vb*	ב.י.ן (הִפְעִיל)
gold *n, m*	זָהָב
set up, prepare *vb*..................	כ.ו.ן (הִפְעִיל)
turn aside *vb*	ס.ו.ר (פָּעַל)
remove, take away *vb*	(הִפְעִיל)
time *n, f*	עֵת, עִתִּים
arise, stand up *vb*	ק.ו.ם (פָּעַל)
cause to stand, set up, establish *vb*	(הִפְעִיל)
return *vb*........................	ש.ו.ב (פָּעַל)
cause to return, bring back *vb*.........	(הִפְעִיל)
chief, officer, captain *n, m*	שַׂר, שָׂרִים

Note: The word זָהָב gold, has no plural form.

Hollow Verbs in the הִפְעִיל Pattern

You have already learned the conjugation of hollow verbs in the פָּעַל pattern. Many of the hollow verb roots which you learned in the פָּעַל pattern are also found in the הִפְעִיל pattern. Such hollow verb roots which can be conjugated in פָּעַל and הִפְעִיל, usually have a causative meaning in the הִפְעִיל pattern.

Examples:	Meaning in הִפְעִיל	Meaning in פָּעַל	Root
	cause to come, bring	come	ב.ו.א
	cause to return, bring back	return	ש.ו.ב

Hollow verb roots in the הִפְעִיל pattern do not necessarily have a causative meaning. They may also have the same simple active meaning as do verbs in the פָּעַל pattern.

Example: understand ב.י.ן (הִפְעִיל)   set up, prepare כ.ו.ן (הִפְעִיל)

The middle root letter ו or י, which causes major variations in the conjugation of the פָּעַל pattern, also causes major variations in the הִפְעִיל pattern. In this chapter, you will learn the conjugation of hollow verbs in the הִפְעִיל pattern.

203

The Conjugation of the Hollow Verb in the הִפְעִיל Pattern

Following are charts showing the conjugation of the hollow verb שׁ.ו.ב in the הִפְעִיל pattern. Hollow verbs with the middle root letter י, as well as those with middle root letter ו, usually follow this same conjugation in the הִפְעִיל pattern. Compare the conjugation of the hollow verb שׁ.ו.ב in the הִפְעִיל pattern to its conjugation in the פָּעַל pattern, and to the conjugation of the regular הִפְעִיל verb שׁ.ל.ך.

The Perfect Tense

	(פָּעַל) return — שׁ.ו.ב	(הִפְעִיל) bring back — שׁ.ו.ב		(הִפְעִיל) throw — שׁ.ל.ך
1 c sg	שַׁבְתִּי	הֲשִׁיבוֹתִי/הֲשַׁבְתִּי	הֲאִיאוֹתִי/הֵאֵאתִי	הִשְׁלַכְתִּי
2 m sg	שַׁבְתָּ	הֲשִׁיבוֹתָ/הֲשַׁבְתָּ	הֲאִיאוֹתָ/הֵאֵאתָ	הִשְׁלַכְתָּ
2 f sg	שַׁבְתְּ	הֲשִׁיבוֹת/הֲשַׁבְתְּ	הֲאִיאוֹת/הֵאֵאתְ	הִשְׁלַכְתְּ
3 m sg	שָׁב	הֵשִׁיב	הֵאִיא	הִשְׁלִיךְ
3 f sg	שָׁבָה	הֵשִׁיבָה	הֵאִיאָה	הִשְׁלִיכָה
1 c pl	שַׁבְנוּ	הֲשִׁיבוֹנוּ/הֲשַׁבְנוּ	הֲאִיאוֹנוּ/הֵאֵאנוּ	הִשְׁלַכְנוּ
2 m pl	שַׁבְתֶּם	הֲשִׁיבוֹתֶם	הֲאִיאוֹתֶם	הִשְׁלַכְתֶּם
2 f pl	שַׁבְתֶּן	הֲשִׁיבוֹתֶן	הֲאִיאוֹתֶן	הִשְׁלַכְתֶּן
3 c pl	שָׁבוּ	הֵשִׁיבוּ	הֵאִיאוּ	הִשְׁלִיכוּ

1. Notice that there are two forms for the first person singular and plural and for the second person singular.
2. As in regular הִפְעִיל verbs, the prefix ה appears in all forms.

The Imperfect Tense

	(פָּעַל) return — שׁ.ו.ב	(הִפְעִיל) bring back — שׁ.ו.ב		(הִפְעִיל) throw — שׁ.ל.ך
1 c sg	אָשׁוּב	אָשִׁיב	אָאִיא	אַשְׁלִיךְ
2 m sg	תָּשׁוּב	תָּשִׁיב	תָּאִיא	תַּשְׁלִיךְ
2 f sg	תָּשׁוּבִי	תָּשִׁיבִי	תָּאִיאִי	תַּשְׁלִיכִי
3 m sg	יָשׁוּב	יָשִׁיב	יָאִיא	יַשְׁלִיךְ
3 f sg	תָּשׁוּב	תָּשִׁיב	תָּאִיא	תַּשְׁלִיךְ
1 c pl	נָשׁוּב	נָשִׁיב	נָאִיא	נַשְׁלִיךְ
2 m pl	תָּשׁוּבוּ	תָּשִׁיבוּ	תָּאִיאוּ	תַּשְׁלִיכוּ
2 f pl	תָּשׁוּבֶינָה/תָּשֹׁבְנָה	תָּשֵׁבְנָה	תָּאֵאנָה	תַּשְׁלֵכְנָה
3 m pl	יָשׁוּבוּ	יָשִׁיבוּ	יָאִיאוּ ·	יַשְׁלִיכוּ
3 f pl	תָּשׁוּבֶינָה/תָּשֹׁבְנָה	תָּשֵׁבְנָה	תָּאֵאנָה	תַּשְׁלֵכְנָה

1. The basic vowel pattern for the hollow verbs in the הִפְעִיל is אָאִיX instead of the XאָאִX pattern of regular הִפְעִיל verbs.

2. As in regular הִפְעִיל verbs, the prefix ה disappears, and the regular prefix and suffix consonants are added. The אִי vowel, characteristic of the הִפְעִיל pattern, appears in all forms except the feminine plural.

3. Unlike hollow verbs in the פָּעַל pattern, when the middle root letters י or ו appear, they appear as the אִי vowel.

The Participle

	(פָּעַל) return — שׁ.ו.ב	(הִפְעִיל) bring back — שׁ.ו.ב		(הִפְעִיל) throw — שׁ.ל.ך
m sg	שָׁב	מֵשִׁיב	מֵאִיא	מַשְׁלִיך
f sg	שָׁבָה	מְשִׁיבָה	מְאִיאָה	מַשְׁלִיכָה/מַשְׁלֶכֶת
m pl	שָׁבִים	מְשִׁיבִים	מְאִיאִים	מַשְׁלִיכִים
f pl	שָׁבוֹת	מְשִׁיבוֹת	מְאִיאוֹת	מַשְׁלִיכוֹת

1. As in regular הִפְעִיל verbs, the prefix ה is replaced by the prefix מ in the participle. The אִי vowel, characteristic of the הִפְעִיל pattern, appears in all forms.

2. The endings of the participle of hollow הִפְעִיל verbs are the same as the endings of the participle in the פָּעַל pattern.

The Imperative

	(פָּעַל) return — שׁ.ו.ב	(הִפְעִיל) bring back — שׁ.ו.ב		(הִפְעִיל) throw — שׁ.ל.ך
m sg	שׁוּב	הָשֵׁב	הָאֵXX	הַשְׁלֵך
f sg	שׁוּבִי	הָשִׁיבִי	הָאִיאִי	הַשְׁלִיכִי
m pl	שׁוּבוּ	הָשִׁיבוּ	הָאִיאוּ	הַשְׁלִיכוּ
f pl	שֹׁבְנָה	הָשֵׁבְנָה	הָאֵאְנָה	הַשְׁלֵכְנָה

As in regular הִפְעִיל verbs, the prefix ה appears in the imperative. The אִי vowel, characteristic of the הִפְעִיל pattern, appears in the *f sg* and *m pl* forms.

The Infinitive

	(פָּעַל) return — שׁ.ו.ב	(הִפְעִיל) bring back — שׁ.ו.ב		(הִפְעִיל) throw — שׁ.ל.ך
absolute	שׁוֹב	הָשֵׁב	הָאֵXX	הַשְׁלֵך
construct	לָשׁוּב	(לְ) הָשִׁיב לְהָשִׁיב	לְהָאִיא	לְהַשְׁלִיך

As in regular הִפְעִיל verbs, the prefix ה appears in both infinitives. The אִי vowel, characteristic of the הִפְעִיל pattern, appears in the infinitive construct.

205

The Verb ב.ו.א in the הִפְעִיל Pattern

In the הִפְעִיל pattern, the perfect tense of the verb ב.ו.א differs from the perfect tense of other hollow verbs, because its third root letter is א, one of the throaty five letters. Following is a chart showing the verb roots ב.ו.א and ש.ו.ב, conjugated in the perfect tense of the הִפְעִיל pattern. In all other forms of the הִפְעִיל pattern, the verb ב.ו.א is conjugated the same way as other hollow verbs.

	(הִפְעִיל) bring — ב.ו.א	(הִפְעִיל) bring back — ש.ו.ב
1 c sg	הֵבֵאתִי	הֲשִׁיבֹותִי/הֲשַׁבְתִּי
2 m sg	הֵבֵאתָ	הֲשִׁיבֹות/הֲשַׁבְתָּ
2 f sg	הֵבֵאת	הֲשִׁיבֹות/הֲשַׁבְתְּ
3 m sg	הֵבִיא	הֵשִׁיב
3 f sg	הֵבִיאָה	הֵשִׁיבָה
1 c pl	הֵבֵאנוּ	הֲשִׁיבֹונוּ/הֲשַׁבְנוּ
2 m pl	הֲבֵאתֶם	הֲשִׁיבֹותֶם
2 f pl	הֲבֵאתֶן	הֲשִׁיבֹותֶן
3 c pl	הֵבִיאוּ	הֵשִׁיבוּ

There are no alternate forms for the conjugation of the verb ב.ו.א in the perfect tense of the הִפְעִיל pattern.

Hollow Verbs in the הִפְעִיל with the Reversing Vav

The imperfect tense of hollow verbs in the הִפְעִיל pattern often has a shortened form when the reversing vav is added. Notice the difference between the shortened forms of הִפְעִיל hollow verbs, and the shortened forms of פָּעַל hollow verbs.

Examples:

Imperfect פָּעַל with Reversing Vav	Imperfect הִפְעִיל with Reversing Vav	Imperfect הִפְעִיל	Root
וַיֵּשֶׁב	וַיָּשֶׁב	יָשִׁיב	ש.ו.ב
וַיָּקָם	וַיָּקֶם	יָקִים	ק.ו.ם
וַיָּסַר	וַיָּסַר	יָסִיר	ס.ו.ר

Some verbs, like ס.ו.ר, have the same shortened forms in both the פָּעַל and הִפְעִיל patterns. The correct meaning can usually be determined from the context.

Exercises

Exercise 1. Conjugate the following roots in all forms of the verb pattern given.

3. נ.צ.ל (הִפְעִיל)   2. ס.ו.ר (הִפְעִיל)   1. ס.ו.ר (פָּעַל)

Exercise 2. Rewrite the sentences below, replacing the underlined word with each word in the list that follows. Every word or grammatical form in the sentence that agrees with the underlined word should be changed to agree with the newly substituted words. Read the sentences aloud. Translate.

1. בָּעֵת הַהִיא (אַתֶּם) הֲקִימוֹתֶם בַּיִת חָדָשׁ בָּעִיר.

E. הִיא	D. אֲנַחְנוּ	C. אַתְּ	B. הֵנָּה	A. הוּא
	I. הֵמָּה	H. אַתֵּן	G. אֲנִי	F. אַתָּה

2. הַשַּׂר צִוָּה אֶת אֲנָשָׁיו לְהַצִּיל אֶת אַנְשֵׁי בֵּית לֶחֶם.

E. ס.ו.ר	D. ז.כ.ר	C. ב.ו.א	B. ג.ד.ל	A. שׁ.ו.ב

3. בָּעֵת הַהִיא, הֵמָּה יָסִירוּ אֶת בְּגָדָיו וְיַלְבִּישׁוּ אֹתוֹ בִּגְדֵי שַׂר.

E. הִיא	D. אַתָּה	C. אַתֵּן	B. הוּא	A. אֲנִי
	I. אַתְּ	H. אַתֶּם	G. אֲנַחְנוּ	F. הֵנָּה

4. אֲנַחְנוּ מְכִינִים אֶת הָאֹכֶל לַשַּׂר.

E. אֲנִי	D. אַתָּה	C. הֵנָּה	B. אַתֶּם	A. אַתְּ
		H. הִיא	G. הוּא	F. אַתֵּן

5. הוּא יָשׁוּב מֵהֶהָרִים וְיָבִיא לָנוּ כֶּסֶף וְזָהָב.

E. אַתָּה	D. הִיא	C. אֲנִי	B. הַנָּשִׁים	A. הֵמָּה
	I. אַתֶּם	H. אַתְּ	G. אֲנַחְנוּ	F. אַתֵּן

6. (אַתְּ) שַׁבְתְּ מִמִּצְרַיִם וְהֵשַׁבְתְּ אֶת הַנַּעַר לְמִשְׁפַּחְתּוֹ.

E. הֵנָּה	D. הוּא	C. אֲנַחְנוּ	B. אַתֵּן	A. הֵם
	I. אַתָּה	H. אַתֶּם	G. הִיא	F. אֲנִי

7. אֵינֶנִּי מֵבִין אֶת אֲשֶׁר הֵנָּה סִפְּרוּ לִי.

E. אֵינֵךְ	D. אֵינָן	C. אֵינְךָ	B. אֵינֶנּוּ (הוּא)	A. אֵינְכֶם
	I. אֵינָם	H. אֵינֶנּוּ (אֲנַחְנוּ)	G. אֵינֶנָּה	F. אֵינְכֶן

Exercise 3. Rewrite the following sentences, filling in the blanks with all forms of the verb root shown that will yield a meaningful sentence. Translate.

Example:

כ.ו.ן   (אַתָּה) _____ אֶת הַכֵּלִים בַּמִּשְׁכָּן.

הֲכִינוֹתָ אֶת הַכֵּלִים בַּמִּשְׁכָּן.

תָּכִין אֶת הַכֵּלִים בַּמִּשְׁכָּן.

הָכֵן אֶת הַכֵּלִים בַּמִּשְׁכָּן.

אַתָּה מֵכִין אֶת הַכֵּלִים בַּמִּשְׁכָּן.

הָכֵן הֲכִינוֹתָ אֶת הַכֵּלִים בַּמִּשְׁכָּן.

הָכֵן תָּכִין אֶת הַכֵּלִים בַּמִּשְׁכָּן.

1. ס.ו.ר   (אַתֶּם) _____ לִרְאוֹת אֶת רֹאשׁ הָהָר וְ_____ אֶת הָאֲבָנִים מֵהַדֶּרֶךְ.

2. ש.ו.ב   (אַתֶּן) _____ לְאֶרֶץ אֲבוֹתֵיכֶן וְ_____ עִמְּכֶן אֶת הַזָּהָב וְאֶת הַכֶּסֶף.

3. ב.ו.א   (אַתְּ) _____ לִרְאוֹת אֶת אָבִי וְ_____ לוֹ פְּרִי וְיַיִן.

4. ק.ו.ם   (הֵמָּה) _____ וְ_____ אֶת שַׁעַר עִירָם.

5. נ.ג.ד   הַשַּׂר _____ לַאֲנָשָׁיו מָה עֲלֵיהֶם לַעֲשׂוֹת.

6. ב.ק.שׁ   (הִיא) _____ לָדַעַת אֶת הָאֱמֶת.

7. ב.י.ן   (אֲנַחְנוּ) _____ אֶת דִּבְרֵי הַשּׁוֹפֵט.

Exercise 4. Read and translate the following sentences. Underline all verb forms that are shortened by the addition of a reversing vav.

1. וַיָּבוֹא הָאִישׁ הֶחָכָם בָּעֵת הַהִיא מֵרֹאשׁ הָהָר וַיָּבֵא אֶת בְּנוֹ עִמּוֹ.

2. וַיֵּשֶׁב הַשַּׂר מִכְּנַעַן וַיָּשֶׁב עִמּוֹ אֶת הַזָּהָב וַיַּגֵּד לָנוּ אֶת כָּל אֲשֶׁר שָׁמַע שָׁם.

3. וַיְבַקְשׁוּ הָאֲנָשִׁים הָרָעִים לְהָסִיר אֶת הַשַּׂר וַיַּצֵּל דָּוִד אֹתוֹ.

4. וַיֹּאכַל וַיֵּשְׁתְּ הָאִישׁ לְעֵת עֶרֶב וַתָּסַר הָאִשָּׁה אֶת הָאֹכֶל.

5. וַיֵּלֶךְ הָאִישׁ יְרוּשָׁלַיְמָה וַיִּבֶן אֶת בֵּיתוֹ שָׁם וַיְגַדֵּל אֶת מִשְׁפַּחְתּוֹ.

Exercise 5. Identify the root and the verb pattern of the following verb forms. Translate.

16. קָמוּ	11. בָּאוּ	6. אוֹכַל	1. בָּחַרְתִּי
17. רָאוּ	12. בּוֹא	7. יָשַׁבְתִּי	2. תִּגְנֹב
18. רְאוּ	13. יָבִיאוּ	8. שַׁבְתִּי	3. זוֹכְרִים
19. מְכִינוֹת	14. מֵבִיא	9. יָשִׁיב	4. לָדַעַת
20. אָכִין	15. לְהָקִים	10. תָּשֵׁבְנָה	5. אוֹכֵל

Exercise 6. Read and translate.

Vocabulary for Reading Selection

tower............	מִגְדָּל	Simon *man's name*........	שִׁמְעוֹן
another..............	אַחֵר, אַחֶרֶת	strong..............	חָזָק
all of them...........	כֻּלָּם	but..............	אַךְ
one another..........	אִישׁ אֶת אָחִיו	Babel..............	בָּבֶל

הָיָה אִישׁ אֲשֶׁר יָשַׁב בְּמוֹאָב וּשְׁמוֹ שִׁמְעוֹן. הוּא הָיָה חָזָק מְאֹד אַךְ לֹא חָכָם מְאֹד.

וַיְבַקֵּשׁ שִׁמְעוֹן לְהַגְדִּיל אֶת שְׁמוֹ. וַיִּשְׁמַע כִּי אַנְשֵׁי בָּבֶל בּוֹנִים מִגְדָּל וְרֹאשׁוֹ בַּשָּׁמָיִם. וַיֹּאמֶר שִׁמְעוֹן בְּלִבּוֹ: "אֵלֵךְ אֶל בָּבֶל וְאֶבְנֶה אֶת הַמִּגְדָּל. אוּכַל לְצַוֹּת אֶת הָאֲנָשִׁים לַעֲשׂוֹת אֶת הַכֹּל כִּי אֲנִי חָזָק מְאֹד."

וַיֵּלֶךְ שִׁמְעוֹן וַיָּבוֹא אֶל בָּבֶל וַיַּרְא אֶת הָאֲנָשִׁים הַבּוֹנִים אֶת הַמִּגְדָּל.

וַיֹּאמֶר לָהֶם שִׁמְעוֹן: "אֲנִי שִׁמְעוֹן! בָּאתִי לִהְיוֹת שַׂר עֲלֵיכֶם. אוּכַל לְהָקִים אֲבָנִים גְּדוֹלוֹת לַמִּגְדָּל כִּי אֲנִי חָזָק מְאֹד."

"¡Buenos dias!" :וַיַּעַן אִישׁ אֶחָד

וַיֹּאמֶר שִׁמְעוֹן: "מַה?"

"Aloha!" :וַיַּעַן אִישׁ אַחֵר

וַיֹּאמֶר שִׁמְעוֹן: "מַה?!"

"I can't understand a word you're saying, :וַיֹּאמֶר אִישׁ אַחֵר
why don't you just speak in English?"

וַיֹּאמֶר שִׁמְעוֹן: "מַה אַתֶּם אוֹמְרִים? אֵינֶנִּי מֵבִין אֶתְכֶם."

וַיִּשְׁמַע זָקֵן אֶחָד אֶת דִּבְרֵי שִׁמְעוֹן וַיָּרָץ אֵלָיו וַיֹּאמֶר: "אַתָּה מְדַבֵּר כָּמוֹנִי! אֵין אֲנָשִׁים בַּמָּקוֹם הַזֶּה הַמְדַבְּרִים כָּמוֹנוּ!"

וַיְסַפֵּר הַזָּקֵן לְשִׁמְעוֹן לֵאמֹר: "כַּאֲשֶׁר קַמְתִּי בַּבֹּקֶר וְשָׁמַעְתִּי אֶת דִּבְרֵי אִשְׁתִּי, לֹא הֵבַנְתִּי אֶת אֲשֶׁר אָמְרָה. בִּקַּשְׁתִּי לְדַבֵּר עִם בָּנַי וְהֵמָּה לֹא הֵבִינוּ אֶת דְּבָרַי. צִוִּיתִי אֹתָם לִבְנוֹת אֶת הַמִּגְדָּל עִם אַנְשֵׁי הָעִיר וְהֵם לֹא שָׁמְעוּ בְּקוֹלִי. הָלַכְתִּי לְסַפֵּר לְאַנְשֵׁי עִירִי עַל מַעֲשֵׂי בְּנֵי הָרָעִים וְכֻלָּם לֹא הֵבִינוּ אֹתִי. כָּל אַנְשֵׁי הָעִיר הַזֹּאת אֵינָם מְבִינִים אִישׁ אֶת אָחִיו."

וַיֹּאמֶר שִׁמְעוֹן: "בָּאתִי לִהְיוֹת שַׂר עַל הָאֲנָשִׁים הַבּוֹנִים אֶת הַמִּגְדָּל. אַךְ לֹא אוּכַל לְצַוֹּת אֹתָם אִם הֵם לֹא יָבִינוּ אֶת אֲשֶׁר אֹמַר לָהֶם. אֵלֵךְ אֶל עִיר אַחֶרֶת לְהַגְדִּיל שָׁם אֶת שְׁמִי."

וַיֹּאמֶר שִׁמְעוֹן: "שָׁלוֹם" וַיֵּלֶךְ.

וַיַּעַן הַזָּקֵן: "שָׁלוֹם!".

"¡Adios!" :וַיַּעַן אִישׁ אַחֵר

"Bon voyage!" :וַיַּעַן אִישׁ אַחֵר

"Ciao!" :וַיַּעַן אִישׁ אַחֵר

"See you later!" :וַיַּעַן אִישׁ אַחֵר

Exercise 7. Fill in the proper form of the verb in the last column and translate.

Root	Number	Gender	Person	Tense	Pattern	Word
שׁ.כ.ח	sg	f	2	perfect	פָּעַל	1
ז.כ.ר	sg	m	2	perfect	פָּעַל	2
ז.כ.ר	sg	m	2	perfect	הִפְעִיל	3
נ.צ.ל	sg	m	2	perfect	הִפְעִיל	4
ב.ו.א	pl	m	2	perfect	פָּעַל	5
ב.ו.א	pl	m	2	perfect	הִפְעִיל	6
כ.ו.ן	pl	m	2	perfect	הִפְעִיל	7
שׁ.ו.ב	pl	c	1	perfect	הִפְעִיל	8
ר.א.ה	pl	c	1	perfect	פָּעַל	9
שׁ.ת.ה	pl	c	1	imperfect	פָּעַל	10
ס.פ.ר	pl	c	1	imperfect	פָּעַל	11
ס.פ.ר	pl	c	1	imperfect	פִּעֵל	12
ד.ב.ר	sg	c	1	imperfect	פִּעֵל	13
צ.ו.ה	sg	c	1	imperfect	פִּעֵל	14
ג.ד.ל	sg	c	1	imperfect	פָּעַל	15
ג.ד.ל	sg	c	1	imperfect	הִפְעִיל	16
שׁ.ל.ך	sg	f	—	participle	הִפְעִיל	17
ס.ו.ר	sg	f	—	participle	הִפְעִיל	18
ק.ו.ם	sg	m	—	participle	הִפְעִיל	19
ק.ו.ם	sg	m	—	participle	פָּעַל	20
ק.ו.ם	sg	m	—	imperative	פָּעַל	21
ק.ו.ם	sg	m	—	imperative	הִפְעִיל	22
ק.ו.ם	sg	f	—	imperative	הִפְעִיל	23
ק.ו.ם	pl	f	—	imperative	הִפְעִיל	24

From the Prayerbook

Prayerbook Vocabulary

pleasantness	נֹעַם	grasp, take hold of	ח.ז.ק (הִפְעִיל)
pathway	נָתִיב	support, hold up	ת.מ.ך (פָּעַל)
make new	ח.ד.ש (פִּעֵל)	happy	מְאֻשָּׁר
	in ancient times, in the past	קֶדֶם	

Selection from the Prayerbook (from the conclusion of the Torah service)

עֵץ חַיִּים הִיא לַמַּחֲזִיקִים בָּהּ וְתֹמְכֶיהָ מְאֻשָּׁר:
דְּרָכֶיהָ דַרְכֵי נֹעַם וְכָל נְתִיבוֹתֶיהָ שָׁלוֹם:
הֲשִׁיבֵנוּ יְיָ אֵלֶיךָ וְנָשׁוּבָה חַדֵּשׁ יָמֵינוּ כְּקֶדֶם:

First translate the prayer into your own words, then read the translations quoted below.

Prayerbook Translations

"It is a Tree of Life to them that hold fast to it,
And everyone that upholds it is happy.
Its ways are ways of pleasantness,
And all its paths are peace.
Turn us unto Thee, O Lord, and we shall return;
Renew our days as of old."

Sabbath and Festival Prayer Book, Morris Silverman, 1946, p. 136

"It is a tree of life to those who hold it fast, and all who cling to it find happiness. Its ways are ways of pleasantness, and all its paths are peace. Help us to return to You, O Lord; then truly shall we return. Renew our days as in the past."

Gates of Prayer, The New Union Prayerbook, 1975, p. 436

1. The word הִיא "it" in this prayer refers to the Torah.
2. Notice in the last line that the hollow verb ש.ו.ב is conjugated in both the פָּעַל pattern and the הִפְעִיל pattern.
3. Notice the direct object endings attached to the verbs ת.מ.ך and ש.ו.ב (see Chapter 19).

הֲשִׁיבֵנוּ = הָשֵׁב אֹתָנוּ
תֹמְכֶיהָ = תֹמְכִים אֹתָהּ

211

Guided Reading from Ruth

	Ruth 3:12 1.
	אָמְנָם truly
	כִּי, כִּי אִם *best left untranslated*
	ג.א.ל redeem, act as kinsman
	וְעַתָּה כִּי אָמְנָם כִּי אִם גֹּאֵל אָנֹכִי
1. "And now, truly I am a redeemer,	וְ־ but 2.
	קָרוֹב near, close, related
	וְגַם יֵשׁ גֹּאֵל קָרוֹב מִמֶּנִּי:
2. but there is also a redeemer who is a closer relative than I.	Ruth 3:13 3.
	ל.י.ן (פָּעַל) lodge, spend the night
	לִינִי הַלַּיְלָה
3. Lodge (here) tonight,	יִגְאָלֵךְ = יִגְאַל אֹתָךְ 4.
	וְהָיָה בַבֹּקֶר אִם יִגְאָלֵךְ טוֹב יִגְאָל
4. and it shall come to pass in the morning, if he will act as a kinsman to you, good, let him act as a kinsman.	ח.פ.ץ be pleased 5.
	לְגָאֳלֵךְ = לִגְאַל אֹתָךְ
	וְאִם לֹא יַחְפֹּץ לְגָאֳלֵךְ
5. But if he is not pleased to act as a kinsman to you,	וּגְאַלְתִּיךְ = וְגָאַלְתִּי אֹתָךְ 6.
	חַי יהוה "as the Lord lives"
	oath formula
	וּגְאַלְתִּיךְ אָנֹכִי חַי יהוה
6. I will act as a kinsman to you, as the Lord lives!	שִׁכְבִי עַד הַבֹּקֶר: 7.
7. Lie down until morning."	Ruth 3:14 8.
	מַרְגְּלוֹת place of the feet
	וַתִּשְׁכַּב מַרְגְּלוֹתָו עַד הַבֹּקֶר
8. And she lay down (at) the place of his feet until morning.	בְּטֶרֶם before 9.
	נ.כ.ר (הִפְעִיל) recognize
	רֵעֵהוּ another (person)
	וַתָּקָם בְּטֶרֶם יַכִּיר אִישׁ אֶת רֵעֵהוּ
9. And she arose before a man could recognize another. (before daylight)	יִוָּדַע it will be known 10.
	גֹּרֶן threshing-floor
	וַיֹּאמֶר אַל יִוָּדַע כִּי בָאָה הָאִשָּׁה הַגֹּרֶן:

10. And he said: "Let it not be known that the woman came (to) the threshing floor."	11. Ruth 3:15 הָבִי *Give! f sg imperative* מִטְפַּחַת cloak וַיֹּאמֶר הָבִי הַמִּטְפַּחַת אֲשֶׁר עָלַיִךְ
11. And he said: "Give (me) the cloak that is upon you	12. א.ח.ז (פָּעַל) hold וְאֶחֳזִי בָהּ וַתֹּאחֶז בָּהּ
12. and hold it." And she held it.	13. וַיָּמָד and he measured שֵׁשׁ six שְׂעֹרִים barley וַיָּמָד שֵׁשׁ שְׂעֹרִים
13. And he measured six (measures) of barley,	14. וַיָּשֶׁת and he set וַיָּשֶׁת עָלֶיהָ וַיָּבֹא הָעִיר:
14. and he set (it) upon her, and he came (to) the city.	

Ruth 3:12 וְעַתָּה כִּי אָמְנָם כִּי אִם גֹּאֵל אָנֹכִי וְגַם יֵשׁ גֹּאֵל קָרוֹב מִמֶּנִּי:

Ruth 3:13 לִינִי הַלַּיְלָה וְהָיָה בַבֹּקֶר אִם יִגְאָלֵךְ טוֹב יִגְאָל וְאִם לֹא יַחְפֹּץ לְגָאֳלֵךְ וּגְאַלְתִּיךְ אָנֹכִי חַי יהוה שִׁכְבִי עַד הַבֹּקֶר:

Ruth 3:14 וַתִּשְׁכַּב מַרְגְּלוֹתָו עַד הַבֹּקֶר וַתָּקָם בְּטֶרֶם יַכִּיר אִישׁ אֶת רֵעֵהוּ וַיֹּאמֶר אַל יִוָּדַע כִּי בָאָה הָאִשָּׁה הַגֹּרֶן:

Ruth 3:15 וַיֹּאמֶר הָבִי הַמִּטְפַּחַת אֲשֶׁר עָלַיִךְ וְאֶחֳזִי בָהּ וַתֹּאחֶז בָּהּ וַיָּמָד שֵׁשׁ שְׂעֹרִים וַיָּשֶׁת עָלֶיהָ וַיָּבֹא הָעִיר:

Chapter 28
The Nif'al נִפְעַל Pattern

Vocabulary

ram *n, m*	אַיִל, אֵילִים
strong, mighty *adj*	גִּבּוֹר, גִּבּוֹרִים
blood *n, m*	דָּם, דָּמִים
strength, army *n, m*	חַיִל, חֲיָלִים
sword *n, f*	חֶרֶב, חֲרָבוֹת
fight, do battle *vb*	ל.ח.ם (נִפְעַל)
messenger, angel *n, m*	מַלְאָךְ, מַלְאָכִים
battle, war *n, f*	מִלְחָמָה, מִלְחָמוֹת
pour out, pour *vb*	ש.פ.ך (פָּעַל)
be poured out *vb*	(נִפְעַל)

Idioms

shed blood	ש.פ.ך דָּם
mighty man of valor	גִּבּוֹר חַיִל
woman of valor	אֵשֶׁת חַיִל

Note: There are no feminine forms of the adjective גִּבּוֹר — strong, mighty — in the Bible.

Active and Passive Verb Patterns

An active verb is a verb which describes an action that the subject of the sentence **does**.

Example: The lad **takes** the book.

The verb **takes** describes what the subject **lad** does.

A passive verb is a verb which describes an action that **is done** to the subject of the sentence.

Example: The book **is taken**.

The verb **is taken** describes what is done to the subject **book**.

214

Hebrew, like English, has both passive and active verb forms. There are three active verb patterns and three passive verb patterns. You have already learned the three active verb patterns: the פָּעַל, the פִּעֵל, and the הִפְעִיל. Verbs conjugated in these patterns have an active meaning; they describe action that the subject of the sentence does.

Examples:	Translation	Verb	Pattern
	he guarded	שָׁמַר	פָּעַל
	he recounted	סִפֵּר	פִּעֵל
	he reminded	הִזְכִּיר	הִפְעִיל

Each of these three active patterns has a corresponding passive pattern. Verbs conjugated in the three passive patterns have a passive meaning; they describe action that is done to the subject of the sentence.

The following chart shows the three active verb patterns, and the three corresponding passive verb patterns.

Hif'il הִפְעִיל	Pi'el פִּעֵל	Pa'al פָּעַל	Active
Hof'al הֻפְעַל	Pu'al פֻּעַל	Nif'al נִפְעַל	Passive

The Nif'al נִפְעַל Pattern

In this chapter, you will learn the conjugation of the נִפְעַל pattern, which is the passive pattern corresponding to the active פָּעַל pattern. Below is a list of the verbs you have learned in the פָּעַל pattern which also appear in the נִפְעַל pattern.

Meaning in נִפְעַל	Meaning in פָּעַל	Root
be chosen	choose	ב.ח.ר
be stolen	steal	ג.נ.ב
be remembered	remember	ז.כ.ר
be written	write	כ.ת.ב
be taken	take	ל.ק.ח
be opened	open	פ.ת.ח
be forgotten	forget	ש.כ.ח
be sent	send	ש.ל.ח
be heard	hear	ש.מ.ע
be guarded	guard	ש.מ.ר
be judged	judge	ש.פ.ט
be poured out	pour out	ש.פ.ך

Some verb roots appear in the נִפְעַל pattern but do not have a passive meaning. Such נִפְעַל verbs often have the same simple active meaning as do verbs in the פָּעַל pattern.

Example: fight, do battle ל.ח.ם (נִפְעַל)

The Conjugation of Verbs in the נִפְעַל Pattern

Following are charts showing the conjugation of the regular verb ש.מ.ר in the נִפְעַל pattern. Compare this to the conjugation of the same root in the פָּעַל pattern. The important characteristic of the נִפְעַל pattern is the prefix נ with the X vowel — נַ. This prefix appears in the perfect tense, the participle, and the infinitive absolute. Read aloud the conjugations of the verb ש.מ.ר in both the נִפְעַל and the פָּעַל patterns, so that you can hear the differences between the two patterns.

The Perfect Tense

	be guarded — (נִפְעַל) ש.מ.ר		guard — (פָּעַל) ש.מ.ר
1 c sg	נִשְׁמַרְתִּי	נִֽXXXְתִּי	שָׁמַרְתִּי
2 m sg	נִשְׁמַרְתָּ	נִXXXְתָּ	שָׁמַרְתָּ
2 f sg	נִשְׁמַרְתְּ	נִXXXְתְּ	שָׁמַרְתְּ
3 m sg	נִשְׁמַר	נִXXX	שָׁמַר
3 f sg	נִשְׁמְרָה	נִXXְXָה	שָׁמְרָה
1 c pl	נִשְׁמַרְנוּ	נִXXXְנוּ	שָׁמַרְנוּ
2 m pl	נִשְׁמַרְתֶּם	נִXXXְתֶּם	שְׁמַרְתֶּם
2 f pl	נִשְׁמַרְתֶּן	נִXXXְתֶּן	שְׁמַרְתֶּן
3 c pl	נִשְׁמְרוּ	נִXXְXוּ	שָׁמְרוּ

1. The prefix נַ, characteristic of the נִפְעַל pattern, appears in all the forms of the perfect tense.

2. The endings in the perfect tense of the נִפְעַל pattern are exactly the same as the endings in the perfect tense of the פָּעַל pattern.

The Imperfect Tense

	be guarded — (נִפְעַל) ש.מ.ר		guard — (פָּעַל) ש.מ.ר
1 c sg	אֶשָּׁמֵר	אֶXָּXֵX	אֶשְׁמֹר
2 m sg	תִּשָּׁמֵר	תִּXָּXֵX	תִּשְׁמֹר
2 f sg	תִּשָּׁמְרִי	תִּXָּXְXִי	תִּשְׁמְרִי
3 m sg	יִשָּׁמֵר	יִXָּXֵX	יִשְׁמֹר
3 f sg	תִּשָּׁמֵר	תִּXָּXֵX	תִּשְׁמֹר
1 c pl	נִשָּׁמֵר	נִXָּXֵX	נִשְׁמֹר
2 m pl	תִּשָּׁמְרוּ	תִּXָּXְXוּ	תִּשְׁמְרוּ
2 f pl	תִּשָּׁמַרְנָה	תִּXָּXַXְנָה	תִּשְׁמֹרְנָה
3 m pl	יִשָּׁמְרוּ	יִXָּXְXוּ	יִשְׁמְרוּ
3 f pl	תִּשָּׁמַרְנָה	תִּXָּXַXְנָה	תִּשְׁמֹרְנָה

1. The basic vowel pattern of נִפְעַל is X̱X̱X̣X̱ , instead of the X̱X̱X̱X̱ or the X̱X̱X̱X̱ pattern of regular פָּעַל verbs.

2. The prefix נִ disappears and is replaced by a dagesh in the first root letter in all the forms of the imperfect tense.

The Participle

	guard — (פָּעַל) ש.מ.ר		be guarded — (נִפְעַל) ש.מ.ר	
m sg	שׁוֹמֵר/שֹׁמֵר	נָX̱X̱	נִשְׁמָר	
f sg	שׁוֹמֶרֶת/שֹׁמֶרֶת, שׁוֹמְרָה/שֹׁמְרָה	נָX̱X̱ת/נָX̱X̱ה	נִשְׁמֶרֶת/נִשְׁמָרָה	
m pl	שׁוֹמְרִים/שֹׁמְרִים	נָX̱X̱ים	נִשְׁמָרִים	
f pl	שׁוֹמְרוֹת/שֹׁמְרוֹת	נָX̱X̱וֹת	נִשְׁמָרוֹת	

1. The prefix נ, characteristic of the נִפְעַל pattern, appears in all the forms of the participle.

2. The only difference between the *m sg* participle and *3 m sg* perfect tense of the נִפְעַל pattern is the vowel of the second root letter. The *m sg* participle takes the X̱ vowel — נִX̱X̱ , while the *3 m sg* perfect tense takes the X̱ vowel — נִX̱X̱.

3. The endings of the participle in the נִפְעַל pattern are exactly the same as the endings of the participle in the פָּעַל pattern.

The Imperative

	guard — (פָּעַל) ש.מ.ר		be guarded — (נִפְעַל) ש.מ.ר	
m sg	שְׁמֹר	הִX̱X̱	הִשָּׁמֵר	
f sg	שִׁמְרִי	הִX̱Xִ̱י	הִשָּׁמְרִי	
m pl	שִׁמְרוּ	הִX̱X̱וּ	הִשָּׁמְרוּ	
f pl	שְׁמֹרְנָה	הִX̱Xְ̱נָה	הִשָּׁמַרְנָה	

1. The imperative takes the prefix ה with the X̱ vowel — הִ.

2. The prefix נ disappears and is replaced by a dagesh in the first root letter in all the forms of the imperative.

The Infinitive

	guard — (פָּעַל) ש.מ.ר		be guarded — (נִפְעַל) ש.מ.ר	
absolute	שָׁמוֹר	נָX̱X̱	נִשְׁמֹר	
construct	לִשְׁמֹר	לְהִX̱X̱	(לְ) הִשָּׁמֵר לְהִשָּׁמֵר	

1. The prefix נ, characteristic of the נִפְעַל pattern, appears in the infinitive absolute.

2. The prefix נ disappears and is replaced by a dagesh in the first root letter in the infinitive construct, and the ה is added as a prefix.

The Verbs ל.ח.ם and ב.ח.ר

The conjugation of the verbs ל.ח.ם and ב.ח.ר in the נִפְעַל pattern is slightly irregular because their middle root letter is ח, one of the throaty five letters. This letter usually does not take a sheva. Therefore, whenever a sheva appears under the second root letter in the regular conjugation, the combination vowel X appears under the letter ח in the verbs ל.ח.ם and ב.ח.ר.

Verbs in the נִפְעַל with ח or ע as Final Root Letter

When the final root letter of a verb is ח or ע, it is conjugated somewhat differently than the regular נִפְעַל verb. The verbs ש.מ.ע, ש.ל.ח, ש.כ.ח, פ.ת.ח, and ל.ק.ח, are examples of this type of verb. Following are charts showing the conjugation of the regular verb ש.מ.ר and the somewhat irregular verb ש.ל.ח in the נִפְעַל pattern. The dots point out the forms that are different. All the verbs listed above are conjugated the same way as the verb ש.ל.ח in the נִפְעַל pattern.

The Perfect Tense

	be sent — ש.ל.ח (נִפְעַל)	be guarded — ש.מ.ר (נִפְעַל)
1 c sg	נִשְׁלַחְתִּי	נִשְׁמַרְתִּי
2 m sg	נִשְׁלַחְתָּ	נִשְׁמַרְתָּ
2 f sg	• נִשְׁלַחַתְּ	נִשְׁמַרְתְּ
3 m sg	נִשְׁלַח	נִשְׁמַר
3 f sg	נִשְׁלְחָה	נִשְׁמְרָה
1 c pl	נִשְׁלַחְנוּ	נִשְׁמַרְנוּ
2 m pl	נִשְׁלַחְתֶּם	נִשְׁמַרְתֶּם
2 f pl	נִשְׁלַחְתֶּן	נִשְׁמַרְתֶּן
3 m pl	נִשְׁלְחוּ	נִשְׁמְרוּ
3 f pl	נִשְׁלְחוּ	נִשְׁמְרוּ

The Imperfect Tense

	be sent — (נִפְעַל) ש.ל.ח	be guarded — (נִפְעַל) ש.מ.ר
1 c sg	• אֶשָּׁלַח	אֶשָּׁמֵר
2 m sg	• תִּשָּׁלַח	תִּשָּׁמֵר
2 f sg	תִּשָּׁלְחִי	תִּשָּׁמְרִי
3 m sg	• יִשָּׁלַח	יִשָּׁמֵר
3 f sg	• תִּשָּׁלַח	תִּשָּׁמֵר
1 c pl	• נִשָּׁלַח	נִשָּׁמֵר
2 m pl	תִּשָּׁלְחוּ	תִּשָּׁמְרוּ
2 f pl	תִּשָּׁלַחְנָה	תִּשָּׁמַרְנָה
3 m pl	יִשָּׁלְחוּ	יִשָּׁמְרוּ
3 f pl	תִּשָּׁלַחְנָה	תִּשָּׁמַרְנָה

The Participle

	be sent — (נִפְעַל) ש.ל.ח	be guarded — (נִפְעַל) ש.מ.ר
m sg	נִשְׁלָח	נִשְׁמָר
f sg	• נִשְׁלַחַת/נִשְׁלָחָה	נִשְׁמֶרֶת/נִשְׁמָרָה
m pl	נִשְׁלָחִים	נִשְׁמָרִים
f pl	נִשְׁלָחוֹת	נִשְׁמָרוֹת

The Imperative

	be sent — (נִפְעַל) ש.ל.ח	be guarded — (נִפְעַל) ש.מ.ר
m sg	• הִשָּׁלַח	הִשָּׁמֵר
f sg	הִשָּׁלְחִי	הִשָּׁמְרִי
m pl	הִשָּׁלְחוּ	הִשָּׁמְרוּ
f pl	הִשָּׁלַחְנָה	הִשָּׁמַרְנָה

The Infinitive

	be sent — (נִפְעַל) ש.ל.ח	be guarded — (נִפְעַל) ש.מ.ר
absolute	• נִשְׁלוֹחַ	נִשְׁמֹר
construct	• (לְ) הִשָּׁלַח	לְהִשָּׁמֵר

Exercises

Exercise 1. Conjugate the following roots in all forms of the verb pattern given.

.1 ג.נ.ב (פָּעַל)   .2 ג.נ.ב (נִפְעַל)   .3 ש.כ.ח (נִפְעַל)

Exercise 2. Rewrite the sentences below, replacing the underlined word with each word in the list that follows. Every word or grammatical form in the sentence that agrees with the underlined word should be changed to agree with the newly substituted words. Read the sentences aloud. Translate.

.1 כַּאֲשֶׁר (אֲנַחְנוּ) נִלְחַמְנוּ בַּמִּלְחָמָה, נִשְׁפַּךְ דָּם רַב.

A. אַתֶּם   B. אֲנִי   C. הֵמָּה   D. אַתֶּן   E. הוּא

F. אַתְּ   G. הִיא   H. אַתָּה   I. הֵנָּה

.2 דָּוִד יִזָּכֵר כִּי הוּא הָיָה אִישׁ גִּבּוֹר וְהָיוּ לוֹ חֲרָבוֹת רַבּוֹת.

A. אַתֶּם   B. הֵמָּה   C. הוּא   D. אֲנַחְנוּ   E. אַתָּה

F. אֲנִי

.3 אִישׁ מִמִּשְׁפַּחְתֵּנוּ יִשָּׁלַח כִּי הוּא מַלְאַךְ הַמֶּלֶךְ.

A. ב.ח.ר   B. ל.ק.ח   C. ש.כ.ח   D. ז.כ.ר

.4 אֵינָם נִשְׁכָּחִים כִּי הֵם נָתְנוּ אֵילִים רַבִּים לְמַלְכָּם כְּמִנְחָה.

A. אֵינֶנִּי   B. אֵינֶנּוּ (הוּא)   C. אֵינֵךְ   D. אֵינְכֶם   E. אֵינָן

F. אֵינֶנּוּ (אֲנַחְנוּ)   G. אֵינְכֶן   H. אֵינְךָ   I. אֵינֶנָּה

.5 אִישׁ גִּבּוֹר בָּא אֶל הַשַּׂר לְהִבָּחֵר.

A. ש.מ.ר   B. ש.מ.ע   C. ש.פ.ט   D. ז.כ.ר   E. ל.ח.ם

.6 הַנְּעָרִים נִשְׁלְחוּ לְהָבִיא חֲרָבוֹת לָאֲנָשִׁים הַנִּלְחָמִים בַּמִּלְחָמָה.

A. אֲנַחְנוּ   B. אַתֶּן   C. אַתָּה   D. הַשַּׂר   E. נָשִׁים

F. אֲנִי   G. אַתְּ   H. אַתֶּם   I. שָׂרָה

.7 הַמַּלְאָךְ מִבֵּית לֶחֶם רָאָה אֶת הַדָּם אֲשֶׁר נִשְׁפַּךְ עַל הָאָרֶץ וְרָץ מֵהַמָּקוֹם הַהוּא.

A. אַתֶּם   B. אֲנַחְנוּ   C. הֵנָּה   D. אֲנִי   E. אַתָּה

F. אַתְּ   G. הֵמָּה   H. אַתֶּן   I. הִיא

Exercise 3. Rewrite the following sentences, changing the active verbs to passive verbs. Translate.

Example: I stole the sword.   גָּנַבְתִּי אֶת הַחֶרֶב.

             The sword was stolen.   **הַחֶרֶב נִגְנְבָה.**

1. אִישׁ יִקַּח אֶת הָאַיִל מֵהַשָּׂדֶה.

2. נִשְׁמַע אֶת דִּבְרֵי הַשַּׂר כִּי הוּא אִישׁ גִּבּוֹר חַיִל.

3. הָאִישׁ בּוֹחֵר בְּאִשְׁתּוֹ מִבֵּין נְשֵׁי מִצְרַיִם.

4. הֵן תִּזְכֹּרְנָה אֶת הַחַיִל הַגָּדוֹל אֲשֶׁר הָיָה בָּעִיר.

5. שְׁלַחְתֶּם מַלְאָךְ לְסַפֵּר לַמֶּלֶךְ אֶת מִסְפַּר חַיְלֵי מוֹאָב.

6. הוּא שָׁפַךְ אֶת דַּם חַיִל מִצְרַיִם בַּמִּלְחָמָה.

Exercise 4. Rewrite the following sentences, changing the passive verbs to active verbs. Use the word shown as the subject of the active sentence. Translate.

Example: הַזָּהָב נִשְׁמָר. אַתָּה **שׁוֹמֵר אֶת הַזָּהָב.**

1. הַמִּצְוֹת נִכְתְּבוּ. הֵמָּה. ____   4. בָּעֵת הַהִיא הַנָּשִׁים תִּשָּׁפַטְנָה. אַתֶּם ____

2. שַׁעֲרֵי הָעִיר נִפְתָּחִים כָּל בֹּקֶר. אֲנַחְנוּ ____   5. הַמַּיִם בַּכְּלִי נִשְׁפְּכוּ עַל הָאֲדָמָה. אֲנִי ____

3. מַעֲשֶׂיךָ הַטּוֹבִים יִשָּׁכְחוּ. הִיא ____   6. סְפָרִים יִכָּתְבוּ עַל חַיִל דָּוִד. הוּא ____

Exercise 5. Translate the following sentences into Hebrew.

1a. Boaz will remember a woman.

1b. Boaz will remember his mother.

1c. Boaz remembered the mother of Ruth.

1d. The mother of Ruth was remembered.

1e. The father of Ruth will be remembered as a strong man.

1f. We will be remembered in the land of Judah as a holy people.

2a. Ruth forgot the ram in the field.

2b. Ruth will not forget the fields of Boaz.

2c. The ram in the field was forgotten.

2d. The ram has no food to eat and no water to drink because he is forgotten.

2e. Ruth remembered the ram in the field of Boaz and the ram was not forgotten.

3a. The captain fought in the battle.

3b. There was blood on the sword of the captain after the battle.

3c. The captain chose the men who will fight in the battle.

3d. You are the captain of the army and you will fight in the battle.

3e. I will not fight in this battle because I am very old.

Exercise 6. Fill in the proper form of the verb in the last column and translate.

Root	Number	Gender	Person	Tense	Pattern	Word
ר.פ.ס	sg	m	3	perfect	פָּעַל	1
ר.פ.ס	sg	m	3	perfect	פִּעֵל	2
ר.כ.ז	sg	m	3	perfect	הִפְעִיל	3
ר.כ.ז	sg	m	3	perfect	נִפְעַל	4
ר.פ.ס	pl	c	1	imperfect	פָּעַל	5
ר.פ.ס	pl	c	1	imperfect	פִּעֵל	6
ר.כ.ז	pl	c	1	imperfect	הִפְעִיל	7
ר.כ.ז	pl	c	1	imperfect	נִפְעַל	8
ר.פ.ס	sg	m	2	perfect	פָּעַל	9
ר.פ.ס	sg	m	2	perfect	פִּעֵל	10
ר.כ.ז	sg	m	2	perfect	הִפְעִיל	11
ר.כ.ז	sg	m	2	perfect	נִפְעַל	12
ר.פ.ס	sg	f	3	perfect	פָּעַל	13
ר.פ.ס	sg	f	3	perfect	פִּעֵל	14
ר.כ.ז	sg	f	3	perfect	הִפְעִיל	15
ר.כ.ז	sg	f	3	perfect	נִפְעַל	16
ר.פ.ס	pl	m	—	participle	פָּעַל	17
ר.פ.ס	pl	m	—	participle	פִּעֵל	18
ר.כ.ז	pl	m	—	participle	הִפְעִיל	19
ר.כ.ז	pl	m	—	participle	נִפְעַל	20
ר.פ.ס	sg	m	—	imperative	פָּעַל	21
ר.פ.ס	sg	m	—	imperative	פִּעֵל	22
ר.כ.ז	sg	m	—	imperative	הִפְעִיל	23

Exercise 7. Identify the root and the verb pattern of the following verb forms. Translate.

16. נִשְׁכַּחַת	11. נְבַקֵּשׁ	6. נָתְנָה	1. נִשְׁמָר
17. נִשְׁכַּח	12. נְצֻוֶּה	7. נִלְקְחוּ	2. נִשְׁמֹר
18. תִּשָּׁכַחְנָה	13. נִרְאָה	8. נִקַּח	3. נַגִּיד
19. תִּשְׁכַּחְנָה	14. אֶשְׁכַּח	9. בִּקַּשְׁתִּי	4. נָבִין
	15. נִשְׁכַּח	10. בָּנִיתִי	5. נָשִׁיר

Exercise 8. The following lines are taken directly from the Bible. You now know enough Hebrew to understand them. Read and translate.

Vocabulary for Reading Selection

where? . . . . אֵי	Cain *man's name* . . . . קַיִן
cry out. . . . . צ.ע.ק (פָּעַל)	Abel *man's name* . . . . הֶבֶל

Notice the use of the interrogative הַ in the second part of the first verse.

from the Cain and Abel narrative — Genesis 4:9-10

וַיֹּאמֶר יהוה אֶל קַיִן אֵי הֶבֶל אָחִיךָ וַיֹּאמֶר לֹא יָדַעְתִּי הֲשֹׁמֵר אָחִי אָנֹכִי:

וַיֹּאמֶר מֶה עָשִׂיתָ קוֹל דְּמֵי אָחִיךָ צֹעֲקִים אֵלַי מִן הָאֲדָמָה:

From the Prayerbook

Selection from the Prayerbook (from the conclusion of the "Aleinu")

וְנֶאֱמַר: וְהָיָה יְיָ לְמֶלֶךְ עַל כָּל הָאָרֶץ: בַּיּוֹם הַהוּא יִהְיֶה יְיָ אֶחָד וּשְׁמוֹ אֶחָד.

First translate the prayer into your own words, then read the translations quoted below.

Prayerbook Translations

"And it is said: 'The Lord shall be King over all the earth; on that day the Lord shall be One, and his name One.' "

Daily Prayer Book, Philip Birnbaum, 1977, p. 414

"And it has been foretold: The Lord shall be King over all the earth; on that day the Lord shall be One, and His name One."

Sabbath and Festival Prayer Book, Morris Silverman, 1946, p. 158

Notice the use of the נִפְעַל form of the verb root א.מ.ר.

223

Guided Reading from Ruth

	Ruth 3:16 .1
	mother-in-law חָמוֹת
	וַתָּבוֹא אֶל חֲמוֹתָהּ וַתֹּאמֶר מִי אַתְּ בִּתִּי
1. And she came to her mother-in-law and she said: "Who (how) are you, my daughter?"	וַתַּגֶּד לָהּ אֵת כָּל אֲשֶׁר עָשָׂה לָהּ הָאִישׁ: .2
2. And she told her all that the man had done for her.	Ruth 3:17 .3 six (measures) שֵׁשׁ barley שְׂעֹרִים וַתֹּאמֶר שֵׁשׁ הַשְּׂעֹרִים הָאֵלֶּה נָתַן לִי
3. And she said: "These six (measures) of barley he gave to me,	empty רֵיקָם .4 כִּי אָמַר אַל תָּבוֹאִי רֵיקָם אֶל חֲמוֹתֵךְ:
4. for he said: 'Don't go empty to your mother-in-law.' "	Ruth 3:18 .5 תֵּדְעִין = תֵּדְעִי וַתֹּאמֶר שְׁבִי בִתִּי עַד אֲשֶׁר תֵּדְעִין
5. And she said: "Stay, my daughter, until you will know	how אֵיךְ .6 it will fall יִפֹּל *best translated as* matter, affair דָּבָר אֵיךְ יִפֹּל דָּבָר
6. how (the) matter will fall (turn out),	ש.ק.ט (פָּעַל) be quiet .7 unless כִּי אִם finish כ.ל.ה (פָּעֵל) כִּי לֹא יִשְׁקֹט הָאִישׁ כִּי אִם כִּלָּה הַדָּבָר הַיּוֹם:
7. for the man will not be quiet unless he has finished the matter today."	Ruth 4:1 .8 וּבֹעַז עָלָה הַשַּׁעַר וַיֵּשֶׁב שָׁם
8. And Boaz went up (to) the gate and sat there,	redeemer, kinsman גֹּאֵל .9 pass by ע.ב.ר (פָּעַל) וְהִנֵּה הַגֹּאֵל עֹבֵר אֲשֶׁר דִּבֶּר בֹּעַז

9. and behold, the kinsman (of) whom Boaz had spoken was passing by.	10. שָׁבָה = שֵׁב סוּרָה = סוּר פֹּה here פְּלֹנִי אַלְמֹנִי an unnamed person, "so-and-so" or "you there!" וַיֹּאמֶר סוּרָה שְׁבָה פֹּה פְּלֹנִי אַלְמֹנִי וַיָּסַר וַיֵּשֵׁב:
10. And he said: "Turn aside! Sit here, you there!" And he turned aside and he sat.	11. Ruth 4:2 עֲשָׂרָה ten וַיִּקַּח עֲשָׂרָה אֲנָשִׁים מִזִּקְנֵי הָעִיר וַיֹּאמֶר שְׁבוּ פֹה וַיֵּשֵׁבוּ:
11. And he took ten men from the elders of the city and he said: "Sit here!" And they sat.	

Ruth 3:16 וַתָּבוֹא אֶל חֲמוֹתָהּ וַתֹּאמֶר מִי אַתְּ בִּתִּי וַתַּגֶּד לָהּ אֵת כָּל אֲשֶׁר עָשָׂה לָהּ הָאִישׁ:

Ruth 3:17 וַתֹּאמֶר שֵׁשׁ הַשְּׂעֹרִים הָאֵלֶּה נָתַן לִי כִּי אָמַר אַל תָּבוֹאִי רֵיקָם אֶל חֲמוֹתֵךְ:

Ruth 3:18 וַתֹּאמֶר שְׁבִי בִתִּי עַד אֲשֶׁר תֵּדְעִין אֵיךְ יִפֹּל דָּבָר כִּי לֹא יִשְׁקֹט הָאִישׁ כִּי אִם כִּלָּה הַדָּבָר הַיּוֹם:

Ruth 4:1 וּבֹעַז עָלָה הַשַּׁעַר וַיֵּשֶׁב שָׁם וְהִנֵּה הַגֹּאֵל עֹבֵר אֲשֶׁר דִּבֶּר בֹּעַז וַיֹּאמֶר סוּרָה שְׁבָה פֹּה פְּלֹנִי אַלְמֹנִי וַיָּסַר וַיֵּשֵׁב:

Ruth 4:2 וַיִּקַּח עֲשָׂרָה אֲנָשִׁים מִזִּקְנֵי הָעִיר וַיֹּאמֶר שְׁבוּ פֹה וַיֵּשֵׁבוּ:

Chapter 29
The Pu'al פֻּעַל Pattern
Numbers

Vocabulary

praise *vb*	ה.ל.ל (פִּעֵל)
be praised *vb*	(פֻּעַל)
honor *vb*	כ.ב.ד (פִּעֵל)
be honored *vb*	(פֻּעַל)
comfort, console *vb*	נ.ח.ם (פִּעֵל)
be comforted, be consoled *vb*	(פֻּעַל)
repay, make whole *vb*	ש.ל.ם (פִּעֵל)
be repaid *vb*	(פֻּעַל)
completeness, peace *n, m*	שָׁלוֹם

Numbers

two	שְׁנַיִם , שְׁתַּיִם
three	שְׁלֹשָׁה , שָׁלֹשׁ
four	אַרְבָּעָה , אַרְבַּע
five	חֲמִשָּׁה , חָמֵשׁ

Note: The plural form of the word שָׁלוֹם, peace, is very rarely used.

The פֻּעַל Pu'al Pattern

Below is a chart of the verb patterns that you have already learned.

הִפְעִיל	פִּעֵל	פָּעַל	Active
		נִפְעַל	Passive

In this chapter, you will learn the conjugation of the Pu'al פֻּעַל pattern. The פֻּעַל is the passive pattern corresponding to the active פִּעֵל pattern.

Following is a list of verbs included in this book which appear in both the פִּעֵל and the פֻּעַל patterns.

Meaning in פֻּעַל	Meaning in פִּעֵל	Root
be sought	seek	ש.ק.ב
be spoken	speak	ד.ב.ר
be brought up	cause to grow, bring up	ג.ד.ל
be praised	praise	ה.ל.ל
be honored	honor	כ.ב.ד
be comforted	comfort	נ.ח.ם
be recounted, be related	recount, relate	ס.פ.ר
be repaid	repay, make whole	ש.ל.ם

The Conjugation of Verbs in the פֻּעַל Pattern

Following are charts showing the conjugation of the regular verb ב.ק.ש in the פֻּעַל pattern. Compare this to the conjugation of the same root in the פִּעֵל pattern. The two important characteristics of the פֻּעַל pattern are the X vowel, which appears under the first root letter in all forms of the conjugation, and the dagesh which appears in the second root letter, as in the פִּעֵל pattern.

Read aloud the conjugations of the verb ב.ק.ש in both the פִּעֵל and the פֻּעַל patterns, so that you can hear the differences between the two patterns.

The Perfect Tense

	be sought — (פֻּעַל) ש.ק.ב		seek — (פִּעֵל) ש.ק.ב
1 c sg	בֻּקַּשְׁתִּי	XֻּXַּXְתִּי	בִּקַּשְׁתִּי
2 m sg	בֻּקַּשְׁתָּ	XֻּXַּXְתָּ	בִּקַּשְׁתָּ
2 f sg	בֻּקַּשְׁתְּ	XֻּXַּXְתְּ	בִּקַּשְׁתְּ
3 m sg	בֻּקַּשׁ	XֻּXַּX	בִּקֵּשׁ
3 f sg	בֻּקְּשָׁה	XֻּXְּXָה	בִּקְּשָׁה
1 c pl	בֻּקַּשְׁנוּ	XֻּXַּXְנוּ	בִּקַּשְׁנוּ
2 m pl	בֻּקַּשְׁתֶּם	XֻּXַּXְתֶּם	בִּקַּשְׁתֶּם
2 f pl	בֻּקַּשְׁתֶּן	XֻּXַּXְתֶּן	בִּקַּשְׁתֶּן
3 c pl	בֻּקְּשׁוּ	XֻּXְּXוּ	בִּקְּשׁוּ

1. The X vowel, characteristic of the פֻּעַל pattern, appears under the first root letter in all forms.

2. The dagesh, characteristic of both the פִּעֵל and the פֻּעַל patterns, appears in the second root letter in all forms.

227

The Imperfect Tense

	be sought — (פֻּעַל) ב.ק.ש			seek — (פִּעֵל) ב.ק.ש
1 c sg	אֲבֻקַּשׁ	אֲXֻXַّX		אֲבַקֵּשׁ
2 m sg	תְּבֻקַּשׁ	תְּXֻXַّX		תְּבַקֵּשׁ
2 f sg	תְּבֻקְּשִׁי	תְּXֻXְّXִי		תְּבַקְּשִׁי
3 m sg	יְבֻקַּשׁ	יְXֻXַّX		יְבַקֵּשׁ
3 f sg	תְּבֻקַּשׁ	תְּXֻXַّX		תְּבַקֵּשׁ
1 c pl	נְבֻקַּשׁ	נְXֻXַّX		נְבַקֵּשׁ
2 m pl	תְּבֻקְּשׁוּ	תְּXֻXְّXוּ		תְּבַקְּשׁוּ
2 f pl	תְּבֻקַּשְׁנָה	תְּXֻXַّXְנָה		תְּבַקֵּשְׁנָה
3 m pl	יְבֻקְּשׁוּ	יְXֻXְّXוּ		יְבַקְּשׁוּ
3 f pl	תְּבֻקַּשְׁנָה	תְּXֻXַّXְנָה		תְּבַקֵּשְׁנָה

1. The basic vowel pattern of פֻּעַל is XֻXַّX.
2. The Xֻ vowel, characteristic of the פֻּעַל pattern, appears under the first root letter.
3. The dagesh, characteristic of both the פֻּעַל and the פִּעֵל patterns, appears in the second root letter in all forms.
4. The prefix and suffix consonants in the imperfect tense of the פֻּעַל pattern are exactly the same as the prefix and suffix consonants in the imperfect tense of the פִּעֵל pattern.

The Participle

	be sought — (פֻּעַל) ב.ק.ש			seek — (פִּעֵל) ב.ק.ש
m sg	מְבֻקָּשׁ	מְXֻXָّX		מְבַקֵּשׁ
f sg	מְבֻקֶּשֶׁת	מְXֻXֶّXֶת		מְבַקֶּשֶׁת
m pl	מְבֻקָּשִׁים	מְXֻXָّXִים		מְבַקְּשִׁים
f pl	מְבֻקָּשׁוֹת	מְXֻXָّXוֹת		מְבַקְּשׁוֹת

1. The participle in both the פֻּעַל and the פִּעֵל patterns always begins with the prefix מְ.
2. The Xֻ vowel, characteristic of the פֻּעַל pattern, appears under the first root letter.
3. The dagesh, characteristic of both the פֻּעַל and the פִּעֵל patterns, appears in the second root letter in all forms.

The Imperative and the Infinitive

No imperative form exists in the פֻּעַל pattern. The infinitive of the פֻּעַל pattern is rarely used; we will not include it in this book.

Numbers in Hebrew

In Hebrew, most numbers have both a masculine and a feminine form. Following is a chart showing the masculine and feminine forms of the numbers two through five. Notice the unusual fact that the masculine forms of the numbers "three", "four", and "five" take the הָ ending, which is normally a feminine ending.

	Feminine	Masculine
2	שְׁתַּיִם	שְׁנַיִם
3	שָׁלֹשׁ	שְׁלֹשָׁה
4	אַרְבַּע	אַרְבָּעָה
5	חָמֵשׁ	חֲמִשָּׁה

How to Use Numbers in Hebrew

Numbers in Hebrew, like adjectives, must agree in gender with the nouns they describe. However, unlike Hebrew adjectives, numbers appear in a sentence immediately before the nouns that they describe. The number "one" is the only exception. As you have already learned, the number "one" appears after the noun it describes.

Examples:

one man	אִישׁ אֶחָד
three messengers	שְׁלֹשָׁה מַלְאָכִים
five mothers	חָמֵשׁ אִמּוֹת

Construct Forms of Numbers

In Hebrew, there is a construct form for the numbers "two" through "ten." Following is a chart of the numbers "two" through "five" with their construct forms.

	Feminine Construct	Feminine Number	Masculine Construct	Masculine Number
2	שְׁתֵּי	שְׁתַּיִם	שְׁנֵי	שְׁנַיִם
3	שְׁלֹשׁ	שָׁלֹשׁ	שְׁלֹשֶׁת	שְׁלֹשָׁה
4	אַרְבַּע	אַרְבַּע	אַרְבַּעַת	אַרְבָּעָה
5	חֲמֵשׁ	חָמֵשׁ	חֲמֵשֶׁת	חֲמִשָּׁה

The use of the construct form of a number is not always distinct from the use of the regular form of the number. Sometimes the two forms can be used interchangeably. However, the construct form of a number usually appears before a definite noun.

Examples:

the five books	חֲמֵשֶׁת הַסְּפָרִים
his two wives	שְׁתֵּי נָשָׁיו

The Verb נ.ח.ם

The conjugation of the verb נ.ח.ם is slightly irregular because the middle root letter is ח, one of the throaty five letters. This letter usually does not take a sheva. Therefore, whenever a sheva appears under the second root letter in the conjugation, the combination vowel ﹱ appears under the letter ח in the verb נ.ח.ם.

Exercises

Exercise 1. Conjugate the following roots in all forms of the verb pattern given.

1. ד.ב.ר (פָּעַל)   2. ד.ב.ר (פִּעֵל)   3. ב.י.ן (הִפְעִיל)

Exercise 2. Rewrite the sentences below, replacing the underlined word with each word in the list that follows. Every word or grammatical form in the sentence that agrees with the underlined word should be changed to agree with the newly substituted words. Read the sentences aloud. Translate.

1. הַמַּלְאָךְ מִירוּשָׁלַיִם כֻּבַּד בְּבֵית לֶחֶם.

   A. אֲנַחְנוּ   B. חֲמִשָּׁה מְלָכִים   C. נְשֵׁי מִצְרַיִם   D. הֶחָיִל   E. אַתְּ

   F. בַּת אַבְרָהָם   G. אַתֶּם   H. אַתָּה   I. אֲנִי   J. אַתֶּן

2. הָאִישׁ מְהֻלָּל כִּי הוּא עָשָׂה שָׁלוֹם בֵּין שְׁנֵי הָאַחִים.

   A. נָעֳמִי   B. שְׁלֹשָׁה שָׂרִים   C. שְׁתֵּי נְעָרוֹת   D. אַתֶּם   E. אַתְּ

   F. אֲנִי   G. אַתָּה

3. (אֲנִי) אֲדַבֵּר עִם הָאִישׁ עַל כַּסְפִּי וַאֲשַׁלֵּם.

   A. הַקָּצֵר   B. אַתְּ   C. דּוֹדָתִי   D. אַתֶּן   E. אַתָּה

   F. אֲנַחְנוּ   G. הַזְּקֵנִים   H. אַתֶּם   I. שָׁלֹשׁ הַמִּשְׁפָּחוֹת

4. בַּלַּיְלָה הַהוּא שָׁתָה בֹּעַז יַיִן רַב וְנֻחַם וְשָׁכַב בְּשָׁלוֹם.

   A. אַתָּה   B. אֲנַחְנוּ   C. רוּת   D. אַנְשֵׁי בֵּית לֶחֶם   E. אַתְּ

   F. אַרְבַּע בְּנוֹת מוֹאָב   G. אַתֶּם   H. אֲנִי   I. שְׁתַּיִם נָשִׁים

5. הַשַּׂר בֻּקַּשׁ בְּכָל אֶרֶץ יִשְׂרָאֵל.

   A. שְׁנֵי הַמַּלְאָכִים   B. אָנֹכִי   C. נַעֲרָה אַחַת   D. חֲמֵשׁ הַנָּשִׁים   E. אֲנַחְנוּ

   F. אַרְבַּעַת הַסְּפָרִים   G. אַתֶּן   H. שְׁלֹשָׁה אֵילִים   I. הֵנָּה

Exercise 3. In the following sentences, circle the correct form of the Hebrew number shown in parenthesis. Pay attention to gender.

1. דָּוִד אָהַב (שְׁלֹשָׁה, שָׁלֹשׁ) נָשִׁים.

2. בַּלַּיְלָה הַהוּא יָסְפְרוּ (אַרְבַּעַת, אַרְבַּע) הַמַּעֲשִׂים.

3. אֲנַחְנוּ רוֹאִים אֶת (חֲמֵשֶׁת, חָמֵשׁ) הָאֹהָלִים בַּמִּדְבָּר.

4. תֶּן לִי (אַחַת, אֶחָד) מִבְּנוֹתֶיךָ וְתָמִיד אֲכַבֵּד אַתָּה.

5. הָיוּ (שְׁנֵי, שְׁתֵּי) מִלְחָמוֹת בֵּין יִשְׂרָאֵל וּבֵין מוֹאָב.

6. תָּבִיאוּ אִישׁ אֶחָד מֵהַשָּׂדֶה וּ(שְׁנַיִם, שְׁתַּיִם) מֵהָעִיר.

Exercise 4. Translate the following English phrases into Hebrew. Pay attention to gender and word order.

1. three rams
2. one battle
3. five captains
4. two swords
5. four commandments
6. five beasts
7. two numbers
8. four utensils
9. one week
10. three families

Exercise 5a. Rewrite the following sentences, changing the active verbs to passive verbs. Translate.

Example: The mother brought up her sons.   הָאֵם גִּדְּלָה אֶת בָּנֶיהָ.

Her sons were brought up.   בָּנֶיהָ גֻּדְּלוּ.

3. אַבְרָהָם שָׁפַךְ יַיִן מֵהַכְּלִי.

4. יַעֲקֹב בִּקֵּשׁ אֶת בְּנוֹ בְּכָל הָעִיר.

5. רוּת נִחֲמָה אֶת אִישָׁהּ.

1. הַמַּלְאָךְ יְהַלֵּל אֶת הַמֶּלֶךְ.

2. הַשַּׂר שִׁלֵּם לוֹ כֶּסֶף.

Exercise 5b. Rewrite the following sentences, changing the passive verbs to active verbs. Use the word shown as the subject of the active sentence. Translate.

Example: You are still sought.   עוֹדְךָ מְבֻקָּשׁ. אֲנַחְנוּ

We are still seeking you.   אֲנַחְנוּ עוֹד מְבַקְשִׁים אֹתְךָ.

3. שְׁנֵי הַשְּׁעָרִים נִפְתָּחִים לְפָנַי. הֵמָּה

4. קוֹלוֹ נִשְׁמַע וּדְבָרָיו נִזְכְּרוּ. אֲנַחְנוּ

1. דִּבְרֵי שָׁלוֹם דֻּבְּרוּ אֵלַי. הֵן

2. אֶזָּכֵר וַאֲנֻחַם. אַתֶּם

Exercise 6. Identify the root and the verb pattern of the following verb forms. Translate.

16. גֻּדְּלוּ	11. כָּבְדָה	6. יִשָׁפֵךְ	1. יָשַׁב
17. הִגְדַּלְתִּי	12. מְכֻבֶּדֶת	7. יְשֻׁלַּם	2. שָׁב
18. מַגְדִּילוֹת	13. מְדֻבֶּרֶת	8. יְשַׁלֵּם	3. נָשׁוּב
19. מְגֻדָּל	14. מַגְדִּילִים	9. לְהִגָּנֵב	4. נָשִׁיב
20. מְשֻׁלָּם	15. גֻּדְּלָה	10. נִגְנַב	5. נִשְׁפַּךְ

Exercise 7. Fill in the proper form of the verb in the last column and translate.

Root	Number	Gender	Person	Tense	Pattern	Word	
ג.ד.ל	pl	m	—	participle	פָּעַל		1
ג.ד.ל	pl	m	—	participle	הִפְעִיל		2
ג.ד.ל	pl	m	—	participle	פָּעַל		3
ג.ד.ל	pl	m	—	participle	פָּעַל		4
נ.ח.ם	sg	f	2	perfect	פִּעֵל		5
נ.ח.ם	sg	f	2	perfect	פִּעֵל		6
נ.ח.ם	pl	c	1	imperfect	פִּעֵל		7
נ.ח.ם	pl	c	1	imperfect	פִּעֵל		8
ה.ל.ל	pl	m	3	imperfect	פִּעֵל		9
ה.ל.ל	pl	m	3	imperfect	פִּעֵל		10
ב.ק.שׁ	sg	m	3	perfect	פִּעֵל		11
ב.ק.שׁ	sg	m	3	perfect	פִּעֵל		12
ל.ח.ם	sg	m	3	perfect	נִפְעַל		13
שׁ.פ.ט	sg	m	2	perfect	נִפְעַל		14
שׁ.פ.ט	sg	m	—	imperative	פָּעַל		15
שׁ.פ.ט	pl	m	—	imperative	פָּעַל		16
שׁ.ו.ב	sg	m	—	imperative	הִפְעִיל		17
שׁ.ו.ב	pl	c	1	imperfect	הִפְעִיל		18
שׁ.ו.ב	pl	c	1	imperfect	פָּעַל		19
י.שׁ.ב	pl	c	1	imperfect	פָּעַל		20
ע.ל.ה	pl	c	1	imperfect	פָּעַל		21
ע.ל.ה	pl	c	1	perfect	פָּעַל		22
ע.ל.ה	pl	m	—	participle	פָּעַל		23
צ.ו.ה	pl	m	—	participle	פִּעֵל		24

Exercise 8. The following reading is taken directly from Genesis 3:1-5, the account of the Garden of Eden. In this passage, Eve encounters the serpent. Read and translate.

Vocabulary for Reading Selection

touch *2 m pl imperfect*	תִּגְּעוּ	serpent	נָחָשׁ
lest	פֶּן	crafty	עָרוּם
you *pl* will die	תְּמֻתוּן	animal	חַיָּה
infinitive absolute of מ.ו.ת — die	מוֹת	indeed	אַף כִּי
open . . . . (פָּעַל) פ.ק.ח		garden	גַּן

Genesis 3:1 וְהַנָּחָשׁ הָיָה עָרוּם מִכֹּל חַיַּת הַשָּׂדֶה אֲשֶׁר עָשָׂה יהוה אֱלֹהִים וַיֹּאמֶר אֶל הָאִשָּׁה אַף כִּי אָמַר אֱלֹהִים לֹא תֹאכְלוּ מִכֹּל עֵץ הַגָּן:

Genesis 3:2 וַתֹּאמֶר הָאִשָּׁה אֶל הַנָּחָשׁ מִפְּרִי עֵץ הַגָּן נֹאכֵל:

Genesis 3:3 וּמִפְּרִי הָעֵץ אֲשֶׁר בְּתוֹךְ הַגָּן אָמַר אֱלֹהִים לֹא תֹאכְלוּ מִמֶּנּוּ וְלֹא תִגְּעוּ בּוֹ פֶּן תְּמֻתוּן:

Genesis 3:4 וַיֹּאמֶר הַנָּחָשׁ אֶל הָאִשָּׁה לֹא מוֹת תְּמֻתוּן:

Genesis 3:5 כִּי יֹדֵעַ אֱלֹהִים כִּי בְּיוֹם אֲכָלְכֶם מִמֶּנּוּ וְנִפְקְחוּ עֵינֵיכֶם וִהְיִיתֶם כֵּאלֹהִים יֹדְעֵי טוֹב וָרָע:

From the Prayerbook

Prayerbook Vocabulary

forever	לְעוֹלָם	saviour	מוֹשִׁיעַ
Zion	צִיּוֹן	proclaim, make known . . . . . (הִפְעִיל) ש.מ.ע	
all generations	דֹר וָדֹר	again, a second time	שֵׁנִית
Halleluia	הַלְלוּיָהּ	holiness	קֹדֶשׁ

Selection from the Prayerbook (from the Kiddusha service)

הוּא אֱלֹהֵינוּ, הוּא אָבִינוּ, הוּא מַלְכֵּנוּ, הוּא מוֹשִׁיעֵנוּ, וְהוּא יַשְׁמִיעֵנוּ בְּרַחֲמָיו שֵׁנִית לְעֵינֵי כָּל חָי: לִהְיוֹת לָכֶם לֵאלֹהִים — אֲנִי יְיָ אֱלֹהֵיכֶם. וּבְדִבְרֵי קָדְשְׁךָ כָּתוּב לֵאמֹר: יִמְלֹךְ יְיָ לְעוֹלָם, אֱלֹהַיִךְ צִיּוֹן לְדֹר וָדֹר: הַלְלוּיָהּ.

Prayerbook Translation

"He is our God; he is our Father; he is our King; he is our Deliverer. He will again in his mercy proclaim to us in the presence of all the living: '. . . to be your God — I am the Lord your God.' And in the holy Scriptures it is written: 'The Lord shall reign forever, Your God, O Zion, for all generations. Praise the Lord!' " *Daily Prayer Book, Philip Birnbaum, 1977, p. 394*

Notice that the word הַלְלוּיָהּ, Halleluia, is formed from the *m pl* imperative form of the פָּעַל verb ה.ל.ל. A shortened form of the divine name, יָהּ, is attached. If translated literally, הַלְלוּיָהּ means "Praise the Lord!"

Guided Reading from Ruth

	Ruth 4:3 .1 ג.א.ל redeem, act as kinsman חֶלְקָה portion וַיֹּאמֶר לַגֹּאֵל חֶלְקַת הַשָּׂדֶה אֲשֶׁר לְאָחִינוּ לֶאֱלִימֶלֶךְ
1. And he (Boaz) said to the kinsman: "The portion of the field that was our brother Elimelech's,	(פָּעַל) מ.כ.ר sell .2 מָכְרָה נָעֳמִי הַשָּׁבָה מִשְּׂדֵה מוֹאָב:
2. Naomi, who returned from the field of Moab, sold. (often translated: is selling)	Ruth 4:4 .3 (פָּעַל) ג.ל.ה uncover אֹזֶן ear וַאֲנִי אָמַרְתִּי אֶגְלֶה אָזְנְךָ לֵאמֹר
3. And I said I will uncover your ear (reveal to you), saying:	(פָּעַל) ק.נ.ה buy .4 נֶגֶד in front of קְנֵה נֶגֶד הַיֹּשְׁבִים וְנֶגֶד זִקְנֵי עַמִּי
4. Buy (it) in front of those who are sitting (here) and in front of the elders of my people,	*another m sg imperative* .5 *form of* נ.ג.ד הַגִּידָה אִם תִּגְאַל גְּאָל וְאִם לֹא יִגְאַל הַגִּידָה לִּי וְאֵדְעָה
5. if you will act as kinsman, act as kinsman! but if he will not act as kinsman, tell me so I will know;	זוּלָתְךָ except for you .6 כִּי אֵין זוּלָתְךָ לִגְאוֹל וְאָנֹכִי אַחֲרֶיךָ
6. for there is none except for you to act as kinsman, and I am after you."	וַיֹּאמֶר אָנֹכִי אֶגְאָל: .7
7. And he said: "I will act as kinsman."	Ruth 4:5 .8 וַיֹּאמֶר בֹּעַז בְּיוֹם קְנוֹתְךָ הַשָּׂדֶה מִיַּד נָעֳמִי
8. Then Boaz said: "On the day of your buying (when you buy) the field from the hand of Naomi,	מֵאֵת from .9 מוֹאָבִיָּה Moabitess מֵת dead man וּמֵאֵת רוּת הַמּוֹאֲבִיָּה אֵשֶׁת הַמֵּת
9. and from Ruth the Moabitess, the wife of the dead man,	נַחֲלָה inheritance .10 קָנִיתָ לְהָקִים שֵׁם הַמֵּת עַל נַחֲלָתוֹ:

10. you have bought (in order) to establish the name of the dead man on his inheritance."	Ruth 4:6 .11 וַיֹּאמֶר הַגֹּאֵל לֹא אוּכַל לִגְאָל לִי
11. And the kinsman said: "I will not be able to act as kinsman myself	.12 פֶּן lest ש.ח.ת (הִפְעִיל) spoil, ruin פֶּן אַשְׁחִית אֶת נַחֲלָתִי
12. lest I ruin my inheritance.	.13 גְּאֻלָּה right of redemption גְּאַל לְךָ אַתָּה אֶת גְּאֻלָּתִי כִּי לֹא אוּכַל לִגְאָל:
13. You yourself redeem my right of redemption, for I will not be able to redeem (act as kinsman)."	

Ruth 4:3 וַיֹּאמֶר לַגֹּאֵל חֶלְקַת הַשָּׂדֶה אֲשֶׁר לְאָחִינוּ לֶאֱלִימֶלֶךְ מָכְרָה נָעֳמִי הַשָּׁבָה מִשְּׂדֵה מוֹאָב:

Ruth 4:4 וַאֲנִי אָמַרְתִּי אֶגְלֶה אָזְנְךָ לֵאמֹר קְנֵה נֶגֶד הַיֹּשְׁבִים וְנֶגֶד זִקְנֵי עַמִּי אִם תִּגְאַל גְּאָל וְאִם לֹא יִגְאַל הַגִּידָה לִּי וְאֵדְעָ כִּי אֵין זוּלָתְךָ לִגְאוֹל וְאָנֹכִי אַחֲרֶיךָ וַיֹּאמֶר אָנֹכִי אֶגְאָל:

Ruth 4:5 וַיֹּאמֶר בֹּעַז בְּיוֹם קְנוֹתְךָ הַשָּׂדֶה מִיַּד נָעֳמִי וּמֵאֵת רוּת הַמּוֹאֲבִיָּה אֵשֶׁת הַמֵּת קָנִיתָ לְהָקִים שֵׁם הַמֵּת עַל נַחֲלָתוֹ:

Ruth 4:6 וַיֹּאמֶר הַגֹּאֵל לֹא אוּכַל לִגְאָל לִי פֶּן אַשְׁחִית אֶת נַחֲלָתִי גְּאַל לְךָ אַתָּה אֶת גְּאֻלָּתִי כִּי לֹא אוּכַל לִגְאָל:

Chapter 30
The Hof'al הָפְעַל Pattern

Vocabulary

thousand *n, m* . . . . אֶלֶף, אֲלָפִים, אַלְפַּיִם

hundred *n, f* . . . . מֵאָה, מֵאוֹת, מָאתַיִם

occurrence, time *n, f* . . . . פַּעַם, פְּעָמִים

    two times, twice . . . . פַּעֲמַיִם

Numbers

six . . . . שִׁשָּׁה, שֵׁשׁ

seven . . . . שִׁבְעָה, שֶׁבַע

eight . . . . שְׁמֹנָה, שְׁמֹנֶה

nine . . . . תִּשְׁעָה, תֵּשַׁע

ten . . . . עֲשָׂרָה, עֶשֶׂר

Names of Women

Rebecca . . . . רִבְקָה

Rachel . . . . רָחֵל

Leah . . . . לֵאָה

Miriam . . . . מִרְיָם

Note: The words פַּעֲמַיִם, מָאתַיִם, and אַלְפַּיִם are all dual forms.

The Hof'al הָפְעַל Pattern

Below is a chart of the verb patterns that you have already learned.

הִפְעִיל	פִּעֵל	פָּעַל	Active
	פֻּעַל	נִפְעַל	Passive

In this chapter you will learn the conjugation of the Hof'al הָפְעַל pattern. The הָפְעַל is the passive pattern corresponding to the active הִפְעִיל pattern.

The following two verbs are the only regular verbs you have learned in the הִפְעִיל pattern which also appear in the הָפְעַל pattern in Biblical Hebrew.

Meaning in הָפְעַל	Meaning in הִפְעִיל	Root
be made king	cause to reign, make king	מ.ל.ך
be thrown, be cast	throw, cast	ש.ל.ך

The Conjugation of Verbs in the הָפְעַל Pattern

Following are charts showing the conjugation of the regular verb ש.ל.ך in the הָפְעַל pattern. Compare this to the conjugation of the same root in the הִפְעִיל pattern. The important characteristic of the הָפְעַל pattern is the X vowel, which appears under the attached prefix in all forms of the verb. This X vowel is a qamets chatuf, and is pronounced **o** as in d**o**g (see Chapter 2). The הָפְעַל pattern is sometimes conjugated with an X vowel in place of the X vowel. However, in this book we will use the X vowel only.

Read aloud the conjugations of the verb ש.ל.ך in both the הָפְעַל and the הִפְעִיל patterns, so that you can hear the differences between the two patterns.

The Perfect Tense

	be thrown — (הָפְעַל) ש.ל.ך		throw — (הִפְעִיל) ש.ל.ך	
1 c sg	הָשְׁלַכְתִּי	הָאָאַכְתִּי	הָאָאְתִּי	הִשְׁלַכְתִּי
2 m sg	הָשְׁלַכְתָּ	הָאָאַכְתָּ	הָאָאְתָּ	הִשְׁלַכְתָּ
2 f sg	הָשְׁלַכְתְּ	הָאָאַכְתְּ	הָאָאְתְּ	הִשְׁלַכְתְּ
3 m sg	הָשְׁלַךְ	הָאָאַךְ	הָאָא	הִשְׁלִיךְ
3 f sg	הָשְׁלְכָה	הָאָאְכָה	הָאָאָה	הִשְׁלִיכָה
1 c pl	הָשְׁלַכְנוּ	הָאָאַכְנוּ	הָאָאְנוּ	הִשְׁלַכְנוּ
2 m pl	הָשְׁלַכְתֶּם	הָאָאַכְתֶּם	הָאָאְתֶּם	הִשְׁלַכְתֶּם
2 f pl	הָשְׁלַכְתֶּן	הָאָאַכְתֶּן	הָאָאְתֶּן	הִשְׁלַכְתֶּן
3 c pl	הָשְׁלְכוּ	הָאָאְכוּ	הָאָאוּ	הִשְׁלִיכוּ

1. The prefix ה appears in the perfect tense in both the הִפְעִיל and the הָפְעַל patterns.
2. The X vowel, characteristic of the הָפְעַל pattern, appears under the prefix ה.
3. The endings in the perfect tense of the הָפְעַל pattern are exactly the same as the endings in the perfect tense of the הִפְעִיל pattern.

The Imperfect Tense

	throw — (הִפְעִיל) ש.ל.ך	pattern	be thrown — (הֻפְעַל) ש.ל.ך
1 c sg	אַשְׁלִיךְ	אָXXX	אֻשְׁלַךְ
2 m sg	תַּשְׁלִיךְ	תָXXX	תֻּשְׁלַךְ
2 f sg	תַּשְׁלִיכִי	תָXXXִי	תֻּשְׁלְכִי
3 m sg	יַשְׁלִיךְ	יָXXX	יֻשְׁלַךְ
3 f sg	תַּשְׁלִיךְ	תָXXX	תֻּשְׁלַךְ
1 c pl	נַשְׁלִיךְ	נָXXX	נֻשְׁלַךְ
2 m pl	תַּשְׁלִיכוּ	תָXXXוּ	תֻּשְׁלְכוּ
2 f pl	תַּשְׁלֵכְנָה	תָXֵאXָנָה	תֻּשְׁלַכְנָה
3 m pl	יַשְׁלִיכוּ	יָXXXוּ	יֻשְׁלְכוּ
3 f pl	תַּשְׁלֵכְנָה	תָXֵאXָנָה	תֻּשְׁלַכְנָה

1. The basic vowel pattern of הֻפְעַל is XֻXְXַX.
2. The X vowel, characteristic of the הֻפְעַל pattern, appears under the imperfect tense prefixes in all forms.
3. The prefix and suffix consonants in the imperfect tense of the הֻפְעַל pattern are exactly the same as the prefix and suffix consonants in the imperfect tense of the הִפְעִיל pattern.

The Participle

	throw — (הִפְעִיל) ש.ל.ך	pattern	be thrown — (הֻפְעַל) ש.ל.ך
m sg	מַשְׁלִיךְ	מָXXX	מֻשְׁלָךְ
f sg	מַשְׁלִיכָה/מַשְׁלֶכֶת	מָXXָה/מָXֶאXֶת	מֻשְׁלָכָה/מֻשְׁלֶכֶת
m pl	מַשְׁלִיכִים	מָXXִים	מֻשְׁלָכִים
f pl	מַשְׁלִיכוֹת	מָXXוֹת	מֻשְׁלָכוֹת

1. The prefix מ appears in the participle of both the הִפְעִיל and the הֻפְעַל patterns.
2. The X vowel, characteristic of the הֻפְעַל pattern, appears under the prefix מ.
3. The endings of the participle in the הֻפְעַל pattern are exactly the same as the endings of the participle in the הִפְעִיל pattern.

The Imperative and the Infinitive

No imperative form exists in the הֻפְעַל pattern. The infinitive of the הֻפְעַל pattern is rarely used; we will not include it in this book.

The Hebrew Numbers "six" through "ten"

Following is a chart of the numbers "six" through "ten" with their construct forms.

	Feminine		Masculine	
	Construct	**Number**	**Construct**	**Number**
6	שֵׁשׁ	שֵׁשׁ	שֵׁשֶׁת	שִׁשָּׁה
7	שְׁבַע	שֶׁבַע	שִׁבְעַת	שִׁבְעָה
8	שְׁמֹנֶה	שְׁמֹנֶה	שְׁמֹנַת	שְׁמֹנָה
9	תְּשַׁע	תֵּשַׁע	תִּשְׁעַת	תִּשְׁעָה
10	עֶשֶׂר	עֶשֶׂר	עֲשֶׂרֶת	עֲשָׂרָה

The Numbers "hundred" and "thousand"

The numbers "hundred" מֵאָה and "thousand" אֶלֶף do not have masculine or feminine forms. They remain the same whether they appear before a masculine noun or a feminine noun.

Examples: a hundred women   מֵאָה נָשִׁים   a hundred men   מֵאָה אֲנָשִׁים

a thousand maidens   אֶלֶף נְעָרוֹת   a thousand lads   אֶלֶף נְעָרִים

The construct forms of מֵאָה and אֶלֶף are included in the glossary.

Exercises

Exercise 1. Conjugate the following roots in all forms of the verb pattern given.

1. שׁ.ל.ך (הִפְעִיל)   2. שׁ.ל.ך (הָפְעַל)   3. ב.נ.ה (פָּעַל)

Exercise 2. Rewrite the sentences below, replacing the underlined word with each word in the list that follows. Every word or grammatical form in the sentence that agrees with the underlined word should be changed to agree with the newly substituted words. Read the sentences aloud. Translate.

1. הַכֶּסֶף הֻשְׁלַךְ אֶל תּוֹךְ הַיָּם.

A. אַתָּה   B. אֲנַחְנוּ   C. אַתְּ וְלֵאָה   D. אֲנִי   E. מֵאָה אִישׁ

F. אַתְּ   G. נַעֲרָה אַחַת   H. שֵׁשׁ נָשִׁים רָעוֹת   I. אַתֶּם

2. עַתָּה אַתֶּם מָמְלָכִים עַל כָּל הָאָרֶץ מֵהֶהָרִים עַד הַיַּרְדֵּן.

A. אֲנִי   B. הַשָּׂר   C. אַתְּ   D. אַתֶּן   E. שְׁמֹנַת הַשֹּׁפְטִים

F. אֲנַחְנוּ   G. לֵאָה   H. אַתָּה   I. תֵּשַׁע בְּנוֹת רִבְקָה

3. אֶלֶף אֲבָנִים תָּשְׁלַכְנָה מֵרֹאשׁ הָהָר.

E. אֲנַחְנוּ   D. אַתָּה   C. רָחֵל וּמִרְיָם   B. הַחֶרֶב   A. הָאַיִל

4. בַּפַּעַם הַזֹּאת הוּא יִשָּׁפֵט בְּבֵית לֶחֶם.

E. אַתְּ   D. אֲנַחְנוּ   C. הַגּוֹי   B. אַתְּ וְרִבְקָה   A. אֲנִי

     H. אַתָּה   G. אַתֶּם   F. רָחֵל

5. מִרְיָם לֹא הֵבִינָה אֶת דִּבְרֵי הַמַּלְאָךְ.

E. שְׁנֵי דּוֹדַי   D. אֲנַחְנוּ   C. אַתֶּן   B. אַתְּ   A. לֵאָה וְרָחֵל

     I. אֲנִי   H. אַתָּה   G. רֹאשׁ הָעִיר   F. אַתֶּם

6. רִבְקָה שָׂמָה אֶת הָאֹכֶל וְאֶת הַמַּיִם לְפָנַי וַאֲנִי שָׁתִיתִי וְאָכַלְתִּי.

E. לְפָנֵינוּ   D. לְפָנֶיךָ   C. לִפְנֵיהֶם   B. לִפְנֵיכֶן   A. לְפָנֶיךָ

     I. לְפָנֶיהָ   H. לִפְנֵיכֶם   G. לְפָנָיו   F. לִפְנֵיהֶן

Exercise 3. Fill in the following blanks with the Hebrew number which correctly completes the equation.

Example: חָמֵשׁ = שָׁלֹשׁ + שְׁתַּיִם

7. אַרְבַּע + שְׁתַּיִם =   1. שְׁמֹנֶה + אַחַת =

8. אַרְבַּע + שֵׁשׁ =   2. חָמֵשׁ + שָׁלֹשׁ =

9. חָמֵשׁ – תֵּשַׁע =   3. שְׁתַּיִם – שֶׁבַע =

10. שֵׁשׁ – שֶׁבַע =   4. שֵׁשׁ – תֵּשַׁע =

11. שְׁמֹנֶה – עֶשֶׂר =   5. שָׁלֹשׁ – עֶשֶׂר =

12. אֶלֶף + אֶלֶף =   6. מֵאָה + מֵאָה =

Exercise 4. In the following sentences, circle the correct form of the Hebrew number shown in parenthesis. Pay attention to gender.

1. נִבְטַח בְּרָחֵל וּבְ(שֵׁשׁ, שֵׁשֶׁת) אַחְיָה.

2. סְפַרְתֶּם (עֶשֶׂר, עֲשָׂרָה) בְּהֵמוֹת בַּשָּׂדֶה.

3. אַצִּיל (שֶׁבַע, שִׁבְעָה) אֲנָשִׁים כִּי אֲנִי גִבּוֹר חַיִל.

4. הַשַּׂר יִתֵּן (תֵּשַׁע, תִּשְׁעָה) חֲרָבוֹת לַשּׁוֹפֵט.

5. לְקַחְתֶּם אֶת (שְׁמֹנֶה, שְׁמֹנַת) כְּלֵי הַיַּיִן מֵהַנְּעָרִים וְהֵם לֹא יָכְלוּ לִשְׁתּוֹת.

Exercise 5. Rewrite the following sentences, changing the active verbs to passive verbs. Translate.

1. חֵיל מוֹאָב הִמְלִיךְ אֶת שָׂרוֹ אַחֲרֵי הַמִּלְחָמָה.

2. רִבְקָה וּמִרְיָם מַשְׁלִיכוֹת אֲבָנִים אֶל תּוֹךְ הַיַּרְדֵּן.

3. תִּגָּנֵב אֶת הַזָּהָב מֵהַמִּשְׁכָּן בָּעֶרֶב.

4. מֵאָה פְּעָמִים שָׁלַחְנוּ אֶת מַלְאֲכֵי הַמֶּלֶךְ יְרוּשָׁלַיְמָה.

5. לֵאָה תַּלְבִּישׁ אֶת בְּנוֹתֶיהָ בַּבֹּקֶר.

Exercise 6. Translate into Hebrew.

1a. The three judges went to Jerusalem.
2a. The four judges took the fruit to Jerusalem.
3a. The fruit was sent to the people of Jerusalem.
4a. The fruit will be sent to seven judges in Jerusalem.
5a. Fruit is taken from the tree and is sent to the eight judges.

1b. Sarah has two pairs of shoes.
2b. Rachel chose these shoes today.
3b. Six women from Sarah's family were chosen because they are wise.
4b. Sarah is wiser than the five women in her home.
5b. Eight women from Moab will choose clothes from Jerusalem.

1c. The son of Jacob counted ten rams.
2c. The nine sons of Jacob will count the rams on the mountain.
3c. Jacob will not be able to count the rams on the mountain.
4c. Jacob did not forget that he saw a thousand rams on the mountain.
5c. The mountain in Judah was not forgotten because it is like the mountain in Moab.

Exercise 7. Fill in the proper form of the verb in the last column and translate.

Root	Number	Gender	Person	Tense	Pattern	Word	
מ.ל.ך	pl	m	2	perfect	פָּעַל		1
מ.ל.ך	pl	m	2	perfect	הִפְעִיל		2
מ.ל.ך	pl	m	2	perfect	הָפְעַל		3
מ.ל.ך	pl	f	2	imperfect	פָּעַל		4
מ.ל.ך	pl	f	2	imperfect	הִפְעִיל		5
מ.ל.ך	pl	f	2	imperfect	הָפְעַל		6
ז.כ.ר	sg	c	1	perfect	פָּעַל		7
ז.כ.ר	sg	c	1	perfect	נִפְעַל		8
ז.כ.ר	sg	c	1	perfect	הִפְעִיל		9
ז.כ.ר	sg	f	—	participle	פָּעַל		10
ז.כ.ר	sg	f	—	participle	נִפְעַל		11
ז.כ.ר	sg	f	—	participle	הִפְעִיל		12
ש.ל.ך	pl	m	—	participle	הִפְעִיל		13
ש.ל.ך	pl	m	—	participle	הָפְעַל		14
ש.ו.ב	pl	m	3	imperfect	פָּעַל		15
ש.ו.ב	pl	m	3	imperfect	הִפְעִיל		16
ש.ו.ב	pl	m	—	imperative	פָּעַל		17
ש.ו.ב	pl	m	—	imperative	הִפְעִיל		18
ש.ו.ב	—	—	—	infinitive construct	פָּעַל		19
ש.ו.ב	—	—	—	infinitive construct	הִפְעִיל		20
ז.כ.ר	—	—	—	infinitive construct	פָּעַל		21
ז.כ.ר	—	—	—	infinitive construct	נִפְעַל		22
ז.כ.ר	—	—	—	infinitive construct	הִפְעִיל		23
ז.כ.ר	sg	f	2	imperfect	נִפְעַל		24

From the Passover Haggadah

In this chapter we are including two excerpts from the Passover Haggadah, in place of the Hebrew reading and the prayerbook selection. Since the Haggadah was compiled in post-Biblical times, some of the Hebrew forms will be unfamiliar to you. These forms are listed with the vocabulary. Read and translate.

A Song from the Passover Haggadah — Vocabulary

the five books of Torah ...... חֲמִשֵּׁי תוֹרָה

orders of the Mishnah .... סְדְרֵי מִשְׁנָה
(Jewish law code)

the Sabbath .... שַׁבַּתָּא = שַׁבָּת

shortened form of אֲשֶׁר .... שֶׁ

tablets of the covenant...... לְחוֹת הַבְּרִית
(the ten commandments)

אִמָּהוֹת = אִמּוֹת

אֶחָד מִי יוֹדֵעַ?
אֶחָד אֲנִי יוֹדֵעַ:
אֶחָד אֱלֹהֵינוּ שֶׁבַּשָּׁמַיִם וּבָאָרֶץ!

שְׁנַיִם מִי יוֹדֵעַ?
שְׁנַיִם אֲנִי יוֹדֵעַ:
שְׁנֵי לְחוֹת הַבְּרִית,
אֶחָד אֱלֹהֵינוּ שֶׁבַּשָּׁמַיִם וּבָאָרֶץ!

שְׁלֹשָׁה מִי יוֹדֵעַ?
שְׁלֹשָׁה אֲנִי יוֹדֵעַ:
שְׁלֹשָׁה אָבוֹת,
שְׁנֵי לְחוֹת הַבְּרִית,
אֶחָד אֱלֹהֵינוּ שֶׁבַּשָּׁמַיִם וּבָאָרֶץ!

אַרְבַּע מִי יוֹדֵעַ?
אַרְבַּע אֲנִי יוֹדֵעַ:
אַרְבַּע אִמָּהוֹת,
שְׁלֹשָׁה אָבוֹת,
שְׁנֵי לְחוֹת הַבְּרִית,
אֶחָד אֱלֹהֵינוּ שֶׁבַּשָּׁמַיִם וּבָאָרֶץ!

חֲמִשָּׁה מִי יוֹדֵעַ?
חֲמִשָּׁה אֲנִי יוֹדֵעַ:
חֲמִשָּׁה חֻמְשֵׁי תוֹרָה,
אַרְבַּע אִמָּהוֹת,
שְׁלֹשָׁה אָבוֹת,
שְׁנֵי לְחוֹת הַבְּרִית,
אֶחָד אֱלֹהֵינוּ שֶׁבַּשָּׁמַיִם וּבָאָרֶץ!

שִׁשָּׁה מִי יוֹדֵעַ?
שִׁשָּׁה אֲנִי יוֹדֵעַ:
שִׁשָּׁה סִדְרֵי מִשְׁנָה,
חֲמִשָּׁה חֻמְשֵׁי תוֹרָה,
אַרְבַּע אִמָּהוֹת,
שְׁלֹשָׁה אָבוֹת,
שְׁנֵי לְחוֹת הַבְּרִית,
אֶחָד אֱלֹהֵינוּ שֶׁבַּשָּׁמַיִם וּבָאָרֶץ!

שִׁבְעָה מִי יוֹדֵעַ?
שִׁבְעָה אֲנִי יוֹדֵעַ:
שִׁבְעָה יְמֵי שַׁבַּתָּא,
שִׁשָּׁה סִדְרֵי מִשְׁנָה,
חֲמִשָּׁה חֻמְשֵׁי תוֹרָה,
אַרְבַּע אִמָּהוֹת,
שְׁלֹשָׁה אָבוֹת,
שְׁנֵי לְחוֹת הַבְּרִית,
ETC ...   אֶחָד אֱלֹהֵינוּ שֶׁבַּשָּׁמַיִם וּבָאָרֶץ!

The Four Questions — Vocabulary

bitter (herbs)	מָרוֹר	differentiates	נִשְׁתַּנָּה
dipping *m pl participle*	מַטְבִּילִין	אוֹכְלִין = אוֹכְלִים	
even	אֲפִילוּ	leavened bread	חָמֵץ
יוֹשְׁבִין = יוֹשְׁבִים		unleavened bread	מַצָּה
reclining *m pl participle*	מְסֻבִּין	only	כֻּלוֹ
all of us	כֻּלָּנוּ	all vegetables	שְׁאָר יְרָקוֹת

In post-Biblical Hebrew, the masculine plural ending אִים often changed to אִין.

מַה נִּשְׁתַּנָּה הַלַּיְלָה הַזֶּה מִכָּל הַלֵּילוֹת? שֶׁבְּכָל הַלֵּילוֹת אָנוּ אוֹכְלִין חָמֵץ וּמַצָּה, הַלַּיְלָה הַזֶּה כֻּלוֹ מַצָּה. שֶׁבְּכָל הַלֵּילוֹת אָנוּ אוֹכְלִין שְׁאָר יְרָקוֹת, הַלַּיְלָה הַזֶּה (כֻּלוֹ) מָרוֹר. שֶׁבְּכָל הַלֵּילוֹת אֵין אָנוּ מַטְבִּילִין אֲפִילוּ פַּעַם אֶחָת, הַלַּיְלָה הַזֶּה שְׁתֵּי פְעָמִים. שֶׁבְּכָל הַלֵּילוֹת אָנוּ אוֹכְלִין בֵּין יוֹשְׁבִין וּבֵין מְסֻבִּין, הַלַּיְלָה הַזֶּה כֻּלָּנוּ מְסֻבִּין.

Guided Reading from Ruth

	Ruth 4:7	.1
	formerly לְפָנִים	
	וְזֹאת לְפָנִים בְּיִשְׂרָאֵל	
1. Now this was (the custom) formerly in Israel	redemption גְּאוּלָה	.2
	exchange תְּמוּרָה	
	confirm (פִּעֵל) ק.י.ם	
	עַל הַגְּאוּלָה וְעַל הַתְּמוּרָה לְקַיֵּם כָּל דָּבָר	
2. concerning redemption and exchange to confirm every matter:	draw off (פָּעַל) שׁ.ל.ף	.3
	his fellow citizen רֵעֵהוּ	
	sign תְּעוּדָה	
	שָׁלַף אִישׁ נַעֲלוֹ וְנָתַן לְרֵעֵהוּ וְזֹאת הַתְּעוּדָה בְּיִשְׂרָאֵל:	
3. a man drew off his shoe and gave (it) to his fellow citizen. And this was the sign in Israel.	Ruth 4:8	.4
	redeem, act as kinsman ג.א.ל	
	buy, acquire (פָּעַל) ק.נ.ה	
	וַיֹּאמֶר הַגֹּאֵל לְבֹעַז קְנֵה לָךְ וַיִּשְׁלֹף נַעֲלוֹ:	
4. And the kinsman said to Boaz: "Buy (it) for yourself!" And he drew off his shoe.	Ruth 4:9	.5
	witnesses עֵדִים	
	וַיֹּאמֶר בֹּעַז לַזְּקֵנִים וְכָל הָעָם עֵדִים אַתֶּם הַיּוֹם	

0

5. And Boaz said to the elders and all the people: "You are witnesses today	6. כִּי קָנִיתִי אֶת כָּל אֲשֶׁר לֶאֱלִימֶלֶךְ
6. that I have bought all that was Elimelech's,	7. וְאֵת כָּל אֲשֶׁר לְכִלְיוֹן וּמַחְלוֹן מִיַּד נָעֳמִי:
7. and all that was Kilyon's and Machlon's from the hand of Naomi.	8. Ruth 4:10 מֹאֲבִיָּה Moabitess וְגַם אֶת רוּת הַמֹּאֲבִיָּה אֵשֶׁת מַחְלוֹן קָנִיתִי לִי לְאִשָּׁה
8. And also Ruth the Moabitess, wife of Machlon, I have bought (or acquired) for myself for a wife	9. מֵת dead man נַחֲלָה inheritance לְהָקִים שֵׁם הַמֵּת עַל נַחֲלָתוֹ
9. (in order) to establish the name of the dead man upon his inheritance,	10. כ.ר.ת (נִפְעַל) be cut off מֵעִם from among וְלֹא יִכָּרֵת שֵׁם הַמֵּת מֵעִם אֶחָיו וּמִשַּׁעַר מְקוֹמוֹ
10. so the name of the dead man will not be cut off from among his brothers and from the gate of his place.	11. עֵדִים אַתֶּם הַיּוֹם:
11. You are witnesses today."	

Ruth 4:7 וְזֹאת לְפָנִים בְּיִשְׂרָאֵל עַל הַגְּאוּלָּה וְעַל הַתְּמוּרָה לְקַיֵּם כָּל דָּבָר שָׁלַף אִישׁ נַעֲלוֹ וְנָתַן לְרֵעֵהוּ וְזֹאת הַתְּעוּדָה בְּיִשְׂרָאֵל:

Ruth 4:8 וַיֹּאמֶר הַגֹּאֵל לְבֹעַז קְנֵה לָךְ וַיִּשְׁלֹף נַעֲלוֹ:

Ruth 4:9 וַיֹּאמֶר בֹּעַז לַזְּקֵנִים וְכָל הָעָם עֵדִים אַתֶּם הַיּוֹם כִּי קָנִיתִי אֶת כָּל אֲשֶׁר לֶאֱלִימֶלֶךְ וְאֵת כָּל אֲשֶׁר לְכִלְיוֹן וּמַחְלוֹן מִיַּד נָעֳמִי:

Ruth 4:10 וְגַם אֶת רוּת הַמֹּאֲבִיָּה אֵשֶׁת מַחְלוֹן קָנִיתִי לִי לְאִשָּׁה לְהָקִים שֵׁם הַמֵּת עַל נַחֲלָתוֹ וְלֹא יִכָּרֵת שֵׁם הַמֵּת מֵעִם אֶחָיו וּמִשַּׁעַר מְקוֹמוֹ עֵדִים אַתֶּם הַיּוֹם:

Chapter 31
The Hitpa'el הִתְפַּעֵל Pattern

Vocabulary

seed, offspring *n, m*	זֶרַע
thus *adv*	כֹּה
judgment *n, m*	מִשְׁפָּט, מִשְׁפָּטִים
please	נָא
prophet *n, m*	נָבִיא, נְבִיאִים
comfort, console *vb*	נ.ח.ם (פִּעֵל)
be comforted, be consoled *vb*	(פֻּעַל)
console oneself *vb*	(הִתְפַּעֵל)
slave, servant *n, m*	עֶבֶד, עֲבָדִים
labor, service *n, f*	עֲבֹדָה
pray *vb*	פ.ל.ל (הִתְפַּעֵל)
prayer *n, f*	תְּפִלָּה, תְּפִלּוֹת

Note: The plural form of the word זֶרַע, seed, is rarely used.

Reflexive Verbs

The types of verbs that you have learned thus far have all been either active or passive. However, another type of verb exists which is neither active nor passive, but reflexive. A reflexive verb is a verb which describes action that the subject of a sentence does to **himself**.

Active	He praised.
Passive	He was praised.
Reflexive	He praised **himself**.

There are two reflexive verb patterns in Hebrew. One is the נִפְעַל pattern, which you have already learned as a passive verb pattern. Verbs conjugated in the נִפְעַל pattern may also have a reflexive meaning.

Passive	He was guarded.	
	— or —	הוּא נִשְׁמַר. (נִפְעַל)
Reflexive	He guarded himself.	

246

The other reflexive verb pattern is the Hitpaʻel הִתְפַּעֵל pattern, which is the last Hebrew verb pattern that you will learn. The הִתְפַּעֵל pattern is usually neither active nor passive, but reflexive.

Below is a chart of all seven Hebrew verb patterns.

Hifʻal	הִפְעִיל	Piʻel	פִּעֵל	Paʻal	פָּעַל	Active
Hofʻal	הָפְעַל	Puʻal	פֻּעַל	Nifʻal	נִפְעַל	Passive
		Hitpaʻel	הִתְפַּעֵל	Nifʻal	נִפְעַל	Reflexive

The Hitpaʻel הִתְפַּעֵל Pattern

In this chapter, you will learn the conjugation of the Hitpaʻel הִתְפַּעֵל pattern, which is the reflexive pattern. Following is a list of some verbs you have learned in the פָּעַל and the פִּעֵל patterns which also appear in the הִתְפַּעֵל pattern. This list is included to illustrate the meaning of the הִתְפַּעֵל pattern, although these הִתְפַּעֵל verbs are used very infrequently in the Bible.

Meaning in הִתְפַּעֵל	Meaning in פָּעַל	Meaning in פִּעֵל	Root
praise oneself, boast, glorify	be praised	praise	ה.ל.ל
honor oneself	be honored	honor	כ.ב.ד
comfort oneself, be relieved	be comforted, be consoled	comfort, console	נ.ח.ם

Some verb roots appear in the הִתְפַּעֵל pattern but do not have a reflexive meaning. Such הִתְפַּעֵל verbs often have an active meaning.

Example:

Meaning in הִתְפַּעֵל	Root
pray	פ.ל.ל

The Conjugation of Verbs in the הִתְפַּעֵל Pattern

Following are charts showing the conjugation of the regular verb פ.ל.ל in the הִתְפַּעֵל pattern. The important characteristic of the הִתְפַּעֵל pattern is the two letter prefix which is added in all forms. This prefix is always a complete syllable; therefore, the first root letter will always take a dagesh if it is a BeGeD-KeFeT letter. Another characteristic of the הִתְפַּעֵל pattern is the dagesh which appears in the second root letter, as in the פִּעֵל and the פֻּעַל patterns.

The Perfect Tense

pray — (הִתְפַּעֵל) פ.ל.ל

1 c sg	הִתְפַּלַּלְתִּי	הִתְאַׄאַׄאְתִּי
2 m sg	הִתְפַּלַּלְתָּ	הִתְאַׄאַׄאְתָּ
2 f sg	הִתְפַּלַּלְתְּ	הִתְאַׄאַׄאְתְּ
3 m sg	הִתְפַּלֵּל	הִתְאַׄאֵׄא
3 f sg	הִתְפַּלְלָה	הִתְאַׄאְׄאָה
1 c pl	הִתְפַּלַּלְנוּ	הִתְאַׄאַׄאְנוּ
2 m pl	הִתְפַּלַּלְתֶּם	הִתְאַׄאַׄאְתֶּם
2 f pl	הִתְפַּלַּלְתֶּן	הִתְאַׄאַׄאְתֶּן
3 c pl	הִתְפַּלְלוּ	הִתְאַׄאְׄאוּ

1. The two letter prefix הִתְ–, characteristic of the הִתְפַּעֵל pattern, appears in all forms.

2. The dagesh, characteristic of the הִתְפַּעֵל pattern, appears in the second root letter in all forms.

The Imperfect Tense

pray — (הִתְפַּעֵל) פ.ל.ל

1 c sg	אֶתְפַּלֵּל	אֶתְאַׄאֵׄא
2 m sg	תִּתְפַּלֵּל	תִּתְאַׄאֵׄא
2 f sg	תִּתְפַּלְלִי	תִּתְאַׄאְׄאִי
3 m sg	יִתְפַּלֵּל	יִתְאַׄאֵׄא
3 f sg	תִּתְפַּלֵּל	תִּתְאַׄאֵׄא
1 c pl	נִתְפַּלֵּל	נִתְאַׄאֵׄא
2 m pl	תִּתְפַּלְלוּ	תִּתְאַׄאְׄאוּ
2 f pl	תִּתְפַּלֵּלְנָה	תִּתְאַׄאֵׄאְנָה
3 m pl	יִתְפַּלְלוּ	יִתְאַׄאְׄאוּ
3 f pl	תִּתְפַּלֵּלְנָה	תִּתְאַׄאֵׄאְנָה

1. The basic vowel pattern is XXXXX.

2. The letter ה disappears from the prefix הִתְ–, and is replaced by the regular prefix consonants of the imperfect tense.

3. The dagesh, characteristic of the הִתְפַּעֵל pattern, appears in the second root letter in all forms.

The Participle

	פ.ל.ל (הִתְפַּעֵל) — pray	
m sg	מִתְפַּלֵּל	מִתְאַxxx
f sg	מִתְפַּלֶּלֶת/מִתְפַּלְלָה	מִתְאַxֶxֶת/מִתְאַxxָה
m pl	מִתְפַּלְלִים	מִתְאַxxִים
f pl	מִתְפַּלְלוֹת	מִתְאַxxוֹת

1. The two letter prefix מְת– appears in all forms of the participle.
2. The dagesh, characteristic of the הִתְפַּעֵל pattern, appears in the second root letter in **all** forms.

The Imperative

	פ.ל.ל (הִתְפַּעֵל) — pray	
m sg	הִתְפַּלֵּל	הִתְאַxֵx
f sg	הִתְפַּלְלִי	הִתְאַxxִי
m pl	הִתְפַּלְלוּ	הִתְאַxxוּ
f pl	הִתְפַּלֵּלְנָה	הִתְאַxֵxְנָה

1. The two letter prefix הִת–, characteristic of the הִתְפַּעֵל pattern, appears in all forms.
2. The dagesh, characteristic of the הִתְפַּעֵל pattern, appears in the second root letter in **all** forms.

The Infinitive

	פ.ל.ל (הִתְפַּעֵל) — pray	
construct	(לְ) הִתְפַּלֵּל לְהִתְפַּלֵּל	לְהִתְאַxֵx

1. The two letter prefix הִת–, characteristic of the הִתְפַּעֵל pattern, appears in the infinitive construct.
2. The dagesh, characteristic of the הִתְפַּעֵל pattern, appears in the second root letter in **the** infinitive construct.
3. The infinitive absolute of the הִתְפַּעֵל pattern is rarely used and will not be taught.

The Verb נ.ח.ם

The conjugation of the verb נ.ח.ם is slightly irregular because the middle root letter is ח, one of the throaty five letters. This letter usually does not take a sheva. Therefore, whenever a sheva appears under the second root letter in the conjugation, the combination vowel אֲ appears under the letter ח in the verb נ.ח.ם.

Exercises

Exercise 1. Conjugate the following roots in all forms of the verb pattern given.

1. כ.ב.ד (פִּעֵל)   2. שׁ.פ.ך (נִפְעַל)   3. כ.ב.ד (הִתְפַּעֵל)

Exercise 2. Rewrite the sentences below, replacing the underlined word with each word in the list that follows. Every word or grammatical form in the sentence that agrees with the underlined word should be changed to agree with the newly substituted words. Read the sentences aloud. Translate.

1. עוֹדֶנִּי מִתְפַּלֵל עַל הַשָּׁלוֹם יוֹם יוֹם.

   A. עוֹדְךָ   B. עוֹדֶנּוּ   C. עוֹדֵנוּ   D. עוֹדֶנָּה   E. עוֹדָם

   F. עוֹדְךָ

2. הַמֶּלֶךְ הִתְהַלֵל וְלֹא הִלֵל אֶת עֲבֹדַת עֲבָדָיו.

   A. אַרְבַּעַת בְּנֵי הַשּׁוֹפֵט   B. בַּת הַנָּבִיא   C. אַתֵּן   D. אֲנַחְנוּ   E. אֲנִי

   F. אַתְּ   G. נְשֵׁי הַשַּׂר   H. אַתֶּם   I. אַתָּה

3. (אַתָּה) תִּתְנַחֵם כַּאֲשֶׁר תִּרְאֶה אֶת עֲבֹדַת בָּנֶיךָ הַטּוֹבִים.

   A. אַתֵּן   B. אֲנִי   C. רִבְקָה   D. הַנָּבִיא   E. שִׁבְעַת הָאָבוֹת

   F. אַתֶּם   G. אֲנַחְנוּ   H. אַתְּ   I. תֵּשַׁע הַמִּשְׁפָּחוֹת

4. הַנָּבִיא יְדַבֵּר אֶת הָאֱמֶת וְהָאֲנָשִׁים לֹא יָשִׂימוּ לִבָּם אֵלָיו.

   A. אֲנִי   B. זֶרַע אַבְרָהָם   C. חֲמֵשֶׁת הַשָּׂרִים   D. אַתֶּם   E. אַתְּ

   F. שְׁלֹשׁ הַבָּנוֹת   G. אֲנַחְנוּ   H. אַתָּה   I. הָעֶבֶד

5. הָאָב צִוָּה אֶת בְּנוֹ לֵאמֹר: "לֵךְ נָא אֶל הַמִּדְבָּר לְהִתְפַּלֵל תְּפִלּוֹת וְלִרְאוֹת אֶת הָעֲבֹדָה בַּמִּשְׁכָּן".

   A. אַתְּ   B. אֲנַחְנוּ   C. שָׂרָה   D. שֵׁשֶׁת הַשּׁוֹמְרִים   E. אַתֵּן

   F. אֲנִי   G. אַתָּה   H. שְׁתֵּי נָשִׁים   I. אַתֶּם

Exercise 3. Rewrite the following sentences, filling in the blanks with all forms of the verb root shown that will yield a meaningful sentence. Translate.

Example:

(ש.כ.ב) (אַתָּה) _____ בַּמִּשְׁכָּב בְּבֵיתֶךָ.

תִּשְׁכַּב בַּמִּשְׁכָּב בְּבֵיתֶךָ.

אַתָּה שׁוֹכֵב בַּמִּשְׁכָּב בְּבֵיתֶךָ.

שָׁכַבְתָּ בַּמִּשְׁכָּב בְּבֵיתֶךָ.

שְׁכֹב תִּשְׁכַּב בַּמִּשְׁכָּב בְּבֵיתֶךָ.

שָׁכוֹב שָׁכַבְתָּ בַּמִּשְׁכָּב בְּבֵיתֶךָ.

שְׁכַב בַּמִּשְׁכָּב בְּבֵיתֶךָ.

1. ש.מ.ע (אַתֶּם) _____ אֶת הַדְּבָרִים מִפִּי זַרְעֲכֶם.

2. ר.א.ה (אֲנִי) _____ אֶת הַמָּקוֹם אֲשֶׁר נִכְתְּבוּ הַמִּשְׁפָּטִים הָאֵלֶּה שָׁם.

3. ב.ו.א (אַתְּ) _____ נָא לִפְנֵי הַשּׁוֹפֵט לִשְׁמֹעַ אֶת מִשְׁפָּטוֹ.

4. ש.ל.ך הָעֶבֶד _____ אֶת הָעֵץ אֶל תּוֹךְ הַיָּם.

5. ל.ח.מ בְּעֵת הָרָעָב, _____ אַנְשֵׁי כְנַעַן בְּעַם יִשְׂרָאֵל וְלָקְחוּ אֹתוֹ כַּעֲבָדִים לְאַרְצָם.

6. פ.ל.ל כֹּה הֵם _____ תְּפִלּוֹת רַבּוֹת בָּעֵת הַהִיא.

7. ש.ו.ב כֹּה אָמַר הַנָּבִיא לְדָוִד: _____ נָא עִם זַרְעֲךָ לְאֶרֶץ יִשְׂרָאֵל.

8. ע.ש.ה הַשֹּׁפֵט _____ מִשְׁפָּט כָּל יְמֵי חַיָּיו.

Exercise 4. In the following sentences, circle the verb form which is conjugated in the pattern that best fits the meaning of the sentence. Translate.

Example:

הַנַּעַר (סִפֵּר, סֻפַּר, סָפַר) אֶת הַבְּהֵמוֹת בַּשָּׂדֶה.

1. הוּא שָׁמַע אֶת תְּפִלַּת עַבְדּוֹ וְ(הִתְנַחֵם, נֻחַם, נִחַם) אֹתוֹ.

2. הַנָּבִיא (יִזְכֹּר, יְזַכֵּר, יַזְכִּיר) לַמֶּלֶךְ כִּי עָלָיו לִשְׁמֹר אֶת הַמִּצְוֹת.

3. תִּשְׁעַת הַזְּקֵנִים (הִלְלוּ, הֻלְּלוּ, הִתְהַלְלוּ) אֶת מַעֲשֵׂי גִּבּוֹר הַחַיִל.

4. עַתָּה הַמֶּלֶךְ (גּוֹדֵל, מְגַדֵּל, מַגְדִּיל) אֶת שְׁמִי בְּכָל הָאָרֶץ כִּי הִצַּלְתִּי אֶת עַמִּי מִיַּד מוֹאָב.

5. כֹּה אָמַר הַנָּבִיא: (הַמְלִיכוּ, הָמְלְכוּ, מָלְכוּ) מֶלֶךְ מִזֶּרַע דָּוִד.

6. הָאָב צִוָּה אֶת בְּנוֹ, לֵאמֹר: (הָשֵׁב, שׁוּב, לָשׁוּב) נָא אֶל אַדְמָתִי.

Exercise 5. Translate the following sentences into Hebrew.

1. What did you m, sg tell (to) the slave?

2. I told (to) the slave to bring the utensils.

3. You m, sg will tell (to) the slaves to bring the bread and wine.

4. The slaves brought the bread and wine to the house of the king.

5. We will put the bread and wine in front of the king.

Exercise 6. The following selection is from the narrative known as "The Binding of Isaac", found in Genesis 22. The section you find here (Genesis 22:1-12) has been slightly edited, but the words you see are taken directly from the Bible. Read and translate.

Vocabulary for Reading Selection

knife	מַאֲכֶלֶת	tested	נִסָּה
the two of them together	שְׁנֵיהֶם יַחְדָּו	here I am	הִנֵּנִי = הִנֵּה + אֲנִי
where?	אַיֵּה	your only one	יְחִידְךָ
sheep	שֶׂה	Moriah *place name*	מֹרִיָּה
altar	מִזְבֵּחַ	raise him up	הַעֲלֵהוּ
lay out	ע.ר.ך	burnt-offering	עֹלָה
bind	ע.ק.ד	get up early	ש.כ.ם
on top of	מִמַּעַל	chop	ב.ק.ע
slaughter	ש.ח.ט	and he lifted up	וַיִּשָּׂא
cry out	ק.ר.א	far away	רָחֹק
anything	מְאוּמָה	fire	אֵשׁ

וַיְהִי אַחַר הַדְּבָרִים הָאֵלֶּה וְהָאֱלֹהִים נִסָּה אֶת אַבְרָהָם וַיֹּאמֶר אֵלָיו אַבְרָהָם וַיֹּאמֶר הִנֵּנִי:

וַיֹּאמֶר קַח נָא אֶת בִּנְךָ אֶת יְחִידְךָ אֲשֶׁר אָהַבְתָּ אֶת יִצְחָק וְלֶךְ לְךָ אֶל אֶרֶץ הַמֹּרִיָּה וְהַעֲלֵהוּ שָׁם לְעֹלָה עַל אַחַד הֶהָרִים אֲשֶׁר אֹמַר אֵלֶיךָ:

וַיַּשְׁכֵּם אַבְרָהָם בַּבֹּקֶר . . . וַיִּקַּח אֶת . . . יִצְחָק בְּנוֹ וַיְבַקַּע עֲצֵי עֹלָה וַיָּקָם וַיֵּלֶךְ אֶל הַמָּקוֹם אֲשֶׁר אָמַר לוֹ הָאֱלֹהִים:

בַּיּוֹם הַשְּׁלִישִׁי וַיִּשָּׂא אַבְרָהָם אֶת עֵינָיו וַיַּרְא אֶת הַמָּקוֹם מֵרָחֹק:

. . . וַיִּקַּח אַבְרָהָם אֶת עֲצֵי הָעֹלָה וַיָּשֶׂם עַל יִצְחָק בְּנוֹ וַיִּקַּח בְּיָדוֹ אֶת הָאֵשׁ וְאֶת הַמַּאֲכֶלֶת וַיֵּלְכוּ שְׁנֵיהֶם יַחְדָּו:

וַיֹּאמֶר יִצְחָק אֶל אַבְרָהָם אָבִיו וַיֹּאמֶר אָבִי וַיֹּאמֶר הִנֶּנִּי בְנִי וַיֹּאמֶר הִנֵּה הָאֵשׁ וְהָעֵצִים וְאַיֵּה הַשֶּׂה לְעֹלָה:

וַיֹּאמֶר אַבְרָהָם אֱלֹהִים יִרְאֶה לּוֹ הַשֶּׂה לְעֹלָה בְּנִי וַיֵּלְכוּ שְׁנֵיהֶם יַחְדָּו:

וַיָּבֹאוּ אֶל הַמָּקוֹם אֲשֶׁר אָמַר לוֹ הָאֱלֹהִים וַיִּבֶן שָׁם אַבְרָהָם אֶת הַמִּזְבֵּחַ וַיַּעֲרֹךְ אֶת הָעֵצִים וַיַּעֲקֹד אֶת יִצְחָק בְּנוֹ וַיָּשֶׂם אֹתוֹ עַל הַמִּזְבֵּחַ מִמַּעַל לָעֵצִים:

וַיִּשְׁלַח אַבְרָהָם אֶת יָדוֹ וַיִּקַּח אֶת הַמַּאֲכֶלֶת לִשְׁחֹט אֶת בְּנוֹ:

וַיִּקְרָא אֵלָיו מַלְאַךְ יְהוה מִן הַשָּׁמַיִם וַיֹּאמֶר אַבְרָהָם אַבְרָהָם וַיֹּאמֶר הִנֵּנִי:

וַיֹּאמֶר אַל תִּשְׁלַח יָדְךָ אֶל הַנַּעַר וְאַל תַּעַשׂ לוֹ מְאוּמָה. . . .

Exercise 7. Fill in the proper form of the verb in the last column and translate.

Root	Number	Gender	Person	Tense	Pattern	Word
ג.נ.ב	sg	c	1	imperfect	פָּעַל	1
ג.נ.ב	sg	c	1	imperfect	נִפְעַל	2
כ.ב.ד	sg	c	1	imperfect	הִתְפַּעֵל	3
ג.נ.ב	sg	m	3	perfect	פָּעַל	4
ג.נ.ב	sg	m	3	perfect	נִפְעַל	5
כ.ב.ד	sg	m	3	perfect	הִתְפַּעֵל	6
ב.ו.א	pl	f	3	perfect	פָּעַל	7
ב.ו.א	pl	f	3	perfect	הִפְעִיל	8
ב.ו.א	pl	m	—	imperative	פָּעַל	9
ב.ו.א	pl	m	—	imperative	הִפְעִיל	10
נ.ח.ם	sg	m	—	participle	פָּעַל	11
נ.ח.ם	sg	m	—	participle	הִתְפַּעֵל	12
ס.פ.ר	sg	f	2	imperfect	פָּעַל	13
ס.פ.ר	sg	f	2	imperfect	פָּעַל	14
ע.ל.ה	sg	f	3	perfect	פָּעַל	15
ל.ק.ח	pl	m	3	perfect	פָּעַל	16
ל.ק.ח	pl	m	3	perfect	נִפְעַל	17
ל.ק.ח	pl	m	3	imperfect	פָּעַל	18
ל.ק.ח	pl	m	3	imperfect	נִפְעַל	19
ל.ק.ח	—	—	—	infinitive construct	פָּעַל	20
ל.ק.ח	—	—	—	infinitive construct	נִפְעַל	21
ז.כ.ר	pl	f	—	participle	פָּעַל	22
ז.כ.ר	pl	f	—	participle	הִפְעִיל	23
ז.כ.ר	pl	f	—	participle	נִפְעַל	24

From the Prayerbook

Prayerbook Vocabulary

remembrance..................	זִכָּרוֹן, זֶכֶר	sanctify	ק.ד.שׁ (פָּעַל)
in the beginning	בְּרֵאשִׁית	take pleasure	ר.צ.ה (פָּעַל)
beginning	תְּחִלָּה	holiness....................	קֹדֶשׁ
festival	מִקְרָא	favor	רָצוֹן
the going out (Exodus)...........	יְצִיאָה	give as an inheritance......	נ.ח.ל (הִפְעִיל)

Selection from the Prayerbook (the Kiddush for Shabbat)

בָּרוּךְ אַתָּה, יְיָ אֱלֹהֵינוּ, מֶלֶךְ הָעוֹלָם, אֲשֶׁר קִדְּשָׁנוּ בְּמִצְוֹתָיו וְרָצָה בָנוּ, וְשַׁבַּת קָדְשׁוֹ בְּאַהֲבָה וּבְרָצוֹן הִנְחִילָנוּ, זִכָּרוֹן לְמַעֲשֵׂה בְרֵאשִׁית. כִּי הוּא יוֹם תְּחִלָּה לְמִקְרָאֵי קֹדֶשׁ, זֵכֶר לִיצִיאַת מִצְרָיִם. כִּי בָנוּ בָחַרְתָּ וְאוֹתָנוּ קִדַּשְׁתָּ מִכָּל הָעַמִּים, וְשַׁבַּת קָדְשְׁךָ בְּאַהֲבָה וּבְרָצוֹן הִנְחַלְתָּנוּ. בָּרוּךְ אַתָּה, יְיָ, מְקַדֵּשׁ הַשַּׁבָּת.

First translate the prayer into your own words, then read the translations quoted below.

Prayerbook Translations

"Blessed are thou, Lord our God, King of the universe, who hast sanctified us with thy commandments and hast been pleased with us; thou hast graciously given us thy holy Sabbath as a heritage, in remembrance of the creation. The Sabbath is the first among the holy festivals which recall the exodus from Egypt. Indeed, thou hast chosen us and hallowed us above all nations, and hast graciously given us thy holy Sabbath as a heritage. Blessed art thou, O Lord, who hallowest the Sabbath."

Daily Prayer Book, Philip Birnbaum, 1977, p. 290

"Blessed is the Lord our God, Ruler of the universe, who hallows us with his Mitzvot and takes delight in us. In His love and favor He has made His holy Sabbath our heritage, as a reminder of the work of creation. It is first among our sacred days, and a remembrance of the Exodus from Egypt. O God, You have chosen us and set us apart from all the peoples, and in love and favor have given us the Sabbath day as a sacred inheritance. Blessed is the Lord, for the Sabbath and its holiness."

Gates of Prayer, the New Union Prayerbook, 1975, p. 719

Guided Reading from Ruth

	Ruth 4:11 .1
	עֵדִים witnesses
	וַיֹּאמְרוּ כָּל הָעָם אֲשֶׁר בַּשַּׁעַר וְהַזְּקֵנִים עֵדִים
1. All the people that were by the gate and the elders said: "(We are) witnesses.	שְׁתֵּיהֶם the two of them .2
	יִתֵּן יהוה אֶת הָאִשָּׁה הַבָּאָה אֶל בֵּיתֶךָ כְּרָחֵל וּכְלֵאָה אֲשֶׁר בָּנוּ שְׁתֵּיהֶם אֶת בֵּית יִשְׂרָאֵל
2. May the Lord grant that the woman who is coming into your house will be like Rachel and Leah, who built, the two of them, the house of Israel.	אֶפְרָתָה Ephrata *place name* .3 קְרָא שֵׁם be famous
	וַעֲשֵׂה חַיִל בְּאֶפְרָתָה וּקְרָא שֵׁם בְּבֵית לָחֶם:
3. Act with strength in Ephrata, and be famous in Bethlehem!	Ruth 4:12 .4
	וִיהִי *indirect imperative* may it be פֶּרֶץ Peretz *man's name* תָּמָר Tamar *woman's name* י.ל.ד give birth, bear
	וִיהִי בֵיתְךָ כְּבֵית פֶּרֶץ אֲשֶׁר יָלְדָה תָמָר לִיהוּדָה
4. May your house be like the house of Peretz, whom Tamar bore to Judah,	מִן הַזֶּרַע אֲשֶׁר יִתֵּן יהוה לְךָ מִן הַנַּעֲרָה הַזֹּאת: .5
5. from the seed that the Lord will give you from this maiden."	Ruth 4:13 .6
	וַיִּקַּח בֹּעַז אֶת רוּת וַתְּהִי לוֹ לְאִשָּׁה וַיָּבֹא אֵלֶיהָ
6. And Boaz took Ruth for himself, and she became his wife, and he came to her (was intimate with her)	הֵרָיוֹן conception .7 תֵּלֵד she will bear
	וַיִּתֵּן יהוה לָהּ הֵרָיוֹן וַתֵּלֶד בֵּן:
7. and the Lord gave conception to her, and she bore a son.	

Ruth 4:11 וַיֹּאמְרוּ כָּל הָעָם אֲשֶׁר בַּשַּׁעַר וְהַזְּקֵנִים עֵדִים יִתֵּן יהוה אֶת הָאִשָּׁה הַבָּאָה אֶל בֵּיתֶךָ כְּרָחֵל וּכְלֵאָה אֲשֶׁר בָּנוּ שְׁתֵּיהֶם אֶת בֵּית יִשְׂרָאֵל וַעֲשֵׂה חַיִל בְּאֶפְרָתָה וּקְרָא שֵׁם בְּבֵית לָחֶם:

Ruth 4:12 וִיהִי בֵיתְךָ כְּבֵית פֶּרֶץ אֲשֶׁר יָלְדָה תָמָר לִיהוּדָה מִן הַזֶּרַע אֲשֶׁר יִתֵּן יהוה לְךָ מִן הַנַּעֲרָה הַזֹּאת:

Ruth 4:13 וַיִּקַּח בֹּעַז אֶת רוּת וַתְּהִי לוֹ לְאִשָּׁה וַיָּבֹא אֵלֶיהָ וַיִּתֵּן יהוה לָהּ הֵרָיוֹן וַתֵּלֶד בֵּן:

Chapter 32
Verb Variations
Using the Verb Charts

Vocabulary

redeem, act as kinsman, *vb*	(פָּעַל)	ג.א.ל
be redeemed *vb*	(נִפְעַל)	
bear, bring forth, give birth *vb*	(פָּעַל)	י.ל.ד
be born *vb*	(נִפְעַל)	
beget *vb*	(הִפְעִיל)	
go out, come out *vb*	(פָּעַל)	י.צ.א
bring out *vb*	(הִפְעִיל)	
go down *vb*	(פָּעַל)	י.ר.ד
bring down *vb*	(הִפְעִיל)	
find *vb*	(פָּעַל)	מ.צ.א
be found *vb*	(נִפְעַל)	
fall *vb*	(פָּעַל)	נ.פ.ל
cause to fall, cast *vb*	(הִפְעִיל)	
lift, carry, take *vb*	(פָּעַל)	נ.ש.א
be lifted up *vb*	(נִפְעַל)	
work, serve *vb*	(פָּעַל)	ע.ב.ד
cause to work *vb*	(הִפְעִיל)	
stand *vb*	(פָּעַל)	ע.מ.ד
cause to stand, set up *vb*	(הִפְעִיל)	
call, proclaim, read *vb*	(פָּעַל)	ק.ר.א
be called, be proclaimed *vb*	(נִפְעַל)	

Names

Moses	מֹשֶׁה
Aaron	אַהֲרֹן
Joseph	יוֹסֵף

256

Verb Variations

You have already learned that certain Hebrew letters cause major variations in verb conjugations when they are part of the verb root. You have learned the variations that occur when the final root letter is a ה or when the middle root letter is a י or ו. However, these are not the only types of variations that can occur in Hebrew verb conjugations.

In this chapter, we introduce ten new verbs. Each of these verbs contains root letters that cause specific variations in the verb conjugation. We are not going to teach you these new variations in detail. Instead, we will use these verbs as examples to teach you how to use the verb charts included in the back of this book. The conjugations of all the verbs introduced in this chapter can be found by using the verb charts.

Using the Verb Charts

There are nine verb charts in the back of this book beginning on page 276. The first chart shows the conjugation of regular verb roots. Each of the other charts shows a particular type of variation. For example the second chart shows the conjugation of final ה verbs, which is a variation you have already learned.

In this chapter you will find brief descriptions of each of the variations shown in the verb charts. These descriptions give the most important features of each variation and list the verbs we have introduced which belong to that variation. After you have read the descriptions, you can see the conjugations of each variation by looking at the appropriate verb chart. Each verb chart shows the conjugation of a model verb root. All other verb roots belonging to that type of variation are conjugated in the same way as the model verb. With the help of the verb charts, you will be able to find *every* form of *every* verb introduced in this chapter.

Note on the Verb Charts

The verb charts included in this book are not complete. They do not show the conjugation of each variation in all the possible verb patterns. Moreover, they do not show every type of variation that exists. We have chosen to present only the most common types of variations, and the most frequently used patterns within those types.

Regular Verbs — Chart #1

Verb Chart #1 shows the regular verb פ.ק.ד. We have chosen the verb root פ.ק.ד because it is a completely regular root and appears in all seven patterns. The general meaning of פ.ק.ד is "attend to," "visit" or "muster," but the specific meanings in each verb pattern are varied. We are not teaching this verb root as part of our active vocabulary because it is a complex verb with many shades of meaning. As you will recall from Chapter 16, there are two possible conjugations for regular verbs in the imperfect tense — one conjugation is used for some verbs, the other conjugation for other verbs. In Chart #1 the verb root שׁ.כ.ב is used to illustrate one conjugation, and the verb root פ.ק.ד the other.

Final ה Verbs — Chart #2

Model Verbs: command — צ.ו.ה   build — ב.נ.ה

Verb Chart #2 lists the conjugation of final ה verbs in the פָּעַל , פִּעֵל and נִפְעַל patterns. The last root letter ה often disappears from these verbs, and vowel pattern changes usually take place. This variation was discussed in Chapters 22 and 25.

Hollow Verbs — Chart #3

Model Verbs: arise — ק.ו.ם   put — שׂ.י.ם

Verb Chart #3 lists the conjugation of hollow verbs in the פָּעַל and הִפְעִיל patterns. The middle root letter ו or י disappears in some forms of the hollow verb. This variation was discussed in Chapters 23 and 27.

Initial י Verbs — Chart #4

Model Verbs: give birth — י.ל.ד   go down — י.ר.ד

Verb Chart #4 lists the conjugation of verbs with י as first root letter in the פָּעַל, נִפְעַל, and הִפְעִיל patterns. The י disappears in almost every form. This variation has not been discussed previously. However, you have already learned most of the פָּעַל forms of the verb י.שׁ.ב, which is an initial י verb.

Initial נ Verbs — Chart #5

Model Verb: fall — נ.פ.ל

Verb Chart #5 lists the conjugation of verbs with נ as first root letter in the פָּעַל and הִפְעִיל patterns. The נ disappears in many forms of these two patterns. This variation has not been discussed previously. However, the verb נ.ת.ן which has the letter נ as first root letter, is irregular, and the conjugation of this verb was listed separately in Chapter 24. In Chapter 26 you also learned the הִפְעִיל forms of the verbs נ.צ.ל and נ.ג.ד, which are initial נ verbs.

Initial א or ע Verbs — Chart #6

Model Verbs: work — ע.ב.ד   say — א.מ.ר

Verb Chart #6 lists the conjugation of verbs with א or ע as first root letter in the פָּעַל and הִפְעִיל patterns. These letters cause some changes in the vowel pattern. There are two variations shown for the פָּעַל pattern. The first includes א.מ.ר and א.כ.ל which were introduced in Chapter 24, and the second variation in the פָּעַל includes the verbs א.ס.ף, ע.ב.ד, and ע.מ.ד.

Verbs with א, ה, ח, or ע as Middle Root Letter — Chart #7

Model Verb: redeem — ג.א.ל

Verb Chart #7 lists the conjugation of verbs with א, ה, ח, or ע as second root letter in the פָּעַל and the נִפְעַל patterns. These letters cause some changes in the vowel pattern. You have already learned how to conjugate the verbs ב.ח.ר, ל.ח.ם, and נ.ח.ם, which are this type.

Final א Verbs — Chart #8

Model Verb: call, read — ק.ר.א

Verb Chart #8 lists the conjugation of verbs with א as third root letter in the פָּעַל and נִפְעַל patterns. The א does not disappear, but there are vowel changes in all patterns.

Dual Variation Verbs — Chart #9

Some verbs belong to two different types of variations. Following are examples.

1. Verbs with י as first root letter and א as third root letter.
    Model Verb: go out — י.צ.א
    The conjugation of this verb in the פָּעַל and the הִפְעִיל patterns is included in Chart #9.
2. Verbs with נ as first root letter and א as third root letter.
    Model Verb: lift, carry — נ.שׂ.א
    The conjugation of this verb in the פָּעַל and the נִפְעַל patterns is included in Chart #9.
3. Verbs with ע as first root letter and ה as third root letter.
    Model Verbs: do, make — ע.שׂ.ה   answer — ע.נ.ה   go up, ascend — ע.ל.ה
    The conjugation of these verbs in the פָּעַל pattern was shown in Chapter 22.
4. Verbs with א as first root letter and one of the "throaty five" as middle root letter.
    Model Verb: love — א.ה.ב
    The conjugation of this verb in the פָּעַל pattern was shown in Chapter 24.
5. Hollow verbs with א as third root letter.
    Model Verb: come, go — ב.ו.א
    The conjugation of this verb in the פָּעַל pattern was shown in Chapter 23 and the conjugation in the הִפְעִיל pattern was shown in Chapter 27.

How to Identify Unfamiliar Verb Forms

In the exercises for this chapter, you will need to be able to identify and translate verb forms that you have not learned by using the verb charts in the back of the book and the vocabulary for this chapter. This is the first step toward learning to translate unfamiliar forms that you will encounter in later reading.

In order to translate any verb form, you must identify:

1. The person, gender, number, and tense of the verb form
2. The verb pattern in which the root appears
3. The verb root

You have already been doing this sort of identifying in the exercises with verbs that you know. The same process is involved in translating unfamiliar verb forms.

When you see a strange verb form, you should go through the following steps to identify and translate it.

1. If there is a suffix, identify it and remove it. The suffix can tell you the person, gender, number, and tense of the verb form.
    Examples: אִים — *m sg* participle   תִּי — *1 c sg* perfect tense
    Removing the suffix brings you closer to discovering the three letter verb root.

2. If there is a prefix, identify it and remove it. The prefix also can tell you the person, gender, number and tense of the verb form.
    Example: א with a vowel (אָ , אֳ , אֶ) — *1 c sg* imperfect tense
    The prefix also may help you distinguish the verb pattern of the form.
    Examples: מ — participle, in the פָּעַל , פֻּעַל , הִפְעִיל, or הָפְעַל pattern
                   הִת — perfect tense, imperative, or infinitive of the הִתְפַּעֵל pattern
    Removing the prefix brings you closer to discovering the three letter verb root.

3. If three letters remain, they are probably the root letters. You can check the glossary to find the meaning of the root. However, if you can't find that three letter root in the glossary, it is possible that one of those three letters is not a root letter. For example, the letters ו and י often appear as vowels in verb conjugations and are not part of the verb root. If this happens, continue with step 4.

4. If fewer than three letters remain, you know that the verb root is one that has disappearing root letters in their conjugations. In this book, you have learned four types of verbs that have disappearing root letters in their conjugations.
    A. Final ה verbs — ה. x.x   C. Initial נ Verbs — x.x.נ
    B. Hollow Verbs — x.ו.x or x.י.x   D. Initial י Verbs — x.x.י
    You can assume that the verb form belongs to one of these types of variations. Check the glossary to see which of the possible verb roots exist and find their meanings.

5. Look up the conjugation of these possible verb roots in the verb charts in order to identify the form correctly. When you have correctly identified the form, you should be able to translate it, using the meaning found in the glossary.

Practice with Unfamiliar Verb Forms

The following examples are included to show you how to identify and translate an unfamiliar verb form, using the steps you have learned.

Identify and Translate the Verb Form מוֹרִידִים.

1. The אִים ending tells you that this form is probably a *m pl* participle. Remove it and you are left with מוֹרִיד.

2. The letter מ could be a root letter or a prefix. If the letter מ is a prefix, then this form must be a participle in the פְּעַל‎, פֻּעַל‎, הִפְעִיל‎, or הֻפְעַל pattern. This agrees with the assumption that you have already made about the אִים ending. Moreover, you already know that the אִי vowel, which appears in this form, is characteristic of the הִפְעִיל pattern. Therefore, you can assume that מוֹרִידִים is a *m pl* participle in the הִפְעִיל pattern. Remove the prefix and the suffix, as well as the אִי vowel characteristic of the הִפְעִיל pattern, and you are left with the letters ד‎, ר‎, and ו.

3. If you check the glossary, you will discover that the root ו.ר.ד does not exist. You can also see that the letter ו appears as a vowel in the form מוֹרִידִים. Therefore, the letter ו is probably not one of the root letters.

4. Now you know that the verb root is one of the four types that have disappearing root letters. Therefore, the root could be either ר.ד.ה (a final ה verb), ר.ו.ד or ר.י.ד (a hollow verb), י.ר.ד (an initial י verb), or נ.ר.ד (an initial נ verb). If you check the glossary, you will find that only one of these four possibilities is listed — י.ר.ד.

5. In order to be certain that your assumptions were correct, you should check Verb Chart #4 — Initial י Verbs. If you look on the chart for the *m pl* participle of י.ר.ד in the הִפְעִיל pattern, you will see the form מוֹרִידִים. From the glossary you learn that the root י.ר.ד in the הִפְעִיל pattern means "bring down." Therefore, you know that the form מוֹרִידִים means "we/you/they (are) bringing down" or "(those who are) bringing down," depending on the context.

Identify and Translate the Verb Form תִּפֹּלְנָה

1. Either the single letter ה or the two letters נָה could be a suffix. If the two letters נָה are the suffix, then this must be a *2 f pl* or *3 f pl* form in the imperfect tense.

261

2. The letter תּ could be an imperfect tense prefix. The prefix תּ together with the suffix נָה indicate that this form is a *2 f pl* or *3 f pl* form in the imperfect tense. Remove the prefix and the suffix and you are left with the letters ל and פ.

3. Since fewer than three letters remain, you know that the verb root is one of the four types that have disappearing root letters.

4. The verb root could be either פ.ל.ה (a final ה verb), פ.ו.ל or פ.י.ל (a hollow verb), י.פ.ל (an initial י verb), נ.פ.ל (an initial נ verb). You may notice that there is a dagesh in the letter פ, which could indicate that a letter has dropped out in front of the פ. In that case, the missing root letter would have to be either an initial י or an initial נ. If you check the glossary, you will find that only one of these possibilities is listed — נ.פ.ל.

5. Look up the conjugation of נ.פ.ל in Verb Chart #5 — Initial נ Verbs. You have assumed that the form תִּפֹּלְנָה is a *2 f pl* or *3 f pl* imperfect tense form. If you check the different patterns, you discover that תִּפֹּלְנָה is the *2 f pl* or *3 f pl* imperfect tense form in the פָּעַל pattern. From the glossary you learn that the root נ.פ.ל in the פָּעַל pattern means "fall." Therefore, you know that the form תִּפֹּלְנָה means "you will fall" or "they will fall."

Identify and Translate the Verb Form נִמְצֵאת

1. The letter ת could be a suffix. Since it does not have a vowel underneath it which can be pronounced, it could be a *2 f sg* perfect tense ending. It could also be a *f sg* participle ending. Remove the suffix and you are left with the letters א, צ, מ, and נ.

2. The prefix נ could indicate either a נִפְעַל form or a *1 c pl* imperfect tense form. However, you know that נִמְצֵאת cannot be a *1 c pl* imperfect tense form, if it has a *2 f sg* perfect tense ending or a *f sg* participle ending. Therefore, the prefix נ probably indicates that this is a נִפְעַל form. Remove the prefix and the suffix and you are left with the letters א, צ, and מ.

3. If you check the glossary, you will discover that the root מ.צ.א is listed.

4. In order to identify this verb form, you should look at the conjugations shown in Verb Chart #8 — Final א Verbs. The verb מ.צ.א follows the same conjugation as the model verb ק.ר.א shown in the chart. If you look on the chart for the *2 f sg* perfect tense form in the נִפְעַל pattern, you find the form נִקְרֵאת. If you look on the chart for the *f sg* participle in the נִפְעַל pattern, you find the same form. Therefore, the word נִקְרֵאת could be either the *2 f sg* perfect tense form or the *f sg* participle, depending on the context.

5. The form נִמְצֵאת is the same as the form נִקְרֵאת, except for the difference in root letters. Therefore, the form נִמְצֵאת must be either the *2 f sg* perfect tense form or the *f sg* participle of the verb מ.צ.א in the נִפְעַל pattern.

6. From the glossary you learn that the root **מ.צ.א** in the נִפְעַל pattern means "be found." Therefore, you know that the form **נִמְצֵאת** means "you were found" if it is a *2 f sg* perfect tense form. It means either "I/you/she (is) being found" or "(the one who is) being found" if it is a *f sg* participle. The correct meaning must be determined from the context.

Exercises

Exercise 1. Conjugate the following roots in all forms of the verb pattern given.

‏1. י.ר.ד (הִפְעִיל)   2. ע.מ.ד (פָּעַל)   3. י.צ.א (פָּעַל)   4. נ.ש.א (נִפְעַל)

Exercise 2. Rewrite the sentences below, replacing the underlined word with each word in the list that follows. Every word or grammatical form in the sentence that agrees with the underlined word should be changed to agree with the newly substituted words. Read the sentences aloud. Translate.

‏1. מִרְיָם יָרְדָה אֶל הַיָּם וּמָצְאָה שָׁם אֶת הַנָּבִיא.

| A. אַתֶּם | B. אַתְּ | C. עֶבֶד אֶחָד | D. רָחֵל וְרִבְקָה | E. אֲנַחְנוּ |
| F. עֲשֶׂרֶת הַשּׁוֹפְטִים | G. אֲנִי | H. אַתֵּן | I. אַתָּה | |

‏2. אִם (אַתְּ) תֵּלְכִי עַל הָאֲבָנִים, תִּפְּלִי.

| A. אֲנִי | B. אַהֲרֹן וְיוֹסֵף | C. הַזְּקֵנָה | D. חֲמֵשׁ הַבָּנוֹת | E. אַתֶּם |
| F. אֲחִי מֹשֶׁה | G. אֲנַחְנוּ | H. אַתָּה | I. אַתֵּן | |

‏3. (אַתָּה) יָצָאתָ מִן הָאֹהֶל בַּבֹּקֶר וְקָרָאתָ לְבָנֶיךָ.

| A. רִבְקָה | B. שֵׁשֶׁת הַשָּׂרִים | C. הַגִּבּוֹר | D. אֲנִי | E. אַתֶּם |
| F. אָנוּ | G. אַתְּ | H. אַתֵּן | I. מִרְיָם וְלֵאָה | |

‏4. כַּאֲשֶׁר אַתֶּם עוֹמְדִים לִפְנֵי הַמֶּלֶךְ, אַתֶּם מְבִיאִים אֵלָיו מִנְחָה.

| A. הָעֲבָדִים | B. רִבְקָה | C. אַתָּה | D. אָנוּ | E. אַבְרָהָם |
| F. הֵנָּה | | | | |

‏5. שָׂרָה תּוֹצִיא אֶת הַכֶּסֶף מִבֵּיתָהּ וּתְשַׁלֵּם לְשָׂרֶיהָ.

| A. אֲנִי | B. דּוֹדוֹ | C. אִמִּי | D. שְׁתֵּי בָנוֹת | E. אַתָּה |
| F. מַלְאֲכֵי הַמֶּלֶךְ | G. אָנוּ | H. אַתֶּם | I. אַתְּ | |

6. אַתָּה תַּעֲלֶה אֶל רֹאשׁ הָהָר וּמִשָּׁם תִּרְאֶה אֶת הַיָּם.

E. מִרְיָם   D. אַתֶּם   C. שָׂרֵי הַמֶּלֶךְ   B. מֵאָה נָשִׁים   A. אֲנִי

I. אַתֶּן   H. הָעֶבֶד   G. אֲנַחְנוּ   F. אַתְּ

Exercise 3. All the verbs in the following sentences are in the פָּעַל pattern. Rewrite the sentences, changing the verbs from the imperfect tense to the perfect tense. Refer to the verb charts for the conjugation of new verbs. Translate.

1. רוּת תִּפֹּל מִן הָעֵץ.
2. אֵצֵא מִן הַבַּיִת וְאֵלֵךְ לְבֵית דּוֹדִי.
3. רִבְקָה תֵּלֵד שְׁנֵי בָנִים וּבַת אַחַת.
4. יוֹסֵף יִגְאַל אֶת שְׂדֵה אָחִיו.
5. אַתָּה תִּמְצָא אֶת הָאֹכֶל בְּכֶלְי.
6. הַבְּהֵמָה תִּשָּׂא אֶת הַמַּיִם.
7. נַעֲמֹד עִם נְשֵׁי מוֹאָב לִרְאוֹת אֶת הַמֶּלֶךְ.
8. תָּמִיד אֶעֱשֶׂה מַעֲשִׂים טוֹבִים.

Exercise 4. All the verbs in the following sentences are in the הִפְעִיל pattern. Rewrite the sentences, changing the verbs from the perfect tense to the imperfect tense. Refer to the verb charts for the conjugation of new verbs. Translate.

1. הוֹצֵאתִי אֶת כָּל הַבְּגָדִים מֵאָהֳלִי.
2. הַשַּׂר הֶעֱבִיד אֶת עֲבָדָיו.
3. הוֹרַדְתֶּם פְּרִי מִן הָעֵץ.
4. יִצְחָק הוֹלִיד שְׁנֵי בָנִים.
5. אֲנַחְנוּ הֶעֱמַדְנוּ אֶת הַכֵּלִים בַּמִּשְׁכָּן.
6. הִצַּלְתָּ אֶת אָחִיךָ מִיַּד מֶלֶךְ מוֹאָב.
7. הִגַּדְתָּ לָנוּ אֶת כָּל אֲשֶׁר כָּתוּב בַּסֵּפֶר.
8. הוֹשַׁבְתֶּם אֹתִי עַל כִּסֵּא גָדוֹל.

Exercise 5. All the verbs in the following sentences are in the נִפְעַל pattern. Rewrite the sentences, changing the verbs from the participle to both the perfect and the imperfect tenses. Refer to the verb charts for the conjugation of new verbs. Translate.

1. בְּנֵי יִשְׂרָאֵל נִגְאָלִים מִמִּצְרַיִם.
2. אֲנִי נִקְרָא אֶל הַמֶּלֶךְ הַיּוֹם.
3. אַתֶּם נִמְצָאִים בְּבֵיתְכֶם בָּעֶרֶב.
4. הוּא נוֹלָד בְּבֵית לֶחֶם.
5. הַמִּשְׁכָּנוֹת נִבְנִים בַּמִּדְבָּר.
6. הַמַּיִם נִשָּׂאִים בְּכֵלִים אֶל הַשָּׂדֶה.

Exercise 6. Identify the roots and the pattern of the following verb forms.

16. תֵּצְאִי	11. תֵּשְׁבִי	6. מַמְלִיכוֹת	1. נִמְצֵאתִי
17. עָשִׂית	12. הִגַּדְתָּ	7. קַמְנוּ	2. רוֹאִים
18. הֶעֱלֵיתִי	13. מוֹרִידִים	8. תִּקַּחְנָה	3. תַּזְכִּירוּ
19. נֹאכַל	14. מוֹצֵא	9. מוֹצִיא	4. תִּפֹּל
20. מַצִּילָה	15. יִקָּרְאוּ	10. הוֹלַדְתֶּם	5. תּוֹדִיעַ

264

Exercise 8. The following reading is taken directly from the Bible, Genesis 28: 11-15. Read and translate.

Vocabulary for Reading Selection

אֶתְּנֶנָּה = אֶתֵּן אֹתָהּ		come upon *vb*	פ.ג.ע.
dust	עָפָר	spend the night *vb*	ל.ו.ן (וַיָּלֶן)
burst forth *vb*	פ.ר.ץ.	*best translated here as* went	בָא
westward	יָמָּה	by his head	מְרַאֲשֹׁתָיו
eastward	קֵדְמָה	dream *vb*	ח.ל.ם.
northward	צָפֹנָה	ladder	סֻלָּם
southward	נֶגְבָּה	stationed	מֻצָּב
bless *vb*	ב.ר.ך.	reach *vb*	נ.ג.ע (מַגִּיעַ)
leave *vb*	ע.ז.ב.	stand *vb*	נ.צ.ב.
until	עַד אֲשֶׁר אִם		

וַיִּפְגַּע בַּמָּקוֹם וַיָּלֶן שָׁם כִּי בָא הַשֶּׁמֶשׁ וַיִּקַּח מֵאַבְנֵי הַמָּקוֹם וַיָּשֶׂם מְרַאֲשֹׁתָיו וַיִּשְׁכַּב בַּמָּקוֹם הַהוּא: וַיַּחֲלֹם וְהִנֵּה סֻלָּם מֻצָּב אַרְצָה וְרֹאשׁוֹ מַגִּיעַ הַשָּׁמָיְמָה וְהִנֵּה מַלְאֲכֵי אֱלֹהִים עֹלִים וְיֹרְדִים בּוֹ: וְהִנֵּה יְהוָה נִצָּב עָלָיו וַיֹּאמַר אֲנִי יְהוָה אֱלֹהֵי אַבְרָהָם אָבִיךָ וֵאלֹהֵי יִצְחָק הָאָרֶץ אֲשֶׁר אַתָּה שֹׁכֵב עָלֶיהָ לְךָ אֶתְּנֶנָּה וּלְזַרְעֶךָ: וְהָיָה זַרְעֲךָ כַּעֲפַר הָאָרֶץ וּפָרַצְתָּ יָמָּה וָקֵדְמָה וְצָפֹנָה וָנֶגְבָּה וְנִבְרְכוּ בְךָ כָּל מִשְׁפְּחֹת הָאֲדָמָה וּבְזַרְעֶךָ: וְהִנֵּה אָנֹכִי עִמָּךְ וּשְׁמַרְתִּיךָ בְּכֹל אֲשֶׁר תֵּלֵךְ וַהֲשִׁבֹתִיךָ אֶל הָאֲדָמָה הַזֹּאת כִּי לֹא אֶעֱזָבְךָ עַד אֲשֶׁר אִם עָשִׂיתִי אֵת אֲשֶׁר דִּבַּרְתִּי לָךְ:

Notice the use of direct object suffixes with these verbs: אֶעֱזָבְךָ, וַהֲשִׁבֹתִיךָ, וּשְׁמַרְתִּיךָ, אֶתְּנֶנָּה (see Chapter 18).

From the Prayerbook

Prayerbook Vocabulary

righteousness, justice	צֶדֶק	find pleasure	ר.צ.ה.

Selection from the Prayerbook (blessing before reading the Haftorah)

בָּרוּךְ אַתָּה יְיָ אֱלֹהֵינוּ מֶלֶךְ הָעוֹלָם אֲשֶׁר בָּחַר בִּנְבִיאִים טוֹבִים וְרָצָה בְדִבְרֵיהֶם הַנֶּאֱמָרִים בֶּאֱמֶת: בָּרוּךְ אַתָּה יְיָ הַבּוֹחֵר בַּתּוֹרָה וּבְמשֶׁה עַבְדּוֹ וּבְיִשְׂרָאֵל עַמּוֹ וּבִנְבִיאֵי הָאֱמֶת וָצֶדֶק.

Prayerbook Translation

"Blessed art Thou, O Lord our God, Ruler of the universe, who hast selected good prophets, taking delight in their words which were spoken in truth. Blessed art Thou, O Lord, who hast chosen Torah, Thy servant Moses, Thy people Israel, and the prophets of truth and righteousness."

Sabbath and Festival Prayer Book, Morris Silverman, 1946, p. 126

Guided Reading from Ruth

	.1 Ruth 4:14 שׁ.ב.ת (הִפְעִיל) leave without וַתֹּאמַרְנָה הַנָּשִׁים אֶל נָעֳמִי בָּרוּךְ יהוה אֲשֶׁר לֹא הִשְׁבִּית לָךְ גֹּאֵל הַיּוֹם
1. And the women said to Naomi: "Blessed is the Lord who has not left you without a kinsman today.	**.2** וַיִּקָּרֵא שְׁמוֹ בְּיִשְׂרָאֵל:
2. May his name be called (may he be famous) in Israel.	**.3** Ruth 4:15 כִּלְכֵּל sustain, support שֵׂיבָה old age וְהָיָה לָךְ לְמֵשִׁיב נֶפֶשׁ וּלְכַלְכֵּל אֶת שֵׂיבָתֵךְ
3. And he will be to you a returner of soul (a restorer of life) and support your old age,	**.4** כַּלָּה daughter-in-law אֲהֵבָתֶךְ = אָהֲבָה אֹתָךְ יְלָדַתּוּ = יָלְדָה אֹתוֹ כִּי כַלָּתֵךְ אֲשֶׁר אֲהֵבָתֶךְ יְלָדַתּוּ הִיא טוֹבָה לָךְ מִשִּׁבְעָה בָּנִים:
4. because your daughter-in-law who loved you, who is better to you than seven sons, bore him."	**.5** יֶלֶד boy וַתִּקַּח נָעֳמִי אֶת הַיֶּלֶד
5. And Naomi took the boy	**.6** Ruth 4:16 שׁ.י.ת put, set חֵיק bosom, breast אֹמֶנֶת foster mother וַתְּשִׁתֵהוּ בְחֵיקָהּ וַתְּהִי לוֹ לְאֹמֶנֶת:
6. and she put him at her breast and she became a foster mother to him.	**.7** Ruth 4:17 שְׁכֵנָה neighbor n, f וַתִּקְרֶאנָה לוֹ הַשְּׁכֵנוֹת שֵׁם לֵאמֹר יֻלַּד בֵּן לְנָעֳמִי
7. And the neighbor women proclaimed for him a name, saying: "A son has been born for Naomi."	**.8** עוֹבֵד Obed יִשַׁי Jesse וַתִּקְרֶאנָה שְׁמוֹ עוֹבֵד הוּא אֲבִי יִשַׁי אֲבִי דָוִד:

8. And they proclaimed his name Obed; he is the father of Jesse, the father of David.	Ruth 4:18 .9 תּוֹלְדוֹת generations פֶּרֶץ Perez חֶצְרוֹן Hezron וְאֵלֶּה תּוֹלְדוֹת פָּרֶץ פֶּרֶץ הוֹלִיד אֶת חֶצְרוֹן:
9. And these are the generations of Perez: Perez begot Hezron;	Ruth 4:19 .10 רָם Ram עַמִּינָדָב Amminadab וְחֶצְרוֹן הוֹלִיד אֶת רָם וְרָם הוֹלִיד אֶת עַמִּינָדָב:
10. and Hezron begot Ram, and Ram begot Amminadab;	Ruth 4:20 .11 נַחְשׁוֹן Nachshon שַׂלְמָה, שַׂלְמוֹן Salmon וְעַמִּינָדָב הוֹלִיד אֶת נַחְשׁוֹן וְנַחְשׁוֹן הוֹלִיד אֶת שַׂלְמָה:
11. and Amminadab begot Nachshon, and Nachshon begot Salmon;	Ruth 4:21 .12 וְשַׂלְמוֹן הוֹלִיד אֶת בֹּעַז וּבֹעַז הוֹלִיד אֶת עוֹבֵד:
12. and Salmon begot Boaz, and Boaz begot Obed;	Ruth 4:22 .13 וְעוֹבֵד הוֹלִיד אֶת יִשַׁי וְיִשַׁי הוֹלִיד אֶת דָּוִד:
13. and Obed begot Jesse, and Jesse begot David.	

Ruth 4:14 וַתֹּאמַרְנָה הַנָּשִׁים אֶל נָעֳמִי בָּרוּךְ יהוה אֲשֶׁר לֹא הִשְׁבִּית לָךְ גֹּאֵל הַיּוֹם וְיִקָּרֵא שְׁמוֹ בְּיִשְׂרָאֵל:
Ruth 4:15 וְהָיָה לָךְ לְמֵשִׁיב נֶפֶשׁ וּלְכַלְכֵּל אֶת שֵׂיבָתֵךְ כִּי כַלָּתֵךְ אֲשֶׁר אֲהֵבַתֶךְ יְלָדַתּוּ אֲשֶׁר הִיא טוֹבָה לָךְ מִשִּׁבְעָה בָּנִים:
Ruth 4:16 וַתִּקַּח נָעֳמִי אֶת הַיֶּלֶד וַתְּשִׁתֵהוּ בְחֵיקָהּ וַתְּהִי לוֹ לְאֹמֶנֶת:
Ruth 4:17 וַתִּקְרֶאנָה לוֹ הַשְּׁכֵנוֹת שֵׁם לֵאמֹר יֻלַּד בֵּן לְנָעֳמִי וַתִּקְרֶאנָה שְׁמוֹ עוֹבֵד הוּא אֲבִי יִשַׁי אֲבִי דָוִד:
Ruth 4:18 וְאֵלֶּה תּוֹלְדוֹת פָּרֶץ פֶּרֶץ הוֹלִיד אֶת חֶצְרוֹן:
Ruth 4:19 וְחֶצְרוֹן הוֹלִיד אֶת רָם וְרָם הוֹלִיד אֶת עַמִּינָדָב:
Ruth 4:20 וְעַמִּינָדָב הוֹלִיד אֶת נַחְשׁוֹן וְנַחְשׁוֹן הוֹלִיד אֶת שַׂלְמָה:
Ruth 4:21 וְשַׂלְמוֹן הוֹלִיד אֶת בֹּעַז וּבֹעַז הוֹלִיד אֶת עוֹבֵד:
Ruth 4:22 וְעוֹבֵד הוֹלִיד אֶת יִשַׁי וְיִשַׁי הוֹלִיד אֶת דָּוִד:

Chapter 33
Using the Dictionary
Further Study

The Biblical Dictionary

In order to begin reading the Bible on your own, you should be aware of some useful study aids. The most important of these aids is a Biblical dictionary, which is usually called a lexicon. In a good lexicon you will find every word that appears in the Bible, its definition, and several examples of how that word is used.

The best Biblical Hebrew lexicon is called the *Hebrew and English Lexicon of the Old Testament* by Brown, Driver, and Briggs (BDB), (Oxford Press, 1907). We recommend this very highly, since it is a very useful aid to Bible reading and study. It is available at most libraries and religious bookstores or you can order it through almost any bookstore.

How to Use BDB

BDB is a very valuable resource, but it is difficult to use without some explanation. As we noted earlier with reference to verbs, Hebrew words — nouns, verbs, adjectives, and others — can be identified by their root. In BDB every word in the Bible is listed by its root, not by the form that actually appears in the Bible. You must be able to determine this root to find the word in BDB. For example, if you were looking for the meaning of the word מִשְׁכָּב "bed" in BDB, you would not find it under מ, but under שׁ, because the root is שׁ.כ.ב. If you were looking for the meaning of the word מִלְחָמָה "battle," you would find it listed under the root ל.ח.ם. In some cases, when the root of the word is difficult to identify, BDB will list the word as it appears in the Bible, with a reference to the correct root.

The only way to really understand BDB is to use it. To help you use it, we have included a short Biblical passage, along with some notes about how to look up the unfamiliar words in the passage in BDB.

The passage we have selected is Genesis 1:1, the first verse in the Bible.

בְּרֵאשִׁית בָּרָא אֱלֹהִים אֵת הַשָּׁמַיִם וְאֵת הָאָרֶץ:

The Word בָּרָא

Let's look at the second word first, because it is a simple three letter form: בָּרָא. The root is probably ב.ר.א, so that is what you should look up in BDB. Roots are arranged alphabetically according to the Hebrew alphabet. (See Chapter 1 for the order of the Hebrew alphabet.) The following is the beginning of the section on ב.ר.א as it appears on page 135 of BDB:

†I. **בָּרָא** 53 **vb.** shape, create (cf. Ar. بَرَى, form, fashion by cutting, shape out, pare a reed for writing, a stick for an arrow; بَرَى, create (loan-word); Ph. הברא CIS[1.347] incisor, a trade involving cutting; As. barû, make, create, COT[Gloss] & Hpt KAT[2 Gloss 1] but dub.; Sab. ברא found, build, DHM[ZMG 1883, 413], synon. בנה; Ba[ZA. 1888, 58], comp. As. banû, create, beget, with change of liquid; Aram. בְּרָא, ܒ݁ܪܳܐ, create)—**Qal** Pf. Gn 1[1]+19 t.; Impf. יִבְרָא Gn 1[21.27] Nu 16[30]; Inf. בְּרֹא Gn 5[1]; Imv. בְּרָא ψ 51[12]; Pt. בּוֹרֵא Is 42[5] +10t.; sf. בֹּרַאֲךָ Is 43[1]; בּוֹרְאֶיךָ Ec 12[1];—shape, fashion, create, always of divine activity, with acc. rei, seldom except in P and Is[2]. **1.** obj. heaven and earth Gn 1[1] 2[3] (P) Is 45[18.18]; mankind Gn 1[27.27.27] 5[1.2] (P) 6[7] (J) Dt 4[32] ψ 89[48] Is 45[12]; the host of heaven Is 40[26]; heavens Is 42[5]; ends of the earth Is 40[28]; north and south ψ 89[13]; wind Am 4[13]; the תַּנִּינִם Gn 1[21](P). **2.** the individual man Mal 2[10] (‖ father) Ec 12[1]; the smith and the waster Is 54[16.16]; Israel as a nation Is 43[15]; Jacob Is 43[1]; the seed of Israel Is 43[7]. **3.** new conditions and circumstances: righteousness and salvation Is 45[8]; darkness and evil Is 45[7]; fruit of the lips Is 57[19]; a new thing חֲדָשָׁה (a woman encompassing a man) Je 31[22]; בְּרִיאָה (swallowing up the Korahites) Nu 16[30] (J); cloud and flame over Zion Is 4[5]. **4.** of trans-

1. The small dagger (†) which appears at the very beginning of the section tells you that all the occurences of this verb, in every form, will be listed somewhere in this section.

2. The I. in front of בָּרָא tells you that this is the first of several meanings which will be given for this root. Another meaning of ב.ר.א, also found on this page in BDB, is "be fat." Since this doesn't seem appropriate to the passage, we can rule it out.

3. The word בָּרָא is the heading of this entry. BDB lists roots with the vowel pattern of the 3rd person masculine singular perfect tense form in the פָּעַל pattern, even when a root does not appear in that pattern.

4. The little "53" next to the בָּרָא is the number of times this word appears in the Bible.

5. The abbreviation **vb.** tells you that this word is a verb.

6. "Shape, create" is the general definition of the word.

7. The next part, in ( ) parentheses, is an analysis of where the word came from, and what it means in similar languages. This section is not very important for you.

8. After the parentheses, the word **Qal** — another name for the Pa'al פָּעַל pattern — tells you that this is the first pattern which will be described. Later in this section **Niph.** נִפְעַל and **Pi.** פִּעֵל are described. The abbreviations BDB uses for the other patterns are **Pu.** פֻּעַל, **Hiph.** הִפְעִיל, **Hoph.** הָפְעַל, and **Hithp.** הִתְפַּעֵל.

9. BDB then lists some of the tenses of this verb in Qal as they appear in the Bible, and some places where they appear. BDB's abbreviations for the different tenses are: pf. — perfect, impf. — imperfect, imv. — imperative, inf. — infinitive, pt. — participle. This list of forms may be useful in helping you determine the form of the verb you are looking up.

10. Biblical references are given by chapter and verse: Gn5[1] means Genesis chapter 5, verse 1. Each book of the Bible has a two letter abbreviation, which is listed at the beginning of BDB.

11. The bold-face numbers indicate the different uses and meanings of the word, in different contexts.

Many of the symbols and abbreviations that appear above are not that important. Once you understand the basic abbreviations, you will be able to use BDB with very little difficulty. From this section of BDB you can tell that the word בָּרָא means "he created;" for now, that is all you need to know.

The Word בְּרֵאשִׁית

Now let's return to the first word: בְּרֵאשִׁית. First of all, you need to find the root. You would not find anything listed in BDB under the word בְּרֵאשׁ, so you can guess that the first letter is probably the preposition–בְּ. You know that the letter ת is sometimes a feminine suffix. So we are left with the root letters ר.א.שׁ. In BDB, we find the word רֹאשׁ "head" followed by other words that come from the root ר.א.שׁ. The word רֵאשִׁית appears on the next page, page 912 in BDB.

> †רֵאשִׁית **n.f.** beginning, chief (for רֵאשִׁית Nö [GGA 1884, 1019], cf. Holz [Hex 465]; Syr. ⟨ﺭ⟩);— abs. ר Dt 33²¹+, cstr. ר Gn 10¹⁰+, רֵשִׁית Dt 11¹²; sf. רֵאשִׁתוֹ Ec 7⁸, רֵאשִׁתוֹ Jb 42¹², etc.;—**1. a.** beginning, of kingdom Gn 10¹⁰ (J), year Dt 11¹², reign Je 26¹ 27¹ 28¹ 49³⁴; =first phase, step, or element in course of events Is 46¹⁰ (opp. אַחֲרִית);

This section looks very much like the section on בָּרָא, except we see the abbreviation **n.f.** (noun, feminine) instead of **vb**. The word רֵאשִׁית means "beginning," so בְּרֵאשִׁית means "in (the) beginning."

So far, we see that בְּרֵאשִׁית בָּרָא means "in the beginning created." The rest of the verse, אֱלֹהִים אֵת הַשָּׁמַיִם וְאֵת הָאָרֶץ . . . contains words that you already know. The whole verse reads "In the beginning God created the heavens and the earth."

Other Study Aids

Index to Brown Driver and Briggs Hebrew Lexicon (Moody Press, 1976), compiled by Bruce Einspahr. Lists every word in the Bible in order, along with the page in BDB.

Hebrew-English Lexicon of the Bible (Schocken Books, 1975). Paperback lexicon with short, simple definitions to Biblical words. Not as complete or accurate as BDB, but easier to use.

Dictionary of the Targumim, the Talmud Babli and Yerushalmi, and the Midrashic Literature (Judaica Press, 1975), by Marcus Jastrow. Dictionary of post-Biblical Hebrew, useful for understanding the prayerbook.

Further Study

It will prove invaluable to continue reading some Hebrew every day.

You may be interested in joining a class or Bible study group. Universities have Jewish Studies, Near Eastern Studies, Religious Studies, and Hebrew departments, all of which may have Hebrew classes. You may be able to join without enrolling as a student full-time.

Synagogues, Temples, and Jewish Community Centers may have Torah study groups.

You may find a havurah in the community that is interested in study, or you might organize one.

We would like to congratulate you for all that you have accomplished. You have learned the basics of Biblical and prayerbook Hebrew. With the knowledge you now possess, a world of ancient writings and wisdom becomes open to you. We strongly encourage you to continue your exploration into these realms.

מַזָּל טוֹב

Notes

<u>Note 1.</u>, from page 15. The pronunciation of the vowel before the consonant sound used to occur also with the consonant ע, when the ע was pronounced as a letter. Since the ע is now silent, we do not hear any difference today. When you see עַ at the end of a word, it is pronounced **a** as in **yacht**. (z'ro/a   זְרוֹ עַ / זְרוֹ עַ = זְרוֹעַ)

<u>Note 2.</u>, from page 22. The pronunciation of this word is a little different than you might expect. According to the rule given in Chapter 3, the sheva in these feminine singular verbs should be a silent sheva. However, this sheva is an exception to that rule and is a short-sound sheva. This is the case with all feminine singular verbs in this verb pattern.

Examples: כָּתְבָה is pronounced ka/th'vah

                                      זָכְרָה is pronounced za/ch'rah

                                      הָלְכָה is pronounced ha/l'chah

Since this is not a silent sheva, there is no dagesh in the BeGeD-KeFeT letter following this sheva.

<u>Note 3.</u>, from page 28. The pronunciation of this sheva too is different than you might have thought. The sheva under the second letter looks like it should be a silent sheva. However, it is a short-sound sheva just like the sheva in the words זָכְרָה , הָלְכָה , כָּתְבָה introduced in Chapter 5. This sheva is almost always pronounced as a silent sheva. Since this is not really a silent sheva, there is no dagesh in the BeGeD-KeFeT letter following this sheva.

<u>Note 4.</u>, from page 65. When the construct state expresses description, it must be translated literally using the word **of**.

Example: A man of kindness   אִישׁ חֶסֶד

This phrase **cannot** be translated as **kindness' man**.

<u>Note 5.</u>, from page 99. If the second root letter of a verb is one of the BeGeD-KeFeT letters, בֶּגֶד–כֶּפֶת, it will take a dagesh in the imperfect tense.

Example: תִּשְׁ/כְּבוּ

Note 6, from page 115. Note also that if the second root letter of a verb is one of the BeGeD-KeFeT letters, it takes a dagesh when an inseparable preposition is added to the infinitive construct.

NOUN CHART #1

The following nouns are irregular in both the singular and the plural when possessive pronoun endings are added.

name — שֵׁם	utensil — כְּלִי	hand — יָד	blood — דָּם	son — בֵּן	brother — אָח	father — אָב

Singular

Plural

NOUN CHART #2

The following nouns are irregular only in the plural when possessive pronoun endings are added. All the nouns with the same pattern are grouped together.

Group I		Group II		Group III		Group IV	
books	סְפָרִים	roads	דְּרָכִים	slaves	עֲבָדִים	lads	נְעָרִים
clothing	בְּגָדִים	kings	מְלָכִים	kindness	חֲסָדִים	shoes	נְעָלִים
things	דְּבָרִים					gates	שְׁעָרִים
	סְפָרִים		דְּרָכִים		עֲבָדִים		נְעָרִים
	סְפָרַי		דְּרָכַי		עֲבָדַי		נְעָרַי
	סְפָרֶיךָ		דְּרָכֶיךָ		עֲבָדֶיךָ		נְעָרֶיךָ
	סְפָרַיִךְ		דְּרָכַיִךְ		עֲבָדַיִךְ		נְעָרַיִךְ
	סְפָרָיו		דְּרָכָיו		עֲבָדָיו		נְעָרָיו
	סְפָרֶיהָ		דְּרָכֶיהָ		עֲבָדֶיהָ		נְעָרֶיהָ
	סְפָרֵינוּ		דְּרָכֵינוּ		עֲבָדֵינוּ		נְעָרֵינוּ
	סִפְרֵיכֶם		דַּרְכֵיכֶם		עַבְדֵיכֶם		נַעֲרֵיכֶם
	סִפְרֵיכֶן		דַּרְכֵיכֶן		עַבְדֵיכֶן		נַעֲרֵיכֶן
	סִפְרֵיהֶם		דַּרְכֵיהֶם		עַבְדֵיהֶם		נַעֲרֵיהֶם
	סִפְרֵיהֶן		דַּרְכֵיהֶן		עַבְדֵיהֶן		נַעֲרֵיהֶן

The following nouns are irregular only in the plural when possessive pronoun endings are added but do not belong in any of the other groups.

face — פָּנִים	trees — עֵצִים	women — נָשִׁים	armies — חֲיָלִים	life — חַיִּים
פָּנַי	עֵצַי	נָשַׁי	חֲיָלַי	חַיַּי
פָּנֶיךָ	עֵצֶיךָ	נָשֶׁיךָ	חֲיָלֶיךָ	חַיֶּיךָ
פָּנַיִךְ	עֵצַיִךְ	נָשַׁיִךְ	חֲיָלַיִךְ	חַיַּיִךְ
פָּנָיו	עֵצָיו	נָשָׁיו	חֲיָלָיו	חַיָּיו
פָּנֶיהָ	עֵצֶיהָ	נָשֶׁיהָ	חֲיָלֶיהָ	חַיֶּיהָ
פָּנֵינוּ	עֵצֵינוּ	נָשֵׁינוּ	חֲיָלֵינוּ	חַיֵּינוּ
פְּנֵיכֶם	עֲצֵיכֶם	נְשֵׁיכֶם	חֵילֵיכֶם	חַיֵּיכֶם
פְּנֵיכֶן	עֲצֵיכֶן	נְשֵׁיכֶן	חֵילֵיכֶן	חַיֵּיכֶן
פְּנֵיהֶם	עֲצֵיהֶם	נְשֵׁיהֶם	חֵילֵיהֶם	חַיֵּיהֶם
פְּנֵיהֶן	עֲצֵיהֶן	נְשֵׁיהֶן	חֵילֵיהֶן	חַיֵּיהֶן

NOUN CHART #3

The following nouns are irregular only in the singular when possessive pronoun endings are added.

field — שָׂדֶה	fruit — פְּרִי	chair — כִּסֵּא
שָׂדִי	פִּרְיִי	כִּסְאִי
שָׂדְךָ	פִּרְיְךָ	כִּסְאֲךָ
שָׂדֵךְ	פִּרְיֵךְ	כִּסְאֵךְ
שָׂדוֹ/שָׂדֵהוּ	פִּרְיוֹ	כִּסְאוֹ
שָׂדָהּ/שָׂדֶהָ	פִּרְיָךְ	כִּסְאָהּ
שָׂדֵנוּ	פִּרְיֵנוּ	כִּסְאֵנוּ
שָׂדְכֶם	פֶּרְיְכֶם	כִּסְאֲכֶם
שָׂדְכֶן	פֶּרְיְכֶן	כִּסְאֲכֶן
שָׂדָם	פִּרְיָם	כִּסְאָם
שָׂדָן	פִּרְיָן	כִּסְאָן

NOUN CHART #4 — REGULAR

Below is a chart comparing the possessive pronoun endings for regular singular and plural nouns.

maidens — נְעָרוֹת	maiden — נַעֲרָה	uncles — דּוֹדִים	uncle — דּוֹד
נַעֲרוֹתַי	נַעֲרָתִי	דּוֹדַי	דּוֹדִי
נַעֲרוֹתֶיךָ	נַעֲרָתְךָ	דּוֹדֶיךָ	דּוֹדְךָ
נַעֲרוֹתַיִךְ	נַעֲרָתֵךְ	דּוֹדַיִךְ	דּוֹדֵךְ
נַעֲרוֹתָיו	נַעֲרָתוֹ	דּוֹדָיו	דּוֹדוֹ
נַעֲרוֹתֶיהָ	נַעֲרָתָהּ	דּוֹדֶיהָ	דּוֹדָהּ
נַעֲרוֹתֵינוּ	נַעֲרָתֵנוּ	דּוֹדֵינוּ	דּוֹדֵנוּ
נַעֲרוֹתֵיכֶם	נַעֲרַתְכֶם	דּוֹדֵיכֶם	דּוֹדְכֶם
נַעֲרוֹתֵיכֶן	נַעֲרַתְכֶן	דּוֹדֵיכֶן	דּוֹדְכֶן
נַעֲרוֹתֵיהֶם	נַעֲרָתָם	דּוֹדֵיהֶם	דּוֹדָם
נַעֲרוֹתֵיהֶן	נַעֲרָתָן	דּוֹדֵיהֶן	דּוֹדָן

VERB CHART #1 — REGULAR VERBS

attend to, visit, appoint — פקד   lie down — שכב

Perfect Tense

	1 c sg	2 m	2 f	3 m	3 f	1 c pl	2 m	2 f	3 c

Imperfect Tense

	1 c sg	2 m	2 f	3 m	3 f	1 c pl	2 m	2 f	3 m	3 f

Participle

Passive Participle

m sg
f
alt. f
m pl
f

m sg
f
m pl
f

Imperative

m sg
f
m pl
f

Infinitive

abs
cs

Indirect Imperative

With Reversing Vav

cs = infinitive construct
abs = infinitive absolute

alt. f = alternate feminine singular form

VERB CHART #3 — HOLLOW VERBS

arise — ק.ו.ם   put — ש.י.ם

Perfect Tense

	הִקְטִיל	קָם	קוֹטֵל
1 c sg			
2 m			
2 f			
3 m			
3 f			
1 c pl			
2 m			
2 f			
3 c			

Imperfect Tense

1 c sg			
2 m			
2 f			
3 m			
3 f			
1 c pl			
2 m			
2 f			
3 f			

VERB CHART #2 — FINAL ה VERBS

command — צ.ו.ה   build — ב.נ.ה

Perfect Tense

Imperfect Tense

Participle

m sg		
f		
m pl		
f		

Imperative

m sg		
f		
m pl		
f		

Infinitive

abs		
cs (לְ)		

With Reversing Vav

alt. *f* = *alternate feminine singular form*

cs = *infinitive construct*

abs = *infinitive absolute*

VERB CHART #4 — INITIAL י VERBS

bear — י.ל.ד   go down — י.ר.ד

Perfect Tense

	הִפְעִיל	נִפְעַל	פָּעַל	
1 c sg	הוֹרַדְתִּי	נוֹלַדְתִּי	יָלַדְתִּי	
2 m	הוֹרַדְתָּ	נוֹלַדְתָּ	יָלַדְתָּ	
2 f	הוֹרַדְתְּ	נוֹלַדְתְּ	יָלַדְתְּ	
3 m	הוֹרִיד	נוֹלַד	יָלַד	
3 f	הוֹרִידָה	נוֹלְדָה	יָלְדָה	
1 c pl	הוֹרַדְנוּ	נוֹלַדְנוּ	יָלַדְנוּ	
2 m	הוֹרַדְתֶּם	נוֹלַדְתֶּם	יְלַדְתֶּם	
2 f	הוֹרַדְתֶּן	נוֹלַדְתֶּן	יְלַדְתֶּן	
3 c	הוֹרִידוּ	נוֹלְדוּ	יָלְדוּ	

Imperfect Tense

	הִפְעִיל	נִפְעַל	פָּעַל	
1 c sg	אוֹרִיד	אִוָּלֵד	אֵרֵד	
2 m	תּוֹרִיד	תִּוָּלֵד	תֵּרֵד	
2 f	תּוֹרִידִי	תִּוָּלְדִי	תֵּרְדִי	
3 m	יוֹרִיד	יִוָּלֵד	יֵרֵד	
3 f	תּוֹרִיד	תִּוָּלֵד	תֵּרֵד	
1 c pl	נוֹרִיד	נִוָּלֵד	נֵרֵד	
2 m	תּוֹרִידוּ	תִּוָּלְדוּ	תֵּרְדוּ	
2 f	תּוֹרֵדְנָה	תִּוָּלַדְנָה	תֵּרַדְנָה	
3 m	יוֹרִידוּ	יִוָּלְדוּ	יֵרְדוּ	
3 f	תּוֹרֵדְנָה	תִּוָּלַדְנָה	תֵּרַדְנָה	

VERB CHART #5 — INITIAL נ VERBS

fall — נ.פ.ל

Perfect Tense

	נִפְעַל	פָּעַל	
1 c sg	נִפַּלְתִּי	נָפַלְתִּי	
2 m	נִפַּלְתָּ	נָפַלְתָּ	
2 f	נִפַּלְתְּ	נָפַלְתְּ	
3 m	נִפַּל	נָפַל	
3 f	נִפְּלָה	נָפְלָה	
1 c pl	נִפַּלְנוּ	נָפַלְנוּ	
2 m	נִפַּלְתֶּם	נְפַלְתֶּם	
2 f	נִפַּלְתֶּן	נְפַלְתֶּן	
3 c	נִפְּלוּ	נָפְלוּ	

Imperfect Tense

	נִפְעַל	פָּעַל	
1 c sg	אֶנָּפֵל	אֶפֹּל	
2 m	תִּנָּפֵל	תִּפֹּל	
2 f	תִּנָּפְלִי	תִּפְּלִי	
3 m	יִנָּפֵל	יִפֹּל	
3 f	תִּנָּפֵל	תִּפֹּל	
1 c pl	נִנָּפֵל	נִפֹּל	
2 m	תִּנָּפְלוּ	תִּפְּלוּ	
2 f	תִּנָּפַלְנָה	תִּפֹּלְנָה	
3 m	יִנָּפְלוּ	יִפְּלוּ	
3 f	תִּנָּפַלְנָה	תִּפֹּלְנָה	

		Participle
m sg		מַקְטִל/מַקְטֵל
f		מַקְטֶלֶת/מַקְטִילָה
alt. f		מַקְטֶלֶת/מַקְטִלָה
m pl		מַקְטִלִים/מַקְטִילִים
f		מַקְטִלוֹת/מַקְטִילוֹת

	Imperative
m sg	הַקְטֵל
f	הַקְטִילִי
m pl	הַקְטִילוּ
f	הַקְטֵלְנָה

	Infinitive
abs	הַקְטֵל
cs	הַקְטִיל (לְ)

With Reversing Vav

וַיַּקְטֵל

Participle

Imperative

Infinitive

With Reversing Vav

		Participle
m sg		נִקְטָל
f		נִקְטֶלֶת
alt. f		נִקְטָלָה
m pl		נִקְטָלִים
f		נִקְטָלוֹת

	Imperative
m sg	הִקָּטֵל
f	הִקָּטְלִי
m pl	הִקָּטְלוּ
f	הִקָּטַלְנָה

	Infinitive
abs	נִקְטוֹל
cs	הִקָּטֵל (לְ)

With Reversing Vav

וַיִּקָּטֵל

---

alt. f = *alternate feminine singular form*

cs = *infinitive construct*

abs = *infinitive absolute*

VERB CHART #6 — INITIAL א OR ע VERBS

work — ע.ב.ד   say — א.מ.ר

	פָּעַל	פָּעַל
	הֶעֱבִיד	

Perfect Tense

1 c sg			
2 m			
2 f			
3 m			
3 f			
1 c pl			
2 m			
2 f			
3 c			

Imperfect Tense

1 c sg			
2 m			
2 f			
3 m			
3 f			
1 c pl			
2 m			
2 f			
3 m			
3 f			

VERB CHART #7 — VERBS WITH א, ה, ח, OR ע AS MIDDLE ROOT LETTER

redeem — ג.א.ל

	נִפְעַל	פָּעַל

Perfect Tense

1 c sg		
2 m		
2 f		
3 m		
3 f		
1 c pl		
2 m		
2 f		
3 c		

Imperfect Tense

1 c sg		
2 m		
2 f		
3 m		
3 f		
1 c pl		
2 m		
2 f		
3 m		
3 f		

Participle / Imperative / Infinitive

	Niphal (גאל)	Niphal (alt.)
Participle		
m sg	נִגְאָל/נִגְאַל	נִגְאָל
f	נִגְאָלָה/נִגְאֶלֶת	נִגְאָלָה
alt. f	נִגְאֶלֶת/נִגְאָל	
m pl	נִגְאָלִים	נִגְאָלִים
f	נִגְאָלוֹת/נִגְאָלֹת	נִגְאָלוֹת
Imperative		
m sg	הִגָּאֵל	הִגָּאֵל
f	הִגָּאֲלִי	הִגָּאֲלִי
m pl	הִגָּאֲלוּ	הִגָּאֲלוּ
f	הִגָּאַלְנָה	הִגָּאַלְנָה
Infinitive		
abs	נִגְאֹל	
cs	(לְ)הִגָּאֵל	הִגָּאֵל

	Qal (עמד)	Niphal
Participle		
m sg	עֹמֵד/עוֹמֵד	נֶעֱמָד/נֶעֱמַד
f	עֹמֶדֶת/עֹמְדָה	נֶעֱמָדָה/נֶעֱמֶדֶת
alt. f	עֹמְדָה/עוֹמְדָה	נֶעֱמֶדֶת/נֶעֱמָד
m pl	עֹמְדִים/עוֹמְדִים	נֶעֱמָדִים
f	עֹמְדוֹת/עוֹמְדוֹת	נֶעֱמָדוֹת/נֶעֱמָדֹת
Imperative		
m sg	עֲמֹד	הֵעָמֵד
f	עִמְדִי	הֵעָמְדִי
m pl	עִמְדוּ	הֵעָמְדוּ
f	עֲמֹדְנָה	הֵעָמַדְנָה
Infinitive		
abs	עָמוֹד	נֶעֱמֹד
cs	(לַ)עֲמֹד	הֵעָמֵד

alt. f = *alternate feminine singular form*

cs = *infinitive construct*

abs = *infinitive absolute*

283

VERB CHART #9 — DUAL VARIATION VERBS

carry — נ.שׂ.א   go out — י.צ.א

Perfect Tense

	פָּעַל	פָּעַל	פָּעַל	פָּעַל
1 c sg				
2 m				
2 f				
3 m				
3 f				
1 c pl				
2 m				
3 f				
3 c				

Imperfect Tense

1 c sg				
2 m				
2 f				
3 m				
3 f				
1 c pl				
2 m				
2 f				
3 m				
3 f				

VERB CHART #8 — FINAL א VERBS

call — ק.ר.א

Perfect Tense

Imperfect Tense

Participle

m sg			
f			
alt. f			
m pl			
f			

Imperative

m sg			
f			
m pl			
f			

Infinitive

abs			
cs (לְ)			

With Reversing Vav

alt. f = alternate feminine singular form

cs = infinitive construct

abs = infinitive absolute

Chapter 1

Exercise 3A. 1. א, ב, ג, ד 2. ה, ו, ז 3. ו, ז, ח 4. א, ב,
ג, ד, ה 5. ד, ה, ו, ז, ח

Exercise 3B. 1. ט, י, כ 2. כ, ל, מ 3. ט, י, כ, ל, מ, ן
4. ד, ה, ו, ז, ח, ט, י, ך, ל 5. א, ב, ג, ד, ה, ו, ז, ח, ט,
י, כ, ל, מ

Exercise 3C. 1. ס, ע, פ, צ 2. ק, ר, ש, ת 3. ס, ע, פ, ץ
4. ס, ע, פ, צ, ק, ר, ש, ת

Exercise 5C. 1. פ 2. ש 3. ע, צ, ר, ת 4. מ, ס, צ, ק, ר, ת
5. ז, ח, י, ל, מ, פ, צ, ר, ת 6. ד, ו, ז, ט, י

Exercise 6C. אב, בחר, גאל, דרך, הנה, וו, זקן, חטא, טוב,
יד, כל, למה, מות, נתן, ספר, עלה, פנים, צד, קול, רק,
שמים, תורה

Exercise 7C. א, ה, ח, ע, ר

Exercise 8C. ב, כ, פ

Exercise 9C. כ–ך, מ–ם, נ–ן, פ–ף, צ–ץ

Chapter 2

Exercise 3. 1. דוֹר 2. לָמָּה 3. שָׁלוֹם 4. אֵם 5. תָּמָר 6. אֹכֶל

Exercise 4a. 1. מָוֶת 2. עֹנֶר 3. וַתָּקָם 4. דָּוִד

Exercise 4b. 1. קָיָם 2. מַיִם 3. יֶלֶד 4. בַּיִת 5. יֵשׁ

Exercise 5. ב, ב, פ, כ

Exercise 6. ע, ר, ח, ה, ר, א, ה, ח, ע, ר, א, ה

Exercise 8. 1. odd 2. seed 3. sheets 4. seen 5. yacht 6. goat 7. doze 8. bed 9. pod 10. lone 11. hate 12. oats 13. name 14. raid 15. net 16. tell 17. bead 18. tar 19. two 20. ooze 21. cave 22. deaf 23. rate 24. loom 25. car 26. meat 27. zoom 28. key

Chapter 3

Exercise 2. 1. בְּ/נוֹת 2. מַ/תִּים 3. שָׁ/פַט 4. נָ/שׁוּב
5. אָכְ/תֹב 6. אַבְ/רָ/הָם 7. אֶרֶץ 8. יִכְ/תְּבוּ 9. הוֹ/לַ/כְת
10. יַ/עֲ/קֹב

Exercise 3. אָלֶף, בֵּית, גִּמֶל, דָּלֶת, הֵא, וָו, זַיִן, חֵית, טֵית,
יוֹד, כַּף, לָמֶד, מֵם, נוּן, סָמֶך, עַיִן, פֵּא, צָדִי, קוֹף,
רֵישׁ, שִׁין, תָּו

Chapter 4

Exercise 1. A. 1. זָכַר דָּוִד. B. זָכַר נַעַר. C. זָכַר הוּא.
D. זָכַר אַבְרָהָם. E. זָכַר יַעֲקֹב. F. זָכַר בֹּעַז. 2. הוּא כָּתַב.
A. הוּא הָלַךְ. B. הוּא זָכַר. C. הוּא כָּתַב.

1. Boaz remembered. A. David . . . B. A lad . . . C. He . . . D. Abraham . . . E. Jacob . . . F. Boaz . . . 2. He wrote. A. . . . went. B. . . . remembered. C. . . . wrote.
Exercise 2. 1. Boaz remembered. 2. Abraham walked. 3. A man wrote. 4. A lad remembered. 5. Jacob wrote. 6. He went. 7. David remembered. 8. He wrote. 9. Abraham remembered.

Exercise 3. בֹּעַז, זָכַר, אַבְרָהָם, הָלַךְ, כָּתַב, יַעֲקֹב, דָּוִד

Exercise 4. בֹּעַז, זָכַר, אַבְרָהָם, הָלַךְ, נַעַר, אִישׁ, יַעֲקֹב, הוּא

Exercise 5. 1. אַבְרָהָם זָכַר. 2. אִישׁ הָלַךְ. 3. הוּא הָלַךְ.
4. זָכַר דָּוִד. 5. כָּתַב בֹּעַז. 6. נַעַר הָלַךְ.

Exercise 6. 1. דָּוִד כָּתַב. 2. הָלַךְ נַעַר. 3. אַבְרָהָם זָכַר.
4. הוּא הָלַךְ. 5. יַעֲקֹב כָּתַב

1. David wrote. 2. A lad went. 3. Abraham remembered. 4. He went. 5. Jacob wrote.

Chapter 5

Exercise 1. 1. A. רוּת כָּתְבָה. B. נַעֲרָה . . . C. הִיא . . .
D. שָׂרָה . . . E. מִשְׁפָּחָה . . . F. הַנַּעֲרָה . . . 2. A. אַבְרָהָם
הָלַךְ. B. דָּוִד . . . C. הוּא . . . D. הָאִישׁ . . . E. בֹּעַז . . .
F. הַנַּעַר . . . 3. A. רוּת כָּתְבָה סֵפֶר. B. אַבְרָהָם כָּתַב . . .
C. הָאִשָּׁה כָּתְבָה. D. בֹּעַז כָּתַב. E. הַנַּעֲרָה כָּתְבָה. F. יַעֲקֹב
כָּתַב. G. הַנַּעַר כָּתַב. H. הַמִּשְׁפָּחָה כָּתְבָה.

1. The woman wrote. A. Ruth wrote. B. A young woman . . . C. She . . . D. Sarah . . . E. A family . . . F. The maiden . . . 2. Jacob went. A. Abraham went. B. David . . . C. He . . . D. The man . . . E. Boaz . . . F. The lad . . . 3. Naomi wrote a book. A. Ruth . . . B. Abraham . . . C. The woman . . . D. Boaz . . . E. The young woman . . . F. Jacob . . . G. The lad . . . H. The family . . .
Exercise 2. 1. The family sent a lad. 2. Boaz walked. 3. Ruth remembered a gift. 4. The woman went. 5. The man remembered a book. 6. She sent a man.

Exercise 3. 1. הַנַּעַר 2. הַסֵּפֶר 3. הַמִּשְׁפָּחָה 4. הָאִישׁ
5. הַמִּנְחָה 6. הָאִשָּׁה 7. הַנַּעֲרָה

1. The lad 2. The book 3. The family 4. The man 5. The gift 6. The woman 7. The maiden

Exercise 4. 1. כָּתַב 2. שָׁלְחָה 3. זָכַר 4. הָלְכָה 5. שָׁלַח
6. הָלַךְ 7. כָּתְבָה 8. זָכְרָה

Exercise 5. 1. נַעַר כָּתַב סֵפֶר. 2. הַנַּעַר כָּתַב סֵפֶר. 3. נָעֳמִי
כָּתְבָה סֵפֶר. 4. הִיא כָּתְבָה סֵפֶר. 5. אִישׁ שָׁלַח מִנְחָה.
6. שָׁלַח הָאִישׁ מִנְחָה. 7. הוּא שָׁלַח סֵפֶר. 8. בֹּעַז שָׁלַח
נַעַר. 9. הַמִּשְׁפָּחָה שָׁלְחָה מִנְחָה. 10. הָלַךְ אַבְרָהָם.

Exercise 6. 1. הַמִּשְׁפָּחָה הָלְכָה. 2. דָּוִד זָכַר סֵפֶר.
3. הָאִשָּׁה שָׁלְחָה מִנְחָה. 4. אַבְרָהָם שָׁלַח נַעַר.

1. The family walked. 2. David remembered a book. 3. The woman sent a gift. 4. Abraham sent a young man.

Exercise 7. 1. שָׂרָה שָׁלְחָה מִנְחָה 2. יַעֲקֹב זָכַר סֵפֶר 3. הוּא
שָׁלַח נַעֲרָה 4. הָאִישׁ זָכַר מִשְׁפָּחָה 5. הַנַּעַר כָּתַב סֵפֶר
6. הִיא שָׁלְחָה אִשָּׁה

1. Sarah sent a gift. 2. Jacob remembered a book. 3. He sent a young woman. 4. The man remembered a family. 5. The young man wrote a book. 6. She sent a woman.

Chapter 6

Exercise 1. 1. A. אַבְרָהָם הָלַךְ וְזָכַר. B. שָׂרָה וְרוּת
הָלְכוּ וְזָכְרוּ. C. הִיא הָלְכָה וְזָכְרָה. D. הָאֲנָשִׁים הָלְכוּ
וְזָכְרוּ. E. הֵמָּה הָלְכוּ וְזָכְרוּ. F. הַנַּעֲרָה הָלְכָה וְזָכְרָה.
G. הַנָּשִׁים הָלְכוּ וְזָכְרוּ. H. הוּא הָלַךְ וְזָכַר. I. הֵנָּה הָלְכוּ
וְזָכְרוּ. J. הַנַּעַר הָלַךְ וְזָכַר. 2. A. הֵם שָׁלְחוּ סְפָרִים
וּנְעָלִים. B. הַנְּעָרוֹת שָׁלְחוּ . . . C. הַמִּשְׁפָּחָה שָׁלְחָה . . .

D. אַבְרָהָם שָׁלַח . . . E. נָעֳמִי שָׁלְחָה . . . F. הֵמָּה

שָׁלְחוּ . . . G. רוּת שָׁלְחָה . . . H. יַעֲקֹב שָׁלַח . . . I. הֵן

שָׁלְחוּ . . . J. הַנְּעָרִים שָׁלְחוּ . . .

1. Jacob and Boaz walked and remembered. A. Abraham walked and remembered. B. Sarah and Ruth . . . C. She . . . D. The men . . . E. They . . . F. The young woman . . . G. The women . . . H. He . . . I. They . . . J. The lad . . . 2. Sarah sent books and shoes. A. They sent . . . B. The maidens . . . C. The family . . . D. Abraham . . . E. Naomi . . . F. They . . . G. Ruth . . . H. Jacob . . . I. They . . . J. The lads . . .

Exercise 2 1. וְאִשָּׁה 2. וְאַבְרָהָם 3. וּמִשְׁפָּחָה 4. וִירוּשָׁלַיִם 5.

וְהִיא 6. וּבָעֲזוּ 7. וְשָׂרָה 8. וּמִנְחָה 9. וְהַמִּשְׁפָּחָה 10. וְהַסֵּפֶר.

Exercise 3. 1. The woman wrote. 2. David wrote. 3. David and the man walked. 4. The family walked. 5. The men and the women remembered. 6. The lads wrote a house. 7. The maiden sent gifts. 8. Naomi remembered a road. 9. Ruth and Boaz sent a pair of shoes. 10. Abraham remembered a woman.

Exercise 4 1. כָּתַב 2. שָׁלְחוּ 3. זָכְרָה 4. הָלְכוּ 5. שָׁלְחָה

6. זָכְרוּ.

Exercise 5 1. הָאֲנָשִׁים שָׁלְחוּ נְעָרוֹת. 2. הַנְּעָרוֹת זָכְרוּ

דְּרָכִים. 3. הֵם כָּתְבוּ סְפָרִים. 4. הַנָּשִׁים שָׁלְחוּ מְנָחוֹת.

Exercise 6 1. הִיא כָּתְבָה סֵפֶר. 2. הָאִשָּׁה וְהָאִישׁ שָׁלְחוּ

מִנְחָה. 3. הַנַּעֲרָה הָלְכָה וְזָכְרָה. 4. הוּא זָכַר דֶּרֶךְ.

Exercise 7 1. הַנַּעַר וְהַנַּעֲרָה הָלְכוּ. 2. הָאֲנָשִׁים שָׁלְחוּ

מְנָחוֹת. 3. הֵנָּה זָכְרוּ מִשְׁפָּחָה. 4. יַעֲקֹב וְאַבְרָהָם שָׁלְחוּ

נַעֲלַיִם. 5. הָאִישׁ כָּתַב סְפָרִים. 6. הַמִּשְׁפָּחוֹת זָכְרוּ בַּיִת.

Exercise 8 1. יַעֲקֹב וּבָעֲזוּ הָלְכוּ. 2. רוּת וְהָאִשָּׁה שָׁלְחוּ

מִנְחוֹת. 3. נָעֳמִי כָּתְבָה סְפָרִים. 4. הַנָּשִׁים זָכְרוּ.

1. Jacob and Boaz went. 2. Ruth and the woman sent gifts. 3. Naomi wrote books. 4. The women remembered.

Chapter 7

Exercise 1 1. A. הַמִּשְׁפָּחָה שָׁלְחָה נַעַר מִבֵּית לֶחֶם אֶל

יְרוּשָׁלַיִם. B. הַנָּשִׁים שָׁלְחוּ. C. אֲנָשִׁים שָׁלְחוּ . . .

D. נָעֳמִי וּבָעֲזוּ שָׁלְחוּ . . . E. הֵן שָׁלְחוּ . . . F. שָׂרָה

שָׁלְחָה . . . G. אִשָּׁה שָׁלְחָה. 2. A. אַבְרָהָם וְדָוִד הָלְכוּ

לַבַּיִת. B. יַעֲקֹב הָלַךְ . . . C. הֵמָּה הָלְכוּ . . . D. רוּת

הָלְכָה . . . E. הוּא הָלַךְ . . . F. הֵנָּה הָלְכוּ . . . G. הִיא

הָלְכָה . . . 3. A. הַמִּשְׁפָּחוֹת כָּתְבוּ עַל דָּוִד. B. הַנְּעָרִים

כָּתְבוּ . . . C. הָאִישׁ כָּתַב . . . D. רוּת וְנָעֳמִי כָּתְבוּ

. . . E. שָׂרָה וּבָעֲזוּ כָּתְבוּ . . . F. הַנָּשִׁים כָּתְבוּ . . . G. יַעֲקֹב

כָּתַב . . . 4. A. הַנְּעָרוֹת הָלְכוּ כְּאַבְרָהָם. B. הוּא

הָלַךְ . . . C. הֵנָּה הָלְכוּ . . . D. הִיא הָלְכָה . . . E. הֵם

הָלְכוּ . . . F. הַנַּעַר וְהַנַּעֲרָה הָלְכוּ . . . G. יַעֲקֹב

הָלַךְ . . .

1A. The family sent a lad from Bethlehem to Jerusalem. B. The women . . . C. The men . . . D. Naomi and Boaz . . . E. They . . . F. Sarah . . . G. A woman . . . 2. A. Abraham and David went to the house. B. Jacob . . . C. They . . . D. Ruth . . . E. He . . . F. They . . . G. She . . . 3A. The families wrote about David. B. The lads . . . C. The man . . . D. Ruth and Naomi . . . E. Sarah and

Boaz . . . F. The women . . . G. Jacob . . . 4A. The young women walked like Abraham. B. He . . . C. They . . . D. She . . . E. They . . . F. The lad and the maiden . . . G. Jacob . . .

Exercise 2 1. אֶל הַבַּיִת 2. בִּירוּשָׁלַיִם 3. עִם הַנְּעָרוֹת 4. מִן

בֵּית לֶחֶם 5. עַל אַבְרָהָם 6. לַבַּיִת 7. בַּדֶּרֶךְ.

1. Ruth walked to the house. 2. The man in Jerusalem wrote a book. 3. The lads walked with the maidens to the road. 4. The families from Bethlehem sent gifts. 5. Sarah wrote about Abraham. 6. The people sent women to the house. 7. David and Boaz remembered maidens on the road.

Exercise 3 1. בְּמִשְׁפָּחוֹת, כְּמִשְׁפָּחוֹת, לְמִשְׁפָּחוֹת 2. בְּמִנְחָה,

כְּמִנְחָה, לְמִנְחָה 3. בַּסֵּפֶר, כַּסֵּפֶר, לַסֵּפֶר 4. בִּדְרָכִים,

כִּדְרָכִים, לִדְרָכִים 5. בְּנַעֲלַיִם, כְּנַעֲלַיִם, לְנַעֲלַיִם

6. בַּאֲנָשִׁים, כַּאֲנָשִׁים, לַאֲנָשִׁים 7. בִּירוּשָׁלַיִם, כִּירוּשָׁלַיִם,

לִירוּשָׁלַיִם 8. בַּבָּתִּים, כַּבָּתִּים, לַבָּתִּים

1. with families, as, like families, to, for families 2. with, in a gift, as, like a gift, to, for a gift. 3. in the book, as, like the book, to, for the book 4. in, with roads, as, like roads, to, for roads 5. with, in the pair of shoes, as, like the pair of shoes, to, for the pair of shoes 6. with people, as, like people, to, for people 7. in Jerusalem, as, like Jerusalem, to, for Jerusalem 8. in the houses, as, like the houses, to, for the houses.

Exercise 4. 1a. Boaz wrote a book. 1b. Boaz wrote to the maiden. 1c. Boaz wrote to the maiden in Jerusalem. 1d. Boaz wrote about the family to the maiden in Jerusalem. 1e. Ruth and Boaz wrote about the family to the maiden in Jerusalem. 2a. Sarah walked to the road. 2b. Sarah walked from the house to the road. 2c. Sarah and Jacob walked from the house to the road. 2d. Sarah and Jacob walked with David from the house to the road.

Exercise 5 1. הַמִּשְׁפָּחָה בְּבֵית לֶחֶם שָׁלְחָה מִנְחָה.

2. הַמִּשְׁפָּחָה בְּבֵית לֶחֶם שָׁלְחָה מִנְחָה לְאִישׁ בִּירוּשָׁלַיִם.

3. הַמִּשְׁפָּחָה בְּבֵית לֶחֶם שָׁלְחָה מִנְחָה מִן רוּת לְאִישׁ

בִּירוּשָׁלַיִם. 4. הַמִּשְׁפָּחָה בְּבֵית לֶחֶם שָׁלְחָה נַעַר עִם

מִנְחָה מִן רוּת לְאִישׁ בִּירוּשָׁלַיִם. 5. הַמִּשְׁפָּחָה בְּבֵית לֶחֶם

שָׁלְחָה נַעַר עִם סְפָרִים כְּמִנְחָה לְאִישׁ בִּירוּשָׁלַיִם.

Exercise 6 1. דָּוִד זָכַר דֶּרֶךְ לִירוּשָׁלַיִם. 2. הֵנָּה כָּתְבוּ

לַנָּשִׁים בְּבֵית לֶחֶם. 3. הֵם שָׁלְחוּ נַעֲרָה מִן הַבַּיִת. 4. נָעֳמִי

הָלְכָה כְּאִשָּׁה.

Exercise 7 1. מִבֵּית לֶחֶם, אֶל יְרוּשָׁלַיִם. 2. עִם בֹּעַז

3. לְאַבְרָהָם 4. כִּנְעָרוֹת, עַל הַנְּעָרִים 5. מִמּוֹאָב, אֶל

יְהוּדָה 6. בִּירוּשָׁלַיִם.

Chapter 8

Exercise 2 1. A. אַתָּה הָלַכְתָּ אֶל הַבַּיִת. B. אַתְּ הָלַכְתְּ . . .

C. הוּא הָלַךְ . . . D. הִיא הָלְכָה . . . E. אֲנַחְנוּ הָלַכְנוּ . . .

F. אַתֶּם הֲלַכְתֶּם . . . G. אַתֶּן הֲלַכְתֶּן . . . H. הֵם . . .

הָלְכוּ . . . I. הֵנָּה הָלְכוּ . . . 2. A. הֵם שָׁלְחוּ נַעֲלַיִם אֶל

הַנָּשִׁים. B. אַתְּ שָׁלַחַתְּ . . . C. אָנוּ שָׁלַחְנוּ . . . D. אַתֶּן

שְׁלַחְתֶּן . . . E. הִיא שָׁלְחָה . . . F. אַתָּה שָׁלַחְתָּ . . .

G. הֵנָּה שָׁלְחוּ . . . H. אֲנִי שָׁלַחְתִּי . . . I. הֵמָּה שָׁלְחוּ . . .

J. אָנֹכִי שָׁלַחְתִּי . . . 3. A. אַתֶּם זְכַרְתֶּם אִישׁ מִבֵּית לֶחֶם.

B. אָנוּ זָכַרְנוּ . . . C. הוּא זָכַר . . . D. הֵם זָכְרוּ . . .

E. אַתָּה זָכַרְתָּ ... F. הֵן זָכְרוּ ... G. אֲנִי זָכַרְתִּי ...
H. אַתֵּן זְכַרְתֶּן ...

1A. You went to the house. B. You ... C. He ... 2A. They sent a pair of shoes to the women. B. You ... C. We ... 3A. You remembered a man from Bethlehem. B. We ... C. He ...

Exercise 3a. 1. הָלַכְנוּ מִן הַדֶּרֶךְ אֶל הַבַּיִת. 2. הֵן שָׁלְחוּ נַעַר אֶל בֹּעַז. 3. אַתֶּם כְּתַבְתֶּם סֵפֶר עַל מוֹאָב. 4. הֵמָּה זָכְרוּ נַעֲרָה. 5. כְּתַבְתֶּן אֶל הַנָּשִׁים וְאֶל הָאֲנָשִׁים מִבֵּית לָחֶם. 6. הֵם שָׁלְחוּ סְפָרִים לְרוּת.

Exercise 3b. 1. כָּתַבְתְּ עַל בֹּעַז וְעַל נָעֳמִי. 2. הִיא שָׁלְחָה נַעֲלַיִם אֶל הַנַּעַר מִן מוֹאָב. 3. זָכַרְתָּ דֶּרֶךְ אֶל הַבַּיִת. 4. הָלַכְתִּי עִם הָאֲנָשִׁים מִירוּשָׁלַיִם. 5. הוּא כָּתַב אֶל הַנָּשִׁים עַל בֵּית לָחֶם. 6. זָכַרְתִּי אִישׁ כְּבֹעַז.

Exercise 4. 1. הָלַכְתִּי 2. שָׁלְחָה 3. זְכַרְתֶּם 4. כָּתְבָה 5. הָלַכְנוּ 6. שָׁלְחוּ 7. זָכַר 8. כָּתַבְתָּ 9. הָלְכוּ 10. שְׁלַחְתֶּן

Exercise 5. 1. אֲנַחְנוּ שָׁלַחְנוּ נַעֲלַיִם. 2. אַתֶּם זְכַרְתֶּם אִישׁ. 3. אַתֵּן כְּתַבְתֶּן אֶל דָּוִד. 4. הֵנָּה הָלְכוּ אֶל הַבַּיִת. 5. הֵם שָׁלְחוּ נְעָרִים מִמּוֹאָב. 6. הֵם זָכְרוּ מִנְחָה.

Exercise 6. 1. שָׁלַחְנוּ נַעֲלַיִם מִמּוֹאָב. 2. שָׁלַחְתָּ סְפָרִים לְמִשְׁפָּחָה. 3. זָכַרְתִּי אִישׁ וְאִשָּׁה. 4. כְּתַבְתֶּם לְאִשָּׁה עַל הַמִּנְחָה. 5. הֵם הָלְכוּ עִם שָׂרָה וְיַעֲקֹב לִירוּשָׁלַיִם.

Exercise 7. 1. הֵם כָּתְבוּ עַל הָאִישׁ. 2. אַתֶּם זְכַרְתֶּם סְפָרִים. 3. הִיא הָלְכָה אֶל הַבַּיִת. 4. שָׁלַחְתְּ מִנְחָה עִם אַבְרָהָם.

1. They wrote about the man. 2. You remembered books. 3. She went to the house. 4. You sent a gift with Abraham.

Chapter 9

Exercise 1. 1. A. בֹּעַז שָׁלַח אֶת הַסֵּפֶר אֶל מוֹאָב. B. ... שָׁלַח נַעֲלַיִם. C. ... אֶת רוּת. D. ... אֶת הַנְּעָרִים ... E. ... שָׁלַח בַּת. F. ... אֶת נָעֳמִי ... G. ... שָׁלַח אֲנָשִׁים ... H. ... אֶת הַבָּנִים ...

2. A. ... שָׁלַח דָּבָר. B. ... הַבֵּן. C. ... בֵּית לָחֶם. D. ... הַדֶּרֶךְ. E. ... יְהוּדָה. F. ... נַעַר. G. ... הַבָּנוֹת. H. הִיא הָלְכָה אֶל הָעִיר. I. ... הַשָּׂדֶה.

3. A. הַנַּעַר זָכַר אֶת הַדְּבָרִים בָּאָרֶץ. B. ... זָכַרְתִּי. C. ... זָכַרְתָּ. D. הֵם זָכְרוּ. E. הֵנָּה זָכְרוּ. F. ... זְכַרְתֶּם. G. ... זָכַרְתָּ. H. ... זָכַרְנוּ ... I. ... זְכַרְתֶּן.

4. A. ... כָּתַבְתִּי אֶת הַסֵּפֶר וְלֹא שָׁלַחְתִּי אֶת הַסֵּפֶר לְרוּת. B. כְּתַבְתֶּן אֶת הַסֵּפֶר וְלֹא שְׁלַחְתֶּן אֶת הַסֵּפֶר לְרוּת. C. הִיא כָּתְבָה אֶת הַסֵּפֶר וְלֹא שָׁלְחָה אֶת הַסֵּפֶר לְרוּת. D. כָּתַבְנוּ אֶת הַסֵּפֶר וְלֹא שָׁלַחְנוּ אֶת הַסֵּפֶר לְרוּת. E. כָּתַבְתָּ אֶת הַסֵּפֶר וְלֹא שָׁלַחְתָּ אֶת הַסֵּפֶר לְרוּת. F. כְּתַבְתֶּם אֶת הַסֵּפֶר וְלֹא שְׁלַחְתֶּם אֶת הַסֵּפֶר לְרוּת. G. הֵן כָּתְבוּ אֶת הַסֵּפֶר וְלֹא שָׁלְחוּ אֶת הַסֵּפֶר לְרוּת. H. כָּתַבְתְּ אֶת הַסֵּפֶר וְלֹא שָׁלַחְתְּ אֶת הַסֵּפֶר לְרוּת.

1. הֵמָּה כָּתְבוּ אֶת הַסֵּפֶר וְלֹא שָׁלְחוּ אֶת הַסֵּפֶר לְרוּת.

1. Boaz sent the maidens to Moab. A. Boaz sent the ... 2. She went to the house. A. ... 3. The daughter remembered the things in the land. A. ... 4. He wrote the book and he did not send the book to Ruth. A. I wrote the book and I did not send ...

Exercise 2. 1. הִיא כָּתְבָה אֶת הַסְּפָרִים. 2. הָאִישׁ שָׁלַח אֶת הַנַּעֲרָה אֶל בֵּית לָחֶם. 3. רוּת וְאַבְרָהָם זָכְרוּ אֶת הַדֶּרֶךְ. 4. שָׁלַחְתְּ אֶת הַנַּעֲלַיִם לְרוּת. 5. הוּא זָכַר אֶת הַשּׁוֹפֵט מִן הָאָרֶץ. 6. זְכַרְתֶּם אֶת הָאִשָּׁה מִן הַבַּיִת. 7. הַיּוֹם זָכַרְתִּי אֶת הַשָּׂדוֹת בְּמוֹאָב.

Exercise 3. 1. – 2. – 3. – 4. אֶת. 5. – אֶת הַנַּעַר וְאֶת הַנַּעֲרָה.

1. Boaz sent a lad to the field. 2. Ruth wrote a book about Judah. 3. The man sent the family to Moab. 4. The son remembered a road and a city. 5. Naomi sent the lad and the maiden.

Exercise 4. 1a. רוּת הָלְכָה לָעִיר. 1b. רוּת הָלְכָה לָעִיר. 1c. רוּת הָלְכָה בָּעִיר. 1d. רוּת הָלְכָה בְּעִיר. 1e. רוּת לֹא הָלְכָה בָּעִיר. 1f. לֹא רוּת הָלְכָה בָּעִיר. 1g. לֹא בָּעִיר הָלְכָה רוּת. 2a. בֹּעַז כָּתַב סֵפֶר עַל בָּתִּים. 2b. בֹּעַז כָּתַב אֶת הַסֵּפֶר עַל בָּתִּים. 2c. בֹּעַז לֹא כָּתַב אֶת הַסֵּפֶר עַל בָּתִּים. 2d. לֹא בֹּעַז כָּתַב אֶת הַסֵּפֶר עַל בָּתִּים. 2e. לֹא עַל בָּתִּים כָּתַב בֹּעַז.

Exercise 5. 1. רוּת וְנָעֳמִי הָלְכוּ מִן הָעִיר. 2. רוּת כָּתְבָה לַבָּנִים וְלַבָּנוֹת. 3. הָאִישׁ זָכַר אֶת הַדָּבָר. 4. יַעֲקֹב הָלַךְ אֶל הָעִיר. 5. הִיא זָכְרָה אֶת בֵּית לָחֶם.

1. Ruth and Naomi went from the city. 2. Ruth wrote to the sons and to the daughters. 3. The man remembered the word. 4. Jacob walked to the city. 5. She remembered Bethlehem.

Exercise 6. 1. רוּת וְנָעֳמִי לֹא הָלְכוּ ... 2. רוּת לֹא כָּתְבָה ... 3. הָאִישׁ לֹא זָכַר ... 4. יַעֲקֹב לֹא הָלַךְ ... 5. הִיא לֹא זָכְרָה אֶת בֵּית לָחֶם.

Exercise 7. 1. The son remembered the woman and the lad today. 2. He sent a pair of shoes and a book to the maidens. 3. They did not go with Naomi and Ruth from the house to the road today. 4. The judge, and not David, wrote the words. 5. The woman remembered the days in Jerusalem.

Exercise 8. 1. definite direct object = הָאִישׁ, הַנַּעַר 2. נַעֲלַיִם,
indefinite direct object = סֵפֶר, object of preposition = הַנְּעָרוֹת
3. נָעֳמִי, רוּת, הַבַּיִת, הַדֶּרֶךְ = object of preposition
4. הַדְּבָרִים 5. definite direct object = הַיָּמִים
definite direct object, object of preposition = יְרוּשָׁלַיִם

Exercise 9. We remembered the days in Bethlehem. I remembered the city and the fields. You remembered the people and the families. Abraham and Boaz didn't remember the city and they didn't remember the people; they remembered the young women.

Chapter 10

Exercise 2. 1. A. אֲנִי הָיִיתִי עִם הַשֹּׁפֵט ... B. רוּת הָיְתָה ... C. אַתָּה הָיִיתָ ... D. בֹּעַז וְנָעֳמִי הָיוּ ... E. אֲנוּ הָיִינוּ ... F. הַנְּעָרִים הָיוּ ... G. אַתֶּן הֱיִיתֶן ... H. אַתְּ הָיִית ... I. אַתֶּם הֱיִיתֶם ... J. הַבֵּן הָיָה ... 2. A. אֲנוּ שָׁמַרְנוּ אֶת

C. הִנֵּה ... הָאֹכֶל כִּי הָיָה רָעָב בָּעִיר. B. אַתָּה שָׁמַרְתָּ ...

שָׁמְרוּ ... D. הִיא שָׁמְרָה ... E. הָאֲנָשִׁים שָׁמְרוּ ...

F. אַתֵּן שְׁמַרְתֶּן ... G. אָנֹכִי שָׁמַרְתִּי ... H. אַתֶּם

שְׁמַרְתֶּם ... 3. A. אַתָּה אָמַרְתָּ: "הַמִּנְחָה הָיְתָה בַּבַּיִת."

B. רוּת אָמְרָה ... C. אֲנַחְנוּ אָמַרְנוּ ... D. הֵנָּה אָמְרוּ ...

E. הוּא אָמַר ... F. הֵם אָמְרוּ ... G. אָנֹכִי אָמַרְתִּי ...

H. אַתְּ אָמַרְתְּ ... 4. A. אַבְרָהָם אֲשֶׁר הָיָה מִמּוֹאָב אָכַל

אֶת הַלֶּחֶם הַיּוֹם. B. אֲנִי אֲשֶׁר הָיִיתִי מִמּוֹאָב אָכַלְתִּי ...

C. אַתֶּן אֲשֶׁר הֱיִיתֶן מִמּוֹאָב אֲכַלְתֶּן. D. אַתְּ אֲשֶׁר הָיִית

מִמּוֹאָב אָכַלְתְּ. E. אֲנַחְנוּ אֲשֶׁר הָיִינוּ מִמּוֹאָב

אָכַלְנוּ. F. ... G. הֵמָּה אֲשֶׁר הָיוּ מִמּוֹאָב אָכְלוּ. ... אַתָּה

אֲשֶׁר הָיִיתָ מִמּוֹאָב אָכַלְתָּ. H. הַבָּנוֹת אֲשֶׁר הָיוּ מִמּוֹאָב

אָכְלוּ ...

1. The man was with the judge. A. I was ... B. Ruth was ... C. You were ...... 2. The judge guarded the food because there was a famine in the city. A. We guarded ... B. You ... 3. The women said: "The gift was in the house." A. You said ... B. Ruth said ... C. We said ... D. They ... 4. The family that was from Moab ate the bread today. A. Abraham, who was from Moab, ate ... B. I, who was from Moab, ate ... C. You, who were ...

Exercise 3 1. אַתֶּן —2 f, pl 2. הִיא —3 f, sg

3. הֵם, הֵן —3 m or f, pl 4. אֲנִי or אָנֹכִי —1 c, sg

5. אַתְּ —2 f, sg 6. הוּא —3 m, sg 7. אַתָּה —2 m, sg

8. אַתֶּם —2 m, pl 9. אֲנִי or אָנֹכִי —1 c, sg 10. הִיא —3 f, sg

11. הֵמָּה, הֵנָּה —3 m or f, pl 12. אַתֵּן —2 f, pl

13. אָנוּ or אֲנַחְנוּ —1 c, pl 14. אַתֶּם —2 m, pl

15. הֵם, הֵן —3 m or f, pl 16. אָנוּ or אֲנַחְנוּ —1 c, pl

Exercise 4 1. הָלַךְ 2. הָיִינוּ 3. שָׁמְרָה 4. הָיָה, הָיְתָה

5. כָּתְבוּ 6. הֱיִיתֶם 7. שָׁמַרְתָּ 8. אֲכַלְתֶּם 9. הָיוּ 10. זָכַר

11. הָיִיתִי, הָיְתָה 12. אֲכַלְתֶּן 13. אָמַר 14. שָׁמַרְתִּי

1. The judge went from Bethlehem to Moab. 2. We were in the fields. 3. She guarded the road two days. 4. Abraham was a son and Naomi was a daughter. 5. Boaz and David wrote about the food. 6. You were with the judges there. 7. You did not guard the shoes. 8. You ate with the family. 9. They were with the women. 10. The young man remembered the things in Jerusalem. 11. I was not with Ruth in the field because Ruth was in Bethlehem. 12. You ate with David there. 13. Jacob said to the man: "Not today." 14. I did not keep the thing.

Exercise 5. 1. There were no people in the land because there was a famine there. 2. We wrote to Jacob that Abraham was in Jerusalem. 3. David was the man that guarded the cities. 4. Abraham wrote to Boaz because Boaz was a judge. 5. The young woman that was in the house, went to the field. 6. The sons ate in the city because there was bread there. 7. Sarah remembered the lad that went to Bethlehem. 8. The man sent books to the daughter in Jerusalem because there were no books there. 9. The man was like a son to Abraham because he guarded the house.

Chapter 11

Exercise 1 A. 1. אֲנַחְנוּ יָשַׁבְנוּ בְּאֶרֶץ טוֹבָה. B. הַמֶּלֶךְ

יָשַׁב ... C. הֵנָּה יָשְׁבוּ ... D. אַתֵּן יְשַׁבְתֶּן ... E. אַתָּה

וְדָוִד יְשַׁבְתֶּם ... F. יַעֲקֹב וְאַבְרָהָם יָשְׁבוּ ... G. אַתְּ

יָשַׁבְתְּ ... 2. A. הַאִם הַטּוֹבָה הָלְכָה אֶל הָעִיר.

B. הַנְּעָרוֹת הַטּוֹבוֹת הָלְכוּ ... C. הָאָב הַטּוֹב הָלַךְ ...

D. הַבָּנִים הַטּוֹבִים הָלְכוּ ... E. הַבַּת הַטּוֹבָה הָלְכָה ...

3. A. הַשֹּׁפֵט הַזָּקֵן בַּשָּׂדֶה הַגָּדוֹל הַיּוֹם. B. הַשֹּׁפֵט הַזָּקֵן

בָּעִיר הַגְּדוֹלָה. C. הַשֹּׁפֵט הַזָּקֵן בַּשָּׂדוֹת הַגְּדוֹלִים ...

D. הַשֹּׁפֵט הַזָּקֵן בַּדְּרָכִים הַגְּדוֹלוֹת ... 4. A. הָאִשָּׁה מִמּוֹאָב

אִשָּׁה קְדוֹשָׁה B. הָאִמּוֹת מִמּוֹאָב נָשִׁים קְדוֹשׁוֹת C. הַשֹּׁפֵט

מִמּוֹאָב אִישׁ קָדוֹשׁ D. הַמְּלָכִים מִמּוֹאָב אֲנָשִׁים קְדוֹשִׁים

E. הַבָּנוֹת מִמּוֹאָב נָשִׁים קְדוֹשׁוֹת 5. A. אֲנַחְנוּ הָיִינוּ אֲנָשִׁים

רָעִים. B. רוּת וְנָעֳמִי הָיוּ נָשִׁים רָעוֹת. C. הֵמָּה הָיוּ אֲנָשִׁים

רָעִים. D. אַתֶּן הֱיִיתֶן נָשִׁים רָעוֹת. E. הִיא הָיְתָה אִשָּׁה

רָעָה. F. אֲנִי הָיִיתִי אִישׁ רַע. G. אַתָּה הָיִיתָ אִישׁ רַע.

H. אַתֶּם הֱיִיתֶם אֲנָשִׁים רָעִים. I. אַתְּ הָיִית אִשָּׁה רָעָה.

1. She stayed in a good land. A. We stayed ... B. The king stayed ... C. They stayed ...... 2. The good man went to the city. A. The good mother ... B. The good maidens ... 3. The old judge is in the big house today. A. The old judge is in the big field ... B. ... is in the big city 4. The fathers from Moab are holy men. A. The woman from Moab is a holy woman. B. The mothers from Moab ... 5. The king was an evil man. A. We were evil people. B. Ruth and Naomi were evil women.

Exercise 2 1. קָדוֹשׁ 2. זְקֵנוֹת 3. רָעִים 4. גְּדוֹלָה 5. טוֹבוֹת

6. קְדוֹשָׁה 7. גְּדוֹלִים 8. הַטּוֹבִים 9. אֶחָד 10. טוֹבִים

11. זָקֵן

Exercise 3. 1a. an old man or A man is old 2a. The man is old. 3a. the old man 1b. a good gift or A gift is good. 2b. The gift is good. 3b. the good gift 1c. great kings or Kings are great. 2c. The kings are great. 3c. The great kings are evil. 1d. A holy man is in a big house. 2d. The holy man is great. 3d. The great and holy man is in the house.

Exercise 4 1. רוּת הָיְתָה נַעֲרָה וְנָעֳמִי הָיְתָה אִשָּׁה. 2. הַמֶּלֶךְ

וְהַשּׁוֹפְטִים הָיוּ בַּדֶּרֶךְ ... 3. אָנוּ הָיִינוּ בַּבַּיִת וְהֵם הָיוּ

בַּשָּׂדֶה. 4. הִיא הָיְתָה עִם הַנָּשִׁים כִּי אַתֶּם הֱיִיתֶם עִם

הַמֶּלֶךְ. 5. הַלֶּחֶם הַטּוֹב הָיָה בַּבַּיִת. 6. אַתְּ הָיִית כְּאֵם

לְרוּת. 7. אַתָּה הָיִיתָ אָב לְיַעֲקֹב. 8. שָׂרָה הָיְתָה נַעֲרָה ...

9. שׁוֹפֵט אֶחָד הָיָה ...

Exercise 5 1. אָנוּ עִם אַבְרָהָם ... 2. הַדְּבָרִים מֵעִיר ...

3. אַתָּה בְּמוֹאָב כִּי ... 4. אַתֶּן עִם הַנָּשִׁים ... 5. אַתְּ אֵם

לְיַעֲקֹב ... 6. דָּוִד בַּבַּיִת ... 7. אִשָּׁה אַחַת ...

Exercise 7. 1. There was a family that dwelled in Judah. The old mother was Sarah and the old father was Boaz. The daughter in the family, Ruth, was good and the son, Jacob, was bad. There was a great famine in Judah and there was no bread. Sarah and Boaz sent Ruth and Jacob to Moab because there was food there. When Ruth was in Moab, she remembered the family and sent food to the family and the people in Judah. The evil Jacob did not remember the father and the mother and did not send food to Judah. When there was bread in Judah, Ruth went from Moab to the family in Judah. The evil Jacob stayed in Moab.

2. זְקֵנָה, זָקֵן, טוֹבָה, רַע, גָּדוֹל 3. הַאִם הַזְּקֵנָה שָׂרָה וְהָאָב

הַזָּקֵן בְּעוֹ. וְהַבֵּן, יַעֲקֹב, רַע. 4. אֶת רוּת וְאֶת יַעֲקֹב, אֶת

הַמִּשְׁפָּחָה, אֶת הָאָב וְאֶת הָאֵם 5. אֵכֵל

Chapter 12

Exercise 1 A. 1. שׁוֹפֵט הַמָּקוֹם שָׁמַר אֶת שְׂדֵה הָאִשָּׁה

הַזְּקֵנָה מְאֹד B. נַעֲרֵי הַמָּקוֹם שָׁמְרוּ C. . . . מֶלֶךְ הַמָּקוֹם
שָׁמַר D. . . . נַעֲרוֹת הַמָּקוֹם שָׁמְרוּ E. . . . נַעֲרַת הַמָּקוֹם
שָׁמְרָה 2. . . . A. כָּל הַלַּיְלָה הָיִינוּ בְּבֵית אַבְרָהָם. B. כָּל
הַלַּיְלָה בַּת הַמִּשְׁפָּחָה הָיְתָה . . . C. . . . הָיִיתִי . . .
D. . . . הֵמָּה הָיוּ . . . E. . . . הָיִיתָ . . . F. . . . הָיִיתָ . . .
G. . . . הֱיִיתֶן . . . H. . . . הֵן הָיוּ . . . 3. A. . . . אִם יַעֲקֹב
הַזָּקֵן אָכְלָה עִם מִשְׁפַּחַת רוּת כָּל בֹּקֶר B. אִם יַעֲקֹב
הַטּוֹב אָכְלָה . . . C. . . . הָרָעָה אָכְלָה . . . D. . . . יַעֲקֹב
הַגָּדוֹל אָכְלָה . . . E. . . . הַקְּדוֹשָׁה אָכְלָה . . .
4. A. נַעֲרוֹת הָעִיר עוֹד זָכְרוּ אֶת יְמֵי דָּוִד הַמֶּלֶךְ B. עוֹד
זָכַרְתִּי C. . . . עוֹד זְכַרְתֶּם D. . . . עוֹד זָכַרְתָּ E. . . . עַם
יִשְׂרָאֵל עוֹד זָכַר F. . . . עוֹד זָכַרְנוּ G. . . . עוֹד
זָכַרְתְּ H. . . . בַּת הַשֹּׁפֵט עוֹד זָכְרָה 5. A. . . . כָּתַבְנוּ כִּי
רַע הָאִישׁ הַזָּקֵן מִבֹּעַז. B. כָּל נְשֵׁי הַמָּקוֹם כָּתְבוּ . . .
C. . . . כָּתַבְתָּ D. . . . כְּתַבְתֶּן E. . . . כָּתַבְתִּי F. . . . שֹׁפְטֵי
יְהוּדָה כָּתְבוּ G. . . . אֵשֶׁת יַעֲקֹב כָּתְבָה H. . . . כְּתַבְתֶּם
I. . . . בֶּן אַבְרָהָם כָּתַב 6. A. . . . בַּבֹּקֶר לֹא הָלַכְתִּי וְלֹא
יָשַׁבְתִּי כְּאִישׁ זָקֵן. B. . . . לֹא הָלַכְתְּ וְלֹא יָשַׁבְתְּ כְּאִשָּׁה
זְקֵנָה. C. . . . אִם שָׂרָה לֹא הָלְכָה וְלֹא יָשְׁבָה כְּאִשָּׁה
זְקֵנָה. D. . . . נַעַר הַשָּׂדֶה לֹא הָלַךְ וְלֹא יָשַׁב כְּאִישׁ זָקֵן.
E. . . . לֹא הֲלַכְתֶּם וְלֹא יְשַׁבְתֶּם כַּאֲנָשִׁים זְקֵנִים.

Exercise 2 1. בֵּית מֶלֶךְ 2. חֶסֶד מְלָכִים 3. עִיר דָּוִד 4. בֶּן
שֹׁפֵט 5. אֵם נְעָרוֹת 6. שׁוֹפֵט אֲנָשִׁים 7. שׁוֹפֵט אִישׁ 8. אֹכֶל
שָׂרָה 9. בַּת אִשָּׁה 10. בָּתֵּי אֲנָשִׁים 11. דִּבְרֵי שֹׁפְטִים
12. אַנְשֵׁי מָקוֹם 13. מִשְׁפְּחוֹת עָרִים 14. עֵינֵי אַבְרָהָם
15. אֲבוֹת נְעָרִים 16. יְדֵי בֹּעַז 17. חַסְדֵי אָבוֹת 18. מְקוֹם
הַנְּעָרוֹת 19. יַד הַנַּעַר 20. סִפְרֵי הַשּׁוֹפְטִים 21. דִּבְרֵי
הָאָבוֹת 22. נַעֲלֵי הָאִשָּׁה 23. חַסְדֵי הַמֶּלֶךְ 24. בְּנֵי הָעָם
25. דַּרְכֵי הָאָרֶץ

1. a king's house 2. kindness of kings 3. the city of David 4. a son of a judge 5. a mother of maidens 6. a judge of men 7. a judge of a man 8. the food of Sarah 9. a daughter of a woman 10. houses of people 11. words of judges 12. people of a place 13. families of cities 14. the eyes of Abraham 15. fathers of lads 16. the hands of Boaz 17. kindnesses of fathers 18. the place of the maidens 19. the lad's hand 20. the books of the judges 21. the words of the fathers 22. the woman's pair of shoes 23. the kindnesses of the king 24. the sons of the nation 25. the roads of the land.
Exercise 3. 1. the gifts of the women—the women's gifts 2. the cities of Judah 3. days of famine 4. The house of the mother—the mother's house 5. the father of the lad—the lad's father 6. the son of the king—the king's son 7. the wife of Abraham—Abraham's wife 8. the people of Israel 9. the people of the place.

Exercise 4 1. מִנְחוֹת/הַנָּשִׁים 2. עָרִים/יְהוּדָה 3. יָמִים/רָעָב
4. בֵּית/הָאֵם 5. אָב/הַנַּעַר 6. בֶּן/הַמֶּלֶךְ 7. אִשָּׁה/אַבְרָהָם
8. עַם/יִשְׂרָאֵל 9. אֲנָשִׁים/הַמָּקוֹם

Exercise 5. 1. the man's son 2. the good man's son—the good son of the man 3. The man's son is good. 4. The good man's son is in the city—The good son of the man . . . 5. The sons of the good man are in the big city. 6. The man's good sons are in the big city. 7. The sons of the good men are in the big city today.—The men's good sons . . . 8. The sons of the good men are good.

Exercise 6 1. מִשְׁפַּחַת מֶלֶךְ 2. מִשְׁפַּחַת הַמֶּלֶךְ 3. מִשְׁפַּחַת
הַמֶּלֶךְ הַגָּדוֹל 4. מִשְׁפַּחַת הַמֶּלֶךְ הַגְּדוֹלָה 5. מִשְׁפַּחַת
הַמֶּלֶךְ גְּדוֹלָה. 6. מִשְׁפַּחַת הַמֶּלֶךְ הַגְּדוֹלָה לֹא בַּשָּׂדֶה.
7. מִשְׁפַּחַת הַמֶּלֶךְ הַגָּדוֹל, גְּדוֹלָה.

Exercise 7. 1. The place is very good in Ruth's eyes. 2. Holy places were in the hands of the people of Judah. 3. A very great people still stayed in the land of Israel. 4. The food was still in the house because the men were still in the field. 5. Every morning the lads of Boaz ate bread in a good place. 6. At night, all the maidens of the king went to the house of the king. 7. At night, Ruth said ''No'' and in the morning Ruth still said ''No''. 8. All the king's gifts were in the hands of the men of the city. 9. I wrote about the judge's kindness to Sarah. 10. David's wife walked on the road to Bethlehem the whole night. 11. Naomi's eyes were very big.

Construct Units: 1. בְּעֵינֵי רוּת 2. בִּידֵי עַם יְהוּדָה
3. בְּאֶרֶץ יִשְׂרָאֵל 5. נַעֲרֵי בֹּעַז 6. נַעֲרוֹת הַמֶּלֶךְ; בֵּית
הַמֶּלֶךְ 8. מִנְחוֹת הַמֶּלֶךְ, בִּידֵי אַנְשֵׁי הָעִיר 9. חַסְדֵי הַשּׁוֹפֵט
10. אֵשֶׁת דָּוִד 11. עֵינֵי רוּת

Chapter 13

Exercise 2 1. A. מִי בְּבֵיתֵךְ עִם בְּנֵךְ? B. מִי בְּבֵיתוֹ עִם בְּנוֹ?
C. מִי בְּבֵיתֵנוּ עִם בְּנֵנוּ? D. מִי בְּבֵיתְכֶם עִם בְּנֵיכֶם? E. מִי
בְּבֵיתָהּ עִם בְּנָהּ? F. מִי בְּבֵיתְכֶן עִם בְּנֶכֶן? G. מִי בְּבֵיתְךָ
עִם בִּנְךָ? H. מִי בְּבֵיתָן עִם בְּנָן? I. מִי בְּבֵיתָם עִם בְּנָם?
2. A. מַה בְּיָדָם? סְפָרִים בְּיָדָם. B. מַה בְּיָדְךָ? סִפְרְךָ בְּיָדְךָ.
C. . . . בְּיָדֵנוּ? סִפְרֵנוּ . . . D. . . . בְּיָדָן? סִפְרָן . . .
E. . . . בְּיֶדְכֶם? סִפְרְכֶם . . . F. . . . בְּיָדוֹ? סִפְרוֹ . . .
G. . . . בְּיָדֵךְ? סִפְרֵךְ . . . H. . . . בְּיָדָהּ? סִפְרָהּ . . .
I. . . . בְּיֶדְכֶן? סִפְרְכֶן 3. A. . . . לֹא זָכַרְתִּי אֶת בְּנָהּ הַטּוֹב.
B. . . . אִמּוֹ הַטּוֹבָה. C. . . . הַמֶּלֶךְ הַטּוֹב. D. . . . הָאָרֶץ
הַטּוֹבָה. E. . . . מַלְכֵּנוּ הַטּוֹב. F. . . . אֲבִיכֶם הַטּוֹב.
G. . . . הָאֲנָשִׁים הַטּוֹבִים. 4. A. . . . שְׁמֵנוּ גָּדוֹל בָּאָרֶץ כִּי
אֲנַחְנוּ אֲנָשִׁים טוֹבִים. B. . . . שְׁמָהּ . . . כִּי הִיא אִשָּׁה טוֹבָה.
C. . . . שִׁמְךָ . . . D. . . . אַתָּה אִישׁ טוֹב. D. שְׁמִי . . . כִּי אֲנִי אִישׁ
טוֹב. E. שִׁמְכֶם . . . כִּי אַתֶּם אֲנָשִׁים טוֹבִים. F. שְׁמָן . . .
כִּי הֵן נָשִׁים טוֹבוֹת. 5. A. רוּת שָׁכְבָה בְּבֵיתָהּ וְזָכְרָה אֶת
מְקוֹם מִשְׁפַּחְתָּהּ. B. בָּתֵּי שָׁכְבוּ בְּבֵיתָה וְזָכְרוּ . . .
מִשְׁפַּחְתָּה C. . . . בִּנְךָ שָׁכַב בְּבֵיתוֹ . . . מִשְׁפַּחְתּוֹ D. אֲנַחְנוּ
שָׁכַבְנוּ בְּבֵיתֵנוּ . . . מִשְׁפַּחְתֵּנוּ E. . . . דּוֹדְכֶם שָׁכַב בְּבֵיתוֹ . . .
מִשְׁפַּחְתּוֹ F. הַנָּשִׁים שָׁכְבוּ בְּבֵיתָן . . . מִשְׁפַּחְתָּן

1. Who is in my house with my son? A. Who is in your house with your son? B. . . . in his house . . . his son? C. . . . our house . . . 2. What is in my hand? My book is in my hand. A. . . . their hand? Their book . . . B. . . . your hand? Your book . . . C. . . . our hand? Our book . . . 3. I did not remember my good daughter. A. I did not remember her good son. B. . . . his good mother. C. . . . the good king. D. . . . the good land. 4. His name is great in the land because he is a good man. A. Our name is great in the land because we are good people. B. Her name . . . she is a good woman. C. Your name . . . 5. The man lay in his house and remembered his

family's place. A. Ruth lay down in her house and remembered her family's place. B. My daughter lay down in her house and remembered her family's place. C. Your son lay down in his house...

Exercise 3 1. אָכְלוּ 2. דַּרְכְּכֶם 3. סִפְרִי 4. מִשְׁפַּחְתֵּךְ 5. מַלְכְּךָ 6. נַעֲרוֹ 7. בִּתְּכֶם 8. שְׁמָהּ 9. בְּנָה 10. אַרְצָן 11. לַחְמוֹ

Exercise 4. 1. his wife 2. Who is her daughter? 3. my family 4. our king 5. Who is his father? 6. his shoe 7. What is in his hand? 8. their uncle 9. What is your name? 10. my mother's house 11. our good land 12. the voice of their judge

Exercise 5. "Goldilocks and the Three Bears" There were three bears that lived in their house in a big field. In the bears' family there was Father-Bear, Mother-Bear and Son-Bear. In the morning, the bears went to their big field and there was not a bear in the bears' house. In the city there was a maiden and her name was Goldilocks. She went from her house in the city to the fields. She walked and walked and came to the bears' house. In the house was a table and on the table was food. There were also three chairs. Goldilocks sat on one chair and the chair was very big. She sat on the second chair and the second chair was also big. She sat on the third chair and the chair was good. Goldilocks sat on the chair and ate the food that was on the table. In the house were three beds. Goldilocks lay down on one bed and the bed was very big. She lay down on the second bed and it also was big. She lay down on the third bed and the bed was good. Goldilocks slept there. The bears came from their field to their house. They went to the table. Father-Bear said in his very big voice: "Who ate my food?" Mother-Bear said in her big voice: "Who ate my food?" Son-Bear said in a not-big voice: "Who ate my food?" The bears sat on the chairs. Father-Bear said in his very big voice: "Who sat on my chair?" Mother-Bear said in her big voice: "Who sat on my chair?" Son-Bear said in a not-big voice: "Who sat on my chair?" The bears went to the beds. Father-Bear said in his very big voice: "Who's been lying on my bed?" Mother-Bear said in her big voice: "Who's been lying on my bed?" Son-Bear said in a not-big voice: "Who's been lying on my bed? A maiden has been lying on my bed and she's still in my bed!" The bears loved Goldilocks and she lived with the bears' family forever.

Exercise 6 1. זָכַרְתִּי 2. כָּתַבְתִּי 3. יָשַׁבְתִּי 4. אָכַלְתִּי 5. אָמַרְנוּ 6. זָכַרְנוּ 7. כָּתַבְנוּ 8. שָׁלַחְנוּ 9. אֲכַלְתֶּם 10. אֲכַלְתֶּן 11. אֲמַרְתֶּם 12. הֱיִיתֶן

1. I remembered 2. I wrote 3. I sat 4. I ate 5. we said 6. we remembered 7. we wrote 8. we sent 9. you ate 10. you ate 11. you said 12. you were

Chapter 14

Exercise 2 1. A. הַמֶּלֶךְ הַזָּקֵן שָׁמַר וְהוּא עוֹד שׁוֹמֵר. B. ... כָּתַב ... כּוֹתֵב ... C. ... שָׁמַע ... שׁוֹמֵעַ ... D. ... יָשַׁב ... יוֹשֵׁב 2. A. שָׁכַב ... שׁוֹכֵב ... נָעֳמִי פּוֹתַחַת אֶת שַׁעֲרֵי עִירָהּ תַּחַת אַבְרָהָם. B. אֲנַחְנוּ פּוֹתְחִים ... עִירֵנוּ C. אַתָּה פּוֹתֵחַ ... הֵנָּה D. ... עִירְךָ ... פּוֹתְחוֹת ... עִירָן ... E. אֲנִי פּוֹתֵחַ ... עִירִי ... F. אַתֶּן פּוֹתְחוֹת ... עִירְךָ G. ... אַתְּ פּוֹתַחַת ... עִירְכֶן H. ... אַתֶּם פּוֹתְחִים ... עִירְכֶם 3. A. ... הַנְּעָרִים הַקּוֹצְרִים לָקְחוּ אֶת הַמִּנְחָה מִן בְּעוֹ. B. הַבֵּן הַקּוֹצֵר לָקַח ... C. ... הַנָּשִׁים הַקּוֹצְרוֹת לָקְחוּ. D. דָּוִד הַקּוֹצֵר לָקַח ... E. אֲנַחְנוּ הַקּוֹצְרִים לָקַחְנוּ. 4. A. ... בִּתֵּנוּ שׁוֹמַעַת אֶת קוֹלִי כָּל הַלַּיְלָה. B. הֵם שׁוֹמְעִים ... C. הַנַּעֲרָה שׁוֹמַעַת ... D. הַשּׁוֹמֵר שׁוֹמֵעַ ... E. הַנָּשִׁים שׁוֹמְעוֹת ... 5. A. ... שָׂרָה הָרָעָה לוֹקַחַת אֶת הָאֹכֶל מִתַּחַת בֵּיתֵנוּ. B. דּוֹדָתָהּ הָרָעָה לוֹקַחַת ... C. ... הַנְּעָרוֹת

... D. הַשּׁוֹמְרִים הָרָעִים לוֹקְחִים ... E. ... אֲנָשִׁים רָעִים לוֹקְחִים 6. A. ... נַעֲלֵי הַמֶּלֶךְ שְׁמוּרִים כָּל הַיּוֹם וְכָל הַלַּיְלָה. B. שְׂדֵי הַמֶּלֶךְ שְׁמוּרִים ... C. בְּנוֹת הַמֶּלֶךְ שְׁמוּרוֹת ... D. כִּסֵּא הַמֶּלֶךְ שָׁמוּר ... E. מְקוֹם הַמֶּלֶךְ שָׁמוּר ...

Exercise 2. 1. The old king reigned and he is still reigning. A. The old king guarded and he is still guarding. B. ... wrote ... writing 2. Boaz is opening the gates of his city instead of Abraham. A. Naomi is opening the gates of her city instead of Abraham. B. We are opening ... our city ... 3. The harvesting woman took the gift from Boaz. A. The harvesting lads took the gift from Boaz. B. The harvesting son took ... C. The harvesting women took ... 4. My son hears my voice all night. A. Our daughter hears ... B. They hear ...... 5. The evil man is taking the food from under our house. A. Evil Sarah is taking the food from under our house. B. Her evil aunt is taking ... C. The evil young women are ... 6. The king's house is guarded all day and all night. A. The king's shoes are guarded all day and all night. B. The king's fields are guarded ...

Exercise 3 1. לָקוּחַ 2. שְׁלוּחוֹת 3. פְּתוּחִים 4. זָכוּר 5. שְׁמוּרָה 6. זְכוּרוֹת 7. פָּתוּחַ 8. כָּתוּב 9. שְׁמוּרָה 10. זְכוּרִים

Exercise 4 1. דָּוִד שָׁמַר 2. פְּתַחְנוּ 3. הוּא מָלַךְ 4. הָלַכְתָּ 5. הַנָּשִׁים שָׁמְעוּ 6. הַמֶּלֶךְ הַזָּקֵן שָׁפַט 7. הֵנָּה לָקְחוּ 8. הָלַכְתִּי

1. David guarded the house instead of Jacob. 2. We opened the gate in the morning before the people of the city. 3. He ruled over all the land. 4. You went to the city instead of your mother. 5. The women heard the holy man in Bethlehem. 6. The old king judged the evil man before the nation. 7. They took the bread instead of the fruit. 8. I went after the harvesters.

Exercise 5 1. אֲנִי אוֹכֵל עִם אִמִּי 2. אַתָּה כֹתֵב מִבֵּיתוֹ. 3. הִיא זוֹכֶרֶת אֶת הָאֲנָשִׁים בְּעִירָהּ. 4. הָאֹכֶל מֵעִירָה זָכוּר. 5. הָאֹכֶל הַטּוֹב מִבֵּיתֵנוּ שָׁמוּר. 6. רוּת לָקְחָה אֶת דּוֹדָתָהּ לָעִיר הַגְּדוֹלָה. 7. בְּעוֹ לָקַח אֶת בְּנוֹ לְעִירוֹ.

Exercise 6. "The Farmer in the Dell" (Harvester קוֹצֵר = farmer) The farmer in the field, the farmer in the field, Heigh Ho The Dario, the farmer in the field. The farmer takes a wife ... Heigh Ho ... the farmer takes a wife. The wife takes a son ... Heigh Ho ... the wife takes a son. The son takes a maiden ... Heigh Ho ... the son takes a maiden. The maiden takes bread ... Heigh Ho ... the maiden takes bread. The bread stands alone ... Heigh Ho ... the bread stands alone.

Exercise 7 1. כָּתַב 2. כּוֹתֵב 3. כָּתוּב 4. פָּתְחוּ 5. פּוֹתְחִים 6. פְּתוּחִים 7. קָצַרְתָּ 8. זָכַרְתָּ 9. זוֹכְרוֹת 10. אָכְלוּ 11. אֲכָלָה 12. אוֹכֵל 13. שָׁמַרְתִּי 14. שָׁמַרְנוּ 15. שְׁמַרְתֶּן 16. שָׁמוּר 17. שׁוֹלַחַת 18. לוֹקַחַת 19. פָּתַחַת 20. פְּתוּחָה 21. שׁוֹמַעַת 22. שָׁמְעָה 23. שָׁמְעוּ 24. שׁוֹמְעִים

1. he wrote 2. writing—m, sg 3. is written—m, sg 4. they opened 5. opening—m, pl 6. are opened—m, pl 7. you harvested 8. you remembered 9. remembering—f, pl 10. they ate 11. she ate 12. eating—m, sg 13. I guarded 14. we guarded 15. you guarded 16. guarding—f, sg 17. sending—f, sg 18. taking—f, sg 19. opening—f, sg 20. is opened—f, sg 21. hearing—f, sg 22. she heard 23. they heard 24. hearing—m, pl

Chapter 15

Exercise 1 1. A. זֶה מָקוֹם גָּדוֹל וְטוֹב. B. זֹאת אֶרֶץ גְּדוֹלָה וְטוֹבָה. C. זֶה חֶסֶד גָּדוֹל וְטוֹב. D. אֵלֶּה שָׂדוֹת גְּדוֹלִים

וְטוֹבִים. E. אֵלֶּה עָרִים גְּדוֹלוֹת וְטוֹבוֹת. 2. A. אֵין לִי אֹכֶל כִּי יֵשׁ רָעָב בָּעִיר הַהִיא. B. אֵין לָכֶן. C. לוֹ D. לָהֶן E. לָכֶם F. לָהּ G. לְךָ H. לָהֶם I. לָךְ 3. A. יַעֲקֹב שָׁמַע אֶת קוֹל הַמֶּלֶךְ הָרַע הַזֶּה. B. . . . הַשּׁוֹפְטִים הָרָעִים הָאֵלֶּה. C. . . . הַדּוֹדָה הָרָעָה הַזֹּאת. D. . . . הָאָבוֹת הָרָעִים הָאֵלֶּה. E. . . . הַנָּשִׁים הָרָעוֹת הָאֵלֶּה. 4. A. יֵשׁ לִי סְפָרִים אֲשֶׁר אֲנִי לוֹקֵחַ מִמִּשְׁפַּחְתִּי. B. . . . יֵשׁ לַבָּנִים . . . הֵם לוֹקְחִים מִמִּשְׁפַּחְתָּם. C. יֵשׁ לָהּ . . . הִיא לוֹקַחַת מִמִּשְׁפַּחְתָּהּ. D. יֵשׁ לָכֶם . . . אַתֶּם לוֹקְחִים מִמִּשְׁפַּחְתְּכֶם. E. יֵשׁ לָךְ . . . אַתְּ לֹקַחַת מִמִּשְׁפַּחְתֵּךְ. F. יֵשׁ לָהֶן . . . הֵן לוֹקְחוֹת מִמִּשְׁפַּחְתָּן. G. יֵשׁ לְךָ . . . אַתָּה לֹקֵחַ מִמִּשְׁפַּחְתְּךָ. H. יֵשׁ לָכֶן . . . אַתֶּן לוֹקְחוֹת מִמִּשְׁפַּחְתְּכֶן. I. יֵשׁ לָנוּ . . . אֲנַחְנוּ לוֹקְחִים מִמִּשְׁפַּחְתֵּנוּ. 5. A. זֹאת הַבַּת אֲשֶׁר פָּתְחָה אֶת הַשְּׁעָרִים הָהֵמָּה. B. אֵלֶּה הָאֲנָשִׁים אֲשֶׁר פָּתְחוּ . . . C. זֹאת הַמִּשְׁפָּחָה אֲשֶׁר פָּתְחָה . . . D. אֵלֶּה הָאֻמּוֹת אֲשֶׁר פָּתְחוּ . . . E. זֶה הַדּוֹד אֲשֶׁר פָּתַח . . . 6. A. אָמַרְתִּי דְּבָרִים טוֹבִים עַל אִמִּי. B. אֲמַרְתֶּם . . . אֲמַרְתֶּם. C. אֲמַרְתֶּם . . . הִיא אָמְרָה . . . אָמָּה . . . D. הֵנָּה אָמְרוּ . . . E. הוּא אָמַר . . . F. אָמֹר . . . G. אֲמַרְתֶּן . . . אָמַרְתֶּן. H. אָמַרְתְּ . . . אִמֵּךְ . . . I. הֵם אָמְרוּ . . . אִמָּם.

1. This is a great and good nation. A. This is a great and good place . . . 2. We don't have food because there is a famine in that city. A. I don't have food because there is a . . . 3. Jacob heard this evil woman's voice. A. Jacob heard this evil king's voice. B. . . . these evil judges' . . . 4. He has books that he takes from his family. A. I have books that I take from my family. B. The sons have . . . they take from their family. 5. These are the judges that opened those gates. A. This is the daughter that opened those gates. B. These are the men . . . 6. You said nice things about your mother.

Exercise 2 1. יֵשׁ לִי סְפָרִים בַּבַּיִת. 2. יֵשׁ בַּיִת גָּדוֹל לָאֲנָשִׁים הָהֵמָּה. 3. יֵשׁ לַנַּעַר מִמּוֹאָב עֵינַיִם רָעוֹת וְיָדַיִם גְּדוֹלוֹת. 4. כָּל בֹּקֶר וְכָל לַיְלָה יֵשׁ אֲנָשִׁים בַּדֶּרֶךְ. 5. הַיּוֹם אֵין לֶחֶם בָּעִיר. 6. בְּבֵית לֶחֶם יֵשׁ אִשָּׁה אֲשֶׁר יוֹשֶׁבֶת בְּבַיִת גָּדוֹל. 7. יֵשׁ לְדָוִד מִנְחָה מִמִּשְׁפַּחְתּוֹ בִּירוּשָׁלַיִם. 8. אֵין לִי בָּתִּים בְּבֵית לֶחֶם.

1. I have books in the house. 2. Those people have a large house. 3. The lad from Moab has evil eyes and big hands. 4. Every morning and every night there are people on the road. 5. Today there is no bread in the city. 6. In Bethlehem, there is a woman who is staying in a big house. 7. David has a gift from his family in Jerusalem. 8. I don't have houses in Bethlehem.

Exercise 3 1. הָיוּ לָנוּ נַעֲלַיִם גְּדוֹלוֹת מְאֹד. 2. לֹא הָיוּ קוֹצְרִים בַּשָּׂדֶה הַיּוֹם. 3. בַּמָּקוֹם הַהוּא לֹא הָיָה לְנָעֳמִי שָׂדֶה גָּדוֹל. 4. לִפְנֵי אַבְרָהָם הָיָה שַׁעַר פָּתוּחַ. 5. בָּאָרֶץ הַהִיא מֶלֶךְ טוֹב. 6. הָיָה לְךָ שֵׁם טוֹב בַּמָּקוֹם הַזֶּה.

1. We had a very big pair of shoes. 2. There were no harvesters in the field today. 3. Naomi did not have a big field in that place. 4. In front of Abraham was an opened gate. 5. There was a good king in that land. 6. You had a good name in this place.

Exercise 4 1. הָלַךְ 2. אָכְלוּ 3. כָּתְבוּ 4. זָכְרוּ 5. שָׁכַבְתִּי,

שָׁמַעְתִּי .6 אָמַר .7 מָלַךְ

1. Jacob's father went today after his wife. 2. Those harvesters ate bread with those women. 3. Those maidens wrote evil things instead of good things. 4. What did you still remember about this place? 5. When I laid down at night, I heard my mother's voice. 6. Who said a kind thing to that old woman? 7. One king reigned over the holy cities and also over Moab.

1. אֲבִי יַעֲקֹב הֹלֵךְ הַיּוֹם אַחֲרֵי אִשְׁתּוֹ. 2. הַקּוֹצְרִים הָהֵמָּה אֹכְלִים לֶחֶם עִם הַנָּשִׁים הָהֵן. 3. הַנְּעָרוֹת הָהֵנָּה כֹּתְבוֹת דְּבָרִים רָעִים תַּחַת דְּבָרִים טוֹבִים. 4. מַה אַתְּ עוֹד זוֹכֶרֶת עַל הַמָּקוֹם הַזֶּה? 5. כַּאֲשֶׁר אֲנִי שׁוֹכֵב בַּלַּיְלָה, אֲנִי שׁוֹמֵעַ אֶת קוֹל אִמִּי. 6. מִי אוֹמֵר דְּבַר חֶסֶד אֶל הָאִשָּׁה הַזְּקֵנָה הַהִיא? 7. מֶלֶךְ אֶחָד מוֹלֵךְ עַל הֶעָרִים הַקְּדוֹשׁוֹת וְגַם עַל מוֹאָב.

Exercise 5 1. הָאִישׁ הַזֶּה רַע. 2. הָאִישׁ הָרַע הַזֶּה מִמּוֹאָב. 3. הָאִישׁ הָרַע הַהוּא מִמּוֹאָב אָבִיו. 4. אֵלֶּה נָשִׁים טוֹבוֹת. 5. הַנָּשִׁים הַטּוֹבוֹת הָהֵנָּה אִמּוֹת הַנְּעָרִים. 6. יֵשׁ אֲנָשִׁים גְּדוֹלִים בְּעִירִי. 7. אֵין אֲנָשִׁים רָעִים בָּעִיר הַזֹּאת.

Exercise 6. This is the house that's in the field of Judah. This is the man that lives in the house that's in the field of Judah. This is the wife that lives with the man . . . These are the daughters that belong to the wife . . . These are the lads that take the daughters . . . This is the judge that guards the lads . . . This is the famine that kills the judge . . . This is the nation that weeps over the famine that kills the judge that guards the lads that take the daughters that belong to the wife that lives with the man that lives in the house that's in the field of Judah.

Exercise 7 1. אָכַלְתִּי 2. אֹכֵל 3. זָכַרְנוּ 4. זֹכְרִים 5. הָלַכְתָּ 6. הֹלֶכֶת 7. כְּתַבְתֶּן 8. כְּתוּבוֹת 9. כְּתוּבֹתָם 10. שְׁמַעְתָּ 11. שׁוֹמַעַת 12. שְׁלַחְתֶּם 13. שֹׁלְחִים 14. שְׁלוּחִים 15. שָׁפְטוּ 16. קְצַרְתֶּן 17. קְצָרוֹת 18. לָקְחָה 19. לוֹקַחַת 20. מָלַכְתָּ 21. מָלַךְ 22. שׁוֹכֵב 23. שׁוֹכְבִים 24. שָׁכְבוּ

1. I ate 2. are eating—m,sg 3. we remembered 4. remembering—m,pl 5. you walked 6. walking—f,sg 7. you wrote 8. writing—f,pl 9. are written—f,pl 10. you heard 11. hearing—f,sg 12. you sent 13. sending—m,pl 14. they judged 15. you judged 16. you harvested 17. harvesting—f,pl 18. she took 19. taking—f,sg 20. you reigned 21. he reigned 22. lying—m,sg 23. lying—m,pl 24. they lay down

Chapter 16

Exercise 2 1. A. תִּשְׁמֹרְנָה אֶת שַׁעֲרֵי הָעִיר. B. הֵם יִשְׁמְרוּ . . . C. הִיא תִּשְׁמֹר . . . D. אֶשְׁמֹר . . . E. תִּשְׁמְרוּ . . . F. הֵנָּה תִּשְׁמֹרְנָה . . . G. תִּשְׁמֹר . . . H. נִשְׁמֹר . . . I. תִּשְׁמְרִי . . . 2. A. נַעֲלֵי רוּת לֹא כְנַעֲלֵי אִמָּהּ. B. כְּסָאוֹת רוּת . . . כְּכִסְאוֹת . . . C. סֵפֶר . . . כְּסֵפֶר . . . D. קוֹל . . . כְּקוֹל . . . E. אֹכֶל . . . כָּאֹכֶל . . . 3. A. הֲעוֹד תִּזְכֹּרְנָה אֶת שֹׁפְטֵי הַמָּקוֹם הַהוּא? B. הֲעוֹד הַנָּשִׁים תִּזְכֹּרְנָה . . . C. הֲעוֹד הַנַּעֲרָה תִּזְכֹּר . . . D. הֲעוֹד תִּזְכְּרוּ . . . E. הֲעוֹד תִּזְכְּרִי . . . F. הֲעוֹד הָאַחִים יִזְכְּרוּ . . . G. הֲעוֹד נִזְכֹּר . . . H. הֲעוֹד אֶזְכֹּר . . . 4. A. אִם לֹא יִכְתֹּב בַּסֵּפֶר, לֹא יִזְכֹּר אֶת הַדְּבָרִים הָאֵלֶּה. B. אִם לֹא תִּכְתֹּבְנָה . . . לֹא תִּזְכֹּרְנָה . . . C. אִם לֹא

נִכְתַּב . . . לֹא נִזְכֹּר . . . D. אִם לֹא תִּכְתְּבוּ . . . לֹא

תִּזְכְּרוּ . . . E. אִם לֹא אֶכְתֹּב . . . לֹא אֶזְכֹּר . . . F. אִם

לֹא תִּכְתְּבִי . . . לֹא תִּזְכְּרִי . . . G. אִם לֹא יִכְתְּבוּ . . . לֹא

יִזְכְּרוּ . . . 5. A. אֵין לְאַבְרָהָם שָׂדוֹת בֵּין הֶהָרִים הָהֵם

וּבֵין הַמָּקוֹם הַהוּא. B. . . . . וּבֵין הַשָּׂדֶה הַהוּא. C. . . . וּבֵין

הַדְּרָכִים הָהֵם (הָהֵנָּה) D. . . . וּבֵין הַבַּיִת הַהוּא.

6. A. הִנֵּה בְּנוֹת אַבְרָהָם הַיּוֹשְׁבוֹת בִּירוּשָׁלַיִם תִּשְׁלַחְנָה

מִנְחָה אֶל מַלְכָּן. B. הִנֵּה הַמִּשְׁפָּחָה הַיּוֹשֶׁבֶת בִּירוּשָׁלַיִם

תִּשְׁלַח מִנְחָה אֶל מַלְכָּהּ. C. הִנֵּה הָאָבוֹת הַיּוֹשְׁבִים

בִּירוּשָׁלַיִם יִשְׁלְחוּ מִנְחָה אֶל מַלְכָּם. D. הִנֵּה הַשּׁוֹמֵר

הַיּוֹשֵׁב בִּירוּשָׁלַיִם יִשְׁלַח מִנְחָה אֶל מַלְכּוֹ. E. הִנֵּה בְּנֵי

נָעֳמִי הַיּוֹשְׁבִים בִּירוּשָׁלַיִם יִשְׁלְחוּ מִנְחָה אֶל מַלְכָּם.

1. He will guard the gates of the city. A. You will guard the gates of the city. B. They will guard . . . . . . 2. The eyes of Ruth are not like the eyes of her mother. A. The shoes of Ruth are not like the shoes of her mother. 3. Will you still remember the judges of that place? A. Will you still remember . . . . B. Will the women still remember . . . . . . 4. If you do not write in the book, you will not remember these things. A. If he does not write in the book, he will not remember. . 5. Abraham does not have fields between those mountains and that city. A. Abraham does not have fields between those mountains and that place.6. Behold! That man who dwells in Jerusalem will send a gift to his king. A. Behold! The daughters of Abraham, who dwell in Jerusalem, will send a gift to their king. B. Behold! The family who dwells in Jerusalem will . . .

Exercise 3 1. תִּקְצֹר; קְצַרְתָּ, קוֹצֵר. 2. תִּשְׁכַּב, שָׁכַב, שֹׁכְבָה. 3. יִשְׁלְחוּ, שָׁלְחוּ, שׁוֹלְחִים. 4. תִּשְׁמַעְנָה, שָׁמְעוּ, שׁוֹמְעוֹת. 5. יִכְתֹּב; כָּתַב, כּוֹתֵב. 6. תִּזְכֹּרְנָה; זְכַרְתֶּן, זוֹכְרוֹת.

1. You will harvest in the morning in the field. 2. At night the wife of Abraham will lie down on her bed in Ruth's house. 3. After the famine the brothers of Sarah will send food to their father in Judah. 4. The women from Moab will hear these words from the king. 5. Behold, the head of the house will write to those young women. 6. You will remember the name of the woman who is sitting in front of those men.

Exercise 4 1. תִּשְׁמַע 2. הִתְקְצֹר 3. נִזְכֹּר 4. תִּשְׁלַחְנָה 5. יִמְלֹךְ, נִשְׁמַע.

Exercise 5 1. הַנַּעֲרָה תִּזְכֹּר אֶת הָאִישׁ הָרָע. 2. אֲחִי הַנַּעֲרָה יִשְׁמַע אֶת קוֹל הָאִישׁ הָרָע. 3. אֲבִי הַנַּעֲרָה וְדוֹדָהּ יִשְׁמְרוּ אֶת הָאֲנָשִׁים הָרָעִים. 4. הָיָה אִישׁ רַע בָּאָרֶץ הַהִיא. 5. אֵין אֲנָשִׁים רָעִים בְּבֵיתֵנוּ. 6. הֲתִזְכְּרִי אֶת אַנְשֵׁי עִירֵנוּ הַטּוֹבִים?

Exercise 6. 1. If I send Ruth to the top of the mountain, will you send Sarah? 2. If you judge between the brothers, will you also judge between this lad and his father? 3. If we harvest in the field, we will not hear the words of the women in the tent. 4. Will they obey the king, if he is a bad king? 5. If you lie in your bed all day, you will not write your book.
Exercise 7. The lad said: When I will be a man, I will reign over all my land. I will reign from the mountains to the sea in peace. I will send good judges to all the cities, and they will judge the evil men. On that day, they will send those men from the land. I will remember my family: my father and my mother and my brother and my uncle and my aunt. I will send them bread. All the women will obey me. My people will send me gifts. Great men will guard my house. I will lie in a bed better than all the beds in my land. When I will be a man, I will be the king because today I am a lad and my father is the king.

Exercise 8 1. שָׁכַב 2. יִשְׁכַּב 3. שׁוֹכֵב 4. פָּתְחָה 5. תִּשְׁמֹר

6. שׁוֹמֶרֶת 7. שָׁמַעְתָּ 8. תִּשְׁמְעִי 9. שׁוֹמַעַת 10. נִזְכֹּר

11. תִּזְכְּרוּ 12. יִזְכֹּר 13. תִּזְכֹּרְנָה 14. זוֹכְרִים 15. זָכְרוּ

16. תִּשְׁפֹּט 17. תִּשְׁפֹּט 18. שָׁפְטָה 19. שָׁפַטְתִּי 20. כָּתַבְנוּ

21. נִכְתַּב 22. כְּתוּבִים 23. תִּכְתְּבְנָה 24. תִּכְתְּבֶנָה

1. he lay down. 2. he will lie down 3. lying—m, sg 4. she opened 5. she will guard 6. guarding—f, sg 7. you heard 8. you will hear 9. hearing—f, sg 10. we will remember 11. you will remember 12. he will remember 13. they will remember 14. remembering—m, pl 15. they remembered 16. you will judge 17. she will judge 18. she judged 19. you will judge 20. we wrote 21. we will write 22. written—m, pl 23. you will write 24. they will write.

Chapter 17

Exercise 2 1. A. קְחִי אֶת דָּוִד לְמֶלֶךְ תַּחַת הָאִישׁ הָרָע הַזֶּה.
B. קְחֶנָה אֶת דָּוִד . . . C. קְחוּ אֶת דָּוִד . . . 2. A. אַל
תִּבְטַח בְּדִבְרֵי הַשּׁוֹפְטִים. B. אַל תִּבְטְחִי . . . C. אַל
תִּבְטַחְנָה . . . 3. A. נִלְבְּשָׁה בְּגָדִים וְנַעֲלַיִם מִבֵּית
מִשְׁפַּחְתֵּנוּ. B. נִבְחֲרָה . . . C. נִשְׁלְחָה
. . . D. נִזְכְּרָה
. . . 4. A. לְכִי וּשְׁבִי בְּבֵיתֵךְ וְשִׁמְעִי בְּקוֹל אִמֵּךְ.
B. לְכוּ וּשְׁבוּ בְּבֵיתְכֶם וְשִׁמְעוּ בְּקוֹל אִמְּכֶם. C. לֵכְנָה
וְשֵׁבְנָה בְּבֵיתְכֶן וּשְׁמַעְנָה בְּקוֹל אִמְּכֶן. 5. A. הַנַּעֲרָה תִּקַּח
אֶת מִנְחָתָהּ אֶל הָאִישׁ הֶחָכָם הַיּוֹשֵׁב בַּשָּׂדֶה. B. רָאשֵׁי הָעָם
יִקְחוּ אֶת מִנְחָתָם. C. . . . תִּקַּח אֶת מִנְחָתְךָ. D. אֶקַּח
אֶת מִנְחָתִי . . . E. נְשֵׁי יְרוּשָׁלַיִם תִּקַּחְנָה אֶת מִנְחָתָן
F. נִקַּח אֶת מִנְחָתֵנוּ. G. . . . תִּקַּחְנָה אֶת מִנְחַתְכֶן . . .
H. תִּקְחוּ אֶת מִנְחַתְכֶם . . . I. . . . תִּקְחִי אֶת מִנְחָתֵךְ . . .

1. Take David as king instead of this evil man. A. Take David as king instead of this evil man. B. Take David . . . C. Take David . . . 2. Do not trust the words of the judges. A. Do not trust the words of the judges. B. Do not trust . . . C. Do not trust . . . 3. Let us steal clothes and shoes from the house of our family. A Let us put on clothes and shoes from the house of our family. B. Let us . . . 4. Go and sit in your house and obey your mother. A. Go and sit in your house and obey your mother. B. Go and sit in your house . . . 5. Abraham will take his gift to the wise man sitting in the field. A. The maiden will take her gift to the wise man sitting in the field. B.The heads of the people will take their gift . . . C. You will take your gift . . . D. I . . .

Exercise 3 1. לְבַשׁ; אַל תִּלְבַּשׁ 2. אַל תֵּלַכְנָה.
3. גְּנֹבוּ; אַל תִּגְנְבוּ 4. קְחִי; אַל תִּקְחִי 5. שְׁכַחְנָה; אַל
תִּשְׁכַּחְנָה 6. בְּטַח; אַל תִּבְטַח 7. שִׁמְעוּ; אַל תִּשְׁמְעוּ
8. שְׁפֹט; אַל תִּשְׁפֹּט 9. בְּחַר; אַל תִּבְחַר

1. Put on your clothes! 2. Go from your city to that city! 3. Steal the clothes, because the old one is guarding the house! 4. Take the fruit of the land! 5. Forget the words that I said! 6. Trust in the kindness of your brother! 7. Obey him! 8. Judge all the people of the land! 9. Choose that maiden for a wife!

Exercise 4 1. לְכוּ 2. שְׁלַח 3. יִשְׁכַּב 4. תִּקַּחְנָה 5. נִקְצְרָה
6. אֶכְתְּבָה 7. לְכִי 8. דְּעוּ

1. Go to the top of the mountain! 2. Send fruit from the people of the city to the head of the city! 3. May the lad lie down at night in his family's house! 4.Let the wise women take fruit for themselves! 5. Let us harvest in the morning in the big fields! 6. Let me write a book like the book of my beloved! 7. Go on the road between the mountains until the sea! 8. Know the names of the fruit of the land of Israel!
Exercise 5. After King David, Solomon his son reigned over the land of Israel. He was very wise, and he was also a good judge. In those days the people of Israel went to Jerusalem to see Solomon the king.

Among all the people that went to Jerusalem there were two women. The name of the first was Sarah, and the name of the second was Orpah. There was one lad between Sarah and Orpah when they came before the king. Sarah said to Solomon: "This lad is not my son, he is the son of this woman." Sarah said to Orpah: "Take your son." Orpah said: "He is not my son, I don't have sons! Don't you know that he is your son? Don't forget your son." Sarah said: "I remember my family and this lad is not from my family." The two women said to Solomon: "Judge between us; choose the mother of the lad!" King Solomon said to the women: "Trust in the words of your king. Sit down and obey me. There is no mother in my land that does not remember her son. If you do not remember this lad, he is not your son. Go on your way. The lad will live in my house." The king said to the lad: "Forget these evil women! Stay in my house with my family and put on the clothes of a king's son." The two women said together: "He's my son, he's my son!" The king said to the women: "I have judged! The lad will live in my house, go to your homes!"

Exercise 6 ‎1. תִּשְׁפֹּט ‎2. שְׁפֹט ‎3. תִּשְׁלַחְנָה ‎4. שְׁלַחְנָה

‎5. תִּפְתְּחִי ‎6. פְּתַחִי ‎7. תִּגְנְבוּ ‎8. גִּנְבוּ ‎9. יֵלְכוּ ‎10. לְכוּ

‎11. יֵלֵךְ ‎12. יֵשֵׁב ‎13. יִקַּח ‎14. יֵדַע ‎15. לְכִי ‎16. שְׁבִי ‎17. קַח

‎18. דַּע ‎19. שְׁמַעְנָה ‎20. שְׁמַע ‎21. שִׁמְעִי ‎22. שִׁמְעוּ

‎23. לֵכְנָה ‎24. קַחְנָה

1. you will judge 2. judge! 3. you will send 4. send! 5. you will open 6. open! 7. you will steal 8. steal! 9. they will go 10. go!11.he will go 12. he will sit 13. he will take 14. he will know 15. go! 16. sit! 17. take! 18. know! 19. hear! 20. hear! 21. hear! 22. hear! 3. go! 4. take!

Chapter 18

Exercise 1 ‎1. זְכֹר, זָכוֹר ‎2. כְּתֹב, כָּתוֹב ‎3. שְׁפֹט, שָׁפוֹט

‎4. בְּטַח, בָּטוֹחַ ‎5. קְחַת, לָקוֹחַ ‎6. שְׁלַח, שָׁלוֹחַ ‎7. לֶכֶת, הָלוֹךְ ‎8. מְלֹךְ, מָלוֹךְ ‎9. דַּעַת, יָדוֹעַ.

Exercise 2 ‎1. A. הָאַחִים יָכְלוּ לִשְׁמֹר בְּתוֹךְ הַשָּׂדֶה.

B. הָאַחִים יָכְלוּ לִשְׁכַּב ... C. ... לָשֶׁבֶת ...

D. ... לָלֶכֶת. E. ... לִהְיוֹת ‎2. A. שָׁכוֹחַ תִּשְׁכַּח

אֶת בֵּית אָבִיךָ. B. יָדוֹעַ תֵּדַע אֶת בֵּית אָבִיךָ. C. בָּחוֹר

תִּבְחַר. D. ... ‎3. A. שָׁמוֹר תִּשְׁמֹר. B. שָׁמוֹר שְׁמַרְתָּ אֶת

הַדְּבָרִים הָאֵלֶּה. B. שָׁמוֹר שְׁמַרְנוּ ... C. הֵנָּה שָׁמוֹר

שָׁמְרוּ. D. הִיא שָׁמוֹר שָׁמְרָה. E. הֵם שָׁמוֹר

שָׁמְרוּ. ‎4. A. ... כִּלְבֹשׁ אַבְרָהָם אֶת בִּגְדּוֹ, יָשַׁב עַל כִּסְאוֹ.

B. כִּלְבֹשׁ שָׂרָה אֶת בִּגְדָהּ, יָשְׁבָה עַל כִּסְאָהּ. C. כִּלְבֹשׁ

הַזְּקֵנָה אֶת בִּגְדָהּ, יָשְׁבָה עַל כִּסְאָהּ. D. כִּלְבֹשׁ בִּתִּי אֶת

בִּגְדָהּ, יָשְׁבָה עַל כִּסְאָהּ. E. כִּלְבֹשׁ הָעָם אֶת בִּגְדָהּ, יָשְׁבָה

עַל כִּסְאָהּ. ‎5. A. בְּפָתְחָם אֶת הַשַּׁעַר, שָׁמְעוּ אֶת קוֹל

אַנְשֵׁי עִירָם. B. בְּפָתְחֲךָ אֶת הַשַּׁעַר, שָׁמַעְתָּ אֶת קוֹל אַנְשֵׁי

עִירְךָ. C. בְּפָתְחָהּ אֶת הַשַּׁעַר, שָׁמְעָה נַעֲמִי אֶת קוֹל אַנְשֵׁי

עִירָהּ. D. בְּפָתְחֵנוּ אֶת הַשַּׁעַר, שָׁמַעְנוּ אֶת קוֹל אַנְשֵׁי עִירֵנוּ.

E. בְּפָתְחָן אֶת הַשַּׁעַר שָׁמְעוּ הַנְּעָרוֹת אֶת קוֹל אַנְשֵׁי

עִירָן. F. בְּפָתְחֲכֶם אֶת הַשַּׁעַר, שְׁמַעְתֶּם אֶת קוֹל אַנְשֵׁי

עִירְכֶם. G. בְּפָתְחֵךְ אֶת הַשַּׁעַר, שָׁמַעַתְּ אֶת קוֹל אַנְשֵׁי

עִירֵךְ. H. בְּפָתְחֲכֶן אֶת הַשַּׁעַר, שְׁמַעְתֶּן אֶת קוֹל אַנְשֵׁי

עִירְכֶן. I. בְּפָתְחִי אֶת הַשַּׁעַר, שָׁמַעְתִּי אֶת קוֹל אַנְשֵׁי עִירִי.

‎6. A. אֲנִי אוּכַל לִשְׁכַּב תַּחַת הָעֵץ הַקָּטֹן. B. הֵמָּה יוּכְלוּ

לִשְׁכַּב. C. ... תּוּכַלְנָה. D. רוּת תּוּכַל ... E. אַתָּה

‎F. וְדָוִד תּוּכְלוּ ... G. נוּכַל ... תּוּכַל ... H. תּוּכְלִי ...

‎I. הֵן תּוּכַלְנָה ...

1. The brothers were able to harvest in the midst of the field. A. The brothers were able to guard . . . B. to lie down C. to sit D. to walk E. to be 2. You will surely remember the house of your father. A. You will surely forget . . . B. You will . . . know . . . 3. He surely kept these words. A. You surely kept these words. B. We . . . C. They D. She E. They 4.When the maiden put on her garment, she sat in her chair. A. When Abraham put on his garment, he sat in his chair. B. When Sarah put on her garment . . . 5. When he opened the gate, the guard heard the voice of the men of his city. A. When they opened the gate, they heard the voice of the men of their city. 6. The lad will be able to lie down under the little tree. A. I will be able B. They will be able.

Exercise 3 ‎1. הַבָּנִים יָכְלוּ לָלֶכֶת ‎2. יְכָלְתֶּם לִהְיוֹת ‎3. נוּכַל

לִזְכֹּר ‎4. יָכֹלְתָּ לִשְׁכַּב ‎5. הַתּוּכַל לָשֶׁבֶת.

1. The sons were able to walk from the sea until the top of the mountain. 2. You were able to be among the harvesters in that place. 3. We will be able to remember the face of your son. 4. You were able to lie down in the night in the field under the heavens. 5. Will you be able to settle among these people?

Exercise 4 ‎1. לִשְׁכֹּחַ ‎2. לִבְטֹחַ ‎3. לִקְצֹר ‎4. מְלֹךְ ‎5. לִשְׁמֹר

‎6. גְּנֹב ‎7. לָשֶׁבֶת ‎8. פָּתוֹחַ

1. He was not able to forget the face of the young woman. 2. We did not know if we were able to trust this judge. 3. He went in the morning to harvest in the field. 4. You will surely reign over all that is under the heavens. 5. The women were not able to guard their house and the lads stole everything. 6. As the men stole the food, they did not take the fruit. 7. When the sun is in the midst of the sky, our daughter will be able to sit under the tree. 8. You will surely open the gate of the city today—don't forget!
Exercise 5. "The Little Camel That Could" In the city that was on the top of the mountain there was a famine and the people there had no bread. They sent a man from the city on the mountain to a city that was by the sea. When they sent the man they said to him: "Take your camel and go to that city, because we have heard that there is food there. Do not forget that we have trusted in you to bring us bread." The man went with his camel to the city by the sea and took food from there. When he took the food he still remembered the famine in his city, and he did not lie down to rest. He went with his camel on the road to the mountains. And the sun in the heavens was very hot. After he had walked all morning, the camel lay down in the road and couldn't walk any more. The man said to his camel: "Do not lie down in the road! Obey me! The people of the mountain trust you!" The camel said to him: "I can't go." The camel continued to lay down. The man said to himself: "If I do not take food to the people on the mountain, they will die." And behold, a very big camel came down the road. The man said to the big camel: "There is a famine in the city in the mountains, and the people of the city will die if I am not able to bring this food to them. My camel has really laid down in the road, and he is not able to walk. Can you take the food and go to the top of the mountain?" The very great camel opened his mouth and said: "What are you saying to me? I am a very great camel! I go every day and every night to very great cities. I will not go to small towns that are in the mountains!" And he went on his way. And behold, the camel of the king came down the road. The man said to the king's camel: "Listen, camel! There is a famine in the city in the mountains and the people of the city will die if I am not able to bring them this food. My camel has really laid down in the road and is not able to walk. Can you take the food and go to the top of the mountain?" The king's camel opened his mouth and said: "What are you saying to me? I am the camel of the king! I go every day and every night only to take the king." And he went on his way. And behold, a very small camel came down the road. The man said to himself: "My camel is big and he was not able to go on this road. This camel is very small. He will not be able to go to the top of the mountain." But the man opened his mouth and said to the little camel: "Listen, little camel! There is a famine in the city in the mountains. The people of the city will die if you do not go to the top of the mountain to bring them food. Can you go to the top of the mountain with the food?" The little camel said: "I surely can!" The little camel took the food from the camel that was lying down, and he and the man went on the road to the mountains. The sun in the heavens was very hot, and they walked and walked. The little camel said to himself: "I surely can! I surely can!" And the sun in the heavens was very hot, and they still walked. The little camel said in his heart: "I surely can!" But he was very weary. At night they came to the city in the mountains. All the people of the city

294

ate from the food that was upon the little camel. The little camel said to himself: "The big camel couldn't, the very big camel couldn't, even the camel of the king couldn't, but I really could!"

Chapter 19

Exercise 1. 1. his lad 2. your wife 3. their gifts 4. our books 5. your house 6. your dwelling place 7. her stones 8. our land 9. my beasts 10. their fathers 11. your nation 12. her bread 13. your sons 14. his eyes 15. your hands 16. my tents 17. their gate 18. our light 19. your mother 20. my father.

Exercise 2a 1. אַתְּ 2. הֵם 3. הִיא 4. אַתֶּן 5. אֲנִי 6. הֵנָּה

7. הוּא 8. אַתֶּם 9. אַתָּה

Exercise 2b 1. אֹתָךְ 2. אֶתְכֶם 3. אֹתוֹ 4. אֶתֶן 5. אֹתִי

6. אֶתְכֶן 7. אֹתָם 8. אֹתָם 9. אֹתָךְ 10. אֹתָנוּ

Exercise 3 1. A. הוּא רַק שָׁכַח אֶת נְעָלָיו. B. רַק שְׁכַחְתֶּם אֶת נַעֲלֵיכֶם. C. רַק שָׁכַחְתִּי אֶת נְעָלַי. D. רַק שְׁכַחְנוּ אֶת נַעֲלֵינוּ. E. הִיא רַק שָׁכְחָה אֶת נְעָלֶיהָ. F. הֵם רַק שָׁכְחוּ אֶת נַעֲלֵיהֶם. G. רַק שְׁכַחְתֶּן אֶת נַעֲלֵיכֶן. H. הֵנָּה רַק שָׁכְחוּ אֶת נַעֲלֵיהֶן. I. רַק שָׁכַחְתָּ אֶת נְעָלֶיךָ. 2. A. תֵּלְכִי לַמִּדְבָּר לָשֶׁבֶת שָׁם עִם בָּנַיִךְ. B. יֵלְכוּ לַמִּדְבָּר לָשֶׁבֶת שָׁם עִם בְּנֵיהֶם. C. אֵלֵךְ לַמִּדְבָּר לָשֶׁבֶת שָׁם עִם בָּנַי. D. יֵלֵךְ לַמִּדְבָּר לָשֶׁבֶת שָׁם עִם בָּנָיו. E. הָלַכְנוּ לַמִּדְבָּר לָשֶׁבֶת שָׁם עִם בָּנֵינוּ.

F. תֵּלַכְנָה לַמִּדְבָּר לָשֶׁבֶת שָׁם עִם בְּנֵיכֶן-הֶן.

G. הָלַכְתִּי לַמִּדְבָּר לָשֶׁבֶת שָׁם עִם בָּנַי.

3. A. אַבְרָהָם לָקַח רַק אֶת בְּגָדָיו לִשְׁלֹחַ אֹתָם אֶל מִשְׁפַּחְתּוֹ. B. הֵנָּה לָקְחוּ רַק אֶת בִּגְדֵיהֶן לִשְׁלֹחַ אֹתָם אֶל מִשְׁפְּחוֹתֵיהֶן. C. לָקַחְתִּי רַק אֶת בְּגָדַי לִשְׁלֹחַ אֹתָם אֶל מִשְׁפַּחְתִּי. D. לְקַחְתֶּם רַק אֶת בִּגְדֵיכֶם לִשְׁלֹחַ אֹתָם אֶל מִשְׁפְּחוֹתֵיכֶם. E. רוּת לָקְחָה רַק אֶת בְּגָדֶיהָ לִשְׁלֹחַ אֹתָם אֶל מִשְׁפַּחְתָּהּ. F. הַזְּקֵנִים לָקְחוּ רַק אֶת בִּגְדֵיהֶם לִשְׁלֹחַ אֹתָם אֶל מִשְׁפְּחוֹתֵיהֶם. G. לָקַחְנוּ רַק אֶת בְּגָדֵינוּ לִשְׁלֹחַ אֹתָם אֶל מִשְׁפְּחוֹתֵינוּ. H. לָקַחְתָּ רַק אֶת בְּגָדֶיךָ לִשְׁלֹחַ אֹתָם אֶל מִשְׁפַּחְתֶּךָ. I. לְקַחְתֶּן רַק אֶת בִּגְדֵיכֶן לִשְׁלֹחַ אֹתָם אֶל מִשְׁפְּחוֹתֵיכֶן. 4. A. בָּנַי זָכְרוּ אֹתָךְ וְאַתְּ לֹא זָכַרְתְּ אֹתָם. B. זָכַרְנוּ אֹתָךְ וְאַתָּה לֹא זָכַרְתָּ אֹתָנוּ. C. אִמְּךָ זָכְרָה אֹתָךְ וְאַתָּה לֹא זָכַרְתָּ אֹתָהּ. D. הוּא זָכַר אֹתָךְ וְאַתָּה לֹא זָכַרְתָּ אֹתוֹ. E. נְשֵׁי הָעִיר זָכְרוּ אֹתָךְ וְאַתָּה לֹא זָכַרְתָּ אֹתָן. 5. A. כָּל דְּבָרֶיךָ הָיוּ בְּבָתֵּי אֲבָנִים וְאַתָּה לָקַחְתָּ אֹתָם לְבָתֵּי עֵץ. B. כָּל דִּבְרֵיהֶם . . . וְלָקְחוּ . . . C. כָּל דְּבָרָיו . . . וְלָקַח . . . D. כָּל דִּבְרֵיכֶם . . . וּלְקַחְתֶּם . . . E. כָּל דְּבָרַיִךְ . . . וְלָקַחְתְּ . . . 6. A. הֵם יִהְיוּ בְּמִשְׁכָּנָם הַיּוֹם וְיִשְׁמְרוּ אֶת בְּנֵיהֶם. B. תִּהְיִי בְּמִשְׁכָּנֵךְ הַיּוֹם וְתִשְׁמְרִי אֶת בָּנַיִךְ. C. הָיִינוּ בְּמִשְׁכָּנֵנוּ הַיּוֹם וְשָׁמַרְנוּ אֶת בָּנֵינוּ. D. תִּהְיֶינָה בְּמִשְׁכָּנְכֶן הַיּוֹם וְתִשְׁמֹרְנָה אֶת בְּנֵיכֶן. E. הִיא הָיְתָה בְּמִשְׁכָּנָהּ הַיּוֹם וְשָׁמְרָה אֶת בָּנֶיהָ. F. תִּהְיוּ

בְּמִשְׁכַּנְכֶם הַיּוֹם וְתִשְׁמְרוּ אֶת בְּנֵיכֶם. G. תִּהְיֶינָה בְּמִשְׁכָּנָן הַיּוֹם וְתִשְׁמֹרְנָה אֶת בְּנֵיהֶן. H. תִּהְיֶה בְּמִשְׁכָּנְךָ הַיּוֹם וְתִשְׁמֹר אֶת בָּנֶיךָ. I. הוּא יִהְיֶה בְּמִשְׁכָּנוֹ הַיּוֹם וְיִשְׁמֹר אֶת בָּנָיו.

1. You only forgot your shoes. A. He only forgot his shoes. B. You only forgot your shoes. C. I only . . . 2. You will go to the wilderness to settle there with your sons. A. You will go to the wilderness to settle there with your sons. B. They will go to the wilderness to settle there with their . . . 3. The judges took only their clothes to send them to their families. A. Abraham took only his clothes to send them to his family. 4. I remembered you and you did not remember me. A. My sons remembered you and you did not remember them. B. We remembered you and you did not remember us. 5. All things were in houses of stone and they took them to houses of wood. A. All your things were in houses of stone and you took them to houses of wood. B. All their things . . . 6. I will be in my dwelling place today and I will guard my sons. A. They will be in their dwelling place today and they will guard their sons. B. You will be in your

Exercise 4 1. אֹתוֹ 2. אֹתָם 3. אֹתָם 4. אַתָּה 5. אֹתָנוּ

6. אֶתְכֶן 7. אֹתוֹ 8. אֹתוֹ

1. They ate it. 2. Don't forget that I remember them. 3. You will wear them. 4. In the darkness he lay in the wilderness and remembered her. 5. He regularly will guard us. 6. In the midst of that city, there will be wise ones and they will judge you. 7. He wrote it by the light of the sun. 8. The nations chose it and they settled there.

Exercise 5 1A. הוּא שָׁלַח אֶת הָאֲנָשִׁים אֶל בֵּיתוֹ. 1B. הוּא שָׁלַח אֹתָם אֶל בֵּיתוֹ. 1C. הוּא שָׁלַח אֹתָם אֶל בָּתֵּיהֶם. 2A. הַנְּעָרִים לָקְחוּ אֶת מִנְחָתָם וְשָׁלַח אֹתָהּ אֶל אִמָּם. 2B. הַנְּעָרִים לָקְחוּ אֶת מִנְחוֹתֵיהֶם וְשָׁלְחוּ אֹתָן אֶל אִמָּם. 2C. הַנְּעָרִים לָקְחוּ אֶת מִנְחוֹתֵיהֶם וְשָׁלְחוּ אֹתָן אֶל אִמּוֹתֵיהֶם. 3A. הָאִשָּׁה תֵּשֵׁב בִּמְקוֹמָהּ וְתִשְׁמַע אֶת דְּבַר בְּנָהּ. 3B. הָאִשָּׁה תֵּשֵׁב בִּמְקוֹמָהּ וְתִשְׁמַע אֶת דִּבְרֵי בָּנֶיהָ. 3C. הָאִשָּׁה תֵּשֵׁב בִּמְקוֹמָהּ וְתִשְׁמַע אֹתָם. 4A. בַּיּוֹם אוֹר וּבַלַּיְלָה יִהְיֶה חֹשֶׁךְ. 4B. הַגּוֹי הַזֶּה יֵלֵךְ רַק בָּאוֹר וְלֹא יֵלֵךְ בַּחֹשֶׁךְ. 4C. הַגּוֹי הַזֶּה הָלַךְ מֵהַמִּדְבָּר עַד הַיָּם.

Exercise 6. "Little Red Riding Hood" There was a little girl, and her name was Little Red Riding Hood, because she regularly wore a red-riding hood. She living in the midst of the city with her mother and her brothers in a small stone house. Her mother said to her: "Go to the tent of your grandmother in the wilderness, to take to her bread and fruit. Walk only on the road, and not in the fields, and don't trust strangers." Little Red Riding Hood said: "I will obey you," and she went on her way. And behold, an evil beast was in the wilderness. As Little Red Riding Hood walked on the road in the wilderness, the evil beast saw her, and it said to itself: "Who is this little girl? And what are the things that are in her hands?" The beast went up to the girl and said to her: "What are the things that are in your hands? And where are you going?" Little Red Riding Hood forgot all that her mother had told her. She said: "I am going to my grandmother's tent to take bread and fruit to her." The evil beast said to itself: "I will go there to take everything: the grandmother, the food, and Little Red Riding Hood." The beast went on another road to the grandmother's tent. Little Red Riding Hood went on her way, and she came to the tent of her grandmother. She said: "My grandmother! Behold, good food!" She heard a voice from inside the tent. "Little Red Riding Hood! Come in and I will take it from your hands." Little Red Riding Hood did not remember this voice, and said: "Are you my grand-mother?" And behold, she heard a voice from the tent: "Come into the tent, and you will know that I am your grandmother." Little Red Riding Hood went into the middle of the tent. When she went inside the tent, she saw the beast in the bed of her grandmother. Little Red Riding Hood did not know that the beast had eaten her grandmother, and put on her clothes. Little Red Riding Hood said: "How big your eyes are!" The beast said: "With my big eyes I can see you." Little Red Riding Hood said: "How big your hands are!" The beast said: "With my big hands I can take the bread and the fruit that are in your hands." Little Red Riding Hood said: "How big your mouth is!" The beast said: "With my big mouth I can eat the food, and you too! I

295

always eat girls in the morning!'' When Little Red Riding Hood heard these words, she saw that the beast was not her grandmother. The beast got up from the bed and took her in its hands and ate her. When the beast had eaten Little Red Riding Hood, it knew that the thing it had done was not good. The beast said to itself: ''This is not good! My eyes are bigger than my belly! I am very sick. It is not good to eat both a grandmother and a girl in one day.'' And behold, Little Red Riding Hood and her grandmother came out of the beast's mouth. The beast lay down on the ground, and Little Red Riding Hood and her grandmother ran to the city.

Chapter 20

Exercise 1 .1 וַנִּקְצֹר 2. וְגָנַבְתִּי 3. וַתִּלְבַּשׁ 4. וְאָכַל 5. וַיִּזְכְּרוּ
6. וָאֶשְׁמַע 7. וְהָלְכָה 8. וַתִּבְחַרְנָה 9. וְאֶשְׁפֹּט 10. וַיְהִי
11. וְשָׁכַחְתִּי 12. וַאֲמַרְתֶּם 13. וּשְׁמַרְתֶּם 14. וַנִּבְטַח
15. וְיָדְעוּ 16. וִישַׁבְתֶּם 17. וַתִּכְתֹּב 18. וָאֶקַּח 19. וּמָלַךְ
20. וּפָתַחְתָּ 21. וַתִּשְׁכְּבְנָה 22. וָאֶשְׁלַח 23. וְזָכַרְנוּ
24. וַתִּקְצֹרְנָה

1. and we harvested 2. and I will steal 3. and she wore 4. and he will eat 5. and they remembered 6. and I heard 7. and she will go 8. and they chose 9. and I judged 10. And it was 11. and I will forget 12. and you will say 13. and you guarded 14. and we trusted 15. and they will know 16. and you will settle 17. and you wrote 18. and I took 19. and he will rule 20. and you will open 21. and you lay down 22. and I sent 23. and we will remember 24. and they harvested

Exercise 2 .1 A. הֵם שָׁמְעוּ אֶת דִּבְרֵי הַבְּרִית וַיִּזְכְּרוּ אֹתָם וַיִּשְׁמְרוּ אֹתָם. B. שָׁמַעְתִּי אֶת דִּבְרֵי הַבְּרִית וָאֶזְכֹּר וָאֶשְׁמֹר אֹתָם. C. הִנֵּה שָׁמְעוּ . . . וַתִּזְכֹּרְנָה אֹתָם וַתִּשְׁמֹרְנָה אֹתָם. D. שָׁמַעַתְּ . . . וַתִּזְכֹּר אֹתָם וַתִּשְׁמֹר אֹתָם. E. שָׁמַעְנוּ . . . וַנִּזְכֹּר אֹתָם וַנִּשְׁמֹר אֹתָם. F. שְׁמַעְתֶּן . . . וַתִּזְכֹּרְנָה אֹתָם וַתִּשְׁמֹרְנָה אֹתָם. G. שָׁמַעְתָּ . . . וַתִּזְכֹּר אֹתָם וַתִּשְׁמֹר אֹתָם. H. הוּא שָׁמַע . . . וַיִּזְכֹּר אֹתָם וַיִּשְׁמֹר אֹתָם. I. שְׁמַעְתֶּם . . . וַתִּזְכְּרוּ אֹתָם וַתִּשְׁמְרוּ אֹתָם.

2. A. עַתָּה הוּא יִקַּח אֶת הַכֵּלִים וְיֵלֵךְ לְאָהֳלוֹ. B. עַתָּה נִקַּח . . . וְנֵלֵךְ לְאָהֳלֵנוּ. C. עַתָּה תִּקַּחְנָה . . . וְתֵלַכְנָה לְאָהֳלְכֶן. D. עַתָּה תִּקַּח . . . וְתֵלֵךְ לְאָהֳלְךָ. E. עַתָּה הֵם יִקְחוּ . . . וְיֵלְכוּ לְאָהֳלָם. F. עַתָּה תִּקְחִי . . . וְתֵלְכִי לְאָהֳלֵךְ.

3. A. תִּלְבְּשׁוּ אֶת בִּגְדֵיכֶם וּפְתַחְתֶּם אֶת הַשַּׁעַר וַהֲלַכְתֶּם לְבֵיתְכֶם. B. הוּא יִלְבַּשׁ אֶת בְּגָדָיו וּפָתַח אֶת הַשַּׁעַר וְהָלַךְ לְבֵיתוֹ. C. תִּלְבַּשְׁנָה אֶת בִּגְדֵיכֶן וּפְתַחְתֶּן אֶת הַשַּׁעַר וַהֲלַכְתֶּן לְבֵיתְכֶן. D. תִּלְבְּשִׁי אֶת בְּגָדַיִךְ וּפָתַחְתְּ אֶת הַשַּׁעַר וְהָלַכְתְּ לְבֵיתֵךְ. E. הִנֵּה תִּלְבַּשְׁנָה אֶת בִּגְדֵיהֶן וּפָתְחוּ אֶת הַשַּׁעַר וְהָלְכוּ לְבֵיתָן. F. נִלְבַּשׁ אֶת בְּגָדֵינוּ וּפָתַחְנוּ אֶת הַשַּׁעַר וְהָלַכְנוּ לְבֵיתֵנוּ. G. הִיא תִּלְבַּשׁ אֶת בְּגָדֶיהָ וּפָתְחָה אֶת הַשַּׁעַר וְהָלְכָה לְבֵיתָהּ. H. אֶלְבַּשׁ אֶת בְּגָדַי וּפָתַחְתִּי אֶת הַשַּׁעַר וְהָלַכְתִּי לְבֵיתִי. I. תִּלְבַּשׁ אֶת בְּגָדֶיךָ וּפָתַחְתָּ אֶת הַשַּׁעַר וְהָלַכְתָּ לְבֵיתֶךָ.

4. A. תִּהְיוּ מְלָכִים טוֹבִים וּשְׁפַטְתֶּם אֶת עַמְּכֶם. B. הוּא יִהְיֶה מֶלֶךְ טוֹב וְשָׁפַט אֶת עַמּוֹ. C. הֵם יִהְיוּ מְלָכִים טוֹבִים וְשָׁפְטוּ אֶת עַמָּם. D. אֶהְיֶה מֶלֶךְ טוֹב וְשָׁפַטְתִּי אֶת עַמִּי. E. נִהְיֶה מְלָכִים טוֹבִים וְשָׁפַטְנוּ אֶת עַמֵּנוּ.

5. A. הִיא יָשְׁבָה עַל אַדְמָתָהּ וַתִּכְתֹּב סֵפֶר לְמִשְׁפַּחְתָּהּ. B. יָשַׁבְתֶּן עַל אַדְמַתְכֶן וַתִּכְתֹּבְנָה סֵפֶר לְמִשְׁפַּחְתְּכֶן. C. יָשַׁבְתְּ עַל אַדְמָתֵךְ וַתִּכְתְּבִי סֵפֶר לְמִשְׁפַּחְתֵּךְ. D. יָשַׁבְנוּ עַל אַדְמָתֵנוּ וַנִּכְתֹּב סֵפֶר לְמִשְׁפַּחְתֵּנוּ. E. הִנֵּה יָשְׁבוּ עַל אַדְמָתָן וַתִּכְתֹּבְנָה סֵפֶר לְמִשְׁפַּחְתָּן. F. יָשַׁבְתָּ עַל אַדְמָתְךָ וַתִּכְתֹּב סֵפֶר לְמִשְׁפַּחְתְּךָ. G. יְשַׁבְתֶּם עַל אַדְמַתְכֶם וַתִּכְתְּבוּ סֵפֶר לְמִשְׁפַּחְתְּכֶם. H. הֵם יָשְׁבוּ עַל אַדְמָתָם וַיִּכְתְּבוּ סֵפֶר לְמִשְׁפַּחְתָּם. I. הוּא יָשַׁב עַל אַדְמָתוֹ וַיִּכְתֹּב סֵפֶר לְמִשְׁפַּחְתּוֹ.

6. A. עַתָּה אַתֶּם בֹּטְחִים בִּבְנְכֶם בְּכָל לְבַבְכֶם. B. עַתָּה אֲנַחְנוּ בֹּטְחִים בִּבְנֵנוּ בְּכָל לְבָבֵנוּ. C. עַתָּה אַתָּה בֹּטֵחַ בְּבִנְךָ בְּכָל לְבָבְךָ. D. עַתָּה הֵמָּה בֹּטְחִים בִּבְנָם בְּכָל לְבָבָם. E. עַתָּה בֹּעַז בֹּטֵחַ בִּבְנוֹ בְּכָל לְבּוֹ. F. עַתָּה הִיא בֹּטַחַת בִּבְנָהּ בְּכָל לְבָבָהּ. G. עַתָּה אַתְּ בֹּטַחַת בְּבִנְךָ בְּכָל לְבָבֵךְ.

1. She heard the words of the covenant and she remembered them and she kept them. A. They heard the words of the covenant and they remembered them and they kept them. B. I heard the words of the covenant and I remembered them and I kept them. 2. Now I will take the vessels and I will go to my tent. A. Now he will take the vessels and he will go to his tent. B. Now we will take . . . and we will go to our tent. 3. They will put on their clothing and open the gate and go to their house. A. You will put on your clothing and open the gate and go to your house. B. He will put on . . . 4. You will be a good king and you will judge your people. A. You will be good kings and you will judge your people. B. He . . . 5. I stayed upon my land and I wrote a book for my family. A. She stayed upon her land and she wrote a book for her family. B. You stayed upon your land and you wrote a book . . . 6. Now I trust my son with all my heart. A. Now you trust your son with all your hearts. B. Now we trust our son . . .

Exercise 3. 1. And it came to pass in the days of the judges (that) there was a famine in the land. 2. The lad stole all the money and took the money to his brothers. 3. We will remember your kindness and we will choose you to be king. 4. We ate the bread and lay down on our bed. 5. We will send the clothing to our father and he will put it on. 6. The wise men of Judah knew the words of the convenant and kept them.

Exercise 4a .1 וְלָקְחָה 2. וּבָחַר 3. וְשָׁמַעְנוּ 4. וְהָיָה, וְיָדְעוּ.

1. She ate of the fruit of the tree, and also gave of the fruit to her husband. 2. David trusted the words of his fathers and chose a good woman to be a wife for him. 3. We walked to the top of the mountain and heard the voice of the judge. 4. And there was light in the wilderness at night, and the people knew that there was a tent there.

Exercise 4b .1 וְיִקְחוּ 2. וְיִכְתֹּב 3. וְיִשְׁפֹּט 4. וְיִזְכְּרוּ, וְיִבְחֲרוּ

1. The young men will steal the vessels of the tabernacle and will take them to the land of Moab. 2. The old man will sit in his house all night and write his book until morning. 3. The king will reign over all the land and he will judge with kindness. 4. Your sons will be good, and they will remember you, and they will choose to walk in your way.

Exercise 5. 1. your land 2. their vessels 3. his silver 4. my life 5. our covenant 6. his heart 7. her soul 8. your stone 9. their tents 10. your heart 11. your tabernacle 12. his mouth 13. your beast 14. our faces 15. their clothes 16. your brothers 17. his head 18. your places 19. my eyes 20. her hands.

Exercise 6. In the days of the judges an old man lived in the land of Israel and his name was Dan. He had animals and fields and houses, and only one son, and his name was Joseph. Joseph did not have a wife. So Dan sent a man to the land of his fathers to choose a wife for his son. And the man took in his hand gifts, silver and clothes and went to the land of Dan's fathers. In this land there was a woman, and her name was Dinah. She not married, and she lived in her father's house. The man that Dan had sent went to the house of Dinah's family, and the man chose Dinah as a wife for Joseph. Now the father of Dinah heard his words and said to himself. ''The thing is not good. If Dinah goes with the man to the land of Israel, she will not be with her family again all the days of her life.'' And Dinah heard the words of the man, and she knew that Dan had animals and fields and houses. And Dinah knew that Dan was a great man. If she went to be a wife to Joseph, she would have clothes and good food all the days of her life. And Dinah went with the man to the land of Israel, and Joseph took her as a wife for himself. After Joseph took Dinah for a wife, she had clothes and good food, and also sons and daughters.

Exercise 7 ‏1. הֲלַכְתֶּן ‏2. יָדוֹעַ ‏3. לָקַחַת ‏4. תִּהְיֶינָה ‏5. דַּע

‏6. שְׁמַע ‏7. אֵלֵךְ ‏8. אֶהְיֶה ‏9. בְּטַחְנָה ‏10. אָמְרָה ‏11. נִשְׁכַּב

‏12. פָּעַל, ‏—, infinitive, ‏13. פָּעַל, 3, m, pl, imperfect, ב.ט.ח.

‏14. פָּעַל, ל.ק.ח., ‏—,—, ‏15. פָּעַל, 2, f, pl, imperative, ש.מ.ר.

‏16. ה.י.ה. 3, m, pl, imperfect, פָּעַל, 3, c, perfect, ה.ל.ך.

1. you went 2. know 3. taking—f, sg 4. they will be 5. know! 6. hear 7. I will go 8. I will be 9. trust! 10. she said 11. we will lie down 12. they will trust 13. to take 14. guard! 15. they went 16. they will be.

Chapter 21

Exercise 1. 1. in you 2. with you 3. in him 4. in them 5. with me 6. to you 7. with them 8. to you 9. in her 10. to him 11. upon us 12. with us 13. to us 14. in us 15. upon her 16. to me 17. upon you 18. to them 19. from them 20. like me 21. upon you 22. from us 23. like her 24. in you 25. to you 26. from you 27. like him 28. to him 29. upon me 30. from you 31. with us 32. in them 33. like you 34. to them 35. from her.

Exercise 2 A. ‏1. עוֹדְךָ בַּמִּדְבָּר וְאֵינְךָ הוֹלֵךְ מִשָּׁם לַיָּם.

B. עוֹדְכֶן . . . וְאֵינְכֶן הוֹלְכוֹת C. . . . עוֹדֵנוּ . . . וְאֵינֶנּוּ

הוֹלֵךְ . . . D. . . . עוֹדֵנִי . . . וְאֵינֶנִּי הוֹלֵךְ . . . E. . . . עוֹדָם

וְאֵינָם הוֹלְכִים . . . F. עוֹדְךָ . . . וְאֵינֵךְ הוֹלֶכֶת . . .

G. עוֹדְכֶם . . . וְאֵינְכֶם הוֹלְכִים . . . H. . . . עוֹדֶנָּה וְאֵינֶנָּה

הוֹלֶכֶת . . . I. . . . עוֹדָן . . . וְאֵינָן הוֹלְכוֹת . . . 2. A. הֵם

יִבְטְחוּ בָנוּ כִּי הֵם זוֹכְרִים אֹתָנוּ. B. הֵם יִבְטְחוּ בָּךְ כִּי הֵם

זוֹכְרִים אֹתָךְ. C. . . . בָּם . . . אֹתָם D. . . . בּוֹ . . . אֹתוֹ

E. . . . בָּכֶן . . . אֶתְכֶן F. אֹתָךְ . . . בָּךְ G. אֶתָךְ . . . בָּךְ

H. . . . בָּכֶם . . . אֶתְכֶם . . . אַתָּה

‏3. A. הַמֶּלֶךְ יִקַּח אֶת בָּנַי מִמֶּנִּי וְגָנַב גַּם אֶת כַּסְפִּי.

B. . . . בָּנֵינוּ מִמֶּנּוּ . . . כַּסְפֵּנוּ C. . . . בָּנֶיהָ מִמֶּנָּה . . . כַּסְפָּהּ.

D. . . . בָּנֶיךֶן מִכֶּן . . . כַּסְפְּכֶן. E. . . . בְּנֵיהֶם מֵהֶם . . . כַּסְפָּם.

F. . . . בָּנָיו מִמֶּנּוּ . . . כַּסְפּוֹ. G. . . . בָּנֶיךָ מִמֶּךָ . . . כַּסְפֶּךָ.

H. . . . בְּנֵיהֶן מֵהֶן . . . I. בָּנֶיךָ מִמְּךָ . . . כַּסְפְּךָ.

‏4. A. עָלֵינוּ לִבְחֹר נָשִׁים חֲכָמוֹת לִשְׁמֹר אֶת בְּנוֹתֵינוּ.

B. עָלַיִךְ . . . בְּנוֹתַיִךְ . . . C. עֲלֵיכֶם . . . בְּנוֹתֵיכֶם. D. עֲלֵיהֶן

. . . בְּנוֹתֵיהֶן. E. עָלַי . . . בְּנוֹתַי. F. . . . עָלָיו . . . בְּנוֹתָיו.

G. עָלֶיךָ . . . בְּנוֹתֶיךָ. 5. A. הִנֵּה הָלְכוּ אֵלֵינוּ לָשֶׁבֶת עִמָּנוּ

וַתִּשְׁמַעְנָה בְּקוֹלֵנוּ וַתִּשְׁמֹרְנָה אֹתָנוּ. B. הִנֵּה הָלְכוּ אֲלֵיהֶם

לָשֶׁבֶת עִמָּהֶם וַתִּשְׁמַעְנָה בְּקוֹלָם וַתִּשְׁמֹרְנָה אֹתָם. C. הִנֵּה

הָלְכוּ אֵלַי לָשֶׁבֶת עִמִּי וַתִּשְׁמַעְנָה בְּקוֹלִי וַתִּשְׁמֹרְנָה אֹתִי.

D. הִנֵּה הָלְכוּ אֵלֶיהָ לָשֶׁבֶת עִמָּהּ וַתִּשְׁמַעְנָה בְּקוֹלָהּ

וַתִּשְׁמֹרְנָה אֹתָהּ. E. הִנֵּה הָלְכוּ אֲלֵיכֶן לָשֶׁבֶת עִמָּכֶן

וַתִּשְׁמַעְנָה בְּקוֹלְכֶן וַתִּשְׁמֹרְנָה אֶתְכֶן. F. הִנֵּה הָלְכוּ אֵלָיו

לָשֶׁבֶת עִמּוֹ וַתִּשְׁמַעְנָה בְּקוֹלוֹ וַתִּשְׁמֹרְנָה אֹתוֹ. G. הִנֵּה הָלְכוּ

אֲלֵיכֶם לָשֶׁבֶת עִמָּכֶם וַתִּשְׁמַעְנָה בְּקוֹלְכֶם וַתִּשְׁמֹרְנָה

H. . . . אֶתְכֶם. הִנֵּה הָלְכוּ אֵלַיִךְ לָשֶׁבֶת עִמָּךְ וַתִּשְׁמַעְנָה בְּקוֹלֵךְ

וַתִּשְׁמֹרְנָה אֹתָךְ.

1. We are still in the wildnerness, and we are not going from there to the sea. A. You are still in the wilderness and you are not going from there to the sea. B. You are . . . 2. They will trust me because they remember me. A. They will trust us because they remember us. B. They . . . you. 3. The king will take your sons from you and also steal your money. A. The king will take my sons from me and also steal my money. B. . . . our . . . 4. She must choose wise women to guard her daughters A. We must choose wise women to guard our daughters. 5. They went to you to stay with you and they obeyed you and guarded you. A. They went to us to stay with us and they . . .

Exercise 3 ‏2. תֵּלְכִי ‏3. יִגְנֹב ‏4. נִבְחַר ‏5. יֵלְכוּ

1. Now you must write to your mother. 2. You will go with us as far as the city. 3. He will steal everything from me. 4. We will choose you from all the young men. 5. They will go after you on the road to Bethlehem.

Exercise 4a ‏1. אֵינֶנִּי ‏2. אֵינֶנּוּ ‏3. אֵינָן ‏4. אֵינֶנָּה

1. I am not in the tent with them. 2. We are not in the darkness with the beasts in the wilderness. 3. They are not eating the fruit. 4. She does not remember the face of her husband.

Exercise 4b ‏1. עוֹדְכֶם ‏2. עוֹדֶנִּי ‏3. עוֹדֶנּוּ—עוֹדֵנוּ ‏4. עוֹדָם

1. You are still good men. 2. I still know these things. 3. We are-he is still with the holy ones in the tabernacle. 4. They are still lying down in their tents today.

Exercise 5 ‏1. מִמֶּנָּה ‏2. כָּמוֹנִי ‏3. בּוֹ ‏4. עָלֵינוּ ‏5. עִמָּךְ

1. The men went to the young woman's house and they stole money from her. 2. Like me, you are from the family of Jacob. 3. We will trust in him and we will remember his words. 4. He sat upon his chair and he ruled over us. 5. They chose you and they went with you.

Exercise 6 ‏1. עוֹדֵנִי עַל אַדְמָתִי ‏2. עוֹדְךָ עַל אַדְמָתְךָ.

‏3. עוֹדֵנוּ עַל אַדְמָתֵנוּ. ‏4. הִיא יוֹשֶׁבֶת עִמָּנוּ. ‏5. אֲנִי יוֹשֵׁב

עִמָּהֶם. ‏6. אַתֶּן יוֹשְׁבוֹת עִמּוֹ. ‏7. אֵינָם כָּמוֹנִי. ‏8. אֵינֵךְ

כָּמוֹהֶן. ‏9. הָלַכְתִּי לְבֵיתִי עִם אִמִּי וְיָשַׁבְתִּי שָׁם. ‏10. הָלַכְתָּ

לְבֵיתְךָ עִם אִמְּךָ וְיָשַׁבְתָּ בְּכִסְאָךְ. ‏11. הוּא הָלַךְ לְבֵיתוֹ

הַגָּדוֹל עִם אִמּוֹ הַזְּקֵנָה וְאָבִיו הַזָּקֵן. ‏12. הָלַכְנוּ לְבֵית אִמֵּנוּ

הַגָּדוֹל כַּאֲשֶׁר הִיא הָיְתָה שָׁם.

Chapter 22

Exercise 2 ‏1. A. הוּא רָאָה אֶת הַמִּשְׁכָּן אֲשֶׁר בְּנֵי יִשְׂרָאֵל

בָּנוּ בַמִּדְבָּר. B. רָאִית אֶת הַמִּשְׁכָּן . . . C. הַקּוֹצְרִים

רָאוּ . . . D. . . . רָאִתֶן . . . E. . . . רָאִיתִי . . . F. . . . רָאִיתָ . . .

G. שָׂרָה רָאֲתָה . . . H. . . . הִנֵּה רָאוּ . . . I. . . . רְאִיתֶם . . .

‏2. A. בֵּין הָעַרְבַּיִם שָׁתִיתִי יַיִן מֵהַכְּלִי וְאָמַרְתִּי "לְחַיִּים!"

B. . . . הִנֵּה שָׁתוּ . . . וְאָמְרוּ C. . . . וַאֲמַרְתֶּם . . . שְׁתִיתֶם

D. . . . הוּא שָׁתָה . . . וְאָמַר E. . . . שָׁתִית . . . וְאָמַרְתְּ

F. . . . שָׁתִינוּ . . . וַאֲמַרְנוּ G. . . . הֵמָּה שָׁתוּ . . . וְאָמְרוּ

H. . . . שְׁתִיתֶן . . . וַאֲמַרְתֶּן I. . . . שָׁתִית . . . וְאָמַרְתָּ

‏3. A. עָלַי עַל הָאֲדָמָה לִבְנוֹת אֶת בָּתֵּיךְ . . . B. עָלֵינוּ

. . . בָּתֵּיכֶן. C. . . . עָלוּ . . . בָּתֵּיכֶם. D. . . . עָלָה . . . בָּתֵּיךָ.

E. . . . עָלֵינָה . . . בָּתֵּיכֶן. 4. A. תִּרְאֶינָה זָקֵן אֲשֶׁר הָלַךְ בַּדֶּרֶךְ

וּבָטַחְתֶּן בּוֹ וּפָתַחְתֶּן לוֹ אֶת שַׁעֲרֵי עִירְכֶן. B. . . . נִרְאֶה . . .

עִירֵנוּ וּבָטַחְנוּ בּוֹ וּפָתַחְנוּ C. . . . הוּא יָרֵא . . . עִירֵנוּ . . . וּבָטַח

בוֹ וּפָתַח . . . עִירוֹ. D. הֵמָּה יִרְאוּ . . . וּבָטְחוּ בוֹ וּפָתְחוּ

עִירָם. E. תִּרְאִי . . . וּבָטַחְתְּ בוֹ וּפָתַחְתְּ . . . עִירֵךְ.

F. הִיא תִּרְאֶה . . . וּבָטְחָה בוֹ וּפָתְחָה . . . עִירָהּ.

G. תִּרְאוּ . . . וּבְטַחְתֶּם בוֹ וּפְתַחְתֶּם . . . עִירְכֶם. H. הֵנָּה

תִּרְאֶינָה . . . וּבָטְחוּ בוֹ וּפָתְחוּ . . . עִירָן. I. אֶרְאֶה . . .

וּבָטַחְתִּי בוֹ וּפָתַחְתִּי . . . עִירִי . . . 5. A. הָאִישׁ הַקָּדוֹשׁ אָמַר

אֵלַי "תַּעֲשֶׂה חֶסֶד כַּאֲבוֹתֶיךָ" וְשָׁמַעְתִּי בְּקוֹלוֹ. B. . . . .

אֵלֶיךָ "תַּעֲשֶׂה חֶסֶד כַּאֲבוֹתֶיךָ" וְשָׁמַעְתָּ בְּקוֹלוֹ. C. . . . .

אֲלֵיכֶן "תַּעֲשֶׂינָה חֶסֶד כַּאֲבוֹתֵיכֶן" וּשְׁמַעְתֶּן בְּקוֹלוֹ.

D. . . . אֲלֵיהֶם "תַּעֲשׂוּ חֶסֶד כַּאֲבוֹתֵיכֶם" וְשָׁמְעוּ בְּקוֹלוֹ.

E. . . . אֵלַיִךְ "תַּעֲשִׂי חֶסֶד כַּאֲבוֹתַיִךְ" וְשָׁמַעַתְּ בְּקוֹלוֹ.

F. . . . אֲלֵיהֶן "תַּעֲשֶׂינָה חֶסֶד כַּאֲבוֹתֵיכֶן" וְשָׁמְעוּ בְּקוֹלוֹ.

G. . . . אֵלֶיהָ "תַּעֲשִׂי חֶסֶד כַּאֲבוֹתַיִךְ" וְשָׁמְעָה בְּקוֹלוֹ.

H. . . . . אֲלֵיכֶם "תַּעֲשׂוּ חֶסֶד כַּאֲבוֹתֵיכֶם" וּשְׁמַעְתֶּם בְּקוֹלוֹ.

1. We saw the tabernacle that the children of Israel built in the wilderness. A. He saw the tabernacle that . . . 2. At dusk, she drank wine from the vessel and said, "To life!" A. At dusk, I . . . 3. Go up upon the land to build your houses. A. Go up . . . 4. You will see an old man who is walking on the road, and you will trust him and open the gates of your city for him. A. You will see an old man who is walking on the road, and . . . 5. The holy man said to us, "You will do kindness like your fathers" and we obeyed him. A. The holy man said to me, "You will do kindness like your fathers" and I obeyed him.

Exercise 3 1. עָנָה 2. תַּעֲלוּ 3. לִבְנוֹת 4. רְאֵה 5. עָשֹׂה יַעֲשׂוּ

1. You say "All that is under the heavens is evil." and I answer you, "No." 2. You will go up with me in the evening from the sea as far as the mountains of Jerusalem. 3. I will choose these men to build my house. 4. See these words that are written and do not forget them. 5. They will surely do everything that their fathers did.

Exercise 4 1. עָלָה, עוֹלֶה, יַעֲלֶה, עָלֹה עָלָה, עָלֹה

יַעֲלֶה 2. שְׁתִי 3. עֲשִׂיתֶם, עוֹשִׂים, תַּעֲשׂוּ, עָשֹׂה עֲשִׂיתֶם,

עָשֹׂה תַּעֲשׂוּ, עֲשׂוּ 4. עָנָה 5. בָּנִינוּ, בּוֹנִים, נִבְנֶה, בָּנֹה

בָּנִינוּ, בָּנֹה נִבְנֶה 6. עָשִׂיתִי, עוֹשָׂה, אֶעֱשֶׂה, עָשֹׂה עָשִׂיתִי,

עָשֹׂה אֶעֱשֶׂה 7. תִּשְׁתֶּה, שָׁתָה 8. רְאִיתֶן, רוֹאוֹת, תִּרְאֶינָה,

רָאֹה רְאִיתֶן, רָאֹה תִּרְאֶינָה, רְאִינָה

1. All this nation (went up, is going up, will go up, surely went up, will surely go up) from the wilderness to the land of Israel. 2. Sit with your family in the field and (drink) only the water! 3. You (did, are doing, will do, surely did, will surely do, do!) evil in the eyes of the judge. 4. I said to him: "Behold, bread and wine and fruit" and he (answered): "I will remember your kindness." 5. We (built, are building, will build, surely built, will surely build) the gates of our city. 6. I (made, am making, will make, surely made, will surely make) wine from the fruit for my family to drink on Sabbath evening. 7. When you go to Moab, don't (drink) the water. Only (drink) the wine! 8. You (saw, are seeing, will see, surely saw, will surely see, see!) the face of the lad regularly.

Exercise 5. 1. We ate the food and drank water and sat in our tents at dusk. 2. The man went up to Jerusalem and saw his uncle there. 3. And it was dark, and the women went to their house. 4. They must build a city in the midst of the wilderness, and they will build it.

Shortened Verbs: 1. וַנֵּשְׁתְּ 2. וַיַּרְא 3. וַיְהִי

Exercise 6 1. פ.ת.ח. 2. ה.ל.ך. 3. ל.ק.ח 4. ב.נ.ה. 5. שׁ.כ.ח.

6. ר.א.ה. 7. ה.י.ה. 8. ע.שׂ.ה. 9. ע.נ.ה. 10. שׁ.ת.ה.

11. ה.ל.ך 12. ה.י.ה. 13. ב.נ.ה. 14. ל.ק.ח 15. ר.א.ה.

16. שׁ.ת.ה. 17. ע.נ.ה. 18. ע.שׂ.ה.

1. I opened 2. go! 3. you will take. 4. you built 5. and I forgot 6. and she saw 7. be 8. and we did 9. to answer 10. drinking 11. I will go 12. and it was 13. and you built 14. take! 15. see! 16. and I drank 17. We answered 18. do!

Exercise 7. 1. And God saw the light, that it was good. And God divided the light from the darkness. And God called the light day, and the darkness he called night. And there was evening and morning, one day. 2. My beloved is mine and I am his. 3. What has been, that shall be, and there is nothing new under the sun.

Exercise 8 1. כָּתַבְתִּי 2. בָּנִיתִי 3. עָלִיתָ 4. שָׁתִיתֶם

5. שְׁמַרְתֶּם 6. עֲשִׂיתֶם 7. יִשְׁפֹּט 8. יִרְאֶה 9. עָשָׂה 10. הָיָה

11. עוֹשָׂה 12. כּוֹתֶבֶת 13. יָשַׁבְתָּ 14. עָלִיתֶן 15. תִּזְכֹּרְנָה

16. תִּרְאֶינָה 17. תַּעֲנֶינָה 18. בְּטַח 19. שְׁתֵה 20. עֲשֵׂה

21. עֲשׂוֹת 22. לָכֶת 23. בְּנוֹת 24. כְּתֹב

1. I wrote 2. I built 3. I went up 4. you drank 5. you guarded 6. you did 7. he will judge 8. he will see 9. he did 10. he was 11. doing—f, sg 12. writing—f, sg 13. you were sitting 14. you went up 15. you will remember 16. you will see 17. you will answer 18. trust! 19. drink! 20. do! 21. do 22. walk 23. build 24. write.

Chapter 23

Exercise 2 1. A. הִיא קָמָה בַּבֹּקֶר וַתִּשְׁכַּב בָּעֶרֶב. B. קַמְתֶּן

C. . . . קַמְנוּ . . . וַנִּשְׁכַּב D. . . . קַמְתְּ . . . וַתִּשְׁכְּבֶנָה

E. . . . הוּא קָם . . . וַיִּשְׁכַּב F. הֵנָּה קָמוּ . . .

G. . . . קַמְתֶּם . . . וַתִּשְׁכְּבוּ H. . . . קַמְתְּ . . . וַתִּשְׁכַּבְנָה

I. . . . הֵם קָמוּ . . . וַיִּשְׁכְּבוּ 2. A. תָּסוּר אֵשֶׁת

בֹּעַז מֵהַדֶּרֶךְ וְרָצָה לָקַחַת אֶת הָאֹכֶל מֵהָאֹהֶל. B. נָסוּר

מֵהַדֶּרֶךְ וְרָצֹנוּ . . . C. . . . יָסוּרוּ הַנְּעָרִים . . . וְרָצוּ

D. . . . תָּסוּרוּ . . . וְרַצְתֶּם E. . . . תָּסֹרְנָה נְשֵׁי יְרוּשָׁלַיִם . . .

F. . . . תָּסוּר . . . וְרָצְתָ G. . . . תָּסוּרִי . . . וְרָצְתְּ

H. . . . תָּסוּרֶינָה . . . וְרַצְתֶּן I. . . . אָסוּר . . . וְרַצְתִּי

3. A. קַמְנוּ וּבָאנוּ אֶל הָאִישׁ הַקָּדוֹשׁ לִשְׁמֹעַ אֶת דְּבָרָיו.

B. הוּא יָקוּם וְיָבוֹא C. . . . קַמְתֶּם וּבָאתֶם D. . . . אָקוּם

וְאָבוֹא E. . . . תָּקוּמִי וְתָבוֹאִי 4. A. . . . בְּשׁוּב הָאִישׁ

מֵהַשָּׂדֶה אֶל בֵּיתוֹ יָשַׁב וְאָכַל וְשָׁתָה יַיִן וְשָׁר. B. בְּשׁוּבִי

מֵהַשָּׂדֶה אֶל בֵּיתִי יָשַׁבְתִּי וְאָכַלְתִּי וְשָׁתִיתִי יַיִן וְשַׁרְתִּי.

C. בְּשׁוּבְכֶם מֵהַשָּׂדֶה אֶל בָּתֵּיכֶם, יְשַׁבְתֶּם וַאֲכַלְתֶּם

וּשְׁתִיתֶם יַיִן וְשַׁרְתֶּם. D. בְּשׁוּבְךָ מֵהַשָּׂדֶה אֶל בֵּיתְךָ יָשַׁבְתָּ

וְאָכַלְתָ וְשָׁתִיתָ יַיִן וְשַׁרְתָ. E. בְּשׁוּב הַנָּשִׁים מֵהַשָּׂדֶה אֶל

בָּתֵּיהֶן יָשְׁבוּ וְאָכְלוּ וְשָׁתוּ יַיִן וְשָׁרוּ. F. בְּשׁוּבֵנוּ מֵהַשָּׂדֶה

אֶל בָּתֵּינוּ יָשַׁבְנוּ וְאָכַלְנוּ וְשָׁתִינוּ יַיִן וְשַׁרְנוּ. G. בְּשׁוּבָהּ

מֵהַשָּׂדֶה אֶל בֵּיתָהּ יָשְׁבָה וְאָכְלָה וְשָׁתְתָה יַיִן וְשָׁרָה.

H. בְּשׁוּבְכֶן מֵהַשָּׂדֶה אֶל בָּתֵּיכֶן יְשַׁבְתֶּן וַאֲכַלְתֶּן וּשְׁתִיתֶן

וְשַׁרְתֶּן. I. בְּשׁוּבֵךְ מֵהַשָּׂדֶה אֶל בֵּיתֵךְ יָשַׁבְתְּ וְאָכַלְתְּ

וְשָׁתִית . . . 5. A. . . . וְשָׁרְתְּ. הוּא יָשִׂים לְפָנָיו מְנָחוֹת וְכֶסֶף

שָׁנָה בְּשָׁנָה וְהוּא יִשְׁמֹר אֹתוֹ מִכָּל רַע. B. תָּשִׂימוּ . . . וְהוּא

יִשְׁמֹר אֶתְכֶם C. . . . הֵנָּה תְּשִׂימֶינָה . . . אֶתָּן D. . . . תָּשִׂים

אֶתְּךָ E. . . . אָשִׂים אֹתִי F. . . . תְּשִׂמְנָה . . . G. הִיא תָּשִׂים

אֶתְכֶן H. . . . אַתָּה תָּשִׂימִי . . .

אֶתְכָן . . .

אִתָּךְ . . . הֵמָּה יָשִׂימוּ . . . אֹתָם . . . 1.

1. I arose in the morning and lay down in the evening. A. She arose in the morning and lay down in the evening. B. You . . . 2. The man will turn aside from the road and he will run to take the food from the tent. A. The wife of Boaz will turn aside from the road and she will run to take the food from . . 3. I arose and went to the holy man to hear his words. A. We arose and went . . . 4. When the harvesters returned from the field to their houses, they sat and ate and drank wine and sang. A. When the man returned from the field to his house, he sat and ate and drank wine and sang. 5. We will set gifts and silver before him year by year, and he will guard us from all evil. A. He will set gifts and silver before him year by year, and he will guard him from all evil. B. You will set . . . and he will guard you . . .

Exercise 3 1. בָּאוּ, בָּאִים, יָבוֹאוּ, בּוֹא בָּאוּ, בּוֹא יָבוֹאוּ

2. סוּרִי 3. קַמְנוּ, קָמִים, נָקוּם, קוֹם קַמְנוּ, קוֹם נָקוּם

4. שָׂם, שָׁם, יָשִׂים, שׂוֹם שָׁם, שׂוֹם יָשִׂים 5. רַצְתִּי, רָץ,

אָרוּץ, רוֹץ רַצְתִּי, רוֹץ אָרוּץ 6. שָׁרָה, שָׁרָה, תָּשִׁיר,

שָׁרָה שׁוֹר תָּשִׁיר

1. They (came, are coming, will come, surely came, surely will come). 2. (Turn aside) from evil and go the good way. 3. We (arose, arise, will arise, surely arose) to go up on the mountain. 4. He (paid attention, pays attention, will pay attention, surely paid attention, surely will pay attention) to the voice of his mother. 5. When my brothers return(ed) to their land, I (ran, run, will run, surely ran, surely will run) to see them. 6. She regularly (sings, sang, will sing, surely sang, surely will sing) in the evening with her family.

Exercise 4a 1. תָּשִׂימוּ 2. יָשׁוּב, יִבְנֶה 3. יָסוּרוּ, יַעֲשׂוּ

4. נֹאכַל, נִשְׁתֶּה, נָקוּם

1. You will set the words of the covenant upon your hearts and upon your souls. 2. He will return to his land and he will build there a house from stone. 3. They will turn aside from the covenant and do evil in the eyes of their fathers. 4. We will eat and drink and arise to go to our tents.

Exercise 4b 1. עָשִׂינוּ, שַׂמְנוּ 2. עָנוּ, בָּאנוּ 3. שָׁבָה 4. שַׁרְתֶּן

1. We made vessels of silver and we put them in the tabernacle. 2. They answered, ''We came to see you''. 3. She returned to the house of her father year by year. 4. You sang with all the people of the city. Exercise 5. 1. The old man went, and came to the holy mountain and went up on it. 2. You heard the sound of a beast and saw it and turned aside from the road. 3. And Ruth returned with Naomi to the land of Israel, and settled with her there. 4. And he built a chair for himself from wood and put the money under it, and sat on it. 5. And it came to pass in the morning that the maiden got up from her bed and put on her garments and went to the house of her brother. 6. I will pay attention to the words of the wise, and turn aside from wine and women. Shortened Verbs: 1. וַיַּעַל 2. וַתֵּרֶא, וַתָּסַר 3. וַתֵּשֶׁב

4. וַיִּבֶן, וַיָּשֶׂם 5. וַיְהִי, וַתָּקָם

Exercise 6. There was a man who lived in a tent in the wilderness. He had sons and daughters, and he had no money. And the day came when there was no food for his family . . .

Exercise 7 1. שַׁבְתָּ 2. עָשִׂיתָ 3. זָכַרְתָּ 4. בָּאתָ 5. נָרוּץ

6. נַעֲלֶה 7. נָסוּר 8. נִשְׁמֹר 9. בָּאָה 10. בּוֹנָה 11. בָּאָה

12. כָּתְבָה 13. הָיְתָה 14. תִּהְיֶינָה 15. תָּקֹמְנָה/תְּקוּמֶינָה

16. יָשִׁירוּ 17. שַׂמְתָּ 18. שִׁיר 19. קוּמוּ 20. קוּמִי 21. אָבוֹא

1. You returned 2. you did 3. you remembered 4. you went 5. we will run 6. we will go up 7. we will turn aside 8. we will guard 9. goes — f, sg 10. builds — f, sg 11. she came 12. she wrote 13. she was 14. they will be 15. they will get up 16. they will sing 17. you put 18. sing! 19. get up! 20. I will get up 21. I will come.

Chapter 24

Exercise 2 1. A. הוּא אָמַר בְּלִבּוֹ: "אָסוּר מִמַּעֲשַׂי הָרָעִים".

B. . . . "הִיא תָּסוּר מִמַּעֲשֶׂיהָ הָרָעִים". C. . . . "הוּא יָסוּר

מִמַּעֲשָׂיו הָרָעִים". D. . . . "הֵנָּה תָּסֹרְנָה מִמַּעֲשֵׂיהֶן הָרָעִים".

E. . . . "בָּנַי יָסוּרוּ מִמַּעֲשֵׂיהֶם הָרָעִים". 2. A. תִּתְּנוּ לָהֶם

מַיִם מֵהַיַּרְדֵּן בָּעֶרֶב וְהֵם יִשְׁתּוּ אוֹתָם. B. הִנֵּה תִּתְּנָה . . .

C. . . . אַתֶּן . . . D. . . . הוּא יִתֵּן . . . E. . . . תִּתְּנִי . . . F. . . . הֵמָּה יִתְּנוּ

. . . G. . . . תִּתְּנָה . . . H. . . . תִּתֵּן . . . I. . . . נִתֵּן . . . 3. A. וַיֹּאמֶר

דָּוִד אֶל אִמּוֹ לֵאמֹר: "אַבְרָהָם יֹאכַל אֶת הַפְּרִי". B. . . . הַבָּנִים

יֹאכְלוּ . . . C. . . . הַנְּעָרוֹת תֹּאכַלְנָה . . . D. . . . בִּתְּךָ

תֹּאכַל . . . E. . . . נֹאכַל . . . F. . . . אַנְשֵׁי מִצְרַיִם יֹאכְלוּ . . .

G . . . תֹּאכְלִי . . . 4. A. . . . הִיא תֶּאֱהַב אֶת מַלְכָּהּ בְּכָל

לִבָּהּ וְתַעֲשֶׂה מַעֲשִׂים רַבִּים בִּשְׁמוֹ. B. . . . תֶּאֱהַבְנָה אֶת מַלְכְּכֶן

בְּכָל לִבְּכֶן וְתַעֲשֶׂינָה . . . C. . . . הֵמָּה יֶאֱהֲבוּ אֶת מַלְכְּכֶם בְּכָל

לְבַבְכֶם וְיַעֲשׂוּ . . . D. . . . נֶאֱהַב אֶת מַלְכֵּנוּ בְּכָל לִבֵּנוּ וְנַעֲשֶׂה

. . . E. . . . הוּא יֶאֱהַב אֶת מַלְכּוֹ בְּכָל לִבּוֹ וְיַעֲשֶׂה . . .

F. . . . תֶּאֱהֲבִי אֶת מַלְכֵּךְ בְּכָל לִבֵּךְ וְתַעֲשִׂי . . . G. . . . אֹהַב אֶת

מַלְכִּי בְּכָל לִבִּי וְאֶעֱשֶׂה . . . H. . . . הִנֵּה תֶּאֱהַבְנָה אֶת מַלְכָּן

בְּכָל לִבָּן וְתַעֲשֶׂינָה . . . I. . . . תֶּאֱהֲבוּ אֶת מַלְכְּכֶם בְּכָל

לִבְּכֶם וְתַעֲשׂוּ . . . 5. A. נָתַן לַזָּקֵן אֶת הַלֶּחֶם וְאֶת הַיַּיִן.

B. הוּא נָתַן . . . C. . . . נָתַתְּ . . . D. . . . הֵמָּה נָתְנוּ . . . E. . . . הִיא

נָתְנָה . . . F. נָתַתְּ . . . G. . . . נָתַתִּי . . . H. . . . הֵנָּה נָתְנוּ . . . I. . . . נְתַתֶּם

. . . 6. A. . . . שָׂרָה לָקְחָה אֶת סִפְרֵי הַתּוֹרָה וַתִּתֵּן אֹתָם

לְבָנֶיהָ. B. הַנָּשִׁים לָקְחוּ . . . וַתִּתֵּנָה אֹתָם לִבְנֵיהֶן.

C. לָקַחְתִּי . . . וָאֶתֵּן אֹתָם לְבָנַי. D. . . . לָקַחְתְּ . . . וַתִּתְּנִי

אֹתָם לְבָנַיִךְ. E. . . . לְקַחְתֶּם . . . וַתִּתְּנוּ אֹתָם לִבְנֵיכֶם.

F. לָקַחְנוּ . . . וַנִּתֵּן אֹתָם לְבָנֵינוּ. G. הָאֲנָשִׁים לָקְחוּ . . .

וַיִּתְּנוּ אֹתָם לִבְנֵיהֶם. H. . . . לְקַחְתֶּן . . . וַתִּתֵּנָה אֹתָם לִבְנֵיכֶן.

I. . . . לָקַחְתְּ . . . וַתִּתְּנִי אֹתָם לְבָנַיִךְ. 7. A. . . . כָּל הָעָם יֹאמַר:

"בְּנֵי יִשְׂרָאֵל עָשׂוּ מַעֲשֵׂי חֶסֶד וְרַחֲמִים כִּי לָהֶם תּוֹרַת

אֱמֶת". B. נְשֵׁי מוֹאָב תֹּאמַרְנָה . . . C. . . . תֹּאמְרוּ . . .

D. . . . תֹּאמַר . . . E. . . . תֹּאמַרְנָה . . . F. . . . הִיא תֹּאמַר . . .

G. . . . נֹאמַר . . . H. . . . תֹּאמְרִי . . .

1. He said to himself: ''They will turn aside from their evil deeds''. A. He said to himself: ''I will turn aside from my evil deeds.'' 2. She will give water from the Jordan to them in the evening and they will drink it. A. You will give water from the . . . 3. David said to his mother, saying, ''I will eat the fruit''. A. David said to his mother, saying, ''Abraham will eat the fruit''. 4. You will love your king with all your heart and you will do many deeds in his name. A. She will love her king with all her heart and she will do many deeds in his name. B. You will love . . . 5. We gave the bread and the wine to the old man. A. You gave the bread and the wine to the . . . 6. He took the books of the Torah and he gave them to his children. A. Sarah took the books of the Torah and she gave them to her children. B. The women . . . 7. The nations will say, ''The children of Israel did deeds of kindness and compassion because they have a law of truth.'' A. All the people will say, ''The children of Israel did . . .

Exercise 3 1. שָׁמַרְתָּ, שָׁם, תָּשִׂים, שׂוֹם, שַׂמְתָּ, שׂוֹם תָּשִׂים,

שִׂים 2. נָתַן, נוֹתֵן, יִתֵּן, נָתוֹן נָתַן, נָתוֹן יִתֵּן 3. אֲהַבְתָּם,

אוֹהֲבִים, תֶּאֱהַב, אָהוֹב אֲהַבְתָּם, אָהוֹב תֶּאֱהַבוּ, אֶהֱבוּ

4. תֹּאכְלִי 5. עָשִׂיתִי, עוֹשֶׂה, אֶעֱשֶׂה, עָשִׂיתִי, עָשֹׂה
עֲשֵׂה 6. אָמַרְתָּ, אוֹמֶרֶת, תֹּאמְרִי, אָמוֹר אָמַרְתְּ, אָמוֹר
תֹּאמְרִי, אִמְרִי

1. You (set, are setting, will set, surely set, will surely set, set!) the love of the Torah among the children of Israel. 2. He (gave, gives, will give, surely gave, will surely give) many vessels to his wife. 3. You (loved, love, will love, surely loved, will surely love, love!) truth and your mother's food. 4. Week after week, you will come to my house and you (will eat) my food. 5. I (did, do, will do, surely did, will surely do) deeds of kindness and compassion daily, because I am better than all the people of my city. 6. You (said, say, will say, surely said, will surely say, say!) to your sons saying: "You have only heard words of truth from the mouth of your mother."

Exercise 4 1. אֶל יְרוּשָׁלַיִם 2. עַל הָהָר 3. שָׁם 4. אֶל הָעִיר
5. אֶל הָאָרֶץ

1. Next week the young men will run to Jerusalem to give their fathers much money. 2. And Jacob went up to the mountain to forget the love of women. 3. And the old man said to them: "Go there to do deeds of kindness and compassion." 4. And the king sent the judge to the city and said to him: "Pay attention to the deeds of my people, and judge them with kindness." 5. We must return to the land after the famine.

Exercise 5 יָשְׁבָה, אָהֲבוּ, בָּאוּ, רְאוֹת, שָׁמָּה, לְכוּ, סוּרוּ,
שׁוּבוּ, שִׁמְעוּ, הָלְכוּ, שָׁב, אָמַר, אוֹהֵב, אֶתֵּן, אוֹכֵל, לָתֵת,
רָאֲתָה, אָהֲבָה, הָיְתָה.

There was a woman who lived in the land of Canaan, and her name was Sarah. There were many men who loved her. They came daily to see her, and she did not pay attention to their words. Sarah said to them: "Go! Turn aside from me and return to your houses!" They obeyed her and went on their way. One man returned to her house every week. He said to her: "I love you with all my heart! I will give you everything that I can give!" Sarah saw that he was a good man. She loved him and became his wife.

Exercise 6 1. א.ה.ב. 2. כ.ת.ב. 3. א.ה.ב. 4. ק.ו.ם 5. נ.ת.ן.
6. ש.י.ם. 7. ב.ח.ר. 8. ע.נ.ה. 9. א.מ.ר. 10. י.ש.ב. 11. ב.ו.א.
12. א.מ.ר. 13. נ.ת.ן. 14. י.ש.ב. 15. ש.י.ם. 16. ע.נ.ה.
17. כ.ת.ב. 18. ב.ו.א. 19. ב.ח.ר. 20. נ.ת.ן.

1. we loved 2. I will write 3. loving—m, sg 4. arise! 5. you gave 6. set! 7. choosing—f, sg 8. we answered 9. you will say 10. to sit 11. he came/comes—m, s 12. saying—f, pl 13. you/she will give 14. you sat 15. we will put 16. answering—m, sg 17. you/they will write 18. come! 19. you will choose 20. give!

Exercise 7 1. אָמְרָה 2. אָהֲבָה 3. נָתְנָה 4. כָּתְבָה 5. רָאֲתָה 6. שָׁמָּה
7. יֹּאמְרוּ 8. יֶאֱהֲבוּ 9. יִתְּנוּ 10. יִשְׁמְרוּ 11. יַעֲשׂוּ 12. יֵשְׁבוּ
13. א.מ.ר sg, f, 2, imperfect פָּעַל 14. א.ה.ב pl, m, 3, imperfect
פָּעַל 15. י.ש.ב sg, m, 3, imperfect פָּעַל 16. נ.ת.ן infinitive construct, פָּעַל 17. ז.כ.ר sg, f, participle, פָּעַל 18. נ.ת.ן sg, m, participle, פָּעַל 19. נ.ת.ן pl, m, 2, imperfect, פָּעַל 20. נ.ת.ן pl, f, 2, perfect, פָּעַל 21. ש.י.ם pl, c, 1, imperfect פָּעַל 22. ב.נ.ה pl, m, 2, perfect פָּעַל 23. ע.ש.ה pl, f, 2, imperative, פָּעַל 24. ב.נ.ה pl, c, 1, imperfect, פָּעַל

1. she said 2. she loved 3. she gave 4. she wrote 5. she saw 6. she put 7. they will say 8. they will love 9. they will give 10. they will guard 11. they will do 12. they will sit 13. you will say 14. they will love 15. he will sit 16. to give 17. giving—m, sg 18. remembering—f, sg 19. you gave 20. you will set 21. you built 22. do! 24. we will build

Chapter 25

Exercise 2 1. A. גָּדַלְתָּ אֶת הַנַּעַר וְהוּא גָּדַל. B. הָאָבוֹת

C. גָּדְלוּ... D. גָּדַלְתֶּן... E. הָאִישׁ גָּדַל...
F. גָּדַלְתָּ... G. גָּדַלְתִּי... H. גָּדַלְתֶּם... I. הַנָּשִׁים
גָּדְלוּ... 2. A. הָיוּ בְּהֵמוֹת רַבּוֹת בַּשָּׂדֶה וַתִּסְפֹּרְנָה הַבָּנוֹת
אֹתָן... B. וָאֶסְפֹּר... C. ...וַתִּסְפְּרוּ... D....
וַתִּסְפְּרִי... E. ...וַיִּסְפְּרוּ... F. ...וַנִּסְפֹּר...
G.... וַתִּסְפֹּר... H. ...וַתִּסְפֹּרְנָה... I. ...וַתִּסְפֹּר
שָׂרָה... 3. A. הַזְּקֵנִים יִזְכְּרוּ אֶת מַעֲשֵׂיהֶם הַטּוֹבִים וְהֵם
יְסַפְּרוּ לָנוּ עֲלֵיהֶם. B. תִּזְכֹּר אֶת מַעֲשֶׂיךָ הַטּוֹבִים וּתְסַפֵּר
לָנוּ עֲלֵיהֶם. C. הִיא תִּזְכֹּר מַעֲשֶׂיהָ הַטּוֹבִים וְהִיא
תְּסַפֵּר... D. תִּזְכְּרוּ אֶת מַעֲשֵׂיכֶם הַטּוֹבִים וּתְסַפְּרוּ...
E. הֵנָּה תִּזְכֹּרְנָה אֶת מַעֲשֵׂיהֶן הַטּוֹבִים וְהֵנָּה תְּסַפֵּרְנָה...
F. תִּזְכְּרִי אֶת מַעֲשַׂיִךְ הַטּוֹבִים וּתְסַפְּרִי... G. תִּזְכֹּרְנָה
אֶת מַעֲשֵׂיכֶן הַטּוֹבִים וּתְסַפֵּרְנָה... 4. A. וַיֹּאמֶר הָאִישׁ
לֵאמֹר: "הַשּׁוֹפְטִים מְצַוִּים אֶתְכֶם לַעֲשׂוֹת אֶת כָּל הַמִּצְוֹת."
B. ...."הַזְּקֵנוֹת מְצַוּוֹת..." C. ..."אֵשֶׁת דָּוִד מְצַוָּה
..." D. ..."אֲנַחְנוּ מְצַוִּים..." 5. A. בִּקַּשְׁתִּי אֶת הָאֱמֶת
וְצִוִּיתִי אֶת הָאֲנָשִׁים לֵאמֹר, "דַּבְּרוּ אֵלַי". B. בִּקַּשְׁתֶּם
וְצִוִּיתֶם... "דַּבְּרוּ אֵלֵינוּ". C. הֵנָּה בִּקְּשׁוּ... וְצִוּוּ
"דַּבְּרוּ אֵלֵינוּ". D. בִּקַּשְׁתְּ... וְצִוִּית... "דַּבְּרוּ אֵלַי".
E. בִּקַּשְׁנוּ... וְצִוִּינוּ... "דַּבְּרוּ אֵלֵינוּ". F. בִּקַּשְׁתְּ...
וְצִוִּית... "דַּבְּרוּ אֵלַי". G. בִּקַּשְׁתֶּן... וְצִוִּיתֶן... "דַּבְּרוּ
אֵלֵינוּ". H. הוּא בִּקֵּשׁ... וְצִוָּה... "דַּבְּרוּ אֵלַי". I. הֵמָּה
בִּקְּשׁוּ... וְצִוּוּ... "דַּבְּרוּ אֵלֵינוּ". 6. A. דָּוִד סָפַר אֶת
כָּל כֵּלָיו וּמִסְפָּרָם לֹא גָּדוֹל... B. סָפַרְנוּ אֶת כָּל כֵּלֵינוּ...
C. שָׂרָה סָפְרָה אֶת כָּל כֵּלֶיהָ. D. הֵן סָפְרוּ אֶת כָּל
כְּלֵיהֶן... E. סְפַרְתֶּם אֶת כָּל כְּלֵיכֶם... F. סָפַרְתְּ
אֶת כָּל כֵּלַיִךְ... G. סָפַרְתָּ אֶת כָּל כֵּלֶיךָ... H. הֵמָּה
סָפְרוּ אֶת כָּל כְּלֵיהֶם... I. סְפַרְתֶּן אֶת כָּל כְּלֵיכֶן...

1. The mother brought up the lad and he grew up. A. You brought up the lad and he grew up. 2. There were many animals in the field and the lad counted them. A. There were many animals in the field and the daughters counted them. B. ... and I counted ...... 3. Our father will remember his good deeds and he will recount them to us. A. The old men will remember their good deeds and they will recount them to us.4. And the man said, saying, "I am commanding you to do all the commandments." A.And the man said , saying,"The judges are commanding you to do all the ..." 5. She sought the truth, and commanded the people, saying, "Speak to me!" A. I sought the truth and commanded the people, ... 6. I counted all my vessels, and their number was not great. A. David counted all his vessels...

Exercise 3. 1. he will come, she came or is coming—f, sg, to come, I came, coming—m, pl, come! 2. to seek, we sought, they/you will seek, seeking—m, pl, he sought, we will seek 3. you saw, you will see, seeing—f, sg, to see, they saw 4. I will give, give!, you gave, giving—f, pl, she gave, to give 5. you will command, they commanded, commanding—m, sg, to command, command!, you commanded, I will command 6. speaking—f, sg, speak!, you spoke, to speak, speak!, I will speak, you will speak 7. he recounted, he counted, I counted, I recounted, to count, to recount, they will recount, they count, counting—m, sg, recounting—f, sg 8. bringing up—m, pl, you will grow up, you/they will raise, to raise, grow up, grow up! he grew up, he will raise, she raised, we grew up, they grew up

Exercise 4 1. סְפַרְתֶּם, מְסַפְּרִים, תְּסַפְּרוּ, סַפֵּר סִפַּרְתֶּם,

סֵפֶר תְּסַפְּרוּ, סַפְּרוּ 2. בִּקַּשְׁתָּ, מְבַקֵּשׁ, תְּבַקֵּשׁ, בַּקֵּשׁ
בִּקַּשְׁתָּ, בַּקֵּשׁ תְּבַקֵּשׁ 3. צִוָּה, מְצַוֶּה, יְצַוֶּה, צַוֵּה
צַוָּה, צַוֵּה יְצַוֶּה 4. גִּדְּלוּ, מְגַדְּלִים, יְגַדְּלוּ, גַּדֵּל גִּדְּלוּ,
יְגַדְּלוּ 5. סִפַּרְנוּ, מְסַפְּרִים, נְסַפֵּר, סַפֵּר סִפַּרְנוּ, סַפֵּר
נְסַפֵּר; סָפְרוּ, סוֹפְרִים, יִסְפְּרוּ, סְפוֹר סָפְרוּ, סְפוֹר יִסְפְּרוּ
6. בָּנִיתִי, בּוֹנֶה, אֶבְנֶה, בָּנֹה בָּנִיתִי, בָּנָה אֶבְנֶה 7. שָׁבָה,
שָׁבָה, תָּשׁוּב, שׁוֹב תָּשׁוּב, שׁוֹב שָׁבָה 8. בִּקֵּשׁ, מְבַקֵּשׁ,
יְבַקֵּשׁ, בַּקֵּשׁ בִּקֵּשׁ, בַּקֵּשׁ יְבַקֵּשׁ

1. You (related, relate, will relate, surely related, will surely relate, relate!) to the nations about the covenant. 2. Upon your return from the wilderness, you (sought, seek, will seek, surely sought, will surely seek) your family. 3. He (commanded, commands, will command, surely commanded, will surely command) his sons, saying: "Give water from the Jordan to the old men." 4. They (raised, raise, will raise, surely raised, will surely raise) many beasts in Egypt. 5. We (recounted, are recounting, will recount, surely recounted, will surely recount) to them about the people who (counted, are counting, will count, surely counted, will surely count) the money. 6. I (built, am building, will build, surely built, will surely build) a great city in Canaan. 7. She (returned, is returning, will return, surely returned, will surely return) from Egypt to see her mother. 8. Jacob (sought, seeks, will seek, surely sought, will surely seek) to know the number of his tents.

Exercise 5 1. דִּבַּרְתִּי דְּבָרִים רַבִּים אֶל אַנְשֵׁי הָעִיר.
2. דִּבַּרְתָּ דְּבָרִים רַבִּים אֶל אַנְשֵׁי הָעִיר. 3. תְּדַבֵּר דְּבָרִים
רַבִּים אֶל אַנְשֵׁי הָעִיר. 4. עוֹדָן מְבַקְשׁוֹת אֶת הָאֱמֶת.
5. עוֹדֶנּוּ מְבַקְשִׁים אֶת הָאֱמֶת. 6. עוֹדְךָ מְבַקֶּשֶׁת אֶת
הָאֱמֶת. 7. צִוִּיתִי אַתָּה לֵאמֹר: "לְכִי!" 8. הִיא צִוְּתָה אֹתוֹ
לֵאמֹר: "לֵךְ!" 9. צִוִּינוּ אֶתְכֶם לֵאמֹר: "לְכוּ!"

Exercise 6 1. כ.ת.ב. 2. ק.ו.ם. 3. ס.פ.ר. 4. ר.א.ה. 5. ע.ש.ה.
6. א.ה.ב. 7. י.ד.ע. 8. ב.ו.א. 9. צ.ו.ה. 10. ג.ד.ל. 11. נ.ת.ן.
12. ד.ב.ר. 13. א.ה.ב. 14. ע.ש.ה. 15. צ.ו.ה. 16. ג.ד.ל.
17. נ.ת.ן. 18. ר.א.ה. 19. ד.ב.ר. 20. י.ד.ע.

פִּעֵל forms: 3, 9, 12, 15, 16, 19
1. she wrote 2. she arose or arising—f, sg 3. recounting—f, pl 4. see! 5. and she did or you did 6. and I loved 7. to love 8. we will come 9. command! 10. grow up 11. you gave 12. you will speak or they will speak 13. to love 14. you did 15. commanding—m, pl 16. I will bring up 17. give 18. and he saw 19. you spoke 20. you will know

Exercise 7. "The Fisherman and His Wife" There was a fisherman who lived in a very small house with his wife, and they had no money. The man went daily to the sea to fish, and he returned in the evening to his house, to give food to his wife. And it came to pass that one morning the fisherman went to the sea and fished there. And in the evening, the fisherman caught a big fish. And the fish said to the fisherman: "Let me return to my house under the water and I will give you all that you seek from me." The fisherman answered the fish, saying: "I must give my wife food. If you give me food instead of you, I will send you to your house under the water." And the fish gave the fisherman wine and bread and fruit, and the man returned to his house. And his wife said to him: "What is this food?" And he recounted to his wife everything that the fish had done for him. And his wife commanded him: "Go back to the sea! Order the fish to build a big house for us, and to give us money." So the fisherman went to the sea and said: "Fish, come! Come up to me!" And the fish came up and said: "What do you request from me?" And he told the fish everything that his wife had said. The fish said: "Return to your house, I will do all that you have requested." And the fisherman returned to his house and behold, everything was as he had requested from the fish. And his wife said to him: "Go back to the sea! Order the fish to make us like kings, and we will rule over all the land." And the fisherman went, and he came to the sea, and he said: "Fish, come! Come up to me!" And the fish came up and said: "What do you request from me?" And he told the fish everything his wife had said. And the fish said: "Return to your house, and everything will be

as you have requested." So the fisherman returned to his house, and behold, everything was as the fish had said. And the wife of the fisherman said to him: "Now we are like kings. Why should we not be gods? Go back to the sea! Order the fish to make us gods, and we shall rule over both the earth, and heaven too." The fisherman answered his wife: "We are like kings. We must only seek things that belong to people. I will not go to ask this thing from the fish." The woman did not pay attention to his words, and said to him: "Go back to the sea! Do what I have commanded you!" So the fisherman went, and came to the sea, and said: "Fish, come! Come up to me!" And the fish came up and said: "What do you seek from me?" And he told the fish everything his wife had said. The fish said: "You have not sought well! A man is not able to be a god. Now, you will not be gods, and you will not be kings, and I will also take both your house and your money from you. Go back to your wicked wife. You have asked for everything, and now you will not have a thing." So the fisherman went back to his little house, and the fish did not come up to him from the sea again.

Exercise 8 1. שָׁמַרְתָּ 2. דִּבַּרְתָּ 3. כָּתַבְנוּ 4. בִּקַּשְׁנוּ 5. בָּנִינוּ
6. צִוִּינוּ 7. תִּשְׁמֹר 8. תְּדַבֵּר 9. יִכְתְּבוּ 10. יְבַקְשׁוּ 11. תִּבְנוּ
12. תְּצַוּוּ 13. תִּשְׁמְרוּ 14. מְדַבֶּרֶת 15. כּוֹתֶבֶת 16. מְבַקְשִׁים
17. בּוֹנִים 18. תְּצַוֶּה 19. תְּדַבֵּר 20. דִּבְּרָה 21. בִּקֵּשׁ
22. יְבַקֵּשׁ 23. צִוָּה 24. יְצַוֶּה

1. you guarded 2. you spoke 3. we wrote 4. we sought 5. we built 6. we commanded 7. she will guard 8. she will speak 9. they will write 10. they will seek 11. you will build 12. you will command 13. you will guard 14. speaking—f, sg 15. writing—f, sg 16. seeking—m, pl 17. building—m, pl 18. you will command 19. you will speak 20. she spoke 21. he sought 22. he will seek 23. he commanded 24. he will command.

Chapter 26

Exercise 2 1. A. הַנְּעָרוֹת הִשְׁלִיכוּ אֲבָנִים אֶל תּוֹךְ הַיַּרְדֵּן.
B. . . . הִשְׁלַכְתְּ C. . . . הִשְׁלַכְנוּ D. הוּא הִשְׁלִיךְ
E. הִשְׁלַכְתֶּם F. הִיא הִשְׁלִיכָה G. . . . הִשְׁלַכְתִּי . . .
H. . . . הִשְׁלַכְתֶּן I. . . . 2. A. הִשְׁלַכְתָּ אֲנִי מַלְבִּישׁ אֶת
בְּנוֹתַי בַּבֹּקֶר. B. הוּא מַלְבִּישׁ אֶת בְּנוֹתָיו C. . . . אַתֶּן
מַלְבִּישׁוֹת אֶת בְּנוֹתֵיכֶן D. . . . אַתְּ מַלְבִּישָׁה אֶת בְּנוֹתַיִךְ
E. . . . הִיא מַלְבִּישָׁה אֶת בְּנוֹתֶיהָ F. . . . הֵם מַלְבִּישִׁים
אֶת בְּנוֹתֵיהֶם G. . . . אַתֶּם מַלְבִּישִׁים אֶת בְּנוֹתֵיכֶם
H. אֲנַחְנוּ מַלְבִּישִׁים אֶת בְּנוֹתֵינוּ I. אַתָּה מַלְבִּישׁ אֶת
בְּנוֹתֶיךָ . . . 3. A. הָעָם יַמְלִיךְ אֹתוֹ וּמָלַךְ עָלָיו כָּל יְמֵי
חַיָּיו B. אַנְשֵׁי כְּנַעַן יַמְלִיכוּ . . . וּמָלַךְ עֲלֵיהֶם . . .
C. תַּמְלִיכוּ . . . וּמָלַךְ עֲלֵיכֶם D. . . . אַמְלִיךְ . . . וּמָלַךְ
עָלַי . . . E. תַּמְלַכְנָה . . . וּמָלַךְ עֲלֵיכֶן F. תַּמְלִיכִי . . .
וּמָלַךְ עָלַיִךְ . . . G. תַּמְלִיךְ . . . וּמָלַךְ עָלֶיךָ H. . . . הֵנָּה
תַּמְלַכְנָה . . . וּמָלַךְ עֲלֵיהֶן I. . . . הִיא תַּמְלִיךְ וּמָלַךְ
עָלֶיהָ . . . 4. A. . . . הָאָב גִּדֵּל אֶת הַבָּנִים וְכַאֲשֶׁר הַבָּנִים
גָּדְלוּ הֵם הִגְדִּילוּ אֶת בֵּית מִשְׁפַּחְתָּם. B. . . . אֲנִי וְכַאֲשֶׁר
גָּדַלְתִּי הִגְדַּלְתִּי אֶת בֵּית מִשְׁפַּחְתִּי. C. . . . אַתֵּן וְכַאֲשֶׁר
גָּדַלְתֶּן הִגְדַּלְתֶּן אֶת בֵּית מִשְׁפַּחְתְּכֶן. D. . . . אַתָּ וְכַאֲשֶׁר
גָּדַלְתָּ הִגְדַּלְתָּ אֶת בֵּית מִשְׁפַּחְתֶּךָ. E. . . . אֲתָנוּ וְכַאֲשֶׁר
גָּדַלְנוּ הִגְדַּלְנוּ אֶת בֵּית מִשְׁפַּחְתֵּנוּ F. . . . אֶת הַבָּנוֹת וְכַאֲשֶׁר
הַבָּנוֹת גָּדְלוּ הֵנָּה הִגְדִּילוּ אֶת בֵּית מִשְׁפַּחְתָּן. G. . . . אֶתְכֶם
וְכַאֲשֶׁר גְּדַלְתֶּם הִגְדַּלְתֶּם אֶת בֵּית מִשְׁפַּחְתְּכֶם. H. . . .

אִתְּךָ וְכַאֲשֶׁר גָּדַלְתָּ אֶת בֵּית מִשְׁפַּחְתְּךָ. I .... ‏אֶת
הַנַּעֲרָה וְכַאֲשֶׁר הַנַּעֲרָה גָּדְלָה הִיא הִגְדִּילָה אֶת בֵּית
מִשְׁפַּחְתָּהּ. 5. A. וַיַּגֵּד הָאִישׁ לָהֶם לֵאמֹר: "אֶת מַעֲשֵׂי
אֲבוֹתֵיכֶם יַזְכִּירוּ לָכֶם וְזָכֹר תִּזְכְּרוּ אֹתָם". B. .... נַזְכִּיר
לָכֶם .... C. .... הִנֵּה תַּזְכַּרְנָה לָכֶם .... D. .... הִיא
תַּזְכִּיר .... F. .... הוּא יַזְכִּיר .... 6. A. הִצַּלְתִּי אֶת אַנְשֵׁי
הָעִיר הַהִיא. B. הִנֵּה הִצִּילוּ .... C. הִצַּלְתָּ .... D. הִיא
הִצִּילָה .... E. הִצַּלְנוּ .... F. הִצַּלְתֶּן .... G. הֵמָּה הִצִּילוּ
.... H. .... הִצַּלְתָּ .... I. .... הִצַּלְתֶּם

1. The sons threw stones into the Jordan. A. The young women threw stones into the Jordan. 2. These women are dressing their daughters in the morning. A. I am dressing my . . . 3. We will make him king and he will rule over us all the days of his life. A. The nation will make him king and he will rule over it all the days of his life. B. The people of Canaan will make him king . . . and he will rule over them . . . C. You will make . . . 4. The father brought up the lad, and when the lad grew up he made the house of his family great. A. The father brought up the sons, and when the sons grew up they made the house of their family great. B. . . . me, and when I grew up I . . . 5. And the man told them saying, "I will mention to you the deeds of your fathers and you will surely remember them" A. And the man told them, saying: "They will . . . 6. Jacob rescued the people of that city. A. I rescued the people of that city. B. They rescued . . .

Exercise 3 1. הִשְׁלַכְתָּ, מַשְׁלִיכָה, תַּשְׁלִיכִי, הַשְׁלֵךְ הִשְׁלַכְתְּ,
הַשְׁלֵךְ תַּשְׁלִיכִי, הַשְׁלִיכִי. 2. הִצַּלְתֶּם, מַצִּילִים, תַּצִּילוּ,
הַצֵּל הַצַּלְתֶּם, הַצֵּל תַּצִּילוּ, הַצִּילוּ! 3. הִמְלִיךְ, מַמְלִיךְ,
יַמְלִיךְ, הַמְלֵךְ הִמְלִיךְ יַמְלִיךְ 4. הִזְכַּרְתָּ, מַזְכִּיר,
תַּזְכִּיר, הַזְכֵּר הִזְכַּרְתָּ, הַזְכֵּר תַּזְכִּיר, הַזְכֵּר; זָכְרוּ,
זוֹכְרִים, יִזְכְּרוּ, זָכֹר זָכְרוּ זִכְרוּ 5. בְּקַשְׁתֶּן,
מְבַקְשׁוֹת, תְּבַקֵּשְׁנָה, בַּקֵּשׁ בְּקַשְׁתֶּן, בַּקֵּשׁ תְּבַקֵּשְׁנָה,
בַּקֵּשְׁנָה! 6. נָתְנוּ, נוֹתְנִים, יִתְּנוּ, נָתוֹן נָתְנוּ, נָתֹן נָתְנוּ 7. קַמְנוּ,
קָמִים, נָקוּם, קוֹם קַמְנוּ, קוֹם נָקוּם

You (threw, throw, will throw, surely threw, will surely throw, throw!) your shoes on the ground. 2. You (saved, will save, surely saved, will surely save, save!) the women from the evil men. 3. The nation (crowned, is crowning, will crown, surely crowned, surely will crown) David as a king over Israel. 4. You (reminded, are reminding, will remind, surely reminded, will surely remind, remind!) the old ones of Bethlehem and they (remembered, are remembering, will remember, surely remembered, surely will remember) the people there. 5. You (sought, seek, will seek, surely sought, surely will seek!) to save the maiden from the midst of the sea. 6. They (gave, give, will give, surely gave, will surely give) new clothes to the women to dress their sons. 7. We (arose, arise, will arise, surely arose, will surely arise) to tell the truth to all the city.
Exercise 4. 1. And the lad ran to the city and told the people all he had seen. 2. And she saw his good works and made him king. 3. And the mother gave her son water to drink and dressed him in new garments. 4. And he heard the voice of a woman, and he saw her in the water, and he turned aside from the road and saved her, and took her to the house of her father.

Shortened Verbs 1. וַיָּרָץ, וַיַּגֵּד 2. וַתֵּרֶא, וַתַּמְלֵךְ 3. וַתַּלְבֵּשׁ
4. וַיַּרְא, וַיָּסַר, וַיַּצֵּל

Exercise 5 1. ג.ד.ל 2. נ.צ.ל 3. ש.י.ר 4. ב.נ.ה 5. ד.ב.ר
6. ג.ד.ל 7. ש.ל.ך 8. ז.כ.ר 9. ב.נ.ה 10. ג.ד.ל 11. נ.צ.ל
12. ז.כ.ר 13. ש.י.ר 14. ד.ב.ר 15. ש.ל.ך

1. I will grow up 2. saving—m, sg 3. to sing 4. he will build 5. we spoke 6. make great! 7. to throw 8. I reminded 9. building—f, sg 10. making great—m, pl 11. we rescued 12. reminding—f, pl 13. she

sang/singing—f, sg 14. I will speak 15. they threw
Exercise 6. 1. Next week they will make me king because . . . 2. Year by year I will tell my family . . . 3. Daily I make my name great because . . . 4. My brothers threw stones at me because . . . 5. You rescued the lad who . . .

Exercise 7 הָיָה, בִּקֵּשׁ, בָּא, הָיָה, לָבַשׁ, עָשׂוֹת, יוֹכְלוּ,
רְאוֹת, תֵּן, אֶעֱשֶׂה, לָדַעַת, עֲשֵׂה, אַלְבֵּשׁ, אַגְדִּיל, לָקַח,
שָׁלַח, רְאוֹת, הָיוּ, רוֹאֶה, יָדַע, יוֹכְלוּ, רְאוֹת, שָׁב, הִגִּיד,
צַוֶּה, אֶלְבַּשׁ, בּוֹא, רְאוֹת, יָדַע, יוֹכְלוּ, רְאוֹת, בָּא, רָאָה,
אָמַר, הָיְתָה, בָּאָה, הִגִּידָה, רָאָה, צַוֶּה, הָלַךְ

There was an evil man who sought much money, and his name was Aaron. One day, Aaron came to a great city. In this city there was a king who always wore new clothes. So Aaron went to the king's house and said: "I can make clothes for you that are not like any others in all your land. Only wise men can see these clothes. Give me money, and I will make them for you." The king said to himself: "I will be a very great king. I will know who is wise and who is not wise." And the king answered and said: "Behold, the money, and now make for me these clothes, and I will wear them and make my name great in the land." Aaron took the king's money and went to make the clothes for the king. After these things the king sent his lad (servant) to Aaron to see the clothes he was making. When the lad came to Aaron's house, he saw that there were no clothes there. The lad said to himself: "I don't see the clothes." The lad knew that only wise men could see the clothes. So the lad said to Aaron: "I see the new clothes. There are none like them in all the land." The lad returned to his king, and told him that he had seen the king's new clothes. The king commanded all his people, saying: "Next week I will put on my new clothes. You must come to see me." All the people knew that only wise men could see these clothes. On that week, the people came to the house of the king. And behold, all the people saw that there were no clothes on the king. Every man said to himself: "I am not wise, because I don't see the king's clothes." Among all the people there was a young woman that had come with her father. She said: "See! The king doesn't have clothes!" All the people knew that the young woman had told the truth. The king saw that he was naked, and ran inside his house. He commanded his lads to seek Aaron, and to kill him. But Aaron was not in the city. He had gone, and all the king's money with him.

Exercise 8 1. פָּתַחְתָּ 2. הִשְׁלַכְתָּ 3. הִצַּלְתָּ 4. זוֹכְרוֹת
5. מַזְכִּירוֹת 6. מַגִּידוֹת 7. תִּמְלֹךְ 8. תַּמְלִיךְ 9. תַּגִּיד
10. גָּדַל 11. גַּדֵּל 12. הִגְדִּיל 13. לוֹבֵשׁ 14. מַלְבִּישׁ 15. מַצִּיל
16. אֶכְתֹּב 17. אֲסַפֵּר 18. אַשְׁלִיךְ 19. אָסוֹר 20. אֶרְאֶה
21. אֲצַוֶּה 22. אַצִּיל 23. שׁוֹמֵעַ 24. מַמְלִיךְ

1. you opened 2. you threw 3. you saved 4. remembering—f, pl 5. reminding—f, pl 6. telling—f, pl 7. she will rule 8. she will crown 9. she will tell 10. grow up 11. raise 12. make great 13. wearing—m, sg 14. dressing—m, sg 15. saving—m, sg 16. I will write 17. I will recount 18. I will throw 19. I will turn aside 20. I will see 21. I will command 22. I will rescue 23. hearing—m, sg 24. crowning—m, sg

Chapter 27

Exercise 2 1. A. בָּעֵת הַהִיא הוּא הֵקִים בַּיִת חָדָשׁ בָּעִיר.
B. בָּעֵת הַהִיא הִנֵּה הֵקִימוּ בַּיִת חָדָשׁ בָּעִיר. C. ....
D. .... הֲקִימוֹת/הֲקַמְתָּ E. .... הֲקִימוֹנוּ/הֲקַמְנוּ ....
F. .... הִיא הֵקִימָה G. .... הֲקִימוֹת/הֲקַמְתְּ ....
H. .... הֲקִימוֹתֶן/הֲקַמְתֶּן I. .... הֲקִימוֹתִי/הֲקַמְתִּי
הֵקִימוּ 2. A. .... הַשַּׂר צִוָּה אֶת אֲנָשָׁיו לְהָשִׁיב אֶת אַנְשֵׁי
בֵּית לֶחֶם. B. .... לְהַגְדִּיל C. .... לְהָבִיא
D. .... לְהַזְכִּיר E. .... לְהָסִיר
3. A. .... בָּעֵת הַהִיא, אָסִיר אֶת בְּגָדָיו וְאַלְבִּישׁ אֹתוֹ

B. ... הוּא יָסִיר ... וַיַּלְבִּישׁ ... C. ...

D. ... וַתִּלְבַּשְׁנָה ... תָּסִיר ... וַתַּלְבִּישׁ

E. ... הִיא תָּסִיר ... וַתַּלְבִּישׁ ... F. ... הֵנָּה

G. ... וַתִּלְבַּשְׁנָה ... נָסִיר ... וְנַלְבִּישׁ

H. ... תָּסִירוּ ... וְתַלְבִּישׁוּ ... I. ... תָּסִירִי

וְתַלְבִּישִׁי ... 4. A. ... B. אַתְּ מְכִינָה אֶת הָאֹכֶל לַשָּׂר. אַתֶּם

C. ... מְכִינִים D. ... אַתָּה מֵכִין E. אֲנִי

מֵכִין/מְכִינָה F. ... אַתֶּן מְכִינוֹת G. ... הוּא מֵכִין

H. הִיא מְכִינָה 5. A. ... הֵמָּה יָשׁוּבוּ מֵהֶהָרִים וְיָבִיאוּ לָנוּ

כֶּסֶף וְזָהָב. B. הַנָּשִׁים תָּשֹׁבְנָה מֵהֶהָרִים וְתָבֶאנָה לָנוּ

... C. אָשׁוּב ... וְאָבִיא ... D. הִיא תָּשׁוּב ... וְתָבִיא

E. תָּשׁוּב ... וְתָבִיא F. תְּשׁוּבֶינָה ... וְתָבֶאנָה

G. נָשׁוּב ... וְנָבִיא H. תָּשׁוּבִי ... וְתָבִיאִי

I. ... תָּשׁוּבוּ ... וְתָבִיאוּ 6. A. הֵם שָׁבוּ מִמִּצְרַיִם וְהֵשִׁיבוּ

אֶת הַנַּעַר לְמִשְׁפַּחְתּוֹ. B. שַׁבְתֶּן ... וְהֲשִׁיבוֹתֶן

C. שַׁבְנוּ ... וְהֱשִׁיבֹנוּ D. הוּא שָׁב ... וְהֵשִׁיב ...

E. הֵנָּה שָׁבוּ ... וְהֵשִׁיבוּ F. ... שַׁבְתִּי ... וַהֲשִׁיבוֹתִי

G. הִיא שָׁבָה ... וְהֵשִׁיבָה H. ... שַׁבְתֶּם ... וַהֲשִׁיבוֹתֶם

I. ... שַׁבְתָּ ... וְהֵשַׁבְתָּ 7. A. אֵינְכֶם מְבִינִים אֶת

אֲשֶׁר הֵנָּה סִפְּרוּ לָכֶם. B. אֵינֶנּוּ מֵבִין ... לוֹ C. אֵינְךָ

מֵבִין ... לְךָ D. אֵינָן מְבִינוֹת ... לָהֶן E. אֵינֵךְ מְבִינָה

F. ... לָךְ G. אֵינְכֶן מְבִינוֹת ... לָכֶן. G. אֵינֶנָּה מְבִינָה

לָהּ. H. אֵינֶנּוּ מְבִינִים ... לָנוּ. I. אֵינָם מְבִינִים ... לָהֶם.

1. At that time, you established a new house in the city. A. At that time, he established a ... 2. The officer commanded his men to rescue the people of Bethlehem. A. The officer commanded his men to bring back the people of Bethlehem. B. .... to make great ... C. to bring ... 3. At that time, they will remove his clothes and they will dress him in clothes of an officer. A. At that time, I will remove his clothes and I will dress him in clothes of ... 4. We are preparing the food for the chief. A. You are ... 5. He will return from the mountains and will bring us silver and gold. A. They will return ... 6. You returned from Egypt and brought the lad back to his family. A. They returned from Egypt and brought the lad back to his family. B. You ... 7. I do not understand what they recounted to me. A. You do not understand what they recounted to you. B. He does ...

Exercise 3 1. סָרַתֶּם, סָרִים, תָּסוּרוּ, סוֹר סָרַתֶּם, סוֹר

תָּסוּרוּ, סוּרוּ; הֲסִירוֹתֶם, מְסִירִים, תָּסִירוּ, הָסֵר הֲסִירוֹתֶם,

הָסֵר תָּסִירוּ, הָסִירוּ 2. שַׁבְתֶּן, שָׁבוֹת, תָּשֹׁבְנָה, שׁוֹב שַׁבְתֶּן,

שׁוֹב תָּשֹׁבְנָה, שֹׁבְנָה; הֲשִׁיבוֹתֶן, מְשִׁיבוֹת, תָּשֵׁבְנָה, הָשֵׁב

הֲשִׁיבוֹתֶן, הָשֵׁב תָּשֵׁבְנָה, הָשֵׁבְנָה 3. בָּאת, בָּאָה, תָּבוֹאִי,

בּוֹא בָּאת, בּוֹא תָּבוֹאִי, בּוֹאִי; הֲבֵאת, מְבִיאָה, תָּבִיאִי,

הָבֵא הֲבֵאת, הָבֵא תָּבִיאִי, הָבִיאִי 4. קָמוּ, קָמִים, יָקוּמוּ,

קוֹם קָמוּ, קוֹם יָקוּמוּ; הֲקִימוּ, מְקִימִים, יָקִימוּ, הָקֵם

הֲקִימוּ, הָקֵם יָקִימוּ. 5. הִגִּיד, מַגִּיד, יַגִּיד, הַגֵּד הִגִּיד, הַגֵּד

יַגִּיד 6. בִּקְשָׁה, מְבַקֶּשֶׁת, תְּבַקֵּשׁ, בַּקֵּשׁ בִּקְשָׁה, בַּקֵּשׁ תְּבַקֵּשׁ

7. הֲבִינוֹנוּ, מְבִינִים, נָבִין, הָבֵן הֲבִינוֹנוּ, הָבֵן נָבִין

1. You (turned aside, are turning aside, will turn aside, surely turned aside, will surely turn aside, turn aside!) to see the top of the mountain and (removed, are removing, will remove, surely removed, will surely remove, remove!) the stones from the road. 2. You (returned, are returning, will return, surely returned, will surely return, return!) to the land of your fathers and (brought back, are bringing back, will bring back, surely brought back, will surely bring back, bring back!) with you the gold and the silver. 3. You (came, are coming, will come, surely came, will surely come, come!) to see my father and (brought, are bringing, will bring, surely brought, will surely bring, bring!) him fruit and wine. 4. They (arose, are arising, will arise, surely arose, will surely arise) and (set up, are setting up, will set up, surely set up, will surely set up) the gate of their city. 5. The officer (told, is telling, will tell, surely told, will surely tell) his men what they must do. 6. She (sought, is seeking, will seek, surely sought, will surely seek) to know the truth. 7. We (understood, are understanding, will understand, surely understood, will surely understand) the words of the judge.

Exercise 4. 1. And the wise man came at that time from the top of the mountain, and he brought his son with him. 2. And the officer returned from Canaan, and he brought back the gold with him, and he told us all that he had heard there. 3. And the evil men sought to take away the officer, and David saved him. 4. And the man ate and drank at eveningtime and the woman removed the food. 5. And the man went to Jerusalem, and he built his house there, and made his family great.

Shortened Verbs: 1. וַיָּבֹא 2. וַיֵּשֶׁב, וַיָּשָׁב, וַיַּגֵּד 3. וַיַּצֵּל

4. וַיֵּשְׁתְּ, וַתָּסַר 5. וַיִּבֶן, וַיְגַדֵּל

Exercise 5 1. ב.ח.ר–פָּעַל 2. ג.נ.ב–פָּעַל 3. ז.כ.ר–פָּעַל

4. י.ד.ע–פָּעַל 5. א.כ.ל–פָּעַל 6. י.כ.ל–פָּעַל 7. י.שׁ.ב–

פָּעַל 8. שׁ.ו.ב–פָּעַל 9. שׁ.ו.ב–הִפְעִיל 10. שׁ.ו.ב–הִפְעִיל

11. ב.ו.א–פָּעַל 12. ב.ו.א–פָּעַל 13. ב.ו.א–הִפְעִיל

14. ב.ו.א–הִפְעִיל 15. ק.ו.ם–הִפְעִיל 16. ק.ו.ם–פָּעַל

17. ר.א.ה–פָּעַל 18. ר.א.ה–פָּעַל 19. כ.ו.ן–הִפְעִיל

20. כ.ו.ן–הִפְעִיל

1. I chose 2. you/she will steal 3. remembering—m,pl 4. to know 5. eating—m,sg 6. I will be able 7. I sat 8. I returned 9. he will bring back 10. you/they will bring back 11. they came 12. come 13. they will bring 14. bringing—,sg 15. to set up 16. they arose 17. they saw 18. see! 19. preparing—f,pl 20. I will prepare

Exercise 6. There was a man who lived in Moab, and his name was Simon. He was very strong, but he was not very wise. Now Simon sought to make his name great. And he heard that the men of Babel were building a tower, with its top in the heavens. And Simon said to himself: "I will go to Babel, and I will build the tower. I will be able to command the men to do everything, because I am very strong." And Simon went, and he came to Babel, and he saw the men who were building the tower. And Simon said to them: "I am Simon! I have come to be chief over you. I can set up great stones for the tower, because I am very strong." And one man answered: "Buenos Dias!" And Simon said: "What?" And another man answered: "Aloha!" And Simon said: "What?" And another man said: "I can't understand a word you're saying, why don't you just speak in English?" And Simon said: "What are you saying? I don't understand you." And one old man heard Simon's words, and ran to him and said: "You speak like me! There are no men in this place who speak like me!" And the old man related to Simon, saying: "When I got up in the morning, and heard the words of my wife, I didn't understand what she was saying. I sought to speak with my sons, and they didn't understand my words. I commanded them to build the tower with the men of the city, and they did not obey me. I went to relate the evil deeds of my sons to the men of my city, and all of them did not understand me. All the men of this city do not understand one another." And Simon said: "I have come to be chief of the men who are building the tower. But I can't command them if they will not understand what I say to them. I will go to another city, to make my name great there. And Simon said: "Shalom" and went. The old man anwered: "Shalom!" Another man answered: "Adios!" Another man answered: "Bon voyage!" Another man answered: "Ciao!" Another man answered: "See you later!"

Exercise 7 1. שָׁכַחְתָּ 2. זָכַרְתָּ 3. הִזְכַּרְתָּ 4. הִצַּלְתָּ 5. בָּאתֶם

6. הֲבֵאתֶם 7. הֲכִינוֹתָם 8. הֲשִׁיבוֹנוּ/הֵשַׁבְנוּ 9. רָאִינוּ

10. נִשְׁתָּה 11. נִסְפֹּר 12. נְסַפֵּר 13. אֲדַבֵּר 14. אֲצַוֶּה

303

15. מֵקִים 19. מְסִירָה 18. מַשְׁלִיכָה 17. אַגְדִּיל 16. אַגְדֵּל

20. קָם 21. קוּם 22. הָקֵם 23. הַקִּמִי 24 הֲקָמְנָה

1. you forgot 2. you remembered 3. you reminded 4. you saved 5. you came 6. you brought 7. you prepared 8. we brought back 9. we saw 10. we will drink 11. we will count 12. we will recount 13. I will speak 14. I will command 15. I will raise 16. I will make great 17. throwing—f, sg 18. removing—f, sg 19. establishing—m, sg 20. arising—m, sg 21. arise! 22. set up! 23. set up! 24. set up!

Chapter 28

Exercise 2 1. A. כַּאֲשֶׁר נִלְחַמְתֶּם בַּמִּלְחָמָה, נִשְׁפַּךְ דָם רַב. B. כַּאֲשֶׁר נִלְחַמְתִּי . . . C. כַּאֲשֶׁר הֵמָּה נִלְחֲמוּ . . . D. כַּאֲשֶׁר נִלְחַמְתֶּן . . . E. כַּאֲשֶׁר הוּא נִלְחַם . . . F. כַּאֲשֶׁר נִלְחַמְתְּ . . . G. כַּאֲשֶׁר הִיא נִלְחֲמָה . . . H. כַּאֲשֶׁר נִלְחַמְתָּ . . . I. . . . כַּאֲשֶׁר הֵנָּה נִלְחֲמוּ . . . 2. A. תִּזָּכְרוּ כִּי הֱיִיתֶם אֲנָשִׁים גִּבּוֹרִים וְהָיוּ לָכֶם חֲרָבוֹת רַבּוֹת. B. הֵמָּה יִזָּכְרוּ כִּי הָיוּ אֲנָשִׁים גִּבּוֹרִים וְהָיוּ לָהֶם חֲרָבוֹת רַבּוֹת. C. הוּא יִזָּכֵר כִּי הָיָה אִישׁ גִּבּוֹר וְהָיוּ לוֹ חֲרָבוֹת רַבּוֹת. D. נִזָּכֵר כִּי הָיִינוּ אֲנָשִׁים גִּבּוֹרִים וְהָיוּ לָנוּ חֲרָבוֹת רַבּוֹת. E. תִּזָּכֵר כִּי הָיִיתָ אִישׁ גִּבּוֹר וְהָיוּ לְךָ חֲרָבוֹת רַבּוֹת. F. אֶזָּכֵר כִּי הָיִיתִי אִישׁ גִּבּוֹר וְהָיוּ לִי חֲרָבוֹת רַבּוֹת. 3. A. אִישׁ מִמִּשְׁפַּחְתֵּנוּ יָבָּחֵר כִּי הוּא מַלְאַךְ הַמֶּלֶךְ. B. . . . יִלָּקַח . . . C. . . . יִשָּׁכַח . . . D. . . . יִזָּכֵר . . . 4. A. אֵינֶנִּי נִשְׁכָּח כִּי נָתַתִּי אֵילִים רַבִּים לְמַלְכִּי כְּמִנְחָה. B. אֵינֶנּוּ נִשְׁכָּח כִּי הוּא נָתַן אֵילִים רַבִּים לְמַלְכּוֹ. C. . . . אֵינֵךְ נִשְׁכַּחַת כִּי נָתַתְּ אֵילִים רַבִּים לְמַלְכֵּךְ. D. . . . אֵינְכֶם נִשְׁכָּחִים כִּי נְתַתֶּם אֵילִים רַבִּים לְמַלְכְּכֶם. E. . . . אֵינָן נִשְׁכָּחוֹת כִּי הֵנָּה נָתְנוּ אֵילִים רַבִּים לְמַלְכָּן. F. . . . אֵינֶנּוּ נִשְׁכָּחִים כִּי נָתַנּוּ אֵילִים רַבִּים לְמַלְכֵּנוּ. G. . . . אֵינְכֶן נִשְׁכָּחוֹת כִּי נְתַתֶּן אֵילִים רַבִּים לְמַלְכְּכֶן. H. . . . אֵינְךָ נִשְׁכָּח כִּי נָתַתָּ אֵילִים רַבִּים לְמַלְכְּךָ. I. . . . אֵינֶנָּה נִשְׁכַּחַת כִּי נָתְנָה אֵילִים רַבִּים לְמַלְכָּהּ. 5. A. . . . אִישׁ גִּבּוֹר בָּא אֶל הַשַּׂר לְהִשָּׁמֵר. B. . . . לְהִשָּׁמַע. C. . . . לְהִשָּׁפֵט. D. . . . לְהִזָּכֵר. E. . . . לְהִלָּחֵם. 6. A. נִשְׁלַחְנוּ לְהָבִיא חֲרָבוֹת לָאֲנָשִׁים הַנִּלְחָמִים בַּמִּלְחָמָה. B. נִשְׁלַחְתֶּן . . . C. . . . נִשְׁלַחְתְּ D. . . . הַשַּׂר נִשְׁלַח E. . . . נָשִׁים נִשְׁלְחוּ F. . . . נִשְׁלַחְתִּי G. . . . נִשְׁלַחְתָּ H. . . . נִשְׁלַחְתֶּם I. . . . שָׂרָה נִשְׁלְחָה 7. A. . . . רְאִיתֶם אֶת הַדָּם אֲשֶׁר נִשְׁפַּךְ עַל הָאָרֶץ וְרַצְתֶּם מֵהַמָּקוֹם הַהוּא. B. . . . רָאִינוּ . . . וְרַצְנוּ . . . C. . . . הֵנָּה רָאוּ . . . וְרָצוּ . . . D. . . . רָאִיתִי . . . וְרַצְתִּי . . . E. . . . רָאִיתָ . . . וְרַצְתָּ F. . . . רָאִית . . . וְרַצְתְּ G. . . . הֵמָּה רָאוּ . . . וְרָצוּ H. . . . רְאִיתֶן . . . וְרַצְתֶּן I. . . . הִיא רָאֲתָה . . . וְרָצָה

1. When we fought in the battle, much blood was shed. A. When you fought in the battle, much blood . . . 2. David will be remembered because he was a mighty man, and he had many swords. A. You will be remembered. . . 3. A man from our family will be sent because he is the king's messenger. A. A man from our family will be chosen

because he is the king's messenger. B. . . . taken . . . 4. They are not being forgotten because they gave many rams to their king as a gift. A. I am not being forgotten because I gave many rams to my king as . . . 5. A mighty man came to the chief to be chosen. A. A mighty man came to the chief to be guarded. B. . . . heard. 6. The lads were sent to bring swords to the men who were fighting in the battle. A. We were sent to bring swords to the men who . . . 7. The messenger from Bethlehem saw the blood that was spilt on the land and ran from that place. A. You saw the blood that was spilt on . . .

Exercise 3 1. הָאַיִל יִלָּקַח מֵהַשָּׂדֶה. 2. דִּבְרֵי הַשַּׂר יִשָּׁמְעוּ. 3. אִשְׁתּוֹ נִבְחֶרֶת. 4. הַחַיִל יִזָּכֵר. 5. מַלְאָךְ נִשְׁלַח. 6. דַּם חֵיל מִצְרַיִם נִשְׁפַּךְ.

1. A man will take the ram from . . . The ram will be taken from the field. 2. We will hear the words of the officer because he is a mighty man of valor. The words of the officer will be heard. 3. The man chooses his wife from among the women of Egypt. His wife is chosen. 4. They will remember the great army that was in the city. The army will be remembered. 5. You sent a messenger to recount to the king the number of the armies of Moab. The messenger was sent. 6. He shed the blood of the army of Egypt in the battle. The blood of the army of Egypt was shed.

Exercise 4 1. הֵמָּה כָּתְבוּ אֶת הַמִּצְוֹת. 2. אֲנַחְנוּ פּוֹתְחִים אֶת שַׁעֲרֵי הָעִיר כָּל בֹּקֶר. 3. הִיא תִּשְׁכַּח אֶת מַעֲשֶׂיךָ הַטּוֹבִים. 4. תִּשְׁפְּטוּ אֶת הַנָּשִׁים. 5. שָׁפַכְתִּי אֶת הַמַּיִם. 6. הוּא יִכְתֹּב סְפָרִים עַל חֵיל דָּוִד.

1. The commandments were written. They wrote the commandments. 2. The gates. . .are opened . . . We open the gates of the city every morning. 3. Your good deeds will be forgotten. She will forget your good deeds. 4. At that time, the women will be judged. You will judge the women. 5. The water in the vessel was poured out on the ground. I poured out the water. 6. Books will be written about the army of David. He will write books about the army of David.

Exercise 5 1A. בֹּעַז יִזְכֹּר אִשָּׁה. 1B. בֹּעַז יִזְכֹּר אֶת אִמּוֹ. 1C. בֹּעַז זָכַר אֶת אֵם רוּת. 1D. אֵם רוּת נִזְכְּרָה. 1E. אֲבִי רוּת יִזָּכֵר כְּאִישׁ גִּבּוֹר. 1F. נִזְכָּר בְּאֶרֶץ יְהוּדָה כְּעַם קָדוֹשׁ. 2A. רוּת שָׁכְחָה אֶת הָאַיִל בַּשָּׂדֶה. 2B. רוּת לֹא תִּשְׁכַּח אֶת שְׂדוֹת בֹּעַז. 2C. הָאַיִל בַּשָּׂדֶה נִשְׁכָּח. 2D. אֵין לָאַיִל אֹכֶל לֶאֱכֹל וּמַיִם לִשְׁתּוֹת כִּי הוּא נִשְׁכָּח. 2E. רוּת זָכְרָה אֶת הָאַיִל בְּשָׂדֶה בֹּעַז וְהָאַיִל לֹא נִשְׁכָּח. 3A. הַשַּׂר נִלְחַם בַּמִּלְחָמָה. 3B. הָיָה דָם עַל חֶרֶב הַשַּׂר אַחֲרֵי הַמִּלְחָמָה. 3C. הַשַּׂר בָּחַר אֶת הָאֲנָשִׁים אֲשֶׁר יִלָּחֲמוּ בַּמִּלְחָמָה. 3D. אַתָּה שַׂר הַחַיִל וְתִלָּחֵם בַּמִּלְחָמָה. 3E. לֹא אֶלָּחֵם בַּמִּלְחָמָה הַזֹּאת כִּי אֲנִי זָקֵן מְאֹד.

Exercise 6 1. סָפַר 2. סִפֵּר 3. הִזְכִּיר 4. נִזְכַּר 5. נִסְפֹּר 6. נְסַפֵּר 7. נַזְכִּיר 8. נִזָּכֵר 9. סָפַרְתָּ 10. סִפַּרְתָּ 11. הִזְכַּרְתָּ 12. נִזְכַּרְתָּ 13. סָפְרָה 14. סִפְּרָה 15. הִזְכִּירָה 16. נִזְכְּרָה 17. סוֹפְרִים 18. מְסַפְּרִים 19. מַזְכִּירִים 20. נִזְכָּרִים 21. סְפֹר 22. סַפֵּר 23. הַזְכֵּר

1. he counted 2. he recounted 3. he reminded 4. he was remembered 5. we will count 6. we will recount 7. we will remind 8. we will be remembered 9. you counted 10. you recounted 11. you reminded 12. you were remembered 13. she counted 14. she recounted 15. she reminded 16. she was remembered 17. counting—m, pl 18. recounting—m, pl 19. reminding—m, pl 20. being remembered—m, pl 21. count! 22. recount! 23. remind!

Exercise 7 1. ש.מ.ר–נִפְעַל 2. ש.מ.ר–פָּעַל 3. נ.ג.ד–

comforted and lay down in peace. A. On that night, you drank much wine and were comforted and lay down in peace. 5. The chief was sought in all the land of Israel. A. The two messengers . . .

Exercise 3 ‏1. שָׁלֹשׁ 2. אַרְבַּעַת 3. חֲמֵשֶׁת 4. חֲמִשָּׁה 5. שְׁתֵּי‎

‏6. שָׁנַיִם‎

Exercise 4 ‏1. שְׁלֹשָׁה אֵילִים 2. מִלְחָמָה אַחַת 3. חֲמִשָּׁה‎

‏שָׂרִים 4. שְׁתֵּי חֲרָבוֹת 5. אַרְבַּע מִצְוֹת 6. חָמֵשׁ בְּהֵמוֹת‎

‏7. שְׁנֵי מִסְפָּרִים 8. אַרְבָּעָה כֵלִים 9. שָׁבוּעַ אֶחָד 10. שָׁלֹשׁ‎

‏מִשְׁפָּחוֹת‎

Exercise 5a ‏1. הַמֶּלֶךְ יְהֻלַּל. 2. הַכֶּסֶף שֻׁלַּם. 3. הַיַּיִן נִשְׁפַּךְ.‎

‏4. בֶּן יַעֲקֹב בֻּקַּשׁ. 5. אִישָׁהּ נֻחַם.‎

1. The messenger will praise the king. The king will be praised. 2. The chief repaid him (with) silver. The silver was repaid. 3. Abraham poured out wine from the vessel. The wine was poured out. 4. Jacob sought his son in all the city. The son of Jacob was sought. 5. Ruth comforted her husband. Her husband was comforted.

Exercise 5b. ‏1. הֵן דֻּבְּרוּ דִּבְרֵי שָׁלוֹם. 2. (אַתֶּם) תִּזְכְּרוּ אֹתִי‎

‏וּתְנַחֲמוּ אֹתִי. 3. הֲמָה פּוֹתְחִים אֶת הַשְּׁעָרִים. 4. (אֲנַחְנוּ)‎

‏שָׁמַעְנוּ אֶת קוֹלוֹ וַזָּכַרְנוּ אֶת דְּבָרָיו.‎

1. Words of peace were spoken to me. They spoke words of peace. 2. I will remember and comforted. You will remember and comfort me. 3. The two gates are being opened before me. They are opening the gates. 4. His voice was heard, and his words were remembered. We heard his voice and remembered his words.

Exercise 6 ‏1. י.שׁ.ב-פָּעַל 2. שׁ.ו.ב-פָּעַל 3. שׁ.ו.ב-פָּעַל‎

‏4. שׁ.ו.ב-הִפְעִיל 5. שׁ.פ.ך-נִפְעַל 6. שׁ.פ.ך-נִפְעַל‎

‏7. שׁ.ל.ם-פָּעַל 8. שׁ.ל.ם-פָּעַל 9. ג.נ.ב-נִפְעַל 10. ג.נ.ב-‎

‏נִפְעַל 11. כ.ב.ד-פָּעַל 12. כ.ב.ד-פָּעַל 13. ד.ב.ר-פָּעַל‎

‏14. ג.ד.ל-פָּעַל 15. ג.ד.ל-פָּעַל 16. ג.ד.ל-פָּעַל‎

‏17. ג.ד.ל-הִפְעִיל 18. ג.ד.ל-הִפְעִיל 19. ג.ד.ל-פָּעַל‎

‏20. שׁ.ל.ם-פָּעַל‎

1. he sat 2. he returned/returning—m, sg 3. we will return 4. we will bring back 5. it was poured out 6. it will be poured out 7. he will be repaid 8. he will repay 9. to be stolen 10. it was stolen 11. she was honored 12. being honored—f, sg 13. speaking—f, sg 14. raising—m, pl 15. she raised 16. they were raised 17. I made great 18. making great—f, pl 19. being raised—m, sg 20. being repaid—m, sg

Exercise 7 ‏1. גוֹדְלִים 2. מַגְדִּילִים 3. מֻגְדָּלִים 4. מְגֻדָּלִים‎

‏5. נֻחַמְתָּ 6. נֻחַמְתָּ 7. נֻחַם 8. נֻחַם 9. יְהֻלְּלוּ 10. יְהֻלְּלוּ‎

‏11. בֻּקַּשׁ 12. בֻּקַּשׁ 13. נִלְחַם 14. נִשְׁפַּטְתָּ 15. שְׁפֹט 16. שִׁפְטוּ‎

‏17. הָשֵׁב 18. נָשִׁיב 19. נָשׁוּב 20. נֵשֵׁב 21. נַעֲלֶה 22. עָלִינוּ‎

‏23. עֹלִים 24. מְצַוִּים‎

1. growing up—m, pl 2. making great—m, pl 3. raising—m, pl 4. being raised—m, pl 5. you comforted 6. you were comforted 7. we will comfort 8. we will be comforted 9. they will praise 10. they will be praised 11. he sought 12. he was sought 13. he fought 14. you were judged 15. judge! 16. judge! 17. bring back! 18. we will bring back 19. we will return 20. we will sit 21. we will go up 22. we went up 23. going up—m, pl 24. commanding—m, pl

Exercise 8. And the snake was more crafty than all the beasts of the field that the Lord God had made. And he said to the woman: "Indeed, God said 'Do not eat from all the trees of the garden'". And the woman said to the snake: "From the fruit of the trees of the garden we may eat, and from the fruit of the tree that is in the middle of the garden, God said 'Do not eat it, and do not touch it, lest you die.'" The snake said to the woman: "You will surely not die. Because God knows that when you eat from it your eyes will be opened, and you will be like gods, knowing good and evil."

‏4. הִפְעִיל. ב.י.ן-הִפְעִיל 5. שׁ.י.ר-פָּעַל 6. נ.ת.ן-פָּעַל‎

‏7. ל.ק.ח-נִפְעַל 8. ל.ק.ח-פָּעַל 9. ב.ק.שׁ-פָּעַל‎

‏10. ב.נ.ה-פָּעַל 11. ב.ק.שׁ-פָּעַל 12. צ.ו.ה-פָּעַל‎

‏13. ר.א.ה-פָּעַל 14. שׁ.כ.ח-פָּעַל 15. שׁ.כ.ח-פָּעַל, נִפְעַל‎

‏16. שׁ.כ.ח-נִפְעַל 17. שׁ.כ.ח-נִפְעַל 18. שׁ.כ.ח-נִפְעַל-פָּעַל‎

‏19. שׁ.כ.ח-פָּעַל‎

1. being guarded—m, sg 2. we will guard 3. we will tell 4. we will understand 5. we will sing 6. she gave 7. they were taken 8. we will take 9. I sought 10. I built 11. we will seek 12. we will command 13. we will see 14. I will forget. 15. we will forget, he was forgotten 16. being forgotten—f, sg 17. we will be forgotten 18. you/they will be forgotten 19. you/they will forget

Chapter 29

Exercise 2 ‏1. A. כִּבַּדְנוּ בְּבֵית לֶחֶם. B. חֲמִשָּׁה מְלָכִים‎

‏כִּבְּדוּ . . . C. נְשֵׁי מִצְרַיִם כִּבְּדוּ . . . D. הַחַיִל כִּבֵּד‎

‏. . . E. כִּבַּדְתְּ . . . F. בַּת אַבְרָהָם כִּבְּדָה . . . G. כִּבַּדְתֶּם‎

‏. . . H. כִּבַּדְתְּ . . . I. כִּבַּדְתִּי . . . J. כִּבַּדְתֶּן . . . 2. A. נֶעֱמִי‎

‏מְהֻלֶּלֶת כִּי הִיא עָשְׂתָה שָׁלוֹם בֵּין שְׁנֵי הָאַחִים. B. שְׁלֹשָׁה‎

‏שָׂרִים מְהֻלָּלִים כִּי הֵם עָשׂוּ . . . C. שְׁתֵּי נְעָרוֹת מְהֻלָּלוֹת‎

‏כִּי הֵנָּה עָשׂוּ . . . D. אַתֶּם מְהֻלָּלִים כִּי עֲשִׂיתֶם . . . E. אַתְּ‎

‏מְהֻלֶּלֶת כִּי עָשִׂית . . . F. אֲנִי מְהֻלָּל/מְהֻלֶּלֶת כִּי עָשִׂיתִי‎

‏. . . G. אַתָּה מְהֻלָּל כִּי עָשִׂית . . . 3. A. הַקָּצֵר יְדַבֵּר עִם‎

‏הָאִישׁ עַל כַּסְפּוֹ וִישֻׁלָּם. B. תְּדַבְּרִי עִם הָאִישׁ עַל כַּסְפֵּךְ‎

‏וּתְשֻׁלָּמִי. C. דּוֹדָתִי תְּדַבֵּר עִם הָאִישׁ עַל כַּסְפָּהּ וּתְשֻׁלָּם.‎

‏D. תְּדַבֵּרְנָה עִם הָאִישׁ עַל כַּסְפְּכֶן וּתְשֻׁלַּמְנָה. E. תְּדַבֵּר עִם‎

‏הָאִישׁ עַל כַּסְפְּךָ וּתְשֻׁלַּם. F. נְדַבֵּר עִם הָאִישׁ עַל כַּסְפֵּנוּ‎

‏וּנְשֻׁלָּם. G. הַזְּקֵנִים יְדַבְּרוּ עִם הָאִישׁ עַל כַּסְפָּם וִישֻׁלְּמוּ.‎

‏H. תְּדַבְּרוּ עִם הָאִישׁ עַל כַּסְפְּכֶם וּתְשֻׁלָּמוּ. I. שָׁלֹשׁ‎

‏הַמִּשְׁפָּחוֹת תְּדַבֵּרְנָה עִם הָאִישׁ עַל כַּסְפָּן וּתְשֻׁלַּמְנָה.‎

‏4. A. בַּלַּיְלָה הַהוּא שָׁתִיתָ יַיִן רַב וְנֻחַמְתָּ וְשָׁכַבְתָּ בְּשָׁלוֹם.‎

‏B. . . . שָׁתִינוּ וְנֻחַמְנוּ וְשָׁכַבְנוּ . . . C. . . . רוּת שָׁתְתָה‎

‏. . . וְנֻחֲמָה וְשָׁכְבָה . . . D. . . . אַנְשֵׁי בֵית לֶחֶם שָׁתוּ‎

‏. . . וְנֻחֲמוּ וְשָׁכְבוּ . . . E. . . . שָׁתִית וְנֻחַמְתְּ וְשָׁכַבְתְּ‎

‏. . . F. . . . אַרְבַּע בְּנוֹת מוֹאָב שָׁתוּ . . . וְנֻחֲמוּ וְשָׁכְבוּ‎

‏. . . G. . . . שְׁתִיתֶם . . . וְנֻחַמְתֶּם וּשְׁכַבְתֶּם . . . H. . . . שָׁתִיתִי‎

‏. . . וְנֻחַמְתִּי וְשָׁכַבְתִּי . . . I. . . . שְׁתַּיִם נָשִׁים שָׁתוּ‎

‏. . . וְנֻחֲמוּ וְשָׁכְבוּ . . . 5. A. שְׁנֵי הַמַּלְאָכִים בֻּקְּשׁוּ בְּכָל אֶרֶץ‎

‏יִשְׂרָאֵל. B. . . . בֻּקַּשְׁתִּי . . . C. . . . נַעֲרָה אַחַת בֻּקְּשָׁה. D. . . . חָמֵשׁ‎

‏הַנָּשִׁים בֻּקְּשׁוּ . . . E. . . . בֻּקַּשְׁנוּ . . . F. . . . אַרְבַּעַת הַסְּפָרִים‎

‏בֻּקְּשׁוּ . . . G. . . . בֻּקַּשְׁתֶּן . . . H. . . . שְׁלֹשָׁה אֵילִים בֻּקְּשׁוּ‎

‏. . . I. . . . הֵנָּה בֻּקְּשׁוּ . . .‎

1. The messenger from Jerusalem was honored in Bethlehem. A. We were . . . 2. The man is being praised because he made peace between the two brothers. A. Naomi is being praised because she made . . . 3. I will speak with the man about my money and I will be repaid. A. The harvester will speak with the man about his money and he will . . . 4. On that night, Boaz drank much wine and was

Chapter 30

Exercise 2 A. 1. הָשְׁלַכְתָּ אֶל תּוֹךְ הַיָּם. B. הָשְׁלַכְנוּ . . .
C. הָשְׁלַכְתֶּן . . . D. הָשְׁלַכְתִּי . . . E. מֵאָה אִישׁ הָשְׁלְכוּ
. . . F. הָשְׁלַכְתְּ . . . G. נַעֲרָה אַחַת הָשְׁלְכָה . . . H. שֵׁשׁ
נָשִׁים רָעוֹת הָשְׁלְכוּ . . . I. הָשְׁלַכְתֶּם. 2. . . . A. עַתָּה אֲנִי
מָמְלָךְ עַל כָּל הָאָרֶץ מֵהָהָרִים עַד הַיַּרְדֵּן. B. עַתָּה הַשַּׂר
מָמְלָךְ . . . C. עַתָּה אַתְּ מָמְלָכָה . . . D. עַתָּה אַתֶּן
מָמְלָכוֹת . . . E. עַתָּה שְׁמֹנַת הַשֹּׁפְטִים מָמְלָכִים . . .
F. עַתָּה אֲנַחְנוּ מָמְלָכִים . . . G. עַתָּה לֵאָה מָמְלָכָה . . .
H. עַתָּה אַתָּה מָמְלָךְ . . . I. עַתָּה תֵּשַׁע בְּנוֹת רִבְקָה
מָמְלָכוֹת. 3. . . . A. הָאַיִל יָשְׁלַךְ מֵרֹאשׁ הָהָר. B. הַחֶרֶב
תָּשְׁלַךְ . . . C. רָחֵל וּמִרְיָם תָּשְׁלַכְנָה . . . D. תָּשְׁלַךְ . . .
E. נָשְׁלַךְ . . . 4. A. בַּפַּעַם הַזֹּאת אֶשָּׁפֵט בְּבֵית לֶחֶם.
B. . . . תִּשָּׁפֵטְנָה. C. . . . הַגּוֹי יִשָּׁפֵט . . .
E. . . . תִּשָּׁפֵטִי. F. . . . רָחֵל תִּשָּׁפֵט . . .
G. . . . תִּשָּׁפְטוּ. H. . . . תִּשָּׁפֵט . . .
5. A. לֵאָה וְרָחֵל לֹא הֵבִינוּ אֶת דִּבְרֵי הַמַּלְאָךְ.
B. לֹא הֵבַנְתְּ . . . C. . . . לֹא הֲבִינוֹתֶן. D. לֹא הֵבַנּוּ . . .
E. שְׁנֵי דּוֹדַי לֹא הֵבִינוּ. F. לֹא הֲבִינֹתֶם. G. . . . רֹאשׁ הָעִיר
לֹא הֵבִין. H. לֹא הֵבַנְתְּ . . . I. . . . לֹא הֲבִינֹתִי . . .
6. A. רִבְקָה שָׂמָה אֶת הָאֹכֶל וְאֶת הַמַּיִם לְפָנֶיךָ וְשָׁתִיתָ
וְאָכַלְתָּ. B. . . . לִפְנֵיכֶן וּשְׁתִיתֶן וַאֲכַלְתֶּן. C. . . . לִפְנֵיהֶם
וְהֵם שָׁתוּ וְאָכְלוּ. D. . . . לְפָנֶיךָ וְשָׁתִית וְאָכַלְתְּ. E. . . .
לְפָנֵינוּ וְשָׁתִינוּ וְאָכַלְנוּ. F. . . . לִפְנֵיהֶן וְהֵנָּה שָׁתוּ וְאָכְלוּ.
G. . . . לְפָנַי וְהוּא שָׁתָה וְאָכַל. H. . . . לִפְנֵיכֶם וּשְׁתִיתֶם
וַאֲכַלְתֶּם. I. . . . לְפָנֶיהָ וְהִיא שָׁתְתָה וְאָכְלָה.

1. The silver was thrown into the midst of the sea. A. You were thrown into the midst of the sea. B. We were thrown . . . C. You and Leah . . . 2. Now you are being made kings over all the land from the mountains to the Jordan. A. Now I am being made king over all the land from the mountains to the Jordan. B. Now the officer is being made king . . . C. Now you are being made ruler . . . 3. A thousand stones will be thrown from the top of the mountain. A. The ram will be thrown from the top of the . . . 4. At this time, he will be judged in Bethlehem. A. At this time, I will be judged in Bethlehem. B. . . . you and Rebecca . . . C. . . . the nation will . . . 5. Miriam did not understand the words of the messenger. A. Leah and Rachel did not understand the words of the messenger. 6. Rebecca put the food and the water before me, and I drank and ate. A. Rebecca put the food and the water before you, and you drank and ate.

Exercise 3 1. תֵּשַׁע. 2. שְׁמֹנָה. 3. חָמֵשׁ. 4. שָׁלֹשׁ. 5. שֶׁבַע.
6. מָאתַיִם. 7. שֵׁשׁ. 8. עֶשֶׂר. 9. אַרְבַּע. 10. אַחַת. 11. שְׁתַּיִם.
12. אֲלָפִים.

Exercise 4 1. שֵׁשׁ. 2. עֶשֶׂר. 3. שִׁבְעָה. 4. תֵּשַׁע. 5. שְׁמֹנַת.

Exercise 5 1. הַשַּׂר הַמֶּלֶךְ. 2. הָאֲבָנִים מָשְׁלָכִים. 3. הַזָּהָב
יִגָּנֵב. 4. מַלְאֲכֵי הַמֶּלֶךְ נִשְׁלְחוּ. 5. הַבָּנוֹת תָּלְבַּשְׁנָה.

1. The army of Moab made its chief king after the battle. The chief was made king. 2. Rebecca and Miriam were throwing stones into the midst of the Jordan. The stones are being thrown. 3. You/she will steal the gold from the tabernacle in the evening. The gold will be stolen. 4. A hundred times we sent the messengers of the king to Jerusalem. The messengers of the king were sent. 5. Leah will dress her daughters in the morning. The daughters will be dressed.

Exercise 6 1A. שְׁלֹשׁ הַשּׁוֹפְטִים הָלְכוּ יְרוּשָׁלַיְמָה.
2A. אַרְבַּעַת הַשּׁוֹפְטִים לָקְחוּ אֶת הַפָּרִי יְרוּשָׁלַיְמָה.
3A. הַפָּרִי נִשְׁלַח אֶל אַנְשֵׁי יְרוּשָׁלַיִם. 4A. הַפָּרִי יִשָּׁלַח
אֶל שִׁבְעָה שׁוֹפְטִים בִּירוּשָׁלַיִם. 5A. פָּרִי נִלְקַח מֵהָעֵץ
וְנִשְׁלַח אֶל שְׁמֹנַת הַשּׁוֹפְטִים. 1B. לְשָׂרָה שְׁנַיִם עֲלֵיהֶם.
2B. רָחֵל בָּחֲרָה אֶת הַנְּעָלִים הָאֵלֶּה הַיּוֹם. 3B. שֵׁשׁ נָשִׁים
מִמִּשְׁפַּחַת שָׂרָה נִבְחֲרוּ כִּי הֵנָּה חֲכָמוֹת. 4B. שָׂרָה חֲכָמָה
מֵחֲמֵשׁ הַנָּשִׁים בְּבֵיתָהּ. 5B. שְׁמֹנֶה נָשִׁים מִמּוֹאָב תִּבְחַרְנָה
בְּנָדִים מִירוּשָׁלַיִם. 1C. בֶּן יַעֲקֹב סָפַר עֲשָׂרָה אֵילִים.
2C. תִּשְׁעַת בְּנֵי יַעֲקֹב יִסְפְּרוּ אֶת הָאֵילִים בָּהָר. 3C. יַעֲקֹב
לֹא יוּכַל לִסְפֹּר אֶת הָאֵילִים בָּהָר. 4C. יַעֲקֹב לֹא שָׁכַח
כִּי הוּא רָאָה אֶלֶף אֵילִים בָּהָר. 5C. הָהָר בִּיהוּדָה לֹא
נִשְׁכַּח כִּי הוּא כָּהָר בְּמוֹאָב.

Exercise 7 1. מְלַכְתֶּם. 2. הִמְלַכְתֶּם. 3. הָמְלַכְתֶּם.
4. תִּמְלֹכְנָה. 5. תַּמְלֵכְנָה. 6. תָּמְלַכְנָה. 7. זָכַרְתִּי. 8. נִזְכַּרְתִּי.
9. הִזְכַּרְתִּי. 10. זוֹכֶרֶת. 11. נִזְכֶּרֶת. 12. מַזְכִּירָה. 13. מַשְׁלִיכִים.
14. מָשְׁלָכִים. 15. יָשׁוּבוּ. 16. יָשִׁיבוּ. 17. יָשִׁיבוּ. 18. הָשִׁיבוּ.
19. שׁוּב. 20. הָשֵׁב. 21. הָשִׁיב. 22. זְכֹר. 23. הִנָּכֵר. 24. תִּזָּכְרִי.

1. you ruled 2. you made king 3. you were made kings 4. you will rule 5. you will make king 6. you will be made rulers—f,pl 7. I remembered 8. I was remembered 9. I reminded 10. remembering—f,sg 11. being remembered—f,sg 12. reminding—f,sg 13. throwing—m,pl 14. being thrown—pl 15. they will return 16. they will bring back 17. return! 18. bring back! 19. return 20. bring back 21. remember 22. be remembered 23. remind 24. you will be remembered

Who knows one? I know one: One is our God who is in the heavens and on the earth! Who knows two? I know two: Two are the tablets of the covenant, one is our God . . . Who knows three? I know three: Three are the fathers, two . . . Who knows four? I know four: Four are the mothers, three . . . Who knows five? I know five: Five are the five books of the Torah, four . . . Who knows six? I know six: Six are the orders of the Mishnah, five . . . Who knows seven? I know seven: Seven are the days of the Sabbath, six are the orders of the Mishnah, five are the five books of the Torah, four are the mothers, three are the fathers, two are the tablets of the covenant, one is our God who is in the heavens and on the earth! What differentiates this night from all the nights? That on all the nights we eat leavened bread and unleavened bread, (on) this night only unleavened bread. That on all the nights, we eat all vegetables, (on) this night (only) bitter herbs. That on all the nights we do not dip even one time, (on) this night two times. That on all the nights we eat either sitting or reclining, (on) this night all of us are reclining.

Chapter 31

Exercise 2 1. A. עוֹדְךָ מִתְפַּלֵּל עַל הַשָּׁלוֹם יוֹם יוֹם.
B. עוֹדֵנוּ מִתְפַּלְלִים . . . C. עוֹדֵנוּ מִתְפַּלֵּל . . . D. עוֹדֶנָה
מִתְפַּלֶּלֶת . . . E. עוֹדָם מִתְפַּלְלִים . . . F. עוֹדְךָ
מִתְפַּלֶּלֶת. 2. A. אַרְבַּעַת בְּנֵי הַשּׁוֹפֵט הִתְהַלְּלוּ וְלֹא
הִלְלוּ אֶת עֲבֹדַת עַבְדֵיהֶם. B. בַּת הַנָּבִיא הִתְהַלְלָה וְלֹא
הִלְלָה אֶת עֲבֹדַת עֲבָדֶיהָ. C. הִתְהַלַּלְתֶּן וְלֹא הִלַּלְתֶּן אֶת
עֲבֹדַת עַבְדֵיכֶן. D. הִתְהַלַּלְנוּ וְלֹא הִלַּלְנוּ אֶת עֲבֹדַת
עֲבָדֵינוּ. E. הִתְהַלַּלְתִּי וְלֹא הִלַּלְתִּי אֶת עֲבֹדַת עֲבָדַי.

F. הִתְהַלַּלְתָּ וְלֹא הִלַּלְתָּ אֶת עֲבֹדַת עֲבָדֶיךָ. G. נְשֵׁי הַשַּׂר הִתְהַלְלוּ וְלֹא הִלְלוּ אֶת עֲבֹדַת עַבְדֵיהֶן. H. הִתְהַלַּלְתֶּם וְלֹא הִלַּלְתֶּם אֶת עֲבֹדַת עַבְדֵיכֶם. I. הִתְהַלַּלְתָּ וְלֹא הִלַּלְתָּ אֶת עֲבֹדַת עֲבָדֶיךָ. 3. A. תִּתְנַחַמְנָה כַּאֲשֶׁר תִּרְאֶינָה אֶת עֲבֹדַת בְּנֵיכֶן הַטּוֹבִים. B. אֶתְנַחֵם כַּאֲשֶׁר אֶרְאֶה אֶת עֲבֹדַת בָּנַי הַטּוֹבִים. C. רִבְקָה תִּתְנַחֵם כַּאֲשֶׁר תִּרְאֶה אֶת עֲבֹדַת בָּנֶיהָ הַטּוֹבִים. D. הַנָּבִיא יִתְנַחֵם כַּאֲשֶׁר יִרְאֶה אֶת עֲבֹדַת בָּנָיו הַטּוֹבִים. E. שִׁבְעַת הָאָבוֹת יִתְנַחֲמוּ כַּאֲשֶׁר יִרְאוּ אֶת עֲבֹדַת בְּנֵיהֶם הַטּוֹבִים. F. תִּתְנַחֵמוּ כַּאֲשֶׁר תִּרְאוּ אֶת עֲבֹדַת בְּנֵיכֶם הַטּוֹבִים. G. נִתְנַחֵם כַּאֲשֶׁר נִרְאֶה אֶת עֲבֹדַת בָּנֵינוּ הַטּוֹבִים. H. תִּתְנַחֲמִי כַּאֲשֶׁר תִּרְאִי אֶת עֲבֹדַת בָּנַיִךְ הַטּוֹבִים. I. תֵּשַׁע הַמִּשְׁפָּחוֹת תִּתְנַחֵמְנָה כַּאֲשֶׁר תִּרְאֶינָה אֶת עֲבֹדַת בְּנֵיהֶן הַטּוֹבִים. 4. A. הַנָּבִיא יְדַבֵּר אֶת הָאֱמֶת וְלֹא אָשִׂים לִבִּי אֵלָיו. B. ... וְזֶרַע אַבְרָהָם לֹא יָשִׂים לִבּוֹ אֵלָיו. C. ... וַחֲמֵשֶׁת הַשָּׂרִים לֹא יָשִׂימוּ לִבָּם אֵלָיו. D. ... וְלֹא תָשִׂימוּ לִבְּכֶם אֵלָיו. E. ... וְלֹא תָשִׂימִי לִבֵּךְ אֵלָיו. F. ... וּשְׁלֹשׁ הַבָּנוֹת לֹא תָשֵׂמְנָה לִבָּן אֵלָיו. G. ... וְלֹא נָשִׂים לִבֵּנוּ אֵלָיו. H. ... וְלֹא תָשִׂים לִבְּךָ אֵלָיו. I. ... וְהָעֶבֶד לֹא יָשִׂים לִבּוֹ אֵלָיו. 5. A. צִוִּיתָ אֶת בִּנְךָ לֵאמֹר: "לֵךְ נָא אֶל הַמִּדְבָּר לְהִתְפַּלֵּל תְּפִלּוֹת וְלִרְאוֹת אֶת הָעֲבֹדָה בַּמִּשְׁכָּן." B. צִוִּינוּ אֶת בְּנֵנוּ לֵאמֹר: "לֵךְ נָא ... C. ... שָׂרָה צִוְּתָה אֶת בְּנָהּ לֵאמֹר: "לֵךְ נָא ... D. שֵׁשֶׁת הַשּׁוֹמְרִים צִוּוּ אֶת בְּנֵיהֶם לֵאמֹר: "לְכוּ נָא ... E. צִוִּיתֶן אֶת בְּנֵיכֶן לֵאמֹר: "לְכוּ נָא ... F. צִוִּיתִי אֶת בְּנִי לֵאמֹר: "לֵךְ נָא ... G. ... צִוִּיתָ אֶת בִּנְךָ לֵאמֹר: "לֵךְ נָא ... H. שְׁתֵּי נָשִׁים צִוּוּ אֶת בְּנֵיהֶן לֵאמֹר: "לְכוּ נָא ... I. צִוִּיתֶם אֶת בְּנֵיכֶם לֵאמֹר: "לְכוּ נָא ...

1. I am still praying about peace daily. A. You are still praying about peace daily. B. We are still praying . . . C. He is still praying . . . D. She is . . . 2. The king praised himself and did not praise the labor of his servants. A. The four sons of the judge praised themselves and did not praise the labor of their servants. B. The daughter of the prophet praised herself and did not . . . 3. You will comfort yourself when you see the service of your good sons. A. You will comfort yourselves when you see the service of your good sons. B. I will comfort myself when I see the service of my good sons. C. Rebecca will comfort herself when she sees the service of her good sons. 4. The prophet will speak the truth and the people will not pay attention to him. A. The prophet will speak the truth and I will not pay attention to him. B. . . . and the offspring of Abraham will not pay attention to him. 5. The father commanded his son, saying: "Please go to the wilderness to pray prayers and to see the service in the tabernacle." A. You commanded your son, saying: "Please go to the wilderness to pray prayers and to see the service in the tabernacle." B. We commanded our son, saying: "Please go . . . C. Sarah commanded her son, saying: "Please go . . .

Exercise 3. 1. שְׁמַעְתֶּם, שׁוֹמְעִים, תִּשְׁמְעוּ, שָׁמוֹעַ שְׁמַעְתֶּם, שָׁמוֹעַ תִּשְׁמְעוּ, שִׁמְעוּ. 2. רָאִיתִי, רוֹאֶה, אֶרְאֶה, רָאֹה רָאִיתִי, רָאֹה אֶרְאֶה, רְאֵה. 3. בּוֹאִי. 4. הִשְׁלִיךְ, מַשְׁלִיךְ, יַשְׁלִיךְ, הַשְׁלֵךְ הִשְׁלִיךְ, הַשְׁלֵךְ יַשְׁלִיךְ, הַשְׁלֵךְ. 5. נִלְחֲמוּ. 6. הִתְפַּלְּלוּ, יִתְפַּלְּלוּ. 7. שׁוּב. 8. עָשָׂה, יַעֲשֶׂה, עוֹשֶׂה, עָשֹׂה עָשָׂה, עָשֹׂה יַעֲשֶׂה.

---

1. You (heard, are hearing, will hear, surely heard, will surely hear, hear!) the words from the mouth of your offspring. 2. I (saw, am seeing, will see, surely saw, will surely see) the place where these judgements were written. 3. (Come!) please before the judge to hear his judgement. 4. The servant (threw, is throwing, will throw, surely threw, will surely throw) the tree into the midst of the sea. 5. At the time of the famine, the men of Canaan (fought) against the people of Israel and they took them as slaves to their land. 6. Thus they (prayed, will pray) many prayers at that time. 7. Thus said the prophet to David: "(Return) please with your offspring to the land of Israel." 8. The judge (made, will make, is making, surely made, will surely make) a judgement all the days of his life.

Exercise 4. 1. נַחֵם 2. יַזְכִּיר 3. הִלְלוּ 4. מַגְדִּיל 5. הַמְלִיכוּ 6. שׁוּב.

1. He heard the prayer of his slave, and comforted him. 2. The prophet will remind the king that he must keep the commandments. 3. The nine old men praised the deeds of the mighty man of valor. 4. Now the king is making my name great in all the land because I saved my people from the hand of Moab. 5. Thus said the prophet: "Crown a king from the offspring of David." 6. The father commanded his son, saying: "Please return to my land"

Exercise 5. 1. מַה הִגַּדְתָּ לָעֶבֶד? 2. הִגַּדְתִּי לָעֶבֶד לְהָבִיא אֶת הַכֵּלִים. 3. תַּגִּיד לָעֲבָדִים לְהָבִיא אֶת הַלֶּחֶם וְאֶת הַיַּיִן. 4. הָעֲבָדִים הֵבִיאוּ אֶת הַלֶּחֶם וְאֶת הַיַּיִן אֶל בֵּית הַמֶּלֶךְ. 5. נָשִׂים אֶת הַלֶּחֶם וְאֶת הַיַּיִן לִפְנֵי הַמֶּלֶךְ.

Exercise 6. And it came to pass after these things that God tested Abraham. And he said to him: "Abraham!" And he said: "Here I am!" And (God) said: "Take (please) your son, your only son whom you love, Isaac, and go to the land of Moriah. And raise him up there for a burnt-offering upon one of the mountains that I will say to you." So Abraham got up early in the morning . . . and he took . . . Isaac his son, and he chopped the wood of the burnt-offering, and he arose and went to the place that God had said to him. On the third day Abraham lifted up his eyes, and he saw the place from far away. . . . and Abraham took the wood of the burnt-offering, and he set (it) upon his son Isaac, and he took in his hand the fire and the knife. And the two of them went together. And Isaac said to Abraham his father, he said: "My father." And Abraham said: "Here I am, my son." And he (Isaac) said: "Behold, the fire and the wood, and where is the sheep for the burnt-offering?" And Abraham said: "God will see to it, the sheep for the burnt-offering, my son." And the two of them went on together. And they came to the place that God had said to him. And Abraham built there the altar, and he laid out the wood. And he bound Isaac his son, and he set him on the altar, on top of the wood. And Abraham sent (stretched out) his hand, and he took the knife, to slaughter his son. And the messenger of the Lord cried out from the heavens, and he said: "Abraham! Abraham!" And he said: "Here I am!" And (the messenger) said: "Do not stretch out your hand to the young man, and don't do anything to him . . ."

Exercise 7. 1. אֶגְנֹב 2. אֶגָּנֵב 3. אֶתְכַּבֵּד 4. גָּנַב 5. נִגְנַב 6. הִתְכַּבֵּד 7. בָּאוּ 8. הֵבִיאוּ 9. בּוֹאוּ 10. הָבִיאוּ 11. מְנַחֵם 12. מִתְנַחֵם 13. תְּסַפְּרִי 14. תְּסַפְּרִי 15. עָלְתָה 16. לָקְחוּ 17. נִלְקְחוּ 18. יִקְחוּ 19. יִלָּקְחוּ 20. קַחַת 21. הִלָּקַח 22. זוֹכְרוֹת 23. מַזְכִּירוֹת 24. נִזְכָּרוֹת

1. I will steal 2. I will be stolen 3. I will honor myself 4. he stole 5. he was stolen 6. he honored himself 7. they came 8. they brought 9. come! 10. bring! 11. comforting—m, sg 12. comforting oneself—m, sg 13. you will count 14. you will recount 15. she went up 16. they took 17. they were taken 18. they will take 19. they will be taken 20. take 21. be taken 22. remembering—f, pl 23. reminding—f, pl 24. being remembered—f, pl

Chapter 32

Exercise 2. 1. A. יְרַדְתֶּם אֶל הַיָּם וּמְצָאתֶם שָׁם אֶת הַנָּבִיא. B. יָרַדְתָּ ... וּמָצָאתָ C. ... עֶבֶד אֶחָד יָרַד ... וּמָצָא D. ... רָחֵל וְרִבְקָה יָרְדוּ ... וּמָצְאוּ E. ... יָרַדְנוּ ...

F. ...עֲשֶׂרֶת הַשּׁוֹפְטִים יָרְדוּ...וּמָצְאוּ... ...וּמָצָאנוּ

G. ...יָרַדְתִּי...וּמָצָאתִי...H. ...יְרַדְתֶּן...וּמָצָאתֶן...

I. ...יָרַדְתְּ...וּמָצָאת...2. A. אִם אֵלֵךְ עַל הָאֲבָנִים,

אֶפֹּל. B. אִם אַהֲרֹן וְיוֹסֵף יֵלְכוּ עַל הָאֲבָנִים, יִפְּלוּ. C. אִם

הַזְּקֵנָה תֵּלֵךְ...תִּפֹּל. D. אִם חָמֵשׁ הַבָּנוֹת תֵּלַכְנָה...

תִּפֹּלְנָה. E. אִם תֵּלְכוּ...תִּפְּלוּ...F. אִם אֲחִי מֹשֶׁה יֵלֵךְ

...יִפֹּל. G. אִם נֵלֵךְ...נִפֹּל. H. אִם תֵּלֵךְ...תִּפֹּל.

I. אִם תֵּלַכְנָה...תִּפֹּלְנָה...3. A. רִבְקָה יָצְאָה מִן הָאֹהֶל

בַּבֹּקֶר וְקָרְאָה לְבָנֶיהָ. B. שֵׁשֶׁת הַשָּׂרִים יָצְאוּ...וְקָרְאוּ

לִבְנֵיהֶם. C. הַגִּבּוֹר יָצָא...וְקָרָא לְבָנָיו. D. יָצָאתִי...

וְקָרָאתִי לְבָנַי. E. יְצָאתֶם...וּקְרָאתֶם לִבְנֵיכֶם. F. יָצָאנוּ

...וְקָרָאנוּ לְבָנֵינוּ. G. יָצָאת...וְקָרָאת לְבָנַיִךְ.

H. יְצָאתֶן...וּקְרָאתֶן לִבְנֵיכֶן. I. מִרְיָם וְלֵאָה יָצְאוּ

וְקָרְאוּ לִבְנֵיהֶן. 4. A. כַּאֲשֶׁר הָעֲבָדִים עוֹמְדִים לִפְנֵי

הַמֶּלֶךְ, הֵמָּה מְבִיאִים אֵלָיו מִנְחָה. B. כַּאֲשֶׁר רִבְקָה

עוֹמֶדֶת...מְבִיאָה...C. כַּאֲשֶׁר אַתָּה עוֹמֵד...מֵבִיא

...D. כַּאֲשֶׁר אָנוּ עוֹמְדִים...מְבִיאִים...E. כַּאֲשֶׁר

אַבְרָהָם עוֹמֵד...מֵבִיא...F. כַּאֲשֶׁר הֵנָּה עוֹמְדוֹת

...מְבִיאוֹת...5. A. ...אוֹצִיא אֶת הַכֶּסֶף מִבֵּיתִי וַאֲשַׁלֵּם לְשָׂרָי.

B. ...דּוֹדִי יוֹצִיא...מִבֵּיתוֹ וִישַׁלֵּם לְשָׂרָיו. C. אִמִּי תּוֹצִיא

...מִבֵּיתָהּ וּתְשַׁלֵּם לְשָׂרֶיהָ. D. שְׁתֵּי בְּנוֹת תּוֹצֵאנָה...

...מִבֵּיתָן וּתְשַׁלֵּמְנָה לְשָׂרֵיהֶן. E. תּוֹצִיא...מִבֵּיתְךָ וּתְשַׁלֵּם

לְשָׂרֶיךָ. F. מַלְאֲכֵי הַמֶּלֶךְ יוֹצִיאוּ...מִבֵּיתָם וִישַׁלְּמוּ

לְשָׂרֵיהֶם. G. נוֹצִיא...מִבֵּיתֵנוּ וּנְשַׁלֵּם לְשָׂרֵינוּ. H. תּוֹצִיאוּ

...מִבֵּיתְכֶם וּתְשַׁלְּמוּ לְשָׂרֵיכֶם. I. תּוֹצִיאִי...מִבֵּיתֵךְ

וּתְשַׁלְּמִי לְשָׂרָיִךְ. 6. A. אֵלֶּה אֶל רֹאשׁ הָהָר וּמִשָּׁם אֶרְאֶה

אֶת הַיָּם. B. מֵאָה נָשִׁים תַּעֲלֶינָה...תִּרְאֶינָה. C. שָׂרֵי

הַמֶּלֶךְ יַעֲלוּ...יִרְאוּ. D. ...תַּעֲלוּ...תִּרְאוּ...

E. מִרְיָם תַּעֲלֶה...תִּרְאֶה. F. ...תַּעֲלִי...תִּרְאִי...

G. נַעֲלֶה...נִרְאֶה. H. הָעֶבֶד יַעֲלֶה...יִרְאֶה...

I. ...תַּעֲלֶינָה...תִּרְאֶינָה...

1. Miriam went down to the sea and found the prophet there. A. You went down to the sea and found the prophet there. B. You went down...C. One servant went down...and found...D. Rachel and Rebecca went down...and found...E. We went down...and found...F. The ten judges went down...and found...G. I went down...and found...H. You went down...and found...I. You went down...and found...2. If you walk upon the stones, you will fall. A. If I walk upon the stones, I will fall. B. If Aaron and Joseph walk upon the stones, they will fall. C. If the old woman walks...she will fall. D. If the five daughters walk...they will fall. E. If you walk...you will fall. F. If the brother of Moses walks...he will fall. G. If we walk...we will fall. H. If you walk...you will fall. I. If you walk...you will fall. 3. You came out of the tent in the morning and called to your sons. A. Rebecca came out of the tent in the morning and called to her sons. B. The six chiefs came out...and called to their sons. C. The mighty man came out...and called to his sons. D. I came out...and called to my

sons. E. You came out...and called to your sons. F. We came out...and called to our sons. G. You came out...and called to your sons. H. You came out...and called to your sons. I. Miriam and Leah came out...and called to their sons. 4. When you stand before the king, you bring a gift to him. A. When the slaves stand before the king, they bring a gift to him. B. When Rebecca stands...she brings...C. When you stand...you bring...D. When we stand...we bring...E. When Abraham stands...he brings...F. When they stand...they bring...5.Sarah will bring out the money from her house and will repay her officers. A. I will bring out the...   6. You will go up to the top of the mountain, and from there you will see the sea. A. I will go up to the top of the mountain, and from there I will see the sea. B. A hundred women will go up...they will see...C. The officers of the king will go up...they will see...D. You will go up...you will see...E. Miriam will go up...she will see...F. You will go up...and you will...G. We will go up...we will see...H. The slave will go up...he will see...I. You will go up...you will see...

Exercise 3 1. נָפְלָה 2. יָצָאתִי, הָלַכְתִּי 3. יָלְדָה 4. גָּאַל

5. מָצָאתָ 6. נָשְׂאָה 7. עָמַדְנוּ 8. עָשִׂיתִי

1. Ruth fell from the tree. 2. I went out from the house and went to the house of my uncle. 3. Rebecca gave birth to two sons and one daughter. 4. Joseph redeemed the field of his brother. 5. You found the food in the vessel. 6. The beast lifted up the water. 7. We stood with the women of Moab to see the king. 8. I regularly did good deeds.

Exercise 4 1. אוֹצִיא 2. יַעֲבִיד 3. תּוֹרִידוּ 4. יוֹלִיד 5. נַעֲמִיד

6. תַּצִּיל 7. תַּגִּידִי 8. תּוֹשִׁיבוּ

1. I will bring out all the clothes from my tent. 2. The officer will cause his slaves to work. 3. You will bring down fruit from the tree. 4. Isaac will beget two sons. 5. We will set up the vessels in the tabernacle. 6. You will save your brother from the hand of the king of Moab. 7. You will tell us everything that is written in the book. 8. You will seat me on a great chair.

Exercise 5 1. נִגְאֲלוּ, יִגָּאֲלוּ 2. נִקְרֵאתִי, אֶקָּרֵא 3. נִמְצֵאתֶם,

תִּמָּצְאוּ 4. נוֹלַד, יִוָּלֵד 5. נִבְנוּ, יִבָּנוּ 6. נִשְׂאוּ, יִנָּשְׂאוּ

1. The sons of Israel (were redeemed, will be redeemed) from Egypt. 2. I (was called, will be called) to the king today. 3. You (were found, will be found) in your house in the evening. 4. He (was born, will be born) in Bethlehem. 5. The dwelling places (were built, will be built) in the wilderness. 6. The water (was lifted up, will be lifted up) in vessels to the field.

Exercise 6 1. מ.צ.א–נִפְעַל 2. ר.א.ה–פָּעַל 3. ז.כ.ר–

הִפְעִיל 4. נ.פ.ל–פָּעַל 5. י.ד.ע–הִפְעִיל 6. מ.ל.ך–הִפְעִיל

7. ק.ו.ם–פָּעַל 8. ל.ק.ח–פָּעַל 9. י.צ.א–הִפְעִיל

10. י.ל.ד–הִפְעִיל 11. י.שׁ.ב–פָּעַל 12. נ.ג.ד–הִפְעִיל

13. י.ר.ד–הִפְעִיל 14. מ.צ.א–פָּעַל 15. ק.ר.א–נִפְעַל

16. י.צ.א–הִפְעִיל 17. ע.שׂ.ה–פָּעַל 18. ע.ל.ה–הִפְעִיל

19. א.כ.ל–פָּעַל 20. נ.צ.ל–הִפְעִיל

Exercise 7. And he came upon the place and he spent the night there because the sun had gone. And he took (some) of the stones of the place, and set (them) by his head, and lay down in that place. And he dreamed, and behold, a ladder was stationed on the earth, its head reaching the heavens. And behold, messengers of God were going up and down on it. And behold, the Lord was standing on it, and he said: ''I am the Lord, the God of Abraham your father, and the God of Isaac. The land on which you are lying (on it) I will give it to you and to your offspring. And your offspring will be like the dust of the earth; and you will burst forth westward and eastward and northward and southward, and in you and in your offspring will all the nations of the earth be blessed. And behold, I am with you, and I will guard you in every (place) that you will go, and I will bring you back to this land, for I will not leave you until I have done what I have spoken to you.

Glossary
Hebrew to English

This glossary shows every word included in the vocabulary lists of each chapter in this book. Every word is a common word in either the Bible or the prayerbook, and is translated into its most common meanings. Only the most common verb patterns have been introduced for each verb root. This vocabulary is not intended to be complete, but rather to be clear and manageable for the beginner.

Abbreviations Used in the Glossary

adj — adjective   m — masculine

adv — adverb   n — noun

c — common   pl — plural

conj — conjunction   prep — preposition

dem — demonstrative   pro — pronoun

du — dual   sg — singular

f — feminine   vb — verb

irr, p — irregular possessive

irr, pl, p — irregular plural possessive

irr, s, p — irregular singular possessive

Using the Glossary

All the words are listed in the glossary in Hebrew alphabetical order.

Nouns are listed alphabetically by their singular form. The other forms of the noun follow the singular in this order: plural, singular construct, plural construct, singular noun with first person possessive pronoun ending, plural noun with first person possessive pronoun ending. If a noun is irregular when the possessive pronoun endings are added, the abbreviation *irr, p* or *irr, pl, p* appears instead of

these forms. These irregular forms are listed in the noun charts. Examples:

ground, land *n, f* . . . . . . אֲדָמָה, אֲדָמוֹת, אַדְמַת־, אַדְמוֹת־,
אַדְמָתִי, אַדְמוֹתַי

brother *n, m* . . . . *irr, p* , אָח, אַחִים, אֲחִי־, אֲחַי־

All six noun forms may not appear. If a form is not shown, it is either irregular, uncommon, or non-existent in Biblical Hebrew.

Verbs are listed alphabetically by root. The root is followed by a list of verb patterns in which it appears, and the meaning it has in each verb pattern. Only the most common verb patterns are shown for each root.

Adjectives are listed alphabetically by the masculine singular form. The other forms of the adjective follow in this order: feminine singular, masculine plural, feminine plural.

א

father *n, m* . . . . *irr, p* , אָב, אָבוֹת, אֲבִי־, אֲבוֹת־

stone *n, f* . . . . אֶבֶן, אֲבָנִים, אֶבֶן, אַבְנֵי־, אַבְנִי, אֲבָנַי

Abraham *man's name* . . . . אַבְרָהָם

ground, land *n, f* . . . . . . אֲדָמָה, אֲדָמוֹת, אַדְמַת־, אַדְמוֹת־,
אַדְמָתִי, אַדְמוֹתַי

love *vb* . . . . פָּעַל – א.ה.ב.

love *n, m* . . . . אַהֲבָה, אַהֲבַת־, אַהֲבָתִי

tent *n, m* . . . אֹהֶל, אֹהָלִים, אֹהֶל, אָהֳלֵי־, אָהֳלִי, אֹהָלַי

Aaron *man's name* . . . . אַהֲרֹן

light *n, f* . . . . אוֹר, אוֹר־, אוֹרִי

brother *n, m* . . . . *irr, p* , אָח, אַחִים, אֲחִי־, אֲחַי־

one *adj* . . . . אֶחָד, אַחַת

after, behind *prep* . . . . *or.,* אַחַר, אַחֲרֵי

ram *n, m*	אַיִל, אֵילִים, אֵיל, אֵילֵי־, אֵילִי, אֵילַי
there is not	אֵין
man *n, m*	אִישׁ, אֲנָשִׁים, אִישׁ־, אַנְשֵׁי־, אִישִׁי, אֲנָשַׁי
eat *vb*	א.כ.ל – פָּעַל
food *n, m*	אֹכֶל, אֹכֶל־, אָכְלִי
don't	אַל
to, into, towards *prep*	אֶל
these *dem, c, pl*	אֵלֶּה
thousand *n, m*	אֶלֶף, אֲלָפִים, אַלְפַּיִם *du*, אַלְפֵי־
if *conj*	אִם
mother *n, f*	אֵם, אִמּוֹת, אֵם־, אִמּוֹת־, אִמִּי, אִמּוֹתַי
say *vb*	א.מ.ר – פָּעַל
truth, faithfulness *n, f*	אֱמֶת, אֱמֶת־
we *pro, c*	אֲנַחְנוּ *or* אָנוּ
I *pro, c*	אֲנִי *or* אָנֹכִי
four	אַרְבָּעָה, אַרְבַּע, אַרְבַּעַת־, אַרְבַּע־
land *n, f*	אֶרֶץ, אֲרָצוֹת, אֶרֶץ־, אַרְצוֹת־, אַרְצִי, אַרְצוֹתַי
woman, wife *n, f . irr, p, pl*	אִשָּׁה, נָשִׁים, אֵשֶׁת־, נְשֵׁי־, אִשְׁתִּי
that, who, which	אֲשֶׁר
direct object marker	אֵת, אֶת
you *pro, f, sg*	אַתְּ
you *pro, m, sg*	אַתָּה
you *pro, m, pl*	אַתֶּם
you *pro, f, pl*	אַתֵּן

ב

in, with *prep*	בְּ
garment, clothing *n, m*	בֶּגֶד, בְּגָדִים, בֶּגֶד־, בִּגְדֵי־, בִּגְדִּי
irr, pl, p	
beast, animal *n, f*	בְּהֵמָה, בְּהֵמוֹת, בֶּהֱמַת־, בַּהֲמוֹת־, בְּהֶמְתִּי, בַּהֲמוֹתַי
come, go *vb*	ב.ו.א – פָּעַל
cause to come, bring *vb*	הִפְעִיל
choose *vb*	ב.ח.ר – פָּעַל
be chosen *vb*	נִפְעַל
trust *vb*	ב.ט.ח – פָּעַל
understand *vb*	ב.י.ן – הִפְעִיל
between, among *prep*	בֵּין
house *n, m*	בַּיִת, בָּתִּים, בֵּית־, בָּתֵּי־, בֵּיתִי, בָּתַּי
Bethlehem *place name*	בֵּית לֶחֶם
son *n, m . irr, p*	בֵּן, בָּנִים, בֶּן־, בְּנֵי־, בְּנִי
build *vb*	ב.נ.ה – פָּעַל
be built *vb*	נִפְעַל

Boaz *man's name*	בֹּעַז
morning *n, m*	בֹּקֶר, בְּקָרִים, בֹּקֶר־, בָּקְרִי־
seek *vb*	ב.ק.שׁ – פִּעֵל
be sought *vb*	פֻּעַל
covenant *n, f*	בְּרִית, בְּרִית־, בְּרִיתִי
daughter, *n, f*	בַּת, בָּנוֹת, בַּת־, בְּנוֹת־, בִּתִּי, בְּנוֹתַי

ג

redeem, act as kinsman *vb*	ג.א.ל – פָּעַל
be redeemed *vb*	נִפְעַל
strong, mighty *adj*	גִּבּוֹר, גִּבּוֹרִים
big, great *adj*	גָּדוֹל, גְּדוֹלָה, גְּדוֹלִים, גְּדוֹלוֹת
grow up, become great *vb*	ג.ד.ל – פָּעַל
cause to grow, bring up *vb*	פִּעֵל
be brought up, be raised *vb*	פֻּעַל
make great, magnify *vb*	הִפְעִיל
nation, people *n, m*	גּוֹי, גּוֹיִם, גּוֹי־, גּוֹיֵי־
also	גַּם
steal *vb*	ג.נ.ב – פָּעַל
be stolen *vb*	נִפְעַל

ד

speak *vb*	ד.ב.ר – פִּעֵל
thing, word *n, m*	דָּבָר, דְּבָרִים, דְּבַר־,
irr, pl, p	דִּבְרֵי־, דְּבָרִי
David *man's name*	דָּוִד
beloved, uncle *n, m*	דּוֹד, דּוֹדִים, דּוֹד־, דּוֹדֵי־,
	דּוֹדִי, דּוֹדַי
aunt *n, f*	דּוֹדָה, דּוֹדַת, דּוֹדָתִי
blood *n, m . irr, p*	דָּם, דָּמִים, דַּם־, דְּמֵי־, דָּמִי
road, way *n, m or f*	דֶּרֶךְ, דְּרָכִים, דֶּרֶךְ־, דַּרְכֵי־,
irr, pl, p	דַּרְכִּי

ה

interrogative	הֲ
he *pro, m, sg;* that *dem, m, sg*	הוּא
she *pro, f, sg;* that *dem, f, sg*	הִיא
be *vb*	ה.י.ה – פָּעַל
go, walk *vb*	ה.ל.ך – פָּעַל
praise *vb*	ה.ל.ל – פִּעֵל
be praised *vb*	פֻּעַל
praise oneself, boast, glorify *vb*	הִתְפַּעֵל
they *pro, m, pl;* those *dem, m, pl*	הֵם *or* הֵמָּה
they *pro, f, pl;* those *dem, f, pl*	הֵן *or* הֵנָּה

lo! behold!	הִנֵּה
mountain, hill n, m	הַר, הָרִים, הַר־, הָרֵי־, הָרִי, הָרִי
ו	
and conj	וְ
ז	
this dem, f, sg	זֹאת
this dem, m, sg	זֶה
gold n, m	זָהָב, זְהַב־, זָהָבִי
remember vb	ז.כ.ר – פָּעַל
cause to remember, remind, mention vb	הִפְעִיל
old adj	זָקֵן, זְקֵנָה, זְקֵנִים, זְקֵנוֹת
seed, offspring n, m	זֶרַע, זָרַע־, זַרְעִי
ח	
new adj	חָדָשׁ, חֲדָשָׁה, חֲדָשִׁים, חֲדָשׁוֹת
life n, m	חַיִּים, חַיֵּי־, irr, pl, p
strength, ability, army n, m	חַיִל, חֲיָלִים, חֵיל־, חֵילִי, חֵילִי, irr, pl, p
wise adj	חָכָם, חֲכָמָה, חֲכָמִים, חֲכָמוֹת
five	חֲמִשָּׁה, חָמֵשׁ, חֲמֵשֶׁת־, חֲמֵשׁ־
kindness n, m	חֶסֶד, חֲסָדִים, חֶסֶד־, חַסְדֵּי־, חַסְדִּי, irr, pl, p
sword n, f	חֶרֶב, חֲרָבוֹת, חֶרֶב־, חַרְבוֹת־, חַרְבִּי, חַרְבוֹתַי
darkness n, m	חֹשֶׁךְ, חֹשֶׁךְ־
ט	
good adj	טוֹב, טוֹבָה, טוֹבִים, טוֹבוֹת
י	
hand n, f	יָד, יָדַיִם, יַד־, יָדֵי־, du, irr, p
know vb	י.ד.ע – פָּעַל
Judah place name	יְהוּדָה
day n, m	יוֹם, יָמִים, יוֹמַיִם, יוֹם־, יְמֵי־, du
Joseph man's name	יוֹסֵף
wine n, m	יַיִן, יֵין־, יֵינִי
be able vb	י.כ.ל – פָּעַל
bear, bring forth, give birth vb	י.ל.ד – פָּעַל
be born vb	נִפְעַל
beget vb	הִפְעִיל
sea n, m	יָם, יַמִּים, יָם־, יַמֵּי־
Jacob man's name	יַעֲקֹב
go out, come out vb	י.צ.א – פָּעַל
bring out vb	הִפְעִיל
go down, descend vb	י.ר.ד – פָּעַל
bring down vb	הִפְעִיל
Jordan river	יַרְדֵּן
Jerusalem place name	יְרוּשָׁלַיִם or יְרוּשָׁלַם
there is	יֵשׁ
sit, stay, settle vb	י.שׁ.ב – פָּעַל
cause to sit, cause to dwell vb	הִפְעִיל
Israel place or people	יִשְׂרָאֵל
כ	
as, like prep	כְּ
as, when conj	כַּאֲשֶׁר
honor vb	כ.ב.ד – פָּעַל
be honored vb	פָּעַל
honor oneself vb	הִתְפַּעַל
thus adv	כֹּה
set up, prepare vb	כ.ו.ן – הִפְעִיל
that, because conj	כִּי
all, every, the whole n, m	כֹּל, כָּל
utensil, vessel n, m	כְּלִי, כֵּלִים, כְּלִי־, כְּלֵי־, irr, p
Canaan place name	כְּנַעַן
seat, throne n, m	כִּסֵּא, כִּסְאוֹת, כִּסֵּא־, כִּסְאוֹת־, כִּסְאוֹתַי, irr, s, p
silver, money n, m	כֶּסֶף, כֶּסֶף־, כַּסְפִּי
write vb	כ.ת.ב – פָּעַל
be written vb	נִפְעַל
ל	
to, for prep	לְ
not, no	לֹא
Leah woman's name	לֵאָה
heart n, m	לֵב, לֵב־, לִבִּי or לֵבָב, לְבַב־, לְבָבִי
put on, wear vb	ל.ב.שׁ – פָּעַל
cause to wear, dress vb	הִפְעִיל
bread n, m	לֶחֶם, לֶחֶם־, לַחְמִי
fight, do battle vb	ל.ח.ם – נִפְעַל
night n, m	לַיְלָה or לַיִל, לֵילוֹת, לֵיל־, לֵילוֹת־
before, in the presence of prep	לִפְנֵי
take vb	ל.ק.ח – פָּעַל
be taken vb	נִפְעַל
מ	
very adv	מְאֹד
hundred n, f	מֵאָה, מֵאוֹת, מָאתַיִם, מְאַת־, du
wilderness, desert n, m	מִדְבָּר, מִדְבַּר־
what?	מַה, מֶה, מָה

Moab *place name*	מוֹאָב
who?	מִי
water *n, m*	מַיִם, מֵי־, מֵימֵי
messenger, angel *n, m*	מַלְאָךְ, מַלְאָכִים, מַלְאַךְ־, מַלְאֲכֵי־, מַלְאָכִי, מַלְאָכֵי
battle, war *n, f*	מִלְחָמָה, מִלְחָמוֹת, מִלְחֶמֶת־, מִלְחֲמוֹת־, מִלְחַמְתִּי, מִלְחֲמוֹתַי
reign, rule *vb*	מ.ל.ך – פָּעַל
cause to reign, make king *vb*	הִפְעִיל
king *n, m*	מֶלֶךְ, מְלָכִים, מֶלֶךְ־, מַלְכֵי־, מַלְכִּי *irr, pl, p*
from *prep*	מִן
gift *n, f*	מִנְחָה, מְנָחוֹת, מִנְחַת־, מִנְחוֹת־, מִנְחָתִי, מִנְחוֹתַי
number *n, m*	מִסְפָּר, מִסְפָּרִים, מִסְפַּר־, מִסְפְּרֵי־, מִסְפָּרִי, מִסְפָּרַי
deed, work *n, m*	מַעֲשֶׂה, מַעֲשִׂים, מַעֲשֵׂה־, מַעֲשֵׂי־, מַעֲשַׂי, מַעֲשֵׂי
find *vb*	מ.צ.א – פָּעַל
be found *vb*	נִפְעַל
commandment *n, f*	מִצְוָה, מִצְוֹת, מִצְוַת־, מִצְוֹת־, מִצְוָתִי, מִצְוֹתַי
Egypt *place name*	מִצְרַיִם
place *n, m*	מָקוֹם, מְקוֹמוֹת, מְקוֹם־, מְקוֹמוֹת־, מְקוֹמִי, מְקוֹמוֹתַי
Miriam *woman's name*	מִרְיָם
Moses *man's name*	מֹשֶׁה
couch, bed *n, m*	מִשְׁכָּב, מִשְׁכָּבִים, מִשְׁכַּב־, מִשְׁכְּבֵי־, מִשְׁכָּבִי, מִשְׁכָּבַי
dwelling place, tabernacle *n, m*	מִשְׁכָּן, מִשְׁכָּנוֹת, מִשְׁכַּן־, מִשְׁכְּנוֹת־ מִשְׁכָּנִי, מִשְׁכְּנוֹתַי
family *n, f*	מִשְׁפָּחָה, מִשְׁפָּחוֹת, מִשְׁפַּחַת־, מִשְׁפְּחוֹת־, מִשְׁפַּחְתִּי, מִשְׁפְּחוֹתַי
judgement *n, m*	מִשְׁפָּט, מִשְׁפָּטִים, מִשְׁפַּט־, מִשְׁפְּטֵי־, מִשְׁפָּטִי, מִשְׁפָּטַי

נ

please	נָא
prophet *n, m*	נָבִיא, נְבִיאִים, נְבִיא־, נְבִיאֵי־, נְבִיאִי, נְבִיאַי
tell, declare *vb*	נ.ג.ד – הִפְעִיל
console *vb*	נ.ח.מ – פָּעַל
be consoled *vb*	פָּעַל
console oneself *vb*	הִתְפָּעֵל
shoe *n, f*	נַעַל, נְעָלִים, נַעֲלַיִם *du*, נַעַל־, נַעֲלֵי־ *du and pl*, נַעֲלִי *irr, pl, p*
Naomi *woman's name*	נָעֳמִי
lad, young man *n, m*	נַעַר, נְעָרִים, נַעַר־, נַעֲרֵי־, נַעֲרִי *irr, pl, p*
young woman, maiden *n, f*	נַעֲרָה, נְעָרוֹת, נַעֲרַת־, נַעֲרוֹת־, נַעֲרָתִי, נַעֲרוֹתַי
fall *vb*	נ.פ.ל – פָּעַל
cause to fall, cast *vb*	הִפְעִיל
soul, living being *n, f*	נֶפֶשׁ, נְפָשׁוֹת, נֶפֶשׁ־, נַפְשׁוֹת־, נַפְשִׁי, נַפְשׁוֹתַי
deliver, rescue *vb*	נ.צ.ל – הִפְעִיל
lift, carry, take *vb*	נ.שׂ.א – פָּעַל
be lifted up *vb*	נִפְעַל
give *vb*	נ.ת.נ – פָּעַל

ס

turn aside *vb*	ס.ו.ר – פָּעַל
remove, take away *vb*	הִפְעִיל
book *n, m*	סֵפֶר, סְפָרִים, סֵפֶר־, סִפְרֵי־, סִפְרִי *irr, p, pl*
count *vb*	ס.פ.ר – פָּעַל
recount, relate *vb*	פָּעַל
be recounted, be related *vb*	פָּעַל

ע

work, serve *vb*	ע.ב.ד – פָּעַל
cause to work *vb*	הִפְעִיל
slave, servant *n, m*	עֶבֶד, עֲבָדִים, עֶבֶד־, עַבְדֵי־, עַבְדִּי *irr, pl, p*
labor, service *n, f*	עֲבֹדָה, עֲבֹדַת־, עֲבֹדָתִי
as far as, until *prep*	עַד
still, yet *adv*	עוֹד
eye *n, f*	עַיִן, עֵינַיִם *du, pl*, עֵינְ־, עֵינֵי־, עֵינִי
city *n, f*	עִיר, עָרִים, עִיר־, עָרֵי־, עִירִי, עָרַי
upon, about *prep*	עַל
go up, ascend *vb*	ע.ל.ה – פָּעַל
with *prep*	עִם
nation, people *n, m*	עַם, עַמִּים, עַם־, עַמֵּי־, עַמִּי
stand *vb*	ע.מ.ד – פָּעַל
cause to stand, set up *vb*	הִפְעִיל
answer *vb*	ע.נ.ה – פָּעַל
tree, wood *n, m*	עֵץ, עֵצִים, עֵצֵי־, עֵצִי *irr, pl, p*

evening n, m	עֶרֶב, עַרְבַּיִם du עֶרֶב־
do, make vb	ע.שׂ.ה – פָּעַל
ten	עֲשָׂרָה, עֶשֶׂר, עֲשֶׂרֶת־, עֶשֶׂר־
time n, f	עֵת, עִתִּים, עֵת־, עִתֵּי־, עִתִּי, עִתֵּי
now adv	עַתָּה

פ

mouth n, m	פֶּה, פִּי־, פִּי
pray vb	פ.ל.ל – הִתְפַּעֵל
face n, m	irr, p פָּנִים, פְּנֵי־
occurrence, time n, f	פַּעַם, פְּעָמִים, פַּעֲמַיִם du פַּעֲמֵי־
fruit n, m	irr, p פְּרִי, פְּרִי־
open vb	פ.ת.ח – פָּעַל
be opened vb	נִפְעַל

צ

command, order vb	צ.ו.ה – פָּעַל

ק

holy adj	קָדוֹשׁ, קְדוֹשָׁה, קְדוֹשִׁים, קְדוֹשׁוֹת
voice, sound n, m	קוֹל, קוֹל־, קוֹלִי
arise, stand up vb	ק.ו.ם – פָּעַל
cause to stand, set up, establish vb	הִפְעִיל
small adj	קָטָן, קְטַנָּה, קְטַנִּים, קְטַנּוֹת
harvest vb	ק.צ.ר – פָּעַל
call, proclaim, read vb	ק.ר.א – פָּעַל
be called, be proclaimed vb	נִפְעַל

ר

see vb	ר.א.ה – פָּעַל
head n, m	רֹאשׁ, רָאשִׁים, רֹאשׁ־, רָאשֵׁי־, רֹאשִׁי
much, many, great adj	רַב, רַבָּה, רַבִּים, רַבּוֹת
Rebecca woman's name	רִבְקָה
run vb	ר.ו.ץ – פָּעַל
Ruth woman's name	רוּת
Rachel woman's name	רָחֵל
compassion n, m	רַחֲמִים, רַחֲמֵי־, רַחֲמַי
evil, bad adj	רַע, רָעָה, רָעִים, רָעוֹת
famine n, m	רָעָב
only adv	רַק

שׁ

week n, m	שָׁבוּעַ, שָׁבוּעוֹת, שְׁבֻעַיִם du
seven	שִׁבְעָה, שֶׁבַע, שִׁבְעַת־, שֶׁבַע־
field, n, m	irr, s, p שָׂדֶה, שָׂדוֹת, שְׂדֵה־, שְׂדוֹת־, שָׂדוֹתַי
return vb	שׁ.ו.ב – פָּעַל
cause to return, bring back vb	הִפְעִיל

judge n, m	שׁוֹפֵט, שׁוֹפְטִים, שׁוֹפֵט־, שׁוֹפְטֵי־, שׁוֹפְטִי,
or	שׁוֹפְטַי, שֹׁפֵט, שֹׁפְטִים, שֹׁפֵט־, שֹׁפְטֵי־, שֹׁפְטִי, שֹׁפְטַי
put, set, place vb	שׂ.י.ם – פָּעַל
sing vb	שׁ.י.ר – פָּעַל
lie down vb	שׁ.כ.ב – פָּעַל
forget vb	שׁ.כ.ח – פָּעַל
completeness, peace n, m	שָׁלוֹם, שְׁלוֹם־, שְׁלוֹמִי
send vb	שׁ.ל.ח – פָּעַל
be sent vb	נִפְעַל
throw, cast vb	שׁ.ל.ך – הִפְעִיל
repay, make whole vb	שׁ.ל.ם – פָּעַל
be repaid vb	פָּעַל
three	שְׁלֹשָׁה, שָׁלֹשׁ, שְׁלֹשֶׁת־, שְׁלֹשׁ־
there, in that place	שָׁם
name n, m	irr, p שֵׁם, שֵׁמוֹת, שֵׁם־, שְׁמוֹת־, שְׁמִי
heavens n, m	שָׁמַיִם, שְׁמֵי־
eight	שְׁמֹנָה, שְׁמֹנֶה, שְׁמֹנַת־, שְׁמֹנֶה־
hear vb	שׁ.מ.ע – פָּעַל
guard, keep vb	שׁ.מ.ר – פָּעַל
be guarded vb	נִפְעַל
sun n, m or f	שֶׁמֶשׁ
year n, f	שָׁנָה, שָׁנִים, שְׁנָתַיִם du, שְׁנַת־, שְׁנֵי־, שְׁנָתִי, שְׁנוֹתַי
gate n, m	שַׁעַר, שְׁעָרִים, שַׁעַר־, שַׁעֲרֵי־, שַׁעֲרִי, irr, pl, p
judge vb	שׁ.פ.ט – פָּעַל
be judged vb	נִפְעַל
pour out, pour vb	שׁ.פ.ך – פָּעַל
be poured out vb	נִפְעַל
chief, officer n, m	שַׂר, שָׂרִים, שַׂר־, שָׂרֵי־, שָׂרִי, שָׂרַי
Sarah woman's name	שָׂרָה
six	שִׁשָּׁה, שֵׁשׁ, שֵׁשֶׁת־, שֵׁשׁ־
drink vb	שׁ.ת.ה – פָּעַל
two	שְׁנַיִם, שְׁתַּיִם, שְׁנֵי־, שְׁתֵּי־

ת

midst	תָּוֶךְ, תּוֹךְ־
law, Torah n, f	תּוֹרָה, תּוֹרוֹת, תּוֹרַת־, תּוֹרָתִי
under, instead of prep	תַּחַת
regularly adv	תָּמִיד
prayer n, f	תְּפִלָּה, תְּפִלּוֹת, תְּפִלַּת־, תְּפִלּוֹת־, תְּפִלָּתִי, תְּפִלּוֹתַי
nine	תִּשְׁעָה, תֵּשַׁע, תִּשְׁעַת־, תֵּשַׁע־

Glossary
English to Hebrew

A

Aaron	אַהֲרֹן
ability	חַיִל
able	י.כ.ל
about	עַל
Abraham	אַבְרָהָם
after	אַחַר or אַחֲרֵי
all	כֹּל, כָּל
also	גַּם
among	בֵּין
and	וְ
animal	בְּהֵמָה
answer	ע.נ.ה
arise	ק.ו.ם
army	חַיִל
as	כְּ, כַּאֲשֶׁר
ascend	ע.ל.ה
aunt	דּוֹדָה

B

bad	רַע
battle	ל.ח.ם
battle	מִלְחָמָה
be	ה.י.ה
beast	בְּהֵמָה
because	כִּי
bed	מִשְׁכָּב
before	לִפְנֵי
beget	י.ל.ד
behind	אַחַר or אַחֲרֵי
behold!	הִנֵּה
beloved	דּוֹד
Bethlehem	בֵּית לֶחֶם
between	בֵּין
big	גָּדוֹל

blood	דָּם
Boaz	בֹּעַז
book	סֵפֶר
born	י.ל.ד
bread	לֶחֶם
bring	ב.ו.א
bring back	ש.ו.ב
bring down	י.ר.ד
bring forth	י.ל.ד
bring out	י.צ.א
brother	אָח
build	ב.נ.ה

C

call	ק.ר.א
Canaan	כְּנַעַן
carry	נ.ש.א
cast	ש.ל.ך, נ.פ.ל
chief	שַׂר
clothing	בֶּגֶד
choose	ב.ח.ר
city	עִיר
come	ב.ו.א
comfort	נ.ח.ם
command	צ.ו.ה
commandment	מִצְוָה
compassion	רַחֲמִים
completeness	שָׁלוֹם
couch	מִשְׁכָּב
count	ס.פ.ר
covenant	בְּרִית

D

darkness	חֹשֶׁךְ
daughter	בַּת
David	דָּוִד

day	יוֹם
declare	נ.ג.ד
deed	מַעֲשֶׂה
deliver	נ.צ.ל
descend	י.ר.ד
desert	מִדְבָּר
do	ע.ש.ה
don't	אַל
dress	ל.ב.שׁ
drink	שׁ.ת.ה
dwelling place	מִשְׁכָּן

E

eat	א.כ.ל
Egypt	מִצְרַיִם
eight	שְׁמֹנָה, שְׁמֹנֶה
establish	ק.ו.ם
evening	עֶרֶב
every	כֹּל, כָּל
evil	רַע
eye	עַיִן

F

face	פָּנִים
faithfulness	אֱמֶת
fall	נ.פ.ל
family	מִשְׁפָּחָה
famine	רָעָב
father	אָב
field	שָׂדֶה
fight	ל.ח.ם
find	מ.צ.א
five	חֲמִשָּׁה, חָמֵשׁ
food	אֹכֶל
for	לְ

English	Hebrew
forget	ש.כ.ח
four	אַרְבָּעָה, אַרְבַּע
from	מִן
fruit	פְּרִי

G

garment	בֶּגֶד
gate	שַׁעַר
gift	מִנְחָה
give	נ.ת.ן
go	ב.ו.א, ה.ל.ך
go out	י.צ.א
go up	ע.ל.ה
gold	זָהָב
good	טוֹב
great	גָּדוֹל, רַב
ground	אֲדָמָה
grow up	ג.ד.ל
guard	ש.מ.ר

H

hand	יָד
harvest	ק.צ.ר
he	הוּא
head	רֹאשׁ
hear	ש.מ.ע
heart	לֵב
heavens	שָׁמַיִם
hill	הַר
holy	קָדוֹשׁ
honor	כ.ב.ד
house	בַּיִת
hundred	מֵאָה

I

I	אֲנִי, אָנֹכִי
if	אִם
in	בְּ
instead of	תַּחַת
into	אֶל
Israel	יִשְׂרָאֵל

J

Jacob	יַעֲקֹב
Jerusalem	יְרוּשָׁלַיִם
Jordan	יַרְדֵּן

English	Hebrew
Joseph	יוֹסֵף
Judah	יְהוּדָה
judge	ש.פ.ט
judge	שׁוֹפֵט
judgement	מִשְׁפָּט

K

keep	ש.מ.ר
kindness	חֶסֶד
king	מֶלֶךְ
know	י.ד.ע

L

labor	עֲבֹדָה
lad	נַעַר
land	אֲדָמָה, אֶרֶץ
law	תּוֹרָה
Leah	לֵאָה
lie down	ש.כ.ב
life	חַיִּים
lift	נ.שׂ.א
light	אוֹר
like	כְּ
living being	נֶפֶשׁ
lo!	הִנֵּה
love	א.ה.ב
love	אַהֲבָה

M

magnify	ג.ד.ל
maiden	נַעֲרָה
make	ע.שׂ.ה
man	אִישׁ
many	רַב
mention	ז.כ.ר
messenger	מַלְאָךְ
midst	תּוֹךְ (תֶּוֶךְ)
mighty	גִּבּוֹר
Miriam	מִרְיָם
Moab	מוֹאָב
money	כֶּסֶף
morning	בֹּקֶר
Moses	מֹשֶׁה
mother	אֵם
mountain	הַר

English	Hebrew
mouth	פֶּה
much	רַב

N

English	Hebrew
name	שֵׁם
Naomi	נָעֳמִי
nation	גּוֹי, עַם
new	חָדָשׁ
night	לַיְלָה or לֵיל
nine	תִּשְׁעָה, תֵּשַׁע
no, not	לֹא
now	עַתָּה
number	מִסְפָּר

O

occurrence	פַּעַם
officer	שַׂר
offspring	זֶרַע
old	זָקֵן
on	עַל
one	אֶחָד, אַחַת
only	רַק
open	פ.ת.ח
order	צ.ו.ה

P

peace	שָׁלוֹם
people	גּוֹי, עַם
place	ש.י.ם
place	מָקוֹם
please	נָא
pour	ש.פ.ך
praise	ה.ל.ל
pray	פ.ל.ל
prayer	תְּפִלָּה
prepare	כ.ו.ן
proclaim	ק.ר.א
prophet	נָבִיא
put	ש.י.ם

R

Rachel	רָחֵל
ram	אַיִל
read	ק.ר.א
Rebecca	רִבְקָה
recount	ס.פ.ר

English	Hebrew
redeem	ג.א.ל
regularly	תָּמִיד
reign	מ.ל.ך
relate	ס.פ.ר
remember, remind	ז.כ.ר
remove	ס.ו.ר
repay	ש.ל.ם
rescue	נ.צ.ל
return	ש.ו.ב
road	דֶּרֶךְ
rule	מ.ל.ך
run	ר.ו.ץ
Ruth	רוּת

S

English	Hebrew
Sarah	שָׂרָה
say	א.מ.ר
sea	יָם
seat	כִּסֵּא
see	ר.א.ה
seed	זֶרַע
seek	ב.ק.שׁ
send	ש.ל.ח
servant	עֶבֶד
serve	ע.ב.ד
service	עֲבֹדָה
set	שׂ.י.ם
set up	ק.ו.ם, כ.ו.ן, ע.מ.ד
settle	י.שׁ.ב
seven	שִׁבְעָה, שֶׁבַע
she	הִיא
shoe	נַעַל
silver	כֶּסֶף
sing	שׁ.י.ר
sit	י.שׁ.ב
six	שִׁשָּׁה, שֵׁשׁ
slave	עֶבֶד
small	קָטָן
son	בֵּן
soul	נֶפֶשׁ
sound	קוֹל
speak	ד.ב.ר
stand	ע.מ.ד

English	Hebrew
stand up	ק.ו.ם
stay	י.שׁ.ב
steal	ג.נ.ב
still	עוֹד
stone	אֶבֶן
strength	חַיִל
strong	גִּבּוֹר
sun	שֶׁמֶשׁ
sword	חֶרֶב

T

English	Hebrew
tabernacle	מִשְׁכָּן
take	ל.ק.ח, נ.שׂ.א
take away	ס.ו.ר
tell	נ.ג.ד
ten	עֲשָׂרָה, עֶשֶׂר
tent	אֹהֶל
that	אֲשֶׁר, הַהוּא, הַהִיא, כִּי
there	שָׁם
there is	יֵשׁ
there is not	אֵין
these	אֵלֶּה
they	הֵם or הֵמָּה, הֵן or הֵנָּה
thing	דָּבָר
this	זֶה, זֹאת
those	הֵם, הֵמָּה, הֵן, הֵנָּה
thousand	אֶלֶף
three	שְׁלֹשָׁה, שָׁלֹשׁ
throne	כִּסֵּא
throw	ש.ל.ך
thus	כֹּה
time	פַּעַם, עֵת
to	אֶל, ל
Torah	תּוֹרָה
towards	אֶל
tree	עֵץ
trust	ב.ט.ח
truth	אֱמֶת
turn aside	ס.ו.ר
two	שְׁנַיִם, שְׁתַּיִם

U

English	Hebrew
uncle	דּוֹד

English	Hebrew
under	תַּחַת
understand	ב.י.ן
until	עַד
upon	עַל
utensil	כְּלִי

V

English	Hebrew
very	מְאֹד
vessel	כְּלִי
voice	קוֹל

W

English	Hebrew
walk	ה.ל.ך
war	מִלְחָמָה
water	מַיִם
way	דֶּרֶךְ
we	אֲנַחְנוּ or אָנוּ
wear	ל.ב.שׁ
week	שָׁבוּעַ
what?	מַה, מֶה, מָה
when (not as a question)	כַּאֲשֶׁר
which, who	אֲשֶׁר
who?	מִי
wife	אִשָּׁה
wilderness	מִדְבָּר
wine	יַיִן
wise	חָכָם
with	בְּ, עִם
woman	אִשָּׁה
wood	עֵץ
word	דָּבָר
work	ע.ב.ד
work	מַעֲשֶׂה
write	כ.ת.ב

Y

English	Hebrew
year	שָׁנָה
yet	עוֹד
you	אַתָּה, אַתְּ, אַתֶּם, אַתֶּן
young man	נַעַר
young woman	נַעֲרָה